THE FRANK LLOYD WRIGHT COLLECTION OF *Surimono*

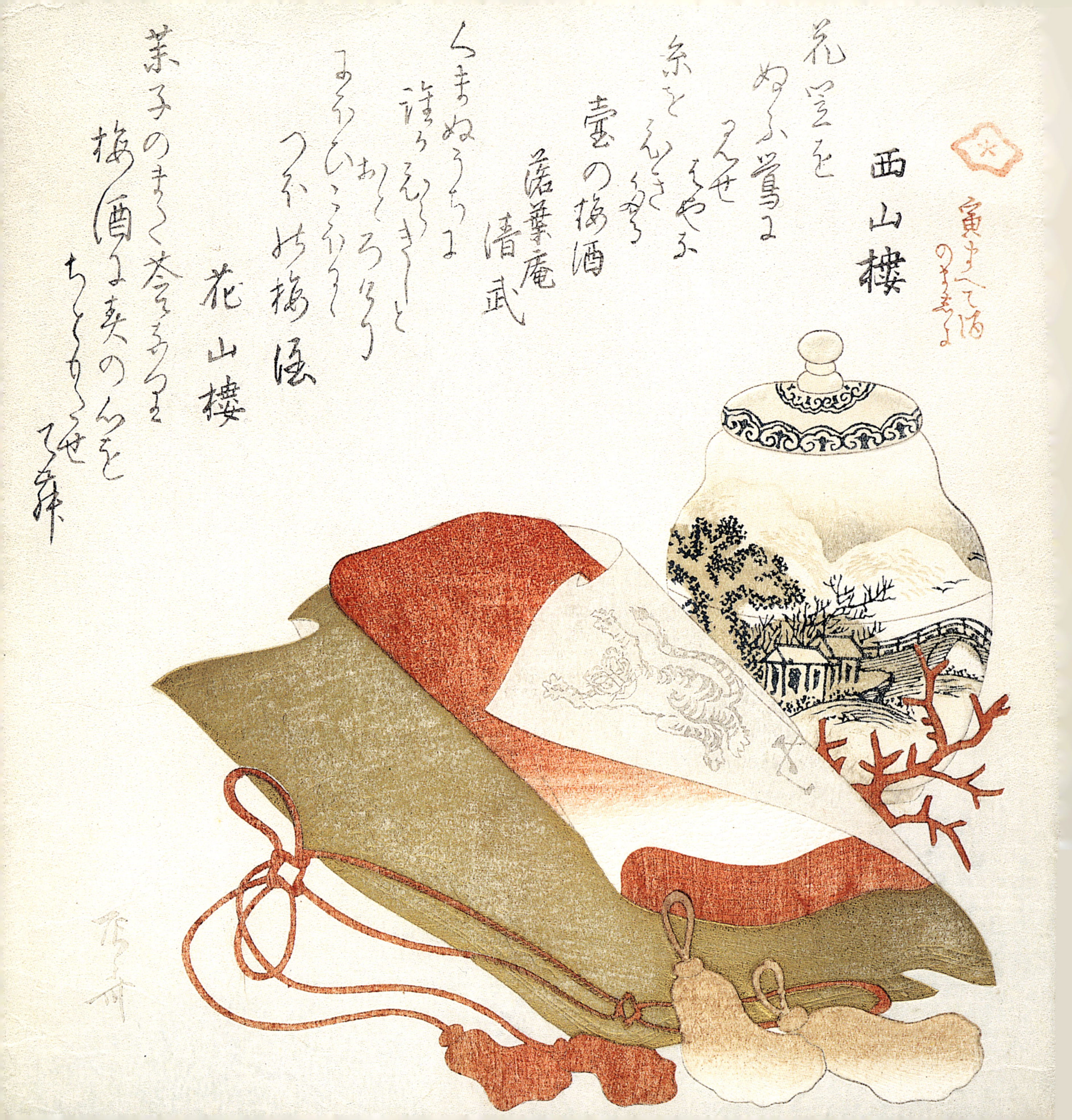
西山楼
壺の梅酒
落葉庵
清武
花山楼

THE FRANK LLOYD WRIGHT COLLECTION OF *Surimono*

JOAN B. MIRVISS

WITH JOHN T. CARPENTER

INTRODUCTION BY

BRUCE BROOKS PFEIFFER

DIRECTOR OF THE FRANK LLOYD WRIGHT ARCHIVES

WEATHERHILL / PHOENIX ART MUSEUM

First edition, 1995

Published jointly by Weatherhill, Inc.
420 Madison Avenue, 15th Floor, New York, NewYork 10017
and Phoenix Art Museum
1625 North Central Avenue, Phoenix, Arizona, 85004.

This volume is published in conjunction with the exhibition *Frank Lloyd Wright and Japanese Art*, organized by the Phoenix Art Museum in cooperation with the Frank Lloyd Wright Foundation and held at Phoenix Art Museum, March 11 through June 11, 1995; and Los Angeles County Museum of Art, September 10, 1995 through January 7, 1996. Major funding for the exhibition and its publication has been provided by the Flinn Foundation.

ISBN 0-8348-0327-5 Weatherhill edition
ISBN 0-910407-32-0 Phoenix Art Museum edition
Printed in Hong Kong

Library of Congress Cataloging in Publication Data:

Mirviss, Joan B.
The Frank Lloyd Wright collection of surimono
by Joan B. Mirviss and John T. Carpenter; and an
introduction by Bruce Brooks Pfeiffer.
p. cm.
Includes bibliographical references (p. 282) and indexes.
—ISBN 0-8348-0327-5
1. Color prints, Japanese—Edo period, 1600-1868—Catalogs.
2. Miniature prints—Japan—Catalogs.
3. Ukiyoe—Catalogs.
4. Wright, Frank Lloyd, 1867-1959—Art collections—Catalogs.
5. Color prints—Private collections—Arizona—Scottsdale—Catalogs.
6. Color prints—Arizona—Scottsdale—Catalogs.
7. Frank Lloyd Wright Archives—Catalogs.
8. Japanese Poetry—Edo period, 1600-1868—History and criticism.
I. Carpenter, John T. II. Phoenix Art Museum.
NE 1321.85.S87M57 1995
769.952'074'79173—dc20 94-41903
CIP

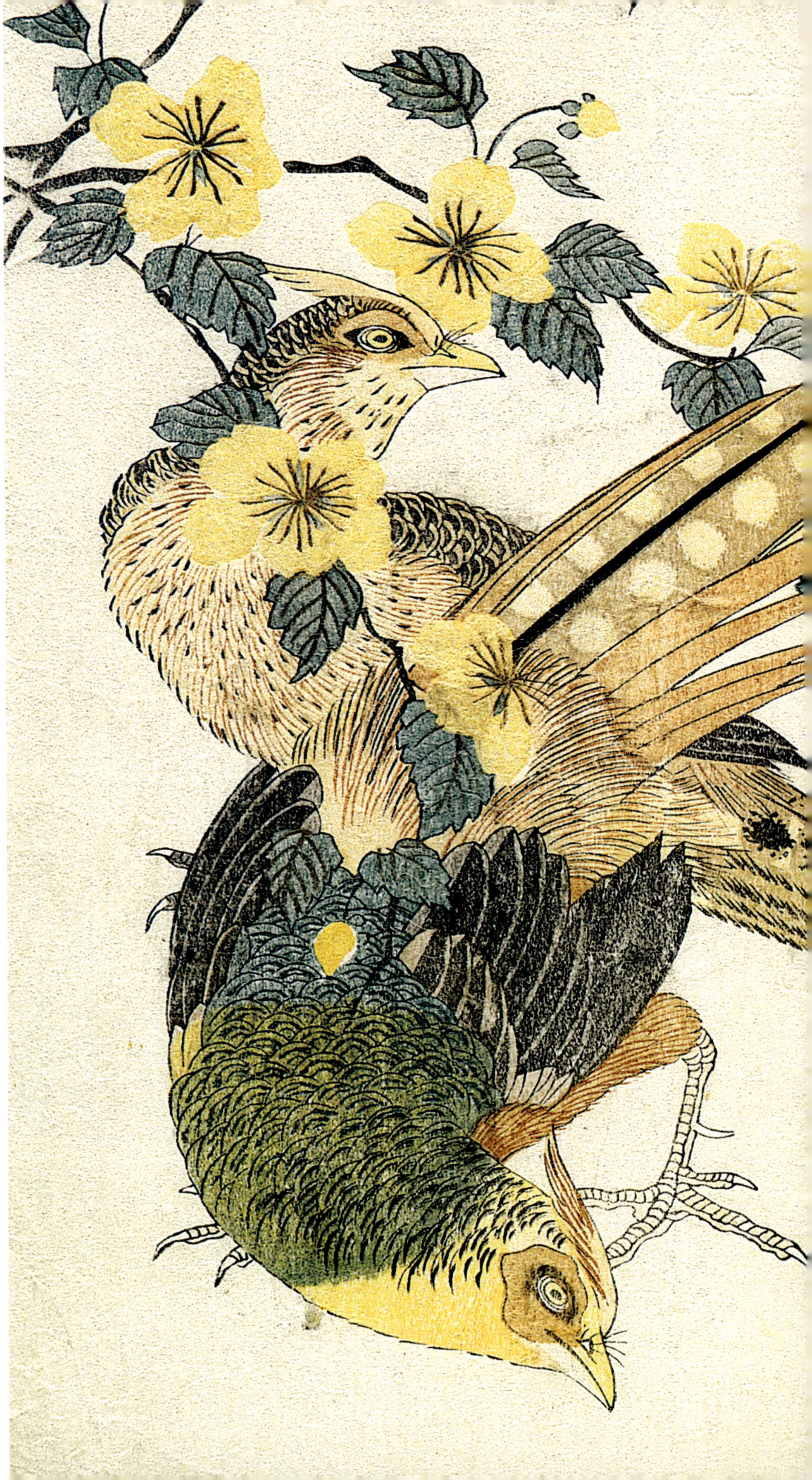

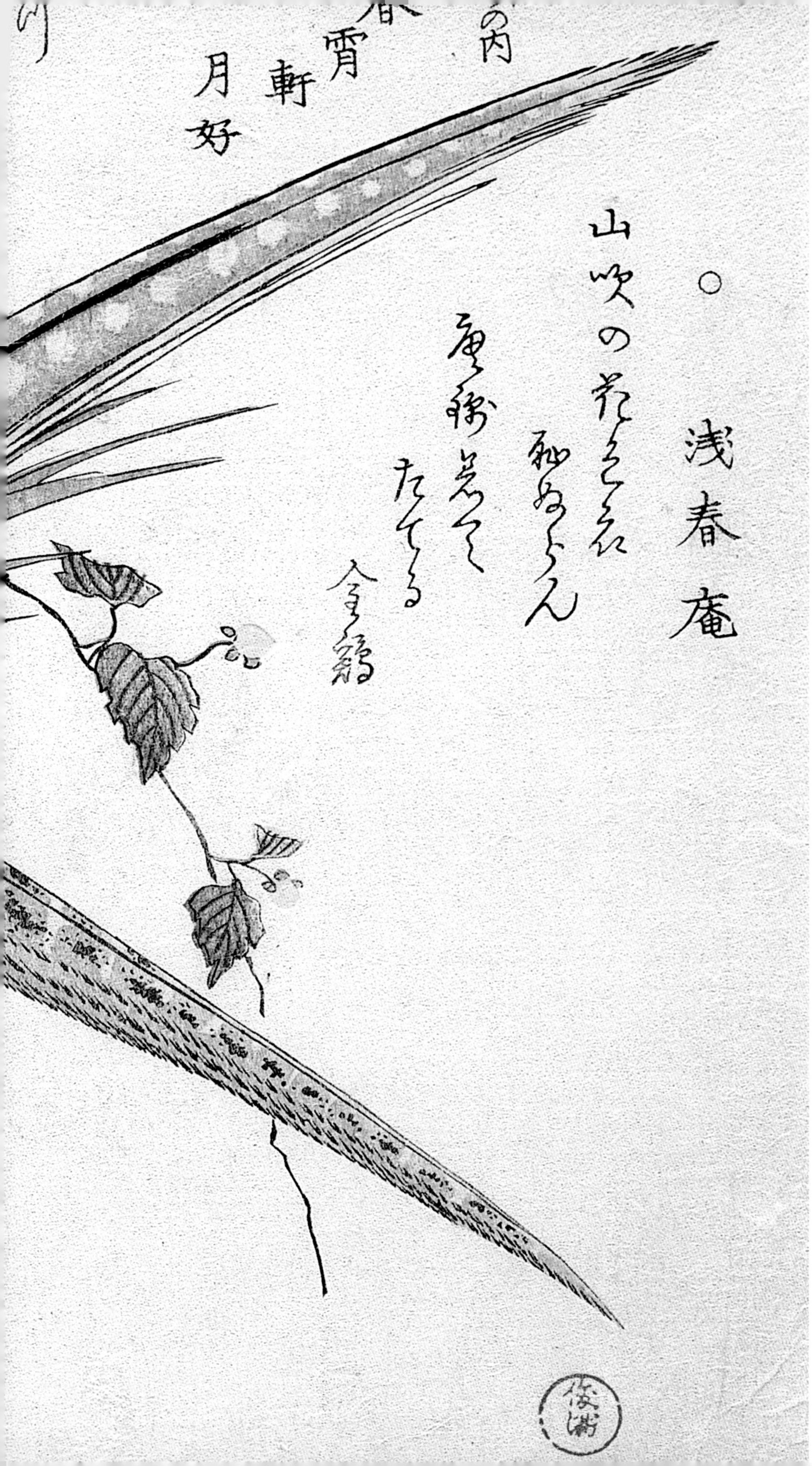

CONTENTS

PREFACE

For more than a decade, the Phoenix Art Museum has enjoyed a remarkable and fruitful relationship with the Frank Lloyd Wright Archives at Taliesin West, Scottsdale. Most notably, in 1990, the two institutions collaborated to produce the first major exhibition of architectural drawings by Wright and his studio from the extensive holdings of the Archives. The resulting display at the Museum of more than three hundred drawings drew more than eighty thousand visitors to see these works on public view for the first time, and a large catalogue, *Frank Lloyd Wright Drawings,* was published in conjunction with the exhibition. In recent years a second ground-breaking collaborative project has been developed by staff members at the Museum and the Archives. Centering on Frank Lloyd Wright's fascination with Asian art, especially Japanese prints, this project has culminated in an exhibition titled *Frank Lloyd Wright and Japanese Art.* The Flinn Foundation of Arizona, through generous grants, has made possible both of these important undertakings.

Internationally known for her work on Wright's collecting of Japanese art, Julia Meech, has served as guest curator for the exhibition. Her scholarly book, *Frank Lloyd Wright and Japanese Art,* will also be published in conjunction with the exhibition. Bruce Brooks Pfeiffer, Director of the Archives, and Claudia Brown, Curator of Asian Art, Phoenix Art Museum, have overseen the process of developing the exhibition. Penny Fowler, Administrator of the Fine Arts Collections at the Archives provided organizational expertise and handled countless requests. Two small preliminary and experimental installations of Japanese art from the Archives were mounted at the Phoenix Art Museum in 1990–91, with the anticipation of initiating the larger project. It soon became clear that the complexities of *surimono* prints demanded the attention of a specialist, and Joan B. Mirviss, noted for her work in this field and already introduced to the collections at Taliesin West, agreed to organize this section of the exhibition. Her enthusiasm and research convinced the project personnel that this remarkable group of prints, the legacy of Wright's collecting still intact at Taliesin West, should become the subject of a full-scale catalogue. John T. Carpenter, a specialist in Japanese poetry, joined in to provide the translations and interpretations of the poems on these highly literary works of art.

The publication of this volume, *The Frank Lloyd Wright Collection of Surimono,* thus coincides with the opening of the exhibition *Frank Lloyd Wright and Japanese Art* at the Phoenix Art Museum. The exhibition will later be shown at the Los Angeles County Museum of Art and a portion of the exhibition will then travel to venues in Japan. We are grateful to The Flinn Foundation for its sponsorship of this project. Our thanks are also due to Douglas Folk and Cynthia Lasko, who contributed toward the photography costs and gave their support and encouragement to the concept of publishing the Japanese print holdings of the Archives.

JAMES K. BALLINGER
DIRECTOR, PHOENIX ART MUSEUM

FOREWORD

The discovery, less than ten years ago, of more than six hundred *surimono*—deluxe, privately-commissioned Japanese prints—that are now in the Frank Lloyd Wright Archives at Taliesin West, Scottsdale, Arizona, has been made available for study and publication. This catalogue illustrates over three hundred of the collection's most interesting and best-preserved surimono.

I initially became involved in this cataloguing project in 1991, when it was suggested that I curate the surimono section of the exhibition being organized by Claudia Brown of the Phoenix Art Museum and Julia Meech, "Frank Lloyd Wright and Japanese Art." It soon became clear, however, that the collection merited fuller treatment, so we decided to do a comprehensive catalogue.To provide the reader with a better understanding of the literary dimensions of surimono, I proposed that translations should be provided for all of the poems on the prints in the color section of the catalogue. For this aspect of the project, I approached John T. Carpenter, an independent scholar specializing in the history of Japanese poetry and calligraphy, whose deep interest in Edo art and culture made him the ideal collaborator. Along with providing full transcriptions and translations of all texts of the prints in the color entries, he also submitted comments on the poems or the interrelationships between texts and images. Also, for the convenience of students of surimono and Japanese poetry, he has compiled an index of the names of all the poets included in the catalogue entries.

Given the extent of the Wright collection—over five hundred and fifty surimono—it was necessary to devise certain criteria for the selection of those to be reproduced in the catalogue. In the case of the color entries, prints were selected primarily from the point of view of connoisseurship, art history, and rarity. We tried to avoid reproducing works that have already been discussed in detail in other publications, but some exceptions were made when the impression in the Wright collection was especially fine. Taken together, the color and black-and-white illustrations highlight the best of the collection and give a representative view of its depth and diversity. Over two hundred surimono were omitted, notably some sixty examples by Hokusai and another seventy-five by his pupils. Many of those were excluded because of inferior condition or duplication. It also should be noted that the collection contains about an additional one hundred small-format prints that are not classifiable as surimono, since they were commercially issued.

Many colleagues and friends have generously contributed their expertise and time to this project. First, I am deeply indebted to Julia Meech, curator of the traveling exhibition "Frank Lloyd Wright and Japanese Art," who knowing of my long-time fascination with surimono, first brought the Wright collection to my attention in 1990. I am also most grateful for her comments on an early draft of the color plate entries. Claudia Brown, Curator of Asian Art at the Phoenix Art Museum and project director for this book and the related exhibition, has with tremendous perseverance found financial support and skillfully handled the innumerable details necessary for such an undertaking. The staff at the Frank Lloyd Wright Archives, led by its vice-president and director, Bruce Brooks Pfeiffer, has always welcomed my extended visits and graciously responded to numerous queries. I am particularly indebted to Penny Fowler, Administrator of the Fine Arts Collections, who has constantly provided able and enthusiastic assistance. She also made available a transcription of recorded remarks made by Roger and Keiko Keyes during a day-long visit to the Frank Lloyd Wright Archives in 1986; their perceptive comments on certain prints were useful in making the initial selection.

For reading over early drafts of the poetry translations and making many valuable suggestions, John Carpenter would like to thank Professor Matsudaira Susumu of Kōnan Women's University and Mutō Junko, Lecturer in Japanese Literature at Gakushūin University. Alexander Brown of the C.V. Starr East Asian Library, Columbia University, also kindly read over the translations and offered much sage advice. He is especially grateful to Kubota Kazuhiro, Research Curator at the Japan Ukiyo-e Museum, for so freely sharing his knowledge and reference materials concerning surimono and Late Edo poetry circles. The Phoenix Art Museum generously covered all of the expenses involved in preparing the translations. Finally, John Carpenter would like to express his gratitude to Zang Toi for his constant encouragement and support.

An ongoing debt of gratitude must be acknowledged to my *sensei* in Japanese art, Professor Miyeko Murase of Columbia University. Through the years, others contributed by allowing me access to their institution's collection of surimono: Barbara Ford Shimizu of the Metropolitan Museum of Art of New York; Money L. Hickman of the Museum of Fine Arts, Boston; Robert D. Mowry of the Arthur M. Sackler Museum, Harvard University Art Museums; Timothy Clark of the British Museum; Robert F. Johnson of the Achenbach Foundation for Graphic Art, San Francisco; and Alice Buse, Head Librarian for the Philosophical Research Society, Los Angeles. Additional information and materials essential to this project were kindly supplied by Robert Smith, Archivist of the Art Institute of Chicago; Virginia M. Krumholz, Archivist of the Cleveland Museum of Art; Asano Shūgō, Curator of the Chiba City Museum of Art; Kubota Kazuhiro, Research Curator of the Japan Ukiyo-e Museum; Ilana Zinger of the Haifa Museum of Art; Barbra T. Okada, specialist in Japanese lacquer and netsuke; Keiko Takahashi, graduate student at Columbia University; Torii Hideo and Matsuoka Haruo, print specialists in Tokyo; and Sebastian Izzard and his staff at Christie's New York. I am most grateful for the perceptive comments and suggestions on early drafts of the manuscript offered by my colleague Gary Levine and for the gracious assistance extended by Sharon Lee Ryder, Richard Bonaparte, and Priscilla Barton. Miyako Yoshinaga, research assistant at The Brooklyn Museum, has diligently worked on this project, practically from the start. Michael Mertz must be singled out for his fine photography, done in the face of a relentless schedule. And finally I must express my profound thanks to my husband, Robert J. Levine, for his unswerving support and advice. He has been involved in the project from its inception, and his contribution is immeasurable.

JOAN B. MIRVISS

ESSAYS

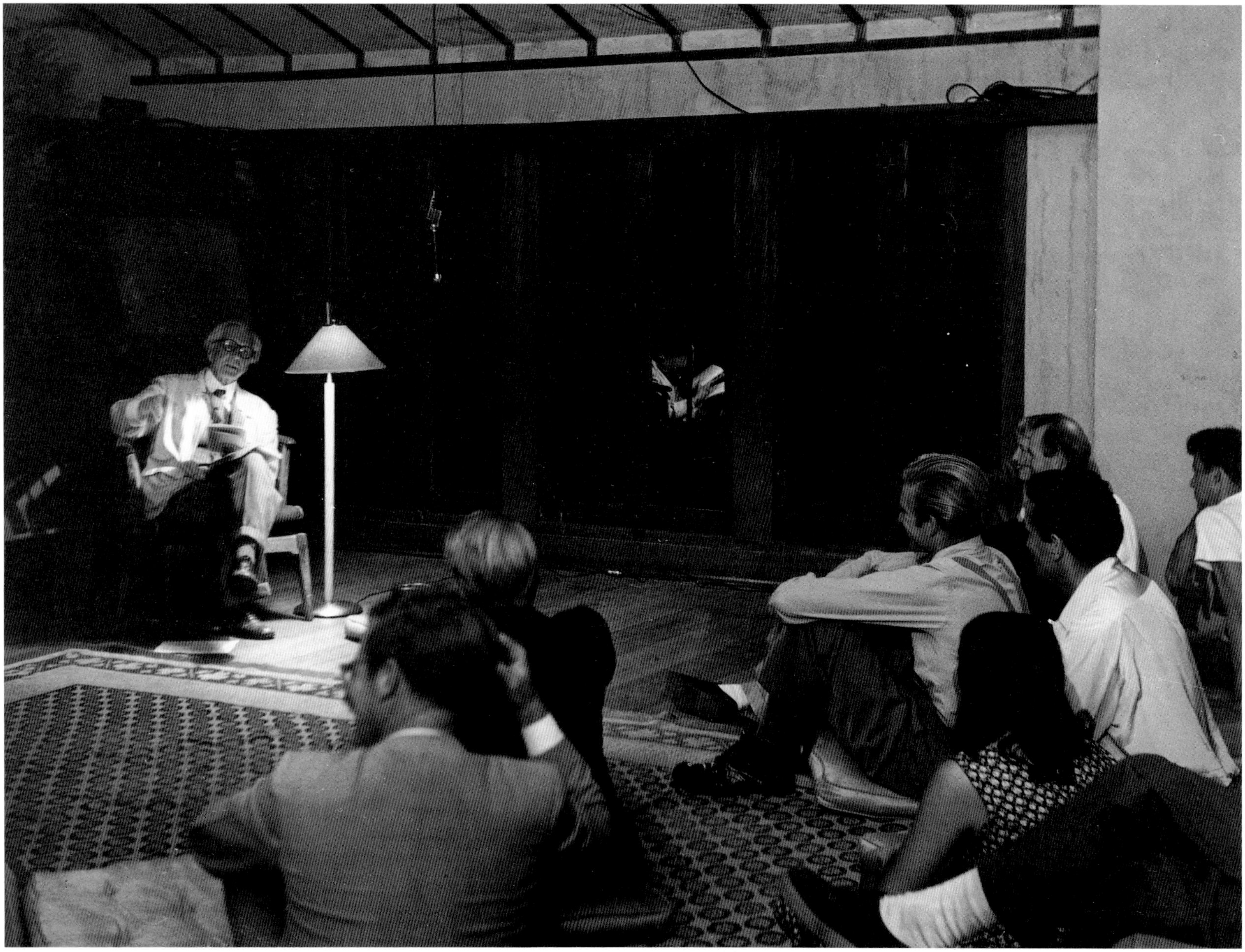

FIGURE 1

Frank Lloyd Wright at a Print Party
at Taliesin in the late 1940s.
Photo by Pedro E. Guerrero

FRANK LLOYD WRIGHT: COLLECTING JAPANESE ART

BRUCE BROOKS PFEIFFER

In a talk to the members of the Taliesin Fellowship, the school for architects that Frank Lloyd Wright and his wife Olgivanna founded in 1932, Wright spoke of Japanese prints:

> I have never confided to you the extent to which the Japanese print per se as such has inspired me. I never got over my first experience with it and I shall probably never recover. I hope I shan't. It was the great gospel of simplification that came over, the elimination of all that was insignificant. . . . We're going to have a print evening where I will show you all these various manifestations of these great artists, probably the greatest the world has ever seen. Hokusai and Hiroshige put on record the entire life of a civilization and the only record of the sort in existence today anywhere. From the smallest act and the most insignificant one to the most important and greatest ones of all. It's all there on record. Beautifully graphic. The architecture of the Japanese is similar—similarly graphic—of their ideology, of their Shintoism. They were the great simplifiers. They were the great discoverers of the essence in whatever they attacked. And if only we could get that quality in our lives again now, come back with it, we could be a great blessing to this confused era in which we live.[1]

Frank Lloyd Wright's strong attraction to the art of Japan began early in the architect's career and persevered until his death in 1959. It was the deep reverence of the Japanese for nature—which Wright chose to spell with a capital "N"—that bound him so firmly to Japanese art and culture. Throughout his life he wrote and lectured on the subject, always in reverent and poetic terms. Coupled with his intense appreciation of the art of Japan, he started to collect it early in life, beginning with the works of the ukiyo-e masters Utamaro, Eishi, Sharaku, Hokusai, and Hiroshige, to cite but a few. He soon expanded his collection to include folding screens, hanging scrolls, sculpture, lacquer, and ceramics. By the time he was in residence in Tokyo designing and supervising the Imperial Hotel from 1916 through 1922, he was buying not only for himself but for other notable collectors in the United States as well. Indeed, during those Tokyo years his profession as architect was supplemented by his role as a procuring agent for other great collections. Towards the end of his stay in Japan he reflected that he was so well known as a buyer of Japanese works of art that dealers and people anxious to sell art works would line up at his studio door.

Of all these works of art—prints, screens, scrolls, sculpture, textiles, ceramics—woodblock prints commanded his greatest respect and were closest to his heart.

> So a fascinating world within a world has grown rapidly among us these past twenty years, increasing steadily in extent and significance as collections have grown richer and as appreciation deepens, and the collections become shrines for the artist pilgrims in need of worship or in search of light.
>
> But still the precious original is all too sacred to the few who, chosen by it, are enslaved by it; because it is no secret that the prints choose whom they love and there is then no salvation but surrender.[2]

In the case of Frank Lloyd Wright and the Japanese print, it was truly an affair of the heart, and he would constantly acknowledge his debt to its masters.

> No more valuable object lesson was ever afforded civilization than this instance of a people who have made of their land and the buildings upon it, of their gardens, their manners and garb, their utensils, adornments and their very gods, a single consistent whole, inspired by a living sympathy with Nature as spontaneous as it was inevitable. To the smallest fraction of Japanese lives what was divorced from Nature was reclaimed by Art and so redeemed.[3]

Wright was well prepared from childhood for his encounter with Japanese art. Born on the Midwest prairie, of English and Welsh ancestry, his attraction to Japan might seem paradoxical. His early training, however, or more precisely the influence of his mother, Anna Lloyd Wright, planted within him the seeds and nourished the conditions that would lead him straight and simply to the art of Japan. Although his mother migrated with her family, the Lloyd Joneses, from Wales to

Wisconsin in 1845, she quickly was drawn to the writings of Emerson. Nature for her was the great truth and benefactor of life, and she instilled in her son that same reverence that consumed her. Toward the end of her life she, too, was taken by the beauty of Japan. While Wright was working on the Imperial Hotel in Tokyo, in 1920, she learned that he was ill and not recovering. At the age of eighty-one, accompanied by a doctor, she journeyed from Oak Park, Illinois, to Tokyo with the express purpose of bringing medical help to him. During the several months she spent in Japan—after his recovery and her own from sciatica—Wright took her on many trips around the countryside to shrines, temples, and monuments. What most deeply impressed her was the constant evidence of the Japanese reverence for nature. Entries in her diary record, "This country is very wonderful. . . . They can learn some things from us but we can learn more from them for they have had time to test things and see failures and successes, learn to know the things of permanence and things of the season. The parks are a dream, the trees are marvels of size and age. I felt like bowing my head in the presence of the Everlasting spirit of life and growth to know the meaning of life, to get hold of the better part . . . the reverence and love of nature! Every little home had its flowers. And cleanliness was met everywhere."[4]

Collecting, for Frank Lloyd Wright, was much more than simply acquisition. He had a consuming passion and desire to live with these objects on an everyday basis.

> A few fresh strawberry leaves laid over them, here comes a heap of noble Taliesin strawberries in a big old Chinese Celadon bowl. The stains of the strawberries are lovely on its cool pale-green surface. Just picked the berries in the garden there below, dew on them, still. . . . And here comes Billy with a wide old Celadon platter of fine asparagus freshly cut—he has just this minute gathered the asparagus. You cannot fail to observe how the color of the asparagus agrees with the Celadon.[5]

When he built his home Taliesin, in Wisconsin, in the valley of his Welsh ancestors, he built his collection of art objects into the home as integral features of the interiors. Outside, on garden walls and in courtyards, he placed bronze and stone sculptures. But as work and sojourn overseas continued, Chinese pottery and sculpture and Momoyama screens overflowed into the rooms where, in a few years, every single object used for decorative accent was an antique of rare quality.

> If the eye rested on some ornament it could be sure of worthy entertainment. Hovering over these messengers to Taliesin from other civilizations and thou-

sands of years ago, must have been spirits of peace and good-will? Their figures seemed to shed fraternal sense of kinship from their places in the stone or from the broad ledges, where they rested.[6]

This passion for spreading these objects generously around the interiors of Taliesin frequently grew to such a degree that a room might resemble an antiquarian's shop more than a residence. His wife, Olgivanna, would occasionally upbraid him for this, saying, "Frank, this room is getting to be such a clutter of Japanese prints, vases, and statuary that there is not a place left to put down a single object. Let's return some of these to the vault, and make more room and space." Together they would carry back woodblock prints, scrolls, vases, bowls, platters, statues, wood objects, and lacquer boxes and carefully set them on the shelves inside the vault in the adjoining studio. "But then, in a few days' time," Olgivanna reflected, "I would spy him carrying back into his bedroom, or the loggia, or the living room, a Han vase, a lacquer box, another Chinese vase, until once again the room was a display and array of fine Japanese and Chinese works of art. He loved them so, he just had to have them around him all the time."[7] In his bedroom he always kept an easel with three Japanese prints on display. Sometimes he would take a brace of prints from the vault to his desk, and study them, print by print, much as one would read a book. They were a constant source of inspiration as well as education for him.

Tragedy in the form of fire struck Taliesin twice, once in 1914 and again in 1925. Each time Wright rebuilt the living quarters that were destroyed. (His studio and work area were miraculously spared. "It was as if God questioned my character, but not my work!" he once remarked.)[8] Following the 1925 fire, he wrote:

> Everything of a personal nature I had in the world, beside my work, was gone. But . . . this time—how thankful—no lives lost except those images whose souls belonged and could now return to the souls that made them—precious works of Art.
>
> Yes . . . poor trustee for posterity, I had not protected them. But they should live in me, I thought. I would prove their life by mine in what I did. And I said so to the suppliant figure [his wife, Olgivanna] standing on the hill-top in the intense dark that now followed the brilliant blaze.[9]

This desire on his part to live with his art collections would also prove hazardous on a less dramatic level. The members of the Taliesin Fellowship as well as the members of his family came to experience the same joy of being surrounded on a daily basis by such beautiful objects. But sometimes a mishap would occur. I was cleaning in the living room at Taliesin, one autumn day in 1951, while Wright was taking a nap on the seat by the fireplace. A large Han bowl filled with antimony was on the ledge behind the piano. As I turned with the wand of the vacuum cleaner, the attached cord caught the bowl and it fell to the flagstone floor. Of a very soft bisque, the bowl crumbled to minuscule pieces and ceramic dust. My face went white. My heart stopped. Mr. Wright opened his eyes, sat up, and said, quite simply, "Bruce, the thing about accidents is that they are so damned accidental. I realize how you must feel, but the fault really lies with me. You see, I prefer to take the chances, have these lovely objects out and about, to storing them or placing them behind glass cases. These were the simple utensils of the people of hundreds of years ago: jars for storing tea, or ginger, or spices; trays and platters for serving food or offerings to the gods; screens and scrolls to adorn the interiors of their homes. Their beauty never ceases to nourish me. But this is the price I must pay—having them about in such profusion and proximity to calamity."

He not only enjoyed these treasures, surrounding himself with them, but also enjoyed sharing them with others. From time to time he would host a "Japanese Print Party" at Taliesin for the members of the Taliesin Fellowship (fig. 1). The evening invariably began with a sukiyaki dinner prepared and served out of doors on the terrace adjacent to his studio. Dinner was prepared on small brass and iron hibachis which he brought back from Japan on his last return voyage in 1922. Four persons, seated on cushions on the flagstone terrace, gathered around each stove, with one person delegated to cooking the prepared meat and vegetables. When dinner was finished, we all filed into the studio and Wright went in and out of the vault carrying both mounted and unmounted Japanese prints. Of all his art collections, it was obvious that these ukiyo-e prints were his favorite.

As he passed them around, or set them on easels, he explained their significance, described the process by which they were made, and their portrayal of the everyday life in Japan at that time.

> You are looking at the work of two of the world's greatest . . . artists in the world: Hokusai and Hiroshige. They are the only two great native sons, as artists, who have made an entire record of everything pertaining to a culture, to a civilization which was one of the few that ever came out of the ground itself, by way of the genius of its own people. . . .[10]
>
> A great craft was being born, probably the greatest handicraft the world has ever seen, because here you have in the first place a marvelous product in the way of paper. Paper sensitive and durable and beautiful beyond any paper that has ever been made; then you have this skilled engraver, beyond skill, beyond almost anything we have ever seen, even Timothy Cole. Then you have the printer—which was a marvelous feat of expertness when he made these prints.[11]

> Now they used to have, in the period that this printing was at its height, what they called the surimono. . . . They would show their skill in printing; where the paper would be rich and thick and they would try all sorts of stunts in printing. They are the master printers in the world today; nothing has gone farther than those surimono of which we have a tremendous box full here. This shows what they could do in the way of printing. There was one style of the thing that Hokusai did, himself. Examine this for printing—silver, lacquer. The mica was put on by mixing it with paste and printing it—they never brushed it on. Some of these things are wonderfully elaborate. Here is a Shumman who was the greatest of all the surimono makers. You see the way they rendered these—masterpieces of printing. . . .
>
> I usually had first call on any prints in Tokyo—because I spent so much money on them, hundreds of thousands of dollars for myself and my friends. And this surimono collection someday is going to be something; get it in order. You wouldn't realize how rare these things are—to see two or three of these in a lifetime is something. . . . These ran the gamut of public taste; they appealed to all sorts and all tastes. Hokusai did beautiful surimono. He did beautiful ladies, graceful figures. Sometimes these drawings were as delicate and perfect as the objects they portrayed. But when the history of printing comes to be written, these people will have a great place in it. Fortunately they keep these surimono, they take good care of them, and you can find them, if you are patient.[12]

Long after Wright died in 1959, that little box of surimono to which he referred in his talk of 1950 remained relatively obscure in the context of the overall collections. The other Japanese prints were carefully set on shelves in the vault at Taliesin, arranged by artist and grouped by "books," or series. Labels on the faces of the shelves carefully identified them. But the surimono seemed almost forgotten. In 1966, when the contents of the vaults at Taliesin were transported to new vaults in Arizona, in keeping with the architect's wishes, the wooden box containing the surimono was among the objects and papers transported to Taliesin West and put away. On opening the box one day, I noticed on the top layer the small prints that we later discovered to be delicate surimono by Hokusai. Unaware of what surimono were at that time, I simply catalogued the collection as "Miscellaneous small Japanese Prints," awaiting the day I would have more time to study them. Eventually the entire contents of the vault were removed to yet a newer and larger vault along with Frank Lloyd Wright drawings, papers, correspondence, and art collections.

At that time, most of our work was consumed by cataloguing and indexing the work of Frank Lloyd Wright: his nearly twenty-two thousand original architectural drawings; a manuscript file of more than six hundred fifty separate books, articles, and periodicals; and the correspondence file—a staggering collection of nearly three hundred thousand documents from 1887 to 1959.

One week during the winter of 1986, T.K. McClintock, who over the years has done conservation work on more than seven hundred Frank Lloyd Wright drawings, was visiting us in Arizona and looking over the contents of our new vault. He pointed to the box of "Miscellaneous small Japanese Prints," and inquired what it contained. I took the box down, placed it on a counter, and opened it. Suddenly T.K. exclaimed, "These are surimono, and what a staggering collection of them!" We spread them out over the other counter tops in the vault and soon discovered a treasure of more than seven hundred. Their storage in the box for more than sixty years had protected them well. It was only a matter of time before an interest in this new find spread across the United States and to Japan. Soon the collection was in demand for exhibitions and publications. It was indeed as if something long lost had surfaced. How gratified Wright would have been to see what he predicted come to be: "This surimono collection someday is going to be something; get it in order. . . . When the history of printing comes to be written, these people will have a great place in it."

NOTES

1 Frank Lloyd Wright to the Taliesin Fellowship, June 20, 1954. AV1014.101.

2 Wright, "Antique Color Prints," The Collected Writings of Frank Lloyd Wright, ed. Bruce Pfeiffer, 2 vols., (New York: Rizzoli, 1992), 1:146–47.

3 Wright, "The Japanese Print: An Interpretation," Collected Writings, 1:119.

4 The Frank Lloyd Wright Foundation is indebted to Franklin Porter, Frank Lloyd Wright's nephew, for recently donating his mother Jane Porter's papers and journals to the Frank Lloyd Wright Archives. Among his mother's papers were the diaries and letters of her mother, Anna Lloyd Wright.

5 Wright, An Autobiography, (New York: Duell, Sloan and Pearce, 1943) 487.

6 Wright, "An Autobiography," Collected Writings, 2:229.

7 Olgivanna Wright to the author, circa 1975.

8 In a talk to the Taliesin Fellowship, during his birthday breakfast in his studio, June 8, 1949.

9 Wright, "An Autobiography," Collected Writings, 3:295.

10 Wright to the Taliesin Fellowship, September 20, 1950, 1, 1014.007.

11 Ibid., 5.

12 Wright to the Taliesin Fellowship, September 20, 1950. AV1014.007, 19–21.

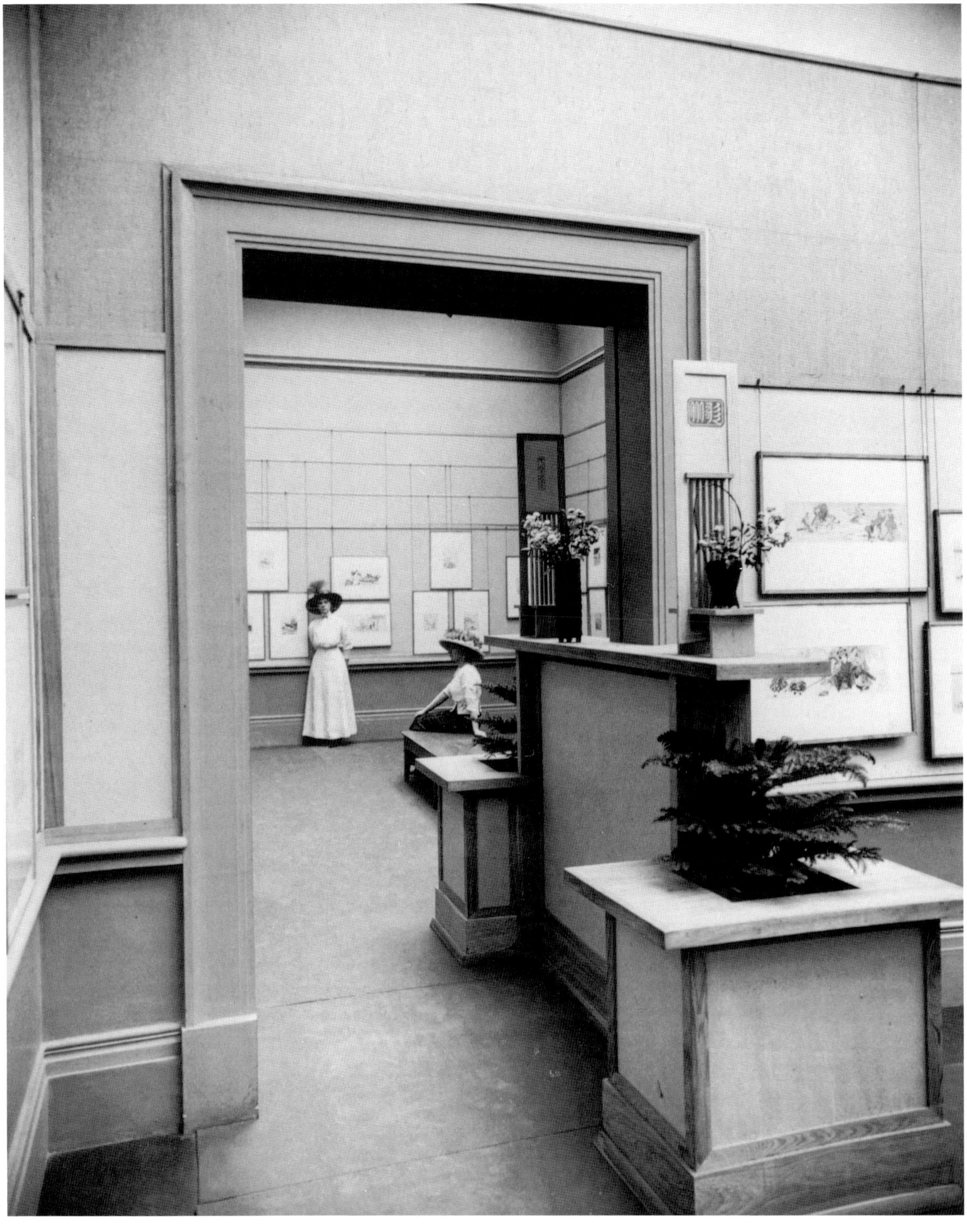

FIGURE 1

View of the display of surimono at the Japanese Print Exhibition, The Art Institute of Chicago, March 1908

A HIDDEN LEGACY:

THE SURIMONO COLLECTION OF FRANK LLOYD WRIGHT

JOAN B. MIRVISS

It is widely known that Frank Lloyd Wright (1867–1959) had a fervent, life-long relationship with Japanese prints, which he understood with an aesthetic intuition shared by few of his contemporaries. As one of the foremost connoisseurs of Japanese prints in his day, Wright was acquainted with collectors, curators, and other devotees of ukiyo-e throughout the United States. His passionate interest in the genre led him to act as a part-time dealer. Travels to Japan in pursuit of architectural commissions and for the supervision of their construction, most prominently that of the Imperial Hotel in Tokyo, afforded Wright access to the major Japanese dealers and collectors. American private collectors and curators became clients, often commissioning Wright to search out fine prints for them. Many thousands of prints once owned by Wright have found their way into public collections throughout the country.

Only recently, however, has Wright's particular interest in a special type of privately published Japanese print known as *surimono* come to light. Less than ten years ago, a large assemblage of small-format prints was "discovered" in the vault of the Frank Lloyd Wright Archives in Scottsdale, Arizona. Stored in an inconspicuous, unmarked Japanese wooden box and ignored for decades, the prints escaped foreclosure actions by the banks and the scrutiny of the tax assessors that had led to the sale of nearly all of the other prints remaining in Wright's estate. When finally examined, the box was found to contain over seven hundred small prints, more than five hundred of which can be classified as surimono. Now stored in the Frank

Lloyd Wright Archives, they have been rescued from obscurity and made available for study and publication for the first time.

Quite apart from their distinguished provenance, these prints amassed by Wright represent one of the finest collections of surimono in the world, both in quality and quantity. These privately published, limited-edition masterpieces of the printer's art are extremely rare. Most are known today by only a few impressions, while others survive as solitary examples. The collection offers a complete range of the genre, from early calendar prints, simply designed and subtly colored, to lavish still lifes printed with the most expensive and luxurious materials. Their soft, fibrous paper, metallic powders, and delicate gradations in tonality, notoriously difficult to capture with the camera, set surimono apart from other prints. As can be seen from so many of the fine examples in the Wright collection, surimono exemplify the acme of the printer's art.

Surimono were usually commissioned by groups of amateur poets, or by individual poets, for special occasions. The poets presented one or more poems that were to be included on the surimono to a professional artist, who conceived the print that was based on or played off the poetic subjects. Most surimono were given as gifts at the New Year, reflecting their origins in the illustrated calendars, or *egoyomi,* customarily given at the New Year. By the beginning of the nineteenth century, egoyomi evolved into the more intricate and highly designed surimono, which frequently retained visual and verbal references to the calendar and the specific years for which they were produced. Because surimono embody a unique collaboration of artist and poet, image and text, each illuminating the other, they are more than just beautiful designs. The poems and the images alike are filled with subtle allusions to past and present events, to literature and to legend. They also reflect the wit, charm, humor, and aesthetic sensibilities of the burgeoning middle-class society of Edo (now Tokyo) in the late eighteenth and early nineteenth centuries.[1]

In order to help the reader appreciate this type of Japanese print, a short introduction will be provided to the techniques and the process by which surimono were produced and the wide array of artistic styles, subjects, and themes engaged. This will be followed by a discussion of the history of the connoisseurship of surimono in the West that will show that Wright was not alone in his pursuit of this type of woodblock print, as French and other European collectors had been acquiring and writing of surimono as early as the 1880s. While it has been assumed in the past that Wright's surimono represent an accumulation of overlooked dealer's stock, it is the thesis of this essay that Wright collected these surimono for himself. Whether initially purchased for his inventory or for his own personal collection, this remarkable group of surimono reflects Wright's intuitive grasp of the surimono aesthetic and his truly fine eye for artistic quality, enabling him to obtain many of the finest impressions known of these rare surimono.

HISTORY AND DEVELOPMENT OF SURIMONO

In the mid-eighteenth century, the financial guarantee of private commissions enabled publishers to experiment with ever-more-costly processes and materials, and facilitated the development of full-color printing (*nishiki-e*). As early as the 1760s, deluxe pictorial calendar prints were privately issued on heavy paper, using a variety of new colors and embossing (*karazuri).* Such prints were called *surimono,* which means simply "printed matter." They are the predecessors of the commercial, multicolored, ukiyo-e prints that were first issued in 1766.[2] Suzuki Harunobu (1724–70), who is recognized as a major innovator in the development of full-color printing, for instance, was commissioned to create many such designs, often at the request of poetry groups. However, poetry was not frequently included with the image until the late 1780s.

Long before the development of surimono, simple illustrated calendars were often privately ordered to be given as gifts. The first such calendars were called egoyomi, or "picture calendars." Calendars played an important part in Japanese society, partly because the calendar system, inherited from China and then adapted, was complex and irregular. Pre-modern Japan employed a lunar calendar with twelve months of either twenty-nine or thirty days. The twenty-nine-day months were called "short months," and the thirty-day months "long months." In order to reconcile the lunar calendar with the solar cycle, an extra, or intercalary month was inserted into the year periodically.

Years were organized into a sixty-year cycle of "ten stems" *(jikkan)* and "twelve branches" *(jūnishi*). The ten stems were named for "major" or "minor" aspects of the five elements (wood, fire, earth, metal, and water), and the twelve branches were identified with the animals of the zodiac (tiger, rabbit, dragon, snake, horse, goat or sheep, monkey, bird, dog, boar, rat, and ox). Each year, month, and day in this sequence was represented by a distinct combination of a stem and a branch. With such a complicated system, calendars were an indispensable tool in Japanese society.

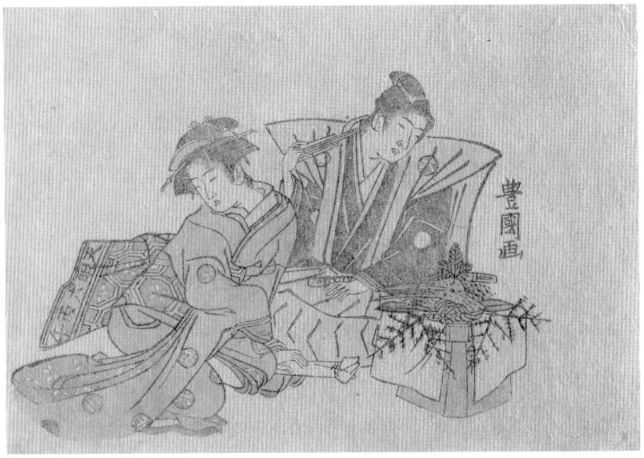

FIGURE 2

Toyokuni I: *Couple with New Year's Arrangement.* 1786, Year of the Horse. (cat. no. 284)

Complete calendars as we think of them today, showing every day of every month, were not commonly used, but at the least it was necessary to know which months were long and which were short. Calendars indicating the length of each month are sometimes called *daishō-goyomi or* "long and short calendars." Egoyomi conveyed the same information, but in a pictorial format providing visual hints as to which months were long and short and what year it was. While the history of printed calendars is indeed a long one, the concept of combining the crucial information with a picture goes back only to the seventeenth century. Few of those issued before the mid-eighteenth century have survived.

One of the earliest prints in the Wright collection is by the celebrated actor-print specialist Utagawa Toyokuni I (1769–1825) and dates to 1786 (fig. 2). In this print the numbers of the relevant months, together with the character for short months, are placed in circular medallions in the textile pattern of the woman's kimono. In other calendar prints, the numerical references are textually interwoven into the poetic inscription accompanying the image (cat. no. 250). The long and short months may also be conveyed simply by alternating large and small objects or design motifs according to the sequence of the long and short months of that year (cat. nos. 155 and 191). Not all egoyomi specify the long and short months; some merely contain a reference to the animal representing a particular zodiac year (for example, the toy tiger in cat. no. 26).

Students of Japanese prints have often surmised that the detailed calendar information was conveyed in cryptic fashion in order to avoid the eye of the censors, because the business of printing calendars was strictly controlled and licensed by the Tokugawa government. But it seems more likely that these "puzzle calendars," which were issued for private circulation and often included the names of the artists, were created to delight and entertain the viewer rather than to avoid the scrutiny of the authorities. Calendars were considered an ideal New Year present for customers, patrons, and associates; and the custom of giving calendars as gifts survives in Japan today.

By the end of the eighteenth century, such prints, usually referred to as *daishō-surimono* (long- and short-month pictorial prints), also typically included poetry by members of the commissioning clubs. Amateur poets made up most of the membership of these poetry groups, which were often divided into subgroups, with branch chapters throughout Japan. The poets most often wrote thirty-one-syllable comic, or "mad," verse (*kyōka*) and became the major patrons of surimono. When commissioning a print, the club or individual poet submitted verses around which a surimono was to be designed to an artist and a publisher. No doubt the proposed design was discussed between the artist and a representative of the poets who commissioned it. The completed surimono were privately distributed to the group members and perhaps to some of their other friends and colleagues.

The production of surimono, like all Japanese prints, was a cooperative effort. The poetry clubs selected the poems before the image was created. The artist allowed adequate space to accommodate the verses on his preparatory drawings, which were executed in ink on thin paper. The publisher, probably a specialist in this genre, coordinated with a calligrapher who transcribed them. The written poems were passed on to a carver to prepare a separate block for the poems, as well as the key block and numerous color blocks. Several distinct styles of calligraphy are evident, and certain hands are identifiable, by style if not by name. Generally speaking, the "key," or outline, block articulated the basic black outline for the entire image. A separate block was carved for each color and material to be used. This complicated process required perfect registration, which in turn necessitated incredibly exact carving. An expert printer assembled these blocks and printed them, using the designated colors and materials, on flexible, fibrous paper that was thick and resilient enough to withstand the embossing process and the application of dense metallic powders.

At this time, with the participation by professional ukiyo-e artists, more sophisticated techniques were employed in the printing of the design, and the calendar references assumed secondary importance. Surimono, like some egoyomi, were printed to commemorate special occasions such as the New Year; to announce a performer's or artist's name change or a musical performance (cat. no. 186); to advertise a shop (cat. no. 291); to serve as a farewell present (cat. no. 146); or to honor the anniversary of a friend's death (cat. no. 218). In addition to relating timely information, the images were typically conceived on a particular theme derived from the poetry on the print. The most common themes were the New Year and the spring season, and their attendant activities, ceremonies, rituals, and symbols.

Paralleling this development toward more complex imagery and the inclusion of poetry, the prints were also changing in size, in the materials used in their production, and in overall aesthetics. The formats used in the 1760s through the 1780s tended to be small, measuring approximately 12 by 9 centimeters. These early forms were generally printed on ordinary paper, with the same materials as those used for standard ukiyo-e but with a slightly paler, more subtle palette. By the late 1790s, however, the most common format measured approximately 14 by 18 cen-

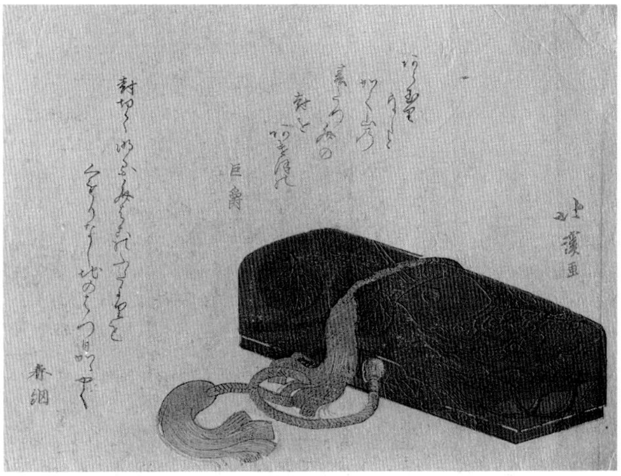

FIGURE 3

Hokkei: *Green-lacquer Letter Box.* early 1810s. (cat. no. 94)

timeters and was termed *koban* (small sheet); if horizontal in format it was called a *yoko-e,* and if vertically composed a *tate-e.*[3] Long surimono (*yokonagaban*) were printed on quite large sheets on which the poetry or inscription appeared upside-down, because the print was intended to be folded in half and then in thirds in order to be presented in an envelope (cat. no. 186).

As the popularity of the koban format was increasing, more sophisticated printing techniques became more prevalent. Initially, expensive metallic powders created from the filings of various metal alloys—often incorporating silver, zinc, tin and copper— were used only as accents. By the end of the first decade of the nineteenth century, however, these metals were applied liberally, along with other expensive pigments and delicate materials such as mother-of-pearl and *gofun,* a gesso-like pigment made of crushed oyster shells. Techniques now included gaufrage (*karazuri*), rubbing to create a lacquerlike effect, and hand-wiping of the blocks before printing. Such precious materials and elaborate processes required thicker, more luxurious paper stock used for both koban and *shikishiban* (approximately 21 by 19 centimeters) formats. The nearly square shikishiban were first issued about 1808, superseding the smaller, rectangular koban, and becoming the most popular format only a few years later; the square configuration predominated until surimono production waned in the 1840s.

Compositions for the shikishi surimono underwent stylistic changes in tandem with these increasingly elaborate technical advances. This is clear when we compare an early still life by Totoya Hokkei (1780–1850), dating to the early 1810s (fig.3), to any of the complicated and ornate compositions of the artist's series of 1823, for the Hanazono-ren (fig.4). From a simple design of a letter box set against a blank background, the artist's work evolved in the course of ten years to a composition overflowing with the patterns and surface detailing of various still-life objects, and even includes a decorative border. Similarly, in many of the later surimono by Gakutei, the border pattern becomes an increasingly elaborate design element (e.g. cat. nos. 80, 81, and 84).

By about 1820, square surimono were frequently commissioned for particular poetry clubs in sets or series. The Shell Series (*Genroku Kasen Kaiawase),* designed by Hokusai and issued in 1821, consists of thirty-six prints and marked his most important work in the genre in many years.[4] This sizable commission underscores the close ties between that artist and the Yomogawa poetry group. Similarly, Yashima Gakutei produced numerous sets for the Hisakataya circle, and Hokkei for the Go-gawa poetry group. Square surimono, perhaps following in the tradition of ukiyo-e, were also designed as diptychs, triptychs, and even larger polyptychs (cat. nos. 7, 10, 59, and 139).

Although surimono, because they were privately commissioned, were not required to list the names of the publisher or craftsmen, the red hand-stamped seals of the technicians involved in their production occasionally appear at the edges of a print (cat. nos. 1, 25, 54, and 285). The best-known example is of the print artist, poet, painter, and publisher Kubo Shumman (1757–1820), who applied a circular red seal reading *Shumman sei* (produced by Shumman), on his own works as well as surimono designed by others.[5] Many of the prints bearing this seal are models of technical refinement. Also an innovator, Shumman created some of the earliest square surimono, using the most subtle techniques (cat. no. 50). Other amateur poets and minor artists likewise designed and published their own surimono, as may been seen in prints by Shushintei Okotaru, poet and leader of the Iwagaki-ren (cat. no. 200), and by Utamasa, a pupil of Utamaro (cat. no. 290).

During the first two decades of the nineteenth century—the golden years of surimono—the majority of the important commissions were given to Katsushika Hokusai (1760–1849) and a number of his pupils who specialized in the genre, most especially Totoya Hokkei (1780–1850), Yashima Gakutei (1786?–1868), and Ryūryūkyo Shinsai (active ca. late 1780s–early 1820s). Hokusai designed numerous surimono beginning in 1798 through about 1809. He became active in the production of surimono again in the 1820s, and his work of that decade is best exemplified by his surimono designs. Hokusai's three pupils, Hokkei, Gakutei, and Shinsai, borrowed many of his aesthetic devices and developed them further, in ever more elaborate and elegant surimono. Other pupils contributed significant and innovative designs, such as Teisai Hokuba (1771–1844), who composed some of the most exquisite floral and still-life designs. The Wright collection contains many superb examples by all these masters of surimono.

While commercial prints were issued in editions of many thousands, private orders for surimono were substantially smaller. For instance, records show that two surimono Kabuki-performance announcements of the late 1780s were issued in an edition of a few hundred.[6] As materials used in the execution of these prints of the early nineteenth century increased in lavishness and expense, editions shrank in size. In any case, compared to the enormous editions of commercial prints, which were printed until the blocks wore out, surimono were issued in extremely limited numbers and are commonly known today through only a handful of extant impressions.

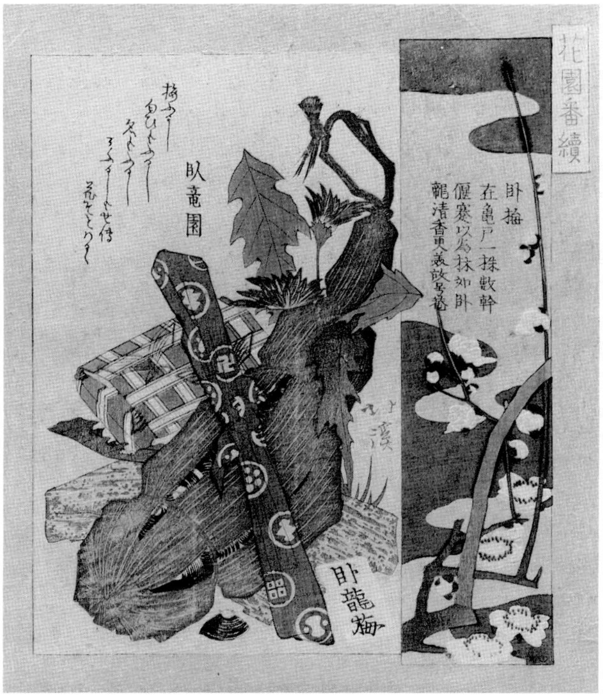

FIGURE 4

Hokkei: *Reclining Plum from a Series for the Hanazono Club (Hanazono Bantsuzuki, Gabai).* 1823. (cat. no. 117)

In another variation from the customary printing process, the text for each surimono was carved onto a block separate from the key block, which resulted in slight discrepancies in the placement of the text from one impression of a design to another. This sometimes leads to the mistaken conclusion that two prints from different editions are being compared. The separation of the poetry and image blocks also enabled surimono publishers to recycle the design blocks in various ways. One of these was the incorporation of different verses, a device that can be seen in two surimono of an amorous couple (figs. 5 and 6) by Yanagawa Shigenobu (1787–1832). Both versions were probably issued for the same year, as the numerical designs on the quilt indicating the long months have been retained. Occasionally second editions were issued with different poems, often supplied by different clubs, sometimes for different years. In such cases, several design details typically had to be changed. In comparing two surimono of travelers by Shinsai (figs. 7 and 8), not only have textile patterns been altered and the rising sun deleted, but the poetry group's emblem has also been replaced. In the square-format version, the crest of the robe of the male figure, and the patterns of the wrapping cloth and obi of the woman standing on the right have been similarly modified.

In addition to allowing publishers to reissue designs with new poetry, the separation of the key block and the poetry block also enabled publishers to issue commercial or later editions of surimono, using the original blocks. Since editions were small, the blocks could be reused; the cherry-tree wood used for the blocks was capable of withstanding printing runs numbering in the thousands. Many long-format surimono by Hokusai originally designed in the first decade of the nineteenth century were reissued with new text in the 1830s (cat. no. 186). The subtle and delicate pigments of the earlier printing were replaced with less costly colors. Sometimes such large-format designs were reissued as commercial prints without the poetry, announcement, or program text. Typically, the quality of the printing in these later editions is not up to the standard of the earlier surimono.

There are several possible explanations for the cessation of surimono production in Edo. Perhaps the custom of distributing such elaborate prints had fallen out of fashion, not only because of strict new government sumptuary regulations which discouraged the printing of luxurious prints and books, but also due to the economic hardships stemming from the Tempō famine in the mid-1830s.[7] There was also a general decline in interest in kyōka and a dramatic reduction in the number of the kyōka groups, who had been the primary patrons of surimono. Surimono continued to be issued after the mid-1830s, but their number drastically decreased, and their publication all but ceased by the early 1840s.

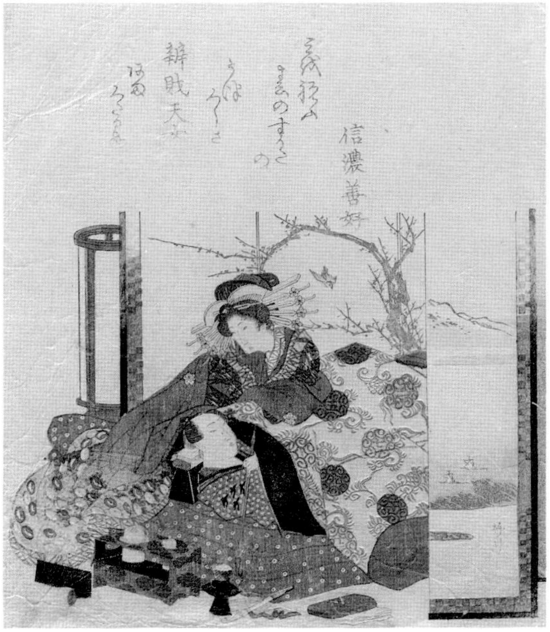

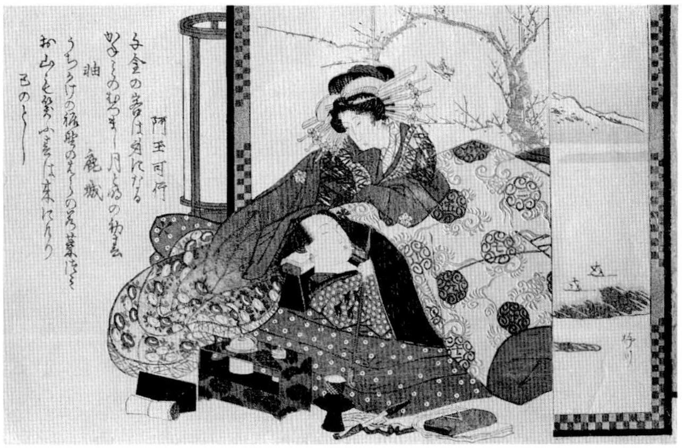

FIGURE 5

Shigenobu: *A Courtesan Reclines Against her Lover* (shikishiban version). 1821, Year of the Snake. (cat. no. 209)

FIGURE 6

Shigenobu: *A Courtesan Reclines Against her Lover* (koban version). 1821, Year of the Snake. (cat. no. 208)

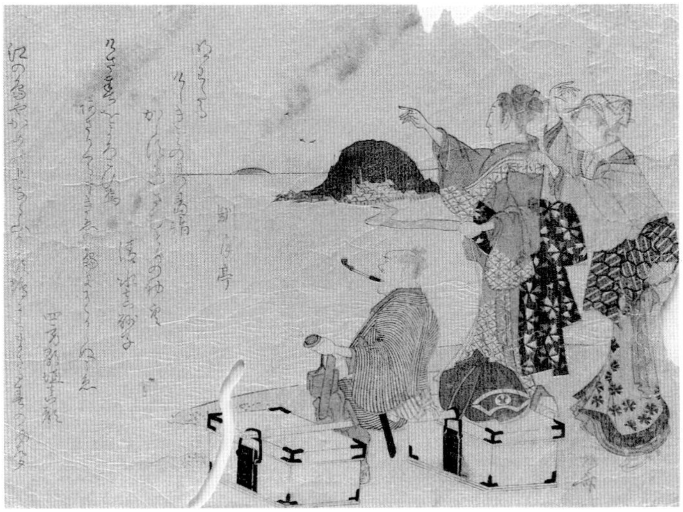

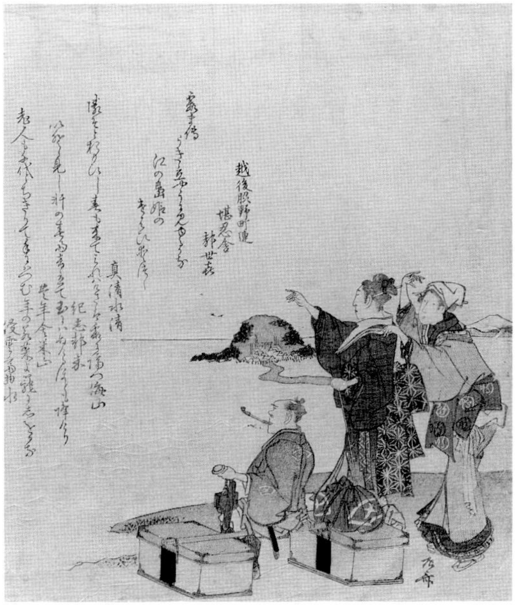

FIGURE 7

Shinsai: *Travelers Pausing to Admire the Rising Sun at Enoshima* (koban version). 1809, Year of the Snake. (cat. no. 219)

FIGURE 8

Shinsai: *Travelers Viewing Enoshima* (shikishiban version). Possibly 1809. (cat. no. 220)

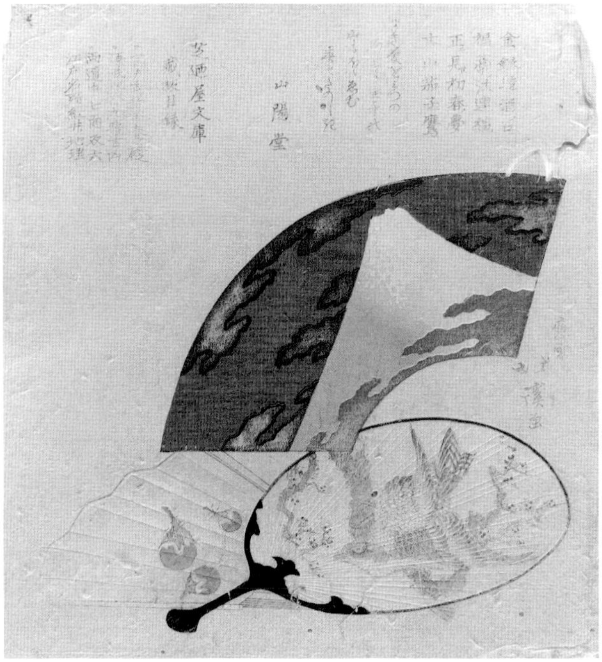

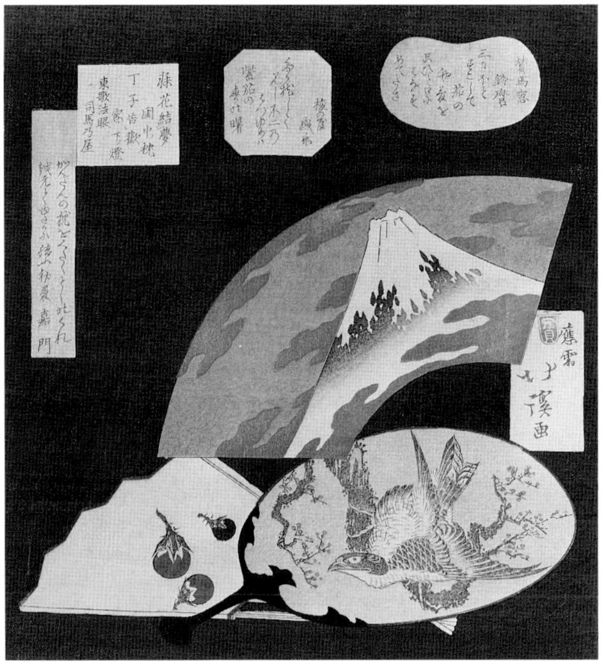

FIGURE 9

Hokkei: *Three Fan Paintings.* ca. 1820. (cat. no. 103)

FIGURE 10

After Hokkei: *Three Fan Paintings.* Facsimile version, late nineteenth century. Arthur M. Sackler Museum, Harvard University Art Museums. Gift of the friends of Arthur B. Duel. 1933.4.1858

Beginning in the last quarter of the nineteenth century, there was a burst of interest from the West in the luxuriously created square prints of the 1810s and 1820s, and these rare, lavish prints captured the eye of numerous European and American collectors of Japanese art. Since the supply could not equal the demand, reproductions, using completely new blocks, were already being produced in the late 1880s and continued to be issued in significant number into the twentieth century. Three albums of nearly five hundred surimono in the collection of the Metropolitan Museum of Art, assembled in 1889 by the well-known dealer Hayashi Tadamasa (1853–1906),[8] includes five facsimiles. Other collections made by less discerning collectors contain a higher proportion of facsimiles. Obviously, the extraordinary demand in the West for surimono was creating a shortage of fine-quality square surimono in Japan. Western demand was so great that, in the late nineteenth century, envelopes for sets of surimono facsimiles were sometimes printed in English!

The quality of the facsimiles varies, and some are much easier to distinguish from originals than others. In such a facsimile version (fig. 10) after an original design by Hokkei (fig. 9), the poetry text and background coloration are obviously different. A close comparison of the facsimile and the original, furthermore, reveals line variations throughout the entire design. However, if one does not have access to examples of both the original and the facsimile, it is necessary to carefully scrutinize several other aspects of the print. A first-hand knowledge of the pigments, paper, and printing techniques employed in the early nineteenth century is crucial, since the best facsimiles are of outstanding quality and difficult to distinguish from genuine surimono. The materials employed—the paper, metallic powders, and pigments—vary according to the time when the copy was issued. The connoisseur, through long experience, acquires a feeling for the coloration and textures of genuine surimono. In the case of the original prints, the paper is generally more pliant, the colors more subtle, the embossing less obvious, and the overall tonality more vibrant. Made on stiffer paper with slightly duller colors, even the best facsimiles tend to have an overall flatness of color and sharpness in execution. Although there is a common misconception that connoisseurship does not play a role in the study of Japanese prints, the complexities in authenticating surimono clearly demonstrate this is not the case.

PATTERNS IN THE HISTORY OF COLLECTING SURIMONO

Originally gifts or announcements, surimono were often saved by their Japanese recipients at the time they were issued. Many of the prints we know today survive because they were assembled and pasted into albums. The existence of several surimono albums in museum collections provides an insight into the manner and style of collecting surimono in Japan in the nineteenth century.

The tradition of collecting calligraphy fragments and pasting them into albums called *tekagami* (literally, "mirrors of the hand") enjoyed a long history in Japan, beginning in the fourteenth century. Assembled accordian-style, albums were artfully arranged and filled with letters, calligraphy, and felicitous poems on paper of various shapes and qualities, occasionally decorated. These collections were passed down as family heirlooms.[9] Because surimono were commissioned and acquired by devotees of Japanese poetry, mounting the prints into similarly constructed albums can be considered an offshoot of that tradition.

Three albums once owned by Théodore Duret, now in the collection of the Bibliothèque Nationale, have surimono mounted in roughly chronological order and decoratively arranged. The compiler of the albums was apparently on close terms with the leaders of the world of kyōka. One of the albums has a preface written by an Osaka *haikai* poet who repeatedly traveled to Edo, Ōtomo no Ōemaru (1722–1805); and the other two albums have prefaces by the well known poets Yomo Magao (1753–1829) and Asakusaan (Sensōan) Ichihito (1755–1821). Given the death dates of the authors of the inscriptions, these volumes must have been assembled soon after the prints were issued.[10] Furthermore Ōemaru's inscription states that the collector, while not a poet himself, was well acquainted with poetry circles of Edo; in the third album, there is a surimono issued in commemoration of the third anniversary of Ōemaru's death, which again indicates a chronological collecting pattern. Since impressions of many of the same surimono designs in these albums are also included in the Wright collection, the two groups are interesting to compare.

Other intact albums of surimono have surfaced. The three volumes assembled by Hayashi, now in the Metropolitan Museum of Art, were reconstituted from two others, as mentioned in his preface. Another album, owned by the Stanford Museum, contains surimono mostly dating to the years 1806 and 1810 and perhaps 1813, and appears to have been assembled during those years.[11] When examined carefully, many loose surimono show traces of glue around the edges on their reverse side, indicating that they were at one time mounted in albums. Undoubtedly, this accounts for the fact that, unlike most ukiyo-e prints, a relatively high proportion have survived in fine state: this pattern of collecting ensured that many surimono escaped repeated handling and the fading and toning caused by the harmful rays of the sun.

When Western collectors began to acquire ukiyo-e in large volume in the Meiji period (1868–1912), there seemed to be little interest in the genre in Japan. During this period, all types of Japanese prints were exported to the West in tremendous quantities. Eventually, the quality of prints reaching the West dwindled. By the early twentieth century, collectors, dealers, and auction houses began to lament the paucity of fine material coming out of Japan. As we shall see, Frank Lloyd Wright played a significant role in this outflow of Japanese prints to the West. In 1925, Arthur Davidson Ficke (1883–1945) wrote a self-serving introduction to the auction catalogue of his prints at Anderson Galleries in New York:

> It has become sufficiently clear to-day that we are quite at the end of that exciting period when superb prints were coming to light, monthly and sometimes weekly, from out [of] the century-old treasure houses of Japan. The supply is now exhausted, and no new discoveries of any importance can be hoped for.[12]

Slightly ahead of the Americans, the French connoisseurs of Japanese prints were already enthusiasts of the surimono genre by the 1880s. Louis Gonse, who in 1883 was the first to organize an exhibition of Japanese art in Paris, wrote in his insightful *L'Art Japonais* in the same year that surimono were among the most seductive marvels of Japanese art, which could astonish even the indifferent viewer. Edmond de Goncourt, one of the earliest proponents of Japanese art in Paris, in his diary entry for May 25, 1888, praises Yashima Gakutei, a pupil of Hokusai, as a master of surimono and likens the charm of his designs to that of Persian and European miniature paintings.[13] Perhaps the meticulous workmanship and attention to detail using luxurious materials in a small format make that comparison inevitable.

Others, such as the extremely influential Parisian dealer Siegfried Bing (1838–1905), actively promoted surimono. Most of the prominent collectors in Paris included significant numbers of surimono among their array of ukiyo-e.[14] By the time of the Paris sale of Hayashi prints at Hôtel Drouot in 1902, Bing, in his brief introduction to the auction catalogue, singled out surimono, describing them as precious objects representing the acme of printing, created with loving care and great imagination.[15] And of the over fifty prints described as "sourimono," fourteen are illustrated in the separate volume of plates, which illustrates only a small percentage of the sale. One of those pictured is in the Wright collection (cat. no. 11). While Wright did not attend any of these European sales, prints were brought to the United States by other collectors and dealers and could easily have passed into his hands.

One may use the prices paid for surimono during these years to ascertain the relative level of desirability among collectors. For example, in 1909, in an Hôtel Drouot auction in Paris, a Hokkei surimono fetched as much as eighty francs, while the average Hokusai landscape brought one hundred francs. At the Javal sale in 1926, the average price paid for surimono was about one hundred and fifty francs, with a particularly dramatic design of Kintoki and the Carp by Hokkei bringing three hundred and ten francs. At the same sale, landscapes of Mount Fuji by Hokusai were averaging two hundred francs.

In 1922, Charles Vignier, another important dealer and collector, wrote in the introduction to the first auction catalogue of the immense Charles Haviland collection of six thousand Japanese prints about the current dispersal of many of the great French collections. He bemoaned the loss of these treasures to the Americans, who were superseding the French in the acquisition of ukiyo-e in general. However, most of the surimono sold in the Parisian auctions during this period remained in Europe.

Despite the enthusiasm for surimono among French devotees, the English and the Americans were not universally enthralled by the genre. William Anderson, an English authority and collector felt surimono to be technically refined but trivial. In Edward Strange's *Japanese Colour Prints,* published in London in 1904 and widely known in America, the subject of surimono received its own chapter, and the author also singled out Gakutei as the equal to Hokusai. This assessment of surimono was endorsed by Arthur Davidson Ficke, a friend of Wright, in his *Chats on Japanese Prints.* His general view of surimono at this time (1915), was:

> the surimono is, in the opinion of many collectors, not as a rule very important as a work of art. In the ordinary surimono the medium employed has outstripped the motive expressed, and what should have been the means has become the sole end. Nevertheless they are unrivalled as specimens of workmanship and printing, and some of the best of them are highly treasured. Some of Hokusai's pupils excelled their master in this form.[16]

In the 1916 auction of the superb collection of prints belonging to Mrs. John Osgood Blanchard, there were nearly thirty prints identified as surimono. Frederick W. Gookin (1853–1936), perhaps the greatest American connoisseur of Japanese prints in his day, repeats this Ficke quotation in his short introduction to the lots of surimono. But he does go on to praise a shikishiban by Hokkei (probably the same image as cat. no. 122) as "undoubtedly one of the gems in the collection," a collection which he had earlier described as of "uniformly fine quality" and unequaled among collections sold publicly in America.

Prices fetched for surimono of fine quality and in excellent condition sold at auction in New York during the 1910s and 1920s also indicate that they were far from ignored. In the auction in 1921 of "duplicates" from the collection of the Spaulding brothers of Boston, a fine bird-and-flower *(kachoga)* surimono by Shumman was purchased for thirty dollars by Arthur B. Duel; at the same sale, a rare Kunimasa bust portrait was sold to the same buyer for thirty-two dollars and fifty cents.[17] Like their French counterparts, American collectors pursued fine-quality surimono, most especially the long-format prints by Hokusai and, to a lesser degree, the more intricate and sumptuous examples in the square format.

With the economic crisis of the 1930s, prices for Japanese prints dropped precipitously; private collections were sold off, and many prints entered into the holdings of American museums. It was not until the late 1960s, and then most dramatically with the sales beginning in 1974 in London of the collection of the Parisian jeweler Henri Vever (1854–1943), that the passion for Japanese prints was rekindled. Having been one of the primary and earliest exponents of Japanese art in Paris, Vever accumulated an exceptional collection.[18] Superb surimono, mostly in excellent condition, came onto the market in the 1970s and sold well. The same design by Hokkei of Kintoki and the Carp, sold in the 1926 Javal auction mentioned above, was sold for one thousand pounds, a price comparable to the average Hokusai landscape. It was not, however, until a few experts, most notably Matthi Forrer, Jack Hillier, and Roger Keyes, turned their attention in the late 1970s to this relatively neglected genre, that a scholarly interest in surimono was reawakened in the West. Since then, several major exhibitions have been held in the United States, Europe, and Japan, and a number of important catalogues devoted to the genre of surimono have been published.

FRANK LLOYD WRIGHT AND SURIMONO

Much has been written about where and when Frank Lloyd Wright may have been initially exposed to Japanese art. It is safe to say that as a young architect in Chicago from 1887 onward he could easily have been introduced to ukiyo-e by the local print fanciers. Perhaps like many others, he had been captivated by the Japanese Pavilion at the 1893 World's Columbian Exposition, held in Chicago.

Clarence Buckingham (1854–1913), whose world-famous collection of Japanese prints is now in the Art Institute of Chicago, began to collect the very next year after the exposition. Frederick W. Gookin (1853–1936), an extremely knowledgeable authority and perceptive collector, served as Buckingham's adviser. Initially a banker, Gookin was one of the first to begin collecting Japanese prints in America and, by about 1902, turned the connoisseurship of Japanese prints into a full-time occupation, as consultant and curator.[19] Gookin was to become Wright's close friend and trusted colleague on matters of print expertise. Buckingham, together with Gookin and several other enthusiasts, made Chicago into a center for the study of ukiyo-e. They held informal "print parties" and often invited visiting out-of-town collectors to participate.[20]

Such enthusiasm and serious interest must have encouraged Gookin and Wright to stage the first Japanese print show at the Art Institute of Chicago, in 1906. Devoted solely to the work of Hiroshige, this exhibition of over two hundred prints consisted of purchases made by Wright on his first trip to Japan, in the spring of 1905. Wright wrote the catalogue for this first-ever show of Hiroshige prints, thereby establishing himself as an authority. He later sold this collection to Buckingham, whose heirs bequeathed it to the Art Institute.

The success of the first show inspired a second, more ambitious exhibition at the Art Institute in 1908. It included loans primarily from the local collectors Gookin, Wright, Buckingham, and Dr. Clarence Webster.[21] This time Gookin coordinated the exhibition and penned the catalogue including the six hundred and forty-nine print entries. Displayed in six rooms designed by Wright, the prints were hung against gray walls on green cords, and simply framed in wood. Potted bonsai trees placed on specially constructed platforms gave the exhibition space a more relaxed and intimate ambience.

At least part of a room was designated exclusively for the display of surimono. All of the more than one dozen prints visible in the often-published photograph of this exhibition are surimono (fig. 1). In the foreground are the long surimono so admired by Wright and his contemporaries, while designs in both square and long formats are displayed in the room beyond. None of the prints visible in this picture is listed in the catalogue, which mentions only three surimono and until now had been thought to be complete.[22] In any case, the photograph demonstrates that at this early date Gookin and Wright, the show's organizers, had significant interest in surimono. In his introduction to the catalogue, Gookin was clearly referring to surimono when he commented:

> Literary men often saved such as were inscribed with odes of especial merit, or had recondite hidden meanings that appealed to them, and to their care we are indebted for the preservation of the majority of those that have survived in perfect or nearly perfect condition.[23]

Just where Wright obtained his immense collection of surimono is not completely clear but, like most of his other major acquisitions of ukiyo-e prints, were for the most part purchased in Japan. This conclusion is supported by the lack of archival references for purchases made elsewhere and the relatively small number of prints bearing the seals of other active dealers in the West such as Hayashi and Wakai. After his initial trip in 1905, Wright returned to Japan six times during the years 1913 through 1922; the last five visits were extended stays for the building of the Imperial Hotel. While he was in Japan in pursuit of the Imperial Hotel architectural commission in 1913, Wright was hired by William Spaulding(1865–1937) and John Spaulding (1870–1948) of Boston to acquire prints for them. Clearly pleased with Wright's purchases, the Spauldings increased their initial investment of twenty thousand dollars after only five months to one hundred and twenty-five thousand dollars, a remarkable sum for that time. Correspondence dating to 1913 between Wright and Shugio Hiromichi (1853–1927), who assisted him in locating prints for the Spauldings, reveals the satisfaction and pleasure with which these prints were greeted upon arriving in Boston.[24] Shugio, an Oxford-educated businessman working in the United States, was also an acknowledged connoisseur of ukiyo-e. He was a founding member of the Grolier Club in New York, where he organized an ukiyo-e exhibition in 1896. Shugio also belonged to the Caxton Club in Chicago, where he might well have made the acquaintance of Wright. After returning to Japan in 1900, Shugio was part of an official commission responsible for arranging loans of Japanese art for exhibitions abroad and was still engaged in such activities when Wright commissioned him to unearth buyable prints in private Japanese collections. At first he accomplished this task with great success, but as early as 1913, in a letter from Tokyo, he complained to Wright:

> Now it is impossible even for money to get such fine collections as you secured [the Spaulding prints]. I find nothing good enough for you now in Japan. All the print dealers say Mr. Wright has taken away all the first class old prints and I think they are nearly right.[25]

Several years later, Shugio appears to have negotiated the purchase of a collection of over eight hundred prints, priced at about twenty-seven thousand dollars, which are described in general in an annotated list by Wright on Imperial Hotel letterhead (dating to about 1920) in the Frank Lloyd Wright Archives.[26] This large group of prints included twenty-six unidentified surimono priced on average at fifteen dollars, and a Hokusai surimono which had cost the noteworthy sum of one hundred dollars. In the acquisition, the average price for a Hiroshige landscape design was about ten dollars and a view of Mount Fuji by Hokusai was one hundred dollars. Thus it appears that surimono were, by this time, far from overlooked or underpriced, even in Japan.

In an undated letter to Wright, probably from 1913, William Spaulding specifically mentions a surimono acquisition. Perhaps a few months later, in a letter to Wright dated February 1914, Spaulding states:

> I am convinced with you that the large, long, Surimono, especially of Hokusai, are to become more and more prized as time goes on—and I feel that we should make a special effort from now on to acquire all that can be obtained perfect in subject, colouring, and condition—perfect in Surimono means more in Surimono than in other prints.

Six weeks later he again corresponds with Wright, reiterating his commitment to "faultless" surimono, and admits that further acquisitions will require patience. He goes on to say:

> We are returning . . . all the Surimono you sent us over except two—$115. and $90.—you can thus see how horridly exacting we are becoming—besides your Japanese friends have placed on them prices in excess of what we personally would be willing or ask to stand for.

According to the card catalogue made by Gookin for the world-famous Spaulding collection of Japanese prints, now in the Boston Museum of Fine Arts, Wright sold the the brothers more than twenty surimono in 1913. When compared to the overall quality of their peerless collection of ukiyo-e, the surimono, including those purchased from other sources, are surprisingly weak. Many of the prints are in less-than-perfect condition, and most of the designs suffer in comparison to those in the Wright collection.

A few years later, in 1916, the Spaulding brothers loaned a group of twenty-six surimono as part of the inaugural exhibition of the Cleveland Museum of Art.[27] According to the correspondence in the museum's archives, William Spaulding was quite concerned about the deleterious effects of light on the "delicate tones" of surimono and requested drapery coverings for the windows. On the walls of the gallery were a set of twelve long landscape surimono by Hiroshige, each hung between a square-format example.[28] Of these fourteen square surimono by various artists, at least six were acquired from Wright in 1913. It is quite likely that this was the first exhibition devoted to the genre of surimono.[29]

Another prominent collector who sought out surimono was Sally Casey Thayer of Kansas City (1856 -1925). An avid student of Japanese prints, Thayer was most concerned with developing a study collection. Her purchasing was done primarily in the United States but also occasionally in Europe. She is known to have acquired many prints from Wright in 1908 and again in 1911.[30] On the whole, her collection of two hundred and sixty-eight surimono, like those owned by the Spauldings and later Edward Burr Van Vleck, is of lesser quality in terms of artistic importance and condition. And despite Mrs. Thayer's goal, her collection is not as comprehensive as that of Frank Lloyd Wright.[31] It does, however, reflect the general quality of surimono available in America at that time.

Wright also used his stock of ukiyo-e, acquired on numerous trips to Japan, as collateral for loans to bail himself out of financial difficulties on several occasions. It was in this manner that surimono once owned by Wright passed into the collection of Edward Burr Van Vleck (1863–1943), a mathematics professor at the University of Wisconsin. In 1928, Wright was hard pressed to avoid bankruptcy as a result of two fires at Taliesin (his home in Spring Green, Wisconsin) and his divorce. The Bank of Wisconsin temporarily took possession of Taliesin. It also seized a group of four thousand prints from Wright and sold them to Van Vleck for the paltry sum of four thousand dollars. As an active ukiyo-e collector, Van Vleck participated in print parties held by fellow mid-westerners Buckingham and Mary Ainsworth of Moline, Illinois. Fortunately, he kept meticulous records of his acquisitions and even of those that he later sold. His records reveal that thirty-five surimono which remained in the collection, now owned by the Elvehjem Museum of Art at the University of Wisconsin-Madison, were acquired in this transaction.[32] Interestingly, like the Spaulding surimono, these are not of the finest condition; nor are they the most beautifully composed. On the bill of sale drafted by the Bank of Wisconsin are notes in Wright's hand stating that the original group included two hundred and fifty surimono. But it is probable, like the contents of the Wright wooden box, that this number included many small Hiroshige landscapes or surimono-style designs, which remain richly represented in the Van Vleck collection; other prints were sold off by Van Vleck, so he more than recouped his initial investment.

But no matter how dire his financial situation, or how important his client, Wright managed to save the best surimono for himself. Always conscious of preserving the prints, unlike other contemporary collectors, dealers, and institutions, he did not place an indelible collector's seal on any of them. Instead, he delicately marked many of the surimono as part of his collection with his initials in lightly drawn pencil on their reverse side.

Wright seems to have ceased his serious print dealing by the mid-1920s. No doubt this was due in part to the scandals resulting from some altered (revamped) prints which he unwittingly purchased in Japan and sold to the Metropolitan Museum of Art.[33] He never returned to Japan after 1922, although he continued to make occasional print purchases in America and Europe. Thereafter, he used Japanese prints primarily for teaching purposes, especially in the informal talks which he gave to his apprentice architects. During one of his talks in 1952 he commented on the subtle beauty of Japanese prints:

> All eloquent, however, in their own peculiar fashion as graven lines should be on sensitive paper which has received the color from various tinted blocks and wherein this process is not only frankly confessed but the confession itself becoming a delightful, poetic circumstance.[34]

Other prints were used to decorate Taliesin. Many were given away as gifts to associates and friends.[35]

After his death in 1959, nearly all of the over five thousand Japanese prints left in his inventory were offered for sale to pay off taxes.[36] Somehow the unmarked wooden box containing this treasure trove of surimono escaped the attention of the creditors and appraisers. In fact, in the appraisals made of the remaining Japanese art in 1961 and again in 1970, no surimono are listed.

Where then, did this surimono collection come from, and why has it remained intact? Like most of his Japanese art, the majority must have come from his vast purchases made during his 1905 trip to Japan and in the course of his numerous lengthy stays there from 1913 through 1922. In a talk given to the Taliesin Fellowship on September 20, 1950, speaking on surimono, Wright stated, "I usually had first call on any prints in Tokyo—because I spent so much money on them, hundreds of thousands of dollars for myself and my friends." Through the years, Wright occasionally acquired prints elsewhere. In a document written by Wright in February of 1925, he listed eighty prints received from an unidentified source, probably Western.[37] On ledger paper, he named most of the artists (sixty-three were by Hiroshige), the series if known, and the price of each print. There are fourteen separately listed surimono, but none is clearly identified. Additional print purchases were made in the late 1930s in Paris, and later in New York; none of the extant correspondence, however, mentions surimono. Wright also acquired prints through trades and purchases from clients and institutions. The sheer size of this collection of over five hundred and fifty surimono argues, however, for a long-term interest, and given the exceptionally high quality of many of these prints, it is likely that the best were acquired early on in Japan.

The relative strengths and weaknesses of the collection support this conclusion. In the 1927 Anderson Gallery auction of ukiyo-e from his "collection," which he was obliged to sell by order of the Bank of Wisconsin, Wright included only five surimono, all of them in the long format. In describing one by Hokusai, he wrote:

> At this period [ca. 1802] the type of female figure as in this print, unsurpassed in grace and delicacy, was brought into being by Hokusai. The figures in this respect have never been excelled by any other artist of the ukiyo-e school.[38]

Wright is known to have sold long surimono to Buckingham, the Spauldings, and Van Vleck, among others. This is the only surimono format included in the Anderson auction and also at the McFettridge sale of Frank Lloyd Wright prints in

1969 at Parke-Bernet Galleries.[39] Long nagaban surimono were clearly sought after by print collectors in this country. It is interesting to note that in Wright's own collection there are only seven long surimono by Hokusai, which are either examples of late editions or in poor condition (see cat. nos. 178 and 186). However, there are scores of smaller koban prints in which Hokusai captured the same sense of feminine beauty, and which his followers imitated with varying degrees of success. Wright was one of the few collectors of his time to appreciate the merits of these small surimono. Indeed, one of the great strengths of this collection is the vast number of koban surimono from this early period (1797–1806). There are nearly seventy examples by Hokusai alone; that number exceeds one hundred and fifty if his pupils are included. Not all in fine condition, many of these rare koban prints are in fair to poor state. Yet, in a way, they exemplify a statement made by Wright in a September 1952 print-party talk:

> Now as you see the prints today, it must be confessed that time has imbued the color with an added charm. The old vegetable dyes saturating and qualified by the soft texture of the wonderful paper all soften and change with sunlight of the moist climate . . . and the tenderness of tone found in fine prints is indescribable. . . .

In the case of his square-format surimono, quite the opposite is true. Most are in fine condition, far exceeding those in the Spaulding and Van Vleck collections. The pigments are strong and the prints are remarkably balanced in artists represented, subject matter, and historic development. The collection includes fine examples by nearly every prominent designer who worked in the surimono genre.

As mentioned above, the collection is richly endowed in works by Hokusai and his followers. Shumman, considered by Wright to be the greatest surimono designer, is represented by numerous examples, spanning his career as both artist and publisher of these special prints.[40] The collection's greatest weakness is the paucity of Utagawa-school prints, notably the absence of surimono by Kunisada and Kuniyoshi. Although Wright actively admired and pursued Kabuki-actor portraits by the late-eighteenth-century Katsukawa-school designers, the bright, bold colors and exaggerated features exemplified in the Kabuki surimono of the Utagawa school active in the late 1820s and 1830s may not have been to his taste. In fact, ukiyo-e prints issued after that time, other than landscapes, have not been widely appreciated in the West until recently. As a whole, though, the collection is extremely well balanced, with many examples of rare egoyomi, early Hokusai works, and a superb group of shikishi by Gakutei and Hokkei. In addition, the seventy surimono by Shinsai probably constitute the largest and finest collection of surimono by this artist. In testament to Wright's fine eye, unlike many other collections formulated at that time, there are only twelve facsimiles among the five hundred and sixty-one surimono.

One may speculate whether Wright actually assembled this vast array of surimono as his personal collection. Several factors indicate that he did, probably early on, in the course of his visits to Japan. The condition of the prints varies tremendously, even within the same series by the same artist. Several of the surimono series are nearly complete, missing only one or two impressions, and clearly originating from different sources. Many display glue residue on their backs from previous album mounts. But even within a series, there appears to be no consistency in this regard. This, too, lends credence to the conclusion that these prints were acquired from numerous sources. The strongest argument for Wright as the actual collector is still that the quality of this collection stands well above the surimono, particularly those in the square format, that Wright sold to others. In the auctions containing Wright prints, only long surimono were included, even though square-format designs would have brought significant prices. Finally, his lightly penciled initials on the back of many of the best prints seems to imply ownership and therefore an intention to collect, especially given that prints sold by him do not bear this identification.

With his keen eye for quality and genius for design, Wright obviously found the genre of surimono highly appealing. He was a man with expensive tastes who often lived beyond his means, and his extravagant style of life often forced him to use Japanese prints as collateral for loans. In fact, he repeatedly claimed that Japanese prints "practically built Taliesin II and III." Given his periodic economic travails and the fact that surimono commanded significant prices at auctions in America and Europe, it must have been difficult to keep this collection intact. Furthermore, although he continued to sell fine-quality long surimono to collectors throughout this country, the square-format prints which passed through his hands were, surprisingly, of only moderate quality. The inevitable inference is that, while acting as a print dealer Wright was simultaneously acting as a sophisticated surimono collector, saving the best koban and shikishiban impressions for himself. In any event, Frank Lloyd Wright's rich and magnificent collection of surimono represents a legacy, hitherto unknown, of rare and delicate beauty.

NOTES

1 For a historical overview of the period during which surimono began to flourish, see Henry D. Smith II, "The Floating World in its Edo Locale 1750–1850," in *The Floating World Revisited,* ed. Donald Jenkins (Portland, Oregon: Portland Art Museum, 1993).

2 In *Kyōjitsu Baka Monogatari* (True Stories of a Fool) as cited by Matthi Forrer, *Egoyomi and Surimono* (Uithoorn, The Netherlands: J.C. Gieben, 1979), 5.

3 For a discussion of surimono formats and their subdivisions according to how they were grouped and printed on large sheets, see Asano Shūgō, *"Dure Kyūzō Surimono-chō no Gaiyō to sono Igi"* (The surimono albums from the Duret Collection and their significance) in *Hizō Ukiyo-e Taikan* (Ukiyo-e masterpieces in European collections), Bibliothèque Nationale (Tokyo: Kodansha, 1990), 300–303.

4 Matthi Forrer and Roger Keyes, "Very Like a Whale?—Hokusai's Illustrations for the Genroku Poem Shells," in *A Sheaf of Japanese Papers* (The Hague: Society for Japanese Arts and Crafts, 1979), 37.

5 Shumman's career as an artist is discussed in Tanaka Tatsuya, *"Shumman no Kenkyū"* (A study of Shumman), 3 parts, *Ukiyo-e Geijutsu,* nos. 107–9 (1993).

6 Roger Keyes, *The Art of Surimono: Privately Published Japanese Woodblock Prints and Books in the Chester Beatty Library, Dublin* (London: Philip Wilson Publishers Ltd., 1985), 20–21.

7 See Matthi Forrer, "The Effects of the Tenpō Crisis upon the Publication of Illustrated Books by Hokusai and his School," *Andon,* no.8, 1982, 31–37.

8 Joan B. Mirviss, "Jewels of *Ukiyo-e:* Hayashi's *Spring Rain Collection* of *Surimono* Albums," *Orientations* 20 (February 1989), 28–29.

9 Miyeko Murase, *Jewel Rivers: Japanese Art from The Burke Collection* (Richmond, Virginia: The Virginia Museum of Fine Arts, 1994), 33.

10 For a thorough discussion of these albums see Eiko Kondō, "Three Volumes of Unpublished Surimono Albums in the Bibliothèque Nationale of Paris (Parts 1–3)," *Ukiyo-e Geijutsu* 80–82, 1984, 28–30, 3–20, 1–23 (in Japanese but a summary in English appears after the final article, 38–39); and Asano Shūgō, *op. cit.,* 300–334.

11 See Roger Keyes, "The Van Reed *Surimono* Album," *The Stanford Museum,* 3 (1974): 3–12.

12 *The Japanese Print Collection of Arthur Davison Ficke,* no. 1915 (New York: Anderson Galleries, January 29–30, 1925).

13 See Siegfried Wichmann, *Japonisme: The Japanese Influence on Western Art in the 19th and 20th Centuries* (New York: Harmony Books, 1981), 12. It is interesting to note that one of the great collectors of Japanese prints, Henri Vever, was also a collector of Persian miniatures.

14 For a discussion of this history see Giovanni Peternolli, *"La Place des surimono dans les premières collections françaises"* in *Les objets tranquilles: Natures mortes japonaises XVIIIe-XIXe Sièles* (Paris: Galerie Janette Ostier, 1978).

15 Collection Hayashi: Dessins, Estampes, Livres illustrés (Paris: Hōtel Drouot, 1902).

16 Arthur Davidson Ficke, *Chats on Japanese Prints* (Rutland, Vermont: Charles E. Tuttle Co., 1958), 373.

17 Today, the Kunimasa portrait would sell for several times more than the Shumman. Arthur B. Duel, a prominent American collector of Japanese prints, owned a superb group of surimono (none of which came directly from Wright as they took an instant dislike to each other), which are now in the collection of the Arthur M. Sackler Museum at the Harvard University Art Museums. See William Green, "Arthur B. Duel (1870–1936), an American Collector of Japanese Prints," *Andon,* no 13 (Spring 1984), 1–10.

18 Vever sold a large group of prints to Matsukata Kōjirō in the 1920s, which became the foundation to the collection of the Tokyo National Museum. It is said that he retained many of the best prints and thereafter added to his collection with purchases made from the important French sales of the 1920s.

19 Julia Meech-Pekarik, "Frank Lloyd Wright's Other Passion," in *The Nature of Frank Lloyd Wright,* Carol R. Bolon, Robert S. Nelson, and Linda Seidel, eds. (Chicago and London: Chicago University Press, 1988), 130 ff. Gookin was also responsible for introducing Wright to Hayashi Aisaku, the future manager of the Imperial Hotel and the supervisor of the building project. Also see Kevin Nute, *Frank Lloyd Wright and Japan* (New York: Van Nostrand Reinhold, 1993), 150–63.

20 Margaret Gentles, "Clarence Buckingham: Collector of Japanese Prints," *Apollo* 84:55 (September 1966), 208–15.

21 For more on this subject see William Green, "A Peerless Pair: Frederick W. Gookin and Frank Lloyd Wright and the Art Institute of Chicago's 1908 exhibition of Japanese prints," *Andon,* no. 14 (Summer 1984), 14–19.

22 The label attached to the back of the copy of this photograph loaned to the author for this publication misidentified the subject as prints by Hiroshige.

23 Frederick W. Gookin, *Catalogue of a Loan Exhibition of Japanese Colour Prints* (Chicago: Art Institute of Chicago, 1908), 20.

24 All of the Spaulding correspondence cited here is in the Frank Lloyd Wright Archives in Scottsdale, Arizona.

25 From the Frank Lloyd Wright Archives where several other letters between Shugio and Wright may also be found.

26 It is of interest to note that the two most outstanding prints in this purchase, by Moronobu and Kaigetsudō, each priced at fifteen hundred dollars (an incredible price at the time), were divided between the two, Wright taking the Moronobu and Shugio the Kaigetsudō. Kobayashi Bunshichi (1861–1923) , who was referred to repeatedly as "K" in this document, appears to have acted as broker in the purchase of this collection. An active dealer in Japan and an important source for Hayashi Tadamasa of Paris, Kobayashi, together with Fenollosa, was also responsible for the first ukiyo-e exhibition in Tokyo in 1898.

27 "Gallery XI—The W.S. and J.T. Spaulding Collection of Surimono," *Catalogue of the Inaugural Exhibition* (Cleveland, Ohio: Cleveland Museum of Art, 1916), 143–45.

28 It is possible that these long surimono were the ones Wright acquired from Katherine Ball, a collector living in California. In correspondence in the Frank Lloyd Wright Archives, Gookin congratulated Wright on his success in obtaining these treasures so reasonably. These Spaulding prints are now in the collection of the Museum of Fine Arts, Boston.

29 Beside the prints, five additional Japanese works of art are listed in the article on the exhibition but mention is not made of them in the title or text of the catalogue, and they do not appear in photograph of the exhibition.

30 Meech-Pekarik, "Frank Lloyd Wright's Other Passion," op. cit., 135.

31 The Thayer surimono collection is published in: Roger Keyes, *Surimono: Privately Published Japanese Prints in the Spencer Museum of Art* (New York: Kodansha, 1984). As yet, it has not been determined which surimono, if any, were purchased from Wright.

32 The Van Vleck Collection is illustrated in *The Edward Burr Van Vleck Collection of Japanese Prints* (University of Wisconsin-Madison: Elvehjem Museum of Art, 1990).

33 For more on this issue see Julia Meech-Pekarik, "Frank Lloyd Wright and Japanese Prints," *The Metropolitan Museum of Art Bulletin,* 40:2 (Fall 1982), 48–57.

34 Taken from a transcribed copy in the Frank Lloyd Wright Archives of a recorded talk given to the Taliesin Fellowship on September 24, 1952.

35 See the introductory essay by Bruce Brooks Pfeiffer.

36 Interview with Bruce Brooks Pfeiffer, December 12, 1993.

37 In the collection of the Frank Lloyd Wright Archives.

38 *The Frank Lloyd Wright Collection of Japanese Antique Prints* (New York: Anderson Galleries, January 6–7, 1927) .

39 This auction of four hundred and thirty-three prints included six long surimono by Hokusai. This group of prints had been the property of Wright but had been given to William McFettridge as agent prior to 1927.

40 Wright discussed Shumman during a talk to the Taliesin Fellowship on September 20, 1950.

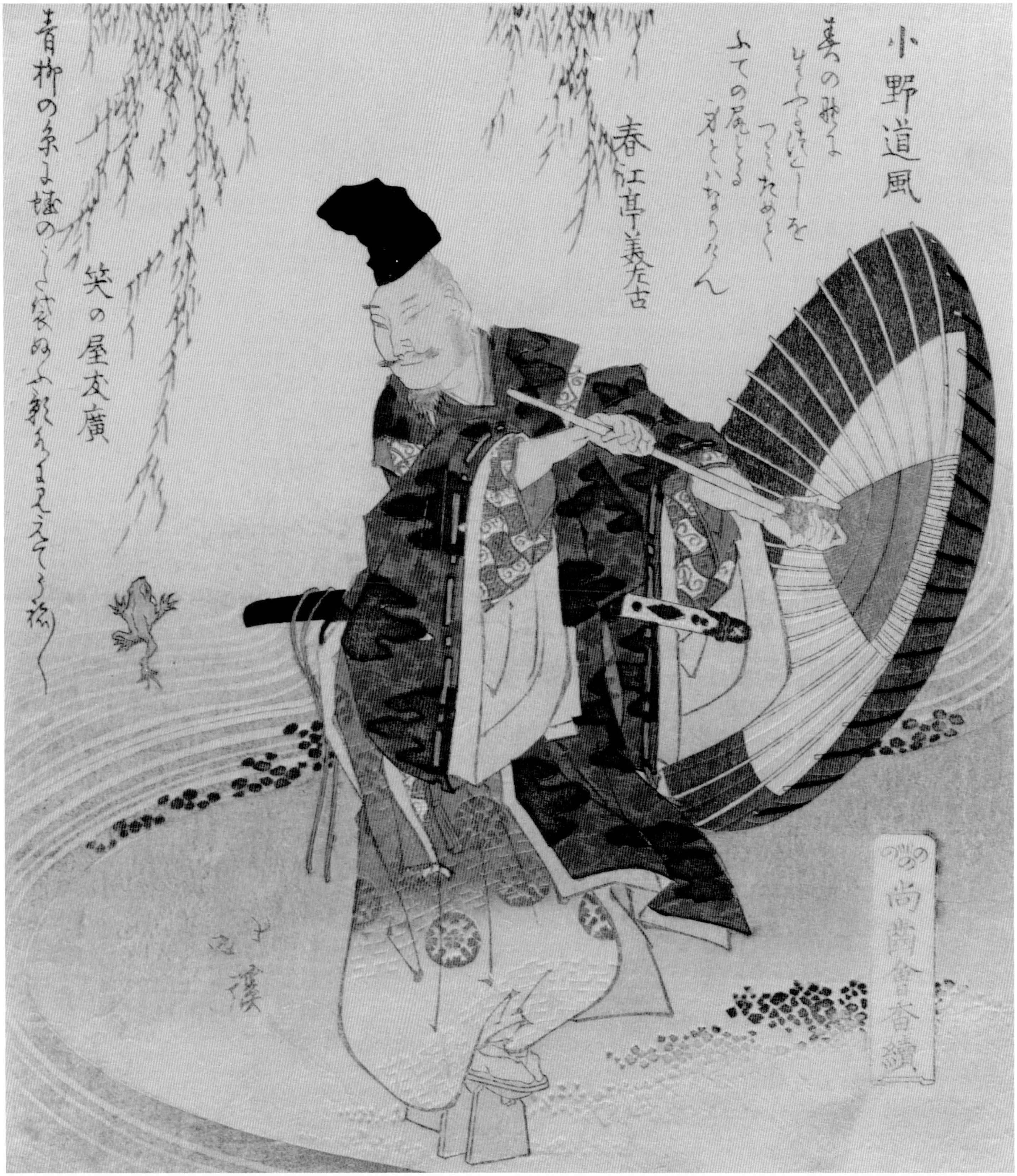

FIGURE 1

Hokkei:
Ono no Tōfū.
ca. 1820.
(cat. no. 101)

WAYS OF READING SURIMONO:

POETRY-PRINTS TO CELEBRATE THE NEW YEAR

JOHN T. CARPENTER

While most *surimono*—privately published Japanese woodblock prints of the late eighteenth and early nineteenth centuries—were printed with one or more of the thirty-one syllable humorous poems called *kyōka,* it was their delightful images and exquisite printing techniques that first caught the eye of Western collectors such as Frank Lloyd Wright, who could not read their playful texts. Likewise, the primary appeal of surimono for modern collectors, both Western and Japanese, lies in their images, which can be enjoyed without an understanding of the literary context that gave them birth.

Nevertheless, an appreciation of poems on surimono can in some cases actually alter or deepen one's perception of the artist's design. Conversely, the reading of the poems is likely to be affected by the accompanying images. Sometimes the artist adds a level of visual punning that gives an unexpected twist to the poem. Even when the verses are conventional New Year greetings or jocular word-puzzles with no direct relationship to the image, the process of reading inscriptions allows one to pause over a print, to hold it longer in the hand or in the eye. For such is the allure of surimono: out of all proportion to their diminutive size and occasional nature, they contain a bounty of subtle meanings and pleasures that are best savored at a leisurely pace or, more ideally, by repeated tastings.

Not all surimono have poems. During the eighteenth century, the term "surimono," which literally means "printed things," was commonly applied to a wide array of privately distributed single-sheet prints, including not only publications of individual poets or poetry clubs but also announcements of musical and stage performances. Nor did the term imply that the prints must have pictures, but unillustrated surimono were rarely saved and have earned little interest from students or collectors. By the early nineteenth century, "surimono" acquired the broader connotation of privately published prints, which is the sense with which the term is used today. According to this broader definition, the genre includes egoyomi (picture calendars), which originally were not considered surimono because they usually lacked texts.[1]

Even without understanding what they wrote, Wright could—as viewers can today—vicariously share the pleasures of the literati who once exchanged these surimono and took delight in their cleverly composed and meticulously printed designs. This essay, however, will focus on that aspect of surimono modern aficionados usually ignore—the texts. After an introduction to the rhetorical devices employed in kyōka and a brief history of kyōka groups, I shall examine a number of poetry-prints from the collection to demonstrate how surimono may be read as a hybrid genre combining art and literature.

POETICAL DEVICES OF KYŌKA

Kyōka are composed in five lines of 5-7-5-7-7 syllables, reflecting the prosody of traditional Japanese court verse, *waka*. While the literal translation of kyōka as "mad poems" might lead one to expect zany or iconoclastic utterances, most are relatively sober, only distinguished from orthodox waka by their disregard of convention in diction and subject matter. What humor they have usually derives from wordplay or the parody of famous verses.

The roots of kyōka can be traced back to the earliest anthologies of Japanese poetry. Examples can be found in humorous poems in the *Man'yōshū* (Collection of Ten Thousand Leaves; ca. 759) and in Book Nineteen of the *Kokinshū* (Collection of Ancient and Modern Poems; ca. 905) in the section titled "Eccentric Poems" (*haikai ka* or *haikai uta*—not to be confused with seventeen-syllable haikai). There remains debate, however, whether these poems earned the designation of "eccentric" because of their unorthodox topics, violation of accepted diction, or merely because they lacked some elusive quality of courtly elegance.[2] The term *odoke uta* (also pronounced *zare uta*), used through premodern times as a synonym for kyōka, literally means "playful poems," which is perhaps the most apt definition of this verse form. The first anthologies devoted exclusively to the genre date to the fourteenth century, by which time the term "kyōka" had become the accepted designation. It could be argued that the kyōka revival of the late eighteenth century, which had a decidedly anti-traditional stance, owed little direct inspiration to ancient and medieval "eccentric poems," but as the genre grew in popularity its exponents looked to these precedents as a source of artistic legitimacy.

Kyōka are reliant on verbal punning techniques that a poet of one of the orthodox schools of waka might have used, but not with such abandon. Perhaps the most common punning technique is the *kakekotoba* (pivot word), a word having one meaning when it is read with the words that precede it and another when read with the words that follow. Homonyms, with which the Japanese language is abundantly blessed, were also used with great relish. Another traditional device found in kyōka, *engo* (association words) are words linked by meaning, sound, or poetic convention. For example, a poem celebrating the New Year attached to a simple but delightful design of tangerines by Hakuga (cat. no. 12) includes association words linked with spring such as *nodokeki,* "tranquil," and *naga no hi,* "long days." Another common poetic device known as *makurakotoba* (pillow words) are stock epithets, often devoid of meaning. For instance, the phrase *murasaki no,* "purple," is often linked with the mention of place names such as Edo (modern Tokyo) because it has the connotation of "majestic" or "highly regarded"; *murasaki no* may also precede *kasumi,* "spring mists," because purple is the conventional color of mist in Japanese poetry. *Senkin no,* "thousand-goldpiece," another overworked pillow word in New Year's kyōka, is invariably followed by the word *haru,* "spring," and derives from a famous stanza by the Chinese poet Su Shi (1037–1101) that laments the ephemerality of a precious ("thousand-goldpiece") spring evening.

To demonstrate more concretely how some of these techniques might operate in a kyōka inscribed on a surimono, let us examine here a typical New Year's poem found on a design by Hokkei, titled *Narumi Shibori,* which belongs to the series "Famous Products of Various Provinces" (fig. 2).[3] Narumi *shibori,* also known as Arimatsu shibori, is a type of tie-dyed cloth made in Narumi, a town on the outskirts of Nagoya and one of the stations of the old Tōkaidō Highway. The image at first glance seems to consist merely of samples of cloth—some already dyed, others awaiting the dyeing process—but the poem by Keijuen invites us to take a closer look at the image:

kesa haru ni
narumi shibori ya
tsuchinoe no
tora mo moyō ni
asobu nodokesa

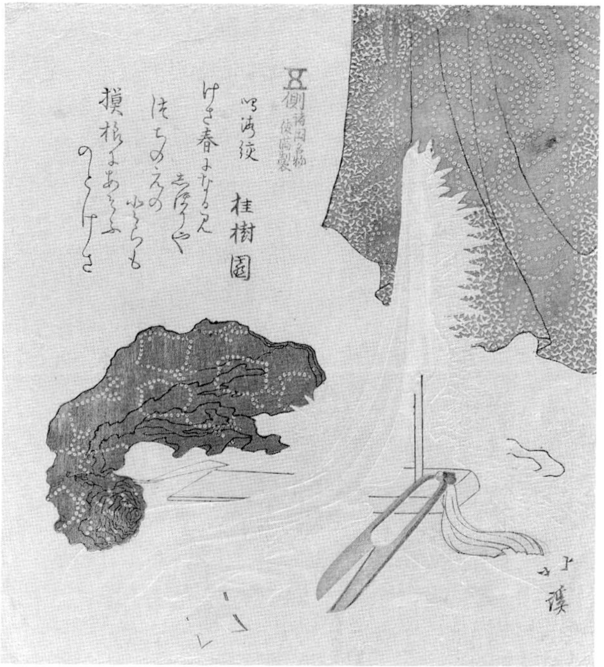

FIGURE 2

Hokkei: *Tie-dyed Fabric from Narumi,* from *Famous Products of Various Provinces for the Go Poetry Group, produced by Shumman (Go-gawa Shokoku Meibutsu, Shumman sei: Narumi Shibori).* 1818, Year of the Tiger. (cat. no. 97)

Because of its wordplay, a literal translation of the poem is impossible, but an attempt at reproducing the effects of pivot words in English results in something like the following:

This morning,
spring arrives i
n
arumi,
where cloth is tie-dyed,
while there is a calmness
in this year of
the tiger
plays in the fabric design.

Association words linked to spring—*nodokesa,* "calmness," and *asobu,* "to play"—contribute a felicitous tone. The place name Narumi serves as a pivot word: *kesa haru ni naru* means "this morning, spring arrives," while the verb *naru* also forms part of the phrase *Narumi shibori,* the theme of the print. Similarly, *tora,* "the tiger," must be read twice. The use of the rather unpoetic phrase *tsuchinoe no tora* (senior-earth tiger), a reference to the cyclical year, allows us to date the print precisely to 1818, but its actual function might be taken as the equivalent of writing "Happy 1818" on a New Year card. The rereading of *tora,* "tiger," with the last line of the poem suggests that there is a tiger playing in fabric designs (*moyō*). Reexamining the image, we can indeed discover the outline of a tiger and bamboo hidden in the patterns on the shibori fabric in the background. Another dimension of visual punning—of a somewhat recondite literary variety—can be discovered if we recall that the place name Narumi is traditionally associated in the Japanese poetic tradition with plovers (*chidori*), which, not coincidentally, are the design motif found on the crumpled panel of red cloth in the foreground.[4] The artist and poet obviously discussed the composition in advance to make image and text work together in a witty fashion.

Another trope commonly used in both waka and kyōka is known as *honkadori* (allusive variation) and refers to the practice of borrowing entire lines or distinctive phrases or words from a well-known classical poem and reweaving them into a new composition. The most common sources of inspiration were the *Kokinshū* (Collection of Ancient and Modern Poems; ca. 905) and the *Hyakunin Isshu* (One Hundred Poets: One Poem Each; thirteenth century). When allusive variation is employed in kyōka, the new poem may be a humorous rendition of the original, or it may simply borrow the mood or associations of an ancient verse. The technique of allusive variation was a hallmark of kyōka of the 1770s and 1780s, but numerous examples can be found in kyōka anthologies and surimono of the early nineteenth century as well.

An example of allusive variation can be found in one of the poems on an image by Gakutei, which was commissioned by members of a poetry circle headed by Shinratei Manzō (fig. 3). The poem on the right, by Natane Shimezuki, reads:

honobono to	Dimly, dimly,
yowa mo Akashi no	night gives way to dawn
uraraka ni	over Akashi Bay
Hitomaro me ni zo	as Hitomaro's eyes mist over
kasumu haru kana	so serenely in the spring.

This is a parody of a famous poem, attributed to the late-seventh-century court poet Kakinomoto no Hitomaro, who was considered through pre-modern times the patron saint of Japanese poetry.[5] The original poem reads:

honobono to	Dimly, dimly,
Akashi no ura no	through the dawn mist
asagiri no	over Akashi Bay—
shima kakure-yuku	my thoughts trail the boat
fune o shi zo omou	fading into the isle's shadow.

As one can see, the kyōka version plays on several phrases from the original, not to mention the name of Hitomaro himself. Both versions use the pillow word *honobono to* (dimly, dimly), and the place name Akashi (which can also mean "has dawned"). *Ura,* which usually means "bay," in the kyōka version becomes a pivot word forming *uraraka ni* (serenely), an association word for spring. The word *kasumu* suggests that the eyesight of the venerable poet is "misting over," while in the context of a spring poem suggests the image of "covered with mist."

In contrast to many of the most beloved waka of the classical canon, which used natural images to express deep feeling, kyōka for surimono rarely convey personal emotions. They voice collectively shared sentiments. Often they are simply New Year's greetings to fellow poets. More complex verses had a display of wit that challenged or flattered the recipient's literary knowledge, as seen in the examples just cited.

Despite their inherent resistance to translation, kyōka can be absorbing for anyone who has an interest in Japanese literature, especially in verse forms such as waka and haikai. The study of surimono as an introduction to the art of kyōka has, however, a limited scope. First, kyōka on surimono are almost without exception

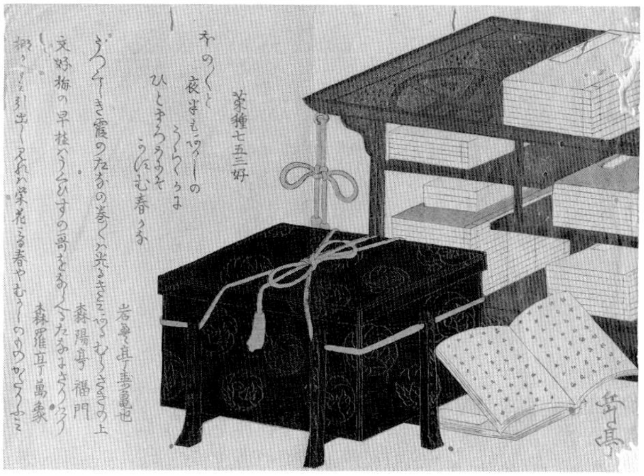

FIGURE 3

Gakutei: *Bookcase, Books, and Document Chest.* ca. 1817. (cat. no. 65)

optimistic and upbeat, which is not true of the genre of kyōka as a whole. Indeed, after encountering a string of blissful poems, one sometimes perversely wishes for a spring dawn that is not calm and peaceful, a plum blossom with a worm, or a warbler that misses a beat or two of its mellifluous song. Another limitation of poems on surimono is a result of their use as greetings for the New Year, which according to the lunar calendar began on the first day of spring. Consequently, poems deal almost exclusively with New Year or spring themes. One might get the impression that Japan is a country of one season—spring; that it has one flower—the plum; and but one bird—the warbler. Yet the same poets who sponsored these deluxe prints to celebrate the New Year also composed playful poems for anthologies on a wide array of themes, including the progression of the seasons, annual events and festivals, travel to famous sites (each seen at the appropriate time of year), the etiquette of love in the pleasure quarters, and day-to-day experiences.

POETS AND POETRY CIRCLES

Kyōka was more than just another literary genre: its popularity engendered a salon culture that involved many of the most prominent writers, artists, and actors of the day. Following the revival of kyōka among wealthy merchants in the Osaka area during the early eighteenth century, a more iconoclastic variety started to flourish in Edo, beginning in the early 1770s, when samurai intellectuals and higher-class *chōnin* ("townspeople"), some still in their early twenties, began hosting parties where kyōka were improvised as parodies of orthodox *waka*. Class distinctions were of little consequence during the early stages of the movement and members of both classes attended the same poetry gatherings.[6]

The Edo kyōka movement reached its peak during the Temmei period (1781–88) under the sponsorship of a group of poetry friends including Karagoromo Kisshū (1749–89), an advocate of traditional kyōka, and Ōta Nampo (1749–1823; who went by the poetry name Yomo no Akara or, later, Shokusanjin), a minor official for the shogunate who sought to invigorate the genre by promoting a humorous, often satirical, approach to classical poetic precedents. Nampo demonstrated his preeminent role in the movement by editing the influential *Manzai Kyōkashū* (Kyōka Anthology of a Thousand Generations; 1783) which, as the title implies, contained not only new poems but ones culled from earlier collections.

Akera Kankō (1740–99), another minor samurai official who joined this circle in the early 1770s, also wrote in a more satiric vein than the conservative Kisshū.

As kyōka soared in popularity among well-educated townspeople, poetry gatherings evolved into more formalized social functions, taking inspiration from the practice of *uta-awase* (poetry contests) that had flourished in the Heian court of a millennium before. Kyōka poets competed and were actually judged, in contrast to *renga* (linked-verse) parties, where cooperation was considered a virtue. Talented poets were appointed judges (*hanja*), and anthologies often indicated which poems were deemed best.

Poems composed during these gatherings were often on set topics (*dai*), and poets competed with each other to come up with the most clever thirty-one-syllable composition. On other occasions, poems were written on themes suggested by sketches or paintings—the reverse of the normal process of producing surimono, in which the poem came first. The movement peaked in the late 1780s, as the emphasis on improvised verses gave way to more carefully wrought verses fit for preservation in anthologies.

By the turn of the century, many of the original leaders of Temmei-era kyōka circles, especially those of the samurai class, bowed out in the wake of the intellectual and artistic repression of the 1790s. During this transitional period, many new kyōka masters came to the fore and formed their own poetry clubs known as *gawa* (groups) or *ren* (circles). These two terms were often used interchangeably during the early stages of the kyōka movement, but as a rule the former was made up of a number of the latter.

In early 1799 Akera Kankō passed away, leaving his wife, Fushimatsu no Kaka (1745–1810), and a handful of other students to lead his followers known as the No-gawa, which soon split into a number of smaller circles. Asakusaan (Sensōan) Ichihito (1755–1821), the head of the Asakusa-gawa, also known as the Tsubo-gawa, played a central role in establishing a network of kyōka circles throughout the various districts of Edo in the late 1790s and early 1800s. Yomo no Utagaki Magao (1753–1829) had taken over the prow of the Yomo-gawa (Four Directions Group) after its founder, Nampo, backed away from center stage of the kyōka movement in the late 1780s. Through the efforts of teachers like Magao, who believed that even an amateur could create acceptable verses if certain rules of traditional waka were respected, interest in kyōka quickly grew in urban centers and eventually in the provinces. The popularity of the Yomo-gawa raised accusations that the quality of kyōka was being compromised and its humor bowdlerized. To counteract the tendency toward the platitudinous, the scholar and popular writer Ishikawa Masamochi

(Yadoya no Meshimori; 1753–1830), better known by his kyōka name Rokujuen, founded the Go-gawa as a rival poetry group, by which he hoped to revive the more witty, satiric tone of Temmei kyōka.

Magao and Rokujuen gradually established themselves as the primary leaders of the kyōka movement in Edo through the period when surimono of high quality were being produced in abundance. Although Rokujuen himself rarely contributed verses to surimono (the one illustrated in fig. 5 is an exception), he remained active in compiling kyōka anthologies. Magao, who referred to the verses he wrote as haikai ka, recalling the ancient name of kyōka, wrote more poems for surimono than any other poet. He established himself as the first professional teacher of kyōka and made his living correcting poems by pupils for a set fee. It can be assumed he likewise collected a small honorarium for verses he submitted to surimono commissioned by pupils. Poets affiliated with the Yomo-gawa or one of its many provincial subgroups were the most frequent sponsors of surimono, and collectively they commissioned many well-known surimono series. By the 1820s, the Go-gawa and Yomo-gawa poetry groups each had an estimated three thousand members, many of whom lived outside the main urban centers of Osaka and Edo. The vast majority of the poets were amateurs, and their output was trite and conventional. Yet there were still a number of kyōka poets who maintained the standards of ingenuity and wit of an earlier era, while others wrote interesting poems in a subdued classical mode.

Although from the point of view of literary innovation the heyday of the kyōka movement was the 1780s, the finest surimono were created during the first third of the nineteenth century. Poets of means commissioned prominent artists, usually of the ukiyo-e school, to provide designs for surimono. Hokusai, who by 1800 had already acquired a reputation as the most brilliant artistic interpreter of kyōka and haikai, was in great demand as a surimono designer. His close connections with authors of illustrated novels had provided him with an entrée to kyōka circles, for most writers were poets as well, under different pen names.[7] Many of Hokusai's pupils, including Sōri, Gosei, Gakutei, Hokuba, Hokkei, and Shinsai, were either kyōka poets themselves or had close connections with poetry circles; many were best known as surimono designers. Artists of the Utagawa lineage of ukiyo-e, including Toyokuni and Kunisada, had close connections with poetry groups that served as *de facto* fan clubs for Kabuki actors; such groups often commissioned surimono to commemorate an actor's adoption of a new stage name or a noteworthy performance.[8] The writer-artist Kubo Shumman, in addition to heading his own group of poets known as the Bakurō-gawa, was involved in the production of surimono for both enjoyment and profit. Although many of the same artists who designed surimono were also involved in commercial printmaking, privately published prints allowed higher standards of production and catered to the more refined tastes of their literati patrons. Commissions from kyōka poets of the early nineteenth century helped perpetuate the technical excellence of Japanese printmaking in an age that saw an overall decline in the quality of prints designed for sale to the public.

After the death of many of its leaders—including Magao in 1829 and Rokujuen the following year—the Edo kyōka movement lost momentum. Gradually the center of kyōka composition returned to Osaka where it had begun in earnest nearly a century before, and where artists of the Shijō school continued to create painterly surimono illustrations for both haikai and kyōka groups. Kyōka continued to be written through the early twentieth century, but by then the next reemergence of thirty-one-syllable Japanese verse in the more vital form of modern *tanka* poetry had already begun to take hold.

FORMATS OF TEXTS

Certain conventions established in kyōka anthologies were respected in verse surimono as well. For instance, poems by the senior poet of a group will usually be found in the position of honor on the far left of the last page of an anthology, or on the far left on a surimono sheet. The other poets who submitted a verse to anthologies or surimono usually contributed a small fee to cover publishing costs. Occasionally a small circle will be found above poems (e.g., cat. nos. 15, 17, 28, 32, 33, 47, and 51). Because similar marks can be found in kyōka anthologies, it is now generally accepted that they indicate poems that were judged the best at kyōka gatherings.

Poems are always signed, but not with the author's real name. Kyōka names are often composed of puns or concentrated poetic expressions; others refer to the poet's real-life profession or place of residence. Pen names of a more prosaic kind may include a character from the studio name of the leader of a poetry circle—hence the clusters of names beginning with "Bun-" (poets in the circle of Bumbunsha), "Shin-" (circle of Shinratei), "Fuku-" (circle of Fukunoya), and so on. Analogously, many members of the Hanazono-ren (Flower Garden Circle) adopted names that included the word "Ume-" (plum), which indicated a close link to their

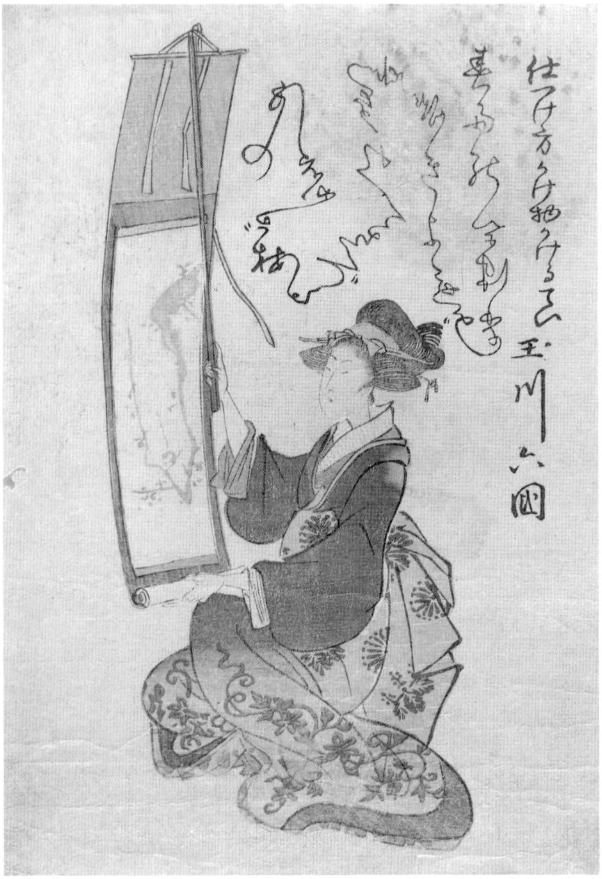

FIGURE 4

Anonymous: *Proper Manners: The Way to Hang a Scroll (Shitsukekata: Kakemono Kakeru Tei)*. ca. 1805. (cat. no. 295)

leader, Garyōen Umemaro. The use of pen names helped to mask official class distinctions between participants at kyōka gatherings, at which samurai, merchant, and artisan poets could mingle. Kyōka names also allowed a convenient separation of a person's sometimes frivolous exercises in verse from their more serious achievements, performed under different names, as writers, scholars, or even government officials.

Whereas poets' names are usually inscribed in a legible formal script, the poems themselves are not easy to decipher, even for those who read Japanese. First of all, Chinese characters in poems are usually written in a cursive or semi-cursive script; yet perhaps a greater obstacle is that phonetic characters (*kana*) are often written in variant forms, and each phoneme can be represented by any one of three, four, or sometimes more variations. Only at the end of the nineteenth century did publishers adopt the standardized kana forms known as *hiragana*.

Still, even to the reader unfamiliar with the conventions of premodern kana and cursive scripts, traditional calligraphy with its flowing ligatures and rhythmical linear expression is more visually appealing than the monotony of typeset characters: without the calligraphy, surimono would lose much of their charm. Although the technology to produce standardized lettering existed during the Edo period, it was not used by publishers of illustrated books and prints, which called for a harmonious integration of text and image. Instead, the hand of the professional calligrapher or of the poet himself was masterfully reproduced by a skilled carver in the woodblock medium.

An idiosyncratic calligraphic style may sacrifice legibility to beauty, an aesthetic effect not limited to surimono. "Anyone who has been asked to read an inscription on a painting or even the text of a printed book of the seventeenth century," Donald Keene has wistfully observed, "will know to what extraordinary extremes of non-communication this love of beauty carried Japanese writing."[9] An extreme instance in the Wright collection is an anonymously designed print that shows a woman hanging a scroll painting of a branch of plum blossoms. The uninterrupted string of calligraphy mimics the unfurling of the scroll as it whirls up and down, at places even turning completely upside down (fig. 4).[10]

Surimono calligraphy usually aims, however, to complement rather than compete with the image. A rare Shigemasa surimono inscribed with poems by Sembakuen Tōzai Namboku, a leading poetry judge of the day, and Rokujuen, the founder of the Go-gawa poetry club, shows how calligraphy can add sophistication to surimono (fig. 5). Both poems link images of spring with the pastime of playing the koto. The calligrapher, perhaps one of the poets himself, complements this elegant theme with a slightly affected writing style quite unlike the more tightly wrought strands found on most prints. Its liberal spacing, heavily brushed horizontal strokes for accent, and overall gentle curving of lines even reflect to a degree the conventions of the Reizei School of court calligraphy—a writing style rarely used in the popular art of woodblock prints.

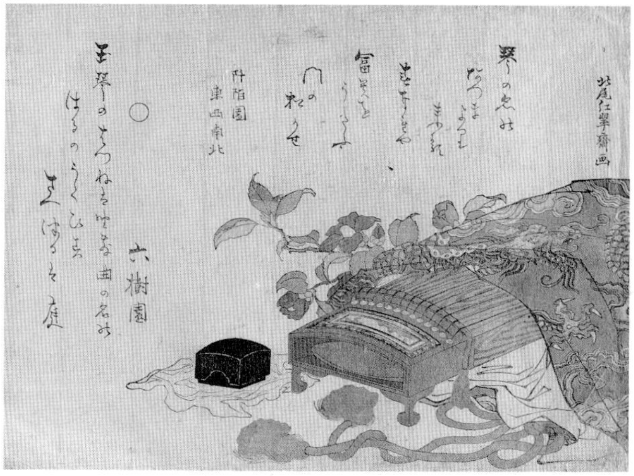

FIGURE 5

Shigemasa: *Koto with Camellia Flowers.* 1808, Year of the Dragon. (cat. no. 207)

STILL LIFE AND LITERATI TASTES

Still life as a distinct subgenre of surimono had no real precedent in the ukiyo-e tradition, which from its earliest stage was concerned primarily with themes and personages of the pleasure quarters and theaters. The art historian will note precedents such as Ming-dynasty woodblock prints of foodstuffs arranged in ornate bowls,[11] but another, perhaps more important inspiration of still-life surimono was the kyōka parties of a previous generation. At these gatherings, poems were composed about exotic or everyday objects that were selected in preparation for the party. Kyōka anthologies often included illustrations of such objects, anticipating the appearance of similar themes in the format of single-sheet or serial surimono.

These images shed light on certain aspects of Edo customs and material culture that historical treatises pass over in silence. They reveal everyday objects in a new light, while the accompanying kyōka also valorize the mundane—as we just saw in the surimono on the theme of Narumi shibori (fig. 2). A person of means might commission a print to celebrate a prized possession. For example, a literatus might request an image of books and writing implements; the man-about-town his stylish pipe and tobacco pouch; the samurai his sword furnishings; and the courtesan her hairpins and mirror. While the inventory of these objects is endless, the most common themes reflect the long tradition in East Asian art of giving honor to the four treasures of calligraphy: writing brush, paper, ink, and inkstone. This reverence is most prominently demonstrated in poems and images on surimono dealing with the *kakizome,* the first writing practice of the year. Shinsai's image of an inkstone and brushes (cat. no. 40), and one from Hokusai's "Horse Series" (cat. no. 34) are examples.

A still life surimono by Hokkei seems at first glance to fall into the category of "famous products" (*meibutsu*), a topic often found in both kyōka anthologies and surimono (fig. 6). The title "Plays of the Ichikawa Family," however, immediately informs the reader that the print is related to Kabuki. The umbrella refers to the

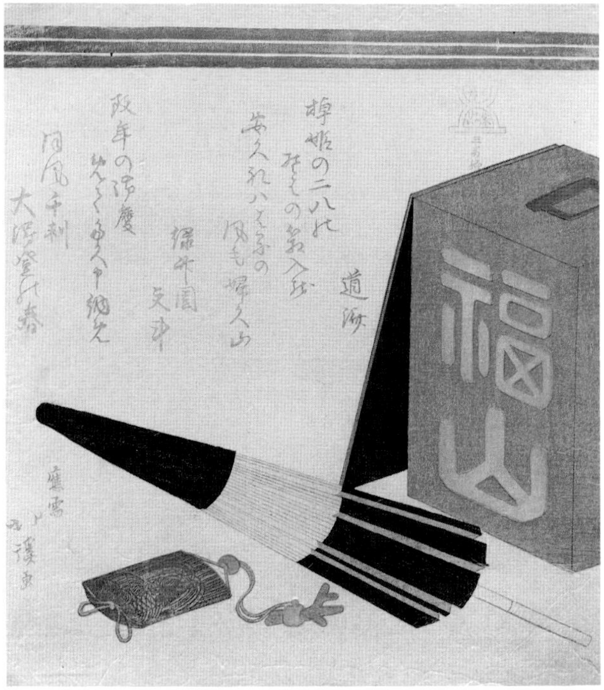

FIGURE 6

Hokkei: *Props for the Kabuki Play "Sukeroku," from Plays of the Ichikawa Family, a set of three (Sanshō Ie no Gei, Samban Tsuzuki)*. ca. 1820. (cat. no. 104)

scene in *Sukeroku,* one of the eighteen famous plays of the Ichikawa Family, in which the dashing young samurai Sukeroku makes a bravado pose, wielding a bull's-eye-patterned umbrella. The delivery boy's box for holding bowls of noodles is also a prop from the play, while the *inrō* case is decorated with a motif of a carp ascending a waterfall, making it a symbol of Ichikawa Danjūrō VII (1791–1859), the most popular Kabuki actor of the day.

While recourse to the text is not needed to identify the themes of the print, the reader can turn to it for other messages. The two poems were provided by members of the Go-gawa poetry club. Their hourglass-shaped emblem forms the title cartouche in the upper right-hand corner of the print. The poem on the left, by Ryokuchikuen Fumimasu, is a standard New Year greeting and has no integral link to the image. In fact, as proof of its all-purpose nature, exactly the same poem—right down to the unorthodox Chinese characters to write Ō-Edo (Great Edo)—is found on a Hokkei landscape of Mount Fuji (for a translation, see cat. no. 13). The poem on the right, however, complements the image in a clever and complex way, although a translation can only convey one level of imagery:

Saohime no	When Princess Sao
nihachi no soba no	opens the delivery box
hakoiri o	of "two-eight" noodles,
akureba haru no	spring winds waft
kaze mo Fukuyama	the scent from Fukuyama.

The mention of "Fukuyama" in the poem, reproducing the characters inscribed on the delivery box in the print, refers to the scene in Sukeroku in which a little boy (a part usually acted by a son or grandson of the reigning Danjūrō) makes an entry with a delivery of noodles from the famous Fukuyama—the name of an actual noodle shop located in the theater district. But a good kyōka has more than one level of imagery. The wit of the poem derives from a secondary series of puns on feminine images, which allude to the heroine of the play, Sukeroku's mistress Agemaki. The punning begins in the first line with the mention of Saohime, the legendary princess of spring. In the next line, nihachi, literally "two-eights," refers to *nihachi soba,* called thus because they cost sixteen *mon* a bowl, but in the argot of Yoshiwara, nihachi also means a young courtesan. Again, in the third line, *hakoiri* (delivery-box) is a common abbreviation for *hakoiri musume,* a young woman who has been overly protected by her parents or guardians as if she were a precious object stored in a box. The wordplay comes to a close with the pivot word *fuku* forming part of *kaze mo fuku,* "the wind blows," and *fuku-yama,* "at Fukuyama" (the *fu* of *fuku* being intentionally miswritten with a Chinese character meaning "woman"). The poet cleverly juxtaposes two entirely different images, one of a young maiden of Yoshiwara and the other of the delivery box of Fukuyama noodles. While the poet shows off his skill in packing multiple meanings into thirty-one syllables, the artist displays equal brilliance in using synecdoche to evoke an entire Kabuki play.

POEMS AND SCENES DRAWN FROM THE PAST

As the surimono just described suggest, Edo literati were conversant with poetry classics as well as the contemporary performing arts such as Kabuki, Jōruri, and Rakugo. Surimono dealing with themes drawn from Japanese history and classical literature were also produced in great number, however, and they are strongly represented in the Wright collection. A survey of these images and poems makes one realize how much the satire that had characterized Temmei intellectual culture had given way to a measured respect for the classics, shown even in the process of spoofing them.

The classics that were best known during the Edo period are also now available in English translations, allowing Western readers to trace the visual and literary references to their sources. *Genji Monogatari* (The Tale of Genji), written nearly a thousand years ago, is widely considered one of the world's great novels; its profound influence on Japanese art is reflected in a number of exquisite designs in the Wright collection (e.g., cat. nos. 23, 29). Allusions to the miscellany of short essays *Tsurezuregusa* (Essays in Idleness) demonstrate that this work, virtually unknown for over three centuries after it was written around 1330, became so well known by the late Edo period that even quotations from trivial chapters would have been recognized by an Edo literatus (see, for instance, cat. nos. 53 and 66). References to famous episodes of medieval war chronicles such as the *Heike Monogatari* (The Tale of the Heike) or the *Taiheiki* (Chronicle of the Great Peace) can be found in both images and poems (e.g., cat. nos. 3, 15, and 55).

Another category of poetry-prints deals with collections of didactic tales whose roots can be traced back to Japan's middle ages, a period when a war-torn nation found solace and moral order in the Buddhist teaching that good deeds would be rewarded. *Uji Shūishū* (A Collection of Tales from Uji; see fig. 7, and cat. nos. 84–85) and *Shasekishū* (Sand and Pebbles; see cat. nos. 75–77) illustrate this law of karma. Later similar tales such as the *Honchō Nijūshikō* (Twenty-four Japanese Paragons of Filial Piety; cat. nos. 4, 67–74) have a more Confucian bent. To the

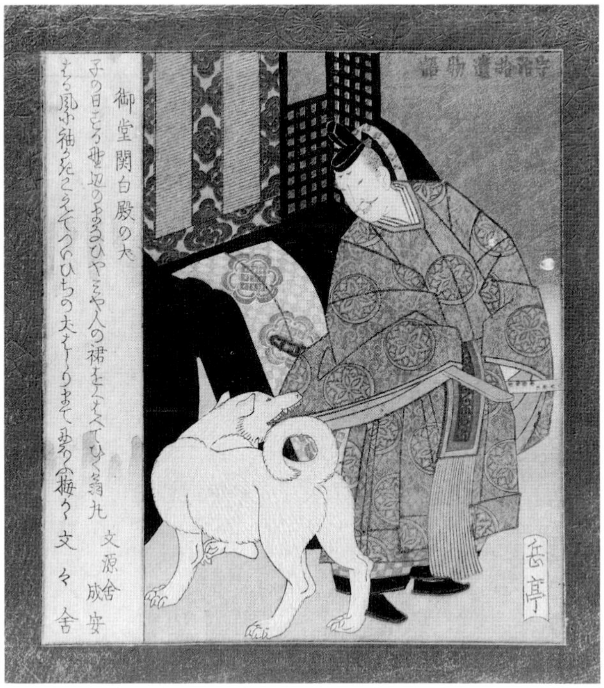

FIGURE 7

Gakutei: *The Dog of Midō Kampaku,* from *A Collection of Tales from Uji (Uji Shūi Monogatari: Midō Kampaku-dono no Inu*). ca. 1830. (cat. no. 86)

modern student, the tales in the latter series seem particularly obscure, and many are derived from sources no longer consulted by anyone except scholars.

In an example of a print on a didactic-tale theme illustrated by Gakutei, we see a dog pulling the sleeve of a courtier's elegant robes—obviously not a scene commonly associated with the auspicious beginning of the New Year (fig. 7). Nor does the title of the print, "The Dog of Midō Kampaku," provide any immediate clue to the meaning of the scene, although it informs us that we are looking at the image of the most powerful man of the early eleventh century court. The series title, *A Collection of Tales from Uji,* however, reveals the source of the imagery, and if we are not familiar with the story—as no doubt most Edo readers were not—we can turn to the work itself. Fortunately Western readers also have ready access to the tale.[12]

In this episode, as Michinaga is about to proceed through the gate of a Buddhist temple his dog grabs his robe and prevents him from entering. Suspecting something is amiss, he calls in a court necromancer to investigate. It is discovered that one of Michinaga's arch-rivals had bribed a miscreant priest to bury an ominous object at the foot of the gateway: had Michinaga walked over it, a curse would have taken effect, endangering his life. An understanding of the historical context changes the way we view the image, giving it another level of meaning. The poem on the left by Bumbunsha, head of the Katsushika circle, translates the ominous episode into the auspicious (albeit elliptical) language of kyōka. Read on a superficial level the poem betrays no direct connection to the image:

harukaze ni	Spring breezes
sodegaki koete	carry the scent of plum
tsuihiji no	over the hedge,
inubashiri made	along narrow paths
niou ume ga ka	beside earthen walls.

The poem, pedestrian at first glance, conceals a hidden level of wit. First, *sode* acts as a pivot word, suggesting that the scent of plum in the wind fills one's "sleeve," but it also forms the word *sodegaki,* which means "hedge." Similarly, the word *inubashiri,* which refers to the narrow dirt path between a canal and a wall, has the literal meaning of "dog run." Read with knowledge of the legend, the buried allusions to Michinaga's robes and his pet dog become clear. The initial ferocity of the image is tamed, and we see how this print could have been intended as a talisman of sorts to ward off nefarious influences from the year before.

Ukiyo-e artists often responded to poems on classical themes by superimposing certain anachronistic characteristics on a historical figure. This technique, called *shukō* had been successfully employed in Kabuki, where plots often had two simultaneous levels of significance—one based on history and legend, the other on current events.[13] Analogously, ukiyo-e artists often presented a poet of ancient times or a fictional character from a classical novel such as *The Tale of Genji* wearing Edo-period dress.

An example of this technique can be found in the print series by Hokkei titled *Shōshikai Bantsuzuki* (Poetry Gatherings to Celebrate Old Age), which represents an imaginary gathering of historical figures of ancient Japan. The example here shows Ono no Tōfū, a talented poet and calligrapher of the tenth-century Heian court, watching a tree frog trying to reach the branches of willow—a symbol of Tōfū's own perseverance (fig. 1).[14] The poem on the right alludes to Tōfū's skills as a calligrapher, while the one on the left, by Eminoya Tomohiro, corresponds more closely to the image. An approximate translation gives one level of meaning:

aoyagi no	A tree frog
ito ni kawazu no	under strands of a willow
utabukuro	bellows out a song,
nuu kage mizu ni	as its reflection in the water
miete une une	appears to twist and turn.

Again, the poem defies precise translation, but the images are connected with "tree frog" (*kawazu*), a standard motif in prints parodying Ono no Tōfū. *Ito,* or "strands," of the willow are linked semantically to the verb *nuu,* "to weave," with the suggestion that they are to be made into an *utabukuro,* a satchel for holding books of poetry. However, *utabukuro* also is the term used to describe the frog's throat sac, which billows out when it croaks. Not everyone's idea of an elegant sentiment, but it is humorous and witty in the original, and it provided the artist with enough keywords to create a splendid design.

For instance, *aoyagi* in the first line, in conjunction with the title of the print, is sufficient hint that this print refers obliquely to the popular Kabuki play *Ono no Tōfū Aoyagi Suzuri* (Ono no Tōfū and the Willow Inkstone). This Kabuki connection helps explain the theatrical pose and the anachronisms of the courtier's costume, which is a hybrid of Heian- and Edo-period styles: high geta, a bull's-eye-patterned umbrella, and a sword are accessories associated with the role in the Edo play, while the courtier's robes and *eboshi* (ceremonial cap), are a tip of the hat to the Heian court.

Finally, even the background of the image was partly inspired by the poem. *Une une* refers to the twisting and turning of the stream which the artist has rendered here with an abstract flourish in Rimpa-school style, complemented by gently swaying strands of willow. The whirl of punning, the poetic ululation of the frog, and the repeated "u" sounds of the last lines of the poem underscore the visual dynamism of the image with allusion and wit.

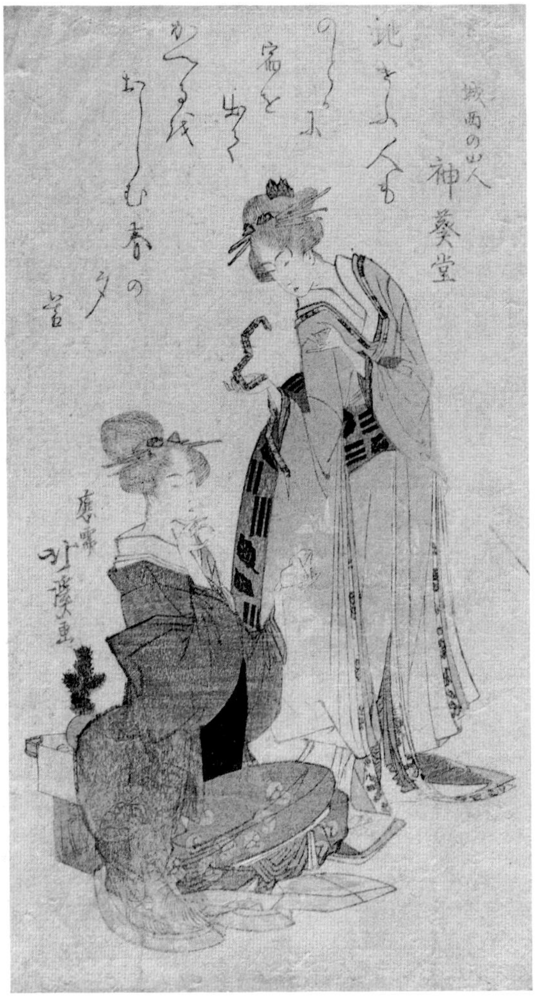

FIGURE 8

Hokkei: *Women with Snake and Frog Toys.* 1809, Year of the Snake. (cat. no. 93)

POEMS ATTACHED TO BEAUTY PRINTS

Even a hasty inventory of surimono with figures reveals that *bijinga* (pictures of beautiful women) dominate the genre, at least until the 1820s, when artists such as Kunisada began creating portraits of male actors in great number.

Even when pictures on surimono portray women, usually shown performing some New Year's activity, the poems themselves often do not specify a female subject. This creates problems for the translator who is forced to make a decision about who, which gender, and how many are doing what in a poem. Here the translator betrays his role as interpreter, and his interpretation of the poem, like any reader's, is unavoidably affected by the image it accompanies.

Two women in a Hokkei design, who may be courtesans, are depicted in the typical style of Hokusai and his pupils of the first decade of the nineteenth century (fig. 8). The standing woman holds a wooden snake, while her seated companion holds a toy frog in one hand and gestures with the other. The image at first glance does not seem to have any clear meaning, except that the snake, one of the symbols of the East Asian zodiac, may indicate the date of issue as the year of the snake. The pine and the arrangement of tangerines in the background are conventional images that merely reinforce the New Year mood.

Let us turn to the text for further clues. The artist Hokkei signed his print "by commission," so we can assume that he designed it on order of the poet Jōsai no Sanjin Shinkidō, who submitted this poem to the illustrator:

hebi tsukau	Even a woman of leisure
hito mo nodoka ni	who leaves the house
yado o dete	so peacefully
kaeru o oshimu	deplores going home
haru no yūgure	at dusk on a spring day.

Again the translation reduces the poem to a literal interpretation. Here the punning relies entirely on homonyms. For instance, in Edo vernacular the opening phrase *hebi tsukau hito* referred to a man or woman of leisure, or someone who is just plain lazy, but it also includes the word *hebi* (snake). In the next-to-last line, *kaeru o oshimu* means both "to regret having to go home" and "to deplore frogs." The word *nodoka* (calm) is an association word for spring and also resonates with the mood of a person of leisure. Just a simple poem, unabashedly frivolous, but the vocabulary provided the artist with a cluster of associations that enliven his innocent image of two beautiful women.

But the print does not yield its full sense until we reflect a bit more on the connections between snakes and frogs in Japanese culture. A theme of popular literature of the time, occasionally depicted in ukiyo-e, is the *san sukumi,* or "three cringing ones," referring to a folk belief that snakes eat frogs, which in turn attack snails, which can poison snakes.[15] Therefore, these three creatures all cringe in each other's presence. Consequently the term *san sukumi* can also be used to describe the kind of deadlock that occurs in human relations when too many people get involved in negotiations. Although the poem does not mention a snail specifically, the phrase *kaeru o oshimu* in its second sense, "to deplore frogs," is a clear reference by omission to a snail.

This reading of the poem is confirmed by a reexamination of the image. We can now see the gestures of the seated woman as representing the shape of a snail with its two antennae. Maybe the snail-gesture visual pun was the artist's own idea, or maybe the poet suggested it. The final composite of poem and image was an attractive, if slightly provocative, greeting card to present to acquaintances the poet had quarrelled with during the preceding year, but now wished to conciliate.

The next print, by Sōri III, another pupil of Hokusai, also depicts women in the master's style—a clear demonstration of Hokusai's role as a shaper of the visual idiom of ukiyo-e (fig. 9). The touching image of a woman breast-feeding her little boy is an uncommon but not unseen theme in ukiyo-e; Utamaro, for instance, created a number of famous images on this theme. Sōri's image does not have, however, the playful or erotic tone of Utamaro's compositions. Although the work is by a male artist and clearly belongs to the imagery of the turn of the century depicting svelte maidens, it offers a sensitive image of motherhood. The accompanying poems confirm this interpretation. (The inscription is slightly abraded here, but legible on an impression in the New York Public Library.)[16] The poem on the right, signed Senrō Notome, reads:

uguisu no	As the warbler sings
koe wa yasashiki	in a gentle voice,
iratsume no	the mother holds her child
komochi karei no	whose teeth are budding
ha sae shiraume	into white plum blossoms.

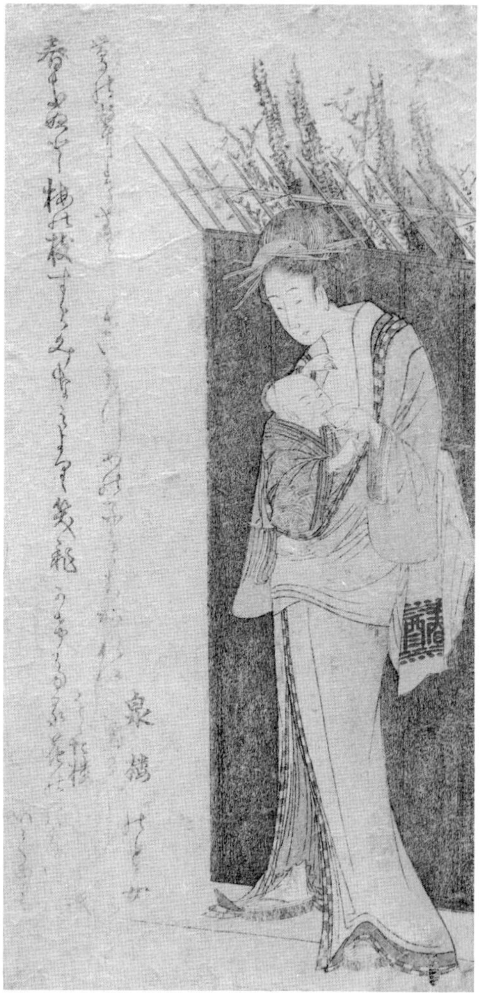

FIGURE 9

Sōri III: *Mother Nursing her Child.* 1801. (cat. no. 273)

It contains allusions to plum blossoms, the most common image in New Year's poems, but this evocation of tactile sensation in the simile of the baby's budding teeth strikes us as a clever break from hackneyed usage. Not surprisingly this intuition comes from a female poet. The second poem, by a male poet, perhaps her husband, uses entirely conventional spring imagery. Incidentally, the final signature on the left, not accompanying any poem, indicates that the calligraphy was by Ikume, which seems to be a girl's name. Perhaps this print was commissioned by a wife and husband who composed the poems and had their young daughter copy out the poems (in competent but slightly cramped textbook style). The delicate image and propitious poems celebrate the birth and growth of a baby, the arrival of a new year, and all the hope, happiness, and prosperity that these events promise.

PARODIC IMAGES OF WOMEN

With notable exceptions such as Gakutei's magnificent pentaptych commissioned by the circle of Hisakataya (cat. no. 7), or Eisen's depiction of a flower-viewing excursion (cat. no. 2), courtesans appearing as courtesans are relatively rare in surimono, in contrast to ukiyo-e, where they are a primary focus of attention. Surimono do employ, however, one of the most prominent devices of Edo literature and art, a form of *mitate* (burlesque or parody) in which male figures are represented as women.

An excellent example in the Wright collection is the series *Hanagasa-ren Shichi Fukujin* (Seven Gods of Fortune for the Hanagasa Circle) designed by Shuntei. The Hanagasa Circle was affiliated with the Taiko-gawa (Drum Group) headed by Dondontei Wataru, whose drum-shaped emblem can be seen in the title cartouche. The theme of the seven gods of fortune is one of the most commonly encountered themes in surimono, but here the poets and artist have given the theme a special twist by portraying the gods as women of different walks of life ranging from prostitutes to palace ladies.

In the example here (fig. 10), Shuntei's design itself provides very few clues to which of the seven gods is represented, but a close examination of the print reveals that there is a mouse in a three-legged cage in the foreground. Since mice are often associated with Daikoku, we can surmise, even without reading the poems, that this is a parodic image of him. A close reading of the poems, however, helps tie the disparate iconography into a more coherent whole.

The first poem, by Yamato no Watamori, gives no hint of the subject of the seven gods of fortune. Instead it is a vehicle of parody, presenting a rarefied image of a Heian court lady:

Saohime no	Mists trail
jūni hitoe ni	like the twelve layers
kasumi hiku	of Princess Sao's robes,
Ōuchiyama no	as spring dawns over
haru no akebono	over the imperial palace.

The poem transforms the legendary Princess Sao, who is usually linked in poems with the mists of spring, into a court lady wearing luxurious *jūni hitoe* (literally, "twelve-layered robes"). The references here clearly gave the artist the inspiration for the image.

The poem on the left by Saieitei Mochimaru, in contrast, provides further clues as to which god of good fortune is represented here:

fukutoku no	The fork-rooted radish
futamata daikon	brings luck when it is plucked
komatsu tomo	along with pine shoots—
hatsune hiku sou	as a warbler in the courtyard
niwa no uguisu	sings its first song.

With the exception of the pine shoots this poem has very little to do with the image; the only suggestion of a warbler is the lacquer bird cage in the foreground. This poem instead confirms what the image only hints at, that it is a parody of Daikoku. The key is the mention of the odd vegetable, a double-rooted radish (*futamata daikon*), which Daikoku, whose name sounds like *daikon,* is often portrayed carrying. The mention of *fukutoku* (good fortune) in the first line also echoes the theme of the print *shichi fukujin* (seven gods of good fortune). *Hatsune,* a reference to the first day of the rat of the year, when pine shoots were plucked for good luck, also means "first song" of a bird at the new year. This pair of poems works well in tandem with the lovely image, demonstrating how the poetic imagination of the artist could cleverly link poems with little direct relationship.

Another type of parody common in kyōka-surimono, and ukiyo-e in general, is transforming a famous warrior figure from Japanese or Chinese legend into a female figure. For instance, a parody print by Shuntei shows the warrior Kajiwara no Kagesue in the pose of a woman flogging a hapless foe with a branch of plum (cat. no. 55). The Wright collection also has a number of prints from two different series by Shumman depicting warriors in the pose of women. One comprises paro-

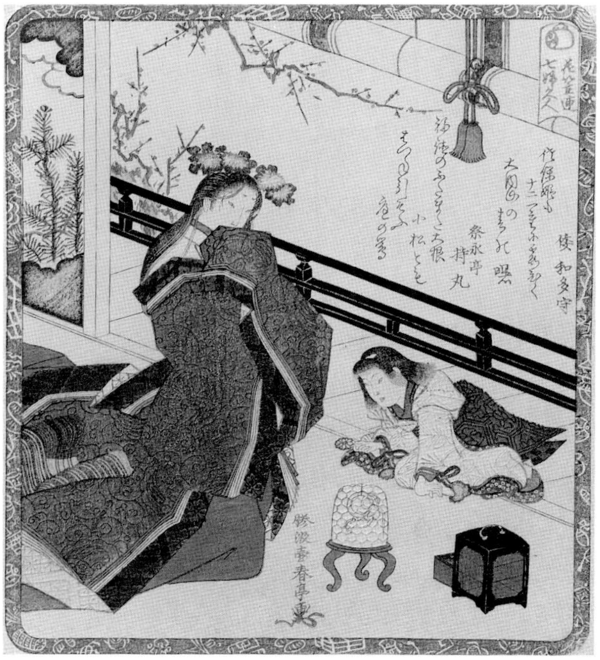

FIGURE 10

Shuntei: *Daikoku as a Palace Lady,* from *Seven Women as the Gods of Good Fortune for the Hanagasa-ren (Hanagasa-ren Shichifukujin).* ca. 1825. (cat. no. 265)

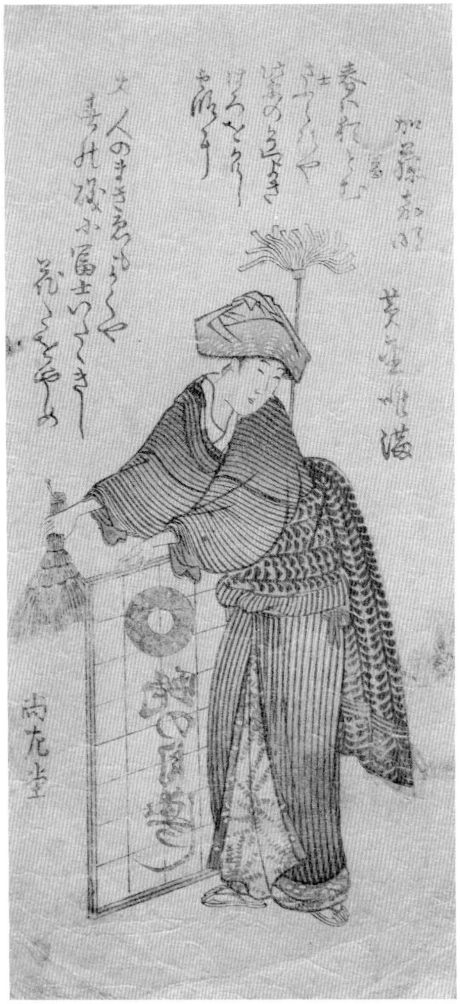

FIGURE 11

Shumman: *The Warrior Katō Yoshiaki as a Cleaning Woman.* ca. 1804. (cat. no. 248)

dies of courtesans as outlaw-warriors from the Chinese classic known as the *Suikoden* in Japanese (cat. nos. 48 and 49); the other series, titled "The Victory of the Seven Spear-Bearers of Yanagase," depicts women in everyday settings as Japanese generals from the late sixteenth century, when Japan was still embroiled in civil war (cat. nos. 247–249).

An example from the latter series is titled "Katō Yoshiaki" after a famous warrior of the sixteenth century, but instead of a fearsome warrior we are presented with an image of a maid dusting a signboard, the spear replaced by a dusting pole slipped into her obi (fig. 11). Both poems draw on images related to Mount Fuji; the one on the left is by the artist Shumman himself, who signs himself Shōsadō. The poem on the right by Kogane Tadamitsu reads:

haru wa nao	Fuji in spring
tomu saburai (Fuji) ya	makes a grand appearance
murasaki no	covered with mist
iro yoki horo o	like a samurai's hood
kakeshi kasumi ni	of rich purple color.

On one level the poem is rather straightforward, simply comparing the majestic mist-covered slopes of Mount Fuji in spring to the hood of a warrior's armor; but a level of wordplay was added by placing the characters for Mount Fuji in the margins of the first two columns, while the primary readings are written in phonetic characters: *tomu* suggests that the spring is abundant, while *saburai* is a verb meaning "to appear" or "to serve," but read in the sense of the character alongside it is the equivalent of *samurai* (warrior). If possible, the reader is to see both readings at the same time as a form of jocular acrostic. The artist seems also to have inserted a visual pun by making the woman's headdress resemble the shape of Mount Fuji. The sign that she is dusting—written in mirror characters just to add to the puzzle—have a bull's-eye (*janome,* literally, "snake's-eye") crest and the name of an actual Edo eatery, Janome Sushi. An Edo samurai reader would have known that this crest was that used by the warriors of the Katō clan, including Yoshiaki and Kiyomasa (also one of the subjects of this series).

Finally, another type of beauty-print parody that is prevalent in surimono, although less so in ukiyo-e generally, presents idealized images of women in beautiful court costume. The Wright collection has a number of such images. One of the most gorgeous depicts the famous woman poet Ono no Komachi (cat. no. 1). The literary interest of the print is deepened by the fact that the poems are both by women, at least one of whom was in the circle of women kyōka poets headed by

Fushimatsu no Kaka, one of the leaders of the Edo kyōka movement after the death of her husband, Akera Kankō, in 1799. Even as they parody the legend of their poetic ancestor they demonstrate a respect for her accomplishments. Furthermore, though only the alphabet places Eisen's image of Ono no Komachi at the fore of the color plate section, it is appropriate that a catalogue dedicated to images inspired by poetry should open with an imaginary portrait of one of Japan's greatest poets.

CONCLUSION

Surimono are the product of imaginative and intellectual collaboration between an artist and one or more poets, rendered in the woodblock-print medium through the skills of an engraver and printer. They were not sold but exchanged as tokens of literary friendship and a shared appreciation of elegant things. Their intimate quality is confirmed by the extreme rarity of original editions of surimono, which is due to their limited distribution at the time of issue. Yet the fact that they were published at all betrays a desire to make a statement that transcends the amateur, exclusive, and ephemeral.

Turning the pages of an old surimono album, leafing through a pile of well-preserved prints, or looking at color reproductions in a catalogue, one can vicariously experience the delight of their original recipients. Though the way we read and enjoy the prints is not the same as that of a past culture, pictorial art can cross the centuries with a direct and profound aesthetic impact. Wright's enthusiastic comments on surimono are records of such an encounter.

Kyōka composed for surimono, which translation can only approximate, cannot communicate to modern audiences as effectively as images. Yet their concern with perennial aspects of experience—appreciation of Nature, enjoyment of everyday life, and literary cultivation—can be conveyed to modern sensibilities.

The metaphors of Nature fundamental to kyōka (as to all Japanese verse), the Edo poet's exuberance on the day he feels something in the air that tells him spring is here, are accessible to all.

Modern in their avoidance of abstract concepts of love, religion, or philosophy, kyōka poets wrote about small things, favorite objects, or famous local products. The celebration of events and objects of everyday life in kyōka and surimono images stimulates us to look at things afresh, to find new ways of viewing things we take for granted.

These poets shared a knowledge of a long and distinguished literary tradition. While thirty-one syllables does not allow elaboration on literary themes, many poems acquire depth through the use of allusion and association. References to classics that surimono poets and artists made with such frequency and ease—analogous to references to Greek and Roman legends in English Romantic poetry—pose an undeniable obstacle to modern readers. Still, the literary and historical references are usually to Japanese and Chinese classics that have now become part of world literature through excellent translations. Our enjoyment of surimono will be enhanced by a greater familiarity with these sources. Conversely, a study of surimono could amount to a wide-ranging, albeit eclectic, survey of premodern Japanese literature and culture.

Surimono is an art of subtle harmonies—between human beings and Nature in the celebration of seasonal renewal and the commonplace objects of everyday life, between past and present in the evocation of old heroes, and between images that please the eye and texts that tease the mind. The reader of this volume is invited to recompose these harmonies.

NOTES

1 A more detailed history of surimono can be found in Roger Keyes, *The Art of Surimono: Privately Published Japanese Woodblock Prints and Books in the Chester Beatty Library, Dublin,* 2 vols. (London: Sotheby, 1985), 13–40; a discussion of the term "surimono" can be found on p. 18. See also Roger Keyes, *Surimono: Privately Published Japanese Prints in the Spencer Museum of Art* (New York: Kodansha, 1984), 11–21.

2 See Helen Craig McCullough, *Brocade by Night: 'Kokin Wakashū and the Court Style in Japanese Classical Poetry* (Stanford: Stanford University Press, 1985), 481–89.

3 This print is also introduced in Suzuki Jūzō, "Edo Kyōka Surimono no Kaishaku to Kanshō" in *Ehon to Ukiyo-e: Edo Shuppan Bunka no Kōsatsu* (Ehon and ukiyo-e: printed pictorial art of the Edo period) (Tokyo: Bijutsu Shuppansha, 1979), 551; and Janette Ostier, ed., *La voix silencieuse des choses: Natures mortes japonaises xviiie-xixe siècles* (Paris: Galerie Janette Ostier, 1989), no. 66.

4 Well-known poems linking Narumi and plovers include *Shinkokinshū,* nos. 648–50.

5 The poem is found in the "Kana Preface" of the *Kokinshū* as well as in the "Travel Poems" section (no. 409) of the same collection, where the attribution to Kakinomoto no Hitomaro is mentioned.

6 For further details concerning the Late Edo kyōka movement, see Donald Keene, *World Within Walls: Japanese Literature of the Pre-Modern Era,* 1600–1867 (New York: Holt, Rinehart and Winston, 1976), 512–24. See also James T. Kenney, "A Brief History of Kyōka and the

Kyōka Movement," in Theodore Bowie, ed., *Art of the Surimono* (Bloomington: Indiana University Art Museum, 1979), 24–42. The best survey in Japanese remains Suga Chikuho, *Kinsei Kyōka Shi* (History of Edo-period kyōka) (Tokyo: Nisshin Shoin, 1940).

7 For further discussion of the links between ukiyo-e artists and popular writers and poets, see Donald Jenkins, ed., *The Floating World Revisited* (Portland, Oregon: Portland Art Museum, 1993); especially see the essay by Haruko Iwasaki, "The Literature of Wit and Humor in Late-Eighteenth-Century Edo," 47–61, and the sections of the catalogue devoted to Ōta Nampo and Santō Kyōden. Also see Carpenter, "Hokusai and Kyōden: Portrayals of Courtesans in Painting and Poetry," in Gian Carlo Calza, ed., *Hokusai Paintings: Selected Essays* (Venice: International Hokusai Research Centre, University of Venice, 1994), 91–116.

8 Unfortunately, theatrical surimono are poorly represented in the Wright Collection. Poems for such prints usually include poems that pun on an actor's name or a particular Kabuki performance. For a brief introduction to this subgenre of kyōka-surimono, see Carpenter, "Kunisada and the Art of Comic Poetry," in Sebastian Izzard, ed., *Kunisada's World* (New York: Japan Society, 1993). The catalogue also includes several translations of kyōka found on surimono related to Kabuki themes.

9 Donald Keene, "Japanese Books and their Illustrations," *Storia dell'arte* (Florence, Italy) 27 (1976), 122.

10 The poem reads: *harusame no / shitsukezama yoki / uguisu wa / saite saezuru / ume ga kakemono* (In the gentle spring rains, the warbler sings as the sweet scent of plum hangs over us like a hanging scroll). There are puns on *shizukesa* (gentleness) and *shitsukezama* (manners), and in the last line, *ka* (scent) forms the first part of *kakemono* (hanging scroll).

11 See Jack Hillier, " Still-life in Surimono," in *A Sheaf of Japanese Papers: In Tribute to Heinz Kaempfer on His 75th Birthday,* Matthi Forrer, Willem R. van Gulik, and Jack Hillier, ed. (The Hague: Society for Japanese Arts and Crafts, 1979) 75–84.

12 D. E. Mills, *A Collection of Tales from Uji: A Study and Translation of Uji Shūi Monogatari* (London: Cambridge University Press, 1970), 411–13.

13 For a succinct discussion of the process of *shukō* and other techniques of parody, see Iwasaki, 51–53.

14 For further discussion of this print, see Julia Meech, *Rain and Snow: The Umbrella in Japanese Art* (New York: Japan Society, 1993), no. 69.

15 For a more typical version of this theme see an illustration by Hokusai in *Ippitsu Gafu;* reproduced in Nagata Seiji, *Hokusai Bijutsukan* (Tokyo: Shūeisha, 1990), vol. 1, pl. 64. This folk tale manifests itself more elaborately in the folk tale and popular Kabuki play *Jiraiya,* which involves characters who invoke the various magical powers of snakes, toads, and snails.

16 Charles Stewart Smith Collection, no. 1051. Another impression in the Duel Collection, Harvard University, is in excellent condition but has an extraneous haikai poem on the theme of a child and plum blossoms brushed in by a poet who signed himself Ippō, no doubt the pen name of the original owner of the print.

A NOTE TO THE READER

Prints in the color entries section of the catalogue were reproduced as close as possible to actual size—with the exception of catalogue numbers 8 and 28, whose formats made this impractical.

The entries in the color and monochrome sections are arranged alphabetically according to artist's most familiar art name, and then in chronological order. It should be noted that the prints reproduced in color are not repeated in the monochrome entries. The dating of the prints has been calculated according to the Japanese lunar calendar in which spring begins in the first month. In entries for calendar prints, intercalcary months are indicated by a capital "I" together with the appropriate number of the month. Dimensions of each print are given in centimeters, height preceding width. References provided in the data section of each entry refer to publications where other impressions of the design have been reproduced or discussed; abbreviated citations are given in full in the Selected Bibliography. The FLLW FDN number provided for each print refers to the registration number assigned to it by the Frank Lloyd Wright Foundation. In the case of the color entries, transcriptions and translations of all of the poems have been provided; they have been transcribed in the sequence they appear on the print, reading from right to left. In the reference section, only the poets' names are provided; once again, listed in the order they appear on the prints.

Japanese names have been given in the Japanese order, surname first, with the exception of individuals who have chosen to use the Western system.

COLOR ENTRIES

KEISAI EISEN

1790–1848

1 Ono no Komachi with her assistant washing a book of poetry

DATE 1825, Year of the Bird
SIGNATURE Keisai
PRINTER'S SEAL Shumpūdō Ryūko
FORMAT Shikishiban (21.8 x 18.5)
REFERENCE Polster, no. 13
FLLW FDN 3020.001

Ōgi no Kaname:

mizukuki no	Spring of the bird year
ato mo nigoranu	arrives under tranquil skies,
kimigayo no	in an imperial reign
nodokeki sora ni	unsullied by any traces
tatsu tori no haru	of the writing brush.

Ayanoya Itome:

kumo no ue	Climbing ever higher
takaku noborite	into the realm of the clouds,
Saohime no	the kite has its writing
kasumi no nami ni	washed away by the waves
arau moji-dako	of Princess Sao's mist.

This lavish print, which aptly reflects the elevated status of its theme, depicts a legend associated with Ono no Komachi (act. mid-ninth century), a lady-in-waiting of the Early Heian court who is generally acknowledged as one of Japan's greatest poets. Through the centuries, numerous legends—based more on imaginative readings of her love poems than on historical fact—have evolved that present her as a woman of great beauty and passion who was afflicted with a melancholy temperament.

The legend alluded to by Eisen is *Sōshi Arai Komachi* (Komachi Washing a Book), a famous Nō play and one of the "Seven Komachi" (*Nana Komachi*) series, themes popularized in the ukiyo-e tradition of *mitate-e* (parody prints). According to legend, Ono no Komachi was accused by a male colleague, Ōtomo no Kuronushi, during a court poetry contest of borrowing a poem unaltered from the famous *Man'yōshū* (Collection of Ten Thousand Leaves), an anthology compiled over a century before. In fact, the night before, the jealous courtier had overheard her reciting this verse, and had transcribed it himself into a copy of this anthology. Komachi proves her innocence by washing off the freshly written verse.

The poems inscribed in the fan-shaped cartouche, notably both by women poets, make subtle allusion to this legend although they do not mention Komachi by name. The opening lines of the first poem play on an old Japanese expression which extols the virtues of calligraphy, "the traces of the writing brush last for a thousand reigns." The world of the court is implied in the first poem by the mention of "imperial reign" and in the second by referring to the "realm of the clouds," an ancient poetic term used to denote the imperial palace, and to the name of the legendary princess of spring, Saohime. The washing away of the writing on a kite is a veiled allusion to the Komachi legend. In the latter poem, *moji* (writing) is used as a pivot word: when combined with the word that follows, it forms part of the compound *ji-dako,* meaning a kite inscribed with auspicious characters. The cartouche may be viewed as a kind of a "kite-with-writing," which cleverly integrates allusions to a classical theme and a popular New Year's pastime.

During the 1820s there was a revived interest in the subject of classical literature in ukiyo-e, and representations of famous poets and writers as we see here were a popular subject with surimono designers. The complexity of this design, the pigments, and the heavy application of brass are also characteristic of prints of this period. Finally, the cyclical year of the bird mentioned in the first poem—which allows us to precisely date the print to 1825—is further suggested through the design of a phoenix rising from the clouds on the curtain-screen of state.

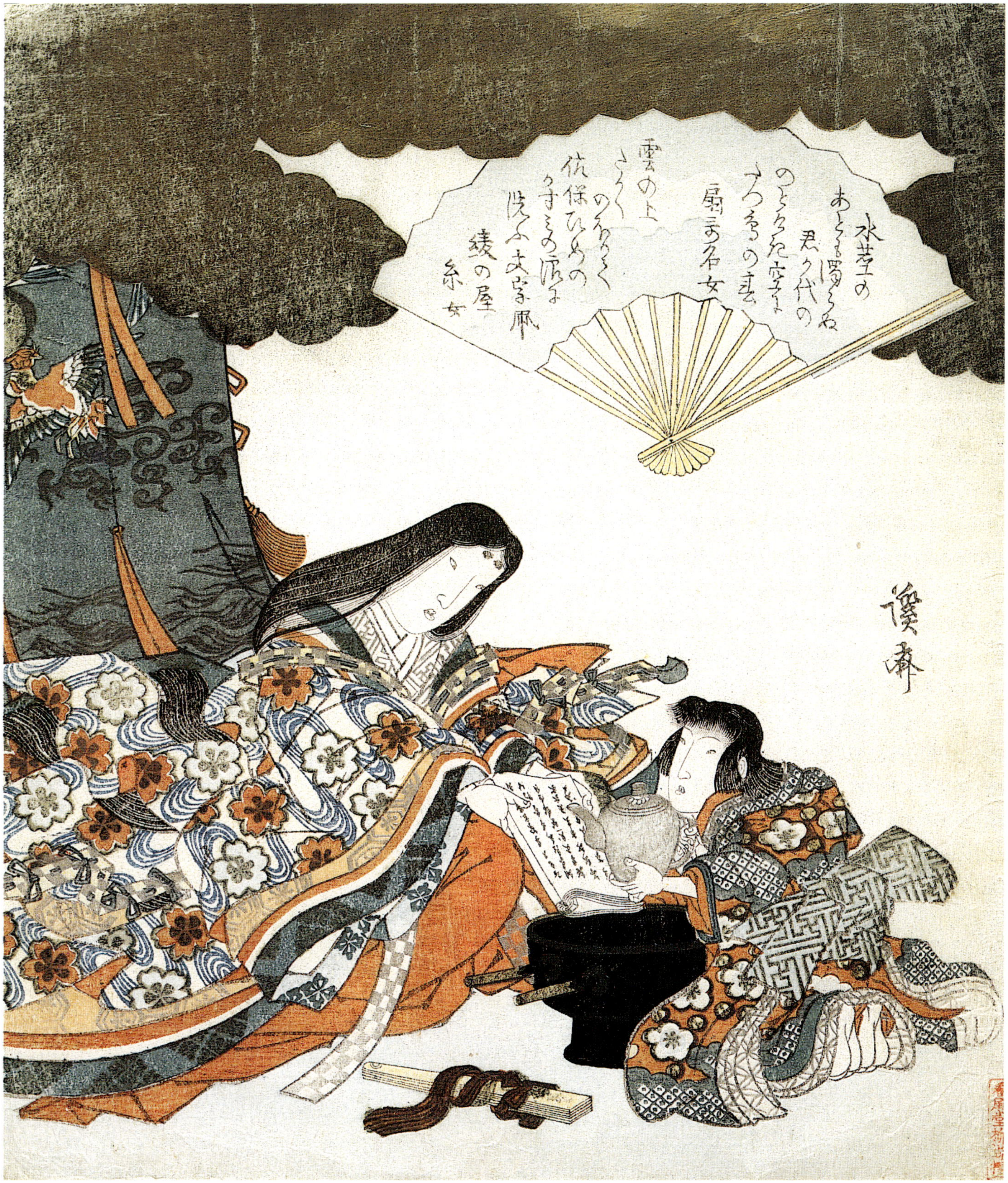

KEISAI EISEN

1790–1848

2 Courtesans on a cherry-viewing excursion to Mount Asuka

DATE ca. 1825
SIGNATURE Keisai
FORMAT Shikishiban (21.2 x 17.9)
FLLW FDN 3020.004

Wakanoya Kazumori:

suitō no	As they tip a flask
sake katabukete	taking sips of wine,
saku hana no	blossoms of snow
yuki ni mo ashi no	flutter around their feet,
akaki yoishire	now all flushed with drink.

Yuminoya Kizuki:

samukaranu	No one feels chilly
sakura no yuki ni	in a snow of cherry blossoms
Asuka-yama	on Mount Asuka—
hinomoto e yoru	as the flower-viewing party
hanami hitomure	gathers around a fire.

This depiction of two courtesans relaxing by a palanquin as they admire the cherry trees in full flower at Mount Asuka owes more to the long tradition of pictures of beauties in classic ukiyo-e than to the usually more refined portrayal of women in surimono. The subject of a cherry-blossom-viewing excursion has been repeatedly portrayed by numerous print designers in the standard ōban and triptych formats. Eisen narrowed the focus to two women, and the blossoming trees have been relegated to the background. The casual, relaxed manner of the women also contrasts sharply with the more formal poses shown in most prints by his predecessors. Eisen was an influential artist whose imagery of beautiful women had an impact on many of his contemporaries.

Because surimono were mainly issued for the New Year, depictions of plum blossoms and allusions to them are pervasive, as the plum is the first flower to open at that time of year. Cherry blossoms, which bloom over a month later, appear only infrequently in surimono. The two courtesans here have no doubt been given the day off, as it was customary for the brothels to close for the day for a cherry-blossom-viewing excursion by the courtesans. The location selected for the outing is Mount Asuka. Now a park in northern Tokyo it has remained a favorite site for cherry-blossom picnics.

Both poems rely on one of the most overworked poetic conceits of traditional Japanese verse that likens cherry blossoms to snowflakes. Draped over the arm of one woman is a polka-dotted coat bearing the emblem of the Honchō poetry club.

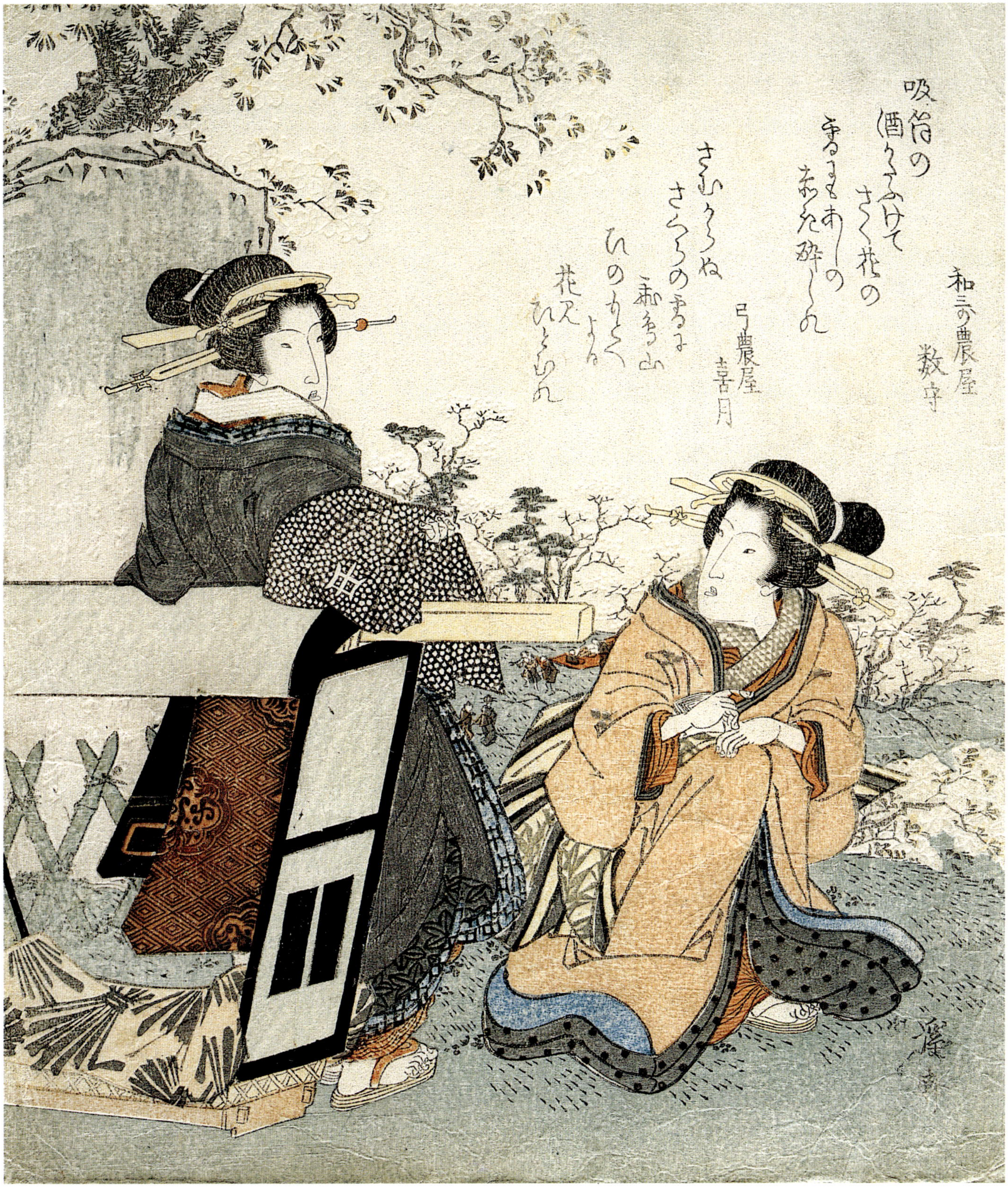

YASHIMA GAKUTEI

1786?–1868

3 A retainer bowing to the shogun

TITLE *Ōkura Umanokami Yorifusa: Taiheiki-dan;* Yorifusa, Counselor of the Right Imperial Stables: A Tale from the *Taiheiki*
SERIES *Honchō-ren: Honchō Nijūshi Kō;* Twenty-four Japanese Paragons of Filial Piety for the Honchō Circle
DATE ca. 1820
SIGNATURE Gakutei
ARTIST'S SEAL Sadaoka
FORMAT Shikishiban (21.2 x 19.1)
REFERENCES Rijksmuseum, *Hokusai,* pl. 213; Hempel, *Scheiwe,* no. 366; Christies, *Scheiwe II,* no. 80; Polster, no. 61
FLLW FDN 3010.015

Shummintei Tanenari:

ne no hi shite	On the day of the rat,
kimi ga tame mata	with both hands he plucks
oya no tame	tiny pines in the field—
ryōte ni hikeru	one for his lordship
nobe no himematsu	and one for his father.

The theme of the Twenty-four Paragons of Filial Piety is based on a Chinese collection of Confucian stories. They were first transposed into Japanese settings during the sixteenth century in anonymous popular stories *(otogizōshi)* that were widely circulated by itinerant storytellers. Confucianism was the prevailing moral and intellectual code of the ruling military class during the Edo period, and its central tenet stressed respect for one's master, ruler, parents, and ancestors. Starting in the late eighteenth century, there was a revival of Confucian classics which were then reinterpreted for popular Japanese taste—as reflected in this set by Gakutei.

This series was commissioned by the Honchō circle, whose name, written with different characters, is also a literary designation for Japan. Based on the theme of filial piety, the subject of each surimono has been drawn from ancient historical and literary treatises. Of the twenty-four prints in this series, fifteen can be found in the Wright collection (see also the following entry and cat. nos. 67–79). For other prints from the series, see Rijksmuseum, *Hokusai,* plates 204–23; and Hempel, *Scheiwe*, numbers 354–77.

The story illustrated here is based on an episode from the *Taiheiki* (Record of Great Peace), an early medieval war tale transmitted orally over the course of several generations. The final version was compiled by the priest Kojima in 1372. During the Edo period, it was a common source of inspiration for writers, playwrights, and artists.

The warrior Yorifusa, the subject of this print, was the son of Ishidō Yoshifusa, who served the shogun Ashikaga Takauji (1305–58). Yoshifusa planned an attack to overthrow his master. On the day prior to the attempted coup, Yoshifusa, knowing this act to be decisive to his family's future, tells his son of his plan. Torn between his filial relationship to his father and his responsibility to his lord, Yorifusa decides that his loyalty to his leader should be absolute. Shown submissively bowing before Takauji with helmet removed, Yorifusa obediently reveals the plot against Takauji formulated by his own father. By foiling Yoshifusa's plans, Yorifusa also indirectly saved his father's life, preventing him from following through with what amounted to a suicide mission.

In a simple but effective way, the poet has used the analogy of plucking auspicious pine shoots in spring to convey a similar message. The reference to the first day of the rat, *ne no hi,* links the scene to the New Year.

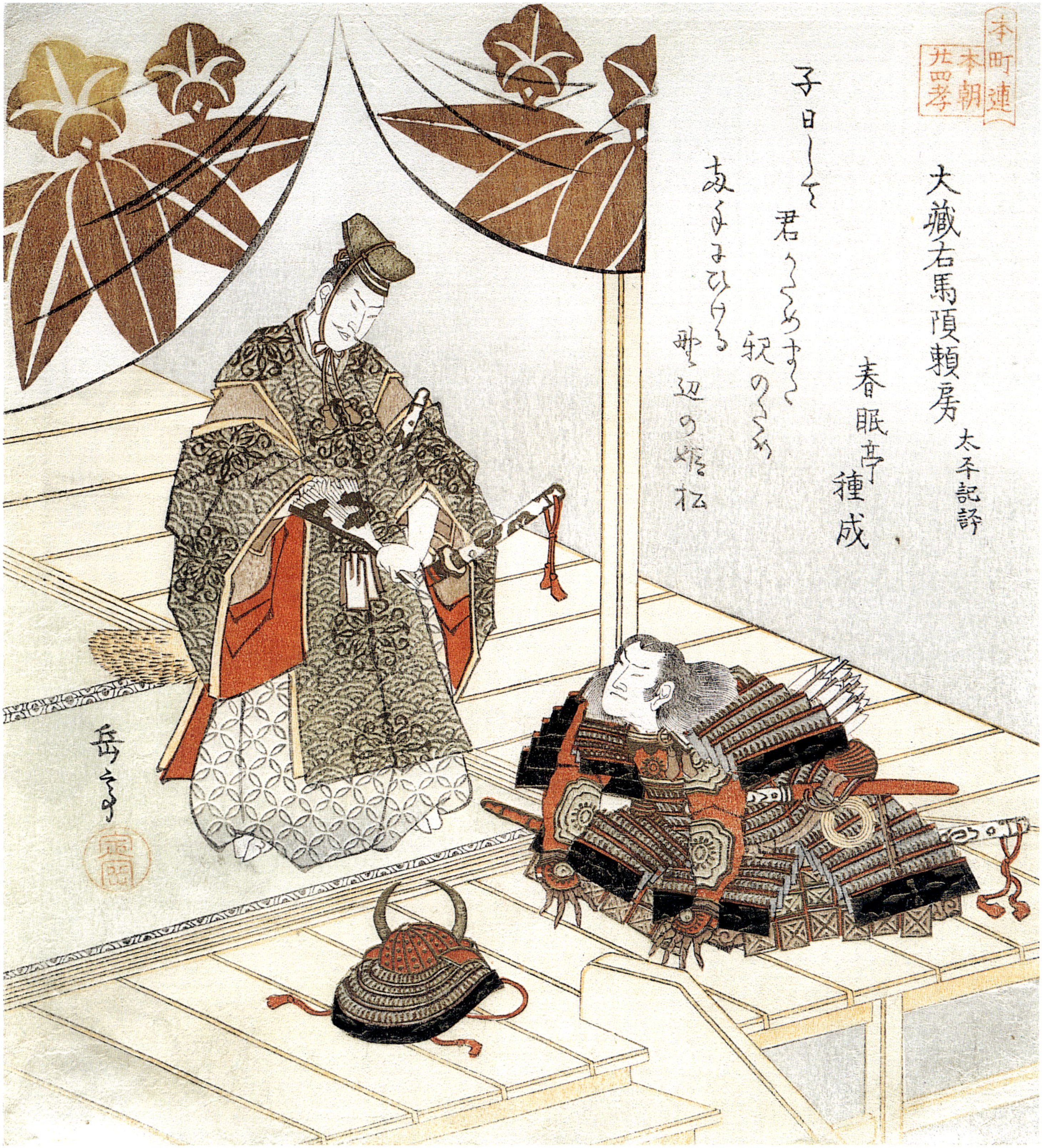
本町連
本朝廿四孝
大藏右馬頭頼房
太平記評
春眠亭種成
岳亭

YASHIMA GAKUTEI

1786?–1868

4 A man hoeing a field

TITLE *Ono no Takamura: Montoku Jitsuroku;* The Tale of Ono no Takamura from *An Official Account of the Montoku Era*
SERIES *Honchō-ren: Honchō Nijūshi Kō;* Twenty-four Japanese Paragons of Filial Piety for the Honchō Circle
DATE ca.1820
SIGNATURE Gakutei
ARTIST'S SEAL Sadaoka
FORMAT Shikishiban (21.3 x 19.0)
REFERENCES Rijksmuseum, *Hokusai*, pl.204; Hempel, *Scheiwe,* no.355
FLLW FDN 3010.024

Hamanoya Masago:

ichinen no	The year is borne
oya naru haru zo	by its mother, Spring,
taisetsu to	under whose care
ue-oki ume no	a plum tree is planted
ka sae takamura	so its fragance may grow.

Sodenoya Furiyoshi:

morokoshi no	On the way to China,
kata o mo haru wa	quarreling through the spring
arasoite	as he set out in a boat,
ogamu ya hatsu no	the thing he admired most
mikazuki no fune	was the first crescent moon.

As a youth, Ono no Takamura (802–52) followed his father on military campaigns in the provinces, and even after returning to the capital continued to hone his martial skills. It was the Emperor Saga who encouraged Takamura to apply himself to literary pursuits. His mastery of the Chinese classics later earned him an appointment as vice ambassador to China. Dissatisfied with the less than seaworthy ship that had been assigned to him for a voyage to China, Takamura quarreled with the chief ambassador, then feigned illness and refused to join the mission. He claimed that if he died along the way that his parents would have no one to care for them in their old age. He also circulated a Chinese poem satirizing the ill-fated mission. For his insubordination he was exiled to the remote island of Oki. Yet, in recognition of his cultural accomplishments and his demonstration of filial piety, he was reinstated at court less than two years later. In the image here, his elderly mother looks on, extending to him a cup of tea.

The first poem reflects the theme of the series, filial responsiblility, through its allusions to parenting. As the spring season is the parent of the year, so too the plum tree gives birth to blossoms whose fragrance attains ever greater strength, like a growing child. The second poem makes oblique reference to Takamura's ill-fated mission to China and his quarrel with the head of the delegation. Countering the seriousness of the theme, the poet alludes to a light-hearted spring boat ride beneath a crescent moon.

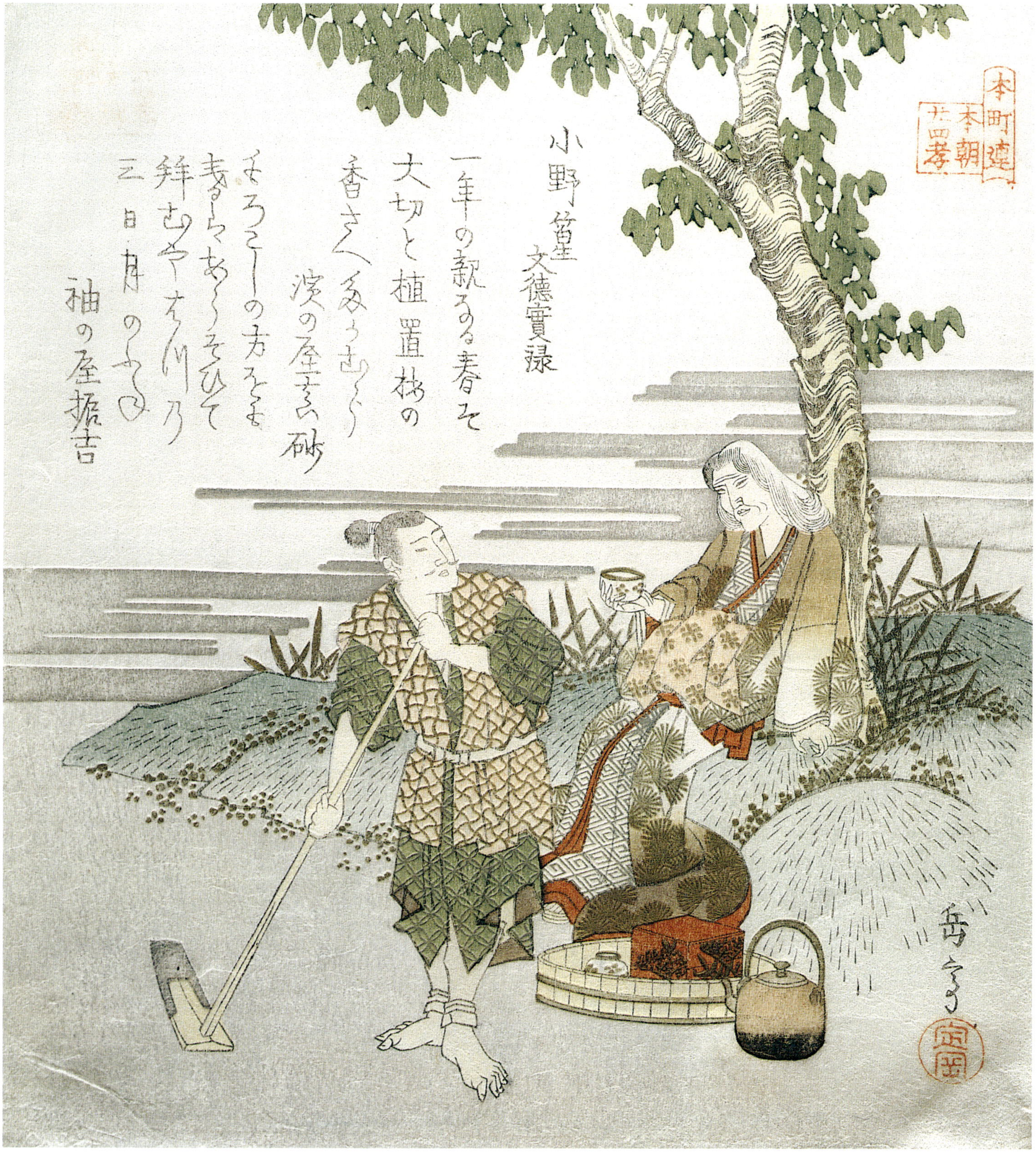
本町連
本朝廿四孝
小野篁
文徳實録

YASHIMA GAKUTEI

1786?–1868

5 A courtesan with a cat

TITLE *Usugumo;* The courtesan Usugumo
SERIES *Katsushika-ren Gakumen Fujin Awase;* Framed Paintings of Women for the Katsushika Circle
DATE ca. 1822
SIGNATURE Gakutei
FORMAT Shikishiban (21.0 x 18.6)
FLLW FDN 3010.029

Matsumado Chieda:

hi o machite	Awaiting the sun
sake yo to megumu	to call the buds to blossom,
haru no yo no	rain on a spring evening
ame to chigiran	promises to burst forth
hana no Usugumo	through a veil of cloud.

Bumbunsha:

murasaki no	Woven with purple
kasumi orikomu	strands of springtime mist,
shikizome no	Usugumo's new bedding
yagu no yama ni mo	forms a mountain covered
kakaru Usugumo	with a light veil of cloud.

This series of at least twelve images includes a wide array of women from Japanese history and legend, including poets, warriors, imperial consorts, high-ranking courtesans, and lowly prostitutes. Their only characteristic in common is their inclusion in the lore of Edo popular culture. Each figure is set against a gold ground and encased within a black and silver frame, as in a votive painting. The poetry appears in a vertical panel at the left, which is heavily embossed to simulate wood grain. These two areas, together with the narrow title cartouche, are juxtaposed against a patterned ground of abstracted blossoms. Gakutei often designed such complex collage-like compositions during the early 1820s (also see cat. no. 8). This is one of three designs in the Wright collection from this series (see cat. nos. 6 and 80; ten other examples from this series are illustrated in Keyes, *Beatty,* pls. 53–62).

Although there were a number of courtesans who used the name Usugumo, the third top-ranked courtesan to use this professional name was famous for her love of cats. She lived in the House of Miura, a Yoshiwara bordello, for twenty-three years beginning in 1693. Her many cats were entertained by her attendants in their free time. She is famous in the annals of the Yoshiwara because she always carried a cat with her during ceremonial processions. Both poems pun on the courtesan's name, Usugumo, which literally means "thin clouds" or "veil of cloud." Harking back to ancient Chinese poetry, the reference to rain and clouds is an allusion to lovemaking. The pledge between the rain and the clouds to make the spring flowers blossom forth is an oblique reference to a patron's pledge of support.

The second poem was written by Bumbunsha Kanikomaru, the leader of the Katsushika-ren poetry group which commissioned the print. *Murasaki* (purple), mentioned in the first line, was the proverbial color of spring mists and was associated with the city of Edo. The term *shikizome* refers in Yoshiwara argot to the ceremony attending the "first setting out" or display of new bedding presented to a courtesan by a devoted patron. For a high-ranking courtesan, such a gift customarily included three sumptuous silk-brocade quilts, which would sometimes be placed on view first at the client's teahouse before being transferred to the brothel. As with many aspects of life in the Yoshiwara, the expense and luxury or ostentation of a courtesan's wardrobe and accoutrements reflected upon the prestige of the courtesan and corresponded to the level of her patronage.

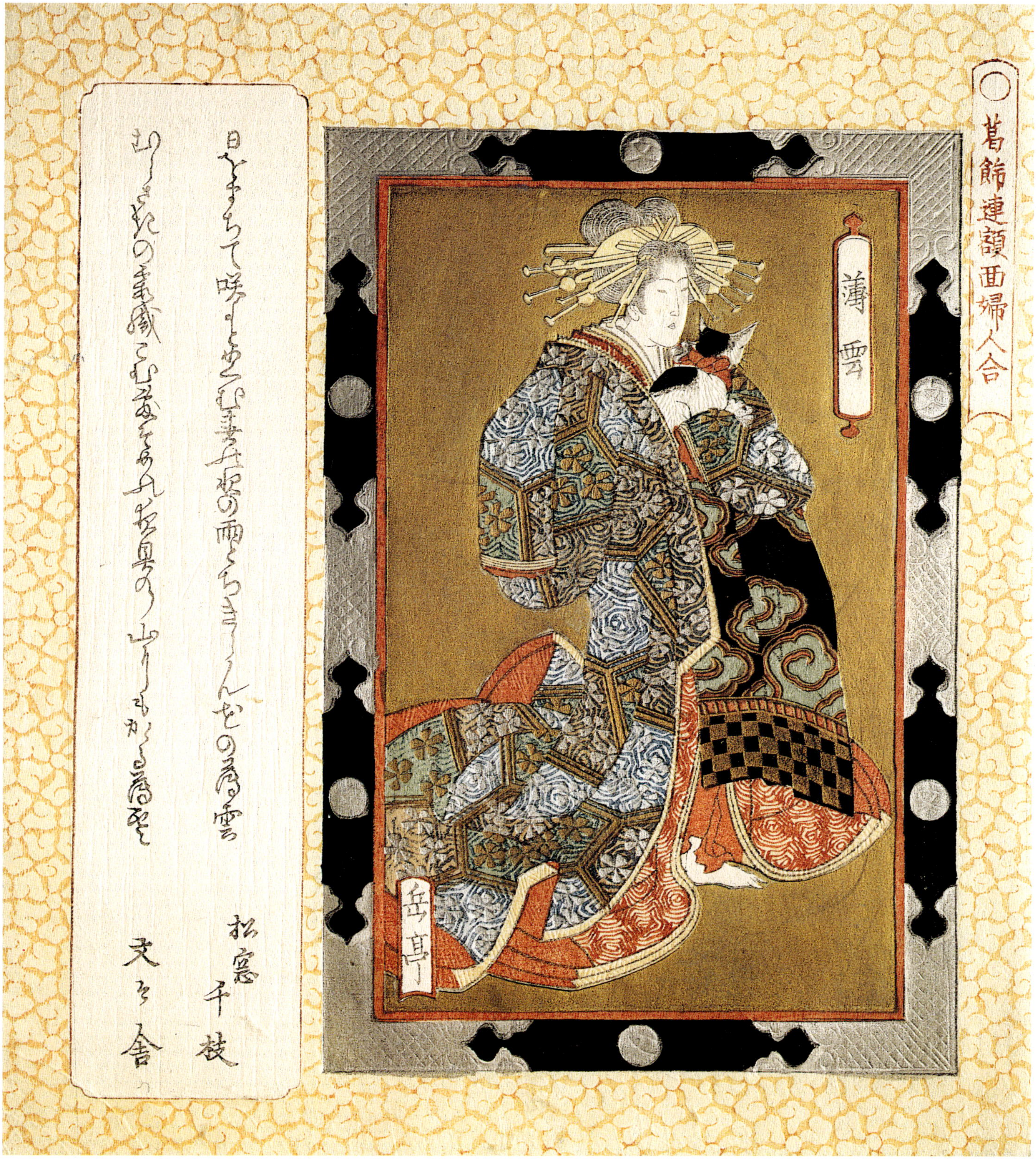
葛飾連頭面婦人合
薄雲
岳亭
松窓 千枝
文々舎

YASHIMA GAKUTEI

1786?–1868

6 A court lady with a koto

TITLE *Kogō no Tsubone;* Lady Kogō
SERIES *Katsushika-ren Gakumen Fujin Awase;* Framed Paintings of Women for the Katsushika Circle
DATE ca. 1822
SIGNATURE Gakutei
FORMAT Shikishiban (21.4 x 18.6)
REFERENCE Narazaki, ed., *Oranda Kokuritsu Raiden Minzokugaku Hakubutsukan,* vol. 1, pl. 116
FLLW FDN 3010.031

Bunkyōsha Hazemaru:

kadomatsu no	So enraptured
koto no shirabe ni	by the sound of a koto
kikihorete	at the pine-laden gate,
hikitodometaru	the young colt of spring
haru no wakagoma	pulls back to stay a while.

Bunkaisha Nazuki:

himematsu ni	Amid small pines
koto o hikasuru	the koto is plucked
harukaze no	by spring breezes
shirabe ni awasu	to the accompaniment
uguisu no fue	of the warbler's flute.

Kogō no Tsubone was a high-ranking lady and talented musician who served in the twelfth-century imperial court. As the favorite consort of Emperor Takakura, who ruled from 1168 to 1180, the beautiful Kogō soon aroused the antipathy of the empress and her circle. She fled, but was forced to return at the command of the emperor; later she gave birth to one of his daughters. She was once again forced out, due to pressure from a male courtier jealous of her position, who made public his knowledge of an illicit affair which had occurred before her tenure at court. She retired to a Buddhist convent at age twenty-three. Her tragic story as related in *The Tale of the Heike* was a source of inspiration for playwrights and raconteurs during the Edo period.

Lady Kogō leans toward her koto, which lies across the trail of her sumptuous robes. The detailing of the floral pattern, printed in copper and gold and set against the checkerboard design of her inner robe, sharply contrasts with the gold-colored ground and intricate frame. In this fine impression, an embossed crosshatch pattern is visible in the silver area of the frame, which also incorporates the character *bun,* the emblem for the Katsushika poetry group.

The first poem hints at the story of the search for Kogō after she had fled the palace in fear of the jealous empress. In the second poem, a type of toy flute made of bamboo called a "warbler's flute" also suggests a warbler singing amid young pines. Pine shoots are traditionally plucked and collected on the first day of the rat after the New Year.

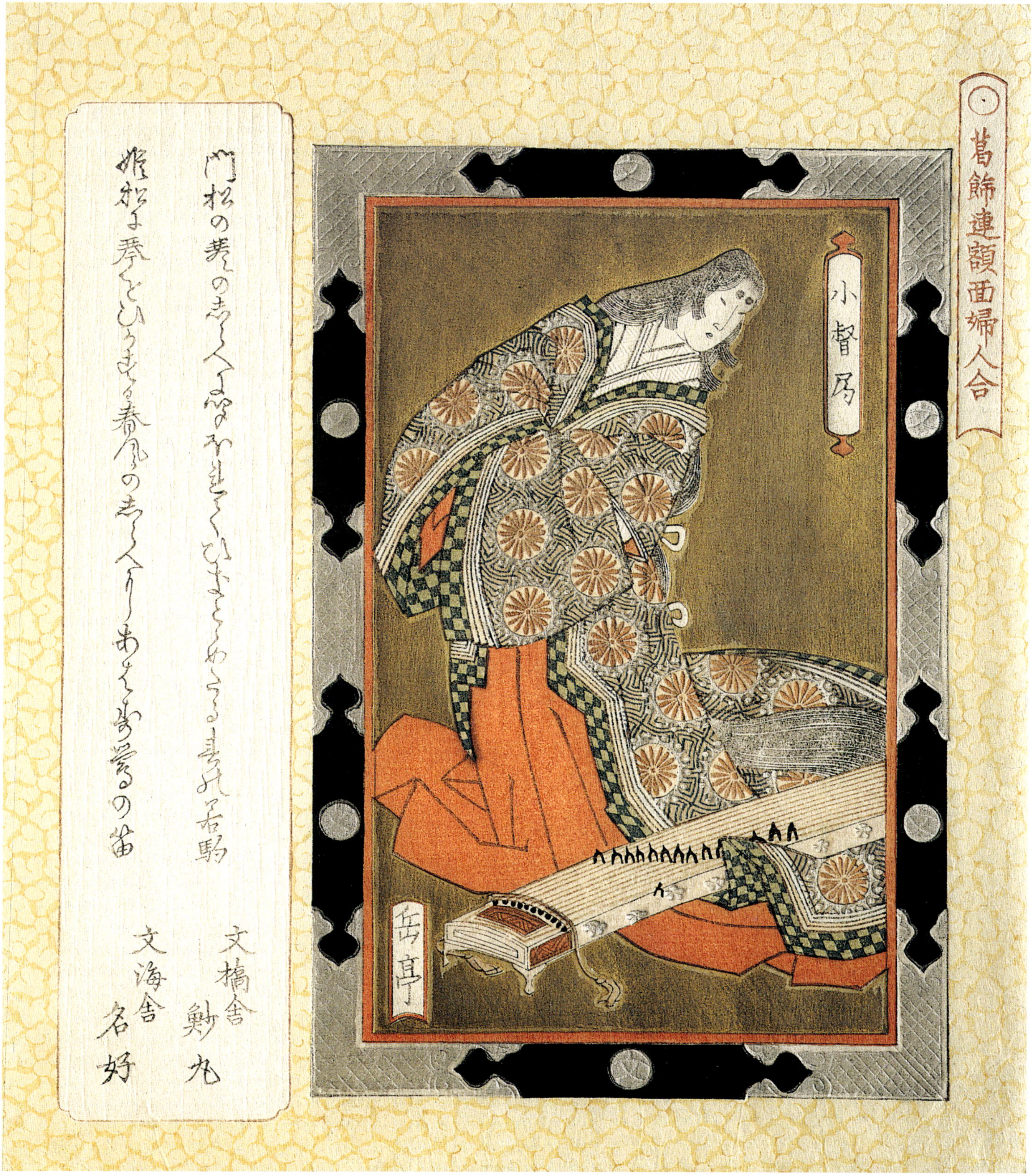
葛飾連額面婦人合
小督局
岳亭
文橋舎
文海舎
名好

YASHIMA GAKUTEI

1786?–1868

7 Pentaptych of strolling courtesans and their apprentices

SERIES *Hisakataya Nakanochō;* Views of Nakanochō for the Hisakataya Club
DATE ca. 1825
SIGNATURE Gakutei Sadaoka (each)
PRINTER'S SEAL Shūgyokudō (each)
FORMAT Shikishiban pentaptych (each 21.4 x 18.8)
REFERENCES Complete set is illustrated in Rijksmuseum, *Hokusai,* pls. 242 a–e; *UT, Pulverer,* pls. 118–22; Pulverer, pl. 2-73; Shimizu, no.35
FLLW FDN 3010.033–37

This richly conceived set of five continuous scenes of courtesans and their apprentices parading on the main street of the Yoshiwara at the New Year is a superb example of the mature style of surimono by Gakutei, whose earlier prints contained a simple, uncluttered ground. Here, the entire surface of the print is filled with decorative details, such as the new bamboo hanging shades, rope curtains with ferns at the top edge, and the bamboo and pine arrangements which tie the designs together. In fact, the only uncolored areas are the poetry cartouches, which are crowded with calligraphy. Despite the complexity of the background, the courtesans in their ornate attire are not upstaged. The lavish kimono and obi are extravagantly printed with thick silver, gold, copper, and richly colored pigments.

The parade through the five districts of the Yoshiwara along its main artery, the Nakanochō, was an annual event staged by the major brothels on the second day of the New Year. Courtesans and their apprentices dressed in their finest new attire, which they personally selected, rather than the house garments that they were required to wear on the first day of the New Year. In a sense this annual parade was a competitive fashion show.

Bordellos with the names mentioned in the titles of each of the prints actually existed, but here it seems they were selected for their playful connections to spring rather than to identify the establishment. Pine and crane are auspicious New Year symbols, and the gathering of herbs and the first writing are traditional activities on that occasion. An open fan is considered an auspicious symbol. Similarly the names of the courtesans are typical but do not seem to refer to actual persons.

The poems are rather staightforward, praising the beauty and talents of the courtesans in a simple fashion, while alluding to New Year customs of the Yoshiwara. In the first print, the name of the brothel the House of the Fan (Ōgiya) is a source of several puns. Terms related to fans are interwoven into the first poem—"tightly shut" (*shimari yoki*), "open" (*hiraku*), and "hinge-pin" (*kaname)*—linking them to the opening of the Great Gate of the Yoshiwara.

In the second print, the allusions are all based on the tradition of collecting young herbs during the New Year season. Wakanaya, the House of Young Herbs, was the actual name of a brothel, and the word *wakakusa,* meaning young grasses, is a common metaphor for a young woman which refers to the *shinzō,* or newly launched young courtesan, shown here dressed in black. In another common poetic conceit, the white-powdered face of a courtesan is frequently likened to snow.

Kite flying, a popular New Year's activity, is the source for the puns in the third surimono. *Hatsusora* refers to the sky on the first day of the New Year. The flying motif is continued in the mention of the auspicious symbol of the crane, a reference to the name of this bordello. The second poem compares the long strides of a courtesan on parade (*ōtori ayumi*) to kites in the shape of large birds (*ōtori hata*).

Because the subject is the Matsubaya or Pine Needle House, the poems for the fourth print revolve around that seasonal theme. Gate decorations made of pine boughs are still used today as doorway ornaments, and in this set of surimono there are large arrangements which also contain tall bamboo. They frame the exterior of the *misezashiki,* or the room for displaying the courtesans, which was traditionally rearranged for special New Year's activities. *Midori* (green), was a generic nickname for a courtesan's girl attendant in the parlance of the Yoshiwara and here refers to the two girls shown beside the high-ranking courtesan.

References in the poems of the fifth print are to "the first shopping," or *hatsugai,* which in the argot of the Yoshiwara means the first visit with a courtesan. *Itsuzuke,* or staying over another day in a bordello, refers to the custom of charging extra for clients staying past six in the morning. Despite the extra fee, such patrons were not encouraged because they allowed the courtesan no time to rest and disrupted the routine of the house.

YASHIMA GAKUTEI

1786?–1868

8 A woman with an umbrella strolling to Marishiten Shrine

TITLE *I, Shitaya:* The Boar, Shitaya District
SERIES *Ichiyō-ren Edo Meisho Mitate Jūnishi;* Famous Places in Edo Compared to the Twelve Animals of the Zodiac for the Ichiyō Circle
DATE ca. 1825
SIGNATURE Gakutei
FORMAT Shikishiban (21.4 x 19.0)
REFERENCES Rijksmuseum, *Hokusai,* pl. 265; Polster, no. 112
FLLW FDN 3010.027

Bunkyosha Takamaru:

kashiwade mo	The sounds of hands
hii fuu mitsu no	clapping, one, two, three,
asa kiyome	on a crisp morning
hibiku ya haru no	echo in the spring air
Marishiten michi	on the way to Marishiten.

Bunshukusha Otoyoshi:

mononofu no	At the shrine
inoru miya-i wa	where warriors worship,
kōin no	time flies
yumiya mo haru no	like an arrow from a bow
Marishiten michi	at Marishiten in spring.

Bunkyōsha Tomomaru:

shinagadori	On festival days
i no hi wa koto ni	dedicated to the boar,
nigiwaite	there's a bustle
ushiro mukarenu	in the presence of a god
kami no hiromae	who never turns her back.

Set against a field of plum blossoms, a woman dressed in kimono and a half-length raincoat holds a bull's-eye-pattern umbrella in the rain. Glancing over her shoulder, she passes by Marishiten, a shrine in the precincts of Tokudaiji, a temple at Shitaya in Edo, near Ueno. Marishiten was originally a male Hindu divinity named Marici Deva. In Japan the deity was worshiped in female form and was considered a guardian of warriors. She is traditionally portrayed with three faces, standing mounted on a boar (see Suzuki, figs. 44–45). During the Edo period, Marishiten worship flourished in conjunction with cults associated with the Seven Gods of Good Fortune. Shrines dedicated to her were visited on the first day of the boar of the New Year; the most popular spots were located within larger temple or shrine complexes in Ueno at Tokudaiji, illustrated here, and at Hachiman Shrine in Fukagawa.

This set was commissioned by the Ichiyō poetry club, which was affiliated with the Katsushika group. Gakutei has again filled the composition with separate cartouches for title, poetry, and image and he has set them against a field of plum blossoms. In this series, the flowers are larger, more fully articulated, and colorful than in the preceding set. Each of the twelve designs from this series juxtaposes contemporary figures with famous shrines, and each alludes to one of the animals of the zodiac. The Wright collection contains three others from the series (see cat. nos. 81, 82, and 83). The Achenbach Foundation for Graphic Arts, San Francisco, has the complete series, illustrated in Polster (nos. 101–12).

The first poem refers to the sound—still familiar to modern-day pilgrims and tourists—of worshipers clapping their hands in front of a shrine to catch the attention of the deity whom they hope will answer their prayers. *Yumiya,* in the second poem, is a reference to *Yumiya kami* (literally "the god of the bow and arrow"), and used to refer to either Marishiten or the better-known Hachiman, the god of war. The poem also puns on an old Japanese proverb still occasionally heard: "time flies like an arrow." Opening with a reference to *shinagadori,* an ancient poetic name for a boar, the third poem links this term to *i-no-hi,* a common expression meaning "the day of the boar." The phrase "never turns her back," is a reminder that Marishiten was said to have three faces, each looking in a different direction. This is charmingly parodied in Gakutei's image by the turned posture of the beauty carrying her umbrella.

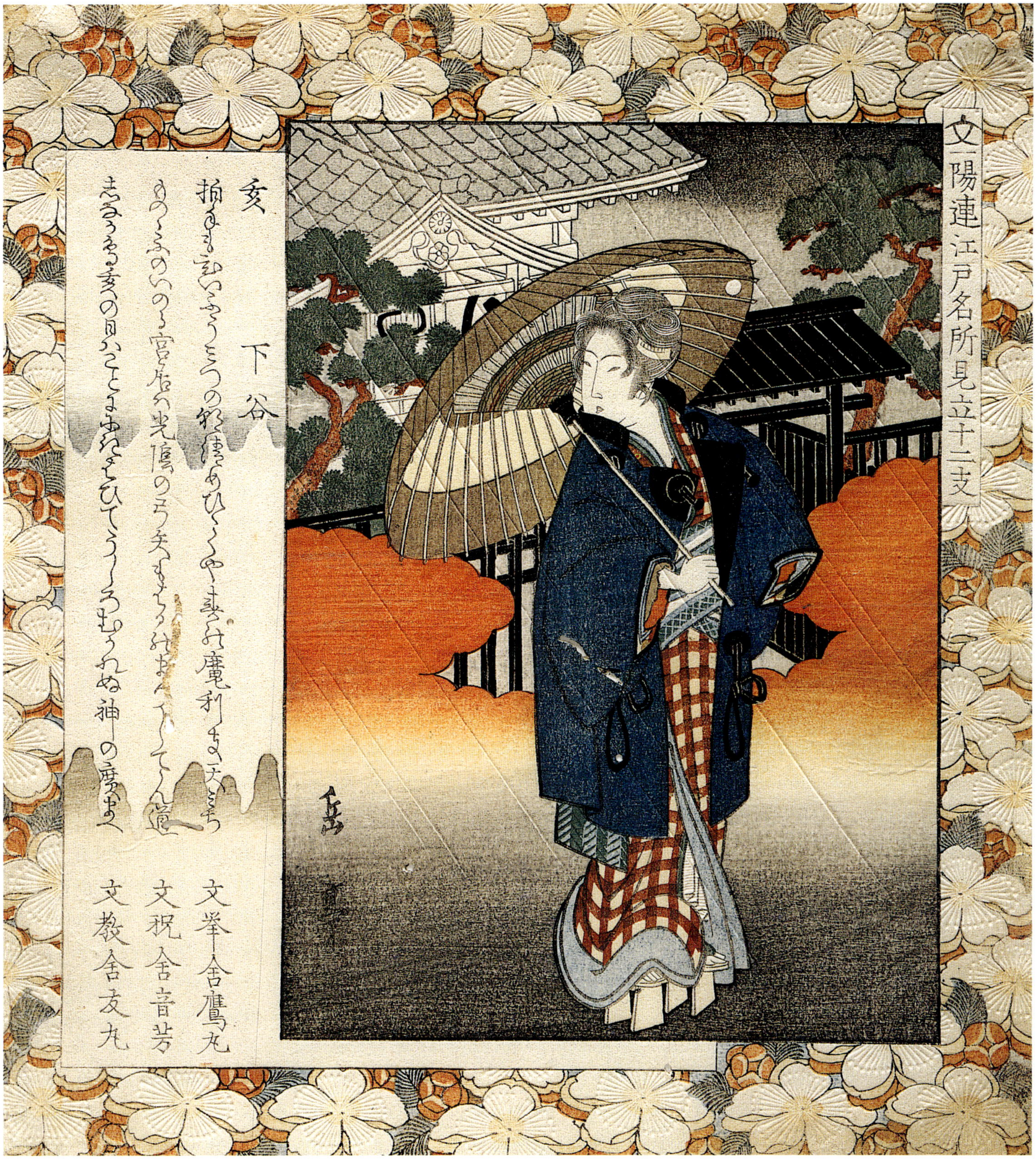
文陽連江戸名所見立十二支
亥
下谷
文挙舎鷹丸
文祝舎音芳
文教舎友丸

YASHIMA GAKUTEI

1786?–1868

9 A woman with a poem card

DATE ca. 1825
SIGNATURE Tōto Gakutei hitsu (Drawn by Gakutei from the Eastern Capital)
FORMAT Shikishiban (20.9 x 18.2)
REFERENCE Rijksmuseum, *Hokusai,* pl. 236
FLLW FDN 3010.032

Reitensha Sodenari:

kogarasu no	Even the color of ink
sumi no iro sae	black as a raven
utsukushiku	appears beautiful,
misuru kasumi no	amid the tinted mists
kinu no tanzaku	of the silk poem card.

Ryūsuitei Sodezumi:

uguisu no	The warbler's song
yomi-izuru uta no	inscribed on a poem card
tanzaku ni	is honed with skill,
kezure furusu no	like bogwood from the valley
tani no umoregi	where it once made its nest.

Senryūtei:

i no naka ni	Even the sound
sumeru kawazu mo	of the song
yomi-izuru	bellowed by a frog
uta no shirabe wa	who lives in a well
kawari tarikeri	is somehow transformed.

The elegant poetess is luxuriously attired in a kimono patterned with stylized plum blossoms and a meandering river, printed with gaufrage. Characters formed with copper powder are graphically integrated within the textile pattern. Her coiffure, as lavish as her dress, is adorned with a profusion of silver hairpins, all in the form of plum blossoms. She prepares to inscribe a narrow poem card. Stacked on the red lacquer desk behind her are piles of books.

All three poets were members of the Sendai branch of the Hanazono Circle, an Edo poetry club. The final poem is by its leader, Senryūtei Karamaro. A close friend of Gakutei, he was featured in the artist's collection of biographies and stylized portraits of contemporary kyōka poets, *Kyōka Genzai Kijin-dan* (Exceptional Kyōka Poets of Recent Times), published in three volumes in 1824.

Each of the poems alludes to the art of composing poetry while suggesting that the efforts of amateur provincial poets—alluded to by mention of a raven, warbler, and frog—are somehow enhanced by being inscribed on beautiful poem card. By extension, there is also a suggestion that the kyōka likewise acquire elegance by being inscribed on a gorgeous surimono designed by a celebrated Edo artist.

In the first poem, *kasumi,* which usually means "spring mist" has another, more specialized meaning of the "blue mist pattern" that was once commonly used to decorate poem cards. The mention of *umoregi* (literally, "buried tree") in the second poem refers to a type of bogwood or fossilized wood found in northeastern Japan. *Umoregi saiku,* "bogwood crafts," were a famous product of Sendai. At the same time the *umoregi* expression connotes a person who lives an obscure life in the countryside. The verb *kezuru* thus refers both to "carving" bogwood and "honing" a poem. The final poem continues the theme of a poet living in obscurity by alluding to the Japanese saying, "The frog who lives in a well can never know the great ocean." Even though the poem does not explicitly mention a poem card, the implication is that the frog's poem, too, is improved by being inscribed in a beautiful format.

The second and third poems in their mention of the songs of a warbler and frog recall the famous lines from the preface to the *Kokinshū* (Collection of Poems Past and Present, ca. 905): "When we hear the warbler singing amidst flowers, or the voice of a frog that lives in the water, we realize there is no living creature that cannot compose poetry." The *Kokinshū,* the first imperially commissioned anthology of waka, was a source of inspiration for waka poets throughout the ages; it was likewise consulted by kyōka poets, who often wrote parodic versions of classical verses.

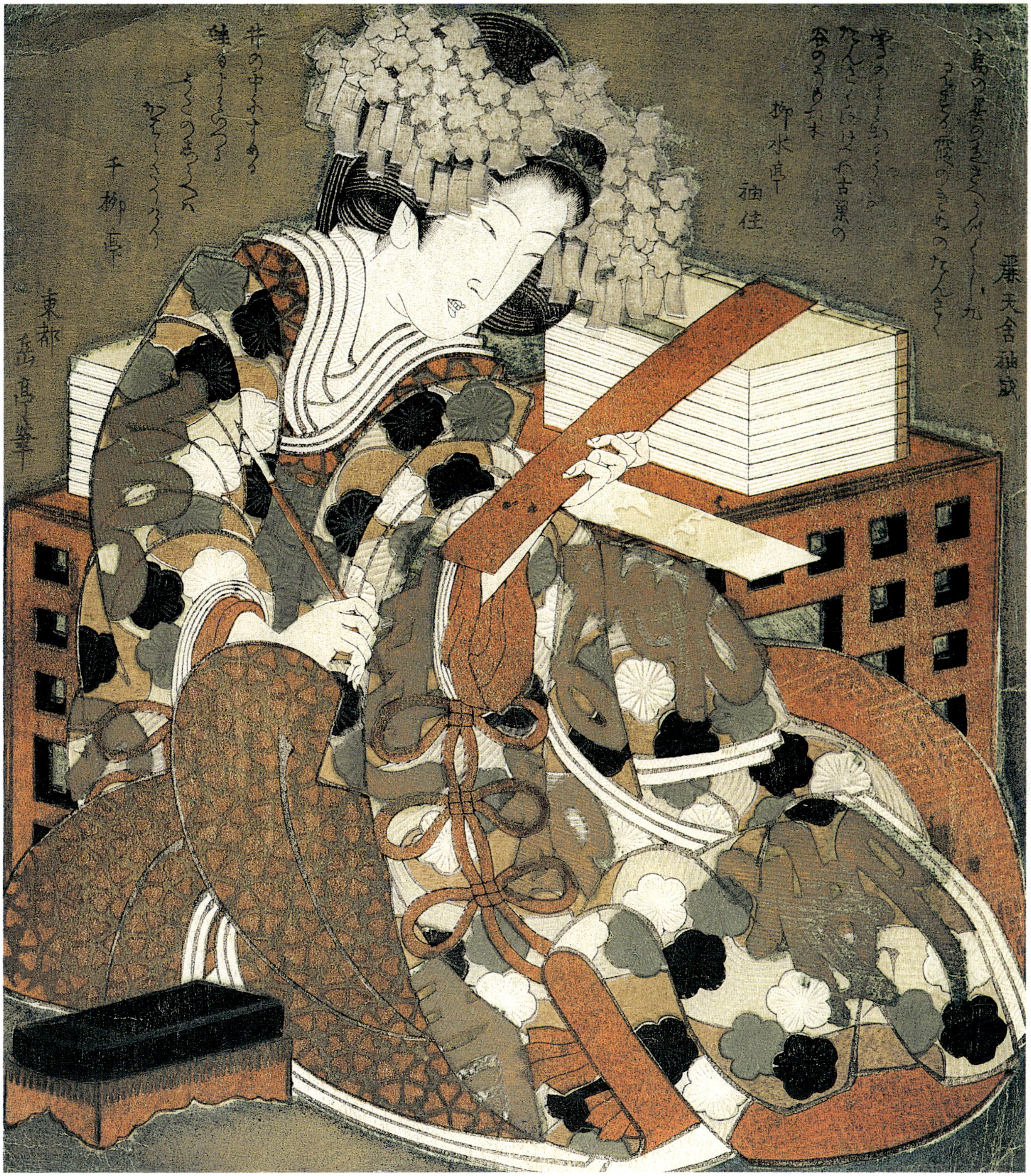

YASHIMA GAKUTEI

1786?–1868

10 Chinese Warriors: The Tiger Generals

SERIES *Suikoden Goko Shōgun;* Five Tiger Generals of the Suikoden
DATE ca. 1828
SIGNATURE Gakutei Sadaoka hitsu (each)
FORMAT Shikishiban (each 21.1 x 18.8)
FLLW FDN 3010.001-.003

(1) Guang Sheng
Fukunoya Uchinari:

toshi no seki	Winning a victory
sugurete hayaku	at the gate between years,
hatsuharu no	we cross over quickly
koeshi o tsuguru	into the advancing spring
niwatori no koe	at the crowing of the cock.

(2) Qin Ming
Arakitei Shikyō:

haru wa kesa	This morning
morokoshi made mo	spring has arrived
yukinu tote	even in faraway China,
hige darake naru	where thick beards
tokoro o zo horu	are so greatly admired.

(3) Lin Chong
Hankotai Atonari:

shihōhai	The rite of the four quarters
sugureba ume no	comes to a close,
uguisu mo	as the plum and warbler
minami ni mukite	turn to the south
hoshi ya tonauru	and praise the stars.

Morinoya Nakanuki:

tsuki hi hoshi	After three mornings
mitsu no ashita ya	of moon, sun, and stars,
saku ume no	plum trees bloom
hana no miyako no	in the flowery capital
uguisu no koe	as the warbler sings.

The Chinese novel titled *The Heroes of the Water Margin* (*Suikoden,* or *Shui Huzhuan* in Chinese) set in the thirteenth century, chronicles the tales of a band of righteous thieves and outcasts who have been forced to flee society and take refuge in the mountains of Shandong Province. First translated into Japanese beginning in 1805, it soon became a popular source of imagery for nineteenth-century ukiyo-e artists (see cat. no. 48).

The Wright collection includes the three right-hand prints of this set of five continuous designs (they are reproduced here in reduced size).Guan Sheng (Japanese: Kanshō), the general in the far right-hand sheet (1), who in the novel is given the nickname "The Great Sword," is seated in an elaborate Chinese chair and has an enormous halberd and a book. An able soldier promoted from within the ranks, he was eventually appointed chief commander. After his capture by this renegade band of outlaws, he was soon converted to their cause of righting injustice. The poem refers to his military skills, punning on his name, which means "barrier gate."

The next figure (2) is the Chinese general Qin Ming (Japanese: Shimmei), nicknamed "The Fire in the Thunder Clap" for his quick temper and loud, rolling voice. Originally an important military figure, he and his army were defeated by Hua Yung, a leader of the band of brigands. Later Qin Ming was converted to their cause and brought others with him. He is shown seated on a scallop-edged carpet with a letter in his hand.

The third print from this set (3) portrays the general Lin Chong (Japanese: Rinchū), nicknamed "Leopard's Head." Initially in charge of eight thousand soldiers, he was forced into exile after offending his commanding officer. Later he joined the group, rising to a high rank. In referring to "three mornings," the second poem perhaps obliquely refers to an episode in the novel when Lin Chong embarks on a three-day search for men sent to assassinate him, yet at the same time recalls a poetic expression that plays on the fact that New Year's day has three mornings—the morning of the first day, the morning of the first month, and the morning of the New Year. The other images of the poem are reconciled if we know that *tsuki hi hoshi,* "moon, sun, stars," according to popular folklore, are the words to the warbler's mellifluous spring song.

All of the prints in the set except the far right-hand print are illustrated in Hempel, *Scheiwe,* number 386. The fourth print, not included in the Wright collection, shows the general Dongping (Japanese: Tōhei) playing a flute. The fifth print, also missing from the collection, portrays Hu Zhuoyan (Japanese: Ko Enshaku) seated in a high-backed throne with a lute balanced on his lap; behind him a long halberd tilts to the right.

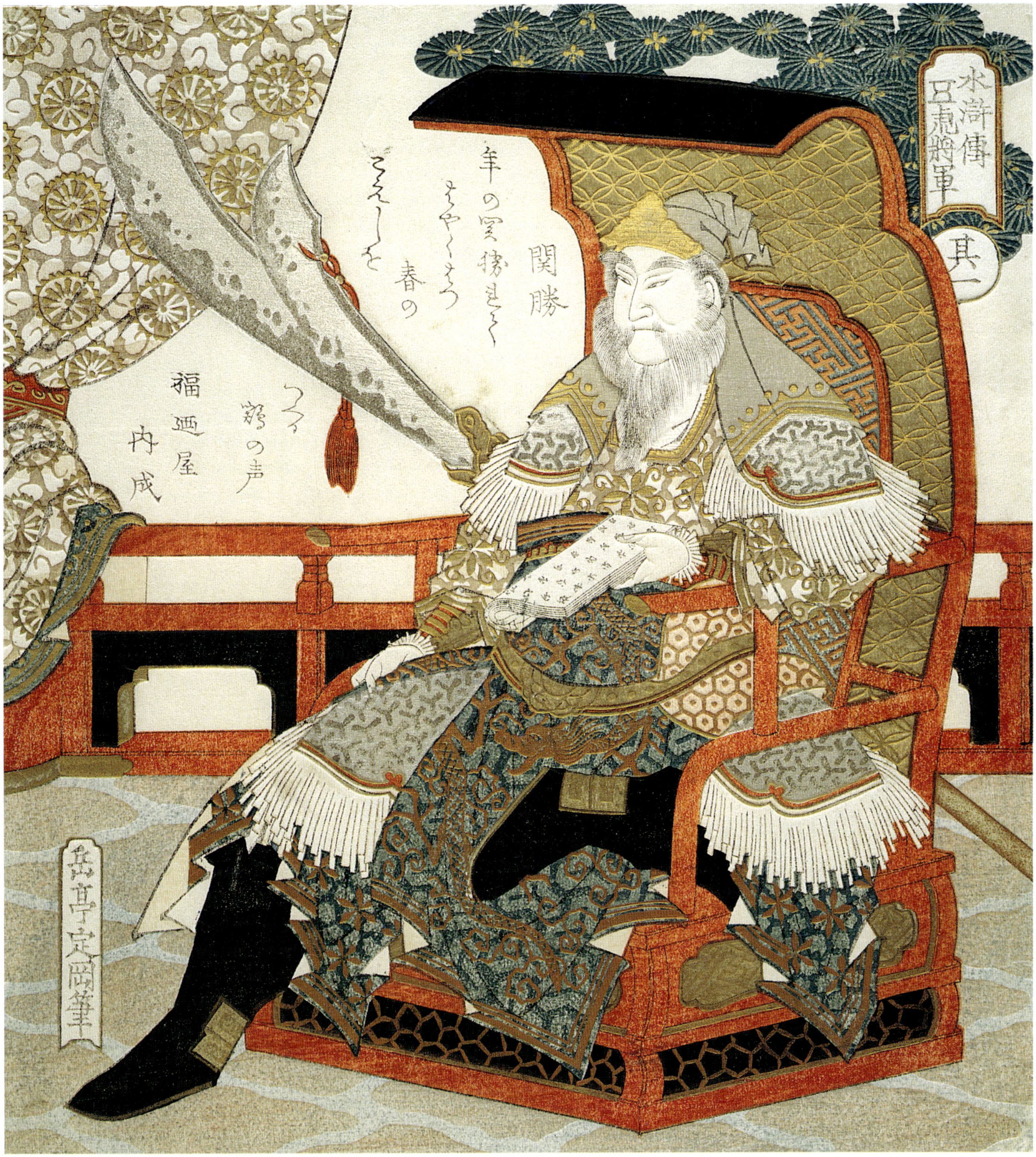

I

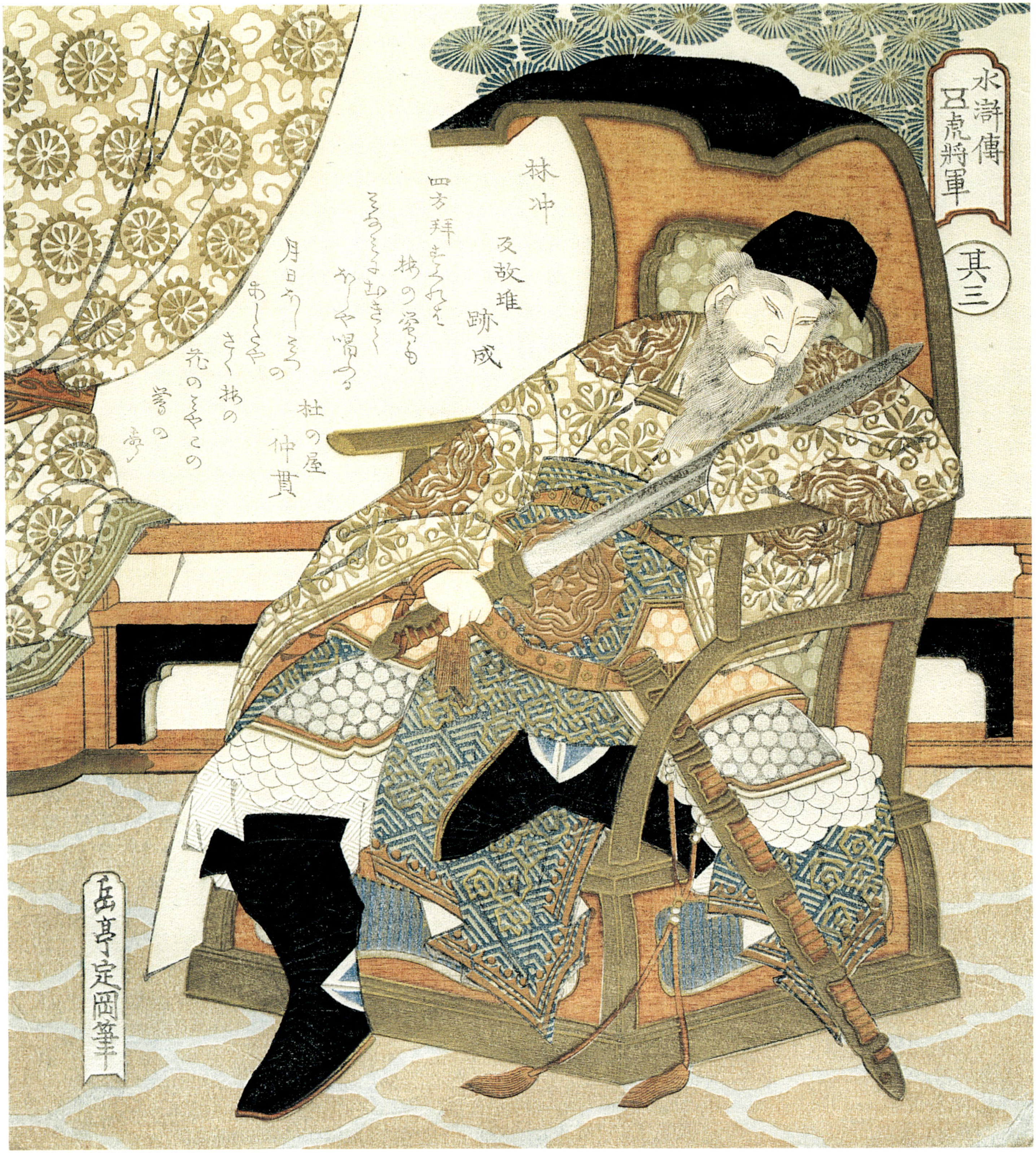

3

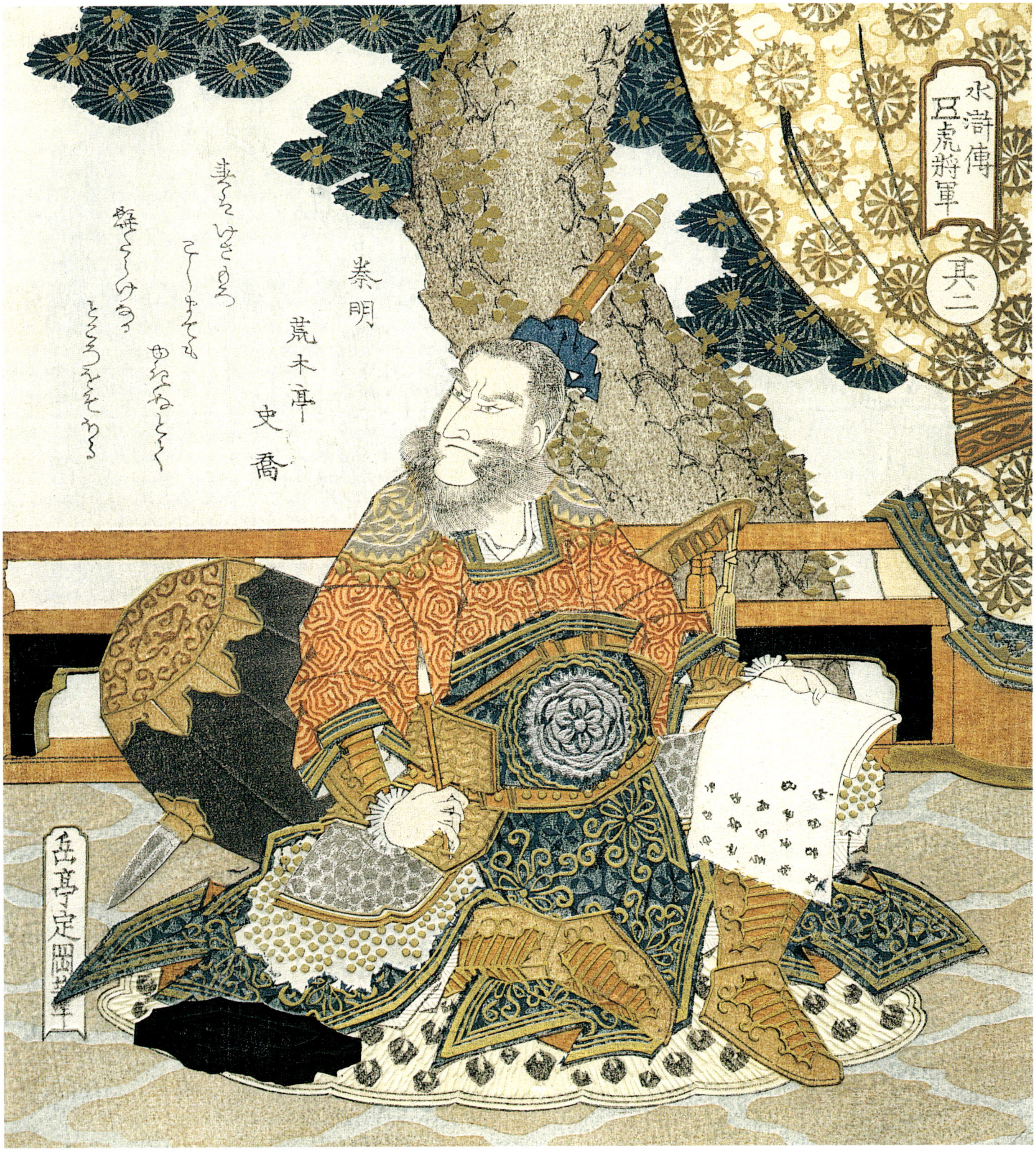
水滸傳
五虎將軍
其二
秦明
荒木亭
史喬
岳亭定岡画

HŌTEI GOSEI

ACT. CA. 1804–35 (d.)

11 A pair of Turtles

TITLE *Shinobazu no Ike;* Shinobazu Pond
SERIES *Tōto Meibutsu Awase;* Famous Attractions of the Eastern Capital
DATE ca. 1820
SIGNATURE Gosei hitsu
ARTIST'S SEAL Gosei
DEALER'S SEAL Hayashi Tadamasa
FORMAT Shikishiban (20.5 x 16.5)
PUBLISHED *Collection Hayashi,* no. 1238
REFERENCES Lane, *Images,* fig. 48; Preetorius, pl. 16.
FLLW FDN 3009.007

Jingairō Kiyozumi:

iwau dani	To celebrate the New Year—
zōni no mochi ni	soup is made with rice cakes
aburiko no	baked on a grill
kikkōgata mo	with a turtle-shell grid
tsukishi medetasa	to bring blessings to all.

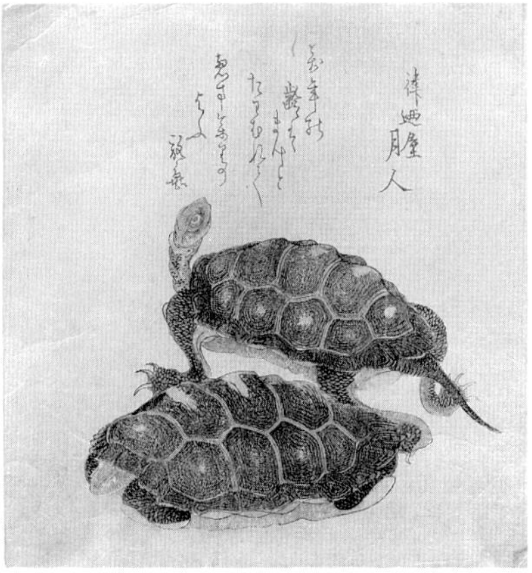

11a. After Gosei: *Two Turtles*
ca. 1890 (cat. no. 91)

Gosei is best known as an ukiyo-e painter of beautiful women and illustrator of kyōka anthologies. First a pupil of Hokusai, from whom he received the name Hokuga, Gosei's early work shows the influence of his teacher. Around 1810, he changed his name to Gosei and produced numerous surimono and illustrated books. This series of surimono is composed predominantly of still lifes based on the theme of Edo specialities. Each print is subtly printed, the central subject often without a black outline, creating a painterly effect. The series title cartouche in the shape of the character *go* representing the Go-gawa circle is next to the title on the left; both are outlined in red with the lettering in gold.

Shinobazu Pond, nearby Ueno Park, is still a popular scenic spot in Tokyo. Much of the pond's surface is covered with lotus plants, which have been growing there since the early nineteenth century. In this set of Edo *meibutsu* (famous attractions or products), Shinobazu Pond is represented by its most noted residents—turtles.

The poem is by Jingairō Kiyozumi, son of Rokujuen, the founder of the Gogawa. The special New Year's soup, *zōni,* is made with vegetables and rice cakes. Rice cakes cooked on a grill bear a pattern that resembles the hexagonal grid of turtle shell. Turtles are considered propitious animals because of their long lifespan.

Hayashi Tadamasa (1853–1906), a prominent dealer who worked predominantly in Paris in the late nineteenth century, once owned this impression and placed his seal in the lower-right corner. Apparently, he had at least one other impression, as another exists with his seal in the lower-left corner (see Lane, *Images*, fig. 48). The popularity of this series is suggested by the existence of numerous facsimile versions of several of the designs issued during the Meiji period. The Wright collection includes one such reproduction of this turtle design, which was published in the early 1890s (see no. 11a, cat. no.91). The poem on the facsimile version, by Inoya Tsukihito, plays on the folk belief that turtles live for ten-thousand years:

mannen no	Turtles set free
yowai wa manto	crawl auspiciously
tawamurete	towards a shrine,
ehō mairi no	and now can play together
hau hanachigame	for ten-thousand years.

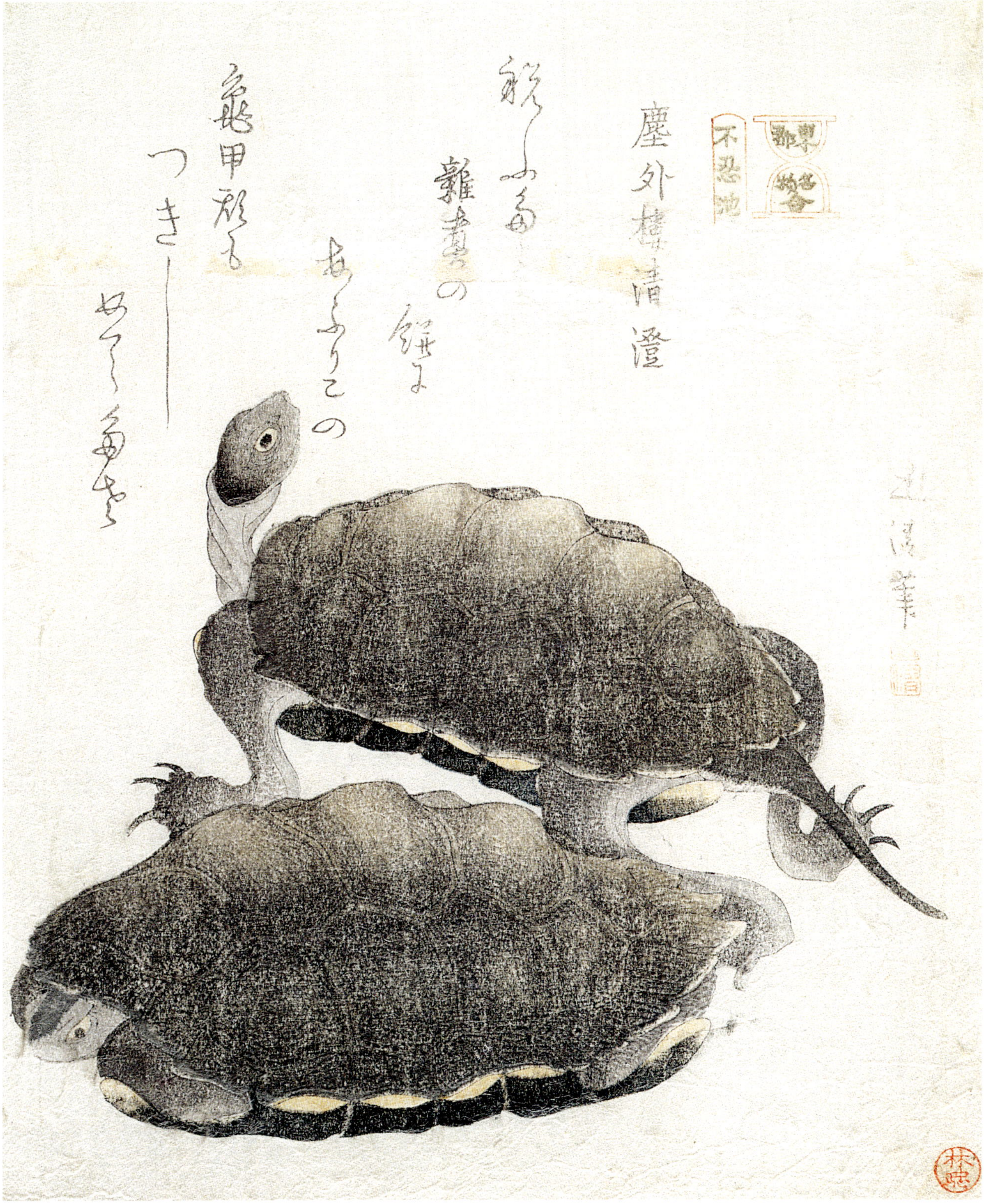
不忍池
塵外樓清澄

KOIKAWA HAKUGA

(ACT. EARLY 19TH CENTURY)

12 Tangerines with sections tied to form monkeys

DATE 1812, Year of the Monkey
SIGNATURE Hakuga; with artist's seal
PUBLISHER'S SEAL Shumman
FORMAT Koban yoko-e (13.3 x 17.8)
FLLW FDN 3040.001

Bempūtei Funaasa:

akete kesa	As the New Year dawns,
nodokeki haru wa	this pleasant spring brings
Kinokuni no	ever longer days—
mikan no saru no	and tangerines from Kinokuni
itodo naga no hi	turn into monkeys on a string.

This animated surimono for the Year of the Monkey is composed simply of tangerines and separated sections. Shaping the inner skins of tangerine sections into tiny monkeys by tying them with string or hair was an idle pastime of the day, especially among courtesans who had to while away time waiting for patrons. Here, the red string may refer to the red leashes used by monkey trainers. In the poem, *ito*, or "string," serves as a pivot word: *saru no ito* refers to "a string of monkeys," while *itodo naga no hi* means "ever longer days."

Tangerines have auspicious connotations and are still used in New Year's decorative arrangements (see cat. nos. 99 and 126). Kinokuni, another name for Kii Province (modern-day Wakayama Prefecture), remains famous to this day for citrus fruit. Another reference may be to Kinokuniya Bunzaemon, the wealthy citrus merchant of the early eighteenth century. Famous in his own time as an entrepreneur and habitué of the Yoshiwara, his name became synonymous with tangerines and he appeared in the popular fiction of the nineteenth century.

The artist Hakuga was an obscure pupil of Koikawa Harumachi I (1744–89), a popular novelist, satirist, and print designer. The style and sophistication of this design, however, relates closely to that of Kubo Shumman, its publisher, who often collaborated with other artists on the production of surimono in the 1810s. The delicate use of gaufrage, sensitive coloration, and the absence of the usual key-block black outline combine to create a naturalistic representation of the fruit; it is an effect often found in Shumman's own designs.

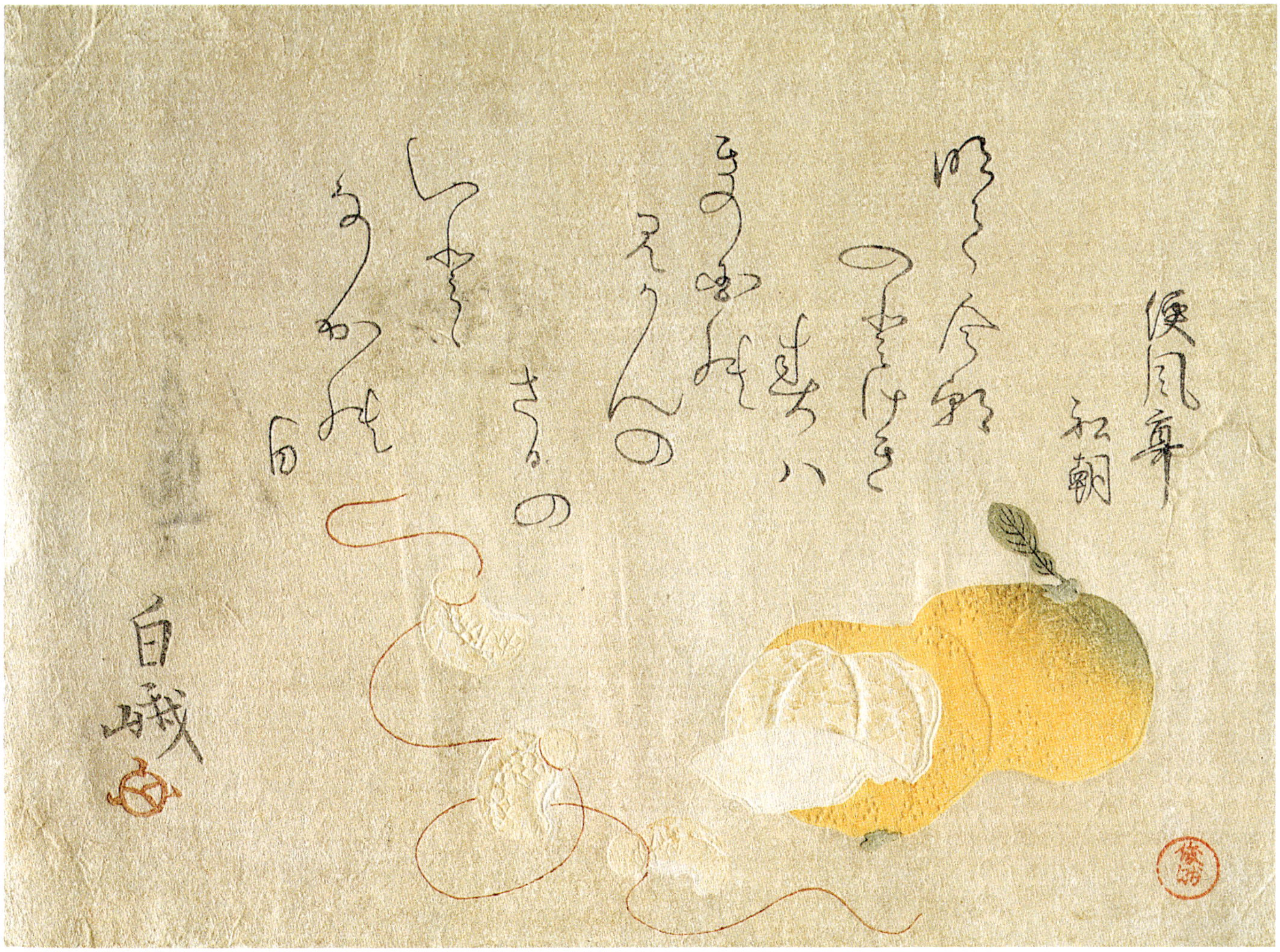

TOTOYA HOKKEI

1780–1850

13 A distant view of Mount Fuji

DATE ca. 1818
SIGNATURE Hokkei
FORMAT Koban yoko-e (13.4 x 18.8)
REFERENCE Polster, no. 241
FLLW FDN 3017.073

Ryokuchikuen Fumimasu:

kainen no	I send my best wishes
gyokei medetaku	as the New Year arrives—
mōshi osame	may auspicious winds
dōfū senri	bring good fortune to all
Ōedo no haru	during spring in Great Edo.

Although landscape had been a mainstay of the Japanese painting tradition for several centuries, the earliest *ukiyo-e* versions date only to the beginning of the nineteenth century. It was not until the late 1820s that Hokusai designed the first major series, "The Thirty-six Views of Mount Fuji." Like the commercial prints, very few landscape surimono were issued prior to that date. This surimono and another by Hokusai also of Mount Fuji represent the only significant examples in the Wright collection (see also cat. no. 37).

This elevated view of Mount Fuji, with its steep road and dotlike figures to the right, reveals the influence of European landscape prints. Despite the ban on foreign contact imposed by the Edo shoguns, the study of Western knowledge was encouraged under certain more permissive shoguns during the mid-eighteenth century. Numerous painters of Kyoto and Edo, most prominently Maruyama Ōkyo (1733–95) and Shiba Kōkan (1747–1818), experimented with these new aesthetics and artistic devices through the study of European prints. Hokusai designed a number of Western-style landscapes in the early 1800s; here, his pupil Hokkei was clearly influenced by his master's experiments in the genre.

Another Hokkei landscape surimono, not in the Wright collection, using the same format, signature, and style, bears a red rectangular hand-stamped title cartouche that reads *Go-gawa Sanyō no uchi: Buyō no Haru* (A Series of Three Provinces for the Go-gawa: Spring in Musashi Province), and depicts a distant view of Edo Castle against Mount Fuji; in the foreground people are shown crossing Nihonbashi in Edo (see Polster, no. 240). Though the poem is the same as that found on this print, the poet signed himself with one of his alternate pen names, Shitsutei Fumimasu. Thus, despite the lack of a cartouche, it is clear that this view of Mount Fuji is from a set of three landscape surimono commissioned by the Go-gawa group.

The poem by Ryokuchikuen, a member of the Go-gawa poetry group established by the poet Rokujuen, is a generic New Year greeting that has little direct relation to the image. In fact, the same poem is found on other prints in this series and at least one other surimono by Hokkei (cat. no. 104; fig 6). The expression *dōfū senri* (usually written as *senri dōfū*) derives from Chinese poetry and literally means "Even though we may be a thousand miles apart, the same wind blows over us." However, here the character *ri,* a measure of distance, has been replaced by a homonym meaning "profit," a reading perhaps more appropriate for an audience of merchant literati. Furthermore, the phrase Ōedo (Great Edo) is written playfully with characters which when combined with *senri* implies that "great profits will arise."

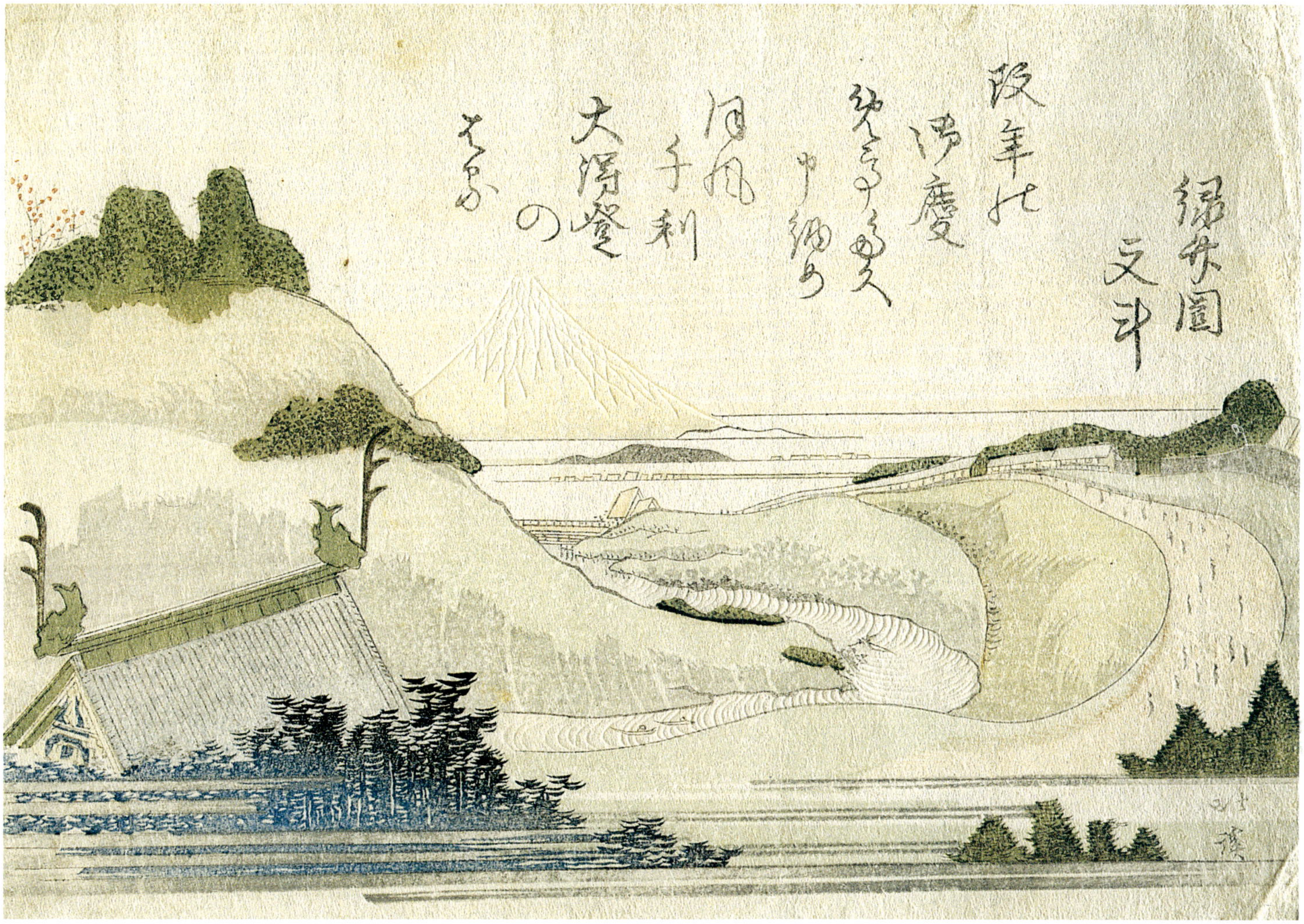

TOTOYA HOKKEI

1780–1850

14 Two dolls and a brocade satchel

SERIES *Ishokujū no uchi;* Clothing, Food, and Shelter
DATE 1818, Year of the Tiger
SIGNATURE Hokkei sha
FORMAT Shikishiban (21.2 x 18.9)
FLLW FDN 3017.060

Kinshitei Orikata:

deku motte	A young maiden
otome wa haru no	holding a wooden doll
hi atari ni	bares her knees
hizakozō made	as she plays in the sun
dashite asoberi	on a fine spring day.

Kashōan Yonemori:

kokimazete	All mixed together
mamoru nishiki no	in a brocade satchel
haru-bukuro	carried by the spring—
yanagi no imoto	little sister willow
ani no ume ga e	and big brother plum.

Perhaps the rarest and certainly the most exquisitely printed surimono in the collection, this design is composed simply of two types of dolls and a brocade satchel. Both dolls are rendered through the elaborate use of gaufrage. The face of the articulated wooden doll, or *deku* (also pronounced *mokugū*), is veiled by a sheet of translucent wrapping tissue. Remarkably, its body is printed with *gofun,* pigment made from crushed oyster shells, a material rarely used in printmaking due to its fragile nature and significant expense. In actuality, such dolls were finished with several layers of this delicate substance. The wooden doll's state of undress is a reference by omission to one of the themes of the series—clothing. The other doll, an *anesama ningyō* (elder sister doll), lies on a diagonal beneath the seated doll and wears a kimono fashioned from folded, textured paper, with hair made from crepe paper.

The brocade satchel for carrying the dolls is decorated with auspicious motifs and a gold disk embossed with the figure of a tiger, which allows the print to be precisely dated to 1818, a tiger year. The bright red silk cord and tassels, along with the black fabric ground of the satchel, sets off the whiteness of the doll's features. The unusual pale yellow background further enhances the subtle interplay of contrasting colors to create a visual tour de force.

Complementing the charm of the image, the first poem describes a young girl who pulls up her robe to kneel on the ground to play with a wooden doll. The second poem likens a springtime vista of plum and willow trees to a doll's brocade carrying case. The inspiration for the poem no doubt derives from a poem by Priest Sosei in the *Kokinshū*:

miwataseba	Seen from afar,
yanagi sakura o	the willow and the cherry
kokimazete	are all mixed together—
miyako zo haru no	like a brocade of spring
nishiki narikeru;	wrapping the capital.

Here the cherry blossoms have been replaced by the more seasonally appropriate plum. The plum tree in kyōka is often referred to as "the elder brother of flowers" since it is the first to bloom. The artist responded to the poem's sibling terminology by depicting an "elder sister doll."

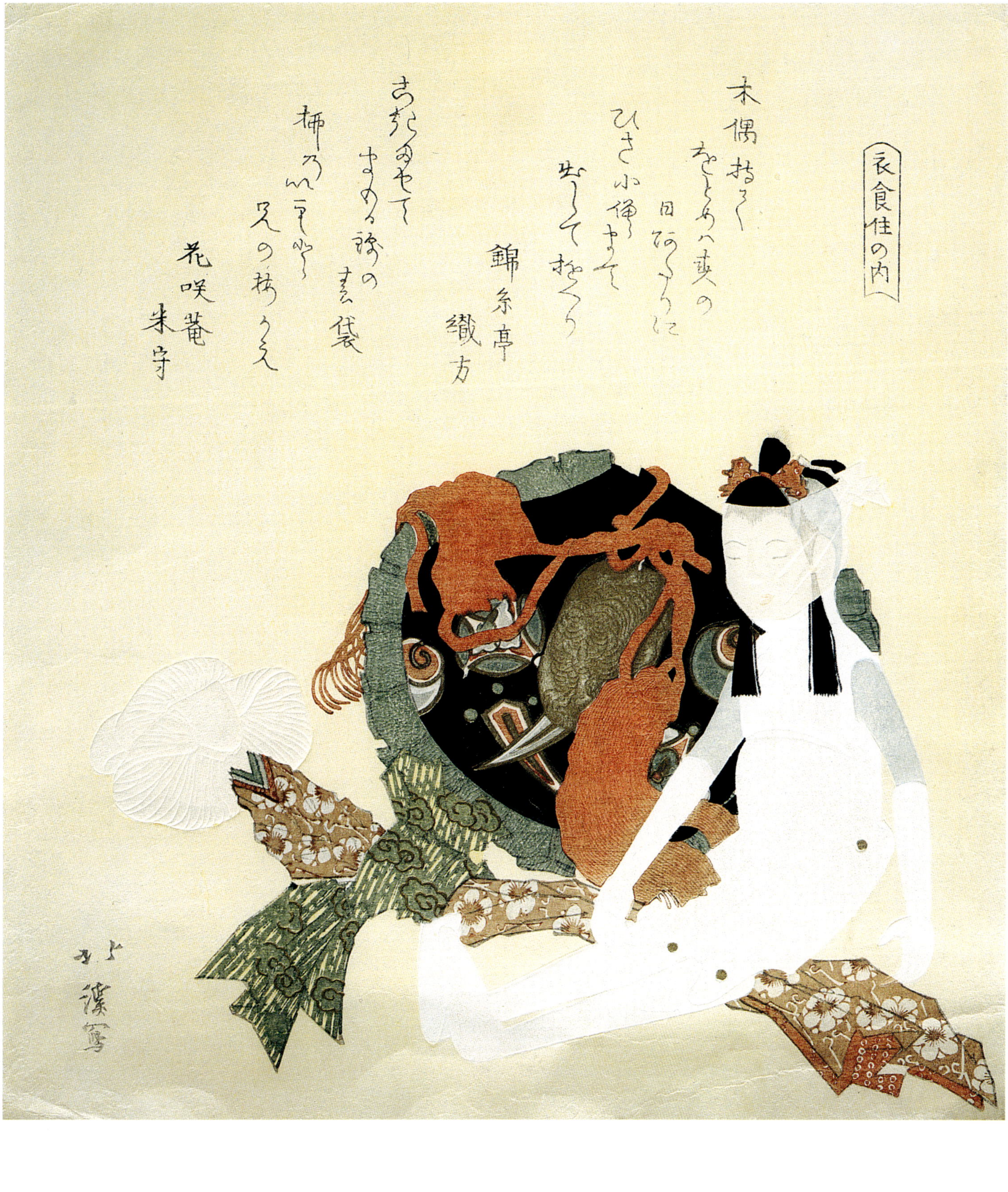
衣食住の内
錦糸亭織方
花咲菴米守
北渓写

TOTOYA HOKKEI

1780–1850

15 Lute with plum branch

TITLE *Ki;* 'Wood'
SERIES *Gogyō;* The Five Elements
DATE ca. 1820
SIGNATURE Hokkei
FORMAT Shikishiban (21.1 x 18.3)
REFERENCE *Japanse Prenten,* pl.6
FLLW FDN 3017.028

Goantei Rakuzumi:

ume yanagi	The Seizan Lute
nueru nishiki no	is wrapped in a satchel
fukuro naru	of spring mist,
kasumi ni tsutsumu	woven with a brocade
Seizan no biwa	of plum and willow.

Sairaikyo:

hatsuyume no	As Fuji arises
Fuji wa nukedashi	in a New Year's dream—
sono ato no	soon afterwards,
kasumi ni uzumu	Lake Biwa appears
Biwa no mizu'umi	buried in spring mist.

Each of the still lifes in this series represents one of the Five Elements *(Gogyō),* an ancient Chinese system of describing the physical world according to five principles: wood, fire, earth, metal, and water. In Japan, such traditional Chinese philosophical concepts were incorporated into Neo-Confucian teachings that flourished during the Edo period. Tradition also links each of the Five Elements with a specific color, but these correspondences were not followed in this set (see cat. no. 43). It is interesting to note that Hokkei also created a set of the Five Elements represented by warriors from the *Suikoden* (see cat. nos. 129–30).

The Wright collection has fine original impressions of four prints from the series; the missing design, "Earth," is only known from late-nineteenth-century facsmile versions (see Keyes, *Beatty,* pl.157; Polster, no. 218). In each print, the Chinese character for the featured element is given in a circular black cartouche. The series title in red appears within a double *no* written in the *kana* syllabary. This was the emblem of the Hyōtan-ren (Gourd Group), a poetry circle headed by Sairaikyō, a medical officer for the Shogunate. Since Sairaikyō was initially affiliated with Akera Kankō's group (the No-gawa) he selected an emblem which integrates the single *no* used by his former teacher. Stacked upon each other, these characters resemble a gourd, an apt symbol for the Hyōtan-ren.

This design representing the element "wood" illustrates a lute (*biwa*) entwined with a branch of budding plum blossoms. The plectrum guard is decorated with a scene of a silver moon rising over a green mountain against a gold background. This can be taken as a literal representation of the famous lute named Seizan (Green Mountains), whose story is told in the seventh chapter of the medieval war tale *The Tale of the Heike* and cited here in the poem by Rakuzumi.

A treasured lute such as Seizan would have been stored in a brocade satchel, but according to the first poem, this instrument is wrapped in a spring mist woven with plum and willow, the two trees most closely associated with early spring.

Dreaming of Mount Fuji, mentioned in the second poem by Sairaikyo, the leader of the Hyōtan Group, is a classic New Year's omen auguring good luck for the forthcoming year. The poem concludes with an allusion to the mythical origins of Mount Fuji, the tallest mountain in Japan and Lake Biwa, the largest lake. The traditional version claims that both were formed in the course of a single night during the fifth year of Kōrei (286 B.C.), when earth flew from Western Japan to the Eastern Plains to form the slightly asymmetrical slopes of Mount Fuji; the enormous cavity left behind became Lake Biwa. More plausible folklore informs us that Lake Biwa acquired its name because its roughly oval shape resembles that of a lute. Hokkei's elegant image cleverly links the two poems whose only connection is the word biwa.

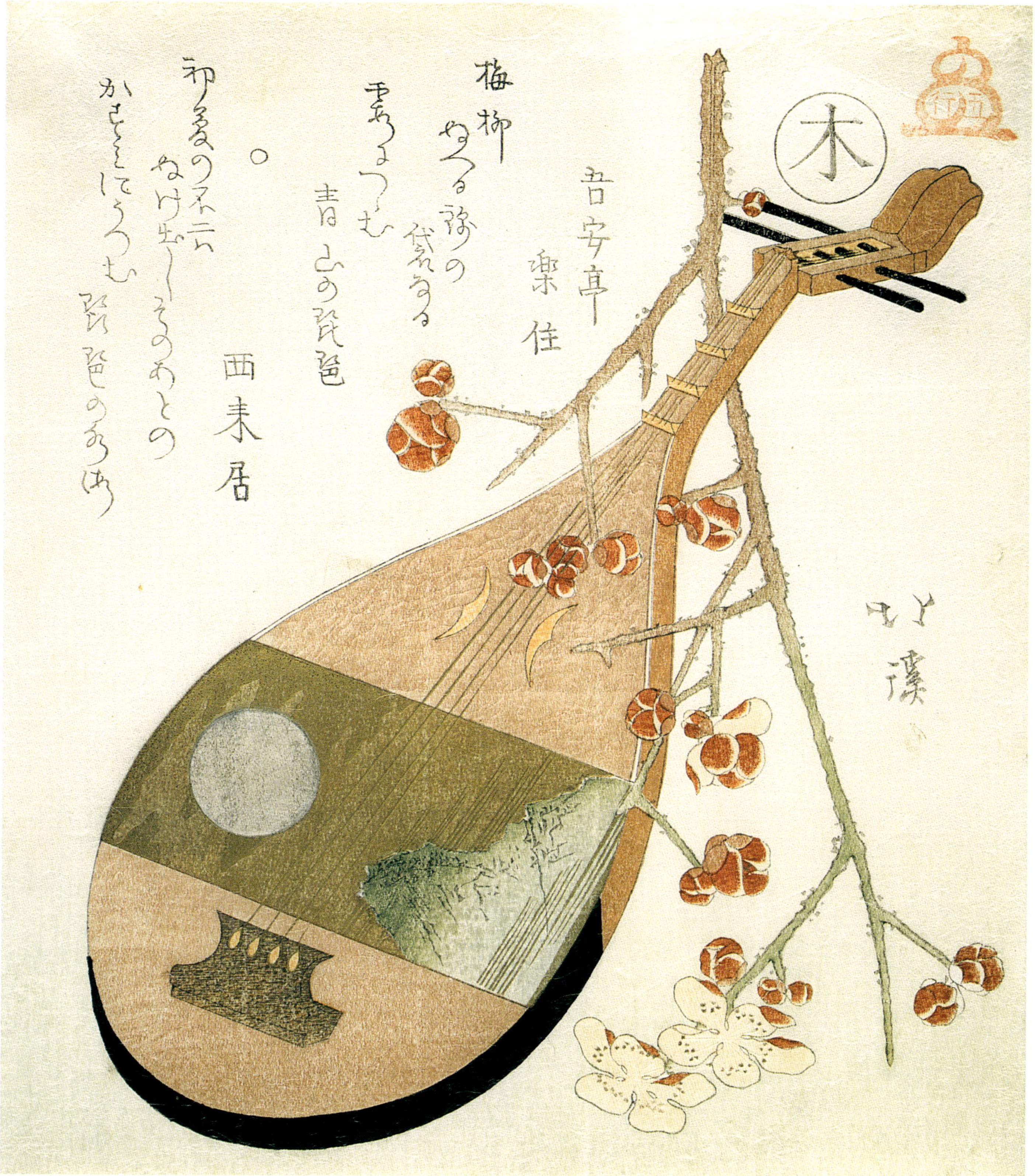
木
吾安亭
楽住
梅柳
青山の琵琶
西来居

TOTOYA HOKKEI

1780–1850

16 A white brazier with a black feather

TITLE *Hi;* 'Fire'
SERIES *Gogyō;* The Five Elements
DATE ca. 1820
SIGNATURE Hokkei
FORMAT Shikishiban (21.1 x 18.3)
REFERENCES Rijksmuseum, *Hokusai,* pl. 145; Ostier, *La voix silencieuse,* pl. 17
FLLW FDN 3017.026

Gosōken Oriyasu:

karasuba no	A blackbird feather
ake o shi tsugete	announces the coming of dawn,
uzumibi mo	as smoldering embers
itadaki shiroku	turn into ash-white peaks
tachikaeru haru	with the return of spring.

The samurai backgrounds of the Hyōtan poetry circle are amply demonstrated by the themes and overall sophisticated tenor of the poems attached to the prints in this series. The "Wood" print, just described, treats the theme of the legend of the Seizan lute from the war saga *The Tale of the Heike,* while the concept of the Five Samurai Virtues provided inspiration for the "Metal" print (cat. no 17). The austere image of implements for the tea ceremony in this design reflects the refined aesthetic sensibilites of both artist and the samurai-literati patrons who commissioned this series. While the tea ceremony is a most unusual theme for a ukiyo-e artist, Hokkei was known to have created a number of surimono images on the subject, and was no doubt conversant in its rituals.

A black crow feather lies in front of a white brazier. Carefully embossed, the wood-grain textured paper wrapped around the brazier is ornamented with crests of stylized chrysanthemums. The silver bracket for the red silk cord repeats this motif. The printer has captured the subtle tonal gradation of the feather through the technique of *bokashi,* the hand-wiping of the color block to create tonal gradations. A crow feather, was used in the tea ceremony to form the ash cone within the brazier.

The element of fire is evoked in the poem's reference to burning embers turning to white ashes. Sunrise is also implied through the mention of a crow feather, since crows in East Asian legend and poetry are said to caw at the break of dawn.

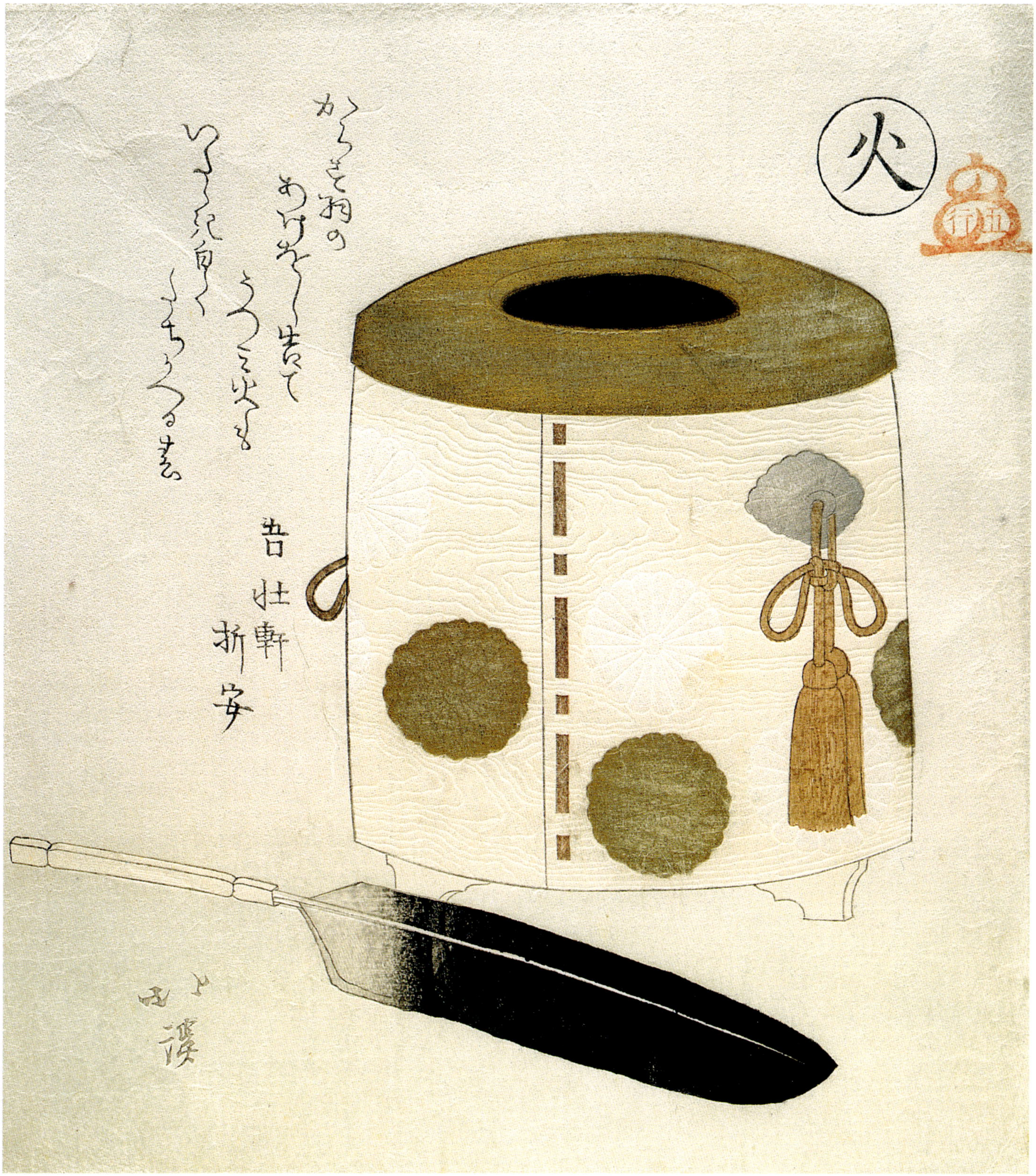
火

TOTOYA HOKKEI

1780–1850

17 A kettle with a trivet

TITLE *Kane;* Metal
SERIES *Gogyō;* The Five Elements
DATE ca. 1820
SIGNATURE Hokkei
FORMAT Shikishiban (21.1 x 18.3)
FLLW FDN 3017.029

Shakudō Maruki:

kurogane no	Made of black iron,
gotoku no tsume mo	the trivet has three talons,
mitsu ashi no	like the three-legged crow
hi no karasu nite	which dwells in the sun
ake no hatsuharu	as the new spring dawns.

Sairaikyo:

kamishimo no	The warrior's formal robes—
gyōgi arare ya	arranged like a kettle
arare-gama	with hailstone texture
gotoku no tsume mo	on a trivet with three fingers
mitsu yubi no haru	stretched out for spring.

In the "Metal" image, a red copper kettle with a silver handle is decorated with a stylized paulownia crest, one of the most prized and popular crests associated with the imperial family and then the Ashikaga shoguns. An *arare-gama,* mentioned in the poem, is a cast-iron pot with an overall texture of raised dots resembling hailstones. A purple cloth is draped over the vessel's cover as protection from the heated silver handle. The bright red, rounded form of the kettle contrasts with the dark gray inverted iron trivet. It is referred to in the poem as *mitsu ashi* (three legs), which is another term for a *gotoku,* a metal or clay support for holding the lid of a kettle during the tea ceremony.

The first poem links *kurogane* (literally "black metal"), an old name for iron, and *karasu* (crow), another black image. The allusion, however, is to the ancient Chinese "crow of the sun," said to be red, have three legs, and reside in the sun. In the second poem, this analogy is continued by the reference to *gotoku,* a homonym for Neo-Confucian concept of the Five Virtues—humanity, righteousness, decorum, wisdom, and faithfulness—which became the basis of the moral code of the samurai. The mention of formal attire worn by the warrior class and the gesture used when bowing at official occasions, placing three fingers of each hand on the tatami mat completes the allusion to the samurai.

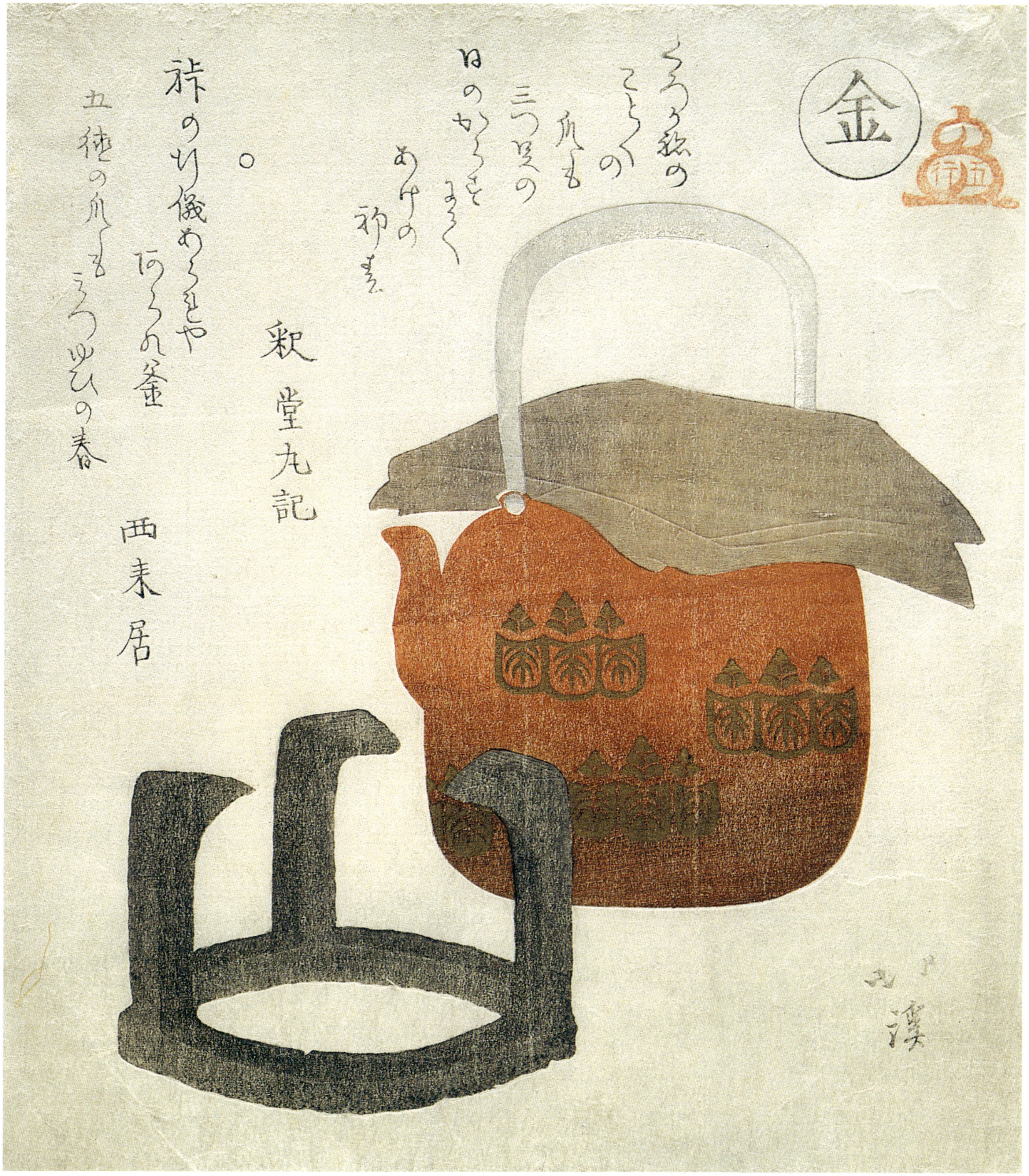

金
釈 堂丸記
西来居

TOTOYA HOKKEI

1780–1850

18 A porcelain bowl with lotion bottle and makeup brush

TITLE *Mizu;* Water
SERIES *Gogyō;* The Five Elements
DATE ca. 1820
SIGNATURE Hokkei
FORMAT Shikishiban (21.1 x 18.3)
FLLW FDN 3017.027

Seishōrō Hisamaru:

hatsu gasumi	The first mists
hitosuji hosoku	over the streams of water
suidō no	flowing in aqueducts
mizu yori Edo no	seem to be the source
haru ya kinuran	of the spring in Edo.

Shunryokuan Mizura:

kage utsuru	Light filtering
kasumi no kinu no	through silken strands
hitohaba wa	of springtime mist
murasaki somuru	gives a purple tinge
Edogawa no mizu	to the waters of Edo River.

A sprig of cherry blossoms floats in a porcelain bowl filled with water. Propped against the black-lacquer mirror cover upon which the bowl rests are a makeup brush and the cover to a wooden box, which stands beside a white bottle. The colorful underglaze-blue and red-enamel Arita porcelain bowl is decorated with gold and green banding in an abstracted wave pattern, a reference to the theme of water. The center blue-and-white medallion shows a shoreline view of Mount Fuji as seen from the beach at Shichirigahama, with Enoshima in the middle ground.

On the box cover is a label reading *Edo no mizu* (literally, "Edo water"), which was a lotion used as a base for makeup. The label also gives the name of the proprietor of the shop where it was sold, Shikitei, who is best known by his pen name Samba (1776–1822). He was one of the most successful writers of the late Edo period. Samba acquired lasting fame for his *Ukiyo-buro* (Bathhouse of the Floating World), written in four parts from 1809 to 1813, a humorous novel based on a day of random meetings at the public bath—a most appropriate theme for a purveyor of "Edo Water."

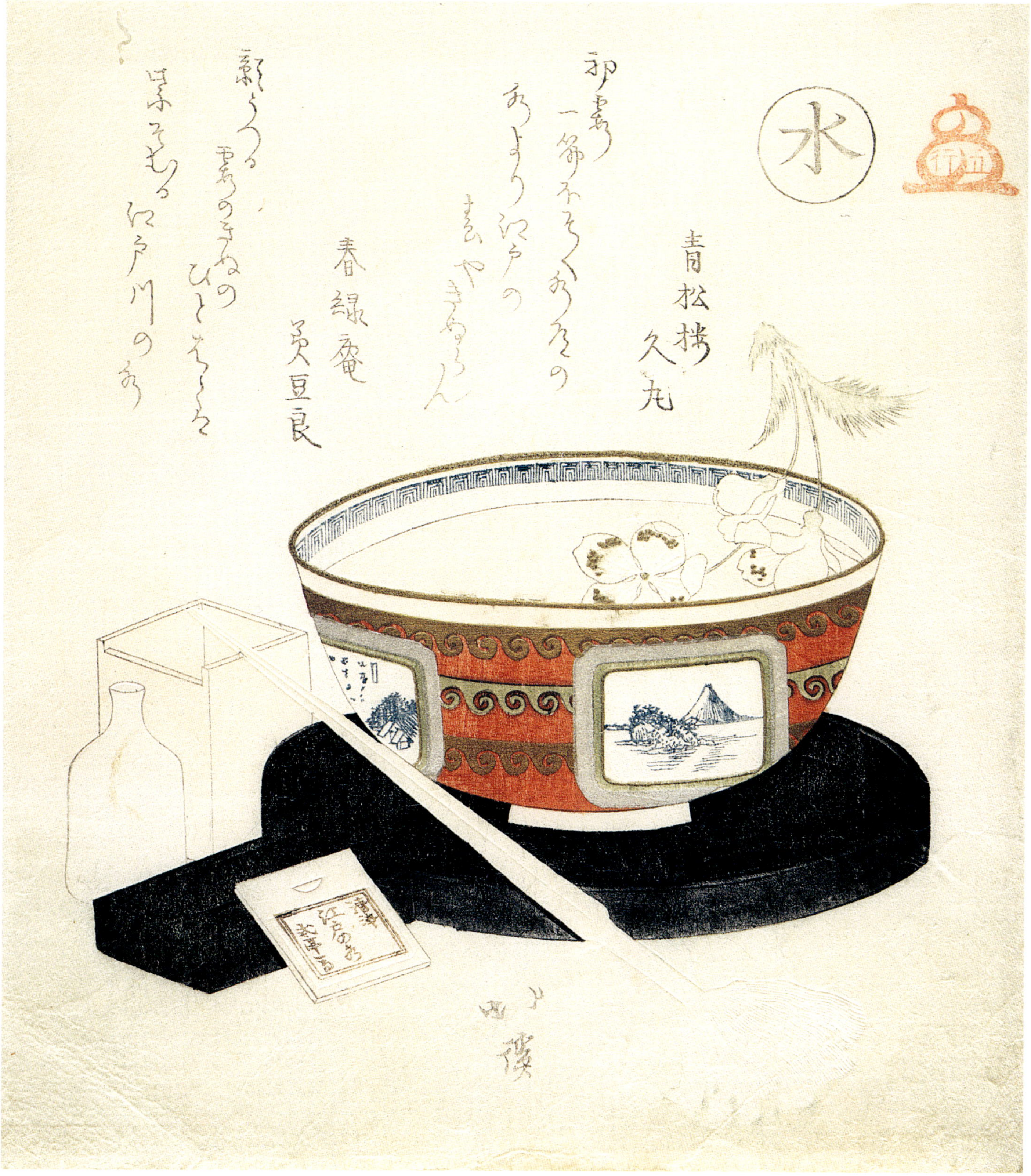
水
青松樓 久丸
春緑庵

TOTOYA HOKKEI

1780–1850

19 A warbler in a cage

TITLE *Ōzetsu ume;* Warbler's Tongue Plum
SERIES *Hanazono Bantsuzuki;* Series for the Hanazono Group
DATE 1823
SIGNATURE Hokkei
FORMAT Shikishi (21.5 x 18.6)
REFERENCE Ostier, *La voix silencieuse,* pl. 145
FLLW FDN 3017.050

Wahōtei Itonaga:

hakaze ni mo	Its blossoms don't scatter
chiranu hana koso	in a feather-light wind,
medetakere	so we praise the plum
ume no makie no	along with the warbler
kago no uguisu	in a lacquered cage.

Fumpunkan Umekaze:

saku hana wa	How grand is the song
monokawa koe no	of the flowers in bloom
Hatsuseyama	on Mount Hatsuse,
ippōguchi no	with its single gateway
kago no uguisu	like a warbler's cage.

One of the most compositionally complex series designed by Hokkei, it was commissioned by the Hanazono-ren, led by Garyōen Umemaro, whose poetry name derives from a variety of flowering plum or *ume* (see cat. no. 47). The theme of each surimono revolves around imaginary and actual varieties of plum. In designing the set, the artist has adapted the *harimaze* format of placing small, cut-up pictures together against a unified ground, a convention which originated as a technique for the decoration of Japanese screens. Here, each central image is flanked by a slightly taller rectangular panel bearing a Chinese-style inscription and an image of a variety of plum. The series cartouche at the far right and the two panels are set against a powder blue background.

The Wright collection includes fifteen different examples and two duplicates (cat. nos. 20, 106–117) from this series of at least twenty surimono (see also Keyes, *Spencer,* cat. nos. 57 and 59; Rijksmuseum, *Hokusai,* pl. 147; Hempel, *Scheiwe,* pl. 342; Kruml, 1978, pl. 48). Included in the design of one print from the series (see cat. no. 106) is an inscription dating the set to the year of the goat (1823). The variations in quality of impression and overall condition of each print, combined with the fact that there are two duplicates, indicates that this group was assembled from different sources.

A warbler peers out from its red lacquer cage at its unmade meal. Resting on the mortar, printed in brass, is a wooden pestle used to grind the leaves for bird feed; the silver cup is the feeder to be placed in the cage.

The Chinese-style inscription in the yellow poem-slip panel states that among the varieties of white plum, this one is unique because when the petals open, the stamen protrudes like a warbler's tongue. The phrase *ōzetsu* (or *uguisu no shita*), the name of this imaginary variety of plum, means "warbler's tongue" or "a beautiful voice." Both poems address the theme of a warbler in a cage. The first praises the plum because it does not lose its blossoms in a light breeze, unlike its more ephemeral cousin, the cherry. *Hakaze* (literally, "feather wind") is the breeze created by the flapping of the wings of a bird—a word that delicately resonates with the image of the warbler. The setting of the second poem is Mount Hatsuse, near Nara, the location of the famous Hasedera Temple. The wit of the poem relies on the conceit that plum blossoms described as having "warbler's tongues" must also have the warbler's lovely voice. The single gateway, likened here to a single-doored cage, no doubt refers to the fact that this temple is surrounded on three sides by mountains and can be approached from only one direction via a long covered stairway.

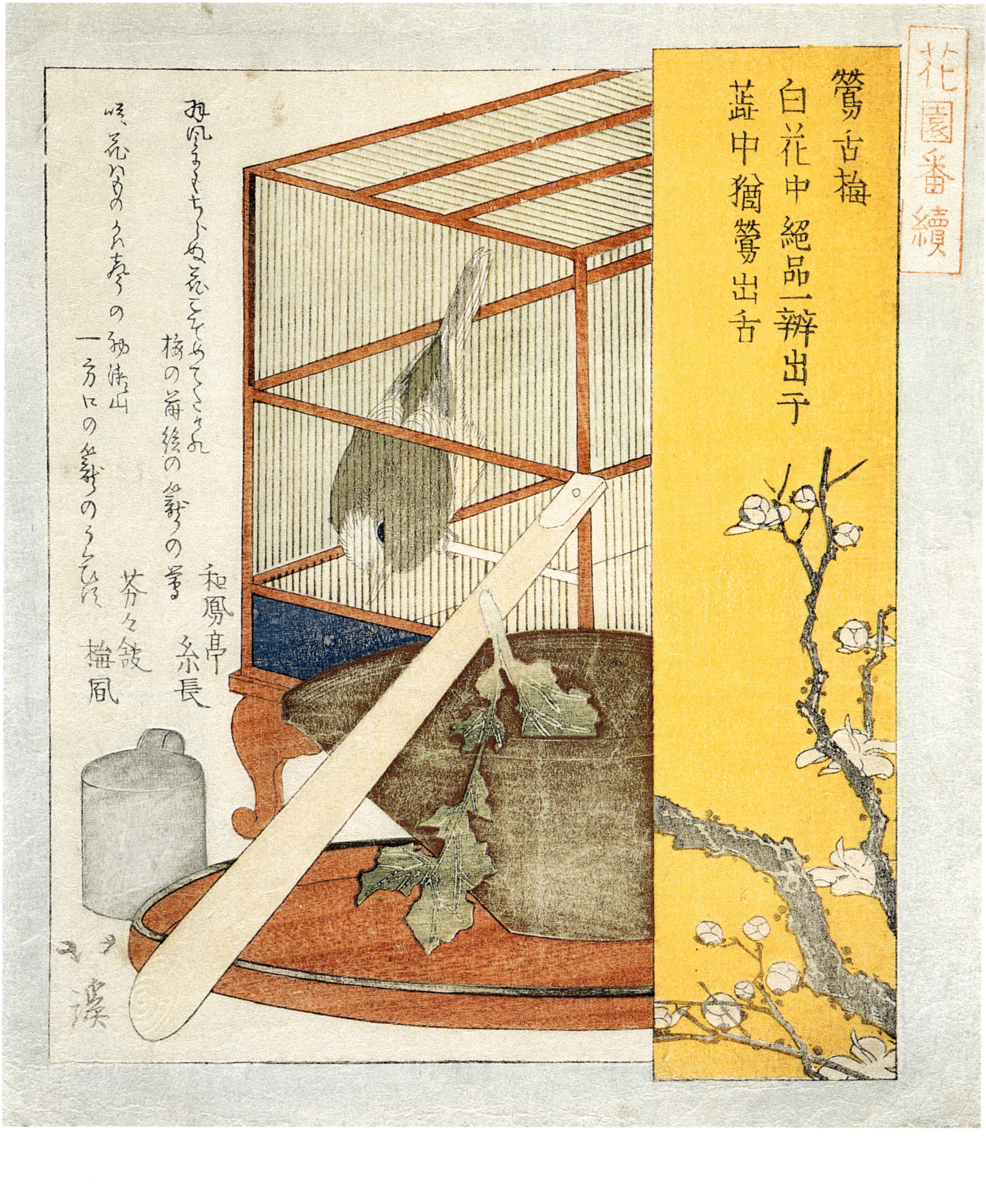
花園番續
鶯舌梅
白花中絶品一瓣出于
蕋中猶鶯出舌
和鳳亭 糸長
梅風
溪

TOTOYA HOKKEI

1780–1850

20 An inkstone and a silver cat

TITLE *Saigyō ume;* Saigyō Plum
SERIES *Hanazono Bantsuzuki;* Series for the Hanazono Group
DATE 1823
SIGNATURE Hokkei
FORMAT Shikishiban (21.5 x 19.0)
REFERENCE Rijksmuseum, *Hokusai,* pl.151
FLLW FDN 3017.045

Kadota Inamura:

fukusa mote	An inkstone
tsutsumu suzuri ga	is wrapped in a cloth
murasaki no	purple in color
kasumi-gakure no	like the mists that veil
Miho no matsukage	the pines of Miho.

Sessōan, from Iinuma:

hikari oba	Even the luster
hatsuhi ni yuzuru	of a cat made of silver
shirogane no	cannot compare in value
neko no atai ya	with sunlight on the first day
senkin no haru	of a priceless spring.

This is another clever surimono from the Hanazono-ren series on the varieties of plum. Here, the Chinese inscription describes a type of plum said to be admired by the famous Zen priest-poet Saigyō (1118–90), who often expressed in his poems an appreciation of cherry blossoms; but we may join the poets who commissioned this series in assuming that he enjoyed plum blossoms as well. This variety has rounded petals that come to a point at the center, and is said to have six petals rather than the typical five.

An unwrapped inkstone and a red lacquer stand upon which sits a silver statue of a cat are pictured on the left, and a woven traveling hat of the kind often worn by itinerant priests lies beside the cat. All three items are clear references to the wandering priest Saigyō. The inkstone alludes to his literary talents. The sculpture refers to an incident in which Saigyō, a supporter of the emperor, was compelled to divulge his knowledge of military arts to the shōgun Yoritomo and was rewarded with the gift of a silver cat. Remorseful over his breach of loyalty to the emperor, upon leaving the palace Saigyō gave the sculpture to a group of frolicking boys. The plum also appears in another Saigyō legend. When asked by the Emperor to rid his garden of a cock that was scattering the blossoms of his plum trees, Saigyō inadvertently slayed the bird with his fan.

In the first poem, the classical allusions are to spring mist and its traditional color, purple. *Tsutsumu,* meaning to wrap, is an association word for mist. A wrapping cloth or *fukusa,* because it includes the word *fuku,* or "good luck," has auspicious connotations.

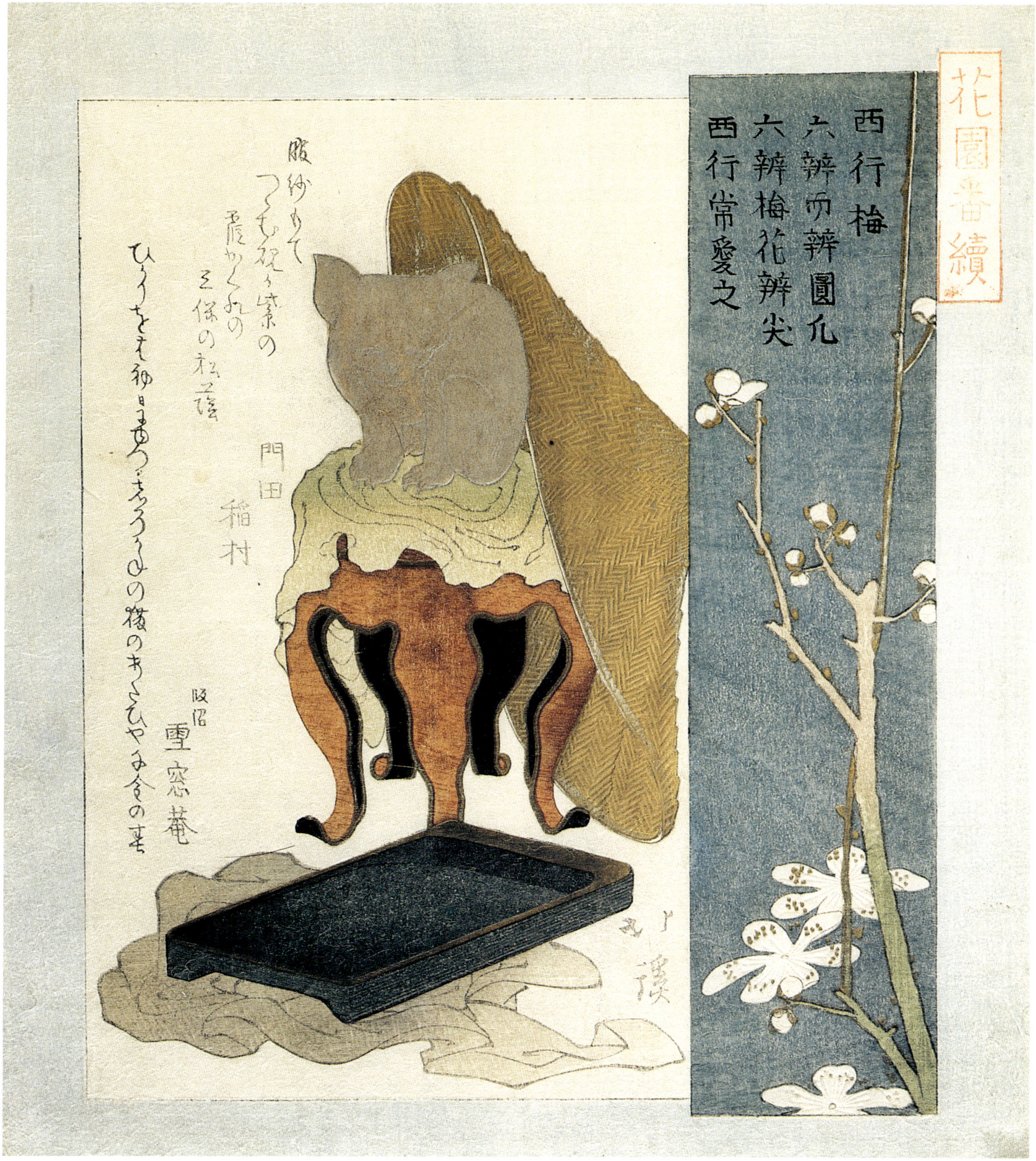
花園番續
西行梅
六瓣而瓣圓几
六瓣梅花瓣尖
西行常愛之
門田
稲村
雪窓菴

TOTOYA HOKKEI

1780–1850

21 Raikō attacks a demon kite

DATE ca. 1825
SIGNATURE Hokkei ga
PRINTER'S SEAL Suri-kō Shinzō (printing studio of Shinzō)
FORMAT Shikishiban (21.4 x 18.6)
REFERENCES Kruml, 1989, pl. 110; Polster, no. 175; Galerie de l'Imagerie, pl. 18
FLLW FDN 3017.012

Soramitsuya Maeda:

sora made ni	A demon kite
ito yarau oni no	trails its string
ikanobori	so high in the sky
wakayagu me ni mo	that even young eyes
miezu kasumeri	lose sight of it in the mist.

During the late Edo period, the supernatural was given wider expression in the popular art forms than it had received in earlier periods. This was due in part to the shogunate's progressively weaker control over the publishing industry and in part to an increasing interest in exotic, "gothic" themes, frequently borrowed from Chinese novels. Depictions of ghosts and demons became especially common in ukiyo-e of the mid-nineteenth century. Surimono, however, rarely depicted such subjects. Clearly the tastes of the individuals who commissioned these prints and the occasions for which they were issued precluded inauspicious themes.

Hokkei portrays the hero Raikō, or Minamoto no Yorimitsu (948–1021). Celebrated as a slayer of monsters, he was requested by the emperor to kill Shuten Dōji, who had been terrorizing the capital, kidnapping young women and devouring townspeople. Together with four retainers disguised as priests, and with the assistance of the gods of three shrines, Raikō gained entry to the demon's castle. Using a magic potion given to him by the gods, he successfully drugged Shuten Dōji. After he and his men decapitated the enormous ogre, the head assumed a life of its own and fell upon Raikō. Fortunately the golden helmet provided by the gods kept him from harm.

The archaic expression *ikanobori* refers to a kite and means "climbing high." The overall feeling of the poem is auspicious, because it connotes banishing demons. At Setsubun, the last day of the lunar year, it was customary to exorcise evil spirits by tossing beans and exclaiming, "Out with demons, in with good fortune." Here, the demon has been banished to the heavens.

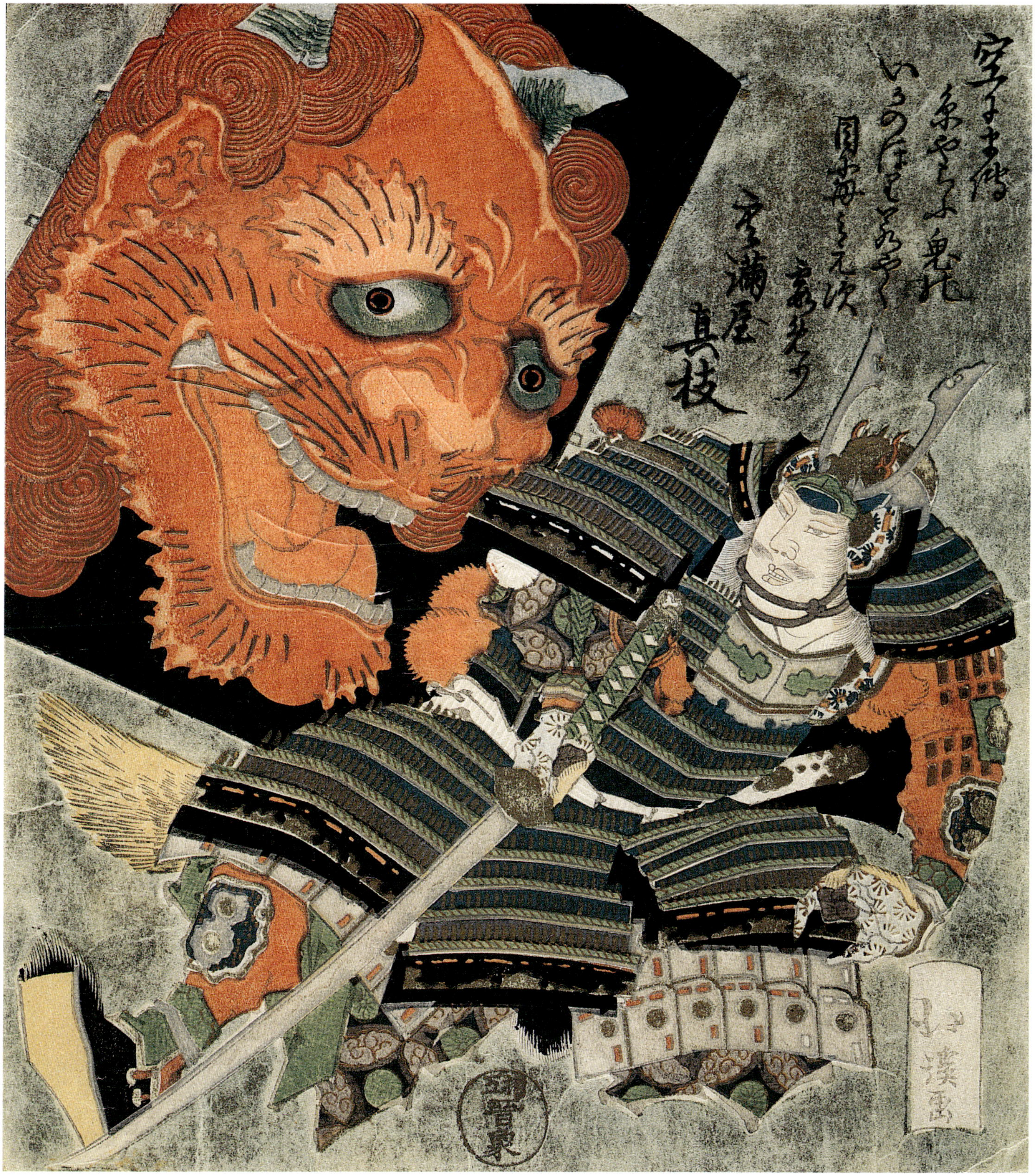

TOTOYA HOKKEI

1780–1850

22 Ushiwakamaru defeats Benkei in a game of *sugoroku*

DATE ca. 1825
SIGNED Hokkei; with artist's seal
FORMAT Shikishiban (21.1 x 18.5)
FLLW FDN 3017.013

Soramitsuya:

wakamusha ni	Refusing to admit defeat
make-oshimi iu	to the young warrior,
Benkei mo	Benkei clenches his fist
kobushi o nigiru	just as a hawk appears
taka no hatsuyume	in a New Year's dream.

Exquisitely printed with a brass ground and various metals throughout, this design portrays two celebrated twelfth-century heroes known for their prowess in the martial arts. Their first encounter took place on Gojō Bridge in Kyoto. At that time the burly, older, and more experienced warrior-priest Benkei was bested in combat by the young Ushiwakamaru, later known as Minamoto no Yoshitsune (1159–89). Here their skill is tested in *sugoroku,* a game of strategy similar to backgammon—and once again youth wins out. Hokkei often used the metaphor of a board game to refer to historical or legendary confrontations. Because the names for the playing pieces of *sugoroku* are called *koma* (colts), images of the game are usually associated with a horse year (see cat. no. 35).

Ushiwakamaru is alluded to as a *wakamusha,* young warrior. The clenched fist (*kobushi*), in addition to emphasizing the frustration of the elder combatant at being outplayed by his young friend, is also a term related to the practice of hunting with hawks. The final line of the poem directly links the image to the New Year, since dreaming of a hawk in the first dream of the New Year was considered to be especially auspicious. On the side of the game board appears the crest of the poetry club which commissioned this surimono, the Yomo-gawa.

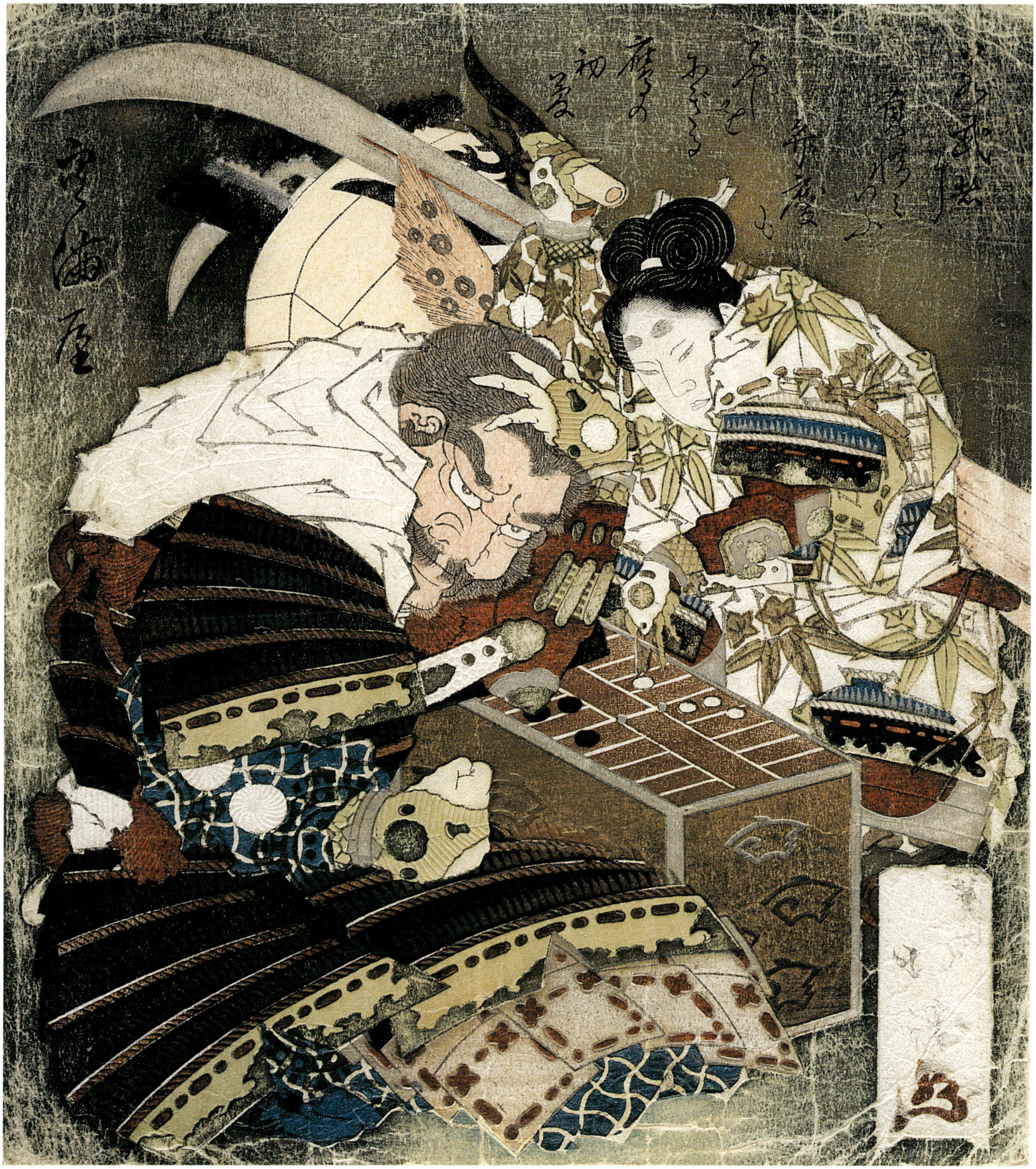

TOTOYA HOKKEI

1780–1850

23 Ukifune

DATE 1826, Year of the Dog
SIGNED Hokkei
FORMAT Shikishiban (21.0 x 18.2)
REFERENCE Rijksmuseum, *Hokusai,* pl. 185; *UT*, *Berès,* pl. 190; Polster, no. 232
FLLW FDN 3017.007

Fukkitei Kanezane:

inudoshi no	When in a boat
haru ni ause no	for a tryst in the spring
ukifune wa	of the year of the dog,
Okinamaru to mo	Ukifune's thoughts
omohoyuru kana	will be with Okinamaru.

Akebono no Haruko:

uruwashiki	Even the dazzling snow
yuki dani haru wa	is fragrant this spring,
Nioumiya	as Prince Niou boards
ume ga kaori o	a boat upon the waters
noseru ukifune	awash with the scent of plum.

Hananomon Masao:

hoshi to yobu	If the fragrance of plum,
ume no kaoreba	which blossoms into stars,
Ukifune no	buffets the boat on the waves,
chigiri ya kataki	Ukifune's pledge of love
ishi to naruramu	will be firm as a rock.

The Tale of Genji, written early in the eleventh century, is generally acknowledged to be the greatest work of Japanese literature and was an important source of inspiration for Japanese artists through the ages. The final chapters, revolving around the life of Ukifune and the later descendants of Prince Genji, were a favorite theme in art (also see cat. nos. 29 and 124), and the scene portrayed here is perhaps the most celebrated (see Meech-Pekarik, "The Artist's View of Ukifune").

The fifty-first chapter, titled "Ukifune" or "Boat Upon the Waters,"concerns a beautiful young woman and her suitors, Prince Niou (Genji's grandson) and Kaoru (Genji's putative son). Prince Niou clandestinely visits Ukifune one winter's evening in Uji and steals off with her to a secret hideaway beyond the river. While in a small boat at the Islet of Oranges (Tachibana no Kojima), he pledges his eternal love.

Several aspects of the composition by Hokkei do not conform to traditional iconography. The artist has not included the moon, which is referred to in the text of the novel. Rather, he has used the stark black ground to contrast with the snowy landscape, creating a dramatic design. The figure of the young boatman, while serving to visually anchor the composition, is given unusual prominence. The pine trees in the background, covered with snow, are a reference to the scene of the pledge. Ukifune is appropriately attired in a robe patterned with silver plum blossoms, nicely complementing the seasonal context.

The first poem reveals that the print was issued for a dog year, which for stylistic and technical reasons must be 1826. It is from a small series commissioned by the Akabane poetry circle, whose bridge-in-a-fan emblem can be seen in the upper right-hand corner. The dog year association led the first poet to recall one of the most famous dogs in classical Japanese literature, Okinamaru, not from *The Tale of Genji* but from the tenth-century *Pillow Book* by Sei Shōnagon (ca. 966–1017). The dog was ostracized from the court for having attacked the emperor's cat. Returning later, Okinamaru was nearly unrecognizable due to repeated beatings, but managed to win the sympathies of the entire court.

Puns on the names of the three central figures Prince Niou, Kaoru, and Ukifune from these final chapters are woven into the second poem. The final poem relies on a conceit sometimes found in kyōka that likens a five-petaled plum blossom to a star. It may also be playing on an old Japanese expression, "a rock in a river turns into a star" *(kawa no ishi hoshi to naru),* which suggests that something one hopes for is actually quite impossible to achieve.

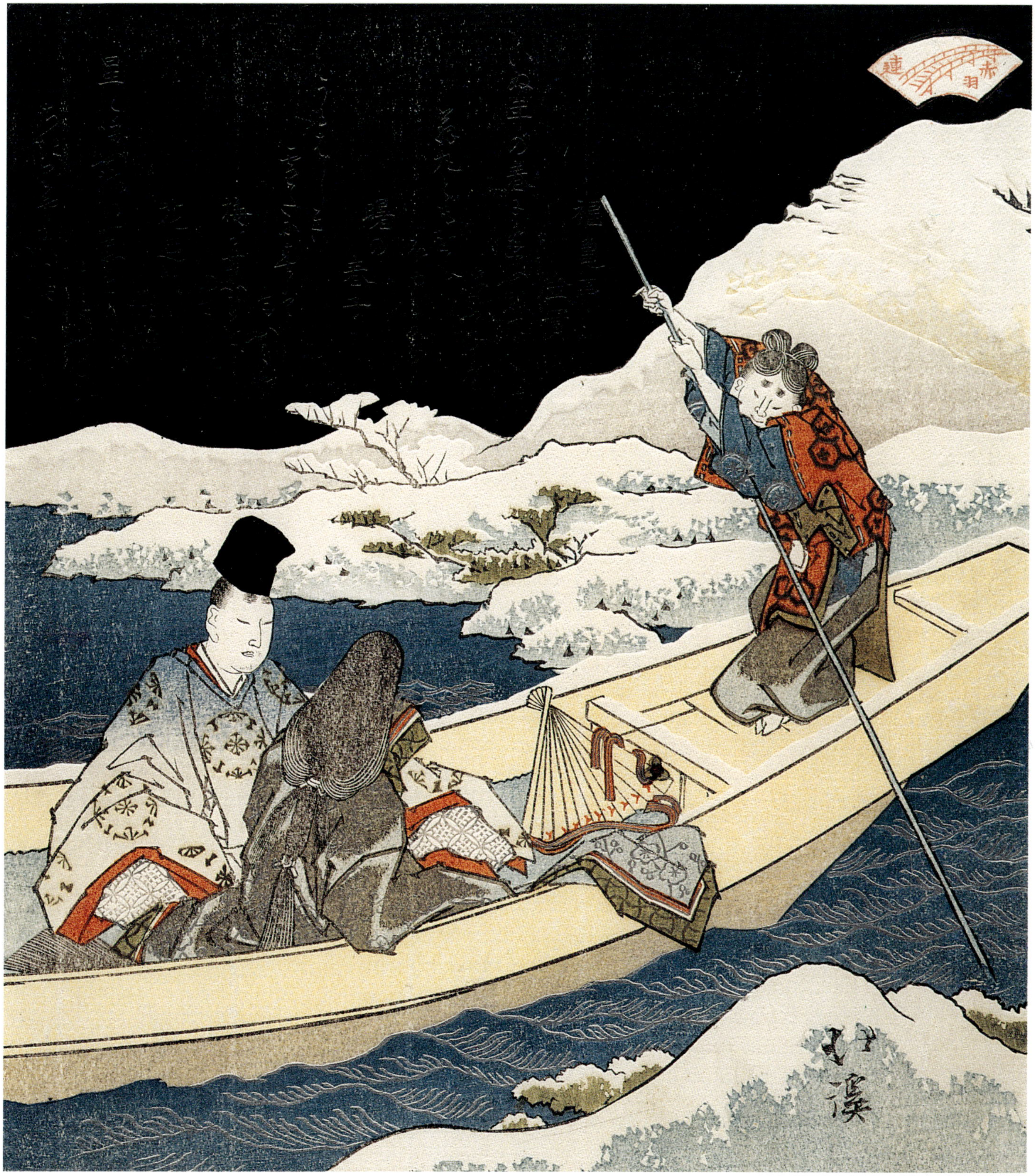
赤羽
連
北渓

TOTOYA HOKKEI

1780–1850

24 Shinozuka Iga no Kami climbing a bamboo

SERIES *Musha shōchikubai bantsuzuki;* A Series of Warriors: Pine, Bamboo and Plum
DATE ca. 1828
SIGNATURE Hokkei
FORMAT Shikishiban (21.0 x 18.5)
REFERENCE Kruml, 1989, pl. 93 (illustrates complete set); Pulverer, pl. 2–45; *UT, Pulverer,* pl. 110
FLLW FDN 3017.011

Kagendō Tsugiho:

musa amata	Among many warriors
aru ga naka ni mo	Shinozuka stands out—
Shinozuka wa	uprooting that bamboo
hikinuku take no	brought glory to his name
yoyo ni nadakashi	through the ages.

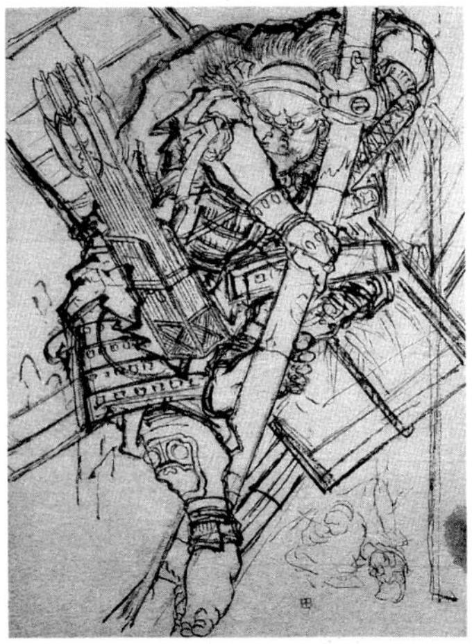

24a. Hokkei: Preliminary drawing of *Shinozuka Iga no Kami*. Collection of the Chiba City Museum of Art.

Shinozuka Iga no Kami climbs a bamboo while carrying an enormous wooden shield strapped to his back. Numerous stories celebrating his feats of strength and his perseverance against great odds surround this early fourteenth-century hero. One of the "four guardians" (*shitennō*) and a retainer of Nitta Yoshisada (1301–38), Shinozuka was known for his skill with a bow and arrow, saving his lord from ten attackers on one occasion. His exploits are chronicled in the *Taiheiki.* At the battle of Onjōji Temple, Shinozuka and another retainer, Kuryū, yanked out a large stupa with their combined brute strength. They then used the stupa as a bridge for their troops to cross a moat and successfully defeat their enemy. Instead of depicting Shinozuka in this dramatic scene, both artist and poet seem to have playfully linked this warrior to the famous hero Shinozuka Gorō—or his theatrical-namesake Takenuki Gorō—who in Kabuki is portrayed uprooting a bamboo.

Hokkei has constructed a surprisingly complex composition, which shows the strong influence of the warrior prints by his mentor Hokusai. The poetry cartouche is integrated into the design through the superposition of the quiver of arrows. A preliminary sketch for this print survives in a drawing album in the collection of the Chiba City Museum of Art, which would have been retraced to create the carefully limned engraver's drawing required for carving the key block (fig. 24a).

The other two subjects in this set of three include the famous warriors Tomoe Gozen (see cat no. 127) and Benkei.

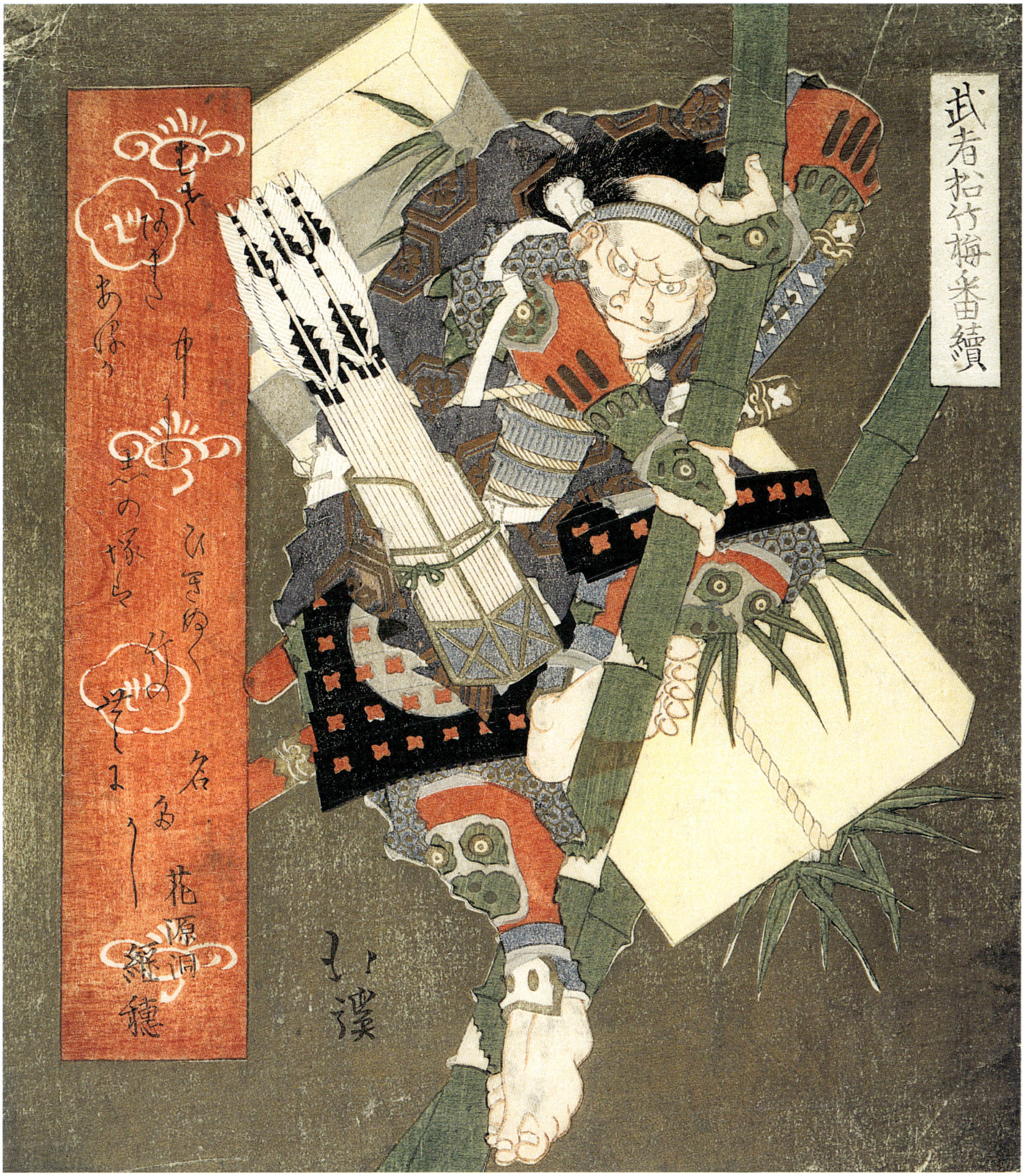
武者揃竹梅番續

TEISAI HOKUBA

1771–1844

25 Two women with a boy and a pet rat

DATE 1804, Year of the Rat
SIGNATURE Hokuba ga
CARVER'S SEAL Tōen ?
FORMAT Koban (14.0 x 9.7)
FLLW FDN 3014.015

26 Two women and a boy with a toy tiger

DATE 1806, Year of the Tiger
SIGNATURE Hokuba ga
FORMAT Koban (15.0 x 10.8)
FLLW FDN 3014.007

Early egoyomi picture calendars of the mid-eighteenth century placed little or no importance on the animals of the zodiac. However, by the end of the century, zodiac symbols typically were a prominent component of the design. These two examples demonstrate that calendar prints listing long and short months were still commissioned at a time when verse-surimono were becoming popular.

In the print on the left, the older woman unrolls a hanging scroll showing Daikoku with his sack of money, tossing coins. (For an egoyomi by Hokusai depicting the same activity, see cat. no 172). Daikoku, one of the Seven Gods of Good Fortune, who was said to confer wealth, was also associated with the rat. A young boy, whose attire is patterned with the auspicious symbols of the raincoat and hat, watches a pet white rat that plays on the arm of the young girl. In the *tokonoma* (alcove) is a bronze vase on a wooden stand with an arrangement of plum branches. On the mounting of the painting are the numbers for the long months of the rat year: *shō* (1), 3, 6, 8, 10, 11, 12. Since the name of Daikoku includes the word *dai* (meaning large), the picture of him can be taken as a clever visual pun to indicate the idea of "long months."

In the design for the year of the tiger on the right, a women carries a little boy who reaches toward a toy tiger held by a young woman. The date is signified not only by the presence of the toy, but also by the numbers for long months—1, 2, 4, 8, 10, 11—which are inscribed on the obi of the standing girl; the character *dai,* indicating the long months, appears on the lower right-hand corner of the trail of the obi. A plum tree peeks in from behind the open sliding doors.

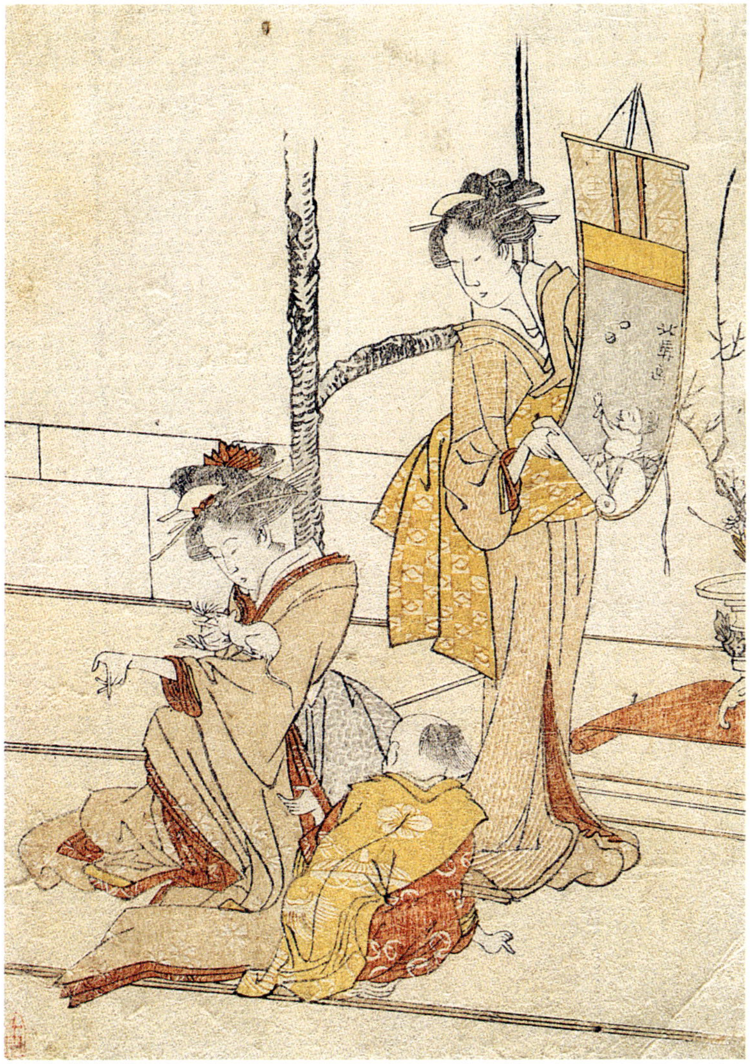

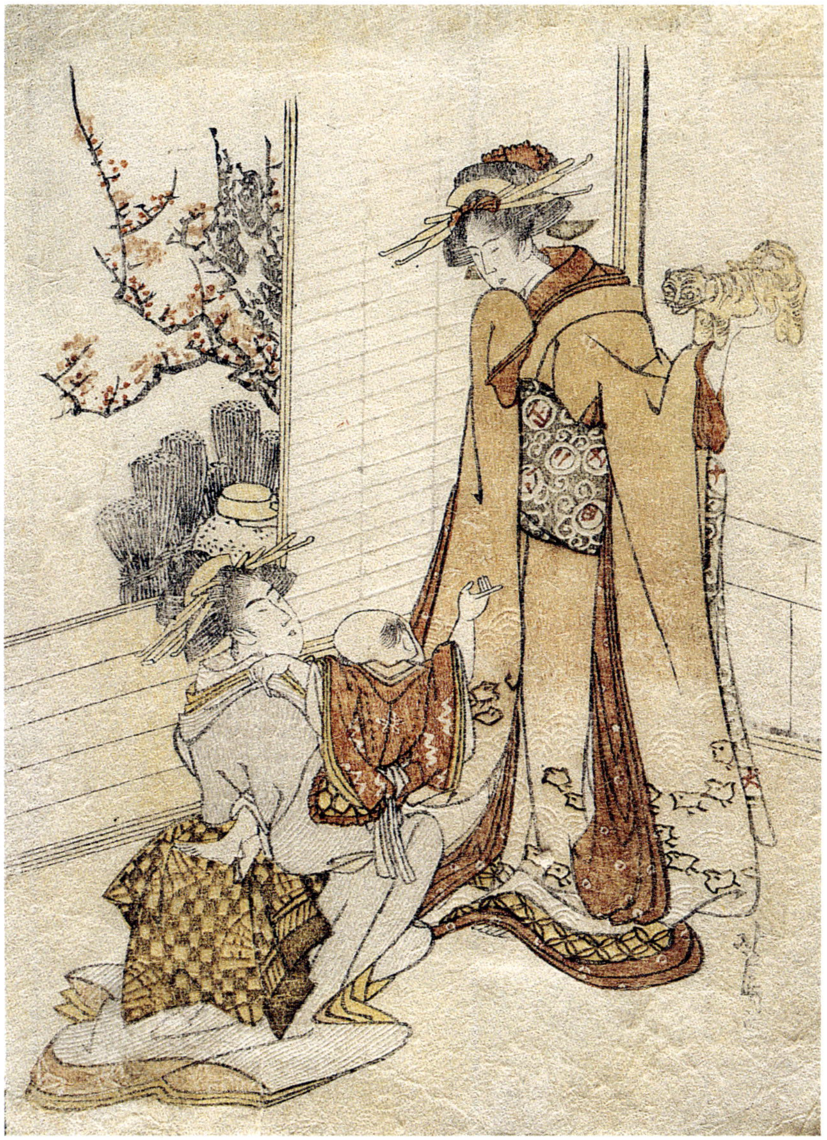

TEISAI HOKUBA

1771–1844

27 Vegetables, greens, and shellfish in an iron skillet

SERIES *Shōutsushi Goban no Uchi;*
Series of Five Drawings from Life
DATE ca. 1808
SIGNATURE Hokuba sha
ARTIST'S SEAL Uma (Ba)
CARVER'S SEAL Horikō Asau
FORMAT Koban yoko-e (14.0 x 18.8)
FLLW FDN 3014.001

Wakayagitei Toshihira:

shita-tsuzumi	Smacking our lips
ute ya hayase ya	as we enjoy a feast
nabeyaki no	cooking in the skillet—
toridori iwau	a host of things to celebrate
kimigayo no haru	this glorious spring.

Senrintei Tsurayoshi:

goshūgi o	When making a spread
narabe tatetsutsu	for a festive meal
shippoku no	of stew with noodles,
kai no hashira mo	shellfish are added
kazou manzai	to bring long life.

As a print designer and painter, Hokuba ranks as one of the top pupils of Hokusai, whose style had a tremendous influence on his depictions of women. He is equally well known for his illustrations for kyōka anthologies and surimono.

The naturalism of this still life of a New Year stew reflects the trend toward "true life" representations first popularized by Maruyama Ōkyo (1733–95). The phrase *shōutsushi* in the series title is meant to suggest that these images were drawn from life; however, it may also be a reference to raw food. In another example from this set, a tray of raw food lies next to a grater (cat. no. 145). Here, the iron skillet overflows with thinly sliced vegetables, octopus, and shellfish resting on top of stiff, uncooked dried greens that poke out of the left edge of the pan. The soup spoon, lying in the foreground, is evidence that there is liquid to be added as well. The wooden cover, resting to the side, will be placed on top of the skillet during cooking.

The first poem uses set phrases all related to eating; *shita-tsuzumi,* for example, means to smack one's lips or eat with gusto. *Toridori* (a host of things) also suggests the image of people eating from a skillet, taking one piece after another without pausing. In the second poem, Senrintei refers to *shippoku,* a vegetable and noodle dish that originated in China and became popular in Nagasaki before spreading throughout Japan. In the print, the noodles have yet to be added, as the seafood and vegetables remain uncooked.

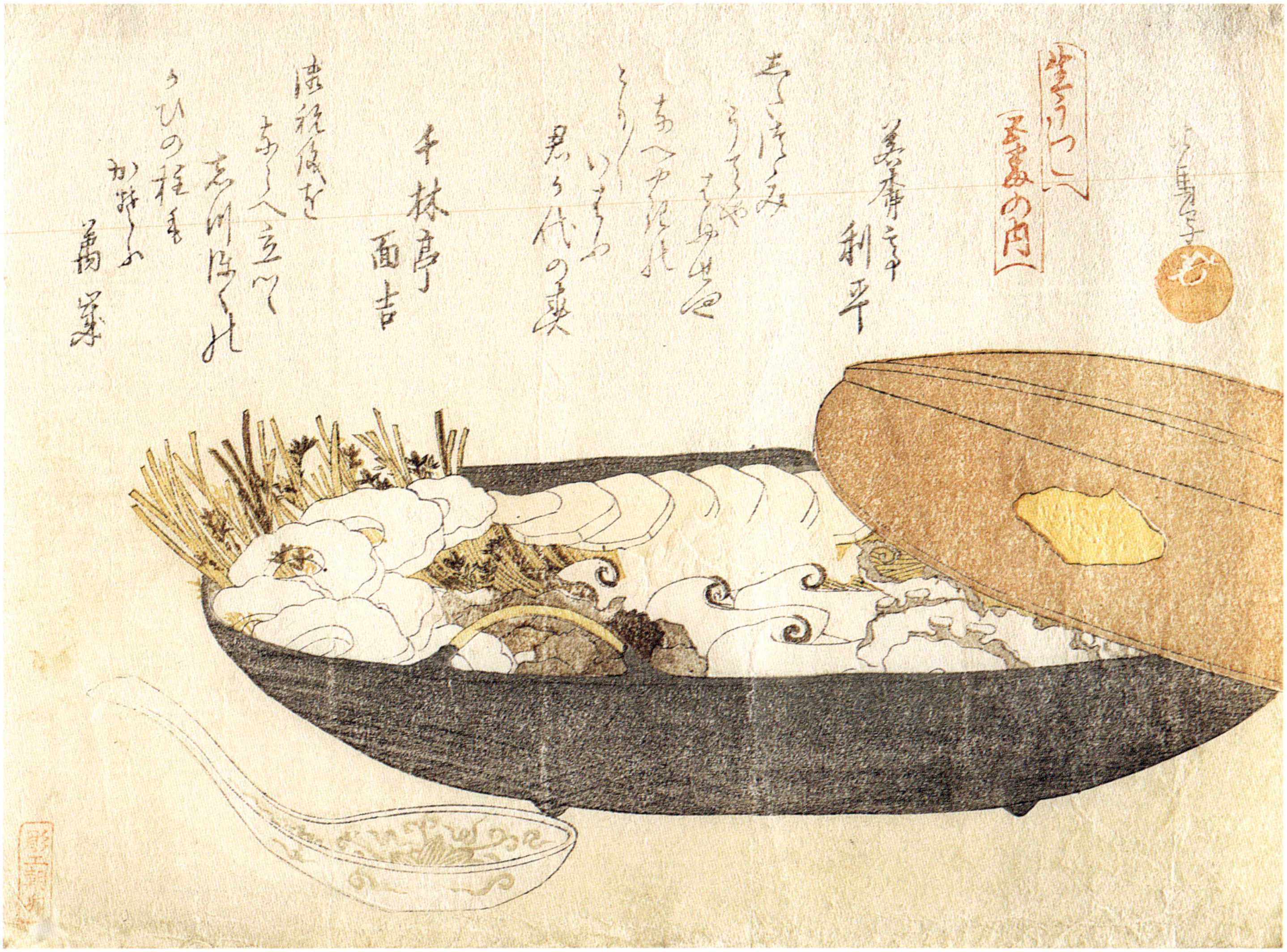
生うつし
五菜の内
利平
千林亭 面吉

TEISAI HOKUBA

1771–1844

28 A mirror with a makeup bowl

DATE ca. 1810
SIGNATURE Teisai Hokuba Fujiwara no Mitsutaka sha
FORMAT Chūban yoko-e (20.6 x 27.6)
REFERENCE Ostier, *Les objets tranquilles,* pl. 85
FLLW FDN 3014.016

Shami Kakusei:

kage utsusu	The hills of spring
ike no kagami ni	reflected in the mirror
haru no yama	of the small lake
waraeba warau	break into laughter
sazanami no ue	as gentle waves ripple.

Naruko Tsunahiko:

itsumoto o	A five-trunked tree
hanada no ito ni	with strands of pale blue
some-agete	gives a certain tinge
yoridokoro aru	to the house of assignation—
kado no aoyagi	the willow near the gate.

Yotsutsuji Kadomori:

kansui ni	The rice-cake mirror
tokite teri aru	when dipped in cold water
kagami mochi	takes on a shine—
utsushi-hajime wa	the first thing it reflects
ume no kaobase	is the face of the plum.

Resting on top of a black-lacquer case adorned with a floral pattern of clematis lies an intricately figured mirror-back. A masterpiece of the printer's art, the configuration of its design is created by extensive gaufrage rising from a monochromatic silver ground. The unseen polished front is protected by a faded red wrapping cloth. Commonly, these mirrors were made from "silver-bronze," and the printer has selected an appropriate metallic powder in order to simulate its surface.

Auspicious symbols such as a pair of cranes, turtle, bamboo, and pine, as in this surimono, were standard motifs for mirrors. In the Edo period, such mirrors were called *hōrai kyō* (paradise mirrors) and were frequently given as wedding gifts. Traditionally, the profession of making mirrors was held to be sacred and the skills were passed down through families. By the eighteenth century, however, the name Fujiwara as part of the artist-craftsman signature on mirrors merely signified high-quality workmanship.

The six poems were composed by poets of the Asakusa group, which at this time was headed by Sembōan (Sensōan II). The first poem likens the surface of a lake to a mirror. Mountains laughing in spring is a common conceit in kyōka. The second poem perhaps refers to the willow near the gate of the Yoshiwara. Returning to the mirror theme, the third poem discusses *kagami mochi,* literally, "mirror rice cakes." Their name came from their flattened circular shape and their polished, smooth surface, created by dipping them into cold water. These cakes

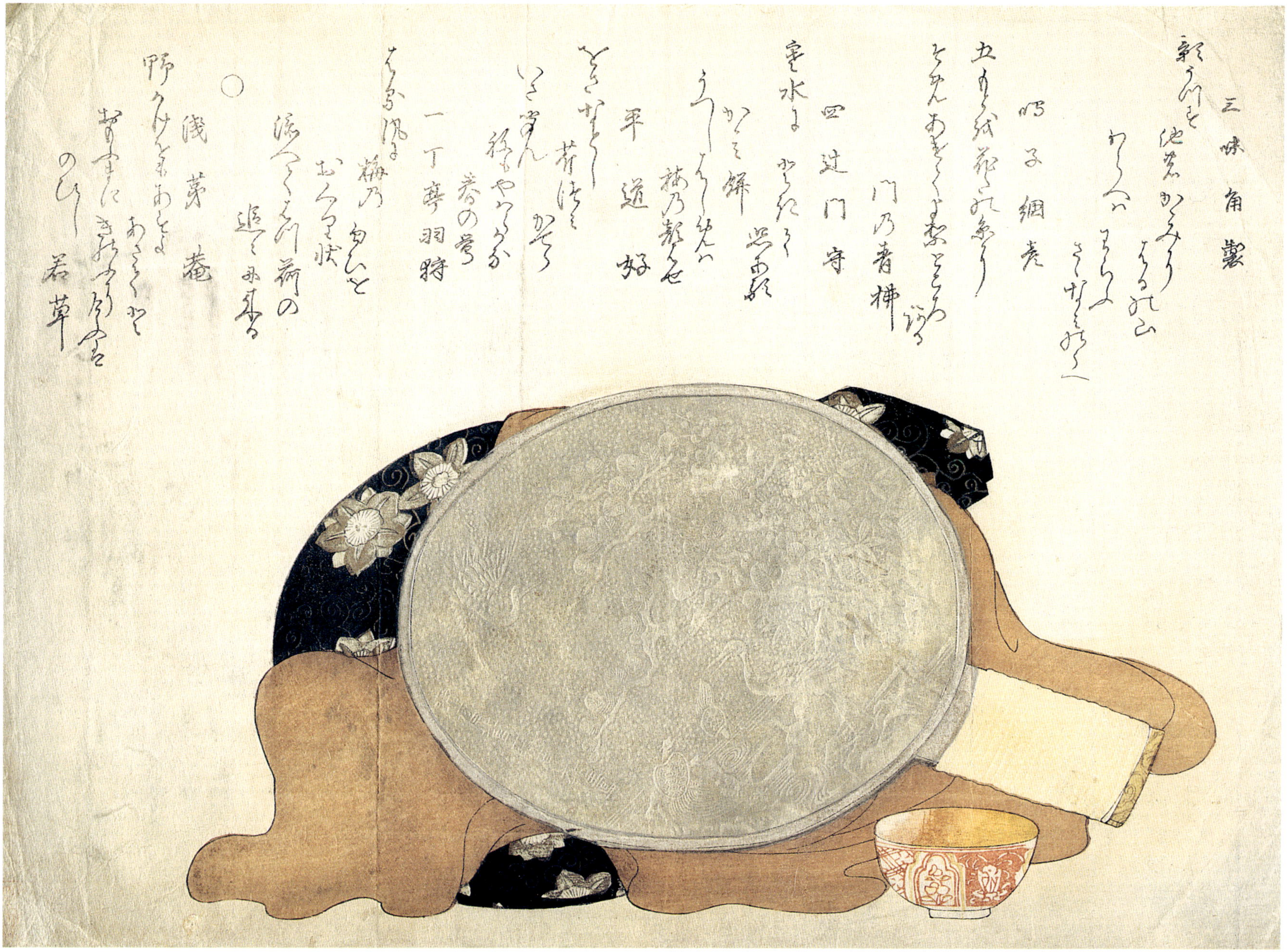

の青柳

守

好

羽特

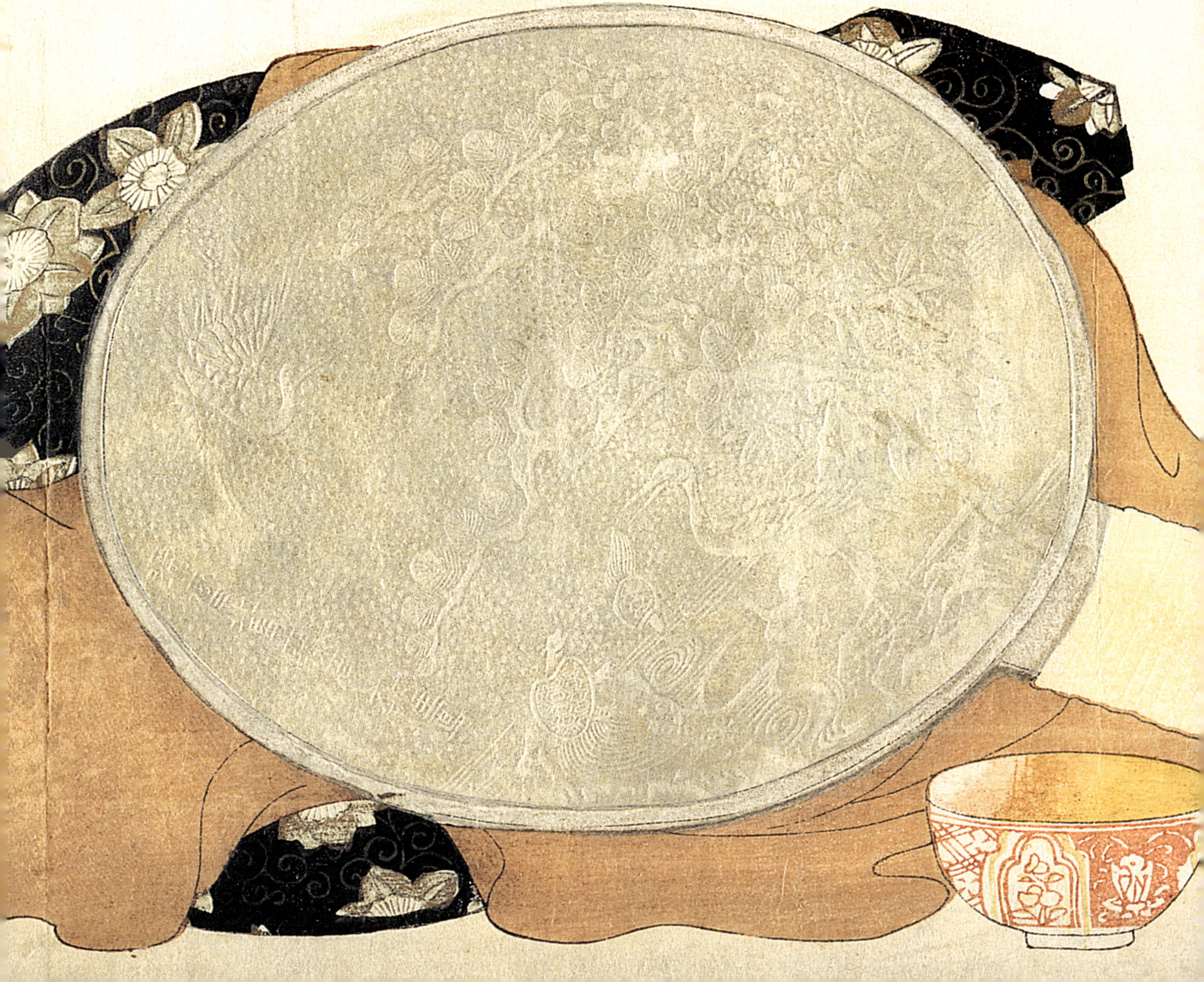

were used for New Year displays and were also eaten, as they were believed to strengthen one's teeth and thus prolong life. In ancient times they were called *mochi kagami* or simply *kagami*. The customary picking of parsley, one of the seven herbs, at the New Year is the seasonal subject of the fourth poem. The subject of the fifth poem is *hatsuni,* another common New Year activity in which wholesalers decorated their goods, piled them on a horse or cart, and sent them to the customer's home. The term also connotes the first delivery of seasonal goods. The final poem by the group leader, Sembōan, takes as its theme the planning of a spring outing. It is a skillful adaption of a poem by Yamabe Akahito that is included in the *Sanjūrokunin Sen* (Anthology of the Thirty-six Poetic Immortals):

asu kara wa	From tomorrow,
wakana tsumamu to	we will pluck young herbs
shimeshi no ni	in the fields—
kinō mo kyō mo	yesterday and today
yuki wa furitsutsu	it continues to snow.

Taira no Michiyoshi:

osana toshi	The year is young
seri tsumi gatera	as we pick wild parsley—
iza kikan	let's listen now
ne mo yawarakana	for the gentle sound
haru no uguisu	of the spring warbler.

Itchōtei Hagari:

harukaze ni	A long-awaited message
ume no nioi o	carried by spring breezes
okurijō	and perfumed with plum,
soete hatsuni no	arrives in due time
oi-oi ni kuru	with the New Year's delivery.

Sembōan:

nogake o mo	From tomorrow
asu yo asate to	or the day after tomorrow
omou ma ni	we can play in the fields,
kinō ni kyō wa	yesterday and today
nobishi wakakusa	young grass has sprouted up.

KARYŌSAI HOKUGA

ACT. CA. 1804–1830

29 Ukifune in Uji

TITLE *Genji Monogatari; The Tale of Genji*
DATE ca. 1828
SIGNATURE Hokuga hitsu
FORMAT Shikishiban (20.7 x 18.5)
REFERENCE Rijksmuseum, *Hokusai,* pl. 117
FLLW FDN 3013.001

Taikōrō Umekage:

tōku kara	Seen dimly from afar,
hono mishi hana o	the flower's fragrance
oboroge ni	as if in a dream
niou ya Uji no	floats in a breeze across
haru no kawakaze	the river at Uji in spring.

Shushintei:

cha no mei ni	Of famous brands of tea
narabu zo Uji no	the best comes from Uji,
hatsu hikage	as the first sun shines
niou miyako no	over the fragrant capital
haru no asaake	at the dawn of the spring.

Karyōsai Hokuga, who specialized in painting and surimono, first studied under Tomikawa Fusanobu (act. 1750–70), an ukiyo-e designer and publisher. He later became a pupil of Hokusai and collaborated with him on an illustrated book of landscape views of Nikkō. In this image, the influence of Hokusai's portrait style of the 1820s can be discerned in both the angular facial features of the woman and the zigzag outlines of the folds of her kimono. Hokusai had two pupils named Hokuga, both of whom are best known as designers of surimono. The other Hokuga, whose name is written with a different character for *ga,* is listed in this catalogue under his later art name, Hōtei Gosei (see cat. nos. 11 and 87–88).

The title cartouche identifies this as a scene from *The Tale of Genji;* the poems mention Uji, which refers to the final section of the novel often called "the Ten Uji Chapters." Ukifune, the central figure in these chapters, is dressed in elaborate Heian court attire. The composition seems to reflect a sub-genre of depictions of beauties in which a small background or separate scene serves as a picture within a picture depicting a scene associated with the main subject of the print. Ukifune is seated before an arched doorway through which can be seen a boatman transporting her and her lover Prince Niou in the scene from the Islet of Oranges (see cat. no. 23). Somewhat downcast in expression, she seems saddened by her recollections. She holds an open folding fan, upon which rests a spray of cherry blossoms. This detail would appear to indicate a specific scene, but in fact does not correlate exactly to traditional iconography. In the late Edo period, well-known scenes from classical literary sources, such as *The Tale of Genji,* were frequently amalgamated in a single composition.

The place name Uji, in Edo parodic verse, is frequently used as an abbreviation for *Uji no Ukifune* (Ukifune at Uji). The name of Ukifune's lover, Prince Niou, is invoked through a string of hidden puns in both poems. The second poem also demonstrates how writers and artists of the late Edo period delighted in anachronisms: tea, a mainstay by this time, was rarely if ever consumed for pleasure during the Heian period. The linking of tea and Ukifune would never have occurred to a *waka* poet.

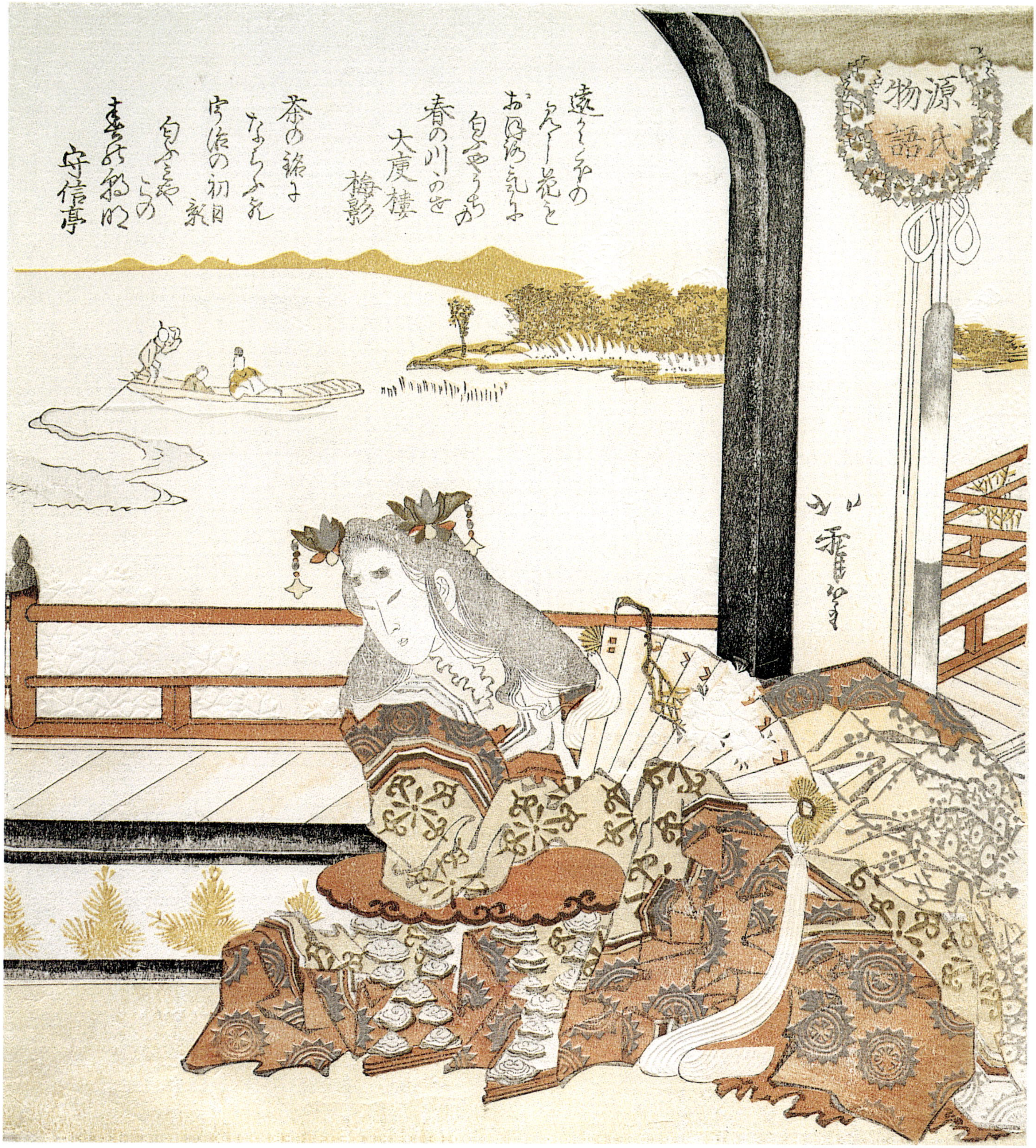
源氏物語

KATSUSHIKA HOKUSAI

1760–1849

30 A courtesan with a boy attendant beneath a willow

DATE ca. 1802
SIGNATURE Gakyōjin Hokusai ga
FORMAT Koban tate-e (20.9 x 9.0)
REFERENCES *UT, Bibliothèque Nationale,* pl. 217
FLLW FDN 3002.144

Kinoe Himada:

harusame no	In a spring drizzle
otonashiyaka ni	so calm and gentle
miru onna wa	the maiden appears—
shittori mono no	though she is slightly damp
koburi made yoshi	the misty rain becomes her.

Beneath a budding willow tree stands a lovely courtesan. She has just closed her bull's-eye-patterned umbrella and her black rain hood has fallen to her shoulders. The treetop is obscured by a band of spring mist. Her boy-attendant carries another umbrella and a straw bundle of herbs. The emblem on the green sack slung across his shoulders indicates the poet's affiliation with one of the poetry circles formed under the aegis of the No-gawa poetry group.

This surimono is closely related to a well-known color painting by Hokusai in the collection of the Hokusai Museum in Obuse (see Lane, *Hokusai,* pl. 109). In both the painting and the surimono, the young beauty is similarly posed with a partially closed umbrella beneath a willow. While the painting does not include a boy, it does contain a large area of mist at the top, suggesting that the painting too was originally designed to accommodate an inscription. The budding willow of the New Year's surimono has been replaced with the tree in full leaf and the blooming flowers of late spring.

A series of rain-related words—*harusame* (spring drizzle), *shittori* (slightly moist), *koburi* (light rain)—all contribute to the misty, impressionistic mood of the image. The suggestion is that a woman appears most beautiful on a misty spring day rather than on a bright sunny day. The last line, *koburi made yoshi,* implies, however, that a light rain is best—that a heavy rain would destroy the effect. One additional series of puns contrasts acting like an adult (*otonashiyaka ni*) to acting like a child (*koburi*), a conceit that gave hints to the artist for the subject of the print.

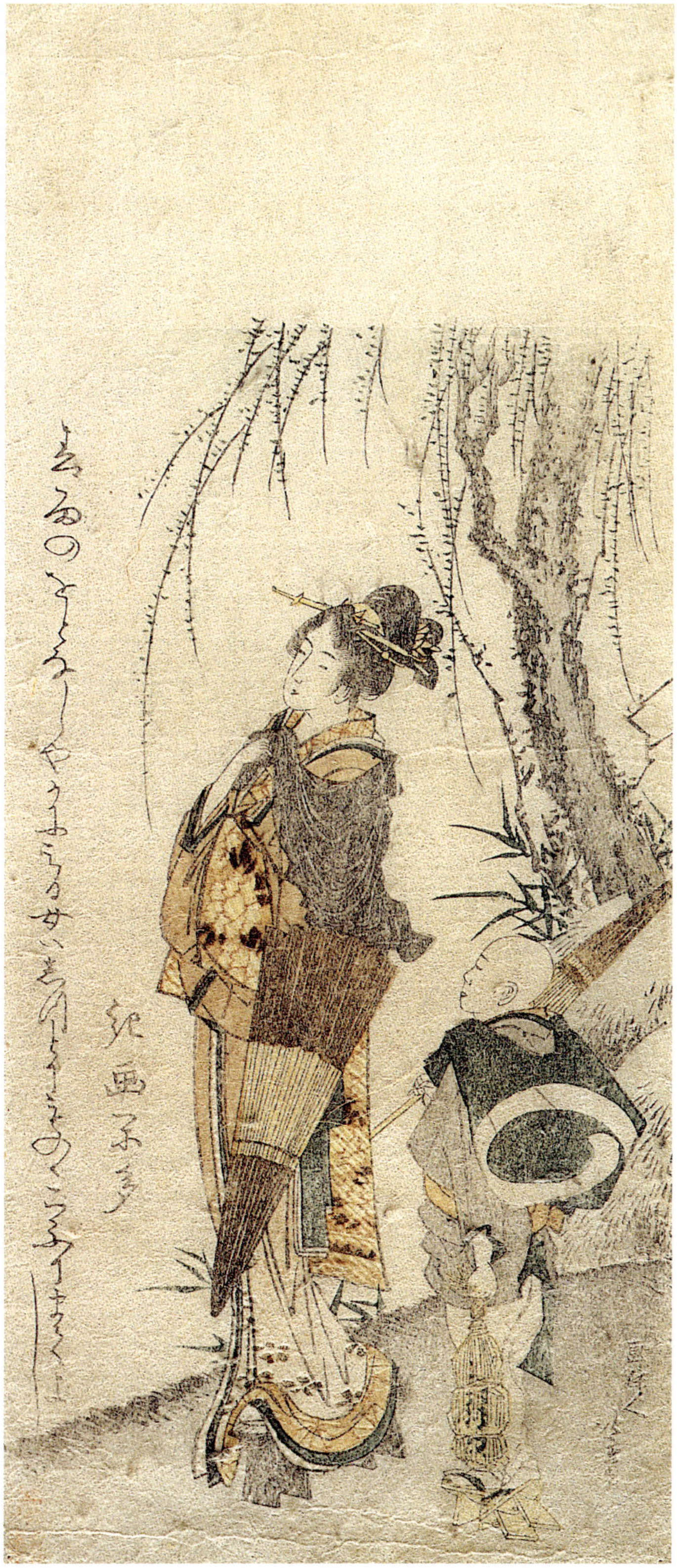

KATSUSHIKA HOKUSAI

1760–1849

31 Two beauties play with puppets

TITLE *Kokaji;* Kokaji—The Blacksmith
SERIES *Noroma Kyōgen;* Humorous Puppet Plays
DATE ca. 1802
SIGNATURE Gakyōjin Hokusai ga
FORMAT Koban yoko-e (14.0 x 18.8)
REFERENCE *UT*, *Bibliothèque Nationale,* pl. 222; Lane, *Hokusai,* 62; Rijksmuseum, *Hokusai,* 18
FLLW FDN 3002.023

Mukō no Yamahiko:

mazu haru no	I'd like to take a nap
yume ni mo chotto	and have a New Year's dream—
nete mitashi	perhaps a fox will appear
izure kitsune no	in the guise of a blacksmith
kaji ga aizuchi	to hammer along with me.

Hanada Sodehiro:

sakumono to	Flowers, crafted by nature,
uguisu mo kesa	blossom as the warbler sings—
ume ga kado	this morning, the plum gate
hirakeba gyokei	opens with felicitations
Sanjō no Kokaji	forged by Sanjō no Kokaji.

Although he was better known as a designer of landscapes, early in his career Hokusai vied with the other major print artists of the late eighteenth century, such as Utamaro, in the depiction of beautiful women. These attenuated, rather delicate ladies appear in genre scenes, paired with effete young dandies, and in theatrical parodies. In a format that also harkens back to Utamaro, Hokusai has placed puppets in the hands of the elegant amateur performers (see also cat. no. 173).

Noroma Kyōgen, the title of this series, refers to plays that were comic interludes between the Jōruri puppet dramas.These amusing skits relied heavily on the Kyōgen repertoire (short plays performed at intervals between Nō). The term *noroma* derives from Noroma Hambei, the founder of this performing art form in Edo around 1670.

The Kyōgen play *Kokaji,* which parallels the plot of the Nō version of the same title, relates a legend surrounding Sanjō no Kokaji (also known as Munechika), the celebrated swordsmith of the late Heian period. Commissioned by the emperor to forge a sword, Kokaji worried because he could not find anyone to assist him, and so he went off to a fox shrine to pray for assistance. At the shrine a child appeared, who encouraged him by telling tales of the virtues of famous swords of the past. The child then told him not to worry and to begin preparations. Upon returning home, a fox-ghost appeared to him and aided in the hammering. The result was the creation of a sword named Kogitsunemaru, Little Fox Blade. Hokusai has selected the scene in which Kokakji, on the right, and the divine-messenger fox, dressed in official costume, alternate hammering the imperial sword.

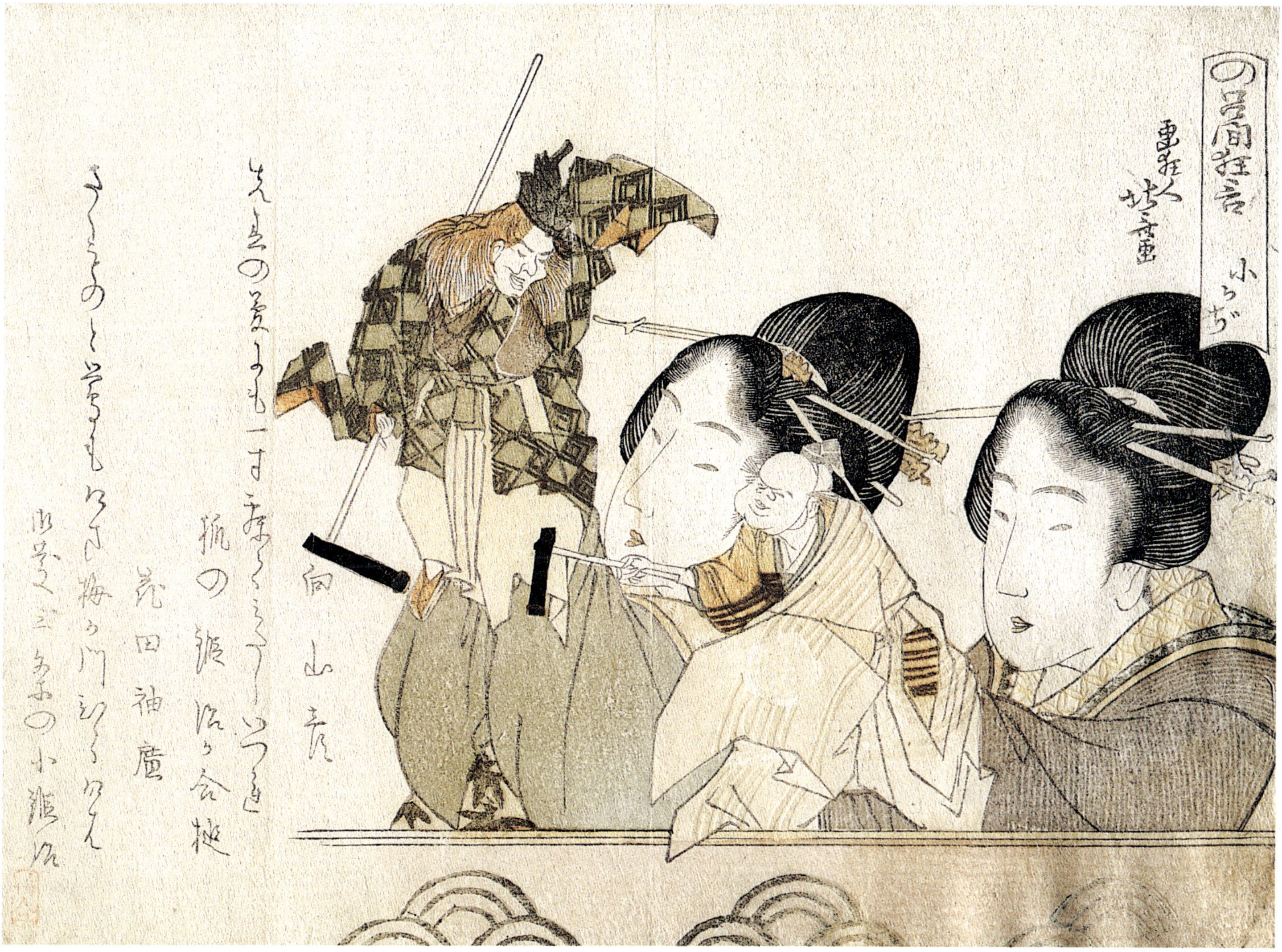

KATSUSHIKA HOKUSAI

1760–1849

32 Two Chinese children watching a mother tiger and cubs cross a river

DATE 1806, Year of the Tiger
SIGNATURE Gakyōjin Hokusai ga
FORMAT Koban yoko-e (14.0 x 19.3)
REFERENCES *Le fou de peinture,* fig. 47; Tōbu Museum of Art, p. 186, pl. 72
FLLW FDN 3002.102

The tiger, a symbol of strength and bravery, was held in great esteem in East Asia. Said to be endowed with magical properties and to live for one thousand years, the tiger is also one of the twelve animals of the zodiac and associated with one of the cardinal directions (west). As tigers were native to the Asian continent but not to Japan, Japanese artists relied upon Chinese renderings and their imaginations as artistic guides.

Hokusai was inspired by a popular Chinese legend that tells of a tiger, mother to three cubs, one of which was always striving to attack the other two. Only the miscreant cub had fur that was spotted. Once, when faced with a river to cross, the mother tiger was in a quandary as to how to get her cubs across without leaving either of the weaker cubs alone with the aggressive one. She decided to bring the spotted cub to the opposite shore before carrying the second across. Then, after returning with the spotted cub to the original shore, she swam across once more with the third. Finally, with the two weaker cubs safely across, she brought over the spotted cub.

In this design, Hokusai has cleverly revised the legend by having the mother tiger make only two trips. By placing the difficult spotted cub on her back, the mother tiger was able to safely transport each striped cub in her mouth on successive trips. Two boys standing on the shore seem delighted by the tiger's ingenuity.

The first poem plays on the image of tigers crossing a river and the common spring theme of the scent of plum blossoms. The second poem recalls the Japanese proverb "the fox borrows the tiger's courage" *(tora no i o karu kitsune),* which refers to those who bask in another person's glory. Additionally, this poem links the bravery of the mother tiger to that of the celebrated general Katō Kiyomasa (1562–1611). From his tiger-hunting exploits in Korea, he was also known as Toranosuke and nicknamed "Tiger."

The final poem links bamboo and tigers, a favorite theme of East Asian painters through the centuries. Here the suggested image is of such a pairing on a huge kite. This allows the poet to allude to an old Japanese saying, "When the tiger howls, the wind will blow"(*tora usobukeba kaze sawagu*), which means that acts of courage and leadership can change the course of human events. Furthermore, according to an old folk belief, winds always rose up at the hour of the tiger (around 4:00 A.M.). Finally, the phrase *hyō-hyō,* onomatopoeia for the sound of wind, is also a pun on the word "*hyō,*" which means a leopard (keeping in mind that in the past tigers and leopards were often confused by Japanese artists and writers).

Sankyōtei Muraji:

mizu o oyogu	Before the tigers
tora yori saki e	can swim across the waters,
saku ume no	the scent of plum
kawa mukō made	has drifted to the far shore
watasu harukaze	carried by spring breezes.

Shingyokutei Toshinami:

tora no i o	A plum tree
karite mo ume wa	in a tiger's skin
mono no fu no	acts like a warrior
yomo ni nioeru	spreading its scent—
haru no kiyomasa	like Kiyomasa in spring.

Shibanoya Sanyō:

karatake ni	A tiger painted
tora o egakeru	amid Chinese bamboo
ōdako mo	on a grand kite
hyō-hyō to fuku	howls at the wind
kaze ni usobuku	as it blows and blows.

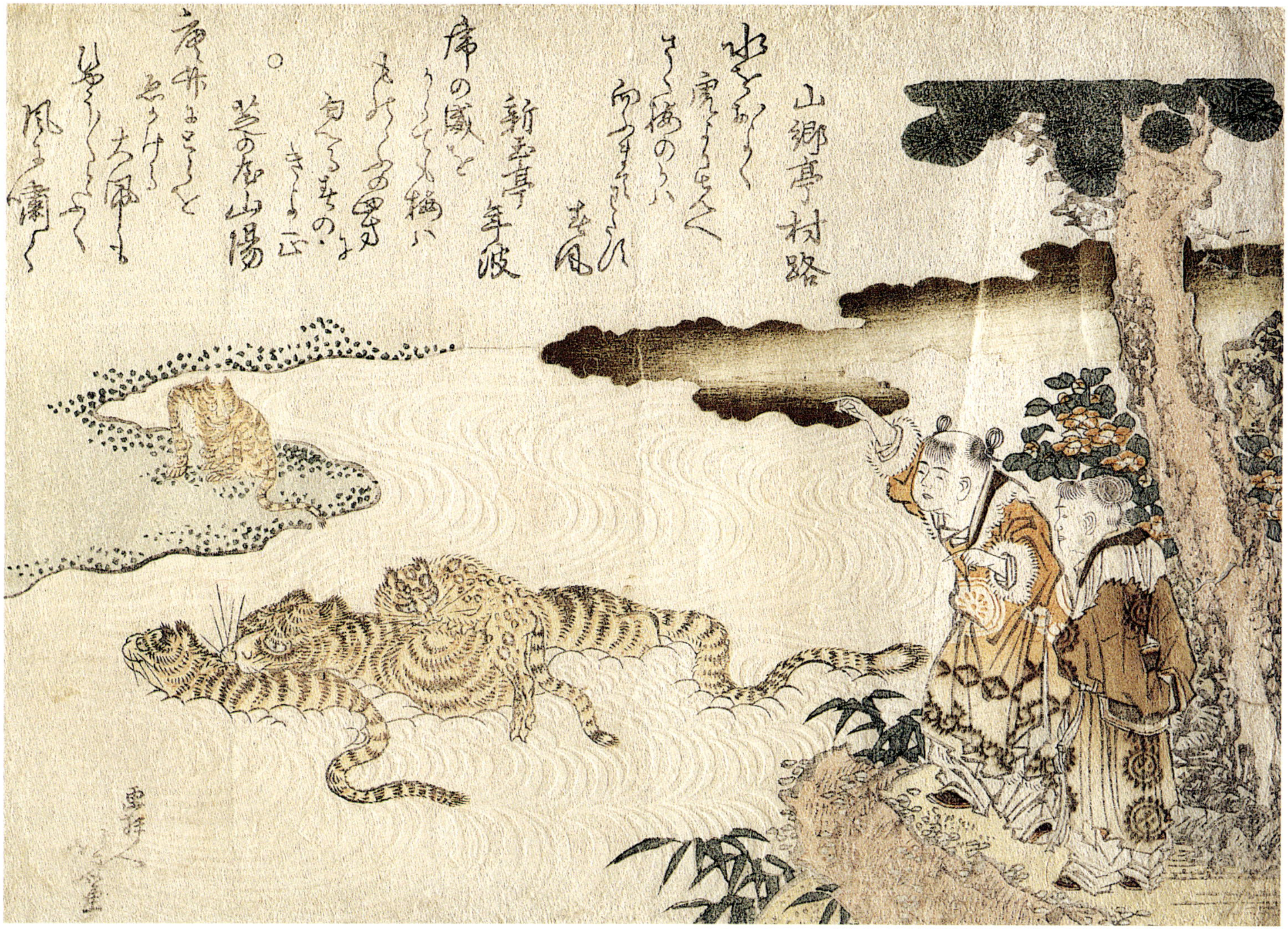
山郷亭村路
新玉亭年波
芝の屋山陽

KATSUSHIKA HOKUSAI

1760–1849

33 A lacquer tray with implements for an incense competition

TITLE *Keibakō;* Incense Horse Race
SERIES *Uma Zukushi;* The Horse Series
DATE 1822
SIGNATURE Fusenkyo Iitsu hitsu
FORMAT Shikishiban (21.3 x 18.8)
REFERENCES Forrer, *Egoyomi and Surimono,* fig. 38; Forrer, *Hokusai,* pl. 267; Polster, no. 265
FLLW FDN 3002.004

Shōryūtei Shigeru:

nioi oba	As its fragrance
sode ni tomeki no	comes to a halt in our sleeves
keibakō	at the incense horse race—
hana ni okurenu	the plum is the front runner,
ume no sakigake	beating out late bloomers.

Seiseisha Fumigaki:

uguisu to	Warbler and plum
ume to irone o	compete in a horse race
kurabe uma	of song versus fragrance—
yanagi no muchi mo	with the wind cracking
ateru harukaze	the whip of the willow.

Yomo Utagaki Magao:

uguisu no	The sweet song of the warbler
koe no nioi ni	enters the horse race—
kurabe uma	but the smell of plum
makezu kazusasu	has never been beaten
eda no ume ga-ka	and takes all of the bets.

This series of at least thirty surimono for the year of the horse represented Hokusai's largest print commission to that time. It was created for the Yomo-gawa poetry group and two of its sub-groups, the Shūchōdō poetry club and the Manji poetry circle. The prints are all connected with equine themes. The kyōka likewise contain numerous puns and references connecting the New Year and horse imagery. The red, gourd-shaped title cartouche on each print alludes to the horse conjured from a gourd by the immortal Chōkarō. With the exception of a triptych of landscape designs, all are still lifes. The Wright collection has seven designs from the series and two duplicates (see also cat nos. 34, 35, and 182–85) and includes another impression of this design FLLW FDN 3002.005.)

Every component of this image relates to the springtime activity of *keibakō,* an incense identification game in which the players' success at recognizing specific scents is played out on a board with horse-and-rider game pieces. On the red-and-black lacquer tray, decorated with the emblem of Yomo-gawa, are other incense game tools, including a gold and silver packet of incense, a feather for sweeping the ashes, small silver incense chopsticks for holding incense chips, and a porcelain incense burner containing ashes to support the incense.

As in the other examples from this series, horse-related puns are abundant. In the first poem, the term *sakigake* can mean the front runner in a horse race or harbinger of things to come. Because the plum is the first flower to bloom each year, it too takes the lead. In fact, there is an old Japanese saying: *ume wa hyakka no sakigake,* "The plum is the first among hundreds of flowers."

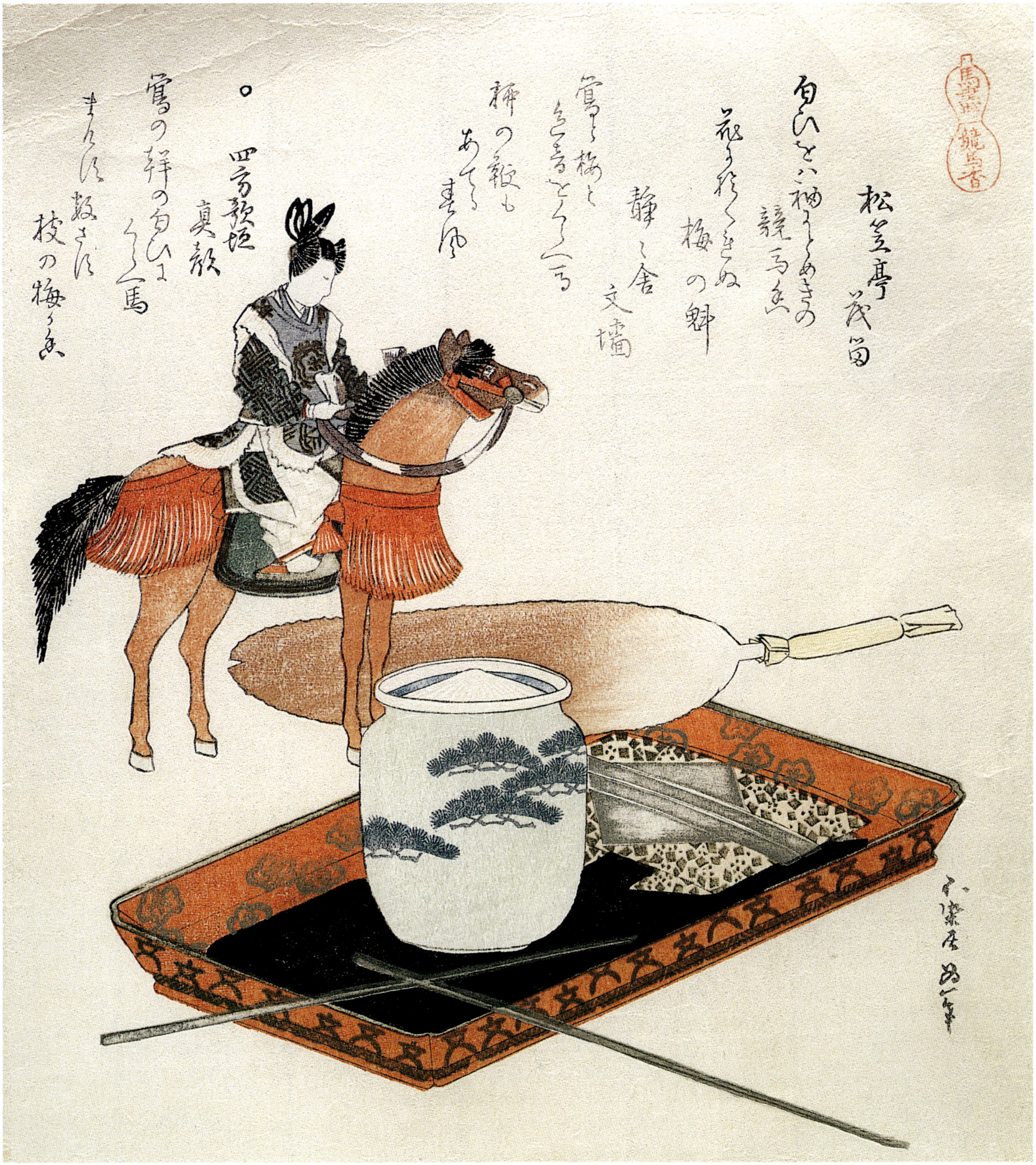

KATSUSHIKA HOKUSAI

1760–1849

34 An inkstone and brushes

TITLE *Bateiseki;* Horse Hoof Inkstone
SERIES *Uma Zukushi;* The Horse Series
DATE 1822
SIGNATURE Fusenkyo Iitsu hitsu
FORMAT Shikishiban (20.3 x 17.8)
REFERENCES Ostier, *Les objets tranquilles,* pl. 1; Bowie, pl. 111
FLLW FDN 3002.001

Tsukihana no Nagame:

haru no hi no	Spring sunlight,
hikari mo eiji	flaring out in eight ways,
happō e	inscribes *Eternity*
haneru hitsui ya	at the first writing practice
uma no kakizome	of the year of the horse.

Gofuku Ayako:

murasaki no	Purple mists trail
kasumi sode hiku	as he tugs at the sleeve
tazuna ni mo	of the shy maiden—
kokoro yurusanu	trying to rein in her heart
imo ga koma geta	as she hoofs along in clogs.

The artist and the five poets have cleverly interwoven horse-related themes with the practice of the first calligraphy of the year. It is a deceptively simple still-life arrangement, composed of writing implements. The central object is a bluish-black inkstone resting on a red lacquer stand, decorated with the flying crane symbol for the Shūchōdō group. The stone is carved into a horseshoe shape which has then been sloped and graded in simulation of an actual hoof. An ink stick is propped against it and a narrow silver paperweight lies beneath the lacquer stand. The small porcelain teapot ornamented with a blue plum-blossom design contains a plum branch; its inverted cover lies in the lower left corner. The octagonal brush container appears to be carved cinnabar lacquer.

The title of this print, *bateiseki,* which literally means horse's-hoof stone, refers to the material from which the inkstone has been fashioned. The stone is a type of obsidian that can be easily carved and is often found with bluish-gray inclusions that resemble snowflakes or horse hooves. During the Edo period, *bateiseki* was also the generic name of a type of inkstone. The rock is also linked to the legend of Sasaki Takatsuna, a warrior under the command of Yoritomo. It is said to have been formed when his mare plunged into a lake in search of her drowning foal; as her hooves touched bottom, *bateiseki* was formed.

The first poem, by the woman poet Tsukihana no Nagame, echoes the theme of calligraphy practice. The rays of light of the spring sun are likened to the brush-work of a calligrapher who has written out the auspicious character *nagaki* or *ei* for

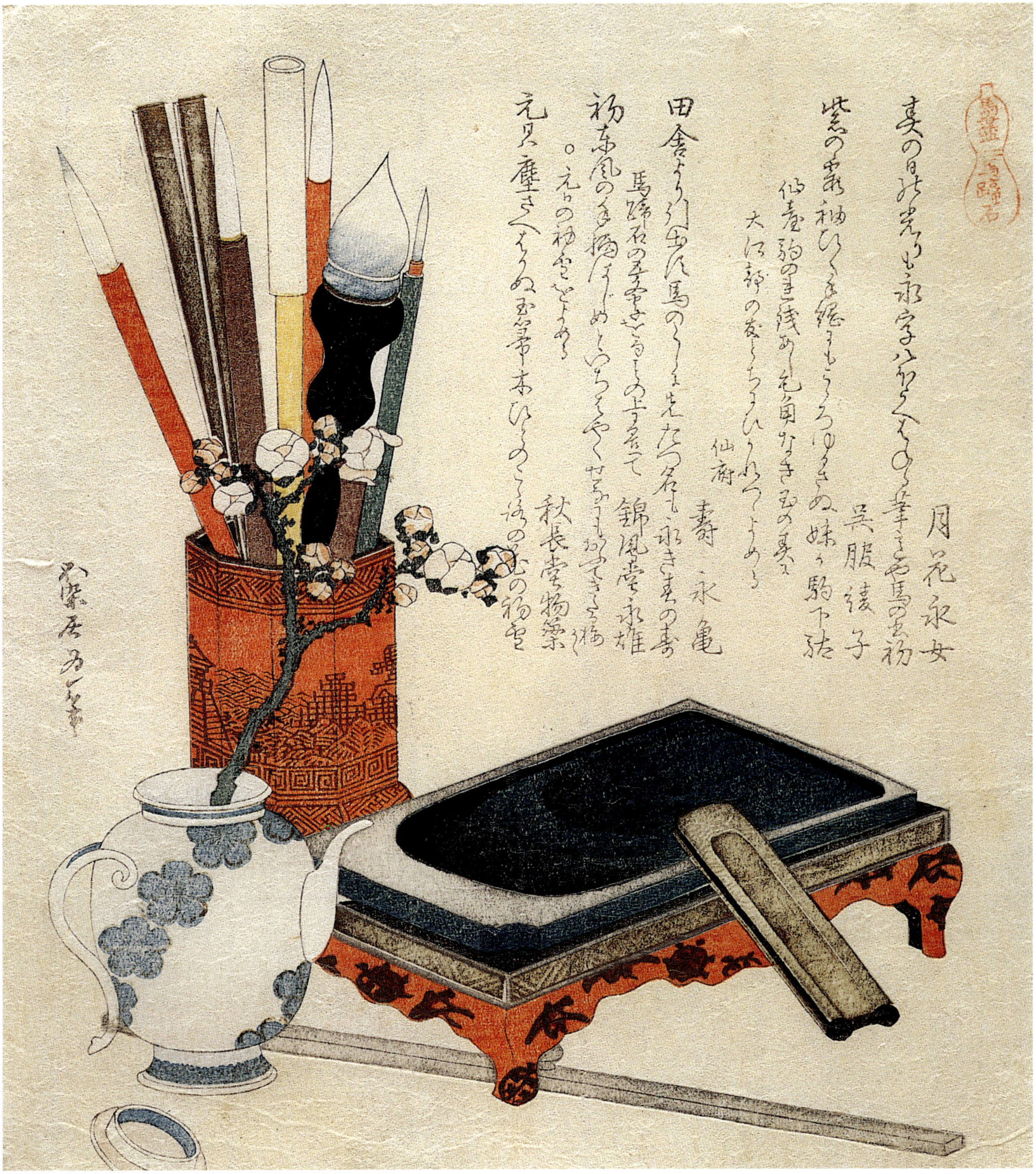

月花永女
呉服綾子
仙府
寿永亀
錦風堂永雄
秋長堂物簗

Kotobuki no Nagaki, Sendai:

Sendai koma no	As I set out from Sendai
renzen ashige kado	this fine spring on a spotted horse,
naki tama no haru ni	I was spurred on by my friends
Ōedo no tomodochi ni	in the great city of Edo
hikaretsutsu yomeru	to compose this verse:

inaka yori	Riding in from the country
hikidasu uma no	as the year of the horse begins—
kura ni saki	my name's *Nagaki,*
tatsu-na mo nagaki	that means *long,* like long reins—
haru no kotobuki	in this spring of good fortune.

Kimpōdō Nagao:

bateiseki no go moji o	The five syllables of "Horse hoof
ku goto no ue ni oite	stone" *(bateiseki)* have been placed
	at the beginning of each line:

hatsukochi ni	A wind from the east
tegara hajime to	on the first mission of the year
ichi hayaku	arrives with dispatch,
sena ni mo oute	carrying along in its trail
kitaru ume ga ka	the scent of plum blossoms.

Shuchōdō Monoyana:

ganjitsu no	A poem about snow on
hatsuyuki o yomeru	the first day of the year—

ganjitsu wa	On New Year's Day
chiri sae hakanu	the jeweled broom
tama-bahaki	sweeps no dust—
hito no kokoro no	as good feelings blossom
hana no hatsuyuki	in the year's first snow.

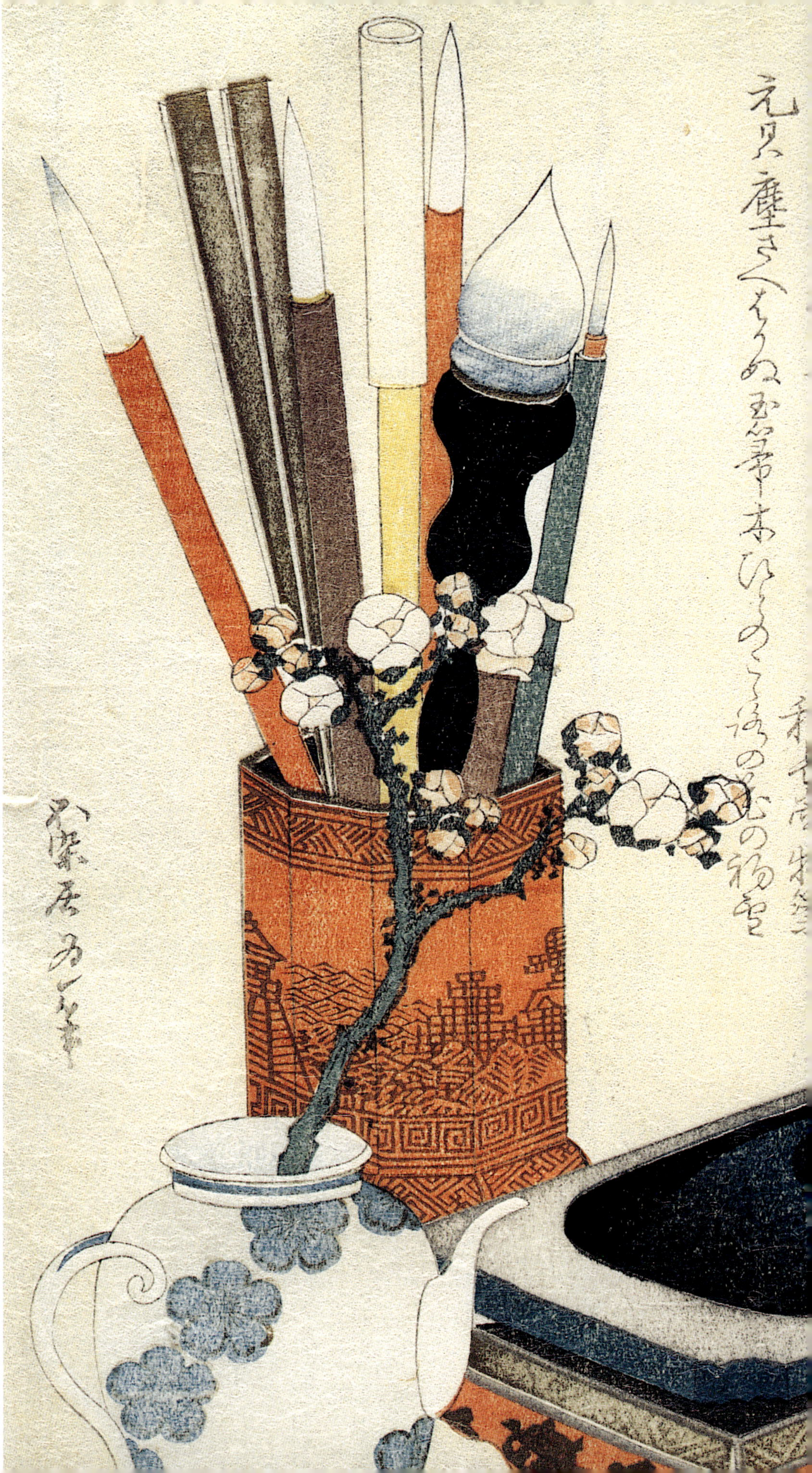

the first writing of the year. *Eiji,* literally "the character *ei* (eternal)" in traditional calligraphy is composed of eight different types of brushstrokes. The character *nagaki,* with all its implications of long life, is often written at the New Year. The horse theme is further intimated through the use of the term *haneru,* which suggests both the prancing of a horse and the sweeping motion of a writing brush.

The next poem by Gofuku Ayako, also a woman, continues with horse-related imagery as it describes a man's amorous approach to a shy maiden. The poet uses the pivot word *hiku* (to pull) in referring both to the "trailing mist" and "pulling on" the sleeve as well as "tugging on the reins" of the horse in the line that follows. *Yurusanu* when referring to reins (*tazuna*) means "not to let up." When describing a person's feelings, however, it means "to be distrustful of." Resembling horse hooves, *koma geta* ("colt clogs") are fashioned from a single piece of wood.

The third poet, in his headnote, mentions that during a visit to Edo, he was invited by his friends in Edo to compose this verse. In the fourth poem, written by the husband of the first poet, the headnote explains that the five syllables comprising *ba-te-i-se-ki* can be found at the beginning of each line (*ba* and *ha* are written with the same phonetic character in Japanese). The fifth poem includes numerous New Year's allusions, as well as plays with the poetic term *tama-bahaki,* traceable to the *Man'yōshū* (Collection of Ten Thousand Leaves), which literally means "jeweled broom." By the Edo period the phrase had taken on the secondary meaning of sake—perhaps implying that drinking wine can sweep away one's worries.

KATSUSHIKA HOKUSAI

1760–1849

35 A *shōgi* game board with a potted adonis plant and miniature plum tree

TITLE *Shōgi koma;* Colts of the Shōgi Board
SERIES *Uma Zukushi;* The Horse Series
DATE 1822
SIGNATURE Fusenkyo Iitsu hitsu
FORMAT Shikishiban (21.2 x 18.6)
REFERENCES Ostier, *Les objets tranquilles,* pl. 99; Rijksmuseum, *Hokusai,* pl. 44; Forrer, *Serial Graphics,* no. 103.7; Polster, no. 269; *UT*, *Rijksmuseum,* pl. 66
FLLW FDN 3002.006

Wakamatsutei Midori:

isami tatsu	The *shōgi* colt,
shōgi no koma ni	showing its mettle
ume no muchi	under the whip of plum,
kachi-iro misuru	smells victory
hana no sakigake	as the flowery front-runner!

[Wakamatsutei Midori:]

kachi shōgi	To win in *shōgi*
te ni wa kingin	one maneuvres
shirogane no	gold and silver pieces,
ume ni kogane no	like the silvery plum
fukujusō kana	and the golden adonis.

Shūchōdō Monoyana:

saku ume no	The plum in bloom
kachi hokoritaru	boasts over its victory
kake shōgi	in a betting game of *shōgi*—
tsuyo shodan naru	a strong beginner
kaze no tenaori	with a handicap from the wind

In another striking still life from the "Horse Series" of 1822, the game of *shōgi* provides an appropriate theme as its game pieces are called *koma,* "colts." This game is believed to have originated in China; the first Japanese references to it are from the twelfth century. Played on a board with eighty-one squares, each player has twenty pieces which are distinguished by the characters written on one side; each can move only in a certain prescribed manner.

The black-lacquer game board in this design is decorated with gold pine saplings and an abstracted silver flying-crane motif that is the symbol of the Shūchōdō poetry club, which commissioned this set. Ten wooden game pieces lie randomly on and near the board, exposing their names; three have fallen to the ground. A blue-and-white porcelain pot contains a blossoming miniature plum tree and an adonis plant, the two most popular flowers of the New Year.

The punning in the poems stems directly from terms used in the game and for horses in general. Most are lighthearted and designed to delight an audience of Edo literati. In the first poem, a plum branch becomes a whip. "Likelihood of victory" and "front runner" allude to both horses and *shōgi;* the latter also can be interpreted as a harbinger of spring. In the third poem, the plum assumes the role of a novice who requires a handicap in the game of *shōgi.*

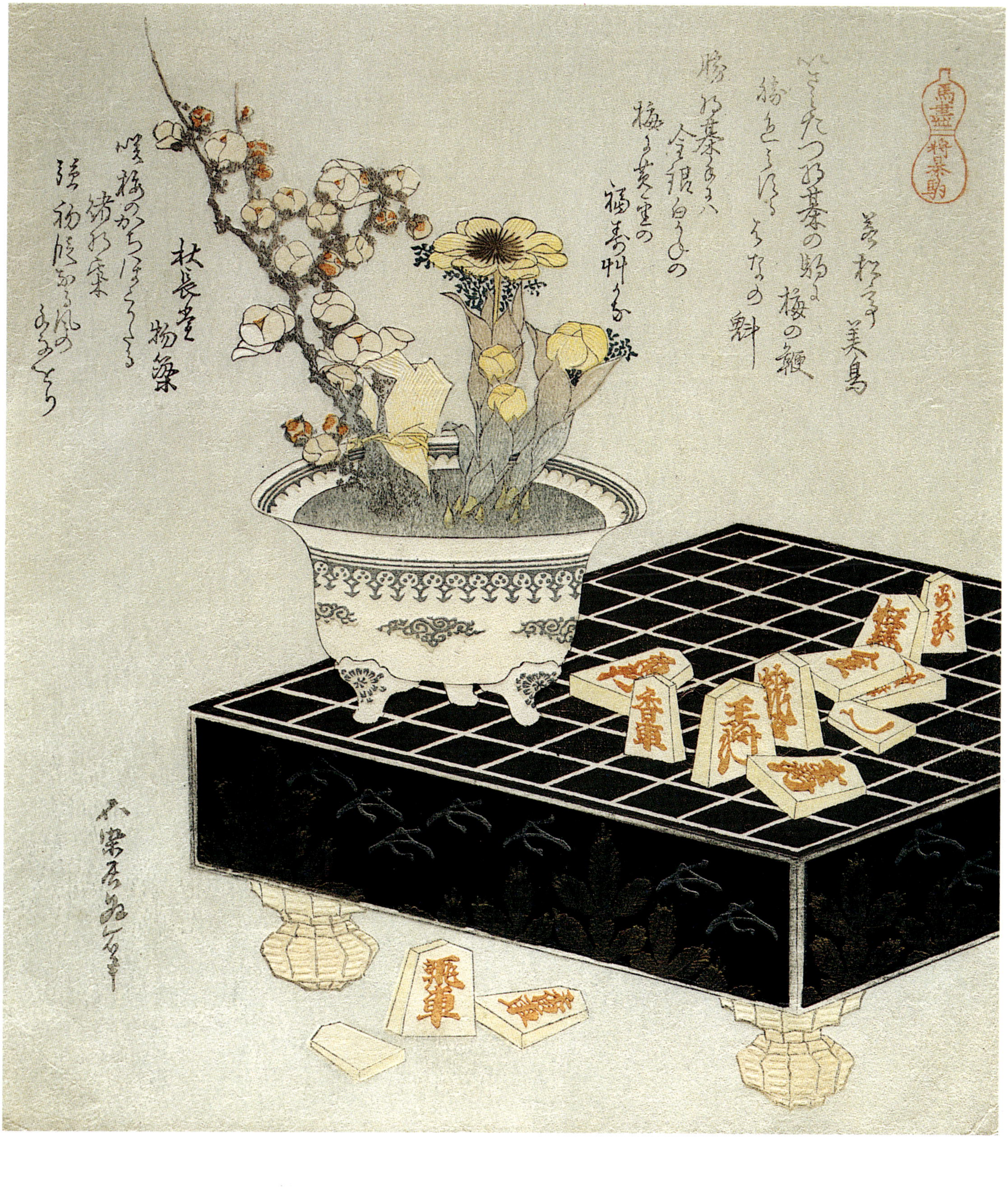
馬盡
将棊駒

KATSUSHIKA HOKUSAI

1760–1849

36 Hair ornaments

DATE Early 1820s
SIGNATURE Hokusai aratame Iitsu hitsu (by Hokusai, now called Iitsu)
FORMAT Shikishiban (22.0 x 18.6)
REFERENCES Ostier, *La voix silencieuse,* pl.65; Ōta Memorial Museum of Art, ed., *Ukiyo-e Yan Būru Korekushon,* sec. 2., pl. 141
FLLW FDN 3002.070

Seiyōen Kagehiro:

kadomatsu ni	As the gate is decked out
take torisoete	with bamboo and pine,
otomego mo	a young maiden wears
haru no hikari no	jewelled hairpins
tama no kanzashi	bright as the spring sun.

Rakuseian:

mage yui no	To her coiffure, entwined
momiji no Tatsuta	with Tatsuta's red leaves,
waga imo ga	my little sister
haru no kazashi no	attaches a flowery array
hana ni soeteki	of springtime spangles.

Silver hairpins with clusters of plum blossom and intertwined cranes lie in translucent tissue and opaque wrapping paper. The red-and-purple puckered fabric used as wadding in the creation of elaborate hair styles contrasts effectively with the flat metallic surfaces of the ornaments. The crinkled texture is the result of a tie-dye process known as *kanoko shibori.* A small amount of fabric is pinched together, then bound tightly with string in concentric circles before final immersion in a dye bath.

Lavish hair decorations such as these were mainly worn by sumptuously attired courtesans and their attendants, especially during New Year celebrations and processions. *Kanzashi,* the ornamental hairpins, are linked in the first poem to decorations of pine and bamboo used to adorn gateways in the New Year season.

The phrase *waga imo,* in the second poem, literally "my little sister," is a term of affection used by a patron to address a young apprentice courtesan. The unseasonal reference to the red maple leaves of Tatsuta River, on the outskirts of Kyoto, is an allusion to the colors of the tie-dyed fabric. Perhaps this pointed, spike-like fabric also serves as a visual allusion to the pointed form of a maple leaf.

This print is one of the rarest in the collection. Facsimile versions of this elegant design appeared in the late 1880s, and the image is known primarily through these later editions.

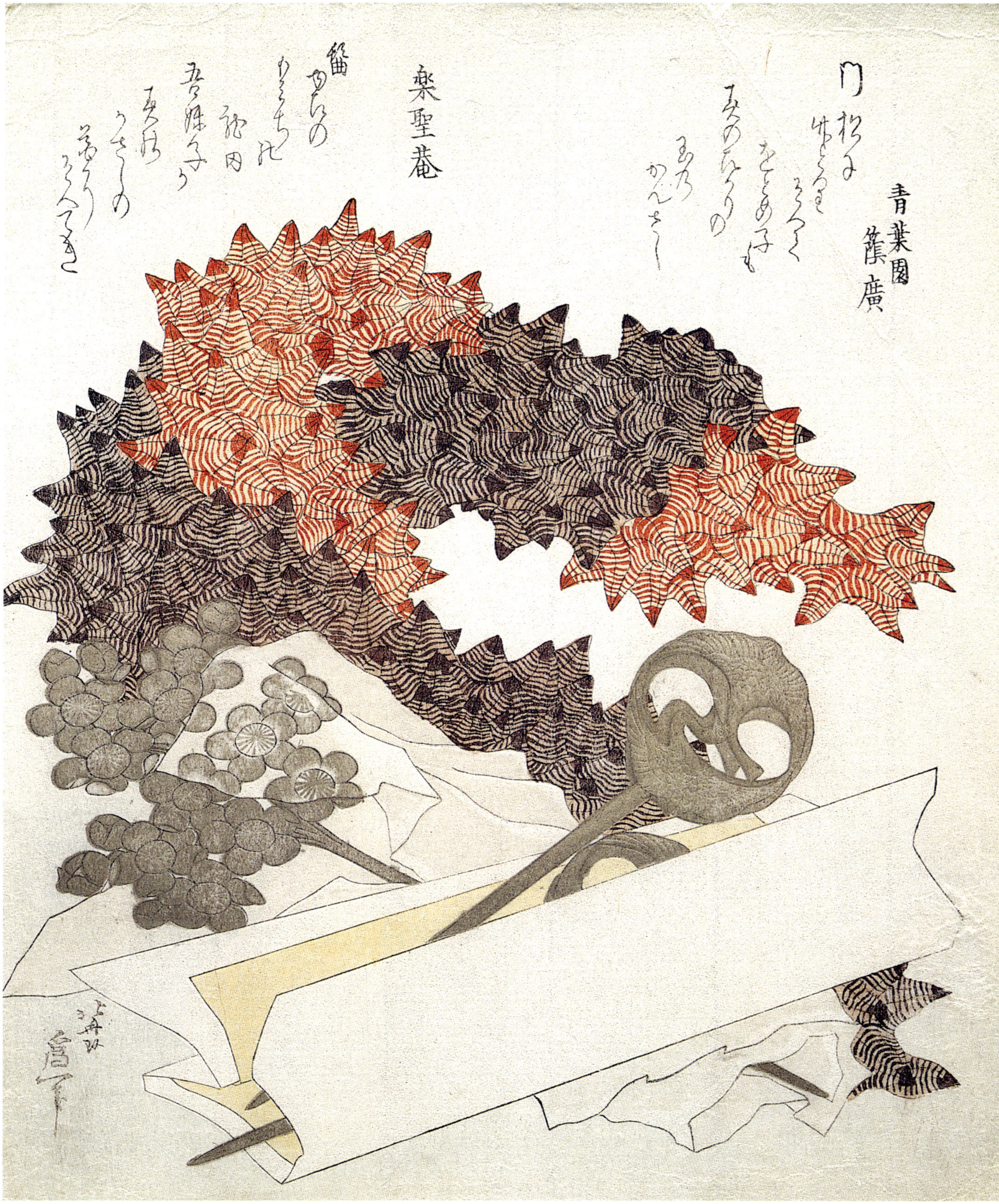
青葉園
蕉廣
楽聖菴

KATSUSHIKA HOKUSAI

1760–1849

37 A view of Mount Fuji

DATE Late 1820s
SIGNATURE Hokusai aratame Iitsu hitsu (by Hokusai, now called Iitsu)
FORMAT Shikishiban (21.9 x 18.4)
REFERENCES Keyes, *Beatty,* pl. 204; Lane, *Hokusai,* fig. 169; *Le fou de peinture,* fig. 103; Forrer, *Hokusai,* pl. 345; Tōbu Museum of Art, 200, pl. 118
FLLW FDN 3002.010

Keika:

mai hibari	Dancing skylarks
koe mo takane to	sing at a pitch as high
seikurabe	as the tallest peak.

Nikyō:

noshime hodo	The hem of its skirt
kasumu susono ya	wrapped in bands of mist—
haru no Fuji	Mount Fuji in the spring.

Best known for his woodblock print series "The Thirty-six Views of Mount Fuji," Hokusai had also focused on the theme of Mount Fuji in book illustrations ("The Hundred Views of Fuji") and Western-inspired landscape scenes. Mount Fuji had long been held in great esteem by the Japanese as a symbol of nature's dominance over the land and its people, while the widespread interest in representations of well-known scenic places during the 1820s contributed to an increased demand for images of this famous mountain (see cat. no. 13). Specific views of Fuji were dictated by custom, but among painters and print designers alike, imaginary representations were also extremely popular. Although the scene here does not correspond precisely to any known vantage point, it may represent a view of Mount Fuji as seen from Lake Ashi in Hakone (Keyes, *Beatty,* no. 204).

This surimono dramatically captures the majesty of this mountain surrounded by golden clouds and patterned rolling hills dotted with pine trees. In place of the traditional horizontal bands of mist, clouds hover around the mountain top in a naturalistic manner. Printed in gaufrage without an outline, the embossed peak appears to push through the clouds.

The design elements complement the allusions of the poems, which are in seventeen-syllable haiku form rather than the more usual kyōka. Keika's poem puns on the word *takane,* which can mean either "high peak" or "high pitch" (if written with other characters). Nikyō's poem likens the image of a dignified Mount Fuji to *noshime* robes, formal underrobes worn by men for occasions such as the New Year. *Susono* means the hem of a kimono or the foot of a mountain.

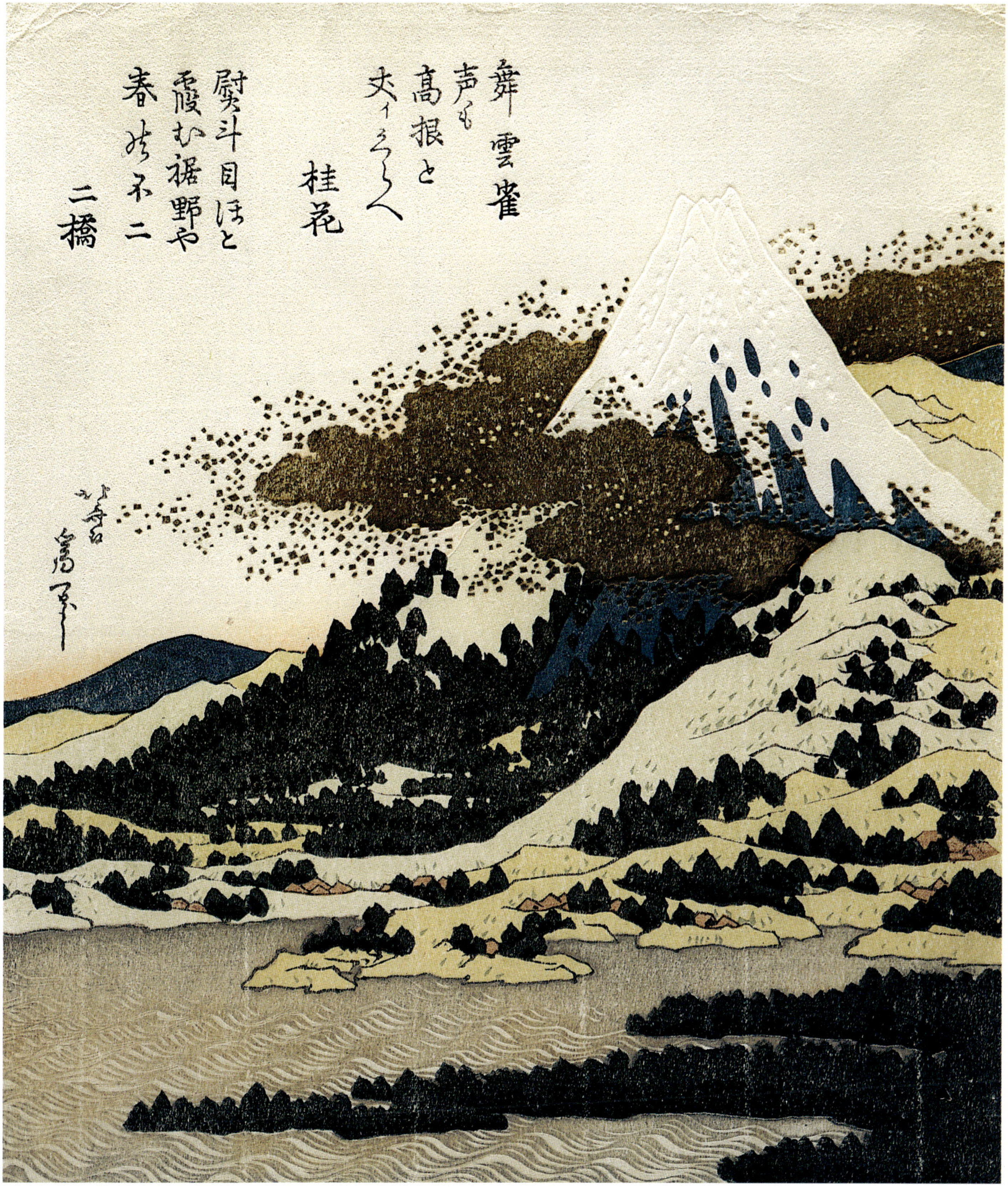
舞雲雀
声も高根と
丈くらへ
桂花
熨斗目ほと
霞む裾野や
春の不二
二橋

AOIGAOKA KEISEI

ACT. CA. 1818–35

38 Two silver decanters and an *uzue* staff

DATE Probably 1831, Year of the Rabbit
SIGNATURE Aoigaoka Keisei
FORMAT Shikishiban (19.8 x 18.3)
REFERENCE Ostier, *La voix silencieuse,* pl. 46
FLLW FDN 3051.001

Gakōen Hanagata:

shiraume no	Reflections of stars
hoshi no kage sae	of white plum blossoms
ari-ari to	glisten as we scoop
kumu wakamizu ni	the first water of the year
hikaru Kameido	at Kameido Shrine.

Keisei, a rather obscure pupil of Hokkei, is known primarily through a few extant surimono. This simple but elegant arrangement is composed of two silver vessels, subtly decorated with a stylized plum-blossom motif. Between them lies an *uzue* ("rabbit stick") a ritual staff with sheets of white paper attached at the top used for celebrating the New Year at a shrine on the first day of the rabbit. A smaller *uzue* was placed on one's head for protection from lightning on rabbit days.

The poem refers to *wakamizu,* the pure spring water customarily drunk on the first day of the year. This tradition had its roots in a court ceremony in which the emperor was presented with water on the first day of spring. Later, it evolved into a popular custom and was said to banish demons for the course of an entire year.

The Kameido Shrine in Edo (modern Tokyo), was widely known for its spring. The shrine is dedicated to the deified Sugawara Michizane (845–903), who is closely associated with plum blossoms. His crest is a stylized plum composed of five circles surrounding a smaller sixth, similar to the motif which adorns the two vessels.

Another impression of this print, published by Janette Ostier, bears an undeciphered artist's seal and a hand-stamped title cartouche in the form of a turtle shell (refering to the literal meaning of the name of Kameido—"Turtle Well Pavilion"), which reads *Kameido mōde niban,* "Two Pilgrimages to Kameido." The Wright collection includes one other design by Keisei, also a still life (cat. no. 204). As both refer to rabbit themes and are similar in style, composition and coloration, perhaps they were issued at the same time for a rabbit year, in this case 1831.

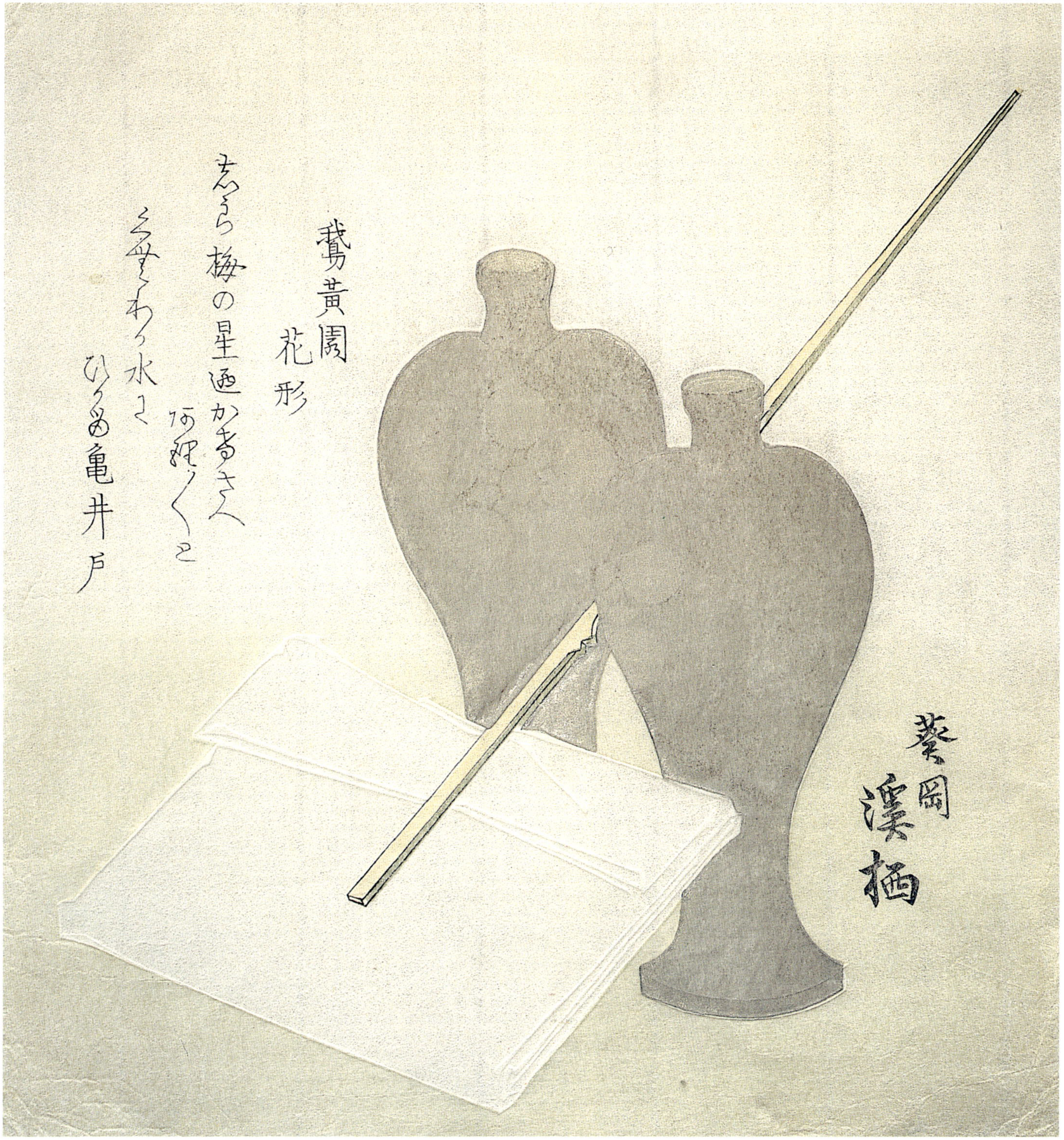
花形
亀井戸
葵岡
溪栖

RYŪRYŪKYO SHINSAI

ACT. CA. LATE 1780S–EARLY 1820S

39 A ferry with a rabbit boatman

SERIES *Usagi no Tegarabanashi: Shichi;*
The Rabbit's Boastful Exploits: Number Seven
DATE 1807, Year of the Rabbit
SIGNATURE Shinsai ga
FORMAT Koban yoko-e (14.1 x 19.4)
REFERENCES *UT, Pulverer,* pl. 110; Forrer, *Egoyomi / Surimono,* pl. 23
FLLW FDN 3003.034

Ise no Hamahito:

mikazuki no	Under a crescent moon
usagi no fune mo	she boards the rabbit's boat
norizome ni	for the first ride of the year,
kumo no namima o	which glides at dusk
hashiru yūgure	through waves of clouds.

Ōe no Ichizumi:

toshinami o	Across waves of time
hashiru usagi no	speeds the rabbit's boat,
fune mo yoi	achieving great feats—
tegara o misuru	during the first ferry ride
haru no norizome	of the New Year.

Shinratei Manzō:

wagimoko ga	I catch a glimpse
sode ka to me ni mo	of my little sister's robes
Tsukubayama	through the mist
hikeru kasumi wa	which trails over Mount Tsukuba
Niibari no kinu	in a skirt around Niibari.

Portrayal of animals performing human activities was a popular artistic device in the Japanese art tradition. Perhaps the most renowned example are the *Chōjū Giga* (Frolicking Animals) scrolls of the twelfth and thirteenth centuries. Such parodies are drawn with a sense of humor and occasionally with satiric intent. In the early nineteenth century there was a revival of interest in folk tales, children's storybooks, and fictional accounts of animals in the role of humans.

Stylistically this print seems to date to the first decade of the nineteenth century; however it should be noted that a novel titled *Usagi no Tegarabanashi,* written by Jippensha Ikku and illustrated by Utagawa Kunimaru, was published in 1816. There is also an *akabon* (children's storybooks of the early eighteenth-century) listed with the title *Usagi no Tegara* with no date given; but given the nature of *akabon,* perhaps there is some other common source for the titles of these books and this print series. For a still life surimono by Shinsai (in shikishiban format) from a series of the same title dating to 1819, a rabbit year, see Keyes, *Beatty,* plate 288.

In this print, the rabbit impersonates a boatman who traditionally ferried customers in slender *chokibune* (boar's-tusk-shaped boats) along the Sumida River in Edo to and from the Yoshiwara. The passenger wears a kimono bearing the emblem of the Manji poetry circle led by Shinratei. This symbol of long life, the *manji* emblem, also appears on the tobacco pouch of a boatman. The well-known landmark Shubi no Matsu pine tree is visible in the distance.

The first poem includes several references to New Year activities and imagery: the first ride of the year, the new moon, and the rabbit in the moon legend. It also plays on the old Japanese expression "a rabbit running across the waves" *(usagi nami o hashiru),* used to describe the effect of moonlight reflected on rippling water.

The reference to *tegara* (merit or exploit) in the second poem alludes to the title of the series. The artist, in addition, seems to have included a visual pun by using a silk ribbon, or *tegara,* as a hair decoration for the young woman. Her erect carriage, staid expression, and distinctive profile are typical of Shinsai's portrayals of women. To her right, the small pine bough is a further reminder of the New Year.

The poem by Shinratei Manzō, a leader of the Manji-ren of the Yomo-gawa, opens with the affectionate form of address used by a man toward a young courtesan (*imo* or *imoko,* little sister). Through the spring mist the poet catches a glimpse of a young courtesan in beautiful robes. Another implication is in the tradition of wearing new attire for the New Year. *Niibari,* meaning "newly sewn," completing the sartorial pun, is also the name of a town at the foot of Mount Tsukuba.

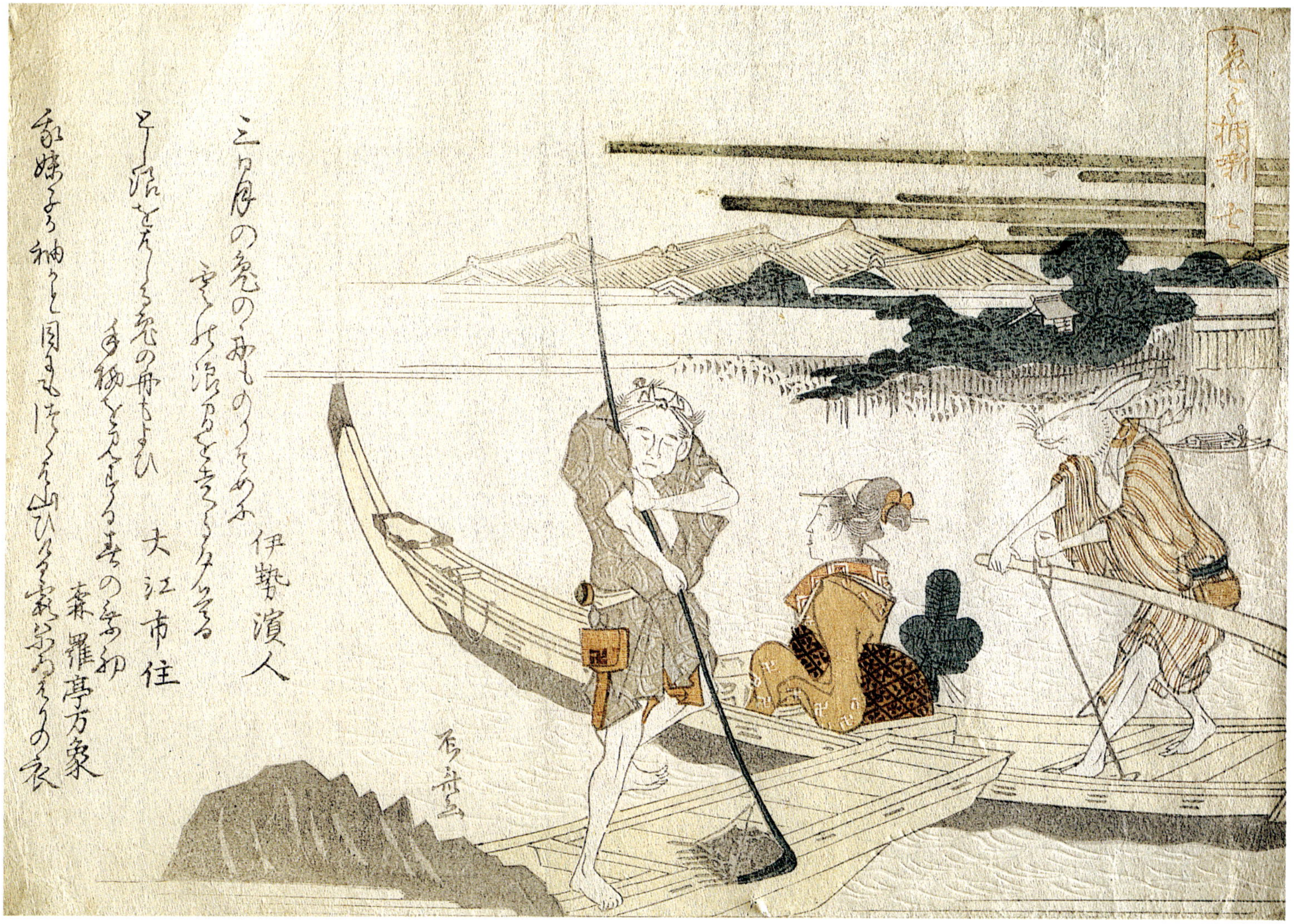
伊勢濱人
大江市住
森羅亭万象

RYŪRYŪKYO SHINSAI

ACT. CA. LATE 1780S–EARLY 1820S

40 A tiered lacquer box, wrapping cloth, and writing implements

TITLE *Toragaishi no Kakizome;* First Writing of the Year at Toragaishi
SERIES From an untitled series on tiger themes
DATE 1818, Year of the Tiger
SIGNATURE Shinsai
FORMAT Shikishiban (21.4 x 18.7)
FLLW FDN 3003.046

Rakuseian:

kokoromiru	As the brushes we use
fude no inochi mo	to write *eternity*
nagaki yo ni	enjoy a long life,
itsumo wakamochi	we always celebrate spring
iwau hatsuharu	with New Year's rice cakes.

Shakusōan:

kakizome no	Brushes just used
fude no futobashi	for the year's first writing
tsukōte wa	now become fat chopsticks
chitose o chigiru	to slice into spring rice cakes
haru no wakamochi	that promise long life.

Each of the five tiers of a layered black lacquer box is lined with white paper, perhaps to prevent New Year rice cakes from sticking to the surface. A design of bamboo in copper and gold enhances the beauty of the lacquer box. Bamboo is often paired with the tiger, and the inkstone is made of a stone similar in appearance to the fur of a tiger—a visual pun on the placename Toragaishi (literally "Tiger Rock") mentioned in the title of the print. The white paperweight in the form of Hotei with his sack and the wrapping cloth decorated with a rain hat, raincoat, and other symbols of good fortune, are all auspicious, auguring well for the New Year.

Repeated as a design element on the poem slip, the plum blossom motif in the upper right corner is the emblem of the poetry circle led by Shakuyakutei Nagane, with which both poets represented here were connected. This crest also appears in combination with themes relating to the tiger on two other surimono by Shinsai (see cat. nos. 41 and 42).

Both poems link two traditional New Year pastimes, namely the first writing of the New Year and the pounding and eating of New Year rice cakes. Customarily, the first writing occurred on the second or third day, while the rice cakes were made and consumed on the following day. The first poem alludes to the practice of writing the character *nagaki* (or *ei*), meaning eternity, at the year's first writing (see also cat. no. 34). The "fat chopsticks" mentioned in the second poem are usually made from willow, and were used during the New Year's season for the eating of *zōni,* a New Year's soup made with rice cakes and vegetables (see cat. nos. 27 and 145).

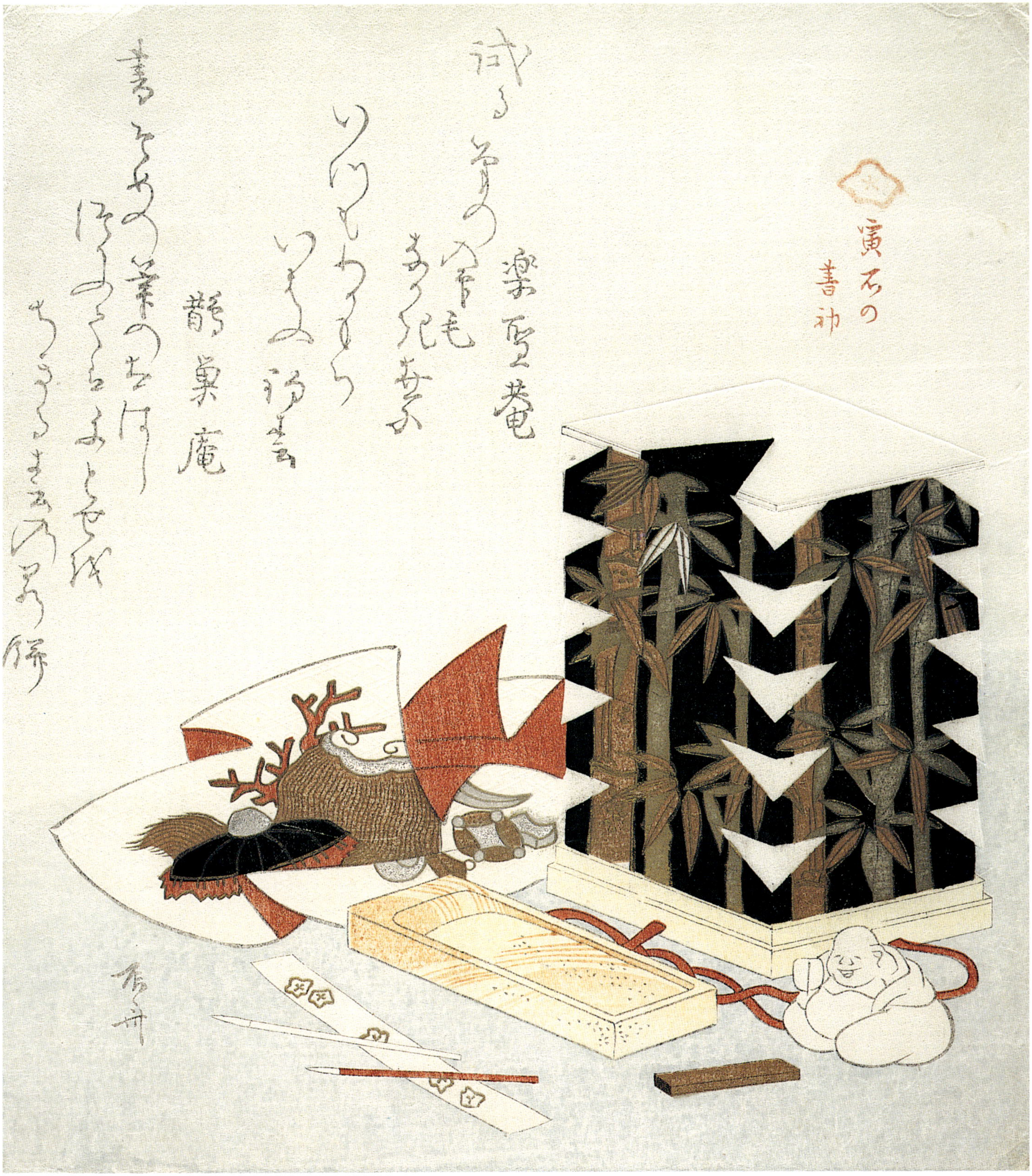

RYŪRYŪKYO SHINSAI

ACT. CA. LATE 1780S–EARLY 1820S

41 A wine pot, coral, and cloth

TITLE *Toramaete sake nomashō;* Let's Nab Someone and Make Him Drink
DATE 1818, Year of the Tiger
SIGNATURE Shinsai
FORMAT Shikishiban (21.5 x 18.8)
REFERENCE Schindler, pl. 47
FLLW FDN 3003.047

Seizanrō:

hanagasa o	As the warbler flies by
nuu uguisu ni	weaving its flowery hat,
misebayana	I'd like to show it
ito o hikitaru	this pot of plum wine
tsubo no umezake	tied up with a string!

Rakuyōan Kiyotake:

kumanu uchi ni	As someone lifts the lid
ta ga hirakishi to	before drinks are scooped—
odorokeri	the fragrance spilling out
nioi koboruru	from the pot of plum wine
tsubo no umezake	packs a pleasant punch.

Kazanrō:

kusuri-ko no	The maid-attendant
mada tsubomi nari	still in the bud of youth
umezake ni	offers plum wine
haru no kokoro o	and carries a small dose
chito motasetemu	of the spirit of spring.

Beside the blue-and-white Arita porcelain wine pot lie a piece of red coral and folds of delicately textured red-dyed crepe. The crepe is partially covered by a sheet of gold wrapping paper, which is decorated on the reverse side with a printed tiger design. Posed like a person standing with raised arms, the tiger seems to mimic a drunken reveler. The designs of both the fabric and the paper are printed with subtle gaufrage. Red-silk cord and pink tassels are draped on the paper.

The title of the print refers to an expression once used to describe a drinking game. As is the case for the other prints in this untitled set (see also cat. nos. 40 and 42), the title incorporates phrases including the word for tiger, *tora*.

One way to interpret the poems on this print is to view them as a series. The first describes a wine pot, still wrapped and tied with cord. In the next poem, the pot has just been opened, the wine as yet untasted; finally, in the third poem, the wine is served. The poet of the first verse seems to suggest that if the warbler would only pull open the string (in order to use the string for its flowery hat), then everyone could enjoy the jar's contents. The second poem extols the fragrance of the plum wine. Using the term *kusuri-ko* for those serving the wine, the poet of the third poem may refer to young women attendants who tasted beverages before they were served to the emperor in New Year rituals. More obvious is the suggestion that one of these young women offers wine at a shrine at the New Year—an image sometimes portrayed in surimono for the New Year. *Haru no kokoro* means both the spirit of spring and spring fever—not inappropriate for a young woman who is likened to a flower bud.

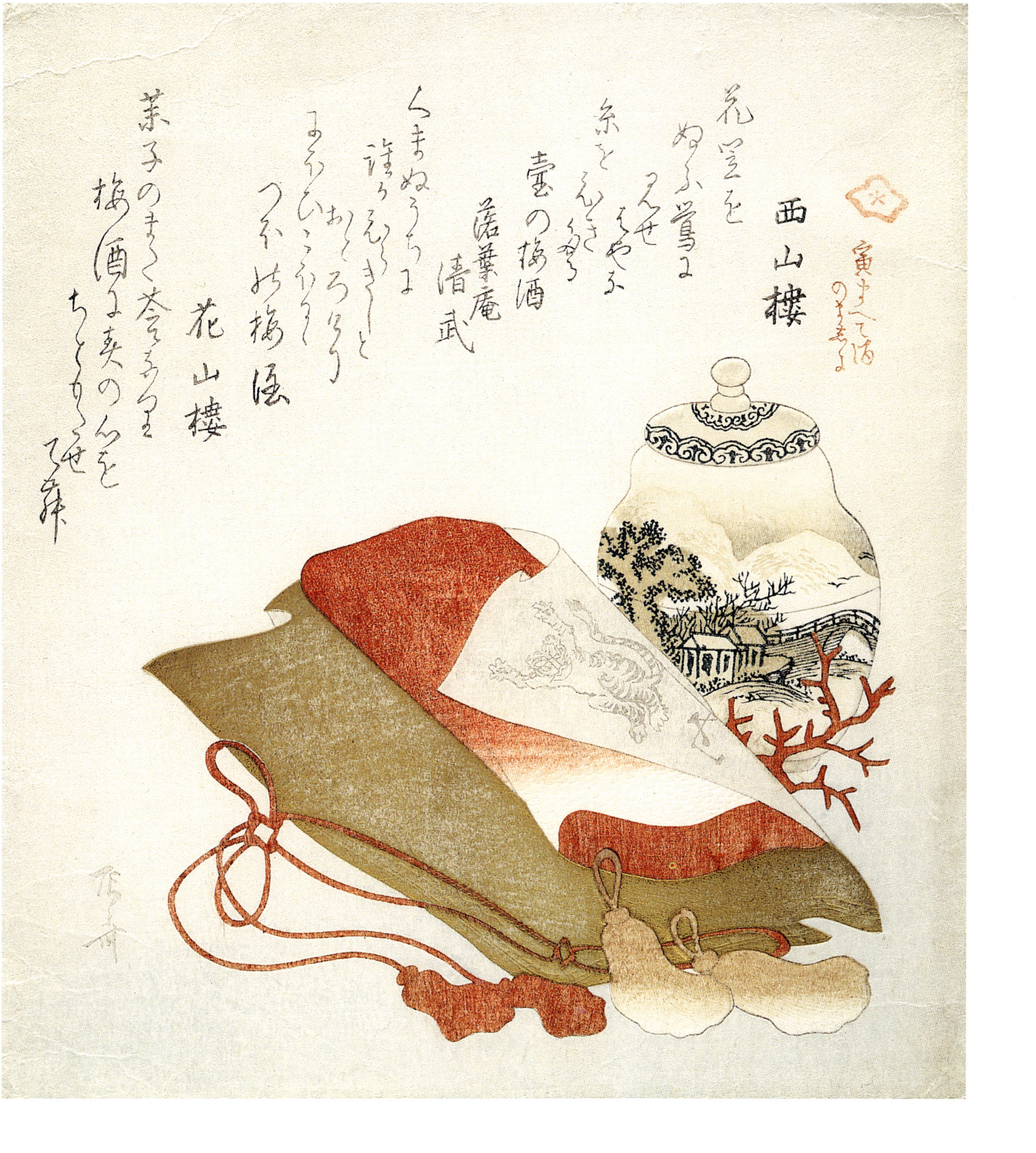
西山樓
落葉庵
清武
花山樓

RYŪRYŪKYO SHINSAI

ACT. CA. LATE 1780S–EARLY 1820S

42 A parody of Yoshitsune receiving a scroll of military secrets from the daughter of Kiichi Hōgen

TITLE *Tora no Maki;* The Tiger Scroll
DATE 1818, Year of the Tiger
SIGNATURE Shinsai
FORMAT Shikishiban (21.5 x 18.8)
FLLW FDN 3003.068

Setsudō Hanakatsura:

aoyagi ni	The willow
narabishi ume no	along with the plum,
wakaeburi	in robes of youth,
doko ga fūfu to	sway together in spring winds
harukaze zo fuku	just like husband and wife.

Baikōsha Chimba, Suifu (Mito):

haru asobi	When dice are tossed
furu sugoroku no	in a *sugoroku* match in spring,
jōzu heta	whether one wins or loses
kore ni mo sukoshi	depends in no small way
denju ya wa aru	on a mastery of secret rules.

Roan Kazuma:

kozo no uchi	What had been mastered
narai ukabete	in the course of the past year
mochi naran	is now bequeathed—
naku uguisu no	the precious legacy
koe no tamamono	of the warbler's song.

The famous warrior Minamoto no Yoshitsune (1159–89) was known for his prowess in the martial arts and warfare. According to legend, at age fifteen he studied with Kiichi Hōgen, a famous teacher of military skills. By seducing his teacher's beautiful daughter through his hypnotic flute playing, Yoshitsune was able to gain access to the much coveted ancient Chinese treatise on martial strategies, here nicknamed the "Tiger Scroll." Knowledge gained from this valuable source propelled him toward his military destiny.

While the themes of the preceding two prints in this series (cat. nos. 40–41) were depicted within elegant still-life compositions, here the artist decided to present a more literal rendition of a legend. The exquisitely attired daughter of Kiichi gazes at Yoshitsune as he reverentially holds the precious scroll, which he has just removed from a green cloth on a small red-lacquer desk. The gold paulownia crest of the Minamoto family seen on his trousers hints at his true identity. A sword sheath cover made of tiger skin extends behind him—and provides another reference to the zodiac year. The small standing screen is decorated with a red sun design that shields their secret activity from view while also serving as a visual reminder of the rising sun of the New Year.

The first poem juxtaposes conventional spring imagery with the pairing of the young Yoshitsune to the daughter of Kiichi Hōgen. In the second poem, martial strategies are compared to the tactics useful in a game of *sugoroku.* In the final poem, the warbler's command of its song is likened to the mastering of the martial arts by Yoshitsune.

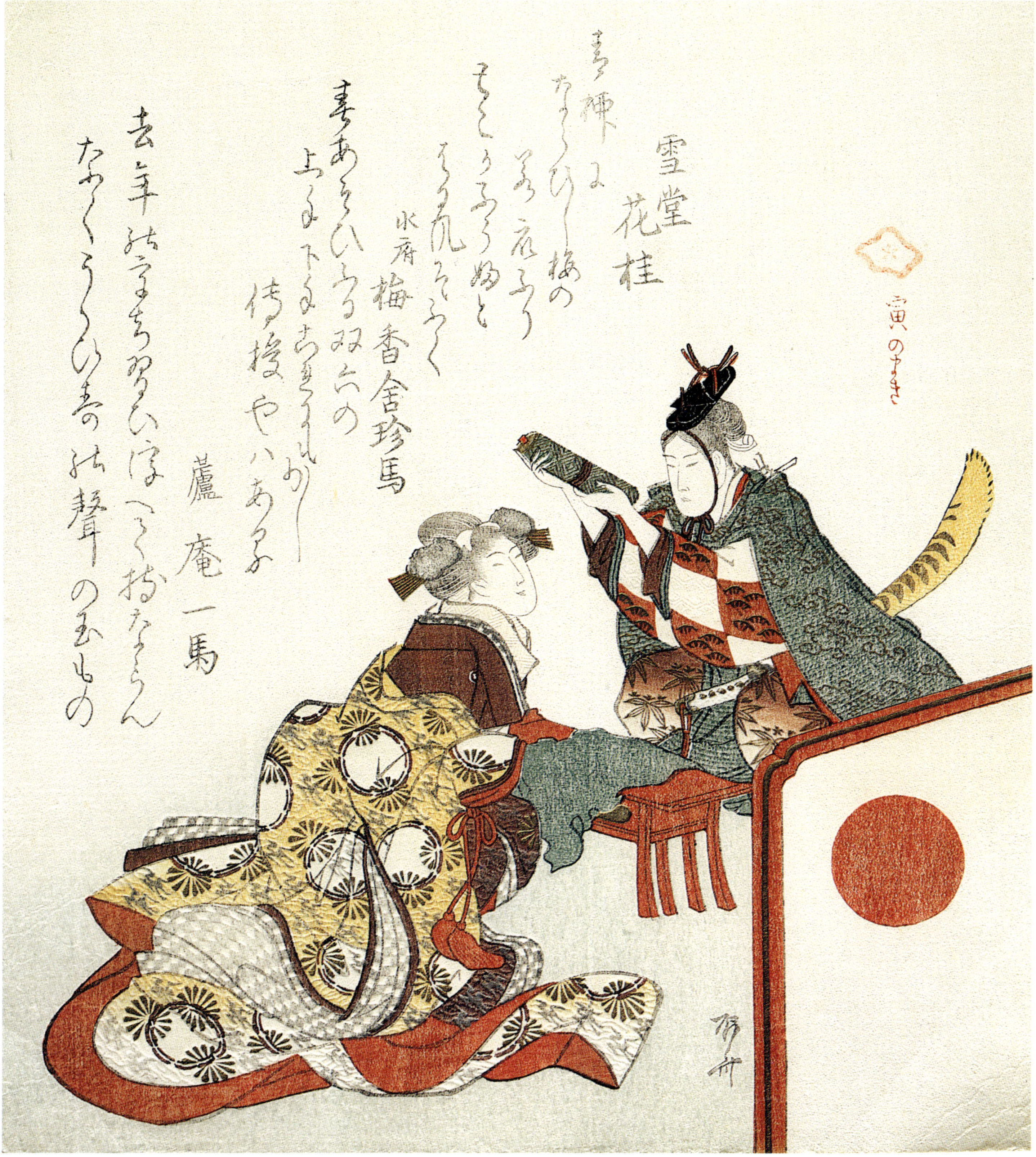

雪堂花桂
氷府梅香舎珍馬
蘆庵一馬

RYŪRYŪKYO SHINSAI

ACT. CA. LATE 1780S–EARLY 1820S

43 A woman and child playing in the snow

TITLE *Shiro;* White
SERIES *Goshiki no Uchi;* The Five Colors
DATE ca. 1820
SIGNATURE Shinsai
FORMAT Shikishiban (21.1 x 18.4)
FLLW FDN 3003.052

Kazanrō:

yuki no uchi ni	A sprig of plum
suwae no nozoku	blossoms peeping out
ume no hana	from the snow
haru no shirushi	serves as a guidepost
sao to koso mire	to the presence of spring.

Shakuyakutei:

uchitsukuru	Because spring is near
soba yori haru no	as soon as I fling
yuki tsubute	snowballs at you,
tokete sonata no	they melt before covering
mon wa kakurezu	the designs of your robe.

Shinsai, another of Hokusai's many pupils, worked under the master at the end of the eighteenth century. His name, Ryūryūkyo, was also used earlier by Tawaraya Sōri I (see cat. no. 57); Shinsai, or "Dragon Studio," derives from Shinsei, a name used by Hokusai. He specialized in surimono—few examples of his work in other genres are known—and was recognized as an innovator in still-life compositions. Since the Wright collection possesses some seventy surimono by Shinsai, his brilliance in this genre can be fully appreciated.

For this design from a series on the theme of the five colors—white, black, red, yellow, and blue—Shinsai selected snow to represent the color white. (Also see cat. no. 236 for "Yellow." Illustrations of "Yellow" and "Blue" may be found in Keyes, *Beatty,* pls. 298 and 299. Impressions of "Red" and "Black" are in the Duel Collection). Set in an appropriately snowy garden with a snow-capped stone lantern, the image portrays a woman attired in an unusual dusty pink-colored kimono playing with a well-dressed barefoot child. The woman—probably a courtesan—and her assistant, no doubt a child raised in the pleasure quarters, are engaged in a lively snowball fight. A newly budding red plum tree adds a colorful accent to the white landscape.

The woman's kimono, exquisitely printed with gold and silver, is adorned with a motif of bracken-fern sprouts, a green collected in early spring. The melting snow indicates that it is a rather warm spring day. This is further suggested in the second poem, where snowballs melt as soon as they hit the woman's robe and cannot cover the design of spring greens.

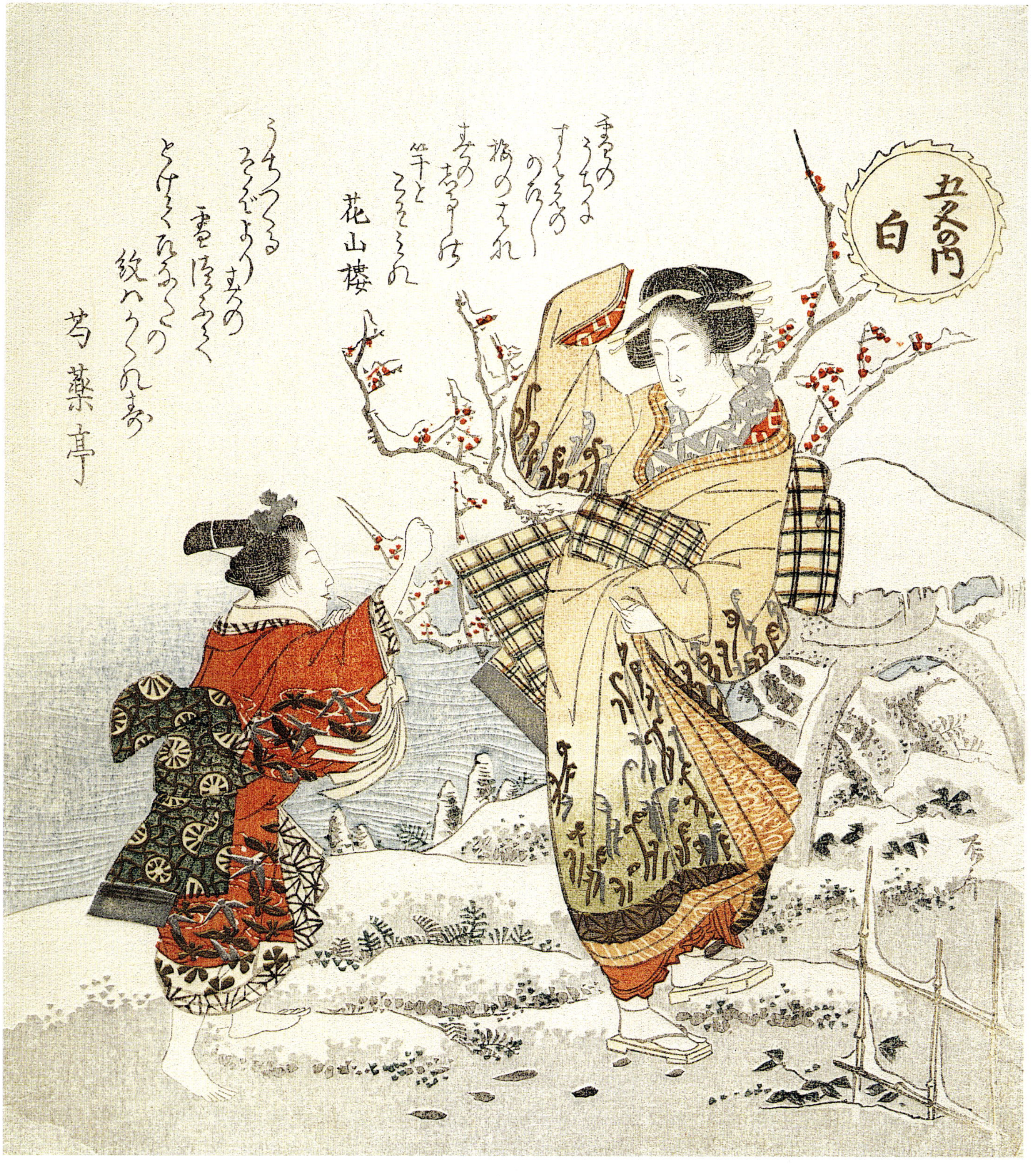

五丈の門
白
花山楼
芍薬亭

RYŪRYŪKYO SHINSAI

ACT. CA. LATE 1780S–EARLY 1820S

44 A woman watching a girl with a lantern

TITLE *Tomoyasu no Musume;* The Daughter of Tomoyasu
SERIES *San Bijin;* Three Beautiful Women
DATE ca. 1820
SIGNATURE Shinsai
FORMAT Shikishiban (21.4 x 18.9)
REFERENCE Polster, no. 415
FLLW FDN 3003.054

Shōjutei Michitomo:

harukaze no	The sound of winds
otozurenureba	announcing spring's arrival
shiorido ni	whispers through boughs
mimikosuri suru	of young willows
aoyagi no eda	at the brushwood gate.

Shakuyakutei:

ume ga ka no	Waiting anxiously
kayoeru kaze o	on the edge of the veranda
machigao ni	for a breeze
hashii yukashiki	carrying the scent of plum—
uguisu no koe	the song of the warbler.

It became increasingly popular in the prints of the early nineteenth century to move from overt representations of courtesans and contemporary beauties to parodies of women from literature and history. As in all three designs from this series, such women are most often attired in the garb of Edo beauties. Empress Kōmyō of the eighth century is portrayed in a blue-and-white bath kimono (see cat. no. 238), and Princess Sotoori of the fifth century appears as a modern woman in current fashion (see Keyes, *Beatty,* pl. 300).

Depicted here is the mid-Heian court lady and poet best known as the mother of Fujiwara no Michitsuna, or, as more flatteringly titled in this print, Daughter of Tomoyasu. Her elegant attire is composed of a purple robe with a gold tortoise-lozenge motif and a plaid obi patterned with gold bats, symbolizing good luck. She looks out her sliding door at her young attendant, who holds a lantern to light the way for a visitor who has just announced his arrival at the gate.

The Mother of Michitsuna is the author of the *Kagerō Nikki* (The Gossamer Years), a diary covering twenty-one years of her life beginning in 954, the year she became the wife of the prominent courtier Fujiwara no Kaneie (929–90). The diary presents a heartrending account of her unhappy marriage, and is noted for its realistic description of court life from a woman's perspective. Both poems here refer obliquely to the opening passage of her diary in which she describes receiving a love note from Kaneie, who was her most persistent suitor. The note was delivered by a messenger who pounded persistently on her gate and consisted simply of a single poem that beseeched her to allow him to hear the "song of the warbler."

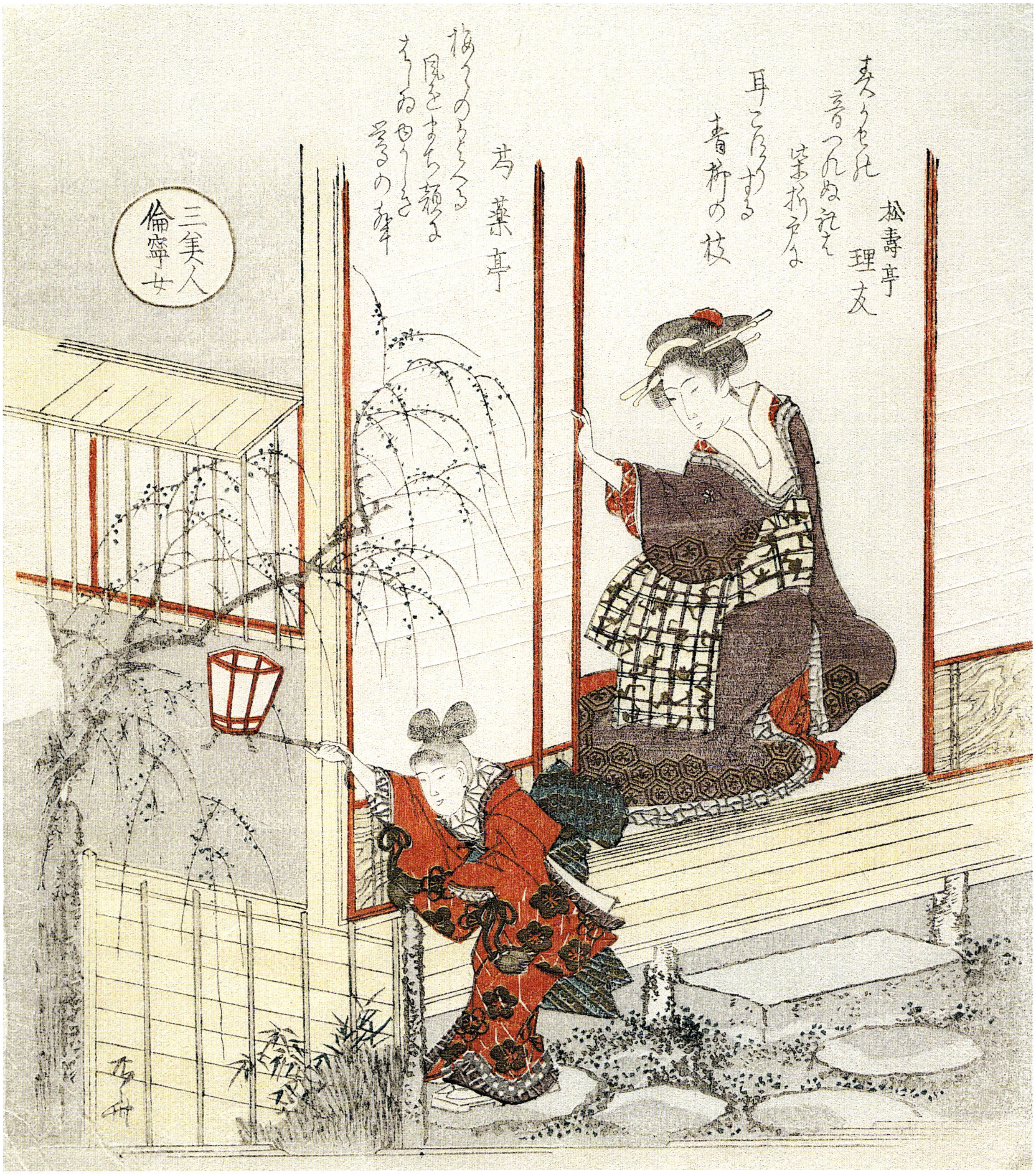

三美人
倫寧女
松壽亭
理友
芍藥亭

RYŪRYŪKYO SHINSAI

ACT. LATE 1780S–EARLY 1820S

45 Setting for a New Year meal

DATE probably 1820
SIGNATURE Shinsai
FORMAT Shikishiban (21.5 x 19.1)
REFERENCE Polster, no. 405
FLLW FDN 3003.045

Hōshūkan Magōri:

hatsuharu wa	As spring begins,
zōni o amata	New Year's soup overflows
Morioka no	Nambu bowls
oka no yō naru	rounded on top
Nambu wan kana	like the hills of Morioka

Yomo Magao:

e o mite wa	Though I cannot spell it out,
mono kakanu mi mo	if you look at the picture
kamiwakuru	and chew a while
Nambu goyomi no	on the Nambu calendar,
hagatame zo yoki	it will be good for your teeth.

This New Year still life consists of famous products of Nambu, another name for Morioka in Iwate Prefecture, renowned for its lacquerware and cast-iron kettles. The lacquer soup bowl in the image typifies this ware, which has a red interior, black exterior, and decorations in gold leaf and multi-colored lacquer. Here the covered bowl, as mentioned in the first poem, contains *zōni,* a special soup for the New Year made of vegetables and rice cakes (see cat. nos. 11 and 27). It rests on a red-lacquer tray with a small dish and a paper-wrapped chopsticks. The kettle, decorated with an unidentified design and adorned with a paper folder, would have been used for the spiced sake prepared for the New Year.

Yomo Magao, a professional kyōka teacher, was one of the most frequent contributors of poetry for surimono. In the second poem, he seems to invite his readers to view the accompanying image as a Nambu *goyomi,* large single-sheet rebus-calendars originally produced in Nambu. Initially issued for the illiterate, these wall calendars were also enjoyed by all as picture puzzles. Thus the viewer must "chew" on the clue in order to discern the zodiacal reference. The answer may be found in the small crackle-glaze porcelain dish of dried sardines (*gomame*), also known as *tatsukuri.* Because *tatsukuri* includes the word *tatsu* (a homonym for the word for dragon), it is not unreasonable to surmise that the poet and artist collaborated to turn this surimono into a Nambu *goyomi,* of sorts, making this their clue for the year of the dragon (1820). The final line of the second poem refers to the custom of hardening the teeth known as *hagatame,* based on the folk belief that chewing tough foods—such as rice cakes or dried sardines—will help bring long life.

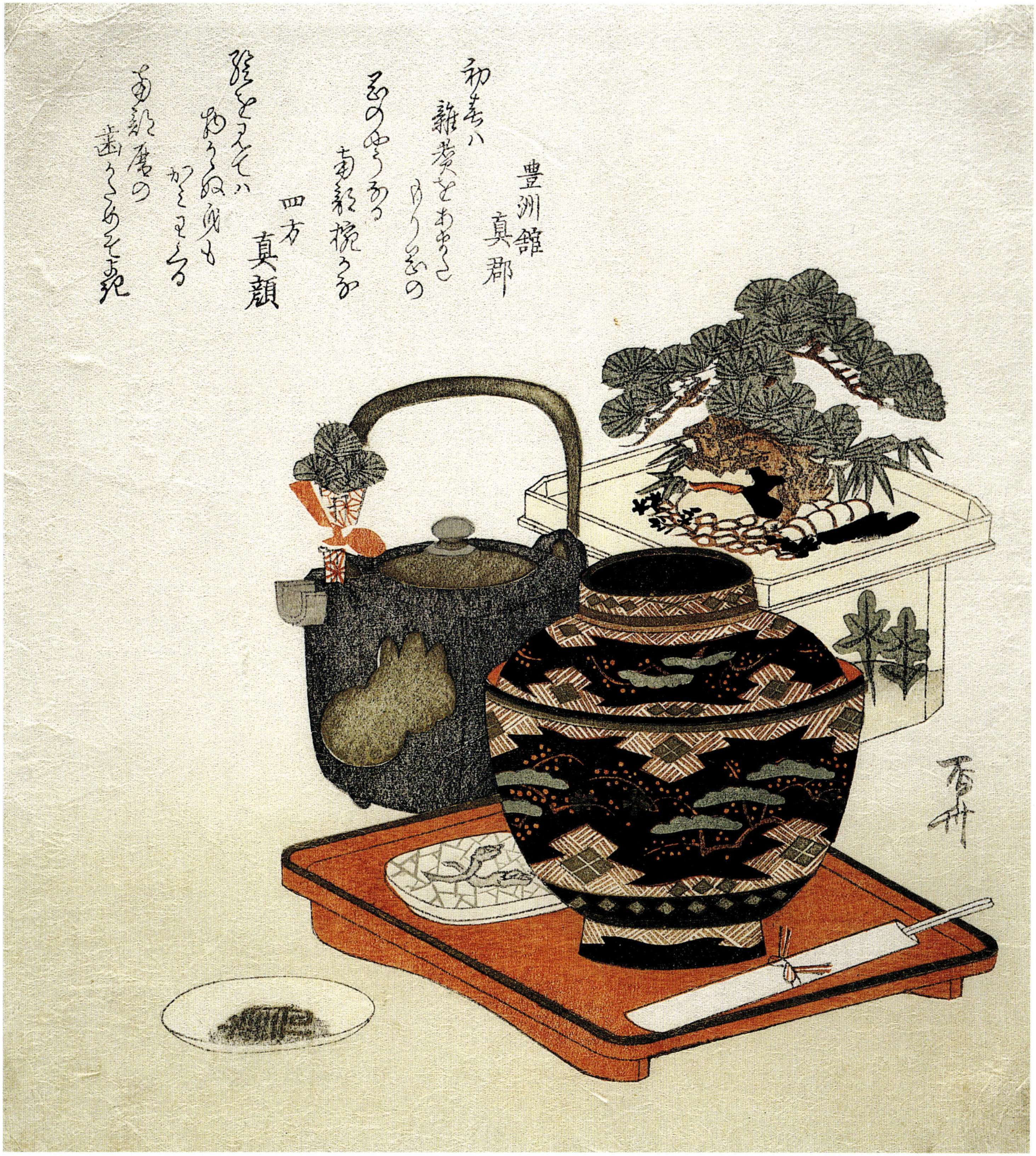

豊洲舘
真郡
四方
真顔

RYŪRYŪKYO SHINSAI

ACT. LATE 1780S–EARLY 1820S

46 Bundles of iron and copper ingots with a potted sago palm, plum, and adonis plant

DATE 1822, Year of the Horse
SIGNATURE Shinsai
FORMAT Shikishiban (21.8 x 19.0)
FLLW FDN 3003.043

Nampōgaki Makaze:

nubatama no	Pitch-black
yami no kurogane	darkness descends
kurashi tote	this iron-grey evening
kasumi ni musubu	as bands of mist entwine
tsuki no akagane	the copper-red moon.

Ryūsai Chimata:

hanaretaru	White horses
yanagi no iro no	tinged willow green
ao-uma wa	are now set free—
onoga ito mote	let's hope we can tether them
toritsunage kashi	with their own willowy strands.

Haikai Utaba:

harusame no	Spring rain drips
tsutau yanagi no	like jewels over a crown
tamakazura	of willow branches
kakete midori no	hanging above the eaves
noki no kanedoi	with green copper gutters.

One of the most interesting and challenging designs in the Wright collection is this still life of seemingly unrelated objects. The traditional New Year plants—the miniature adonis and plum tree—are dwarfed by a potted sago palm tree. Two bound bundles of ingots, one copper colored and the other iron colored, lie near the decorative planters. An unusual subject in Japanese prints, the sago palm, or *sotetsu,* was no doubt selected because its name contains the word for iron (*tetsu*). This is just one clue in revealing the underlying theme of this surimono—copper and iron. The container is decorated with a clematis motif. The name of this flower was once written with characters meaning "iron wire," so it would appear that the artist purposely intended it as a visual and verbal pun.

In the first poem *nubatama*, meaning pitch black, is also a pillow word linked to night, black moon, and nocturnal imagery. Used here to describe dark gray mists, *kurogane* is also an old name for iron, while *akagane* contrasts with this dark imagery since it literally means "red metal," and is the Japanese name for copper. The second poem is perhaps alluding to the *ao-uma sechie* court festival, traditionally held on the seventh day of the New Year, during which white horses are paraded before the emperor. Yomo Utagaki Magao, the leader of the Yomo-gawa through the early nineteenth century, signed the third poem with one of his numerous pen names, Haikai Utaba. The poem by Magao is slightly obscure but it seems he attempted to fashion a link between green oxidized-metal downspouts and willow branches, whose only association is their green color.

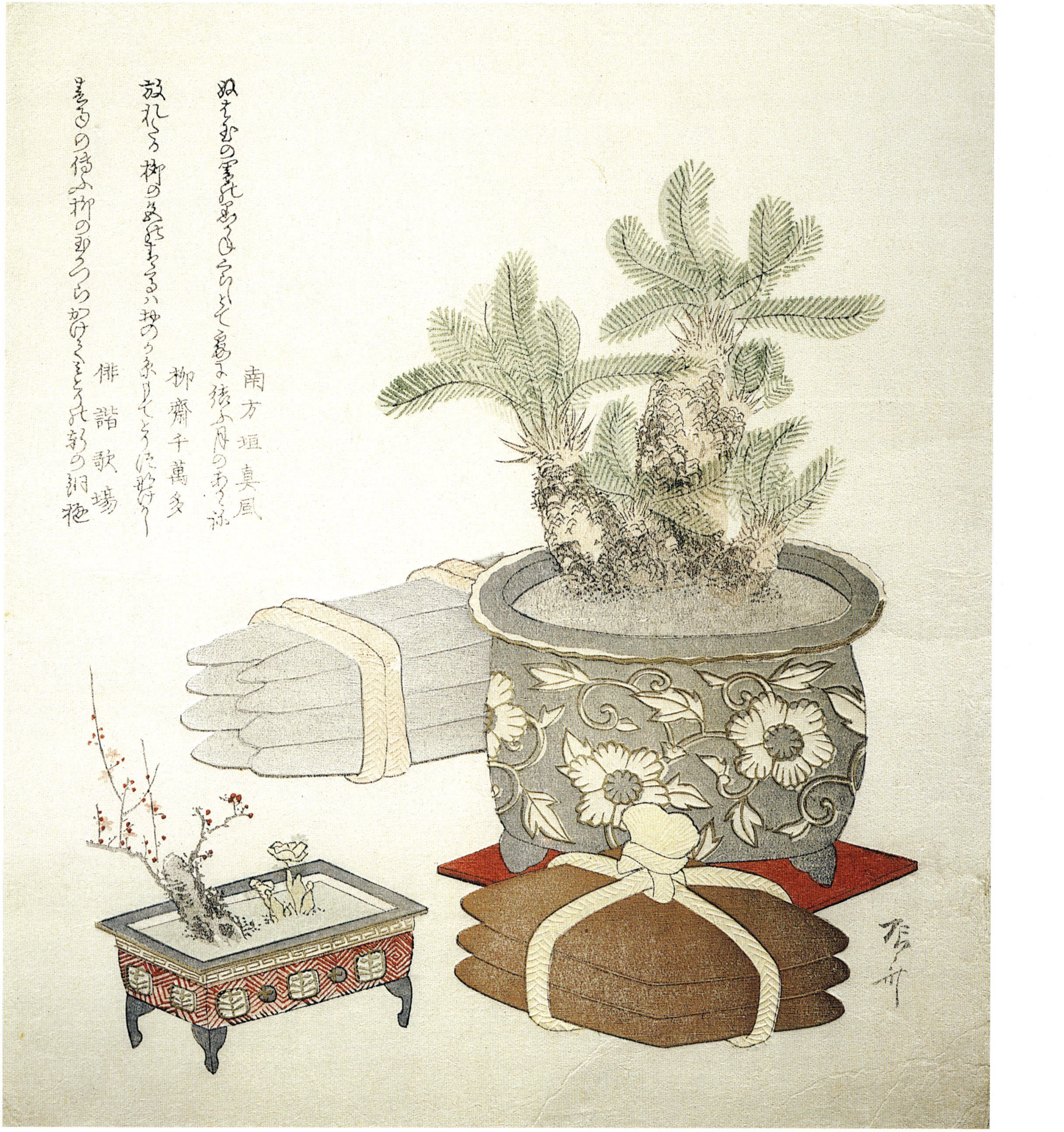
南方垣真風
柳齋千萬多
俳諧歌場

RYŪRYŪKYO SHINSAI

ACT CA. LATE 1780S–EARLY 1820S

47 A mother watching two boys play with a toy horse

DATE 1822, Year of the Horse
SIGNATURE Shinsai
FORMAT Shikishiban (21.5 x 18.8)
FLLW FDN 3003.051

Shōkontei Iwamaru:

shōgatsu no	He cinches in
futae harubi o	the double-saddle girth
hikishimete	on New Year's day
haru no chōshi o	as he mounts his steed
norizome no koma	for the first ride of spring.

Ki no Yasuhima:

kasumi hiku	While mists trail
haru no hajime no	at the dawn of spring,
sometazuna	the striped reins
toru te yutaka ni	of the prancing horse
koma zo isameru	are proudly held in hand.

Kasugano Furusato:

karagoromo	The deep sleeves
tamoto yutaka ni	of his splendid robes
kaze furete	billow in the wind
uraraka narishi	during his first ride
haru no norizome	of a glorious spring.

Kyōkadō:

kono haru zo	Spring is here,
garyō no ume no	and along with the scent
ka ni tsurete	of pink plum blossoms,
nagare o wataru	we cross over the stream
mizunoe no uma	into the year of the horse.

One of the most charming designs in the collection, this domestic scene presents a mother watching her two sons play with a wooden hobbyhorse. One boy holds the striped reins as the other brandishes a toy sword. A branch of plum, symbol of the New Year, is just visible outside the parted shoji door.

The perfect subject for a horse year, the theme is especially relevant because the first ride of the year was an auspicious New Year's activity. In the Edo period there was also a custom for entertainers to ride on horse-head sticks when paying calls in this season.

All of the poems present an image of a samurai or noble mounting his steed for the first ride of the New Year. Perhaps the idea of using a toy horse was the artist's own conception. Each poem is interwoven with equestrian vocabulary. In the first poem, the verb *hikishimeru* refers to "cinching in" a saddle girth, but also has a secondary meaning of "acting with resolve," or as we say in English, "making a New Year resolution." *Harubi* is not only a common alternative reading for *haruobi,* the word for saddle girth, but is also a homonym for *harubi,* meaning "spring day." The striped reins referred to in the second poem are made from intertwined colored cord, often seen in portraits of mounted warriors, votive paintings of horses, and screens of stable scenes.

The *garyō no ume* (or *garyō-bai*), literally "bowing dragon plum," cited in the fourth poem, has pale red blossoms and takes its name from its unusual appearance: its branches droop down and form new roots where they touch the ground. In the last line, *mizunoe no uma* refers to the cyclical year of the horse and allows the print to be precisely dated to 1822. The poem is signed simply Kyōkadō, which is one of the many poetry names used by Yomo Utagaki Magao, one of the most prolific kyōka poets of the early nineteenth century. Other times his styled himself Yomo Magao (see cat. no. 45) or Haikai Utaba (see cat. no. 46). Poetry circles organized under the aegis of the Yomogawa, which was headed by Magao, commissioned surimono in great number. Many of the poets affiliated with these circles lived in the provinces (for instance, the name of the third poet here literally means "Born on the Fields of Kasuga"). Amateur poets often requested their teacher to contribute a poem to add prestige to a surimono. For prominent teachers, it was also a means of supplementing their income.

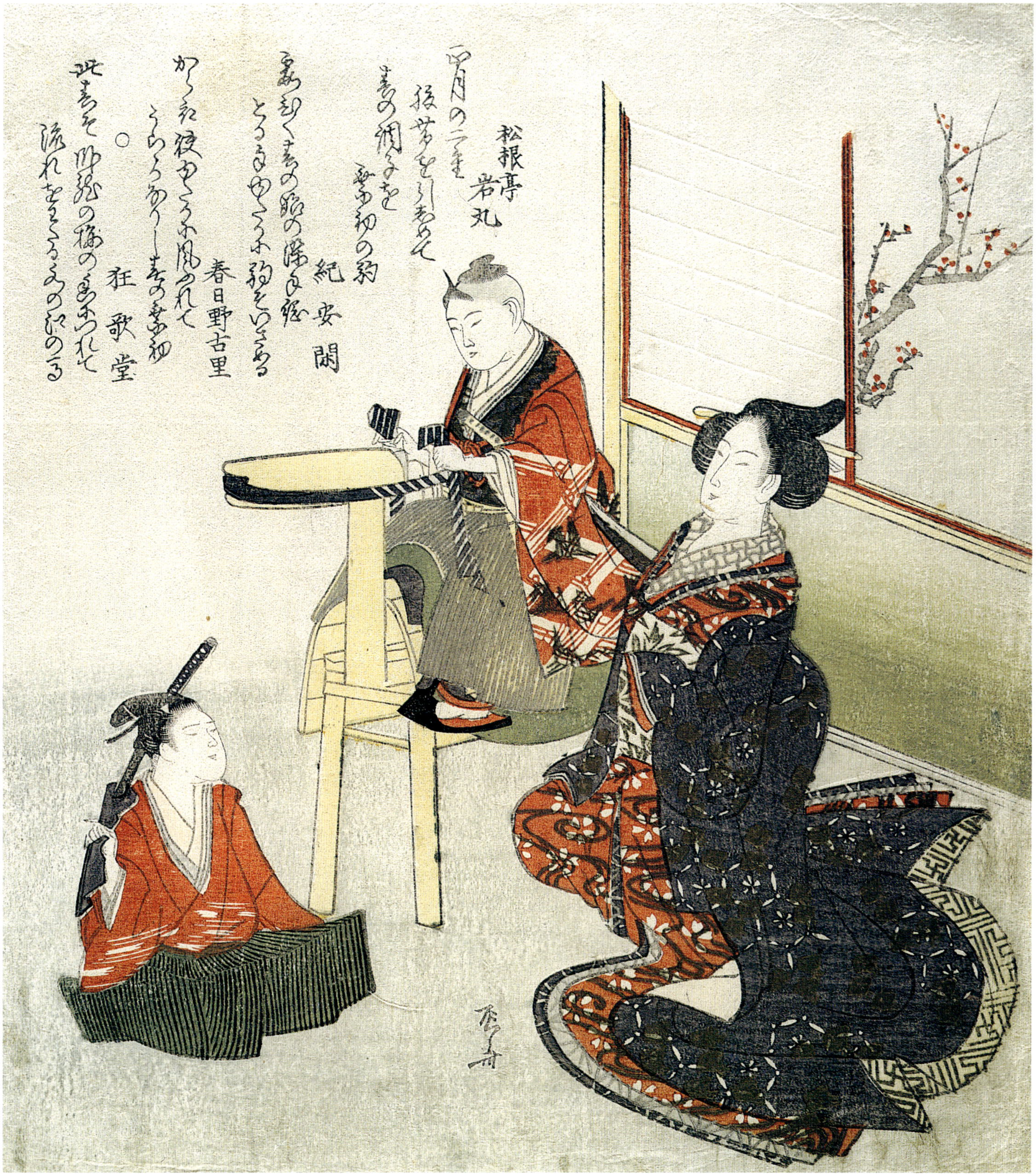
松根亭 岩丸
紀安閑
春日野古里
狂歌堂

KUBO SHUMMAN

1757–1820

48 The Chinese warrior Shandong Jishiyu Hubaoyi Songgongming as a Yoshiwara courtesan

SERIES Untitled series of parodies of *Suikoden* Heroes
DATE ca. 1807
FORMAT Koban tate-e (20.0 x 8.9)
REFERENCE *UT, Bibliothèque Nationale,* pl. 149; Keyes, *Spencer,* cat. no. 203
FLLW FDN 3007.013

Kudanami Shigetoshi:

momo tori no	She is admired
kashira to auge	as the grand dame of birds,
yamagata ni	on top of the mountain
hoshi o saezuru	shining like a star—
sato no uguisu	the warbler in the district.

Shōsadō:

oshoku tote	The head courtesan
kamuro shinzō	looks after her apprentices,
wakakusa no	even as they sleep—
ne-yoke ni oyobi	as the gentle spring rain
megumu harusame	rains kindly on young grasses.

The Chinese novel *The Water Margin* (*Suikoden* in Japanese and *Shui Huzhuan* in Chinese) tells the story of a band of honorable outlaws. It was first translated into Japanese by Kyokutei Bakin (1767–1848) in 1805, and then continued by Takai Ranzan (1762–1838). This series by Shumman pictures Yoshiwara courtesans of various ranks to parody the Chinese heroes (also see the following entry). There is no background design; rather, each figure is surrounded by a field of calligraphy. Metallic powders and gaufrage are used sparingly.

This high-ranking courtesan wears a kimono decorated with peacock feathers of gold and an obi of pine boughs in silver. Her frontal posture and high status parallels the leadership role played by Songgongming in the novel. Originally a virtuous and charitable civil servant in Shandong, he was given the nickname written with Chinese characters that can be read *Oyobi Shigure* in Japanese, meaning "Opportune Rain," because he would always arrive to help in a crisis, like a life-saving rain during a drought. After he accidentally killed a woman who had robbed him, he was put into prison. He succeeded in escaping, however, and went on to join and eventually lead this group.

Praising the warbler, the ubiquitous bird of kyōka surimono, the poet bestows upon it a rank equivalent to that of the highest of courtesans. *Yamagata* (literally, mountain shape), refers to a symbol used to rank courtesans. In the *Yoshiwara Saiken,* a guidebook to the Yoshiwara, mountain-shaped marks were placed above the name of each courtesan, denoting her rank and therefore her price. *Iri-yamagata ni futatsu hoshi* (double mountain with two stars) was the highest level, and it is this class of courtesan which is compared to the Chinese leader. The mention of stars also recalls that each of the *Suikoden* heroes was the human incarnation of a star. *Sato,* "village" or "mountain district," was a common nickname for the pleasure quarters.

The reference to a mountain in the first poem also puns on the first character (*shan,* or mountain) of the hero's hometown, Shandong. Likewise, the second poem, by the artist Shumman himself, plays on the first character of the hero's nickname Jishiyu by using the word *oyobi* (the pronunciation in Japanese). The phrase "spring rain" is a further pun on "Opportune Rain." The word *oshoku,* or "head of a brothel," reflects the high rank of the Chinese warrior she is supposed to represent. Continuing the allusions to the pleasure quarters, Shumman uses the word *wakakusa,* or young grasses, which is a pillow word often associated with beautiful young women.

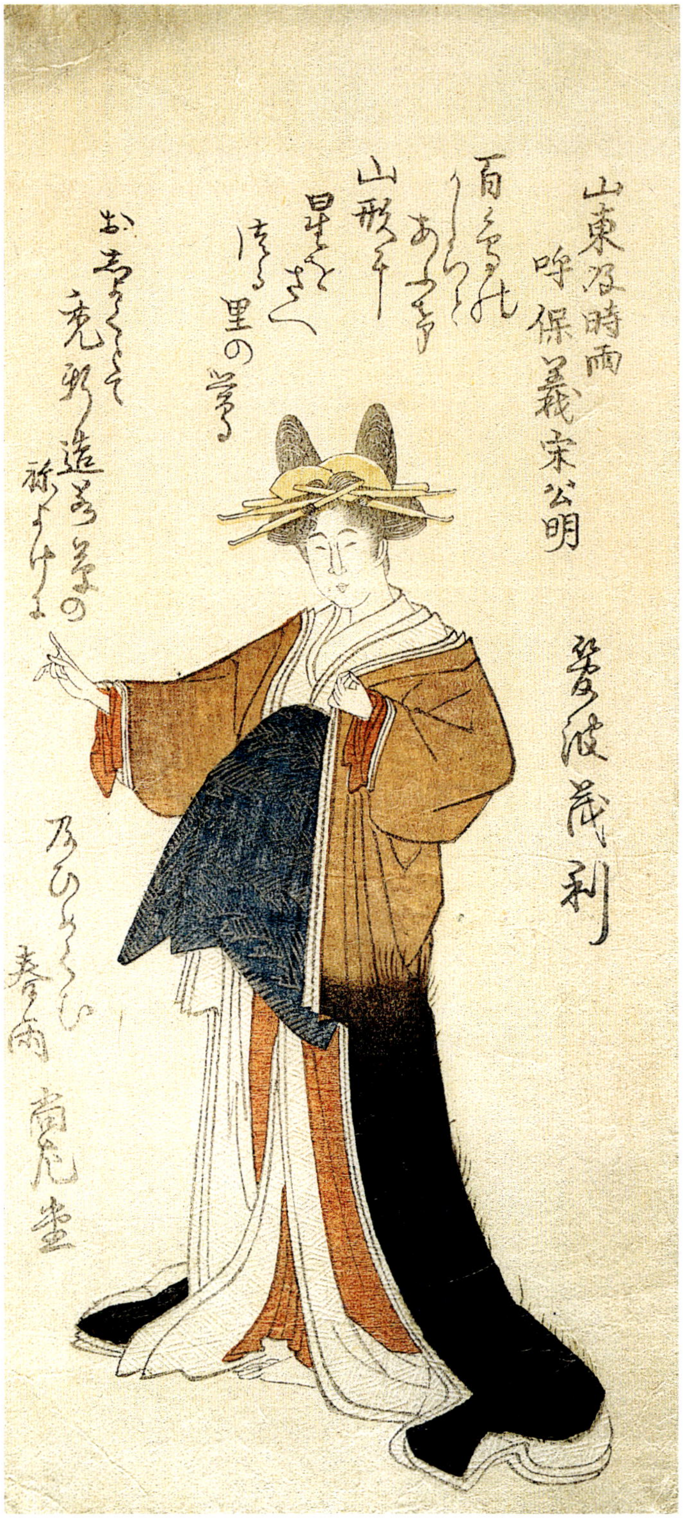
呼保義宋公明

KUBO SHUMMAN

1757–1820

49 The Chinese warrior Gongsunshen as a Yoshiwara courtesan

SERIES Untitled series of parodies of *Suikoden* Heroes
DATE ca. 1807
ARTIST'S SEAL Shumman
FORMAT Koban tate-e (20.1 x 9.0)
REFERENCES *UT, Bibliothèque Nationale,* pl. 151; Polster, no. 449
FLLW FDN 3007.014

Jōben Katatsura:

araigami	Her long wet hair
nagaki hi kasumu	shimmers in the haze
itoyū wa	as days grow longer
shabon no tama no	in a spring as delicate
haru no nodokesa	as crystalline bubbles.

Shōsadō:

hana no kumo	When flowery clouds
okoshi namida no	burst into tears of rain
ame o furase	on festival days,
mombi shimawasu	pulling in customers
keisei no jutsu	requires a madam's magic.

In another elegant parody of a *Suikoden* hero, a courtesan with her newly washed hair is dressed in a green cloak, which protects her kimono from the damp hair and gives the impression of a magician's cape. The large design of the open fans on this garment is the symbol of the Ōgiya bordello in the Yoshiwara.

The title of the print informs us that she represents Gongsunshen, warrior and magician. He was said to be able to summon the winds and rain clouds when attacking his enemy and was often attired as a wandering Taoist ascetic and nicknamed "Dragon in the Clouds." The scene here uses the beauty's blowing of bubbles to parody the magician's ability to create lightning and rain clouds. The fashion of bubble blowing is said to have begun in 1677, when a traveling peddler began marketing soap-bubble liquid.

The second poem refers to the custom in the Yoshiwara of festival days on which clients were charged double fees for the services of a courtesan. If the courtesan's appointment book was not completely filled, she would be severely penalized by the owner of the brothel. The poet intimates that in order to convince their clients to honor their appointments, especially in stormy weather, courtesans needed to have tremendous powers of persuasion. "Clouds" and the word *jutsu* (art, skill, or magic powers) are allusions to the magic powers of Gongsunshen.

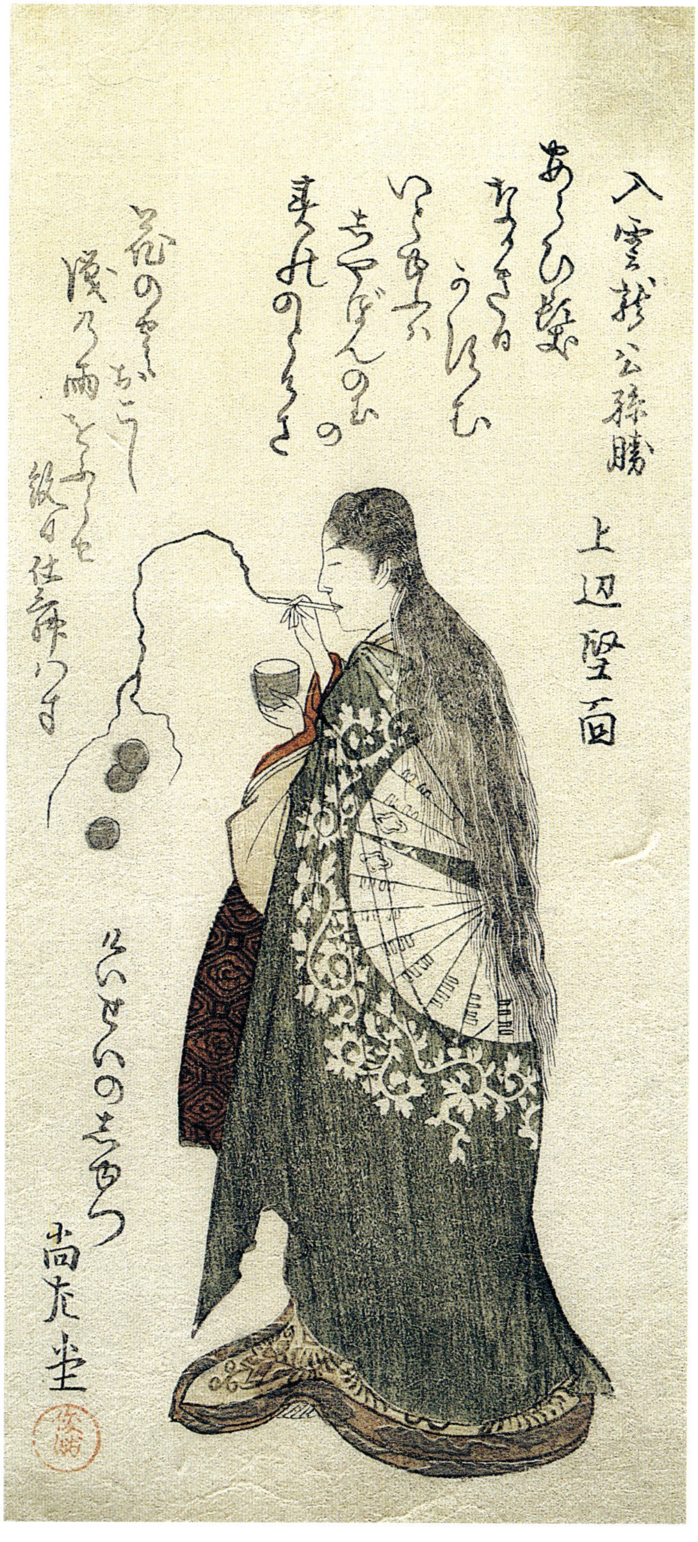
尚左堂

KUBO SHUMMAN

1757–1820

50 A temple bell and an illustrated Nō libretto

TITLE *Banshū Takasago Onoe Kane zu;* Picture of the Bell at Onoe in Takasago, Banshū (Harima) Province
DATE 1809, Year of the Snake
SIGNATURE Shōsadō sha
ARTIST'S SEAL Shumman
FORMAT Shikishiban (20.1 x 18.0)
FLLW FDN 3007.039

Hinokibutei Tsukuru:

Takasago no	The bell on the hill
onoe no kane wa	at Takasago waits—
matsu to tomo ni	together with the pine tree
nagaki tameshi o	an enduring example,
hiku kasumi kana	now wrapped in mist.

Perhaps only Shumman, who was both a talented print designer and a publisher, would have attempted this extraordinary and technically difficult embossed design of a large bronze bell. Almost impossible to capture with the camera, the gradations of tone and high- and low-relief gaufrage combine to reveal a richly patterned surface. The bell is adorned with a pair of flying Buddhist angels with musical instruments, floral scrolls, and geometric banding.

Next to the bell lies a sheet from a libretto for the auspicious Nō play *Takasago.* The protagonists of the play, the elderly husband and wife, Jo and Uba, are pictured with rake and broom in hand, beneath the pine tree at Takasago. According to the legend conveyed in the play, Jo, when a young man, fell in love with and married a beautiful young woman who was actually the spirit of the pine tree. After a long and happy life, they died together at the same moment. On moonlit evenings their elderly forms were said to reappear and continue to rake the pine needles.

The play is considered auspicious because of its theme of eternal marital fidelity, and for that reason was sometimes chanted at wedding ceremonies. In the poem, the phrase *Onoe no kane* (the bell of Onoe, literally, "the bell on the hill") refers specifically to a line in the play and in Edo times came to be associated with a couple's wedding night. The depiction of a temple bell also calls to mind the custom of *joya no kane*—the traditional practice of ringing in the New Year at a Buddhist temple. The bell is struck with a wooden beam one hundred and eight times, each strike symbolically quelling the hundred and eight evil passions of mankind.

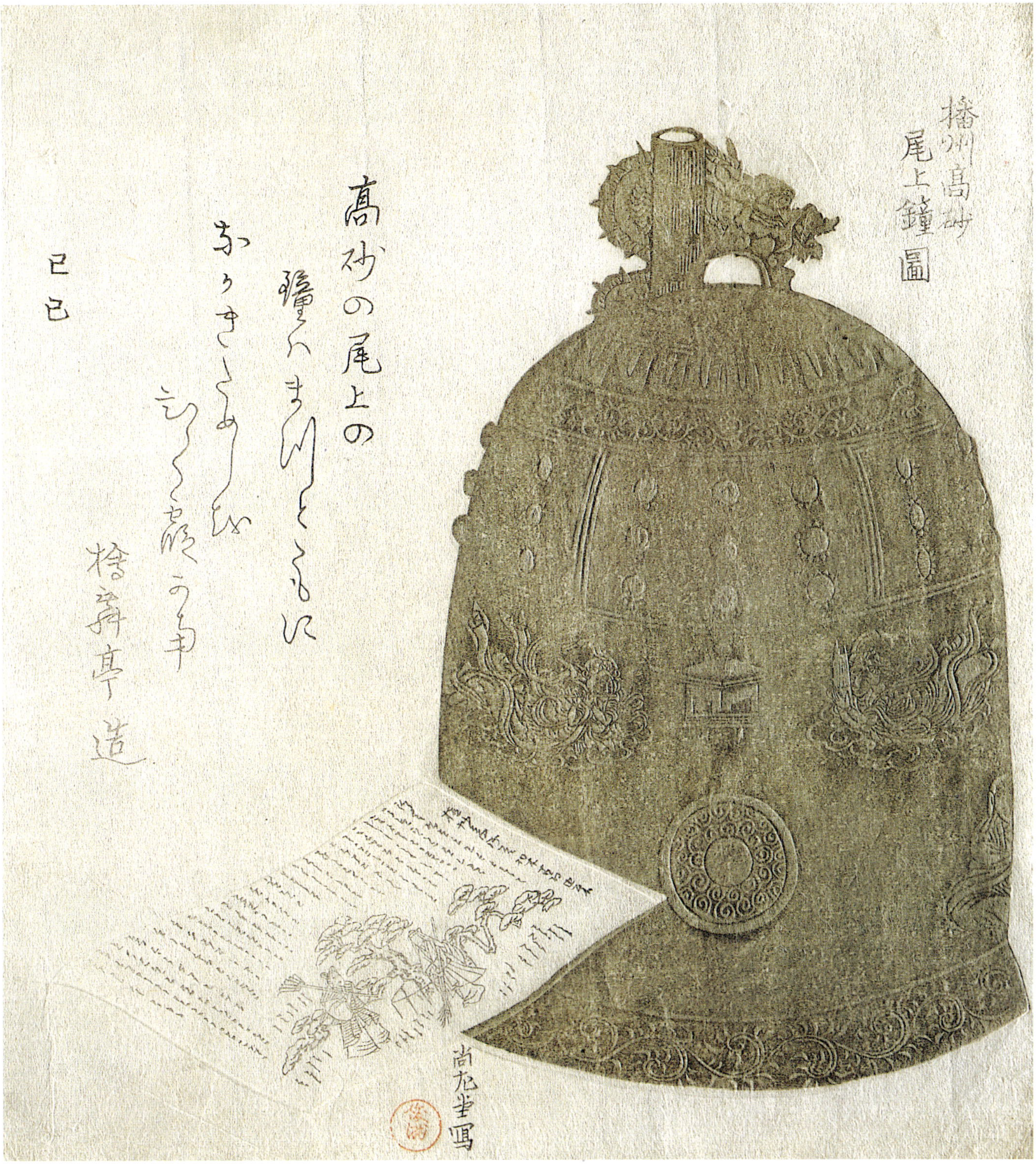
播州高砂
尾上鐘圖
高砂の尾上の
己巳
尚左堂写

KUBO SHUMMAN

1757–1820

51 A pair of Chinese pheasants and *yamabuki* flowers

SERIES *Yamagawa Shimotsuke Kanuma Fuyō-ren Kachō Nana Bantsuzuki no Uchi;* Series of Seven Bird-and-Flower Prints for the Fuyōren of Kanuma in Shimotsuke Province
DATE ca. 1810
ARTIST'S SEAL Shumman
FORMAT Shikishiban (20.6 x 18.6)
FLLW FDN 3007.042

Shunshōken Tsukiyoshi:

yamabuki no	Nestled beneath
yado ni kogane no	*yamabuki* flowers,
niwatori no	the golden bird
minoge wa hitotsu	has a cloak of feathers,
tare ni kasuran	but to whom will he lend it?

Senshun'an:

yamabuki no	The *yamabuki* blossoms,
hanairo-goromo	in robes of flowery color
hajinuran	must feel ashamed
kara nishiki kite	while golden pheasants
tateru kinkei	strut their Chinese brocade.

The subject of birds with flowers and plants is one that has enjoyed a long and rich tradition in the art of the Far East. In the early history of Japanese single-sheet prints, bird-and-flower pictures *(kachōga)* played a minor role, appearing only occasionally in the work of Harunobu, Koryusai, Utamaro, and others. Brilliant designs by Hokusai rekindled a broad interest in this subject in the 1830s. However, a little known but masterful contribution to the genre are the bird-and-flower surimono by Shumman of the 1810s. The Wright collection can boast of only this example. Two other designs from this series are located in the Duel Collection at the Arthur M. Sackler Museum, Harvard University Art Museum.

In this deceptively simple composition, a male and female Chinese pheasant pause before a graceful spray of *yamabuki,* kerria flower or yellow mountain rose. Famous for their colorful plumage, these birds are native to China but have been the subject of Japanese painting through the centuries.

The symbol at the top right is the emblem for a rural branch (*yamagawa*) of the Tsubo-gawa. Both poems refer to the gorgeous plumage of the birds, comparing them to sumptuous textiles and to *yamabuki,* which is a frequent image in traditional Japanese poetry. The first poem refers obliquely to the story of the tenth-century courtier Prince Kaneakira, who presented a spray of *yamabuki* flowers to a woman when she asked to borrow a raincloak. Since *yamabuki* are known to bear "no fruit" (*mi no nashi),* this allowed him an elegant way of telling her that he had "no raincloak" *(mino nashi).*

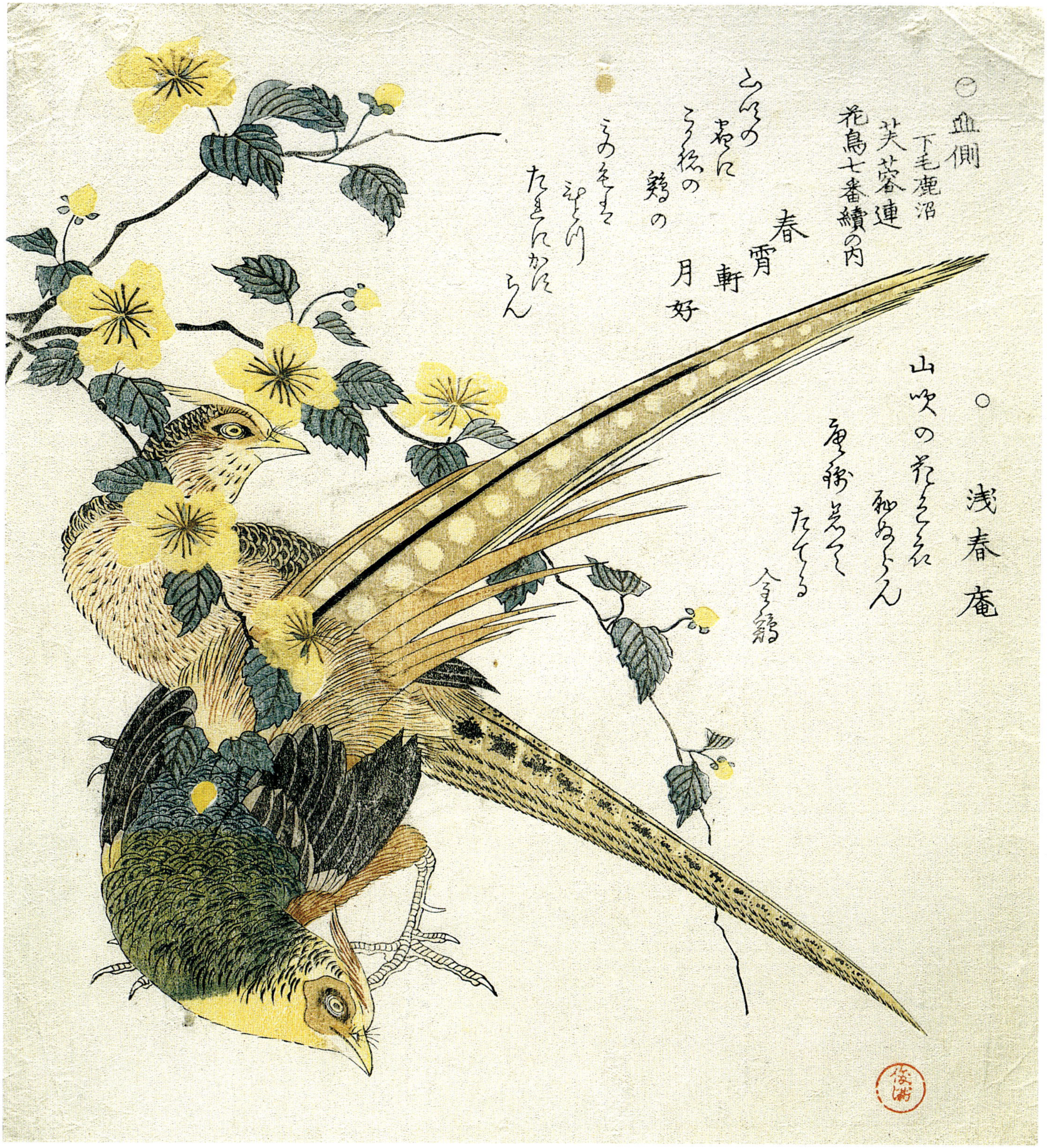

皿側
下毛鹿沼
芙蓉連
花鳥七番續の内
春霄軒
月好
浅春庵

KUBO SHUMMAN

1757–1820

52 A pipe and a tobacco pouch

DATE 1813, Year of the Bird, spring
SEALED Shumman
FORMAT Shikishiban (20.2 x 18.3)
REFERENCE Okada, 16
FLLW FDN 3007.040

Senzaitei Tazu Tomotoshi:

harugasumi	Spring mists spread over
tateru ya Yamana	Kōdaiji Temple in Yamana,
Kōdaiji	while a cloud of smoke
kusa no keburi mo	from burning grasses
yomo ni kunjite	wafts in all directions.

Shōsadō Shumman:

Kasugano no	On the plains of Kasuga
Tobuhino nomori	the Tobuhino watchman
koshisage no	plucks young greens
ha sagu tabako ni	from tobacco leaves
wakana tsumiten	in the pouch around his waist.

Yomo Takisui Komehito:

itsu made mo	It never dies,
oizu shinanu no	never grows stale,
waka tabako	fresh tobacco—
chiyo iku saka ni	nothing surpasses it
kosu mono wa naki	in the long climb of life.

Introduced from the West, probably by the Portuguese in the late sixteenth century, tobacco became an immediate success; recognizing its baneful qualities only twenty years later, the government issued a series of ineffectual edicts forbidding its consumption and sale. By the eighteenth century, however, smoking had become an important part of Edo culture. The etiquette and accouterments that it required were given careful attention by men and women of sophistication. Smoking is often romanticized in Edo popular art and literature, and smoking implements are commonly featured as the subject of still-life surimono compositions.

The pouch illustrated here is an especially fine example of embossed gilt leather, a technique that originated in the Netherlands in the early seventeenth century. In Japan, these Dutch leather samples, termed *kinkarakawa* (gold leather), were cut up and often made into tobacco pouches. By the nineteenth century, a process for producing this crafted leather had been developed in Japan. The design embossed on this pouch is also of European origin. The sumptuous floral motifs and a white squirrel surrounding a stylized figure with a feathered headdress and bare torso was no doubt inspired by a design found in *Sōken Kishō* (Treasury of Sword Fittings and Rare Accessories) compiled by Inaba Tsūryū in 1781. There we find a similar pattern modeled after a European impression of a North American Indian (see Okada, 16). Shumman was known to have relied on this source for a number of surimono designs (see Suzuki, figs. 13–15).

The manner in which a pouch is threaded with a silk cord and held in place with an *ojime,* here a rust-colored bead, and *netsuke* (toggle) is easily discerned in the print. The flat lacquer-and-gold disk with a maple-leaf design is known as a *manjū netsuke* (a round flat toggle named after the similarly-shaped rice cake).

This print was most probably commissioned by the poet Senzaitei, who prefaced his poem with his address, Higashi Ueda (a small village in northeastern Nagano Prefecture), and his age, eighty-one. In fact, he lived to the ripe old age of ninety, a rare feat during this time. The temple and village he mentions in his poem are actually in the neighboring prefecture of Gumma, in the city called Takazaki, which lies somewhat to the east of Higashi Ueda. According to biographical accounts he began his studies of kyōka at the advanced age of seventy with Yomo no Takisui Komehito, a judge of the Yomo-gawa.

Shumman's own poem, in the middle position, reveals his knowledge of and fondness for classical literature. Parodying a spring poem from the *Kokinshū,* the first two lines rely on the ancient verse and refer to the annual fire set on the fields near Kasuga Shrine in Nara. The left-hand poem (in the honored position) by Komehito was no doubt written in tribute to his elderly pupil, who must have been a devotee of smoking; it heartily endorses tobacco as an elixir of long life!

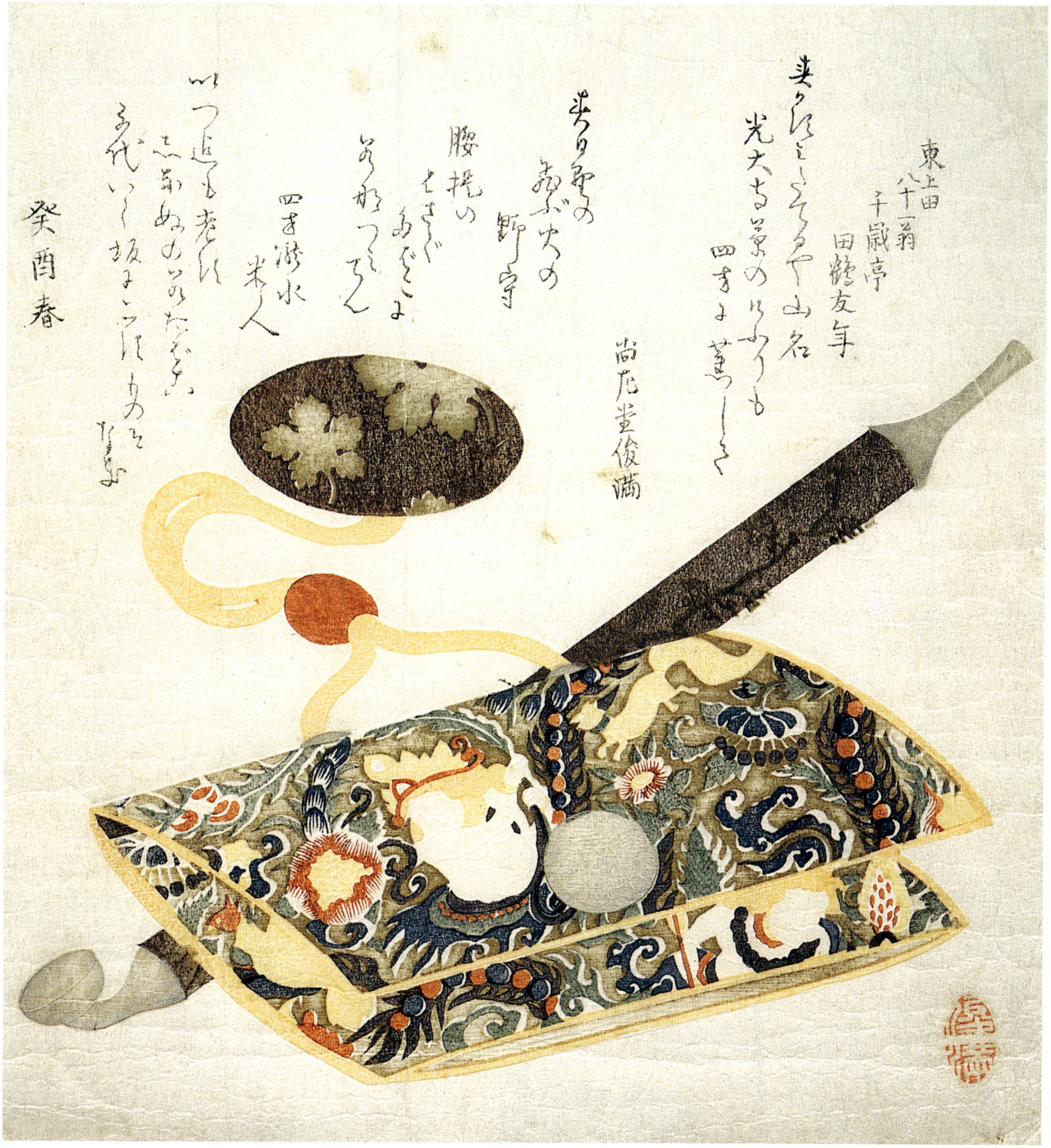
東上田
八十翁
千歳亭
田鶴友年
四方滸水
米人
尚左堂俊満
癸酉春

KUBO SHUMMAN

1757–1820

53 A lacquer picnic box, violets, and dandelions

TITLE *Gojūshi-dan;* Chapter Fifty-four
SERIES *Asakusa-gawa Tsurezuregusa; Essays in Idleness* for the Asakusa Group
DATE ca. 1818
ARTIST'S SEAL Shumman sei (in title cartouche)
FORMAT Shikishiban (trimmed; 20.8 x 15.9)
FLLW FDN 3007.041

Prose preface:

Omuro ni imijiki	There was a handsome young
chigo no arikeru o	acolyte at the temple in Omuro,
ikade sasoi-idashite	and a group of priests were
asoban to takumu	trying to trick him into joining
hōshi domo	their party.

Sengetsuan Haruhito:

imo ga kao	The maiden's face
momiji takasete	turns red as maple leaves
warawabaya	as they heat wine—
sashiai kuwanu	laughing and eating together
no-asobi no kyō	on a picnic in the fields.

[Masagoan Michimori]:

tsuma koedo	Though he loves his wife
ken mo hororo ni	she squawks at him
hagakure no	as she looks for food
esa nomi tazunete	hidden under the leaves—
naku kigisu kana	the cry of the pheasant.

Masagoan Michimori:

noasobi no	Opening the lunch box
warigo hirakan	for a picnic in the fields,
sawamizu no	they find boiled greens
hitashi mono ni wa	from waters of the marsh—
yomena tampopo	asters and dandelions.

A diminutive, red-lacquer, tiered picnic box used for an individual meal is nestled in a purple, gold, and silver draw-string pouch, and decorated with the gold arc-in-a-circle emblem of the Asakusa group. It is surrounded by late-spring flowers, white violets and dandelions. Dandelion leaves were once often prepared as marinated boiled greens, mentioned in the third poem.

Each of the prints in this series are based on a chapter of *Tsurezuregusa* (Essays in Idleness). Often the allusion in the images and the poems are not immediately apparent until the print is carefully examined. It is noteworthy that another print from this series was designed in koban yoko-e format, unlike this example (see Ostier, *Les objets tranquilles,* pl. 14). The prose preface on this print is composed of the opening sentence of chapter fifty-four of the *Tsurezuregusa,* a selection of essays written around 1333 by Yoshida Kenkō. This chapter tells the humorous story of a group of priests from Omuro who persuade a handsome young monk to join them on a picnic. In an attempt to induce him to join them, they concoct an elaborate scheme in which they pack a sumptuous meal in a lunch box and then hide it beneath a cover of autumn leaves. They hope to impress the youth by magically "discovering" this repast while on an outing later in the day. Instead their scheme is foiled by an observer who steals the box before they arrive at the spot. The frustrated priests search the entire hillside in vain.

Each of the poems obliquely refers to phrases or images found in this chapter. In the first poem, reference is made to a once common expression describing a young girl blushing in embarrassment *(kao ni momiji o chirasu); momiji,* or maple leaves, becomes a pivot word for the expression *momiji takasete* (the burning of autumn leaves), a poetic expression for the heating of sake and a phrase found in Kenkō's text. The second poem presents the image of a pair of pheasants whose cry, *ken mo hororo,* is also a phrase meaning to rebuff someone. The implication is that the female ignores her spouse while he searches for food. This parallels the image of the priests in their search for the picnic box. In the third poem, a picnic box is opened to reveal a tasty lunch including boiled greens; this is a humorous allusion to the picnic box in Kenkō's tale.

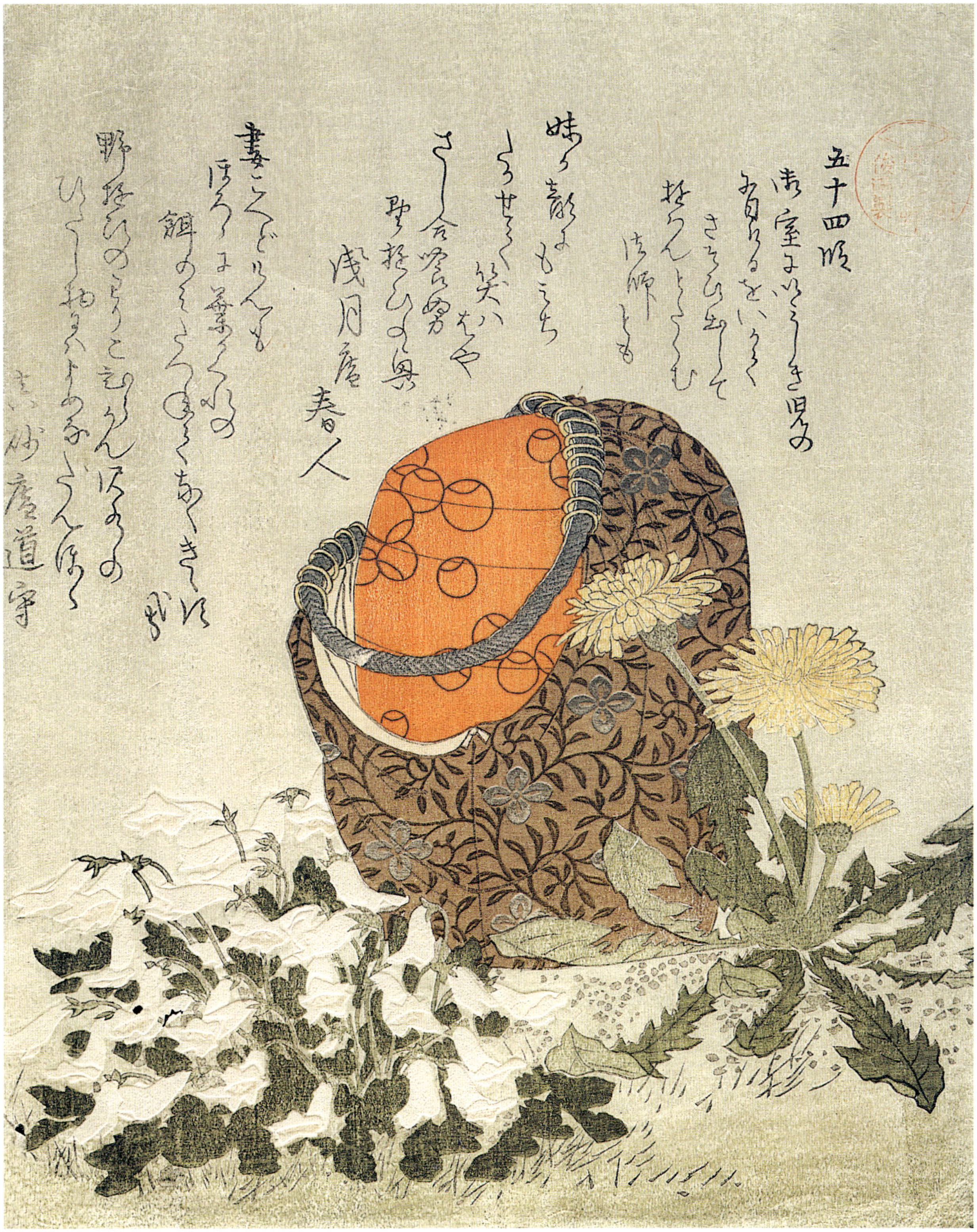
五十四服
春人

KATSUKAWA SHUN'EI

1762–1819

54 A court lady with a koto looks out at the night rain

DATE 1798, Year of the Horse
SIGNATURE Shun'ei ga
CARVER'S SEAL Hōko tō
FORMAT Koban yoko-e (14.0 x 18.3)
FLLW FDN 3004.002

Fuji no Tsuruhito:

koto no sono	Strings of rain
kumoi yori hiku	from the palace of clouds
ito mizu ya	are plucked like a koto,
ne sae shizukeki	and echo softly in the night
yowa no harusame	during a gentle spring drizzle.

Katsukawa Shun'ei, a gifted pupil of Shunshō (1726–92), is best known for his theatre prints and for his individualistic portraits of actors, which greatly influenced other actor-print artists including Sharaku and Toyokuni. By the mid-1790s he was at the height both of artistic powers and popularity. Like many Katsukawa artists, Shun'ei designed prints and illustrated books on themes of classical beauties and poets; surimono by the artist, are, however, extremely rare.

In the early evening, a court lady gazes pensively at a candle flickering in the spring breeze as rain, rendered in gaufrage, slants down beyond the veranda. The curtain of state indicates her status as a high-ranking imperial consort or a lady-in-waiting. The mood created by the misty evening setting and introspective nature of the portrayal is unusual in work of this genre. This atmosphere is further enhanced by the delicate coloration and embossing. The sensibility and refinement are more reminiscent of classical court painting than of the up-to-date, cosmopolitan tastes of Edo. The poem has been interpreted literally by Shun'ei's delicate image. Subtle erotic undertones, however, may be implied in the use of rain and cloud imagery, which in East Asian poetry was traditionally used as a veiled allusion to lovemaking.

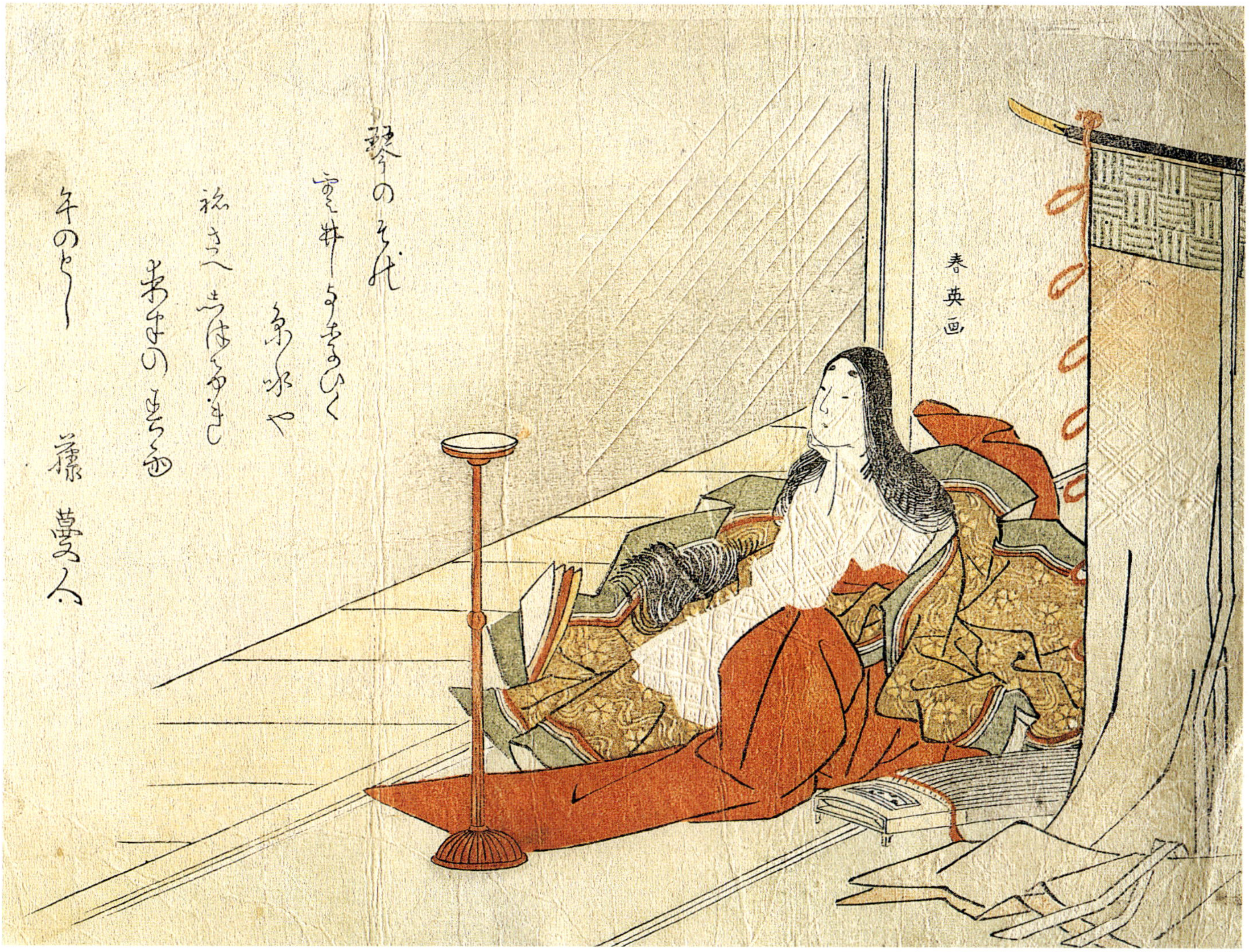
春英画

KATSUKAWA SHUNTEI

1770–1820

55 A parody of Kajiwara no Kagesue

DATE ca. 1818
SIGNATURE Shuntei ga
FORMAT Shikishiban (21.2 x 18.6)
FLLW FDN 3012.007

Senkaen Jobun:

ka ni niou	The young plum
wakaki no ume wa	with fragrant blossoms
taoyagi ni	seems ever so gentle,
makenu sugata ya	but shows great flourish
hana no edaburi	never accepting defeat.

Mitsugian:

ōmisoka	Having swept away
harai-shimōte	the last day of the year,
mada ume ni	we can now enjoy
ukaruru sake no	wine under plum blossoms,
nido no kake ari	and make a second attack.

This dramatic scene is a parody of the story of the warrior Kajiwara no Kagesue at the battle of Ikuta Forest. According to legend, Kagesue, a follower of the general Minamoto no Yoshitsune (1159–89), defiantly placed a blossoming branch in his quiver during battle, making him an easy target for the enemy. In the second foray he narrowly averted death but lost his helmet. In the tale as told in some versions of *The Tale of the Heike,* Kagesue carries a spray of cherry blossoms; however, in the *Gempei Jōsuiki* (An Account of the Gempei Wars),which overlaps in content with its more famous literary predecessor, the cherry branch has been replaced by a plum branch.

The warrior Kagesue, rather than being portrayed as a fierce samurai, has been transformed here into a contemporary beauty brandishing a plum branch as if it were a weapon. The textile pattern of her kimono simulates of a suit of armor. These clues and the lost helmet at her feet provide the visual hints needed to identify the scene.

The first poem combines references to common New Year images and Kagesue. In the second poem, the phrase *nido no kake* refers to the two attacks made by Kagesue and the title of the pertinent section of *The Tale of the Heike.* The last two lines of the poem suggest the custom of cleaning shops and homes, settling debts, and making a clean sweep of the past year on its last day. Of course, the completion of these tasks was often accompanied by a good deal of drinking and celebrating. The "second attack" occurs at the beginning of the New Year, when plum blossoms and rice wine make good companions.

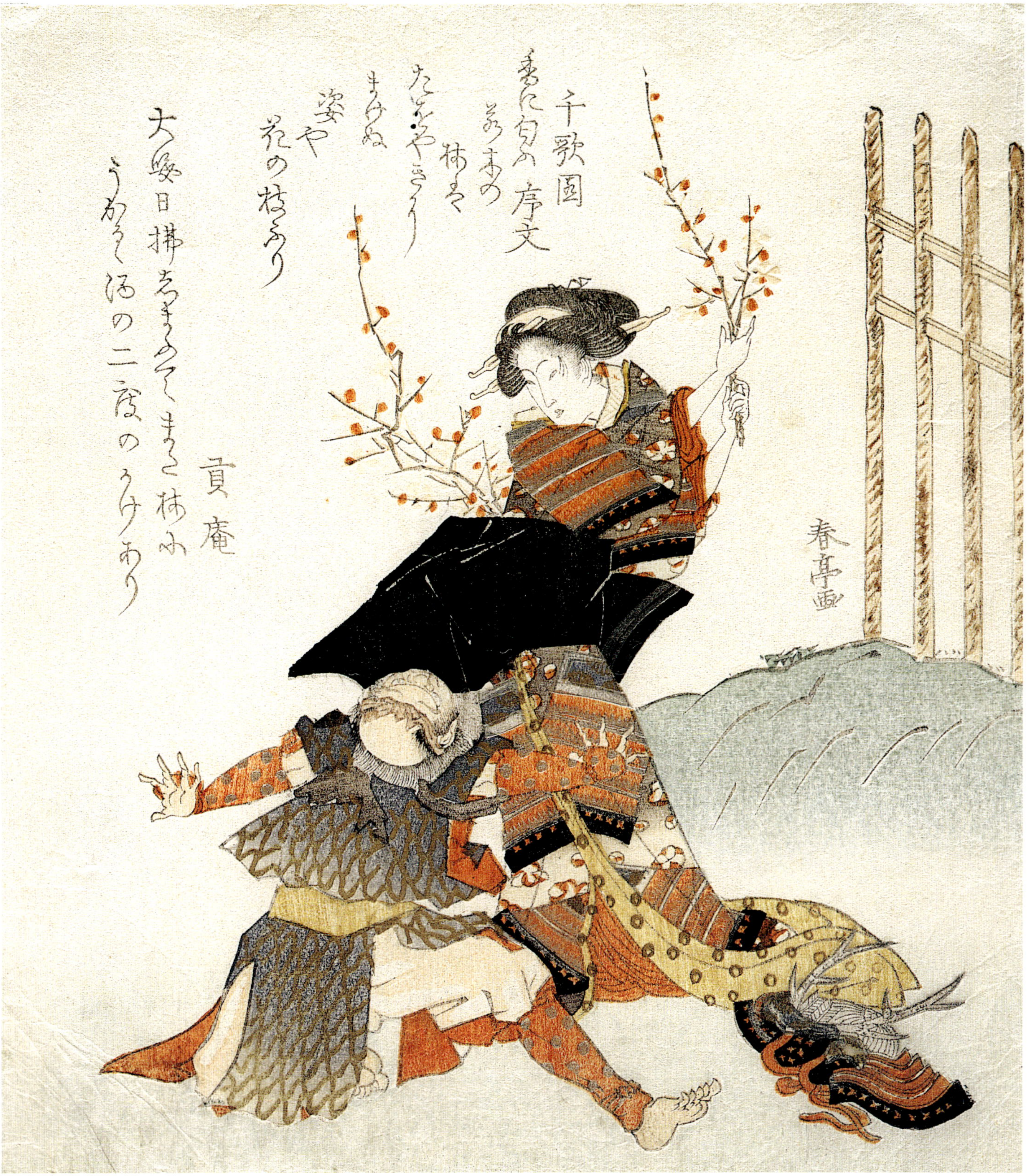
千歌園
貢庵
春亭画

KATSUKAWA SHUNTEI

1770–1820

56 A woman in the pose of Ebisu

SERIES *Hanagasa-ren Shichi Fukujin;*
Seven Women as the Gods of Good Fortune for the Hanagasa Poetry Club
DATE 1823, Year of the Goat
SIGNATURE Shuntei ga
FORMAT Shikishiban (20.5 x 18.4)
FLLW FDN 3012.003

Machigiwa Hayaki:

Fukagawa no	The plum blossoms
Ebisu no miya ni	at Ebisu Shrine in Fukagawa,
kakure mino	first wrapped in cloaks,
kisohajime yoki	now change into new clothes
ume no utsuriga	with a lingering scent.

Kishirō Somenushi:

nodokesa ni	With last year's wintry cold
kozo no samusa mo	gently laid to rest,
ume no hana	the plum blossoms open
hirakuru un no	as Ebisu bestows
haru o Ebisu wa	good fortune this spring.

Yamato no Watamori:

aoyagi o	The willow is like a kept woman
kakoime ni shite	as the scent of plum,
hana no ani	big brother of flowers,
umegaka kayou	comes and goes with the wind
kaze no degōshi	through the latticed doorway.

Kasentei Momobito:

Ebisugami	My mistress stashes
torite tamoto e	Ebisu paper in her sleeves
kakushi tsuma	for the first writing—
hitsuji mo konomu	also the favorite time
toshi no kakizome.	of the year for the goat.

Pastiches of women parodying famous men or legendary figures were popular throughout the history of ukiyo-e. This series represents one of the most common examples of this parody technique by presenting the Seven Gods of Good Fortune as everyday women or courtesans. Of this series of eight designs, six are in the Wright collection (see also cat. nos. 261–65).

Seated by a veranda, a woman entertains a young boy who playfully points to a dangling fish. The woman is a parody of Ebisu, the god of wealth and the patron saint of merchants, who is traditionally shown with a fishing pole in hand. She holds a bamboo branch, to which are attached two symbols of Ebisu—a miniature sea bream and a golden coin. The stand which would support the bamboo branch can be seen in the lower right corner. A potted plum tree is at the far left of the design. The surrounding green border is composed of auspicious symbols associated with the gods.

The first poem is set at an Ebisu Shrine in Fukagawa. The poet likens an unopened plum blossom to a courtesan who wears a cloak; when the plum fully blossoms, the appearance is like their brilliant robes (*kisohajime*) worn for the New Year. A lover's lingering scent in those robes is further implied in the phrase *utsuri ga.* Using *ume* in the third line of the second poem as a pivot word, the poet links the images of "burying" the wintry cold and the blossoming spring "plum."

The third poem mentions a *kakoime,* a type of courtesan, and then uses the term *degōshi,* which as an abbreviation for *degōshi jorō* also refers to a denizen of a bordello. *Ebisugami,* mentioned in the fourth poem, refers to a sheet of paper the folded corner of which remains uncut when a pile is trimmed; this is also called *fukugami,* or "good-luck paper." Juxtaposing this lucky paper and the New Year's first writing, *kakizome,* the poem extols the joy of a goat at finding an abundance of his favorite food, paper. The link between the goat, *hitusji,* and the *kakizome* is further suggested by the alternative meanings of *hitsuji:* "paper," or "writing brush and paper."

This series may be based on the popular New Year tradition of making a pilgrimage to the seven shrines devoted to each of the Seven Gods of Good Luck. Commissioned by the Hanagasa-ren of the Taiko-gawa, the series of probably eight surimono portrays women in the pose of the seven Gods of Good Luck; the collection includes six from the set. The others are Benzaiten, illustrated in *Japanese Prenten,* plate 4, and another which appears to be a cover design as it includes items associated with several of the gods, illustrated in Rijksmuseum, *Hiroshige,* plate 263.

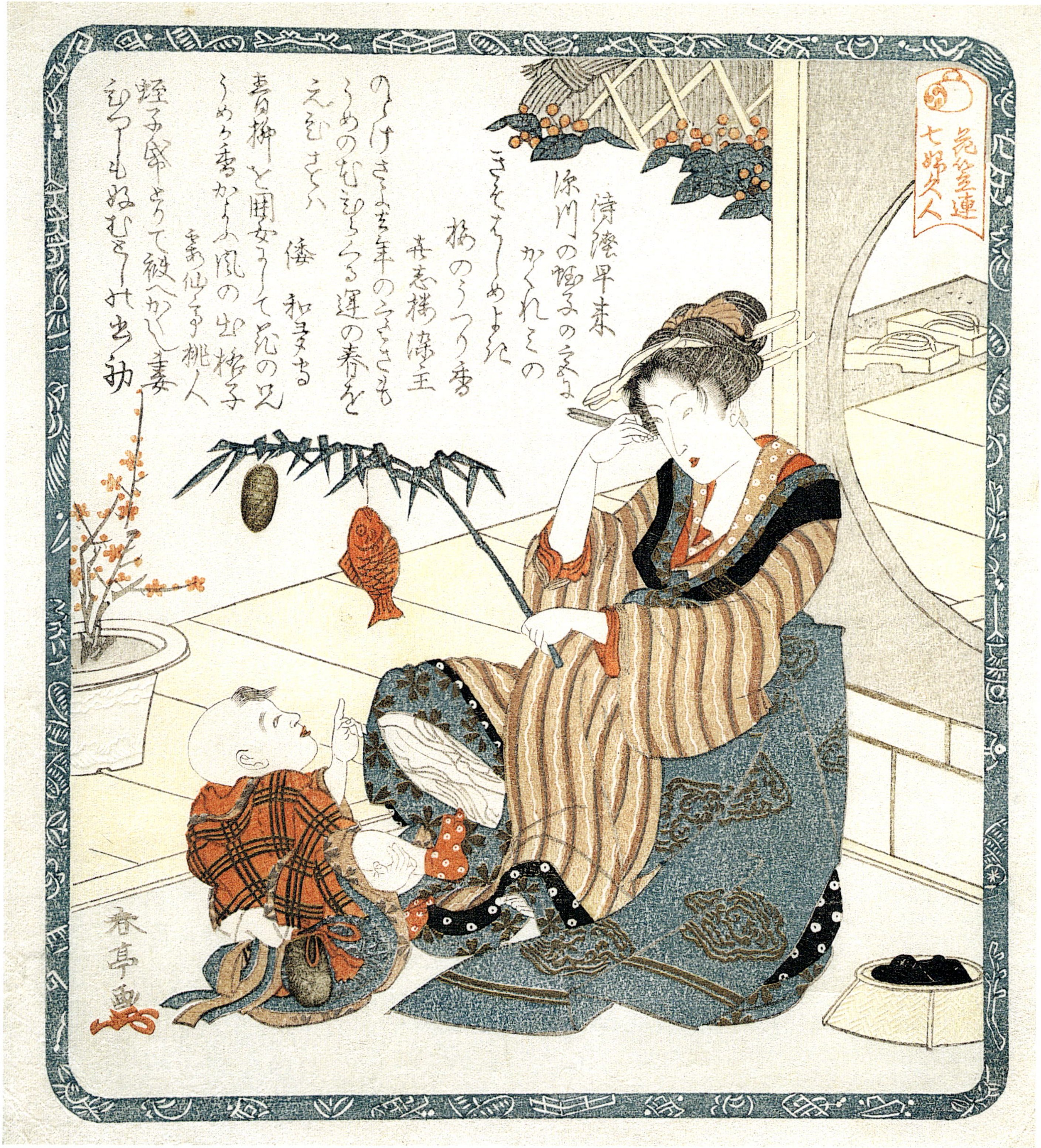
春亭画

HISHIKAWA SŌRI

ACT. 1797–CA. 1813

57 A geisha with a shamisen and her maid

DATE ca. 1800
SIGNATURE Sōri ga
FORMAT Koban yoko-e (14.4 x 19.2)
REFERENCE *UT, Bibliothèque Nationale,* 201, pl. 39
FLLW FDN 3008.048

Karasaki Matsumoto:

haru kinu to	"Spring has come,"
aruji ni tsugete	she announces to her patron,
mado no kuchi	as the fragrance of plum
sotto fukikomu	carried by winds from the east
kochi no ume ga ka	whispers in through the window.

Kashiwauma Mitsunari:

rainen no	If after this morning
koto o iwan to	you talk of "next year,"
kesa yori wa	demons in the hills
onizumi yama no	will begin to laugh
warau hatsuharu	now that spring has come.

Takisui Kiyoki:

ōtori mo	The great bird,
kite wa tomaran	spotting its prey,
kuisashi ni	comes to land
kazarishi ebi no	on a long whisker
nagaki hige ni wa	of the New Year's lobster.

Considerable confusion has persisted over the identities of the artists using the name Sōri. First adopted by Hokusai in 1794 after studying with the Tawaraya school, the name can be clearly associated with this master until late 1798. At that time, he seems to have passed the appellation to his pupil Sōji, who thus became Sōri III. (For a surimono bearing the Sōji signature of Sōri III see cat. no. 271.) Surimono from the late 1790s bearing this signature are quite difficult to attribute when unaccompanied by some means of precise dating such as zodiac references. Scholars are forced to resort to stylistic analysis, comparing the fluid and animated brushwork by Hokusai to the often stiffer and more static expression of Sōri. (For other examples of surimono by Sōri, see cat. nos. 271–78).

In this simply composed design of an elegant young geisha with her older attendant, such distinctions become quite difficult. Perhaps it is the lack of bodily form beneath the kimono of the woman holding the sake pot and cup, or her extremely attenuated wrists and disproportionately small hands, or the unnatural way that the blue robe pools beneath the legs of the attendant, which dictate an attribution to Sōri. The faces of the women, on the other hand, are refined and delicate and could be by either artist. This leads us to surmise that this surimono represents one of finer examples of the work of Sōri III.

Without explicitly indicating the subject, the author of the first poem suggests that spring's arrival can be announced in various ways—by a man's mistress or by the fragrance of plum blossoms. The second poem alludes to the Japanese proverb,

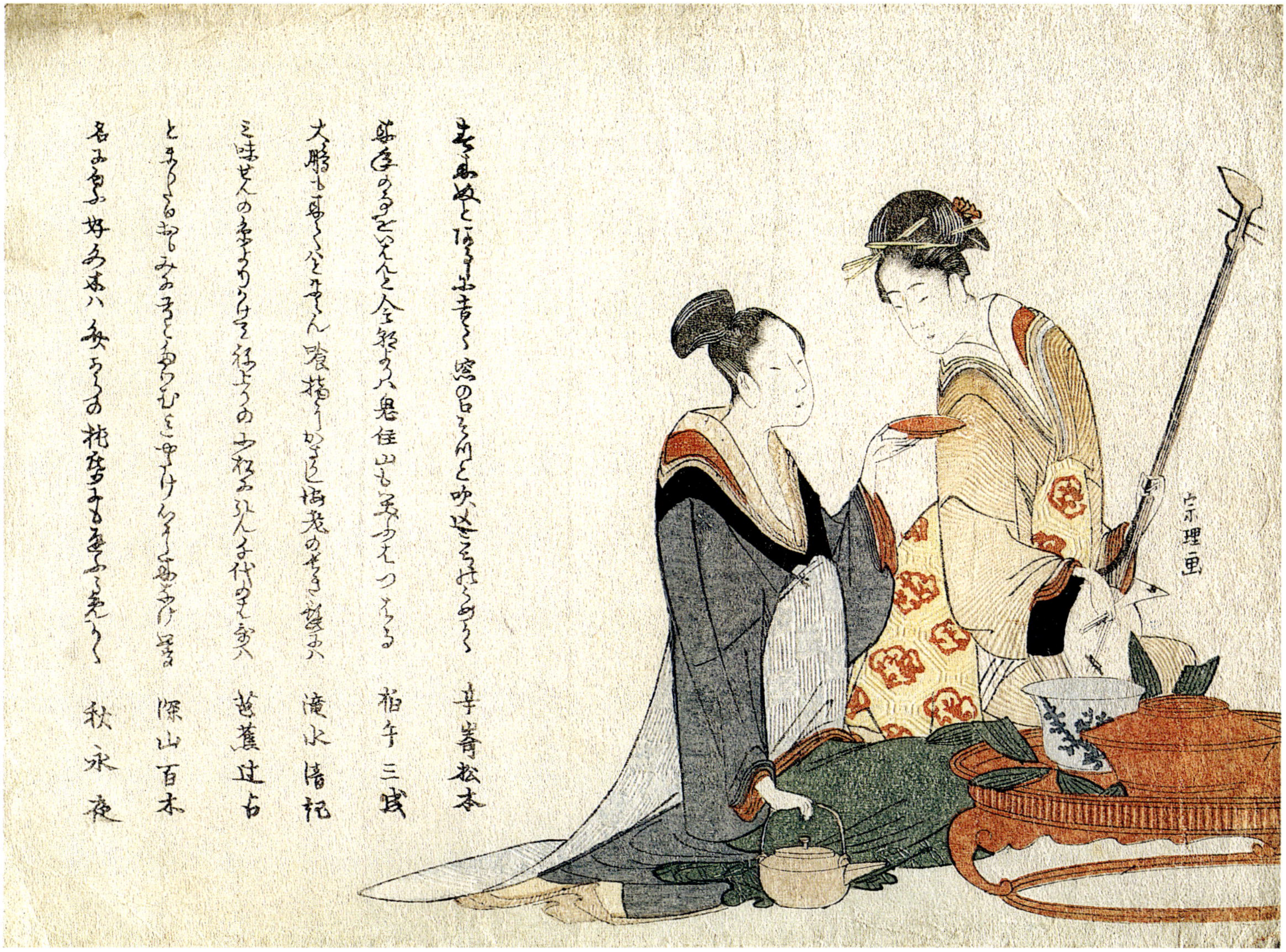
滝水清記
芭蕉辻古
深山百木
宗理画

Bashō Tsujiura:

shamisen no	To the sound of the shamisen
ito yori kakete	strings strumming
neagari no	a tune of celebration,
komatsu ni hikan	we pluck pine shoots
chiyo no hauta wa	to bring us long life.

Miyama Momoki:

tomaritaru	After coming to a stop
omomi ni yumi to	like a stretched bow
tawamu made	bent all the way back—
yatakegokoro ni	come now and sing, warbler,
kinake uguisu	in a full-bodied voice.

Aki no Nagayo:

na ni niou	"Literatus tree"—
kōbunboku wa	even the name has an aroma
fumigara no	of plum blossoms,
makuragami ni mo	which perfume the pillow
kayou ume ga ka	piled with old letters.

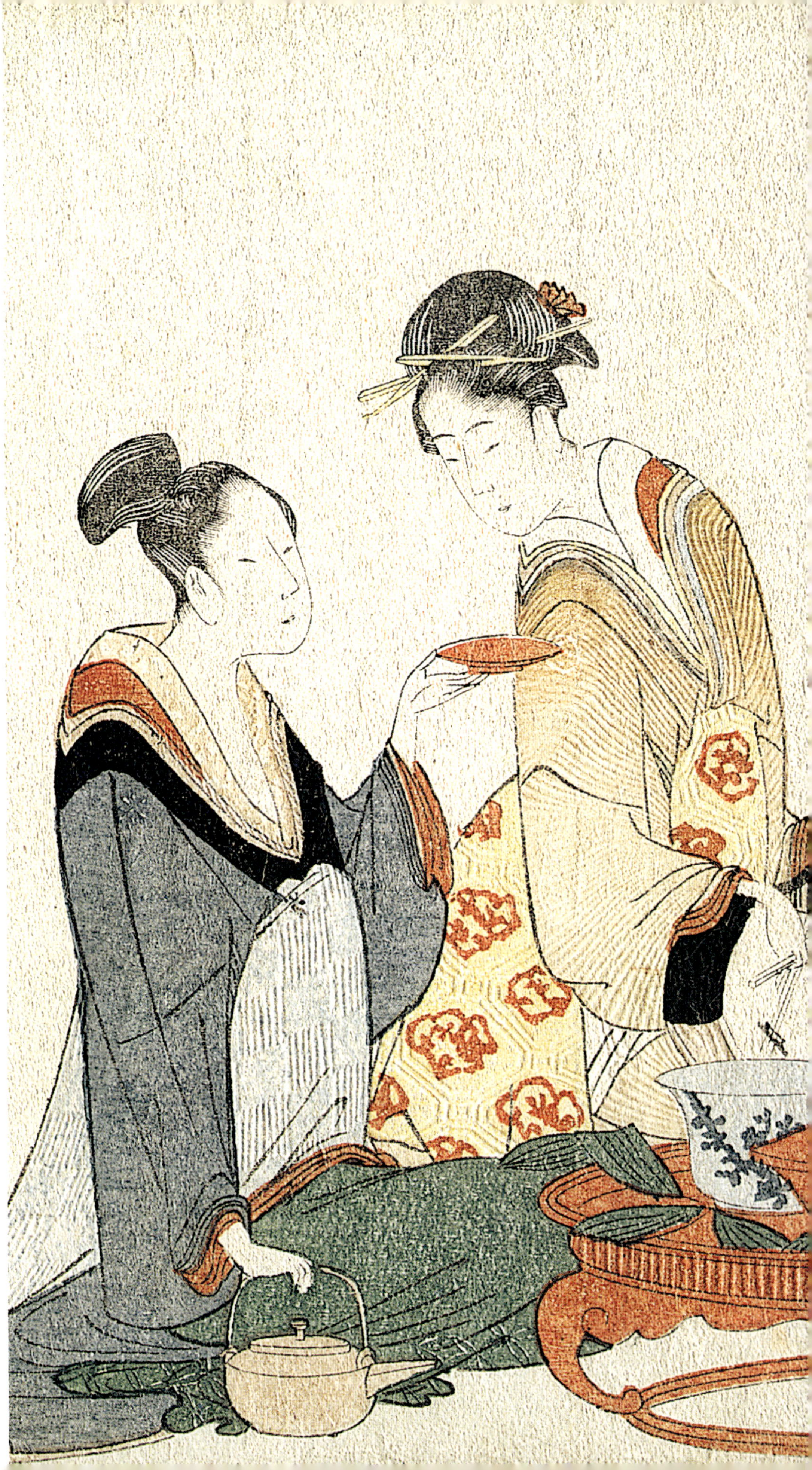

"talk about next year and the demons will laugh" (*rainen no koto o ieba, oni ga warau*). The poem pokes fun at those who continually say "next year," when in fact the new year has already begun. *Yama warau,* "the mountains laugh," is a common poetic conceit for describing the brightly colored mountains in spring, as opposed to the monochromatic landscape of mountains in winter, which are said to be "sleeping."

In the third poem, the "great bird" refers to the Chinese bird of myth said to have a wing span of over three thousand miles and the ability to fly ninety thousand miles before it lands. In the magical world of kyōka surimono, where auspicious images often make strange company, this enormous bird lands on the antennae of a lobster, set out as a New Year's decoration.

The fourth poem most directly evokes the image portrayed by Sōri by comparing the plucking of young pine saplings to the plucking of the strings of a shamisen, as the verbs for both are homonyms reading *hiku.* The collecting of pine saplings traditionally took place on the first rat day of the year and was a popular subject in surimono.

The final poem alludes to the *kōbunboku,* a poetic name for a plum tree which appears to have been derived from an episode in the *Jikkunshō* (Treatise of Ten Rules), a selection of didactic tales collected in the mid-thirteenth century. One tale tells of an emperor who started to doze while reading a book. When plum blossoms fell onto the open pages, he remarked that "this tree enjoys books." Thus the plum came to be known as the "literatus tree."

UTAGAWA TOYOKUNI

1769–1825

58 Twelve calendar prints depicting women

SERIES *Jūni-en no uchi;* A Set of Twelve Lovely Women
DATE 1799, Year of the Goat
SIGNATURE Toyokuni ga
FORMAT Koban tate-e (set of twelve; 13.9 x 9.0 each)
REFERENCE Another complete set is in the collection of the St. Louis Museum of Art
FLLW FDN 3011.005-.015 and .017

Toyokuni was initially known for his prints of beautiful women, much in the style of his contemporaries such as Utamaro and Eishi. His reputation and fame, however, came from his actor portraits of the late 1790s, a field which he dominated for over twenty years, until his death. It is generally thought that his greatest designs were created between the years 1794 and 1804. With the development of shikishiban surimono beginning in the first decade of the nineteenth century, Toyokuni also made important contributions in this genre in his later years.

This set of twelve prints may have been commissioned by a patron or fan club of the Kabuki actor Ichikawa Danzō IV (1745–1808) to which Toyokuni may have belonged. On an inscribed envelope illustrated in the design for the eleventh month is written: *Shin yakusha zuke Ichikawa Danzō*. This indicates that the envelope would have contained a standard folded schedule of the year's Kabuki performances and actors' rankings *(yakusha zuke)*, which was personally sent by Ichikawa Danzō IV to members of his fan club.

In each image, a young woman is posed in a seasonal activity or with an item that is associated with one of the twelve months. Below the signature on each print are two red seals: the upper seal reads *tsuchinoto hitsuji,* indicating the year 1799, year of the goat; one of two seals appear directly beneath, reading either *dai no tsuki* (long month) or *shō no tsuki* (short month). The appropriate numbers for the long months are 2, 3, 4, 7, 9, and 12; and for the short months, 1, 5, 6, 8, 10, and 11. Numbers or characters are cryptically woven into each design, together with references to seasonal symbols and festivals, and in most designs the relevant zodiac animal for the first day of that month.

(1) First Month: The first month is represented by a lavishly attired young woman, carrying a tray bearing a New Year pine sapling. The numbers, appearing as decoration on her kimono, correspond to the short months. There is no animal motif in this design

(2) Second Month: A kneeling courtesan removes a tray of New Year rice cakes as she gazes at a soaring warbler, both symbols of the New Year. Sewing utensils refer to the *hari-kuyō*, or "needle ritual," performed on the eighth day of the second month when bent or broken needles were offered to a shrine. A small sculpture of an ox rests on a pile of cushions; stroking it was said to bring good luck and grant wishes; each time a wish was granted, another pillow was added to the pile. The ox reference is a reminder that the first day of the second month was an ox day.

(3) Third Month: The popular celebration of the third month, the Doll Festival (*hina matsuri*), is indicated here by the courtier doll which the woman has just removed from its storage box. The numbers for the long months are written on the

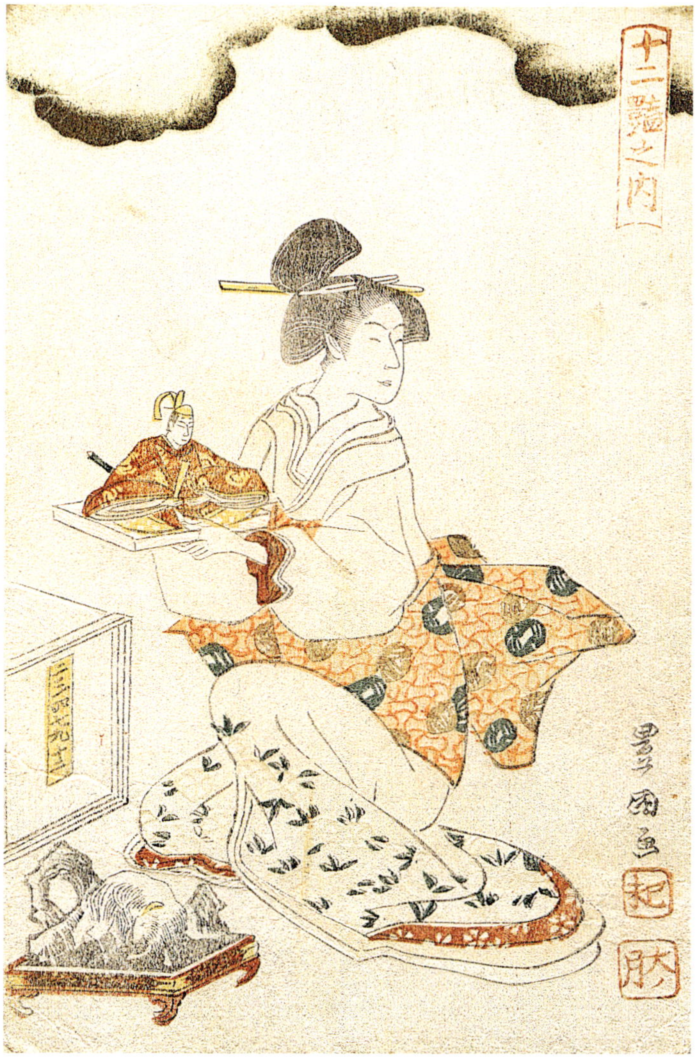

Third Month

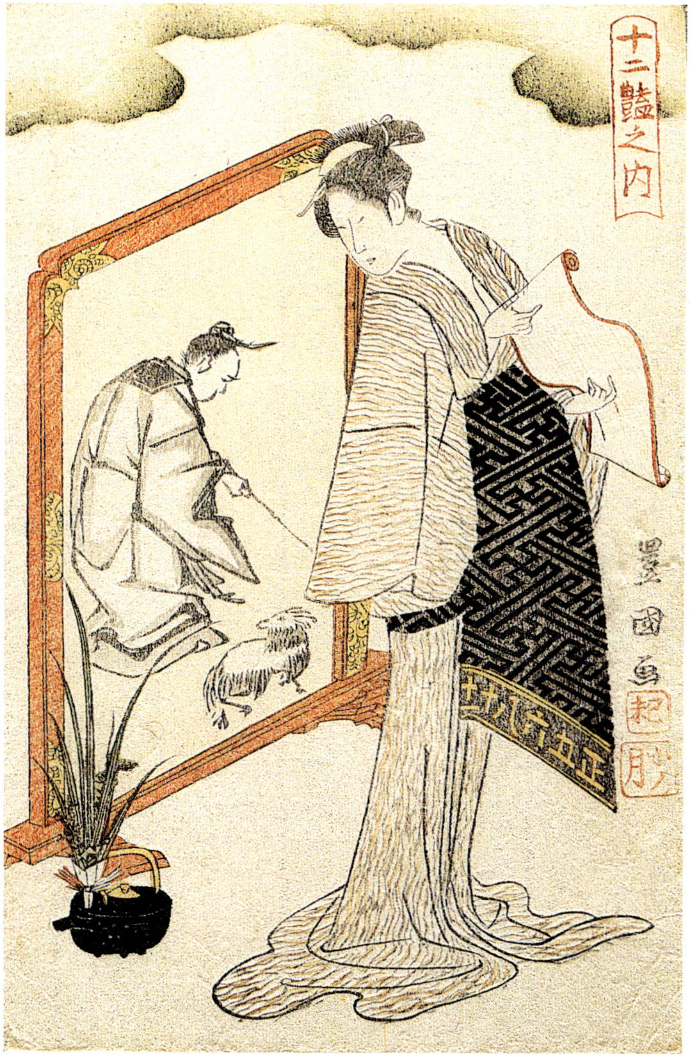

Fifth Month

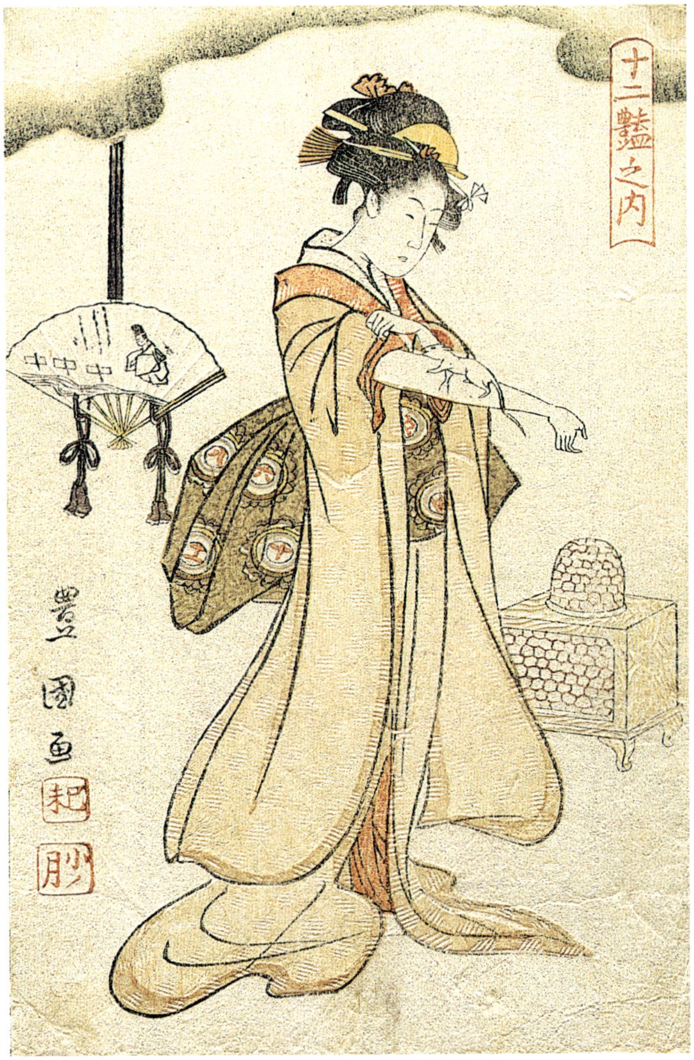

Sixth Month

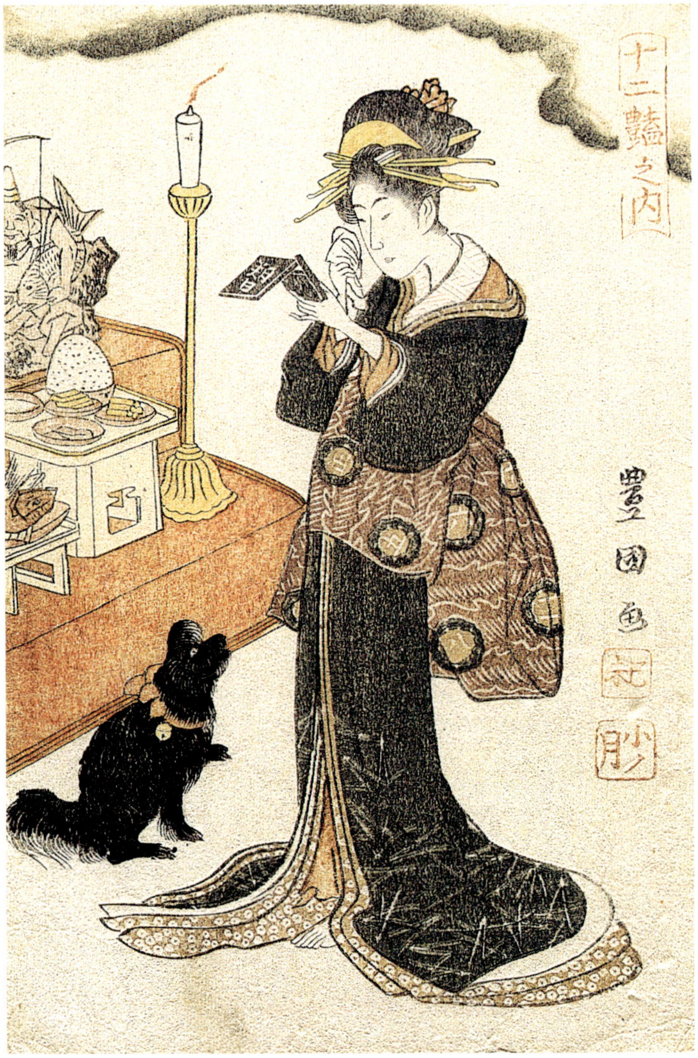

Tenth Month

box, as if a label. In the foreground, a tray garden contains a small sculpture of a goat, the appropriate animal for the first day of that month.

(4) Fourth Month: A court lady is shown dressed in elaborate court robes, a reference to the custom called *koromogae* ("changing clothes"), traditionally celebrated on the first day of the fourth month, when women exchange their winter wardrobe for lighter summer robes. Dating back to a Heian court ritual, the custom was revived by townspeople during the Edo period. The numbers for the long months are inscribed on her fan. A phoenix appears as a bird motif on one of her inner robes, but does not indicate a zodiac symbol here.

(5) Fifth Month: Irises, which bloom in the fifth month, are attached to the handle of a kettle. The artist refers to the horse by depicting the immortal Chokarō with his miniature horse in the ink painting on the standing screen. However, the artist has depicted the horse with a goat-like appearance, perhaps appropriate as the first day of of the fifth month of that year was a goat day. The numbers of the short months are embossed in gold on the edge of the courtesan's obi.

(6) Sixth Month: A young woman plays with her pet rat, an indication that the first day of the sixth month was a rat day. The numbers of the short months are woven into the pattern of her obi. Behind her hangs a fan painting with a scene of a Shinto priest making preparations for the *minazuki-barae,* "Sixth-Month Exorcism." It was customary, on the last day of that month, to visit a shrine near a river and join in purification rites. Sometimes, as illustrated here, white paper strips were attached to bamboo stakes and placed in the water where the purification rites were held.

(7) Seventh Month: A summer lantern sways in the breeze and is linked to Obon, the festival honoring deceased souls, which traditionally was held in the seventh month. Wearing a summer kimono, the waitress carries a fan with a picture of a snake, an indication that the first day of the month was a snake day. Here the numbers for the long months are embossed on the white paper hanging from the lantern.

(8) Eighth Month: A woman kneels with her shamisen resting on her lap and drinks sake from a shallow cup. The large porcelain bowl of cold *somen* noodles bear the numbers of the short months. The late-summer flower arrangement indicates the eighth month. The character *i* (boar) is written on the black storage box and indicates the animal sign for the first day of the month.

(9) Ninth Month: The ninth month is traditionally identified with the chrysanthemum festival. Here a woman carries a formal arrangement of three large flowers. The long months are listed on a package placed on some vegetables. The

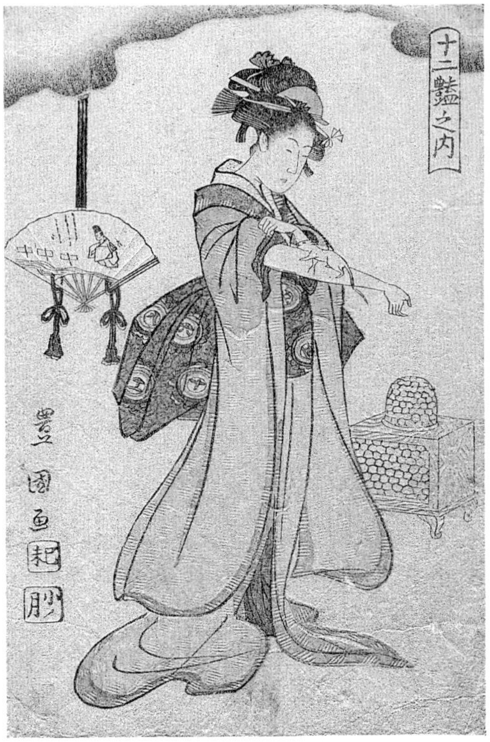

6

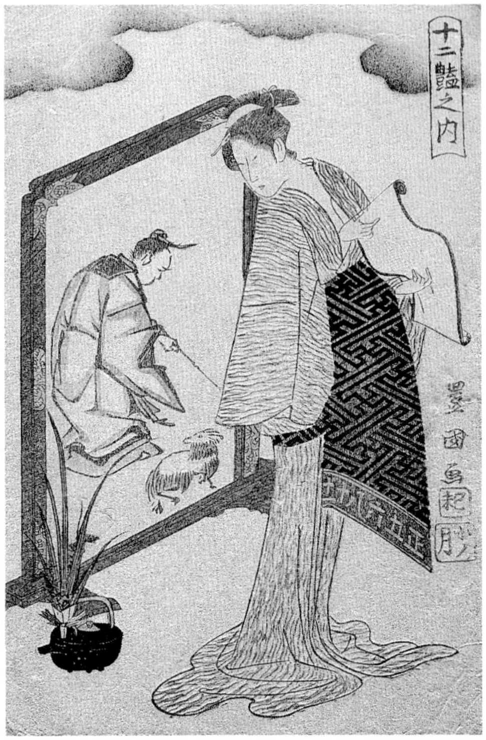

5

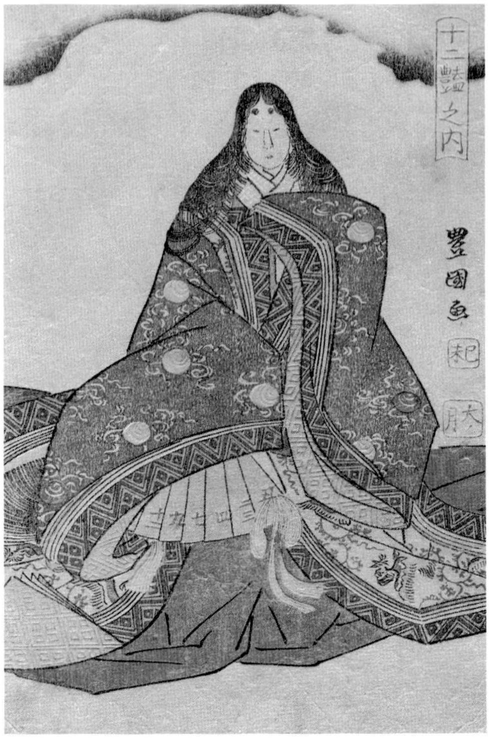

4

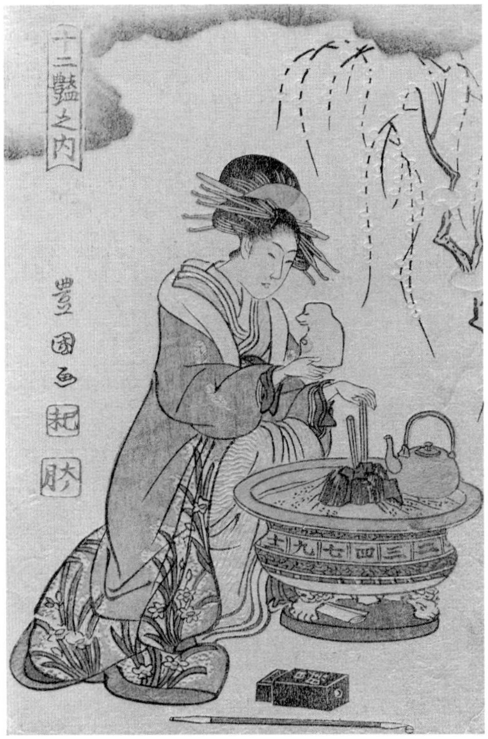

12

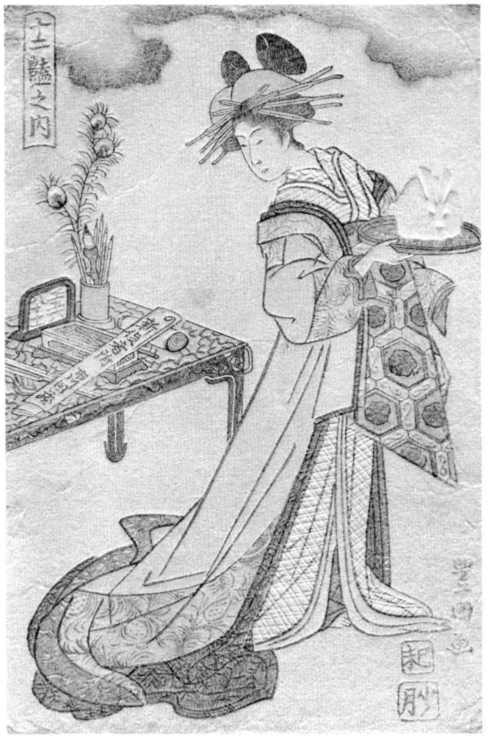

11

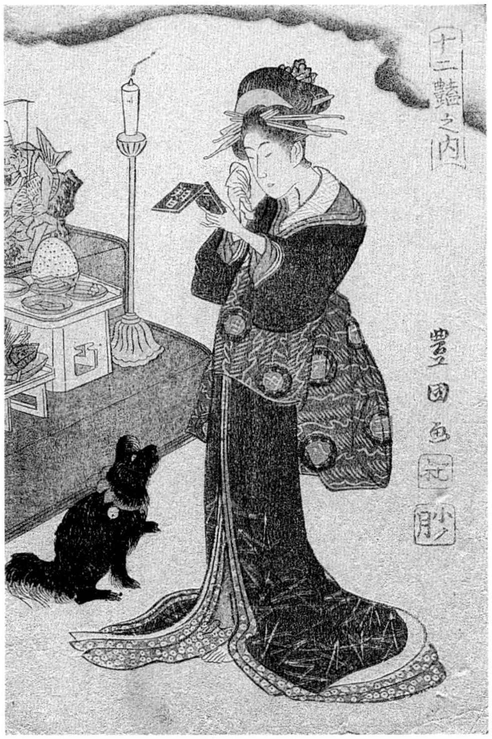

10

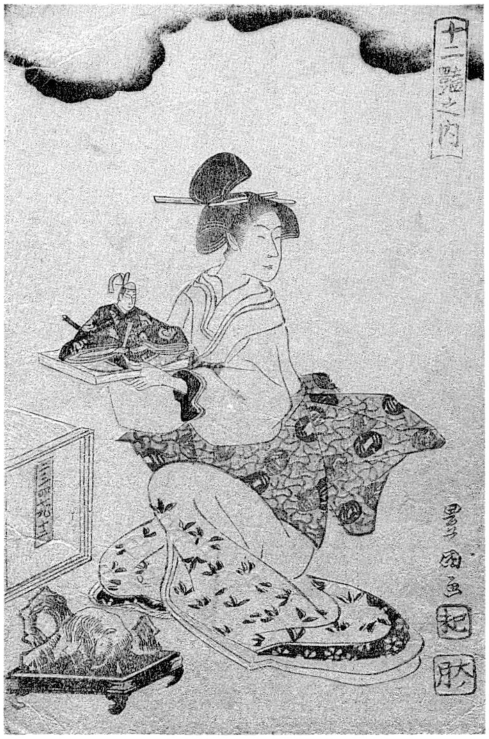

3

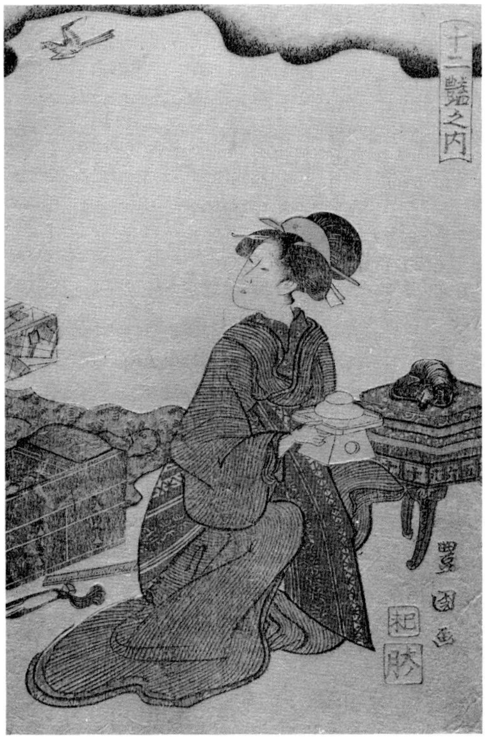

2

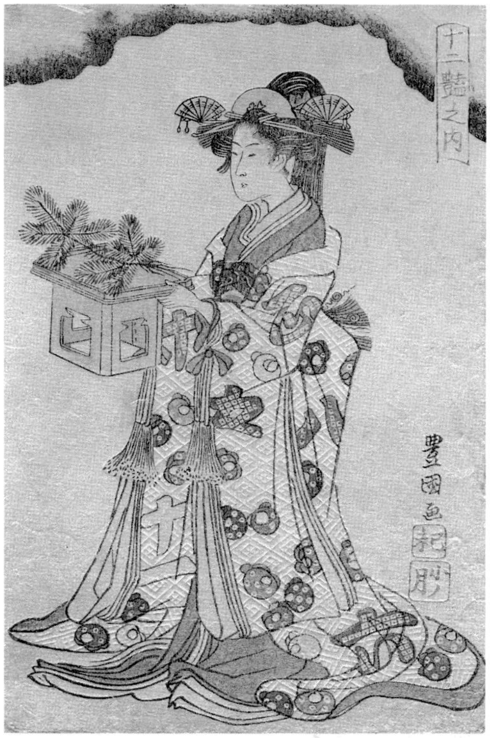

1

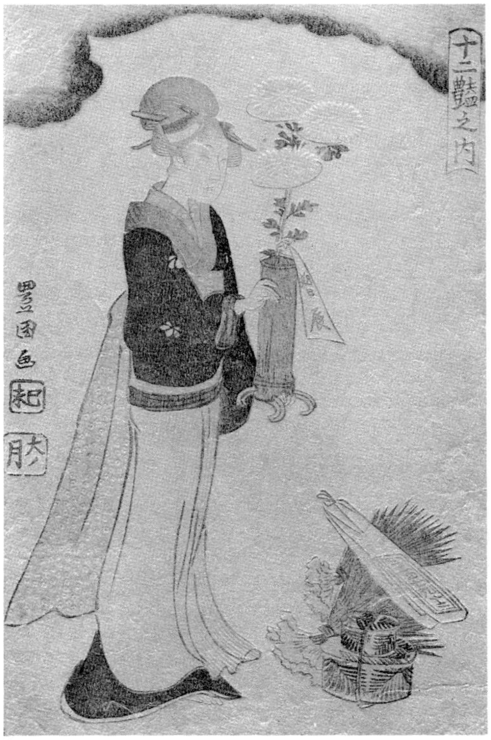

9

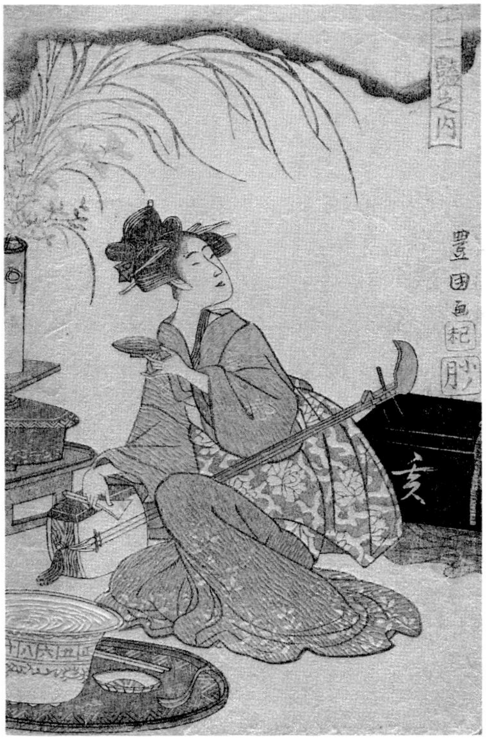

8

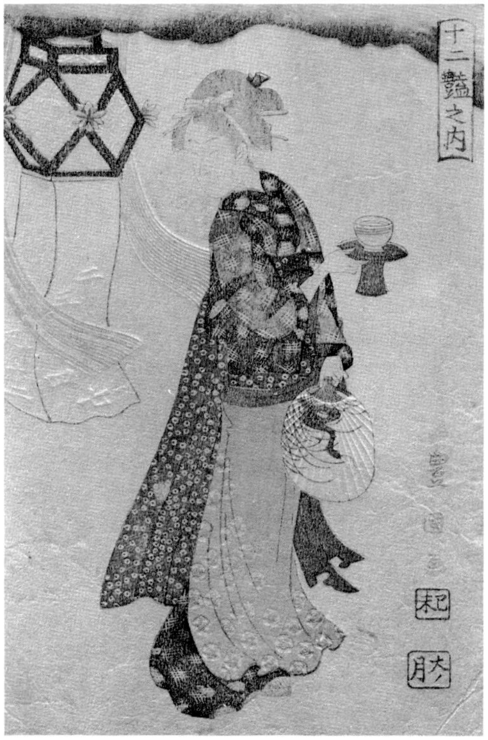

7

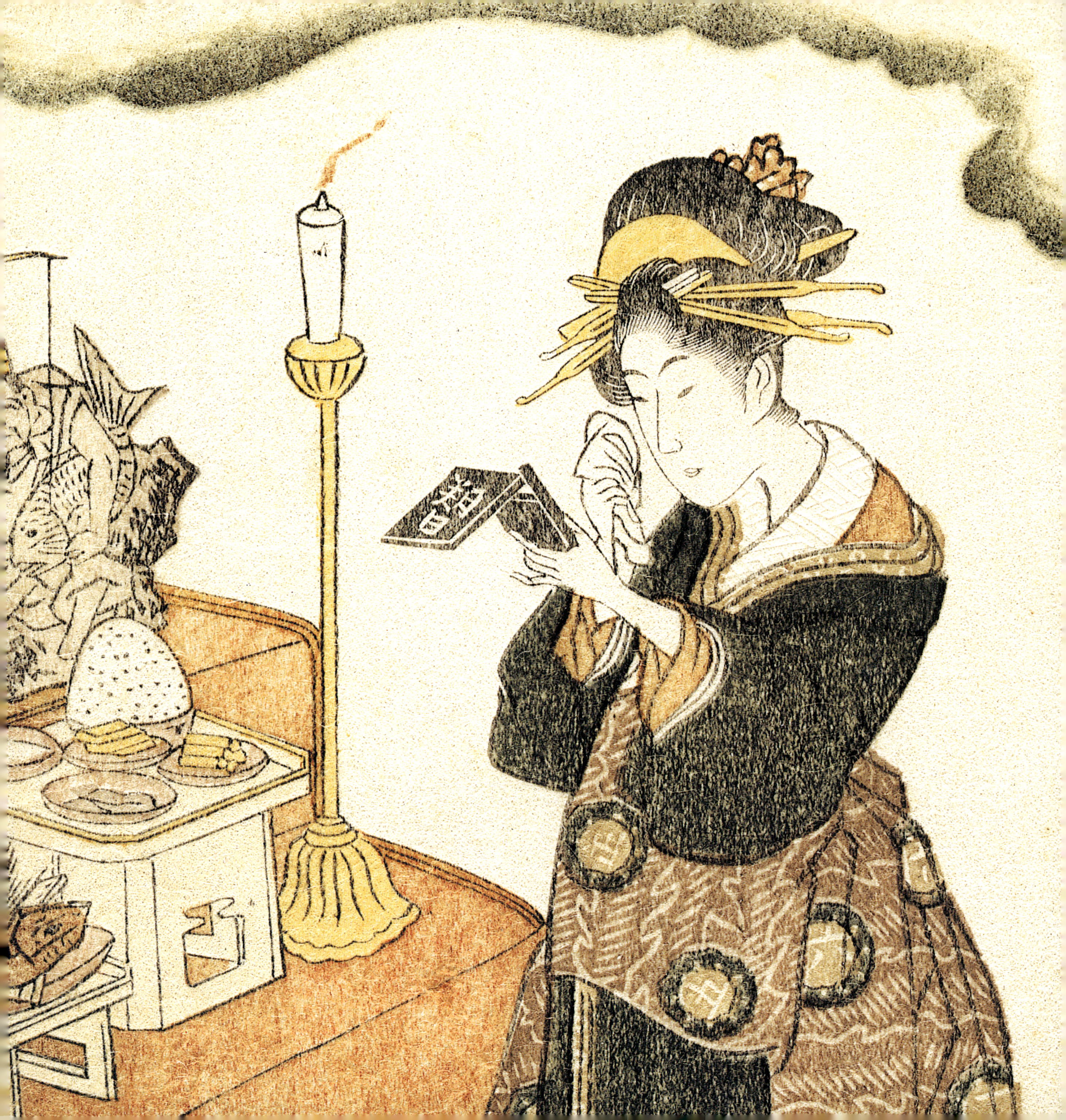

inscription on the strip of paper attached to the flowers reads *tsuitachi tatsu,* which indicates that the first of that month was a dragon day. The base of the flower vase itself may represent the talons of a dragon.

(10) Tenth month: A woman repairs her makeup as a black dog tries to attract her attention. Her mirror reads *tsuitachi* (first day). The tiered arrangement is for the Ebisu Festival, traditionally held in the first and tenth months, which celebrates this god of good luck, usually depicted as a fisherman. Once again the short months are indicated as an obi decoration, and the dog designates the first day of the month.

(11) Eleventh Month: A stately courtesan carries a white-rabbit sculpture on a tray symbolizing the first day of the month in 1799. She glances back at a desk with writing implements and a tablet bearing the numbers of the short months. The inscription on the envelope, as discussed above, announces the new Kabuki program for the year.

(12) Twelfth Month: Holding a toy monkey, a woman stokes a hibachi on which are inscribed the numbers for the long months. Written on a small box, the characters *tsuitachi* (first day) indicate that the month began on the day of the monkey. Narcissus flowers, which bloom through the second month, adorn the edge of her outer cloak. In the background is a branch decorated with rice-cake flowers.

UTAGAWA TOYOKUNI

1769–1825

59 A scene from *Akegarasu*

DATE ca. 1821
SIGNATURE Toyokuni ga
FORMAT Shikishiban diptych
(20.7 x 18.6, left; 20.7 x 18.8, right)
FLLW FDN 3011.001-.002

Ryūotei Hananari:

shirayuki ni	On a branch of plum
uzumu tachi-e no	poking out of the snow—
ume no hana	blossoms release their fragrance
harukaze no te ni	as they melt in the fingers
tokete nioeri	of the spring breeze.

Ryūfūtei Hanagaki:

masurao naru	Using a stick ladder
matsu no udegi o	made of sturdy pine beams—
chikara nite	the strong fragrance
Tsukiji o koeru	of plum blossoms
ume no hana no ka	climbs over into Tsukiji.

This boldly conceived surimono diptych portraying the Kabuki actors Segawa Kikunojō V (1802–32) on the right and Onoe Kikugorō III (1784–1849) holding a child seems to represent an imaginary performance of *Akegarasu Yume no Awayuki;* also known simply as *Akegarasu*. Although this story had already become one of the most popular pieces in the repertory of *shinnaibushi* (a school of narrative music) soon after it was written in 1772, it was not adapted for the Kabuki stage until 1851, over two decades after this print was issued. It was not uncommon, however, for surimono to depict imaginary performances of this sort as a novelty greeting card to be distributed at the New Year among members of an actor's fan club. In 1821, a *ninjōbon* (light romance novel) titled *Akegarasu Nochi no Masayume,* was published with illustrations by Utagawa Kuninao (1793–1854), a pupil of Toyokuni. Thus it is also possible that this surimono diptych was issued to help promote or commemorate his pupil's publication. The debut of the Kabuki version, *Akegarasu Hana no Nureginu,* at the Ichimura-za theatre in Edo in 1851 was commemorated by a triptych by Toyokuni's primary disciple Utagawa Kunisada that is notably similar in composition to this surimono diptych (see Rijksmuseum, *Hiroshige,*pl. 157).

In the later Kabuki version, based on actual events of 1769, the courtesan Urazato falls in love with one of her patrons, Kasugaya Tokijirō, a merchant whose family sold goods to the government. Their daughter, Midori, grew up in the brothel and later served as a *kamuro* (child attendant-apprentice to a courtesan).

Unfortunately, Urazato's passionate involvement with Tokijirō prevents her from attending to her other brothel clients. After catching them during a secret tryst, the owner of the bordello attempts to separate the lovers by punishing Urazato and tying her to a snow-covered pine tree in the courtyard. In the emotional climax depicted here, Tokijirō has secretly climbed the wall into the courtyard. He has untied his lover in order to rescue her and their daughter, before they make their daring escape.

Standing to the right, Urazato, represented by Kikunojō V, seductively clenches in her teeth the cloth which bound her to the pine. Tokijirō, represented by Kikugorō III, has seized Midori and is about to climb back up the green bamboo ladder. The pine tree, stone lantern, and other garden-courtyard elements unify the two sheets of the diptych, and together with the stark contrast provided by the whiteness of the embossed snow and the blackness of the wooden wall add to the dramatic quality of the scene. The poems, printed in gold, brighten the field of black.

Both poems, while introducing spring imagery, refer obliquely to theatrical props used in this performance. Tsukiji, famous today for its fish market, was close to the Edo theatre district.

ANONYMOUS

60 An octopus and its shell

DATE ca. 1830
PRINTER Shinzō
FORMAT Shikishiban
(20.1 x 18.0)
FLLW FDN 3027.002

Irifunetei Ōki:

hatchō no	With eight legs
roashi soroitsu	as oars in the stern
takobune ni	of her octopus boat,
kako bushi iwau	the captain sings to celebrate
haru no norizome	the first voyage of spring.

Takarabunesha:

nakazora no	Like a moon hanging
tsuki ni mo nitari	in the sky,
takobune no	the octopus boat
tayuta ni asobu	drifts playfully in spring
haru no unabara	over the fields of sea.

Floating on a golden sea, a *funedako* ("boat octopus"), an argonaut or paper nautilus, peers out at the viewer with small black eyes. The embossed gray and pink tentacles wind around its shell, which is beautifully articulated with gaufrage and delicate coloration. The female of the species spreads out her primary tentacle to form a webbed, sail-like arm on which it secretes a shell. The eggs are laid in this shell, commonly called *takobune* ("octopus boat"), which is a theme of both poems. *Takarabunesha,* the pen name of the second poet, refers to the boat carrying the Seven Gods of Good Fortune, and plays on the image of the "boat" of the octopus.

The artist of this surimono masterpiece has inexplicably chosen to remain anonymous. As with the Wright example, two other known impressions, each with slight variations in the color blocks, are unsigned. These other impressions are in the Arthur B. Duel Collection at the Arthur M. Sackler Museum, Harvard University Art Museums, and the Art Institute of Chicago. The seal of the printer Shinzō appears on surimono dating from the early 1820s through the mid 1830s (see also cat. no. 21). The delicate line and attention to detail, while reminiscent of the best of the work of Shumman a decade or two earlier, suggests the influence of Hokusai, and may represent the work of one of his top pupils. Certainly, the brilliance and fluidity of the design argue strongly for an attribution to a professional artist rather than to an amateur poet-artist.

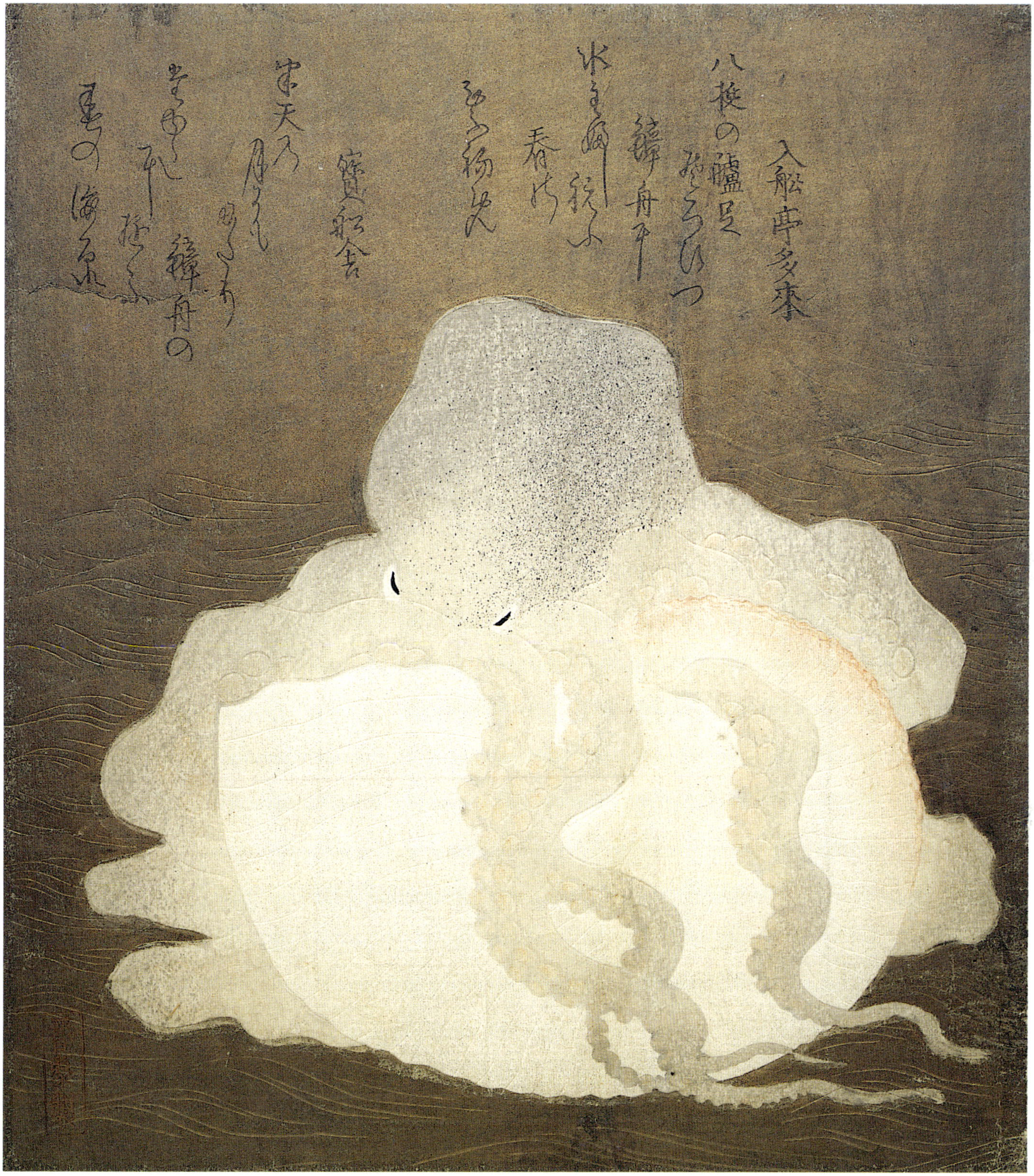
入船亭多楽

MONOCHROME
ENTRIES

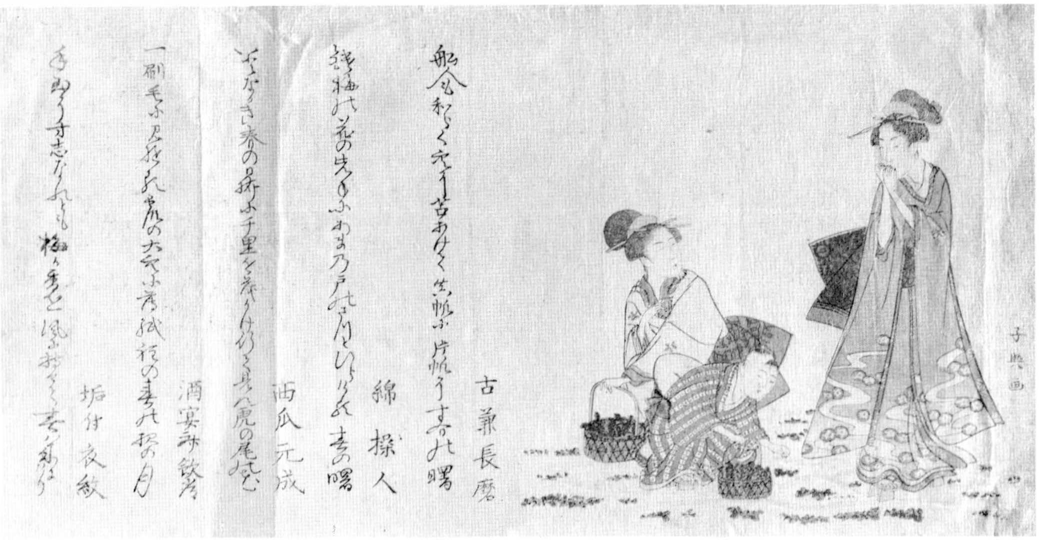

MOMOKAWA CHŌKI

ACT. CA. 1790–1810

61 A woman with a boy collecting herbs

DATE 1806
SIGNATURE Shikō ga
FORMAT Koban yoko-e (12.8 x 25.2)
REFERENCE *UT, Bibliothèque Nationale,* p.187, pl. 12
POETS Kogane Nagamaro, Wata no Kurihito, Suika Motonari, Shuensai Nomimasu, Akatsuki Emon
FLLW FDN 3057.002

Considerable confusion remains concerning the details of the life and works of Momokawa Chōki. Although early sources, including the *Ukiyo-e Ruikō,* clearly state that he also worked under the name Shikō, as seen here, some experts have speculated that works rendered with this artistic name, in a demonstrably different style, were by the hand of another artist. Indeed, it is difficult to detect in this surimono the brilliance that distinguishes the best of his portraits of beautiful women.

Since the third and fourth poems both mention the tiger, a dating to that zodiac year is appropriate.

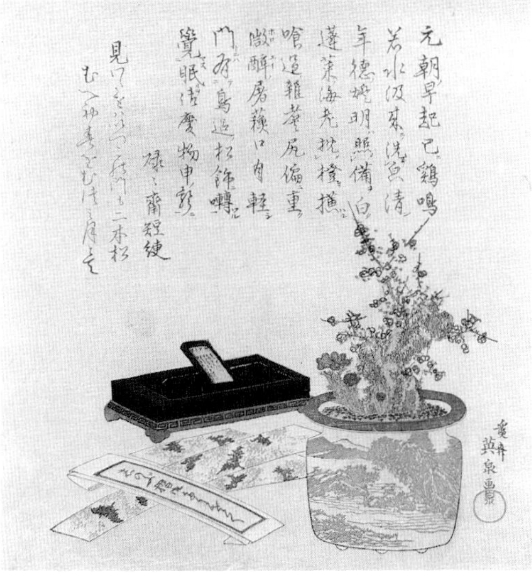

KEISAI EISEN

1790–1848

62 A dwarf plum, adonis plant, inkstone, and envelope

DATE 1825
SIGNATURE Keisai Eisen ga
ARTIST'S SEAL Sen
FORMAT Shikishiban (21.0 x 18.1)
REFERENCE Markus, *I Surimono*, 16 (on 18 there is another print, probably from the same set)
POET Rokurokusai Tankō
FLLW FDN 3020.003

In a blue-and-white porcelain planter is a gnarled minature plum tree and an adonis plant for the New Year. An inkstone and stick rest beside it with poem cards and their envelope on which is written *shinobu-zuri go-tanzaku,* "fern-patterned writing papers."

The opening line of the Chinese-style poem mentions the first crow of the cock of the New Year, perhaps an indication of the zodiac year. The style of the artist's signature is also in accordance with his dated works of the mid-1820s.

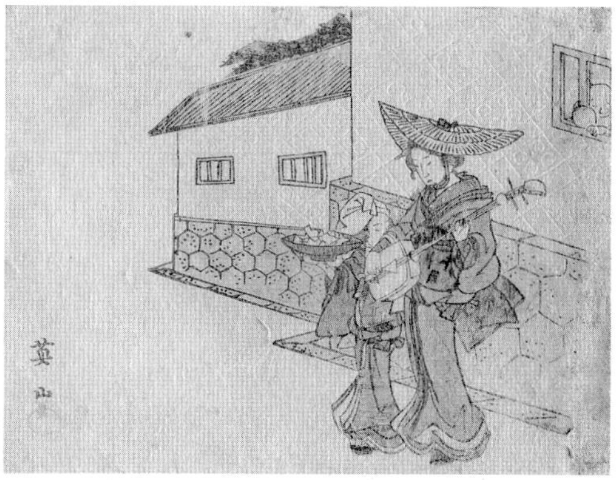

KIKUGAWA EIZAN
1787–1867

63 A child watching a street musician

DATE ca.1810
SIGNATURE Eizan
ARTIST'S SEAL Ei
FORMAT Koban yoko-e (9.5 x 12.4)
FLLW FDN 3018.001

From the window of a mansion, an amused child watches an itinerant woman musician as she plays the shamisen and her assistant carries a large bowl. Written on her obi are the numerals for the months indicating that this print was issued as an egoyomi, but they were printed in brass and are now illegible.

Eizan produced few surimono; rather, he specialized in traditional ukiyo-e prints of beautiful women in the manner of the late work of Utamaro. His pupils included Eisen, Eishō (Kōitsu), and Hidenobu.

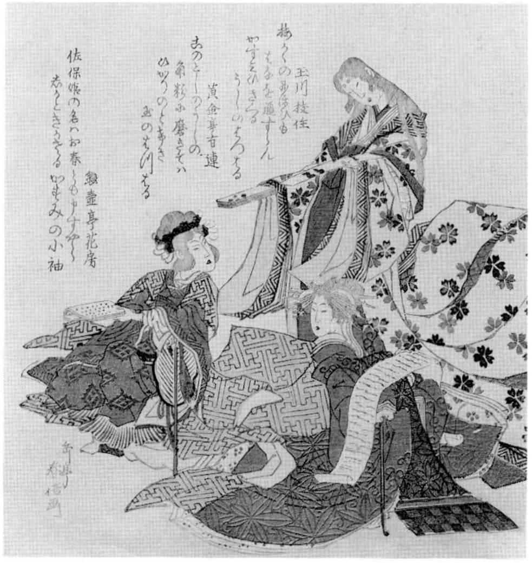

YASHIMA GAKUTEI
1786?–1868

64 Beautiful women of the three capitals

DATE 1817, Year of the Ox
SIGNATURE Gakutei Harunobu ga
FORMAT Shikishiban (21.1 x 18.7)
REFERENCE Keyes, *Beatty*, no.26
POETS Tamagawa Edazumi, Ōgontei Aritsura, Kenkotei Hanabusa
FLLW FDN 3010.009

This image is a clever variation on the popular ukiyo-e theme of the beauties of Edo, Kyoto, and Osaka. Instead of dressing the women in contemporary garb, the artist has given each woman a costume and coiffeur appropriate to one of the "three capitals" of ancient Japan: Nara, Heian-kyō, and Edo. The seated woman at the right is dressed in the Chinese-style robes of a princess or empress of eighth-century Nara. The standing woman wears elegant multi-layered robes and has long trailing hair, identifying her as a lady-in-waiting of the tenth or eleventh-century Heian court. In the foreground, an Edo courtesan holds a long-stemmed pipe and a love letter.

A dating of 1817 is indicated by the mention of an ox in two of the poems.

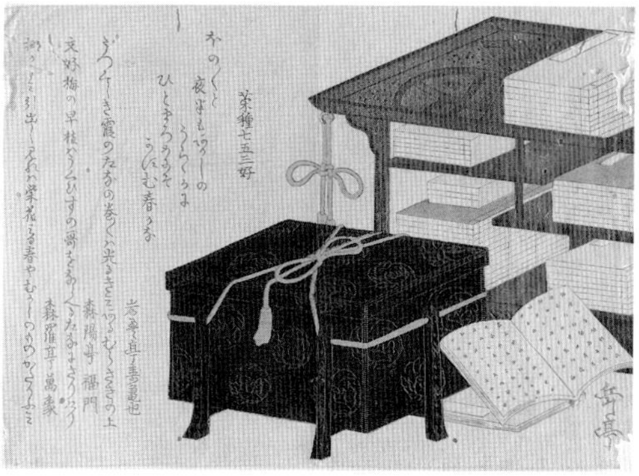

GAKUTEI

65 A bookcase, books, and a document chest

DATE ca. 1817
SIGNATURE Gakutei
FORMAT Koban yoko-e (12.8 x 17.6)
POETS Natane Shimezuki, Ganjōtei Sukinari, Shin'yōtei Fukumon, Shinratei Manzō
FLLW FDN 3010.038

A multi-legged black lacquer chest used for clothing or documents is decorated with the crane design associated with the poet Shinratei Manzō. It sits before a set of shelves filled with books. Each of the four accompanying poems alludes to classical literary themes. The poem by Natane Shimezuki is discussed on page 41.

The "Gakutei" signature on this surimono is an example of the artist's earliest signature style. Initially known as a talented kyōka poet, Gakutei was strongly influenced by Hokusai and turned to book illustrating. Eventually, he made his living as a surimono designer. By the mid-1820s, his surimono had increasingly complex compositions.

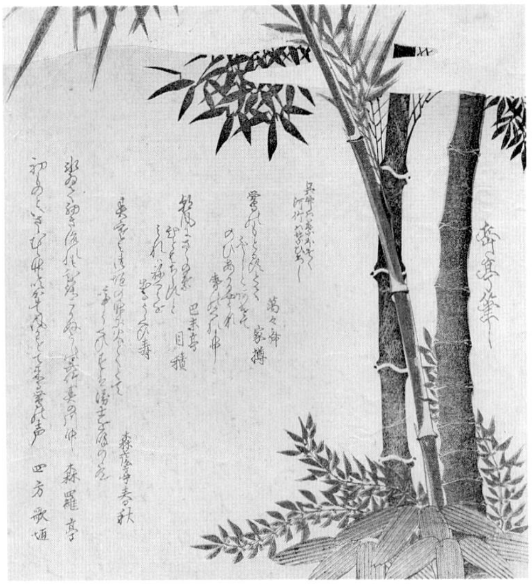

GAKUTEI

66 Varieties of bamboo

DATE ca. 1817
SIGNATURE Gakutei hitsu
FORMAT Shikishiban (21.1 x 18.8)
POETS Mammansai Ietaru, Hazuetei Metsumori, Shin'intei Haruaki, Shinratei, Yomo Utagaki
FLLW FDN 3010.039

Both the subject matter and composition are uncharacteristic of Gakutei's work in the print medium, but demonstrate his awareness of traditional Chinese-style ink painting. Inscribed in two columns to the right, the theme of the poems is a quotation from the *Tsurezuregusa (*Essays in Idleness), a collection of anecdotes and short essays composed around 1330 by the priest-literatus Yoshida Kenkō: *kuretake wa ha hosoku, kawatake wa ha hiroshi,* "Chinese bamboo has narrow leaves, river bamboo has broad leaves." This simple observation on two varieties of bamboo in the precincts of the ancient imperial palace has become the subject for an Edo kyōka-surimono.

Gakutei affected an elegant signature to resonate with the literary purport of the commission.

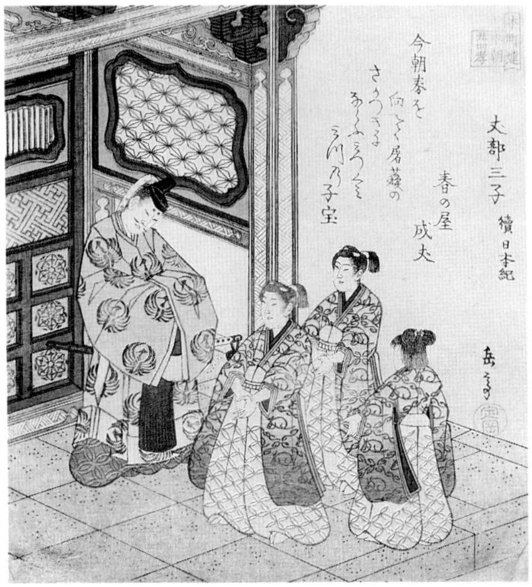

GAKUTEI

67 Three obeisant boys standing before their father

TITLE *Hasetsukabe Sanshi, Shoku Nihongi*; Three Filial Sons of Hasetsukabe from *The Chronicles of Japan Continued*
SERIES *Honchō-ren Honchō Nijūshikō*; Twenty-four Paragons of Filial Piety for the Honchō Circle
DATE ca.1820
SIGNATURE Gakutei
ARTIST'S SEAL Sadaoka
FORMAT Shikishiban (21.0 x 18.9)
REFERENCES Rijksmuseum, *Hokusai,* pl. 211; Polster, no. 64; Hempel, *Scheiwe*, no.361
POET Harunoya Naritake
FLLW FDN 3010.010

The series illustrates stories of filial piety based on Confucian principles (see also cat. no. 3–4). Of the twenty-four surimono in the series, the Wright collection includes fifteen (for the entire series see Hempel, *Scheiwe,* pls. 354–77).

This may be an illustration of the tale of a father and his three sons found in the *Shoku Nihongi*. After each of his sons fails to break an arrow by himself, the father instructs the boys that only if they join forces will they succeed.

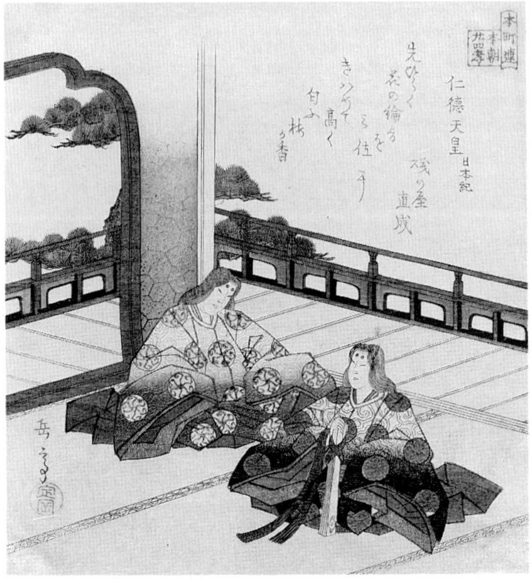

GAKUTEI

68 Prince Nintoku and his brother

TITLE *Nintoku Tennō, Nihongi;* Nintoku from the *Chronicles of Japan*
SERIES *Honchō-ren Honchō Nijūshikō*; Twenty-four Paragons of Filial Piety for the Honchō Circle
DATE ca.1820
SIGNATURE Gakutei
ARTIST'S SEAL Sadaoka
FORMAT Shikishiban (21.2 x 18.9)
REFERENCES Rijksmuseum, *Hokusai,* pl. 219; Hempel, *Scheiwe,* no. 367; Polster, no. 68
POET Isonoya Naonari
FLLW FDN 3010.020

The two young noblemen portrayed in the garb and hairsyles of ancient princes sit on a veranda by an arched doorway. They are Prince Nintoku and his brother, who both initially refused to become emperor. Their story is told in the *Nihongi.*

The poem, in describing a plum that is the first to blossom as "sovereign," alludes to the the elder brother's initial refusal to rule and his eventual acceptance of the position.

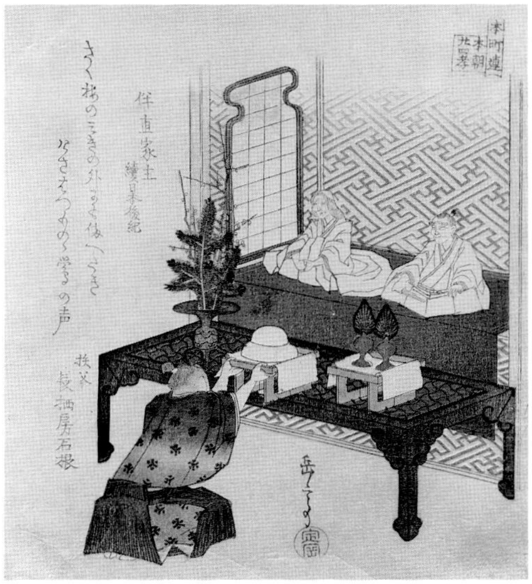

GAKUTEI

69 A man at an altar with an offering

TITLE *Tomo no Naoie Nushi, Shoku Nihonkōki*; Tomo no Naoie Nushi from the *Later Records of Japan*
SERIES *Honchō-ren Honchō Nijūshikō*; Twenty-four Paragons of Filial Piety for the Honchō Circle
DATE ca. 1820
SIGNATURE Gakutei
ARTIST'S SEAL Sadaoka
FORMAT Shikishiban (21.0 x 18.9)
REFERENCES Rijksmuseum, *Hokusai,* pl. 212; Hempel, *Scheiwe,* pl. 357
POET Chōseibō Iwane
FLLW FDN 3010.011

A young man at an altar makes an offering of dried New Year's rice cakes to statues of his deceased parents. Also on the altar is a bronze vase with pine boughs and a serving tray with two ceremonial bottles. The source for this story is the *Shoku Nihonkōki*, which treats the period 833–50.

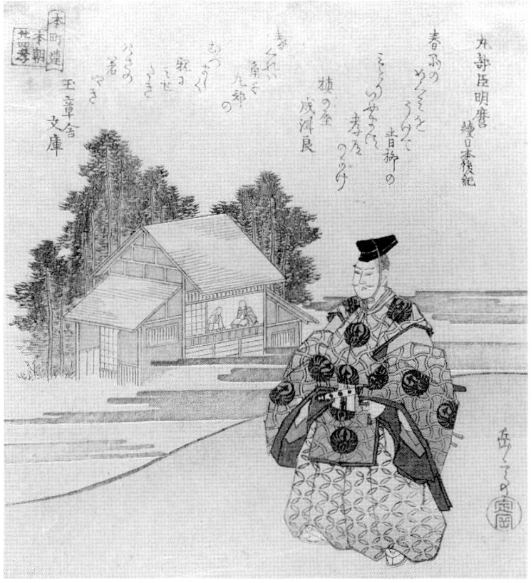

GAKUTEI

70 A courtier in ceremonial robes stands before his parents' house

TITLE *Wanibe Omi Akimaro, Shoku Nihonkōki;* Wanibe Omi Akimaro from the *Later Records of Japan*
SERIES *Honchō-ren Honchō Nijūshikō*; Twenty-four Paragons of Filial Piety for the Honchō Circle
DATE ca. 1820
SIGNATURE Gakutei
ARTIST'S SEAL Sadaoka
FORMAT Shikishiban (21.0 x 18.9)
REFERENCE Hempel, *Scheiwe*, no. 356
POETS Makinoya Naritsura, Gyokushōsha Bunko
FLLW FDN 3010.022

The *Shoku Nihonkōki* covers the reign of Emperor Nimmyō (833–50). According to the entry for the Tenth Month of 848, Wanibe Ōmi Akimaro received a commendation from the palace for his filial devotion, and he was exempted from paying taxes in his old age. Earlier in his career he had relinquished a court-appointed administrative post to his father so that his parents could enjoy the benefits. When they grew old, he visited them every day, morning and evening, even though they lived over ten miles away.

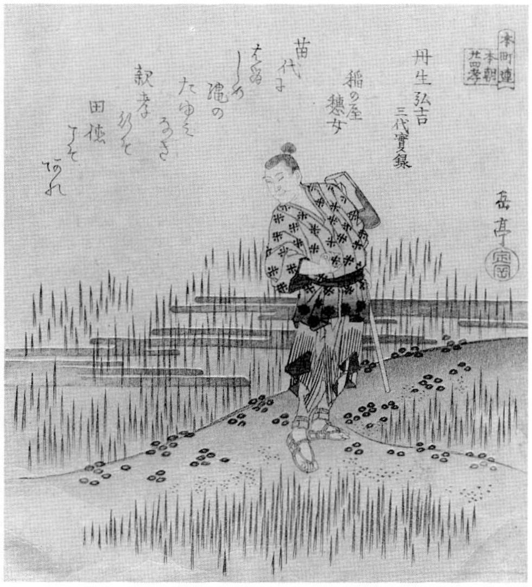

GAKUTEI

71 A farmer holding his hoe on a path between rice fields

TITLE *Nibu Hiroyoshi, Sandai Jitsuroku*; Nibu Hiroyoshi from the *Official Chronicles of Three Imperial Reigns*
SERIES *Honchō-ren Honchō Nijūshikō*; Twenty-four Paragons of Filial Piety for the Honchō Circle
DATE ca. 1820
SIGNATURE Gakutei
ARTIST'S SEAL Sadaoka
FORMAT Shikishiban (21.2 x 19.1)
REFERENCES Keyes, *Beatty*, no. 34; Rijksmuseum, *Hokusai,* pl. 222; Hempel, *Scheiwe,* no. 358
POET Inanoya Home
FLLW FDN 3010.013

The source for this image is the *Sandai Jitsuroku,* which covers the years 858–87 and the reigns of three emperors. The poem likens a sacred rope strung across a newly planted rice field, which never slackens, to the filial piety of the rice farmer.

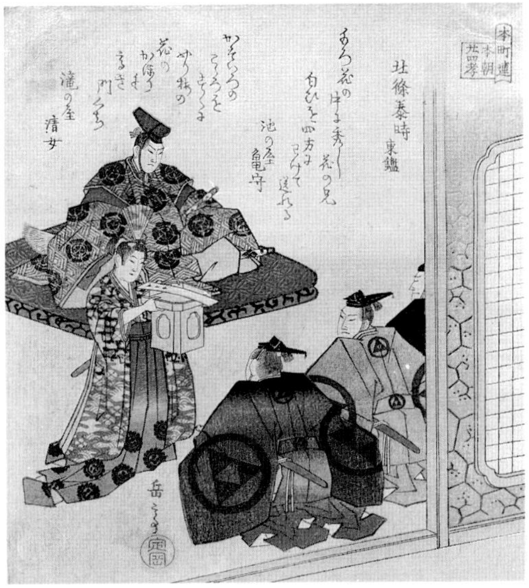

GAKUTEI

72 A seated general facing three retainers

TITLE *Hōjō Yasutoki, Azuma Kagami*; Hōjō Yasutoki from the *Mirror of the East*
SERIES *Honchō-ren Honchō Nijūshikō*; Twenty-four Paragons of Filial Piety for the Honchō Circle
DATE ca. 1820
SIGNATURE Gakutei
ARTIST'S SEAL Sadaoka
FORMAT Shikishiban (21.0 x 18.8)
REFERENCES Rijksmuseum, *Hokusai,* pl. 216; Hempel, *Scheiwe*, no. 354; Polster, no. 91
POETS Ikenoya Kamemori, Takinoya Kiyome
FLLW FDN 3010.021

Three men sit across from their lord as a young servant brings a poem or letter on a tray to the left-hand figure. Yasutoki (1183–1242) was the third Hōjō regent in the lineage of the advisors to the shogun in Kamakura. According to Hempel, *Scheiwe,* number 354, this print shows Yasutoki receiving a commendation for his filial piety from Minamoto no Sanetomo. *Azuma Kagami* is a history of the Kamakura military government covering 1180 to 1266.

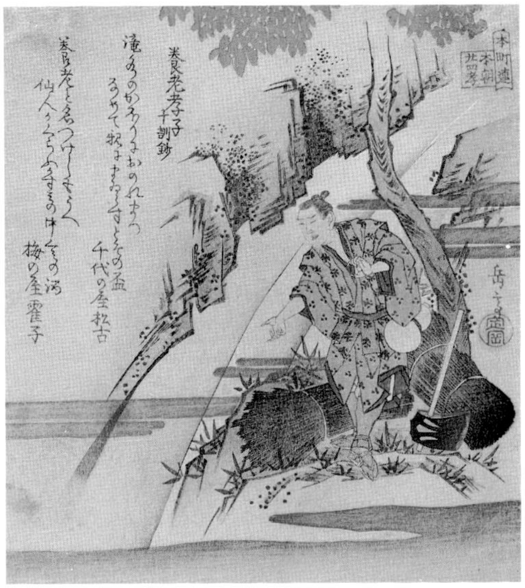

GAKUTEI

73 The woodcutter Kosagi

TITLE *Yōrō Kōshi, Jikkunshō*; Devoted Son at Yōrō Waterfall, from the *Treatise of Ten Moral Teachings*
SERIES *Honchō-ren Honchō Nijūshikō*; Twenty-four Paragons of Filial Piety for the Honchō Circle
DATE ca. 1820
SIGNATURE Gakutei
ARTIST'S SEAL Sadaoka
FORMAT Shikishiban (21.0 x 18.6)
REFERENCES Keyes, *Beatty*, no. 35; Rijksmuseum, *Hokusai*, pl. 220; Hempel, *Scheiwe*, no. 365
POETS Chiyonoya Matsufuru, Umenoya Tsuruko
FLLW FDN 3010.014

This surimono illustrates the story of the poor woodcutter Kosagi, who was unable to afford his father's daily cup of wine. Instead he drew a cup of water from a waterfall. Moved by his filial piety, the gods turned the water into wine. The falls from which the water was taken was renamed Yōrō (Nourishment for Old Age).

The *Jikkunshō* is an anthology of didactic tales (*setsuwa*) completed around 1252.

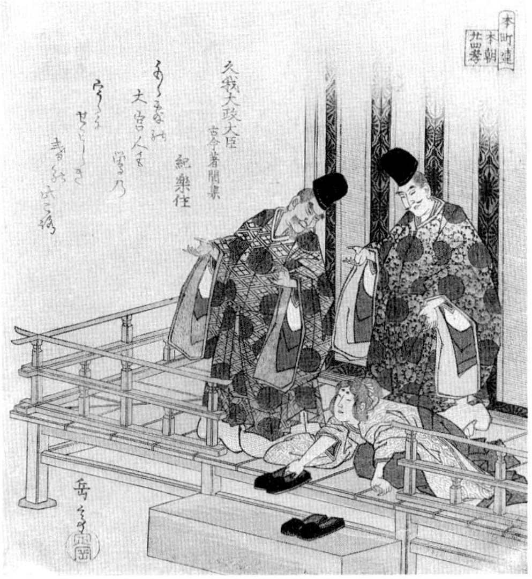

GAKUTEI

74 Two courtiers watch a boy

TITLE *Kuga Dajōdaijin, Kokon Chomonjū*; Prime Minister Kuga from *Stories Heard from Writers Old and New*
SERIES *Honchō-ren Honchō Nijūshikō*; Twenty-four Paragons of Filial Piety for the Honchō Circle
DATE ca. 1820
SIGNATURE Gakutei
ARTIST'S SEAL Sadaoka
FORMAT Shikishiban (19.0 x 18.8)
REFERENCES Rijksmuseum, *Hokusai,* pl. 205; Hempel, *Scheiwe,* no. 377
POET Ki no Rakuzumi
FLLW FDN 3010.023

Minamoto no Masazane (1059–1127) was also known as Kuga Dajōdaijin (the Kuga Prime Minister). *Kokon Chomonjū* (Stories Heard from Writers Old and New), is a collection of didactic tales compiled in 1254 by Tachibana no Narisue. When Masazane was nine years old, his father and grandfather, both high-ranking courtiers, were walking through a palace building and were about to enter a courtyard in their bare feet when Masazane thoughtfully brought them their shoes, which he had been carrying in his robes.

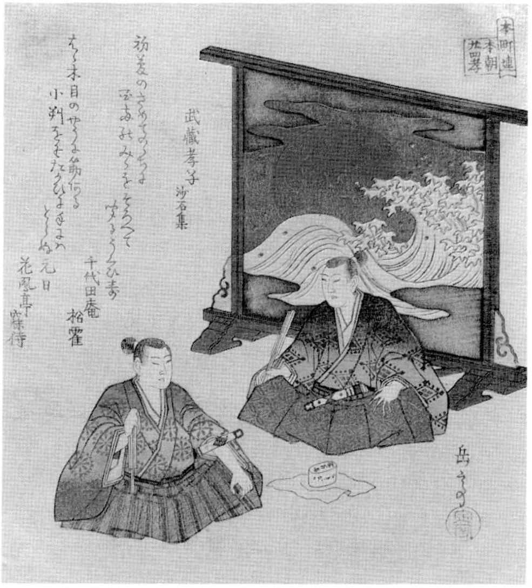

GAKUTEI

75 Two men seated before a screen with a gold piece

TITLE *Musashi Kōshi, Shasekishū*; A Filial Son from Musashi Province from the *Sand and Pebbles*
SERIES *Honchō-ren Honchō Nijūshikō*; Twenty-four Paragons of Filial Piety for the Honchō Circle
DATE ca. 1820
SIGNATURE Gakutei
ARTIST'S SEAL Sadaoka
FORMAT Shikishiban (21.0 x 18.8)
REFERENCES Rijksmuseum, *Hokusai,* pl. 208; Hempel, *Scheiwe*, no. 375; Polster, no. 74
POETS Chiyodaan Matsutsuru, Kahōtei Nemachi
FLLW FDN 3010.017

The story depicted here is that of two friends whose fathers, one rich and one poor, were also close friends. The poor son has a dream in which his deceased father orders him to repay a debt to the rich son, whose father has also died. The poor son tries to fulfill his filial obligation by offering a piece of gold to his friend, but the wealthy son refuses the money from his impoverished comrade. The sons instead decide to make an offering for the repose of both fathers, thus fulfilling their moral responsibilities.

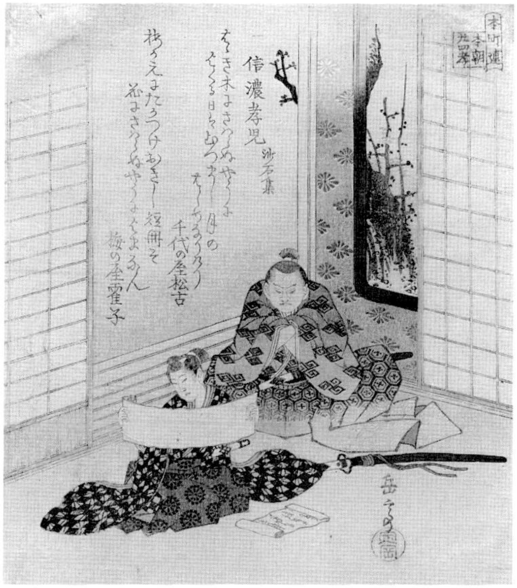

GAKUTEI

76 A young man reading documents as an older samurai watches

TITLE *Shinano Kōji, Shasekishū*; Filial Son from Shinano Province from the *Sand and Pebbles*
SERIES *Honchō-ren Honchō Nijūshikō*; Twenty-four Paragons of Filial Piety for the Honchō Circle
DATE ca. 1820
SIGNATURE Gakutei
ARTIST'S SEAL Sadaoka
FORMAT Shikishiban (21.4 x 18.8)
REFERENCES Rijksmuseum, *Hokusai,* pl. 207; Hempel, *Scheiwe*, no. 363
POETS Chiyonoya Matsufuru, Umenoya Tsuruko
FLLW FDN 3010.019

The source of this story is the *Shasekishū*, a collection of moralizing but often entertaining tales written by the Buddhist priest Mujū Ichien (1226–83). The image is based on the story of a wealthy land steward in Musashi Province who had earlier bought the land of one of his impoverished neighbors. When the man died the wealthy man handed over the deeds to the son who had been left penniless. The sword between them may represent the deceased father.

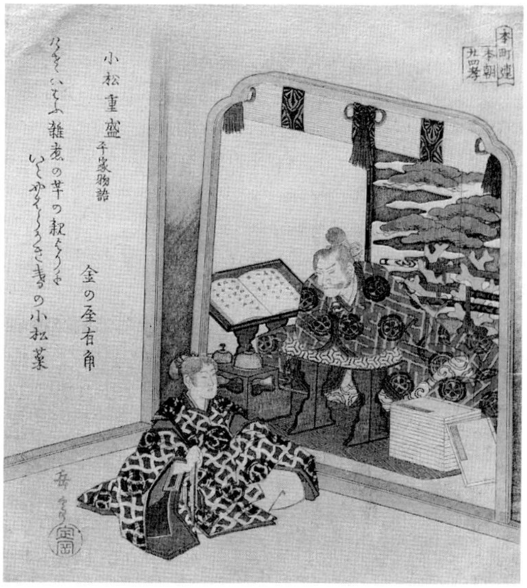

GAKUTEI

77 Taira no Kiyomori and Shigemori

TITLE *Komatsu Shigemori, Heike Monogatari;* Komatsu Shigemori from *The Tale of Heike*
SERIES *Honchō-ren Honchō Nijūshikō*; Twenty-four Paragons of Filial Piety for the Honchō Circle
DATE ca. 1820
SIGNATURE Gakutei
ARTIST'S SEAL Sadaoka
FORMAT Shikishiban (21.0 x 18.9)
REFERENCES Rijksmuseum, *Hokusai,* pl. 223; Hempel, *Scheiwe,* no. 371
POET Kanenoya Arizumi
FLLW FDN 3010.018

Taira no Kiyomori sits in an alcove amongst his books and converses with his son Shigemori (1138–79). Unlike his tyrannical father, Shigemori had a just and honest temperment. He would frequently intervene with sound advice hoping to mitigate against his father's aggressive and despotic tendencies. He supported Emperor Go Shirakawa during insurrections that had resulted from his father's attempt to usurp imperial power. Thus Shigemori is considered the model of fidelity to the emperor.

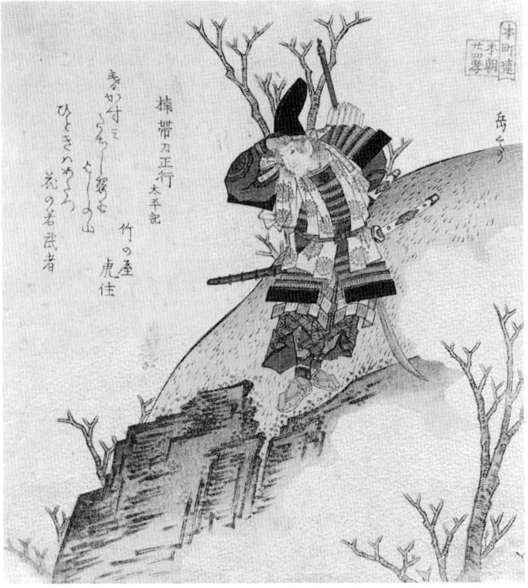

GAKUTEI

78 A warrior on a hill by blossoming cherry trees

TITLE *Kusunoki Tatewaki Masatsura, Taiheiki*; Kusunoki Masatsura, from the *Record of the Great Peace*
SERIES *Honchō-ren Honchō Nijūshikō*; Twenty-four Paragons of Filial Piety for the Honchō Circle
DATE ca.1820
SIGNATURE Gakutei
FORMAT Shikishiban (21.2 x 18.9)
REFERENCES Hempel, *Scheiwe,* no.364; Polster, no.76
POET Takenoya Torazumi
FLLW FDN 3010.012

Masatsura, oldest son of the famous warrior Masashige, was a loyal retainer and brilliant military tactician who fought first for Emperor Go Daigo and then for Emperor Go Murakami against the Hōjō clan. Masatsura is shown here leaving Yoshino, the capital of the Southern Dynasty, for the fatal battle in which he and his younger brother were critically wounded and committed double-suicide. Masatsura was only twenty-three when he died.

The poem mentions Mount Yoshino, famous for its cherry trees, and compares their short-lived flowers to a young warrior.

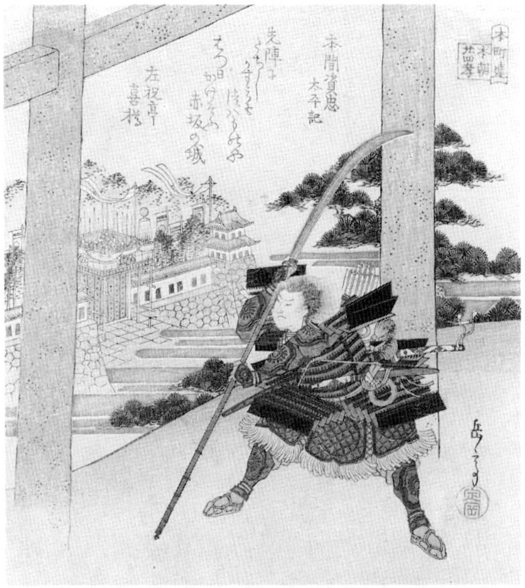

GAKUTEI

79 Suketada in full military attire before a *torii* gate

TITLE *Homma Suketada, Taiheiki*; Homma Suketada from the *Record of the Great Peace*
SERIES *Honchō-ren Honchō Nijūshikō*; Twenty-four Paragons of Filial Piety for the Honchō Circle
DATE ca.1820
SIGNATURE Gakutei
ARTIST'S SEAL Sadaoka
FORMAT Shikishiban (21.2 x 18.8)
REFERENCES Rijksmuseum, *Hokusai,* pl. 215; Hempel, *Scheiwe*, no. 362; Kruml, 1975, pl. 44
POET Sashukutei Kitaru
FLLW FDN 3010.016

Homma Suketada was a loyal retainer of the Hōjō clan, and is best known for his valor at the battle of Akasaka Castle, in which he was slain at age eighteen. Just prior to this battle, Suketada wrote a death poem for his deceased father on the stone torii at Tennōji Temple.

The *Taiheiki,* the source for this story, is a record of military intrigue and political history from 1318 to 1367, when the Emperor Go Daigo attempted to wrest control of the government from the ruling Hōjō regents.

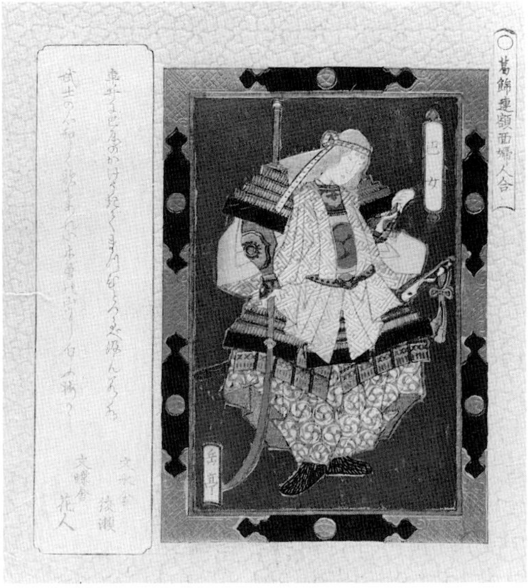

GAKUTEI

80 A woman warrior

TITLE *Tomoe Jo*; Lady Tomoe
SERIES *Katsushika-ren Gakumen Fujin Awase*; Framed Paintings of Women for the Katsushika Circle
DATE ca.1822
SIGNATURE Gakutei
FORMAT Shikishiban (21.1 x 18.6)
REFERENCES Keyes, *Beatty*, no.62; Kruml, 1989, pl.117; Polster, no. 72
POETS Bunsuisha Ayase, Bunchōsha Hanahito
FLLW FDN 3010.030

Tomoe Gozen, a twelfth-century woman warrior renowned for her bravery and beauty, is depicted in full armor with a long-handled halberd and a pair of swords. The *mitsudomoe* (three-comma) pattern on her breastplate derives from her name. She fought bravely beside her husband, Minamoto (Kiso) no Yoshinaka, until he was slain in the epic battle of Uji River in 1184 . She later became the mistress of Wada Yoshinori, with whom she had a son, Asahina no Saburō, who is remembered in legend for his herculean strength (see also cat. no. 127). For a discussion on this series see cat. no. 5.

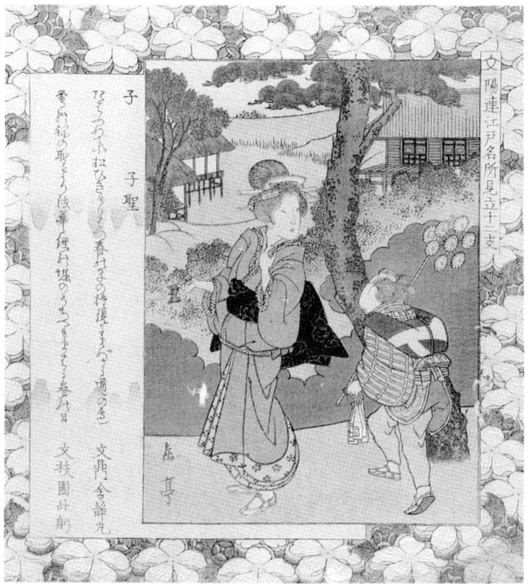

GAKUTEI

81 A woman and a boy with a pinwheel

TITLE *Ne, Ne no Hijiri*; Rat, The Rat Shrine
SERIES *Ichiyō-ren Edo Meisho Mitate Jūnishi*; Famous Places of Edo Compared to the Twelve Animals of the Zodiac for the Ichiyō Circle
DATE ca. 1825
SIGNATURE Gakutei
FORMAT Shikishiban (21.0 x 19.0)
REFERENCE Polster, no. 101
POETS Bunteisha Shizumaru, Bunshien Konomi
FLLW FDN 3010.025

This series of twelve surimono was commissioned by the Ichiyō-ren, a poetry circle affiliated with Katsushika Group, as indicated by the *bun*-character emblem of the group in the title cartouche (see also cat. nos. 8, 82, 83). Each print takes as its theme a famous shrine in Edo that has some connection to a zodiac animal. In each print a beautiful woman, either alone or with a companion, makes a pilgrimage to a shrine. Here, the specific shrine has yet to be identified, but Ne no Hijiri ("the rat saint") refers to ceremonies held at various shrines dedicated to rats and their patron deity Daikokuten. The mention of Hokkekyō no Hori (Lotus Sutra Canal) in the second poem may provide a clue to the location of this particular shrine.

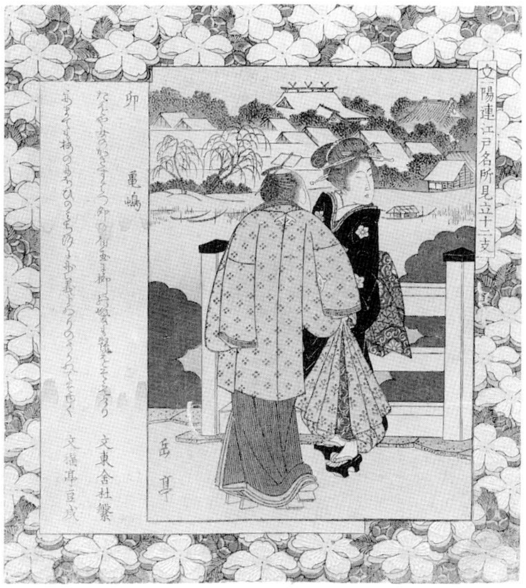

GAKUTEI

82 A man and woman standing on a bridge

TITLE *U, Kamejima*; Rabbit, Kamejima (Bridge)
SERIES *Ichiyō-ren Edo Meisho Mitate Jūnishi*; Famous Places in Edo Compared to the Twelve Animals of the Zodiac for the Ichiyō Circle
DATE ca. 1825
SIGNATURE Gakutei
FORMAT Shikishiban (21.4 x 18.9)
REFERENCES Keyes, *Beatty*, no. 86; Rijksmuseum, *Hokusai,* pl. 263; Polster, no. 104; *Collection Ernest Le Vèel, (3e vente),* no. 155
POETS Buntōsha Morishige, Bumbukutei Mamenari
FLLW FDN 3010.026

A man whose coat bears the emblem of the Ichiyō poetry club stands with a woman on Kamejima Bridge. In his hair is a paper talisman given to visitors at Myōgi Shrine in Kameido on the first rabbit day of the New Year.

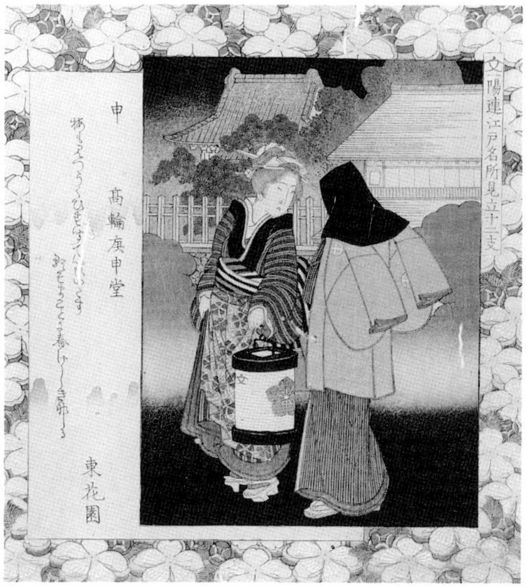

GAKUTEI

83 A man and woman on the street at night

TITLE *Saru, Takanawa Kōshindō*; Monkey, Takanawa Kōshindō
SERIES *Ichiyō-ren Edo Meisho Mitate Jūnishi*; Famous Places in Edo Compared to the Twelve Animals of the Zodiac for the Ichiyō Circle
DATE ca. 1825
FORMAT Shikishiban (21.3 x 19.0)
REFERENCE Hillier, *Japanese Prints and Drawings from the Vever Collection,* vol. 3, no. 786c
POET Tōkaen
FLLW FDN 3010.028

A woman with a lantern bearing the *bun*-character emblem of the Ichiyō poetry club stops in the evening to chat with a hooded man. The Kōshindō Shrine in the Takanawa district of Edo was devoted to the worship of Shōmen Kongō, the Japanese name for a Chinese divinity with a blue, monkey-like face. Pilgrims traditionally visited the shrine on the day of the monkey.

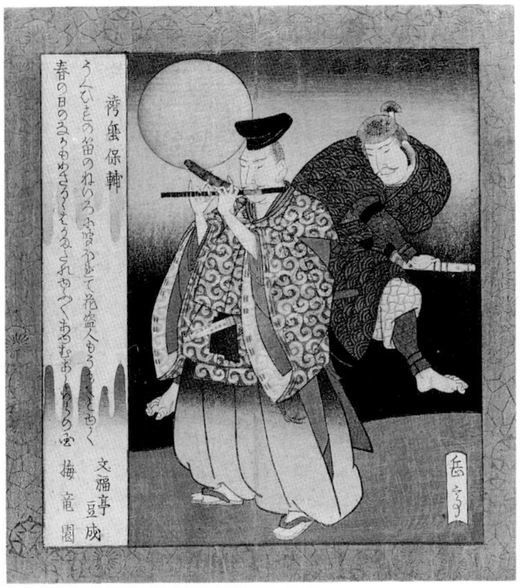

GAKUTEI

84 A thief and a courtier

TITLE *Hakamadare Yasusuke*
SERIES *Uji Shūi Monogatari, A Collection of Tales from Uji*
DATE ca.1830
SIGNATURE Gakutei
FORMAT Shikishiban (21.0 x 19.0)
REFERENCE Keyes, *Beatty*, no.94
POETS Bumbukutei Mamenari, Bairyūen
FLLW FDN 3010.006

This series of at least seven prints is based on the *Uji Shūi Monogatari,* a collection of didactic tales compiled in the late twelfth or early thirteenth century. Here, the thief Hakamadare, who had planned to steal the fine cloak of Fujiwara no Yasumasa (958–1036), is mesmerized by the courtier's flute playing and abandons the attack. Later Yasumasa presents the thief with his warm cloak and admonishes him to give up his evil ways.

Each print in the series has a brown border composed of a cracked-ice pattern with roundels of plum blossoms and a motif of three characters reading *bun*, the emblem of the Katsushika poetry group.

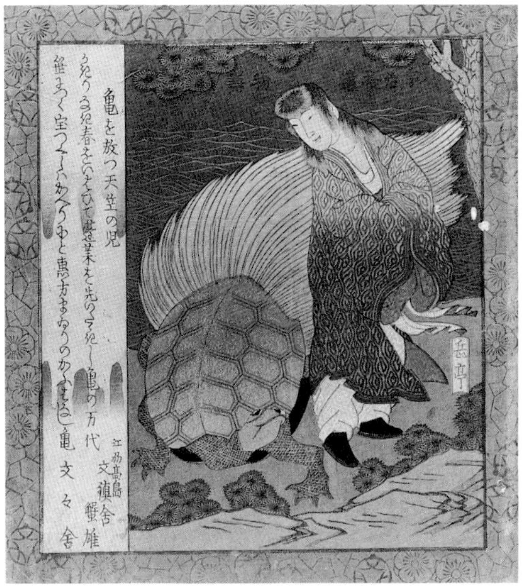

GAKUTEI

85 A boy and a turtle

TITLE *Kame o Hanatsu Tenjiku no Ko*; The Child from India Who Released the Turtle
SERIES *Uji Shūi Monogatari*; *A Collection of Tales from Uji*
DATE ca.1830
SIGNATURE Gakutei
FORMAT Shikishiban (21.2 x 18.4)
REFERENCES Keyes, *Beatty* no.96; Galerie de l'Imagerie, pl. 9; Uhlenbeck, pl.10
POETS Bunchinsha Kanio of Takashima Gōshū (Ōmi, now Shiga Pref.), Bumbunsha
FLLW FDN 3010.007

The story depicted here relates how a boy saved five turtles from death by purchasing them, using money entrusted to him by his father. He returned home empty handed, expecting to be reprimanded by his father. Instead, he learned that the money he had spent on the turtles had been reimbursed by five mysterious men—the turtles in their true form.

Some impressions of this design were mistakenly printed with the wrong title and poetry cartouche (see Keyes, *Beatty*, no.96).

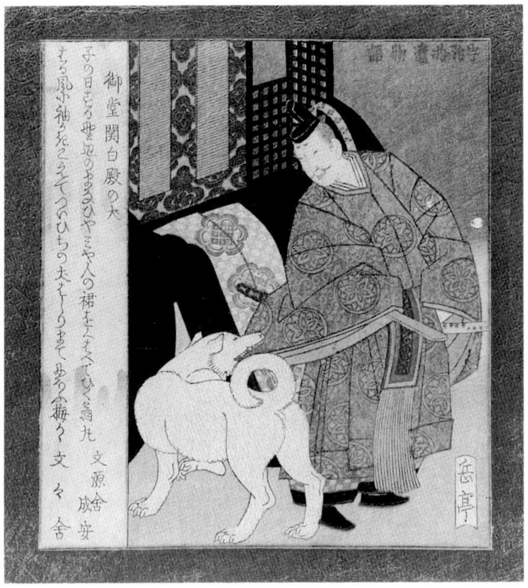

GAKUTEI

86 A white dog nipping at the sleeve of Fujiwara no Michinaga

TITLE *Midō Kampaku-dono no Inu*, The Dog of Midō Kampaku
SERIES *Uji Shūi Monogatari*; *A Collection of Tales from Uji*
DATE ca.1830
SIGNATURE Gakutei
FORMAT Shikishiban (21.2 x 19.1)
REFERENCES *Paul F. Walter Collection of Surimono,* pl. 51; Uhlenbeck, pl. 11
POETS Bungensha Nariyasu, Bumbunsha
FLLW FDN 3010.008

"Midō Kampaku" refers to Fujiwara no Michinaga (966–1027), without question the most powerful man in Japan during his tenure as the chief advisor to the emperors of the mid-Heian period.

The image refers to the tale of Michinaga's white dog, who by biting on the hem of his master's robe, drew his attention to a spot where two cursed vessels lay buried, thereby saving his life. A fuller discussion of the print is given on page 50.

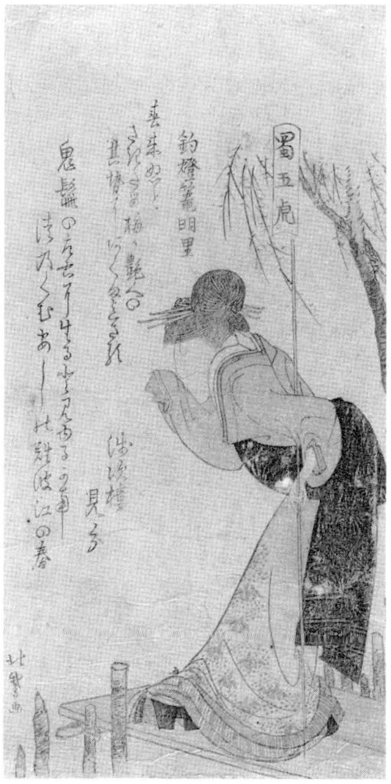

HŌTEI GOSEI

CA. 1804 -1835 (D.)

87 A young woman with a narrow pole standing on the end of a pier

SERIES *Shoku Go Ko*; Five Tiger Generals
DATE Probably 1806, Year of the Tiger
SIGNATURE Hokuga ga
FORMAT Koban tate-e (21.6 x 10.5)
POETS Tsuridōrō Akesato, Senjirō Miwake
FLLW FDN 3009.002

Hōtei Gosei was a minor pupil of Hokusai, who gave him the name Hokuga, which Gosei used until 1810. Consequently, Gosei's early work is frequently confused with that of the lesser-known Karyōsai Hokuga. Gosei specialized in surimono, book illustration, and painting.

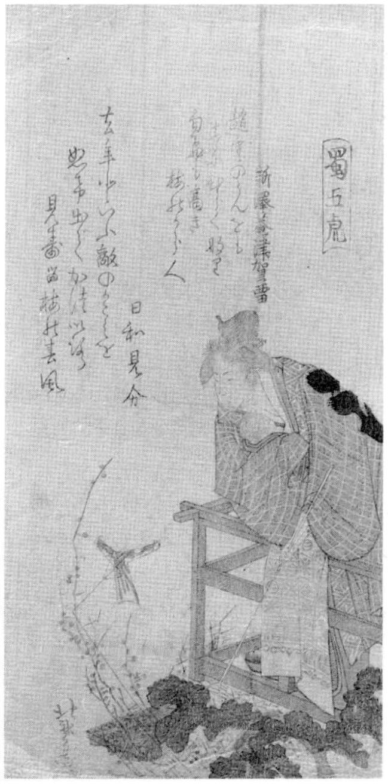

GOSEI

88 A woman on a balcony holding a child

SERIES *Shoku Go Ko*; Five Tiger Generals
DATE Probably 1806, Year of the Tiger
SIGNATURE Hokuga ga
FORMAT Koban tate-e (21.4 x 10.7)
POETS Shintakuan Tsukaru, Hiyori Miwake
FLLW FDN 3009.003

The collection has four of the five designs from this set. Each parodies one of the five famous generals whose stories are told in the Chinese war tale known in Japanese as the *Suikoden*.

A woman holds a child to her breast as she leans out over a veranda. She uses a forked pole to attempt to disentangle a kite from a plum tree, both references to the New Year.

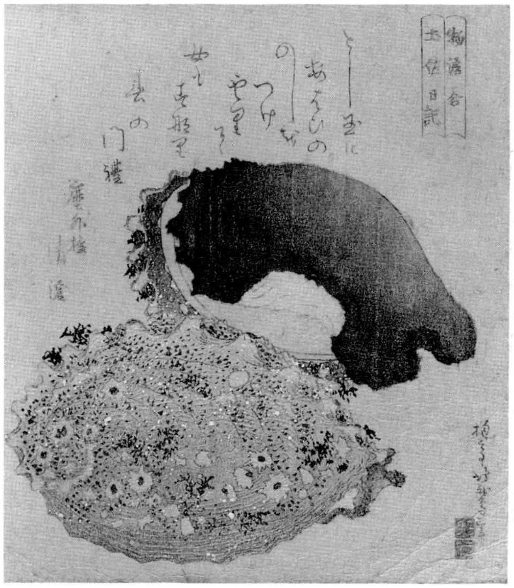

GOSEI

89 An abalone shell

TITLE *Tosa Nikki*; *Tosa Diary*
SERIES *Monogatari Awase*; Selections from Tales
DATE Probably 1809
SIGNATURE Hōtei Hokuga hitsu
ARTIST'S SEAL Hoku; Ga
FORMAT Shikishiban (21.2 x 18.3)
REFERENCES Preetorius, p.15; another impression is in the collection of the Tokyo National Museum
POET Jingairō Kiyozumi
FLLW FDN 3009.005

The title of the print, *Tosa Nikki,* refers to a poetry journal written in about 935 by the courtier poet Ki no Tsurayuki (ca. 872–945), which records the events of his return by ship from Tosa Province to the capital. The poem mentions the dried abalone strip usually tied to gifts at the New Year.

Abalone shells were a famous product of Enoshima and thus perhaps the print dates to 1809, a snake year, because of the traditional associations of the Benzaiten Shrine on Enoshima with snakes. It is also thought that Hōtei Hokuga changed his name to Gosei in 1810.

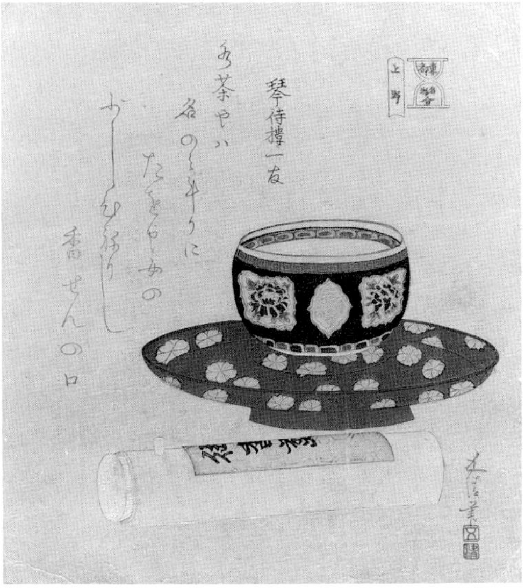

GOSEI

90 A cup and saucer with a *kōsen* powder canister

TITLE Ueno
SERIES *Tōto Meibutsu Awase;* Famous Products of the Eastern Capital
DATE ca. 1820
SIGNATURE Gosei hitsu
ARTIST'S SEALS Go, Sei
FORMAT Shikishiban (20.7 x 18.2)
POET Kinshirō Ichitomo
FLLW FDN 3009.006

An Imari porcelain cup decorated with peony blossoms sits in a lacquer saucer. In the foreground lies a narrow *kōsen* powder container with a wooden peg stopper. *Kōsen* powder is an infusion made of spiced, roasted barley powder. The title of the print refers to the Ueno district in northeastern Edo, which was at one time famous for serving kōsen tea. For other illustrations of this type of canister see cat. no. 201.

Each of the prints from this series commissioned by the Go-gawa poetry group depicts a famous product or special attraction of a particular area of Edo.

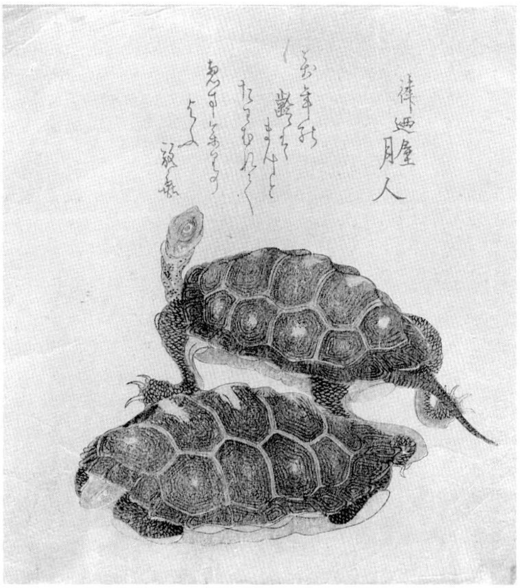

after GOSEI

91 Two turtles

DATE ca. 1890
FORMAT Shikishiban (21.2 x 19.4)
POET Inoya Tsukihito
FLLW FDN 3009.008

This is a late-nineteenth-century reprint of a surimono originally issued about 1820. It employs a new poetry block and lacks the title cartouche or club affiliation found on the original edition. For a more complete discussion of the image and text, see catalogue number 11.

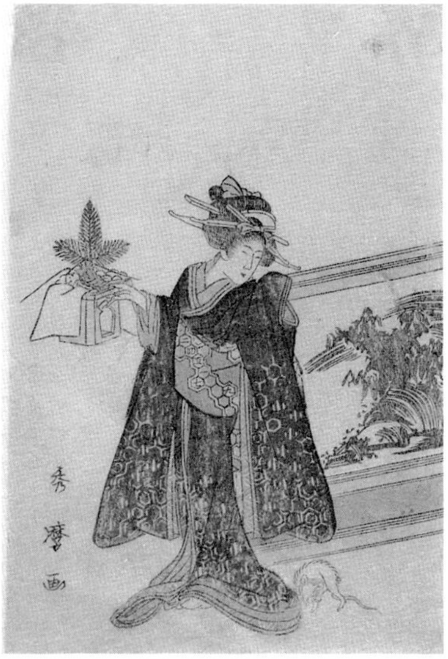

KITAGAWA HIDEMARO
ACT. CA. 1800–1820

92 A woman with a New Year arrangement and a white rat

DATE 1804
SIGNATURE Hidemaro ga
FORMAT Koban tate-e (13.6 x 8.9)
FLLW FDN 3037.001

This well-composed egoyomi shows a young woman glancing down at her pet white rat as she balances in one hand a New Year still life arrangement of a pine sapling and a lobster. Behind her is a standing screen depicting rocks in a rushing river. Scattered through the hexagonal pattern of her obi are the numbers for the short months—2, 4, 5, 7, 9—of the year of the rat, 1804.

Hidemaro was initially a pupil of the bijinga master Utamaro and collaborated with him on the famous illustrated book *Seirō Ehon Nenjū Gyōji* (Picture Book of Annual Events in the Bordellos) in 1804, the year in which this print was issued.

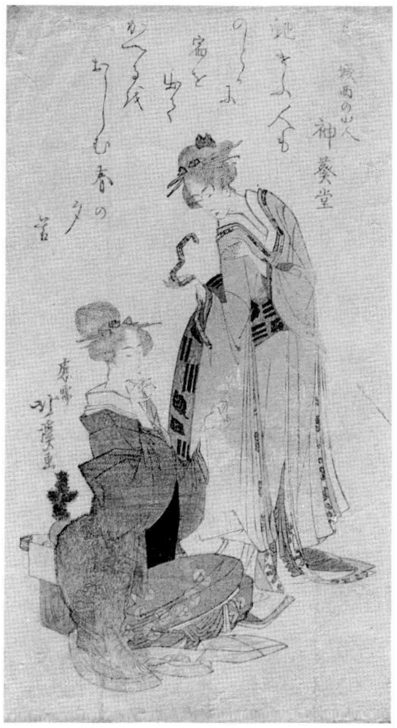

TOTOYA HOKKEI
1780–1850

93 Two women playing a hand game

DATE 1809
SIGNATURE Ōju Hokkei ga
FORMAT Koban tate-e (20.2 x 11.2)
POET Jōsai no Sanjin Shinkidō
FLLW FDN 3017.071

A kneeling woman holds a toy frog and a standing woman plays with a folding snake toy, which no doubt is an indication that this print was commissioned for a snake year. This print and its text are discussed in detail on pages 52–53.

The signature on this print is an example of Hokkei's early style in which the left-hand portion of the "Hoku" character is distinctly smaller than the right side.

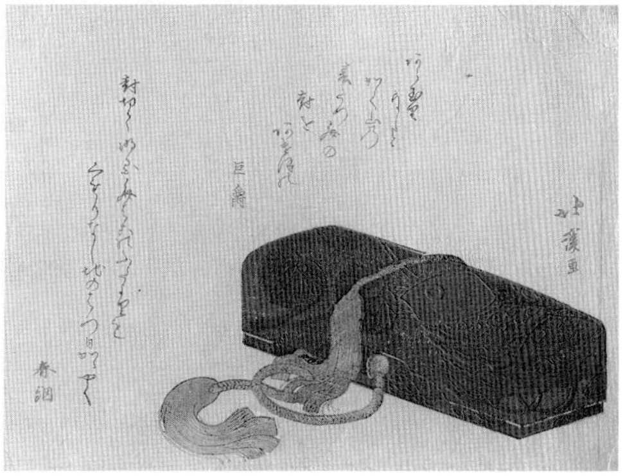

HOKKEI
94 Green-lacquer letter box

DATE Early 1810s
SIGNATURE Hokkei ga
FORMAT Koban yoko-e (14.1 x 18.4)
POETS Kyoshaku, Haruami
FLLW FDN 3017.067

A green-lacquer letter box is decorated with the motifs of an elaborate *torikabuto* hat and hollyhock leaves, printed in gold. *Torikabuto*, literally "bird helmets," were made of paper and silk brocade, and worn by the Bugaku court dancers. Entwined around the hat are hollyhock leaves, a symbol of the Tokugawa clan. For a discussion of this image, see page 16.

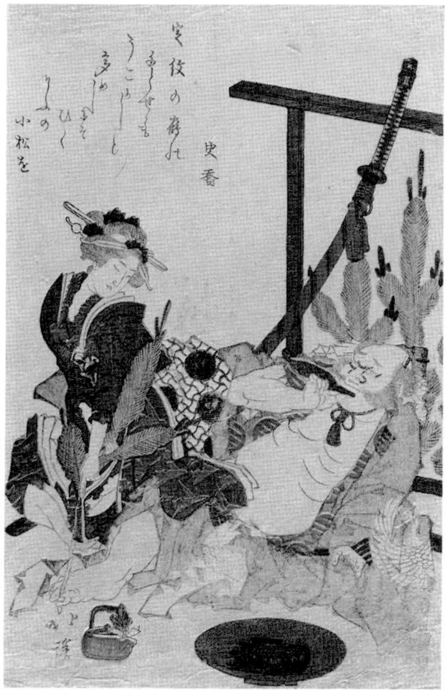

HOKKEI
95 Asahina no Saburō and a serving woman

DATE Mid-1810s
SIGNATURE Hokkei
FORMAT Koban tate-e (21.8 x 13.8)
POET Shikyō
FLLW FDN 3017.070

Asahina no Saburō smokes a small fat pipe as he leans by a standing screen decorated with pine branches. A serving woman pulls out a pine sapling using both arms as he casually yanks with his foot in a mock tug-of-war. This is a parody of the New Year custom of collecting of pine saplings on the first rat day.

It also alludes to a famous scene in the story of the Soga brothers, in which the mistress of the younger brother mistakenly pours sake for her lover before serving the higher-ranking Hatakeyama Shigetada and the strongman Asahina no Saburō (identified here by his crane emblem). This resulted in a contest of strength between the elder brother and Asahina.

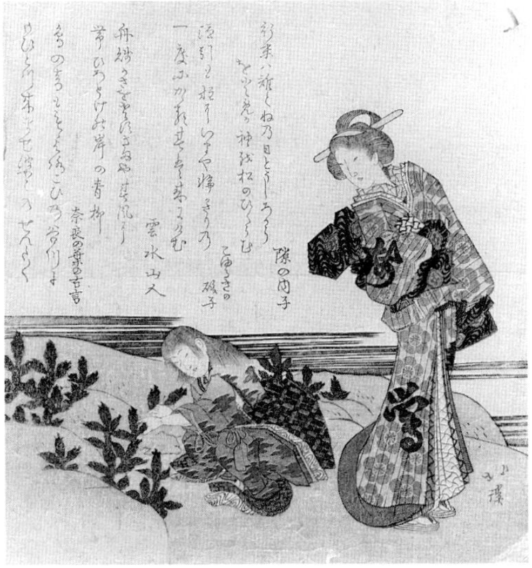

HOKKEI

96 Collecting young pine saplings

DATE Mid-1810s
SIGNATURE Hokkei
FORMAT Shikishiban (19.8 x 18.4)
POETS Hima no Naishi, Koyurugi no Isoko, Unsui Sanjin, Nara no Ha no Furukoto
FLLW FDN 3017.008

On the first rat day of the year, it was customary to go out to the fields and forests to collect pine saplings and young herbs and compose a poem on the theme of longevity. In this New Year scene, a sumptuously dressed woman watches a girl pluck a sapling. On her kimono are the characters *ume* (plum) and *uguisu* (warbler)—both New Year's symbols—written in gold.

The signature used here by Hokkei is an example of the style he used in the mid-1810s.

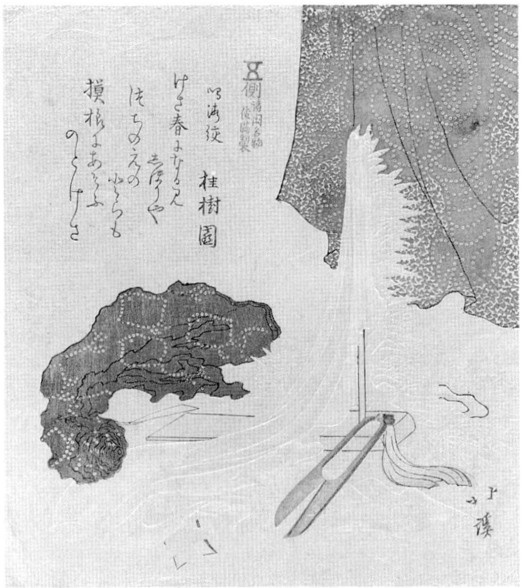

HOKKEI

97 Tie-dyed fabric

TITLE *Narumi Shibori*; Tie-dyed Fabric from Narumi
SERIES *Go-gawa Shokoku Meibutsu Shumman Sei*; Famous Products of Various Provinces, Produced by Shumman for the Go-gawa Group
DATE 1818, Year of the Tiger
SIGNATURE Hokkei
FORMAT Shikishiban (20.2 x 18.0)
REFERENCES Ostier, *La voix silencieuse*, pl. 66; Suzuki, fig. 30
POET Keijuen
FLLW FDN 3017.030

A blue tie-dyed cloth hangs behind a piece of undyed fabric which is draped on a standing pole, ready to be bound for the resist-dying process. A scissors, needle and thread, and another red cloth lie on the ground. Nearly invisible, the pattern of a tiger amidst bamboo may be discerned on the blue tie-dyed fabric, indicating the zodiac year. Narumi *shibori* is a fabric made by a tie-dye resist technique. The print was commissioned by the Go-gawa as indicated by the hourglass emblem in the shape of the character *go* (five). This print is discussed on pages 39–40.

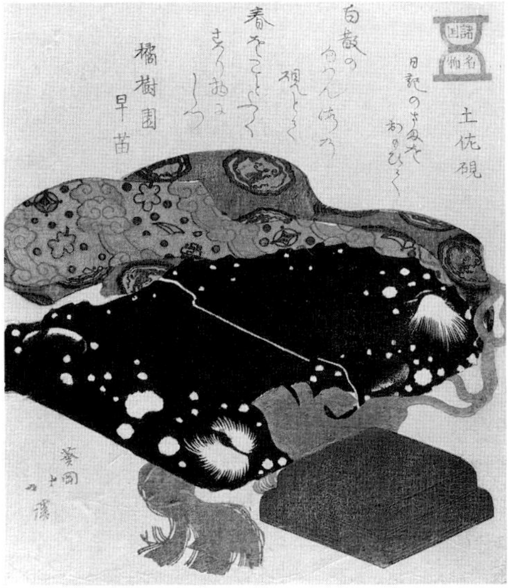

HOKKEI

98 An inkstone and a brocade satchel

TITLE *Tosa Suzuri;* Tosa Inkstone
SERIES *Shokoku Meibutsu*; Famous Products of Various Provinces
DATE Late 1810s
SIGNATURE Aoigaoka Hokkei
FORMAT Shikishiban (20.1 x 16.8)
POET Kitsujuen Sanae
FLLW FDN 3017.032

A blue inkstone from Tosa Province has been partially removed from its brocade drawstring sack. The surface of the inkstone, colored an unusual deep blue, is subtly printed with an incised design in gold and covered with a light silvery wash to create the effect of a polished surface. The random patterning of the white "sprinkled" design may represent flower pollen.

The poem speaks of *byakuzan*—a type of medicinal spice that is used for making New Year's sake, which is mentioned in the *Tosa Nikki (Tosa Diary)*. The crest of the Go-gawa has been integrated into the series-title cartouche.

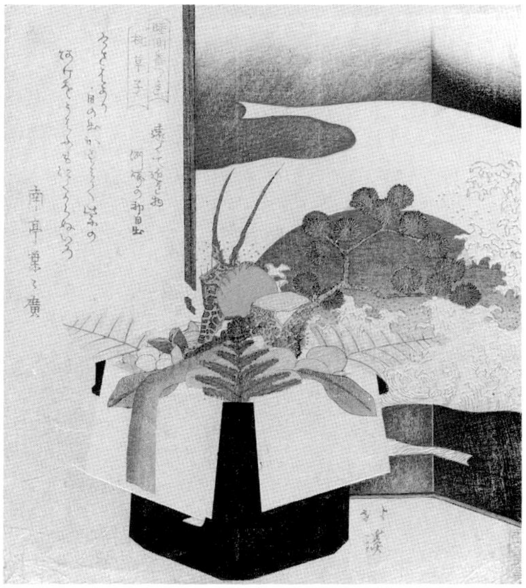

HOKKEI

99 A New Year's arrangement

TITLE *Tōkute Chikaki Mono Susaki no Hatsuhinode;* Things that are Distant Yet Near: New Year Sunrise at Susaki
SERIES *Mutsumigawa Bantsuzuki Makura no Sōshi*; *The Pillow Book* Series for the Mutsumi Group
DATE Late 1810s
SIGNATURE Hokkei
CARVER'S SEAL Gyoku ? sha ?
FORMAT Shikishiban (21.6 x 18.9)
REFERENCE Keyes, *Beatty*, no. 106
POET Nantei Habahiro
FLLW FDN 3017.066

This New Year still life shows a lobster, ferns, bitter oranges, tangerines, pine, and *yuzuri* leaves arranged on a black lacquer tray-table with ceremonial white paper. The series title refers to *Makura no Sōshi* (*The Pillow Book*), a collection of anecdotes and observations of court life compiled by Sei Shōnagon (ca. 966–1017). One of the sections in the volume includes a short list of "things that are distant yet near." The first sunrise of New Year is traditionally viewed from the coast of Susaki near Shinagawa. The folding screen shows the sun rising over the waves off this coast.

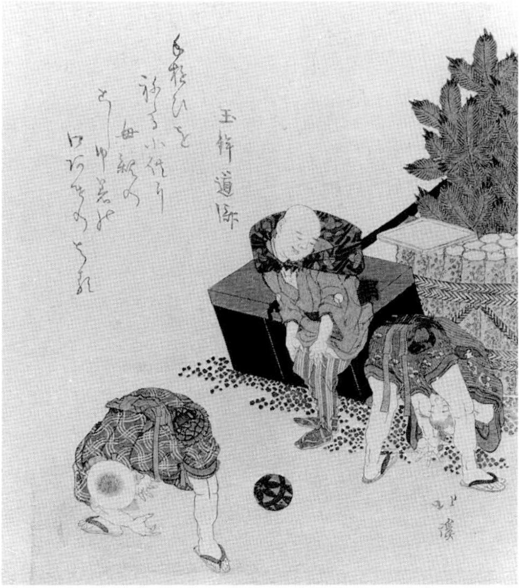

HOKKEI

100 Boys playing catch

DATE Late 1810s
SIGNATURE Hokkei
FORMAT Shikishiban (21.8 x 18.7)
POET Tamahoko Michizumi
FLLW FDN 3017.003

Two boys with their backs to each other toss a ball between their legs. The ball is decorated with multi-colored string, and was no doubt a New Year gift. A young porter has put down his heavy load to watch the New Year game. Behind them is a large seasonal pine arrangement.

This surimono may be from an untitled set based on the theme of children's games. A surimono depicting a boy on stilts and a girl with a jump rope is in the Duel Collection (see Polster, no. 151), which also has another impression of the print shown here.

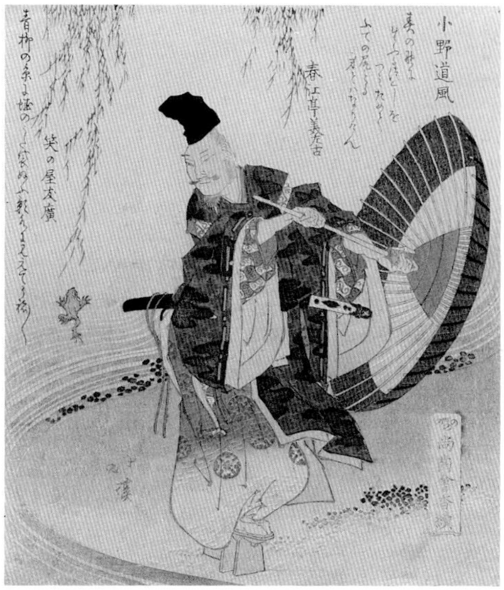

HOKKEI

101

TITLE *Ono no Tōfū*
SERIES *Shōshikai Bantsuzuki;* A Gathering of the Elders of Poetry
DATE ca. 1820
SIGNATURE Hokkei
FORMAT Shikishiban (21.6 x 18.4)
REFERENCES Rijksmuseum, *Hokusai,* pl. 140; Meech, *Rain and Snow,* pl. 69; Polster, no. 168
POETS Shunkōtei Misako, Eminoya Tomohiro
FLLW FDN 3017.001

This series of at least ten prints was commissioned by the Hanazono Circle, whose emblem of three petals of a plum blossom, in the shape of the character *no*, appears at the top of the series-title cartouche in the lower right corner. Each print depicts a famous figure from Japanese history. (Also see the following entry.)

According to legend, the persistent efforts of a frog in its attempts to leap into a willow tree gave inspiration to the celebrated tenth-century calligrapher Ono no Tōfū (894–966). For a discussion of this print see pages 51–52.

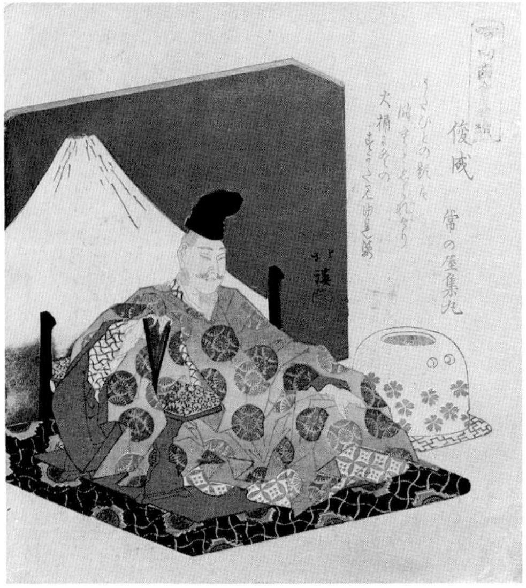

HOKKEI

102 The court poet Fujiwara Shunzei

TITLE Shunzei
SERIES *Shōshikai Bantsuzuki;* A Gathering of the Elders of Poetry
DATE ca. 1820
SIGNATURE Hokkei
SEAL Hoku (on screen)
FORMAT Shikishiban (22.1 x 19.0)
POETS Tsunenoya Atsumaru
FLLW FDN 3017.074

Fujiwara Shunzei (1114–1204), the leading poet in the late twelfth century, compiled the imperially commissioned collection of poetry, *Senzai Wakashū*. He is seated before a screen of Mount Fuji; at his side is a round brazier. He places his fan against an armrest (*dai*), the word for which is a homonym for a poetry topic.

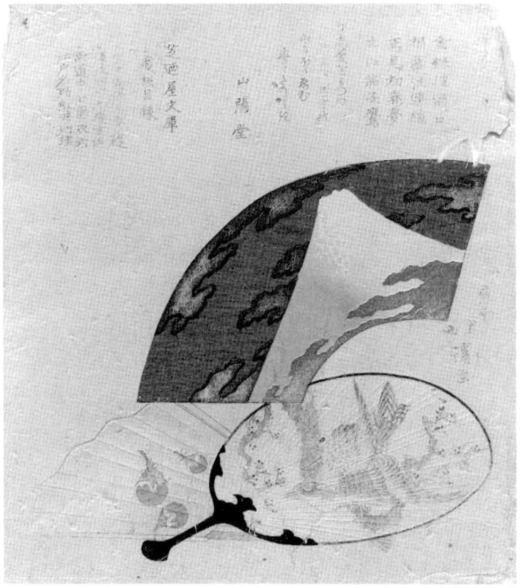

HOKKEI

103 Three fan paintings

DATE ca. 1820
SIGNATURE Ōju Hokkei ga
FORMAT Shikishiban (21.0 x 18.6)
POET Sanyōdō
FLLW FDN 3017.034

Three types of fans each illustrate one of the lucky dreams: an unmounted fan painting of Mount Fuji amid clouds, a round fan with a hawk on a plum branch, and a folding fan with three eggplants. For more on this subject, see Matthi Forrer "Dreaming of Fuji, Falcon and Eggplant," (*Andon,* vol. 6, no. 21, 1986). The inscription includes an advertisement for printed paper gameboards for variations of backgammon.

This print is better known through facsimile editions issued in the Meiji period with a deep blue background and different poems. The two versions are discussed on pages 20–21.

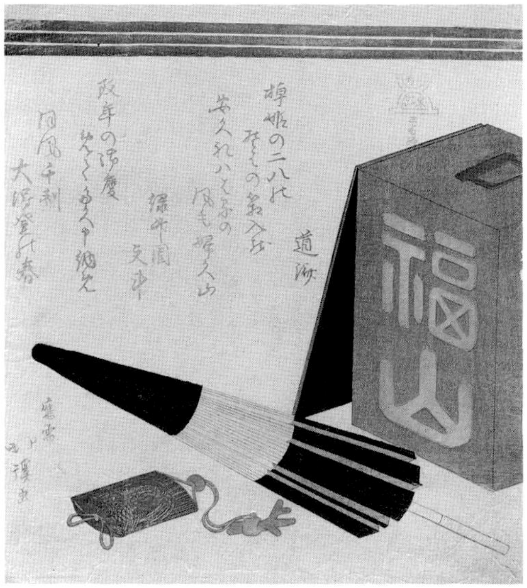

HOKKEI

104 Box, umbrella, and inrō

SERIES *Sanshō Ie no Gei, Samban Tsuzuki*; Plays of the Ichikawa Family, A Series of Three
DATE ca. 1820
SIGNATURE Ōju Hokkei ga
FORMAT Shikishiban (21.6 x 18.3)
REFERENCES Kanagawa Prefectural Museum, ed., *Ukiyo-e Meihin,* pl. 372
POETS Michizumi, Ryokuchikuen Fumimasu
FLLW FDN 3017.033

A red-lacquer noodle-delivery box sits behind an umbrella and an inrō (medicine case), which is threaded with a netsuke of coral. These objects are related to the Kabuki play *Sukeroku Yukari no Edo Zakura* (see cat. no 112) and Ichikawa Danjūrō VII, whose flamboyant personality suited the role of the dashing Sukeroku. The three parallel gold lines at the top edge of the print is a reference to the *mimasu* (three concentric rice-measuring boxes) crest of the Ichikawa family of Kabuki actors. *Sanshō* in the title was an alternative name used by members of this family.

For a more complete discussion of this print see pages 47–49.

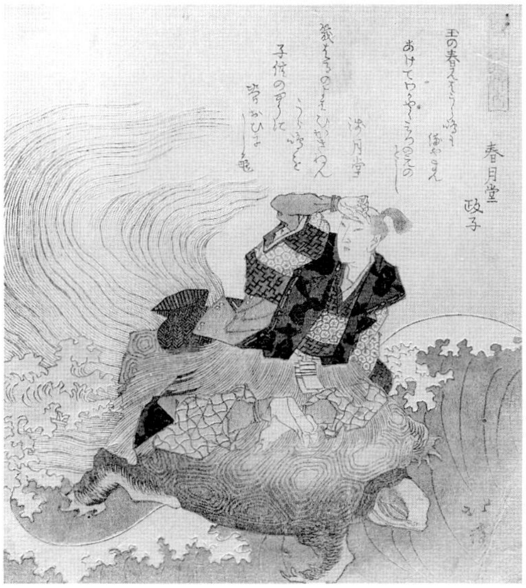

HOKKEI

105 A turtle transporting Urashima Tarō

SERIES *Tsurukame Matsutake no Uchi*; Crane, Turtle, Pine and Bamboo
DATE Perhaps 1822
SIGNATURE Hokkei
FORMAT Shikishiban (21.4 x 18.6)
REFERENCE Polster, no. 160.
POETS Shungetsudō Masako, Sengetsudō
FLLW FDN 3017.017

Urashima Tarō, a fisherman, saved the life of a turtle who turned out to be the daughter of the Dragon King. In gratitude, she took him to her palace beneath the sea, where he lived with her for centuries.

The first poem mentions the cyclical year *mizunoe no toshi*, which accords with 1822. While on this basis and stylistic grounds, a dating to this year seems appropriate, other prints in the series have zodiac allusions that seem to indicate a date of 1821 (see Keyes, *Beatty*, no. 115).

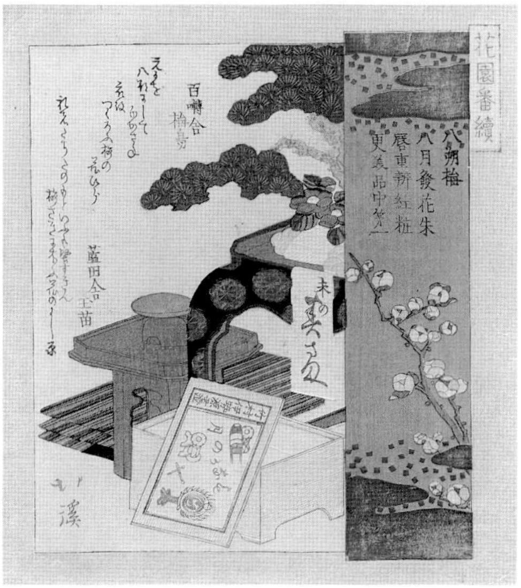

HOKKEI

106 Camellia, pine, and sweets

TITLE *Hassaku Ume*, Plum Dressed in White
SERIES *Hanazono Bantsuzuki*; A Series for the Hanazono Club
DATE 1823, Year of the Goat
SIGNATURE Hokkei
FORMAT Shikishiban (21.2 x 18.8)
REFERENCE Kanagawa Prefectural Museum, ed., *Ukiyo-e Meihin,* pl. 373
POETS Hyakutensha Umedori, Randensha Tamanae
FLLW FDN 3017.054

The first day of the eighth month (*hassaku*) was traditionally celebrated by an exchange of gifts. In the Yoshiwara, all of the courtesans donned white garments.

A black lacquer tray-table holds a camellia, pine branch, and white-wrapped sweets; attached to the tray is a white paper slip which reads *hitsuji no harusama,* "a spring scene for the year of the goat." A red lacquer tray with a sake cup rests on a wooden stand. The label of the up-ended cover of a wooden sweets box is decorated with various musical instruments. For a discussion of this series see catalogue number 19.

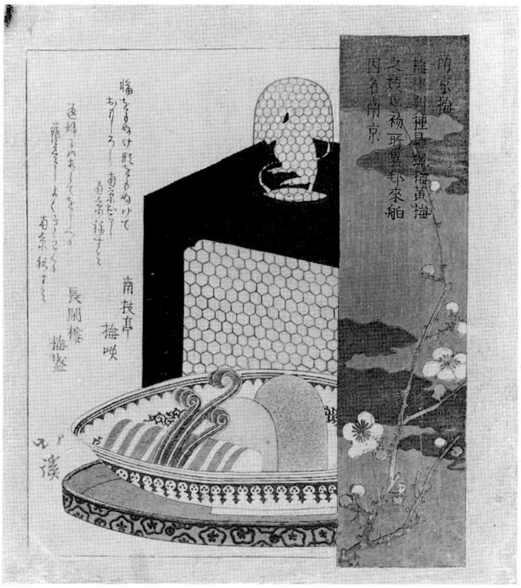

HOKKEI

107 A mouse in a cage and colorful sweets

TITLE *Nankinbai*; Plum of Nanking
SERIES *Hanazono Bantsuzuki*; A Series for the Hanazono Club (missing in this impression)
DATE 1823
SIGNATURE Hokkei
FORMAT Shikishiban (21.1 x 18.6)
POETS Nanshitei Umesaki, Chōkanrō Umemori
FLLW FDN 3017.053

Both poems refer to the variety of white mice imported from Nankin. *Nankin okoshi*, referred to in the first poem, were probably sweets from China, or perhaps it was just a term referring to exotic sweetmeats.

This impression lacks a title cartouche, although the light blue background block was carved to accommodate such a panel. Either the printer neglected to print it or in an oversight it was never completed. Since the impression is weaker than the others in the set, it is possible that it represents a second printing that had no connection to the Hanazono poetry club, whose members commissioned the original printing of the series.

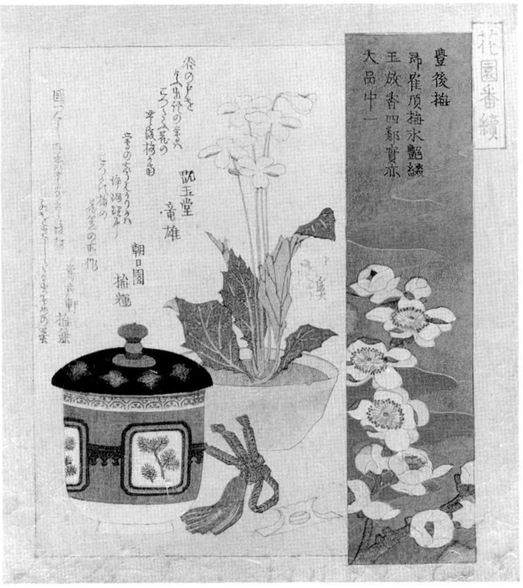

HOKKEI

108 Primroses, a covered teacup, and a shamisen bridge

TITLE *Bungo Ume*; Plums from Bungo
SERIES *Hanazono Bantsuzuki,* A Series for the Hanazono Club
DATE 1823
SIGNATURE Hokkei
FORMAT Shikishiban (21.4 x 18.7)
REFERENCES Keyes, *Spencer*, cat. 58; NUK, *Pulverer,* pl. 2-55: Uhlenbeck, pl. 20
POETS Gangyokudō Tatsuo, Asahien Umeteru, Ōseiken Umekane
FLLW FDN 3017.040

Larger than most varieties, Bungo plum blossoms are pale red or white and have two layers of petals. Bungo, in northeastern Kyūshū, was known for a type of Jōruri music called *bungo-bushi*. The primrose once served as the emblem for musicians from this region. The covered teacup would have been used by singers.

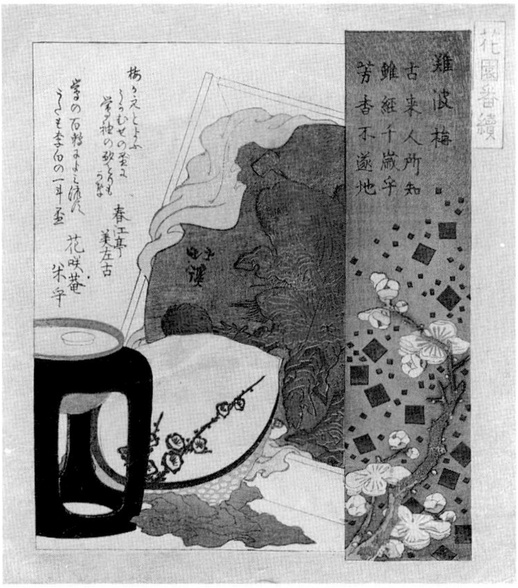

HOKKEI

109 A large sake cup and an abalone shell cup

TITLE *Naniwa Ume;* Plum of Naniwa
SERIES *Hanazono Bantsuzuki;* A Series for the Hanazono Club
DATE 1823
SIGNATURE Hokkei (on cup)
FORMAT Shikishiban (21.0 x 18.7)
REFERENCE Rijksmuseum, *Hokusai,* pl. 149
POETS Shunkōtei Misako, Kashōan Yonemori
FLLW FDN 3017.044

Naniwa (present-day Osaka) was famous in ancient times for its plum trees. To the left, a black lacquer stand supports a silver bowl of hot water containing a floating sake cup. In the foreground sits a cup specially made from an abalone shell for the house sake of an Osaka restaurant, Ukamuse. Nestled in a wooden storage box is an unusually large red lacquer sake cup decorated with two *shōjō;* one dances while the other plays the flute. *Shōjō* are mythical sea creatures with bodies resembling puppies, human faces, long arms, and red hair. Lovers of wine, they are a most appropriate subject for a wine cup.

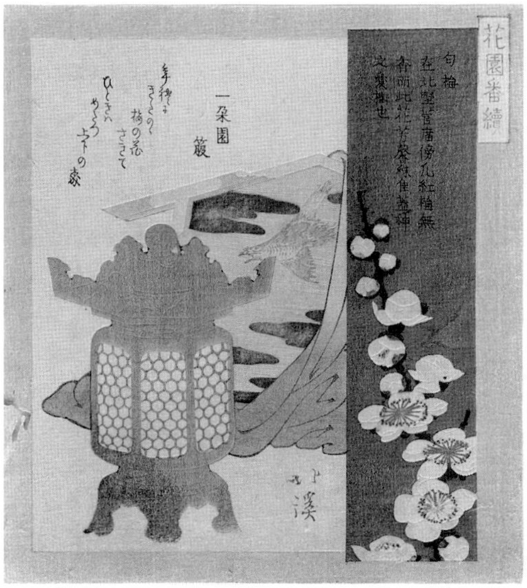

HOKKEI

110 A bronze shrine lantern and a votive painting of a warbler

TITLE *Nioi Ume*; Fragrant Plum
SERIES *Hanazono Bantsuzuki,* A Series for the Hanazono Club
DATE 1823
SIGNATURE Hokkei
FORMAT Shikishiban (20.7 x 18.4)
REFERENCES Keyes, *Beatty*, no. 117; Ostier, *La voix silencieuse*, pl. 59; Schmidt, cat. no. 25
POET Ichidaen Ebira
FLLW FDN 3017.055

Both the Chinese inscription and kyōka mention Kitano Shrine in northern Kyoto, which was constructed in honor of the Early Heian statesman, Sugawara no Michizane (845–903). In the centuries after his death, Michizane came to be revered as the patron saint of scholars, and eventually he was recognized as the Shinto deity known as Tenjin. Legend also holds that Michizane had a passion for plum blossoms.

The bronze lantern in the image, a symbol of Kitano Shrine, is not printed in metal as might be expected, but rather in subtle gradations of an unusual green pigment to suggest a patina.

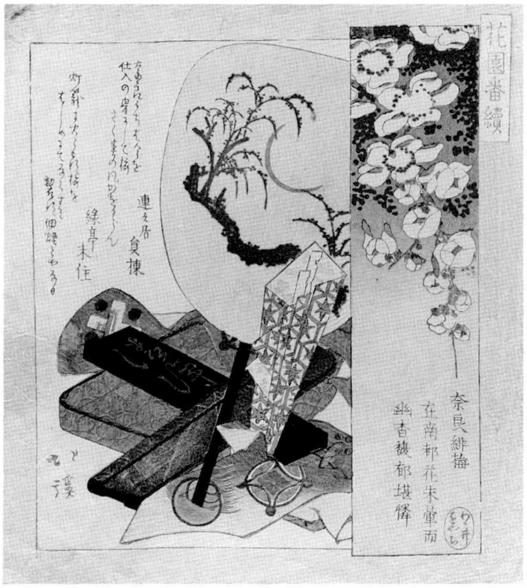

HOKKEI

111 A fan and toothpicks

SERIES *Hanazono Bantsuzuki*, A Series for the Hanazono Club
TITLE *Nara Hibai;* Nara Red Plum
DATE 1823
SIGNATURE Hokkei
DEALER'S SEAL Wakai Oyaji (Old Man Wakai)
FORMAT Shikishiban (21.0 x 18.7)
REFERENCE Polster, no. 176
POETS Renrenkyo Kazumune, Ryokutei Mizumi
FLLW FDN 3017.046

A round fan decorated with a plum branch and moon is propped above an inkstick labeled *seijō* (pure). The lavish wrapping cloth is decorated with a lucky jewel motif, associated with the Seven Gods of Good Luck. Lying against the fan are two toothpicks encased in a paper folder. Fans and inksticks, mentioned in the poems, are both traditional famous products of the Nara area.

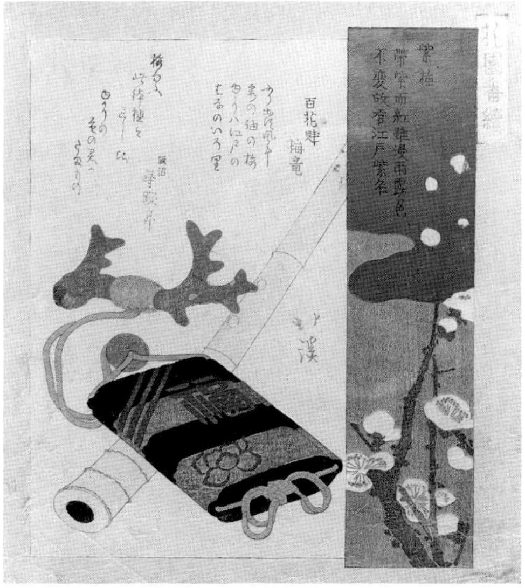

HOKKEI

112 An inrō and flute

TITLE *Shibai;* Purple Plum
SERIES *Hanazono Bantsuzuki*, A Series for the Hanazono Club
DATE 1823
SIGNATURE Hokkei
FORMAT Shikishiban (21.4 x 18.8)
POETS Hyakkakai Umetatsu, Jinjōtei, of Iinuma
FLLW FDN 3017.051

An inrō with a design of the character for luck, a peony, and three stripes is threaded with a netsuke of coral. A flute lies beneath them. All of the items refer to Sukeroku in the famous Kabuki play *Sukeroku Yukari no Edo Zakura* (Sukeroku's Affinity for the Cherry Blossoms of Edo). When this print was issued, the role was played by Ichikawa Danjūrō VII (see also cat. no. 104). The three stripes, referring to the Ichikawa family's *mimasu* (three concentric squares) crest, and the peony flower, an alternative crest, are both connected with the actor. The poems mention part of the play's title in association with spring themes.

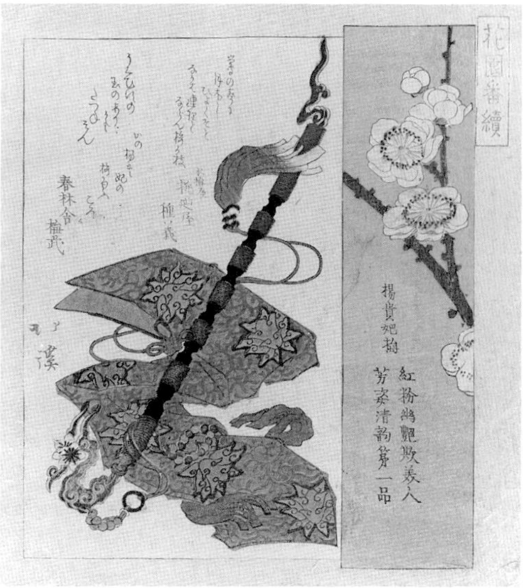

HŌKKEI

113 A Chinese dragon-shaped flute

TITLE *Yōkihibai*; Plum of Yang Guifei
SERIES *Hanazono Bantsuzuki*, A Series for the Hanazono Club
DATE 1823
SIGNATURE Hokkei
FORMAT Shikishiban (21.0 x 18.6)
POETS Momonoya Taneyoshi, Shunrinsha Umetake
FLLW FDN 3017.058

Yang Guifei (719–56), known in Japanese as Yōkihi, was the favorite consort of Emperor Xuan Zong of the Tang dynasty (eighth century). She charmed the emperor with her beauty and musical talents. His infatuation for her caused him to neglect his official duties and the empire was soon beset with civil war. Their tragic story was immortalized in "The Song of Everlasting Sorrow," a romantic ballad by the ninth-century Chinese poet Bo Juyi, which was a favorite source of inspiration to Japanese writers and poets through the centuries.

Another impression of this image in the collection (FLLW FDN 3017.057) is an example of a slightly later printing.

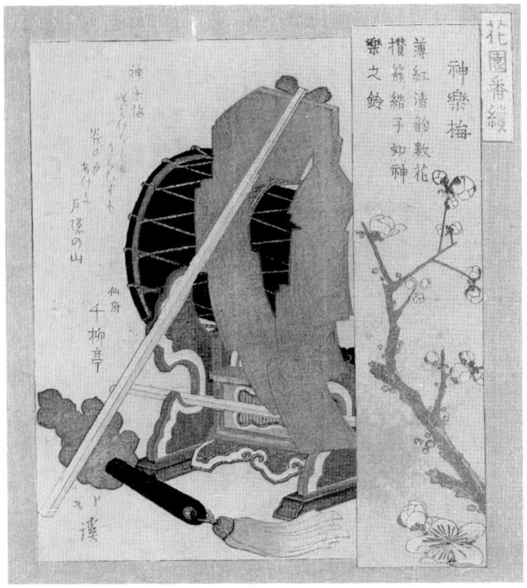

HOKKEI

114 A drum on a stand and silver holy papers

TITLE *Kaguraume*, Shrine-music Plum
SERIES *Hanazono Bantsuzuki*, A Series for the Hanazono Club
DATE 1823
SIGNATURE Hokkei
FORMAT Shikishiban (21.0x 18.2)
POET Senryūtei of Sempu
FLLW FDN 3017.052

This design incorporates musical and religious themes, as the name of this variety of plum refers to the music played in shrines. A stick with silver holy papers leans against a drum set on its stand. Lying on a diagonal is a ceremonial implement with a tassel attached at one end and numerous bells (*kagurasuzu*) to the other.

According to the Chinese inscription in the long yellow cartouche, the buds of the *kagura* plum are said to resemble bells used for the Kagura dance. The kyōka mentions the song of the warbler, which is said to open the door to heaven on the sacred mountain at Togakushi.

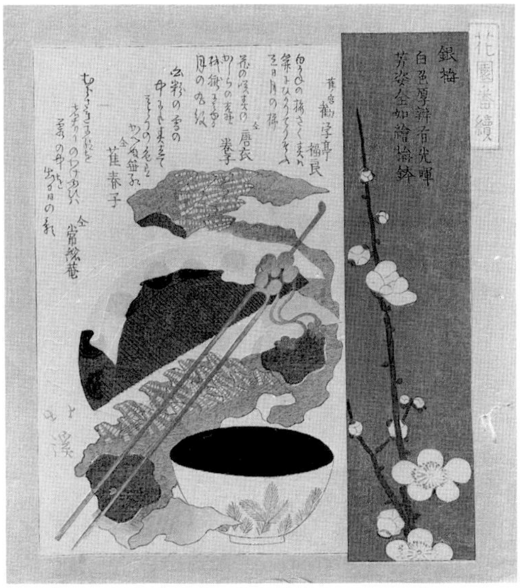

HOKKEI

115 A make-up bowl and hair ornaments

TITLE *Ginbai*; Silver Plum
SERIES *Hanazono Bantsuzuki;* A Series for the Hanazono Club
DATE 1823
SIGNATURE Hokkei
FORMAT Shikishiban (21.1 x18.6)
REFERENCE Rijksmuseum, *Hokusai,* pl.146
POETS Kangakutei Fukuyoshi, Karagoromo Makiko, Tsuru no Haruko, Jōsōsan (all from Tsurunomiya)
FLLW FDN 3017.056

This complex composition includes a bowl for lip-rouge, a tie-dyed cloth surrounding a silver hair pin decorated with a plum motif, and a comb wrapped in a translucent white cloth—all objects connected with the "first makeup" of the New Year.

The obvious connection to the silver plum of the title is the silver hair ornament. There are further allusions to a traditional snow, moon, and flower theme—the snow of the white cloth, the lunar crescent shape of the comb, and the flower of the hairpin.

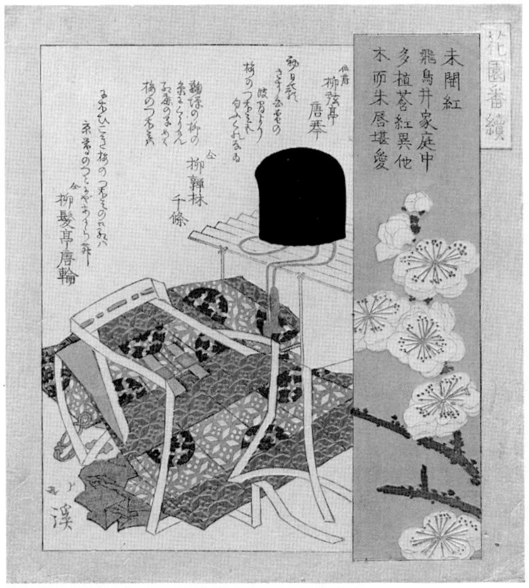

HOKKEI

116 A folded courtier's ceremonial robe and hat

TITLE *Mikai Beni*; Not-Fully-Opened Red
SERIES *Hanazono Bantsuzuki*; A Series for the Hanazono Club
DATE 1823
SIGNATURE Hokkei
FORMAT Shikishiban (21.1 x 18.7)
REFERENCES Rijksmuseum, *Hokusai,* pl. 150; Ostier, *La voix silencieuse*, pl. 44
POETS Ryūgentei Karakoto, Ryūtarin Senjō, Ryūhatsutei Karawa (all from Sempu)
FLLW FDN 3017.047

The title alludes to plum blossoms that remain unopened and are therefore red in appearance. All three kyōka verses were composed on the theme of budding plum blossoms. The Chinese inscription to the right describes the red plum blossoms in the garden of the Asukai family, a noble family which produced many famous poets and *kemari* ("football") experts.

There is another impression of this image in the Wright collection.

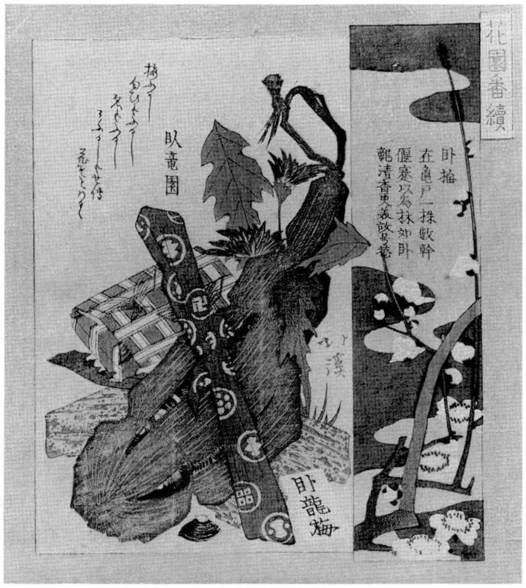

HOKKEI

117 Wrapped packages

TITLE *Gabai*; Reclining Plum
SERIES *Hanazono Bantsuzuki*, A Series for the Hanazono Club
DATE 1823
SIGNATURE Hokkei
FORMAT Shikishiban (21.2 x 18.3)
REFERENCE Rijksmuseum, *Hokusai*, pl. 148
POET Garyōen
FLLW FDN 3017.049

A pipe wrapped in a cloth leans upon a straw carrier containing fresh-water mussels. Behind it is a tobacco pouch made of plaid cotton cloth. The unidentified crests on the wrapping cloth of the pipe are the same as those that appear in catalogue number 128.

The white card at the bottom reads *Garyōbai* ("reclining dragon plum") referring to a variety of a plum named for its unusual downward-curving branches, the silhouette of which is said to resemble a reclining dragon. The leader of the Hanazono-ren poetry club, Garyōen Umemaro, derived his name from this type of plum tree. Also, the Chinese inscription mentions the famous Garyō plum trees at Kameido.

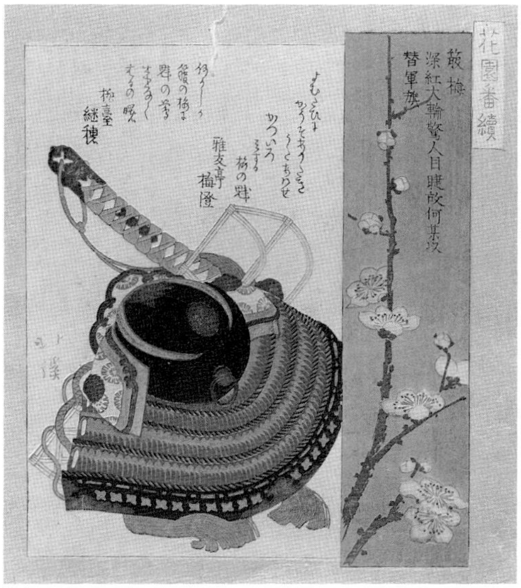

HOKKEI

118 A warrior's helmet and yellow arrow quiver

TITLE *Ebira Ume;* Quiver Plum
SERIES *Hanazono Bantsuzuki;* A Series for the Hanazono Club
DATE 1823
SIGNED Hokkei
FORMAT Shikishiban (21.2 x 18.8)
POETS Gayūtei Umezumi, Momodai Tsugiho
FLLW FDN 3017.076

The composition juxtaposes two separate designs, one of plum blossoms and another of a warrior's helmet, sword, and empty arrow quiver. The visual allusion is to the twelfth-century warrior Kajiwara no Kagesue, who bravely demonstrated his fearlessness at the battle of Ikuta Forest by placing a branch of flowering plum in his quiver to draw the enemy's attention. For a more detailed description of this story see catalogue number 55.

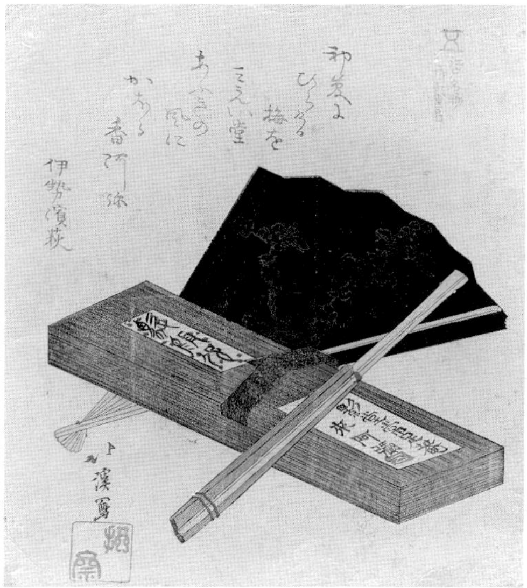

HOKKEI

119 A wooden fan box and two fans

TITLE *Mieidō Ōgi*; Mieidō fans
SERIES *Edo Meibutsu;* Famous Products of Edo
DATE ca. 1824
SIGNATURE Hokkei sha
ARTIST'S SEAL Kyōsai
FORMAT Shikishiban (20.9 x 18.2)
POET Ise no Hamaogi
FLLW FDN 3017.059

On a wooden box for fans lies an unopened folding fan. A black fan is partially unfolded to reveal its golden design of blossoming plum branches.

The emblem for the Go-gawa poetry group appears above the hand-stamped title cartouche as well as beneath the name on the box. The label on the box identifies the source for these fans as the Miedō, a famous fan shop in Kyōbashi, near the present-day Ginza shopping district. The print was probably commissioned by the proprietor of the shop, who seems to have used the poetry name Miedō Sokuan Raiami. The poem also puns on the name of the Miedō fan shop while likening the opening of a budding plum to opening a fan.

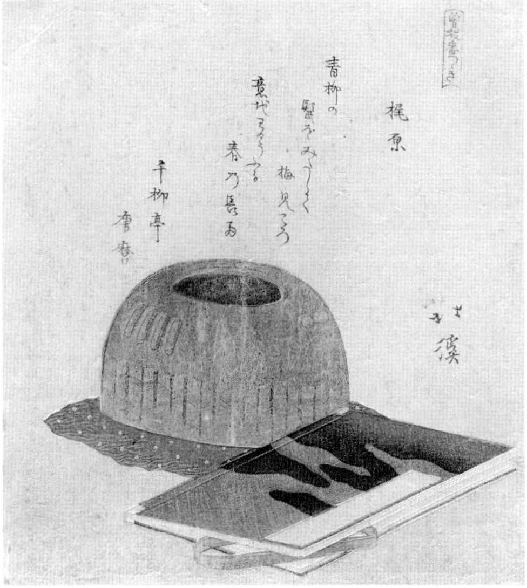

HOKKEI

120 A pair of tweezers with a book and a brazier

TITLE *Kajiwara*
SERIES *Soga Bantsuzuki*; The Soga Brothers Series
DATE ca.1824
SIGNATURE Hokkei
FORMAT Shikishiban (20.8 x 18.4)
REFERENCES *Collection de Monsieur X . . .*, pl.162; Ostier, *Les objets tranquilles*, pl.50
POET Senryūtei Karamaro
FLLW FDN 3017.063

Kajiwara, short for Kajiwara no Kagesue, was ordered by the Shōgun, Yoritomo, to behead the two young Soga brothers, who were the offspring of Kagesue's slain enemy. Only through the intervention of Hatakeyama Shigetada was the command rescinded.

The double arrow-quill crest of Kagesue is used as a repeated decorative element on the round brazier. A scene in the play based on the Soga Brothers' story includes beard plucking, which is referred to by the tweezers. For another image of Kagesue, see catalogue number 55.

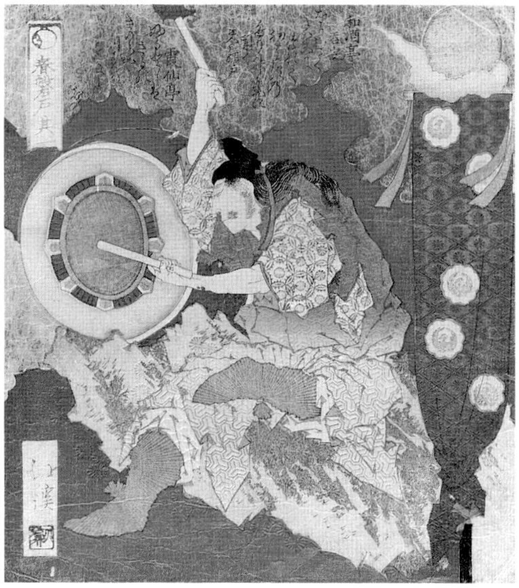

HOKKEI

121 A seated deity playing a drum

TITLE *Sono Ichi*; Number One
SERIES *Haru no Iwato*; The Cave of Spring
DATE 1825, Year of the Bird
SIGNATURE Hokkei
SEAL Hokkei
FORMAT Shikishiban (21.0 x 18.7)
REFERENCES Galerie Zacke, pl.4 (for the fifth sheet see pl. 5)
POETS Washutei Nomiyasu, Kasentei Momohito
FLLW FDN 3017.014

A set of five contiguous prints commissioned by the Taiko-gawa is based on a famous myth about Amaterasu, the sun goddess and divine ancestor of the Japanese emperor. According to this myth, Amaterasu, having been insulted by her brother, flees and hides in a cave, thereby depriving the world of sunlight. Eventually she is lured from the cavern with a dance and music performance by an entourage of her fellow deities outside the cave.

The subject of each print is set against a blue evening sky with gold clouds. At the far right, a silver moon rises through the clouds, a dramatic reminder of the theme of the print.

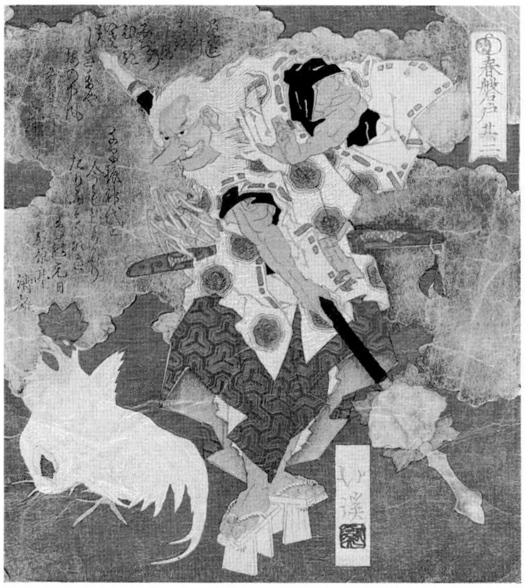

HOKKEI

122 The god Sarutahiko with a rooster and hen

TITLE *Sono Ni*; Number two
SERIES *Haru no Iwato*; The Cave of Spring
DATE 1825, Year of the Bird
SIGNATURE Hokkei
SEAL Hokkei
FORMAT Shikishiban (21.0 x 18.3)
REFERENCES Rijksmuseum, *Hokusai,* pl.172; Polster, no.198
POETS Saireitei Nanao (rubbed, read from another impression), Ishiwaratei Namio
FLLW FDN 3017.016

Sarutahiko, a Shinto deity, is described as having an extremely long nose and shining eyes. As in this pentaptych, he is traditionally portrayed before the cave in which the goddess Amaterasu has hidden herself.

The presence of the cock and hen serves to indicate that this series was commissioned for a bird year. The decorative scalloped medallions on the garments and textiles in some of the prints in this set include stylized bird motifs.

The complete pentaptych is in the collection of the Rijksmuseum voor Volkenkunde, Leiden.

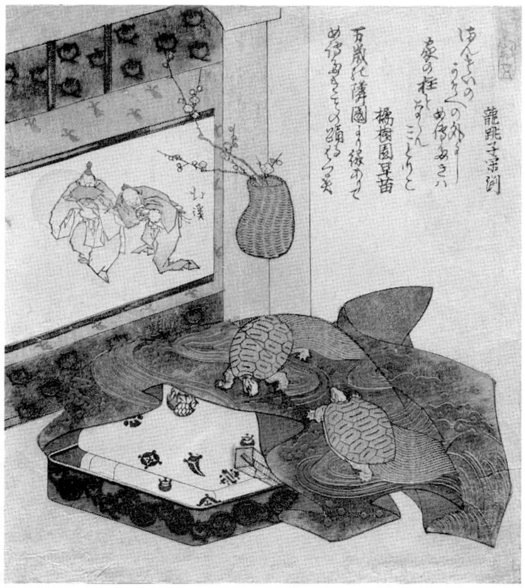

HOKKEI

123 A scroll of two *manzai* dancers and a lacquer tray with fabric

DATE ca. 1825
SIGNATURE Hokkei (in painting)
FORMAT Shikishiban (21.0 x 18.5)
POETS Ryōchōshi Himafuchi, Kitsujuen Sanae
FLLW FDN 3017.064

Manzai is a comical song accompanied by dance performed at the New Year. The word *manzai* also means "ten thousand years" and therefore signifies longevity.

The brocade cloth is decorated with a pair of "long-tailed" turtles, another symbol of long life. The lucky-treasures motif adorns the white fabric. The red seal in the upper right corner bears the hourglass emblem of the Go-gawa poetry group and a mandarin orange motif which is repeated as the brocade pattern for the scroll's mounting.

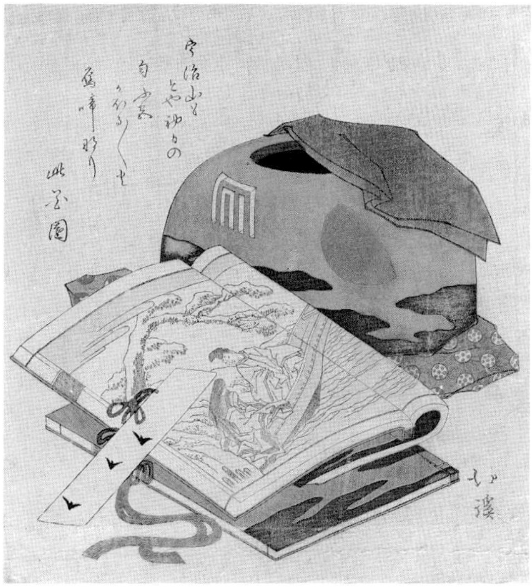

HOKKEI

124 An illustration of *The Tale of Genji* and a brazier

DATE ca. 1825
SIGNATURE Hokkei
FORMAT Shikishiban (20.4 x 18.3)
REFERENCES Ostier, *Les objets tranquilles*, pl. 51; Hillier, *The Japanese Print*, pl. 53; Meech-Pekarik, "The Artist's View of Ukifune," fig. 27
POET Shikaen
FLLW FDN 3017.039

On the small, round brazier is the Genji crest for chapter fifty-one. Beside it is an illustrated version of the *Tale of Genji* opened to the scene of the clandestine meeting between Ukifune and Niou, her secret love (for a discussion of this famous subject see also cat. no. 23).

Mentioned in the poem and alluded to on the bookmark, the cry of the crow, *kaoru*, is also the name of Prince Kaoru, who is not only the close friend and half-brother of Niou, but a rival suitor of Ukifune.

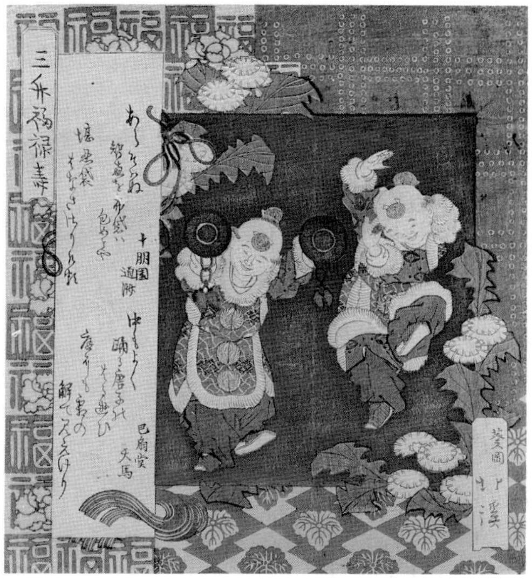

HOKKEI

125 Two Chinese boys

TITLE *Mimasu Fukurokuju*; Long Life, Health, and Happiness for the Mimasu Circle
DATE ca. 1825
SIGNATURE Aoigaoka Hokkei
FORMAT Shikishiban (20.2 x 18.5); left sheet of diptych
REFERENCE Rijksmuseum, *Hokusai*, pl. 170 b; for the right-hand sheet, see pl. 170 a
POETS Tōhōen Michizumi, Hasendō Temma
FLLW FDN 3017.036

A Chinese boy plays the cymbals as another dances. This is the left-hand sheet of a diptych; the other illustrates the god Hotei with a fan, decorated with the emblem of the Go-gawa poetry group. The background is comprised of three textile patterns: the red tie-dyed fabric is of a *mimasu* pattern (three concentric squares), the green area is patterned with the character for luck with peonies, and the purple section has ivy leaves set in a three-layer diamond pattern. All are symbols of the Kabuki actor Ichikawa Danjūrō VII. This surimono was probably commissioned by a patron or fan of the actor.

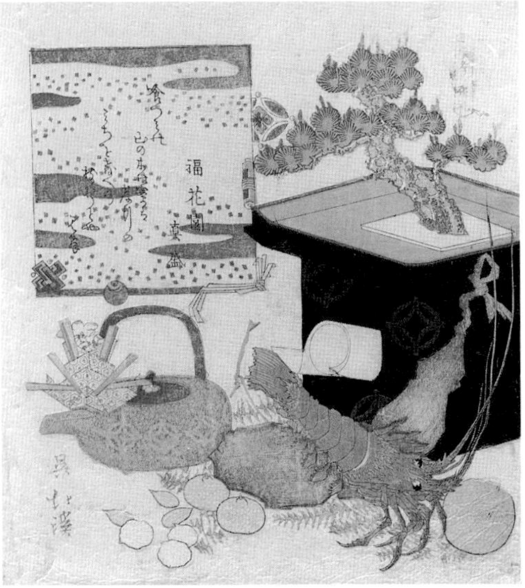

HOKKEI

126 New Year arrangement

TITLE *Chōkō Chōrei;* The Two Brothers Chōkō and Chōrei
SERIES *Shippōren Nijūshikō*; Twenty-four Paragons of Filial Piety for the Shippō-ren
DATE ca. 1825
SIGNATURE Go Hokkei
FORMAT Shikishiban (20.9 x 18.1)
REFERENCES For other prints from the series see Ostier, *Les objets tranquilles*, pl. 19; Keyes, *Beatty*, nos. 126–28
POET Fukkaen Masakari
FLLW FDN 3017.038

The story of filial piety alluded to here tells of two brothers, Chōkō and Chōrei, in search of food for their starving family. When set upon by a murderous robber who threatens to kill them, one son offers himself on the condition that his brother be allowed to return to provide for their mother. Moved by this filial gesture, the robber releases them both and gives them his remaining food.

The emblem of the club appears as the decorative design on the black lacquer planter and above the title.

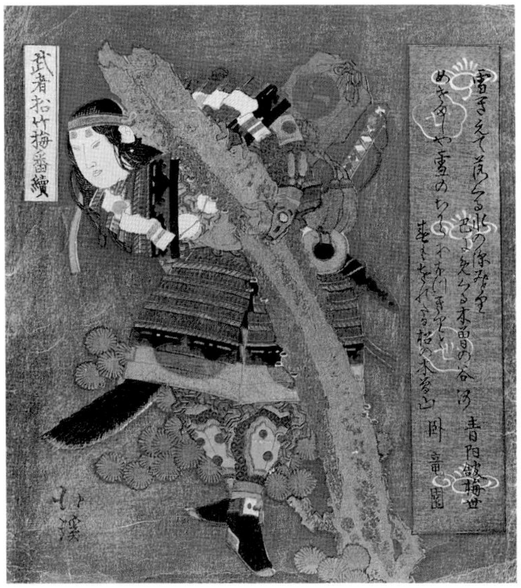

HOKKEI

127 Tomoe Gozen with an uprooted pine tree

SERIES *Musha Shōchikubai Bantsuzuki*; A Series of Warriors: Pine, Bamboo, and Plum
DATE Late 1820s
SIGNATURE Hokkei
FORMAT Shikishiban (21.0 x 18.5)
REFERENCES Mirviss, *Surimono,* pl. 4; Schindler, pl. 108. The complete set is illustrated in Kruml, 1989, pls. 92–94
POETS Seiyōkan Umeyo, Garyōen (Umemaro)
FLLW FDN 3017.010

This print depicts the moment in which the famous woman warrior Tomoe Gozen, identified by the *mitsudomoe* (three-comma) emblem on her sack, wrenches the trunk of a pine tree from the grasp of her attacker, Wada Yoshinori. She later becomes his mistress, bearing him a son, the famous strong man Asahina no Saburō.

For another entry discussing this heroine see catalogue number 80; for another print from this series (bamboo) see catalogue number 24.

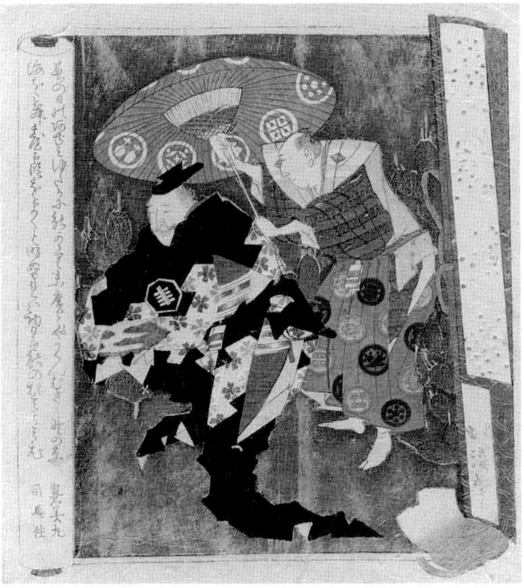

HOKKEI

128 A scene from *Suehiro*

DATE Late 1820s
SIGNATURE Hokkei hitsu ("painted by Hokkei" as if on a handscroll)
FORMAT Shikishiban (21.3 x 18.7)
REFERENCE Rijksmuseum, *Hokusai,* pl. 175
POETS [E]mimaru, [?] Shibazumi
FLLW FDN 3017.009

A scroll opens to a view of *Suehiro,* a Kyōgen play, in which a dancing courtier is shielded by an umbrella held by a servant. The story from which this scene is drawn tells of a master who asks his servant to purchase a *suehiro* fan. In town, the poor fellow is swindled and is tricked into buying an old umbrella instead.

The distinctive circular design elements on the servant's pants and umbrella have yet to be deciphered. Quite possibly, they are clues to the dating since twelve appear on the pants, six in silver, six in gold.

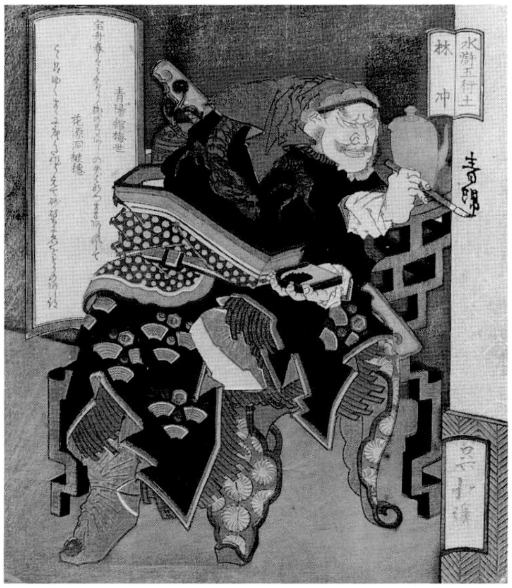

HOKKEI

129 Lin Chong

TITLE *Tsuchi*; Earth
SERIES *Suiko Gogyō*; The Five Elements of the Suikoden
DATE Late 1820s
SIGNATURE Go Hokkei
FORMAT Shikishiban (21.3 x 18.2)
REFERENCE Keyes, *Spencer,* pl. 18, NUK, *Pulverer,* pl.2-51; Hempel, *Scheiwe*, pl. 348
POETS Seiyōkan Umeyo, Kagendō Tsugiho
FLLW FDN 3017.015

Lin Chong, of the group of bandits immortalized in the Chinese novel, *Shui Huzhuan* (J: *Suikoden*), is shown inebriated, writing on an earthen wall. According to the novel, he is wrongfully exiled, after which he endures numerous hardships. Lin Chong manages to escape to a wine shop where his true identity is made known when, befuddled by drink, he writes his name on the wall. In this surimono, he writes the name of the judge of the poetry group, "Seiyō."

The series links the five *Suikoden* heroes to the Five Elements. In this print, the element earth is alluded to by the earthen wall. For another depiction of Lin Chong, see catalogue number 10.

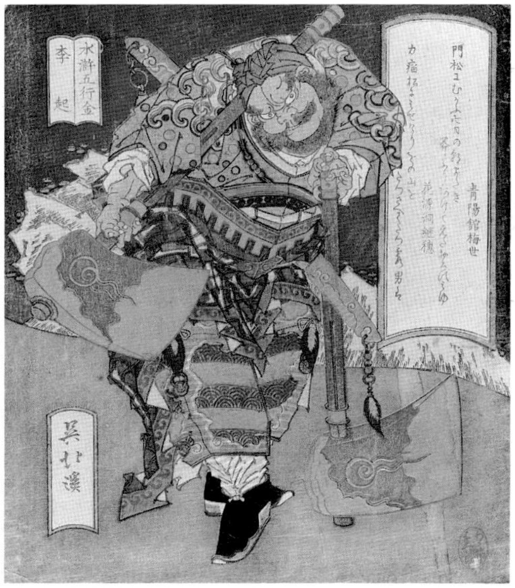

HOKKEI

130 Li Qi, the strong man with two large axes

TITLE *Kane*; Metal
SERIES *Suiko Gogyō*; The Five Elements of the *Suikoden*
DATE ca. 1828
SIGNATURE Go Hokkei
DEALER'S SEAL Wakai Oyaji (Old Man Wakai)
FORMAT Shikishiban (21.1 x 18.3)
REFERENCES Hempel, *Scheiwe,* no.350; Polster, no.147; Ward, no. 85; for the water, fire, and wood designs see Rijksmuseum, *Hokusai,* pls.194–195a
POETS Seiyōkan Umeyo, Kagendō Tsugiho
FLLW FDN 3017.075

Chinese renegades of the *Suikoden* are paired with one of the five elements in each of the five prints from this series. Li Qi is known for having used his large axe to break down a temple door; the first poem parodies this by referring to the New Year *kadomatsu* decoration (literally, pine gate arrangement). In every design in the series, the background is completely filled, using both metals (silver and brass) and a fragile blue pigment.

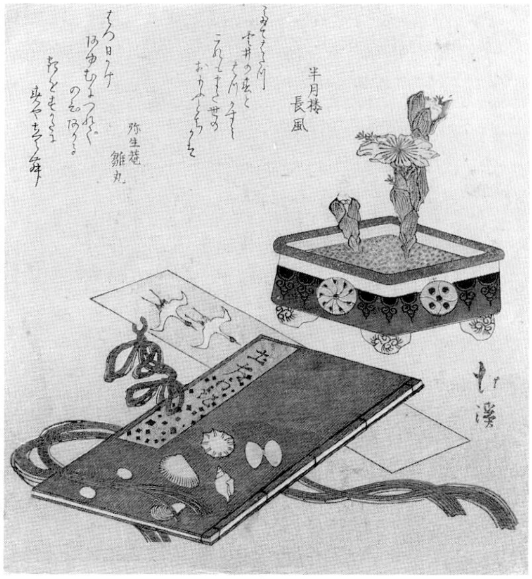

HOKKEI

131 A copy of the *Tosa Nikki* and a potted adonis plant

DATE ca. 1830
SIGNATURE Hokkei
FORMAT Shikishiban (20.0 x 18.3)
REFERENCE Schmidt, pl.31
POETS Hangetsurō Nagakaze, Yayoian Hinamaru
FLLW FDN 3017.024

In this still life a poem card adorned with a pair of cranes in flight lies beneath a volume of the *Tosa Nikki,* the earliest example of a Japanese prose diary, written by Ki no Tsurayuki, ca. 935. A potted adonis plant sits nearby in a square porcelain container. The crane and adonis plant are traditional New Year symbols.

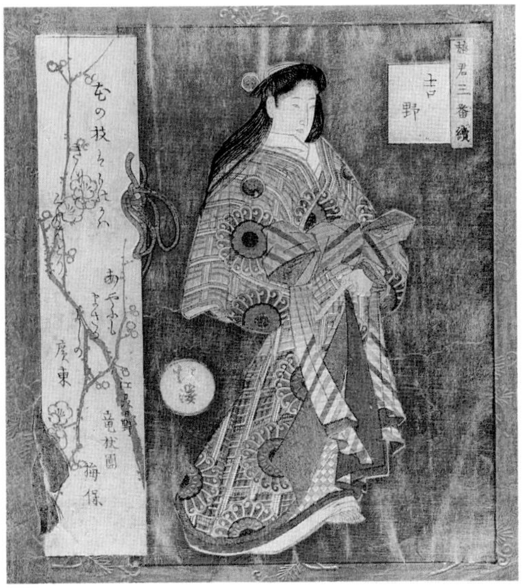

HOKKEI

132 A courtesan in formal attire

TITLE Yoshino
SERIES *Yūkun Samban Tsuzuki*; Series of Three Prints of Courtesans
DATE ca. 1830
SIGNATURE Hokkei
FORMAT Shikishiban (21.0 x 18.2)
REFERENCE Kruml, 1989, pl. 106; Schindler, pl. 96
POET Ryōjōen Umeyasu of Hino, Gōshū
FLLW FDN 3017.006

Each of the three designs from this set shows a woman placed against a brass ground and framed with a delicate blue border with silver pines; this print and the next two constitute the complete set. Yoshino was perhaps the most famous courtesan of the Shimabara pleasure quarters of Kyoto during the seventeenth century, and was renowned for her musical skills and artistic achievements, including a mastery of the arts of koto playing, poetry, tea ceremony, and flower arrangement. In the print, she is portrayed wearing an elaborate plaid kimono patterned with floral roundels; her obi is tied as a bow in the front in the manner of a high-ranking courtesan.

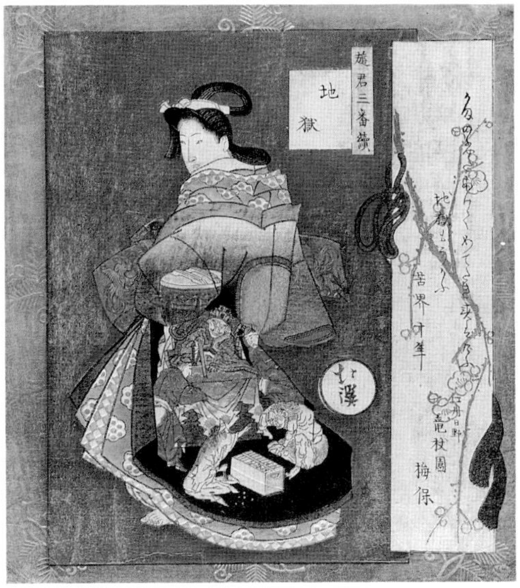

HOKKEI

133 A courtesan in formal attire

TITLE Jigoku
SERIES *Yūkun Samban Tsuzuki*; Series of Three Prints of Courtesans
DATE ca. 1830
SIGNATURE Hokkei
FORMAT Shikishiban (21.1 x 18.3)
REFERENCE *Collection Ernest Le Vèel (3e, vente)*, pl. 162
POET Ryōjōen Umeyasu of Hino, Gōshū
FLLW FDN 3017.005

Jigoku (whose name means "Hell"), a renowned courtesan of the fifteenth century, wears an elaborate kimono adorned with the design of the King of Hell watching demons play backgammon. Much of Jigoku's fame is due to her legendary encounter with the poet-priest Ikkyū (1394–1481).

Kukai jūnen (ten years of of servitude) mentioned in the poetry refers to the ten-year contract made between a courtesan and her brothel. It also alludes to a "harsh world" as in *jigoku* or hell.

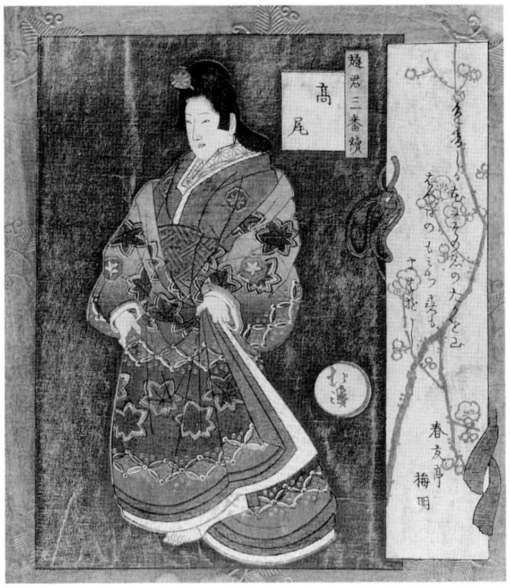

HOKKEI

134 A courtesan in formal attire

TITLE *Takao*
SERIES *Yūkun Samban Tsuzuki*; Series of Three Prints of Courtesans
DATE ca. 1830
SIGNATURE Hokkei
FORMAT Shikishiban (21.1 x 18.0)
REFERENCES Forrer, *Surimono/Egoyomi*, pl. 142; *Paul F. Walter Collection of Surimono*, pl. 30; Schindler, pl. 97; *Collection de Monsieur X . . .*, pl. 167
POET Shun'yūtei Umeaki
FLLW FDN 3017.004

There were several courtesans who used the name Takao, but the best known, and the one depicted here, is Takao II, a courtesan of the Miuraya bordello in the Yoshiwara, who according to most accounts died in 1659. She wears a maple-leaf patterned coat over her kimono. The maple leaf also appears as her crest and hair-pin ornament. The *tanzaku* poem panel at the right has a seasonal plum motif and the border contains pine boughs.

This is probably the right-hand sheet of the set of three prints.

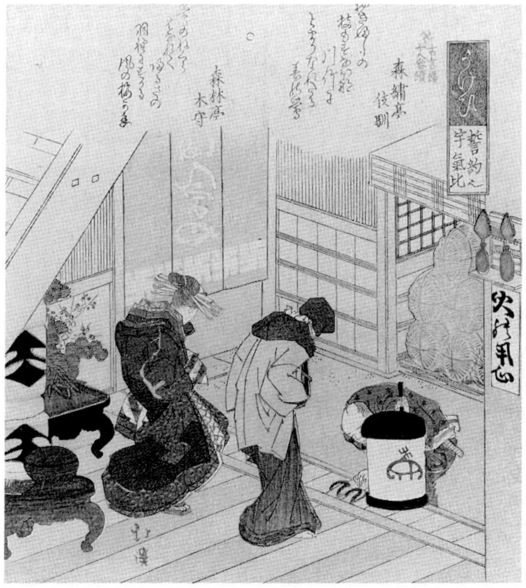

HOKKEI

135 A courtesan and her patron

TITLE *Seiyaku no Ukei*; Promise
SERIES *Kogentei Jūhachiban Tsuzuki*; Eighteen Illustrations for "The Staircase of Ancient Words"
DATE 1831
SIGNATURE Hokkei
FORMAT Shikishiban (20.7 x 17.8)
POETS Shinshūtei Tsuenare, Shinrintei Komori
FLLW FDN 3017.002

A courtesan with her disguised patron depart from her brothel, Manjiya; the *manji* (reversed swastika) is also the emblem for the poetry group led by Shinratei which commissioned this series. A servant places sandals before the honored customer.

The *Kogentei,* published by Kadori Nabiko in 1764, was a study of the development of the Japanese phonetic script viewed from classical sources (Keyes, *Beatty*, no. 139).

This set of at least eighteen prints focuses on the syllable "u," which can be interpreted as "rabbit" and therefore indicates the date of this series, 1831, year of the rabbit. In this case, the "u" is for the word *ukei* or promise.

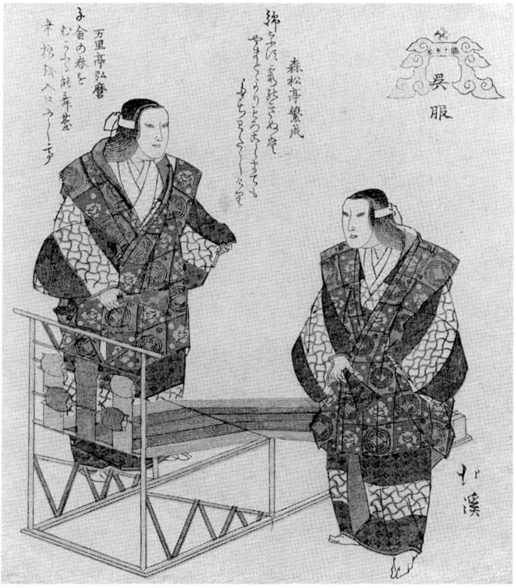

HOKKEI

136 Two Chinese weavers

TITLE *Kureha*; The Weavers
SERIES *Nō Jūgoban;* Fifteen Nō Plays
DATE Early 1830s
SIGNATURE Hokkei
FORMAT Shikishiban (21.2 x 18.7)
REFERENCE Kruml, 1975, pl.34
POETS Shinshōtei Shigenari, Manritei Hiromaro
FLLW FDN 3017.061

Commissioned by the Manji circle, as indicated by the reversed swastika crest above the title cartouche, this series of fifteen designs depicts scenes from prominent Nō dramas. Here, two Nō performers play the roles of Kurehatori and Ayahatori, Chinese weavers who came to Japan during the reign of Emperor Yūryaku (456–79).

For thirteen other designs from this series see Kruml, 1975, plates 26–39. The fifteenth design may be found in Keyes, *Spencer*, catalogue number 71.

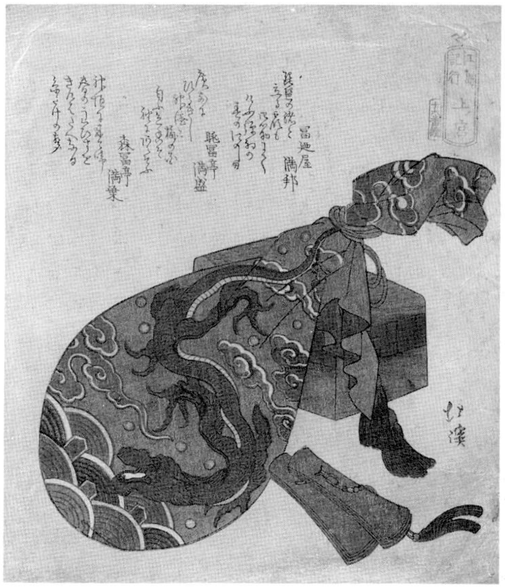

HOKKEI

137 A lute and brocade satchel

TITLE *Uenomiya*
SERIES *Enoshima Kikō Jūrokuban Tsuzuki*; A Series of Sixteen Designs of Travel to Enoshima
DATE 1833
SIGNATURE Hokkei
FORMAT Shikishiban (20.9 x 18.0)
REFERENCES Ostier, *Les objets tranquilles*, pl.103; Kruml 1975, pl.19
POETS Tominoya Mitsukuni, Chōfutei Mitsumori, Shimputei Mitsuba
FLLW FDN 3017.037

A lute encased in a brocade sack decorated with a Chinese-dragon design leans against a storage box with a reversed swastika motif for the Manji poetry circle. Beside it are a pair of castanets.

According to legend, Benzaiten, the goddess of arts and learning, was able to quell a serpent that was destroying the island of Enoshima through the mesmerizing power of her lute. A temple was built in her honor and has remained a center for her worship. The image of the lute combined with the reference to Enoshima are links to Benzaiten and the snake year.

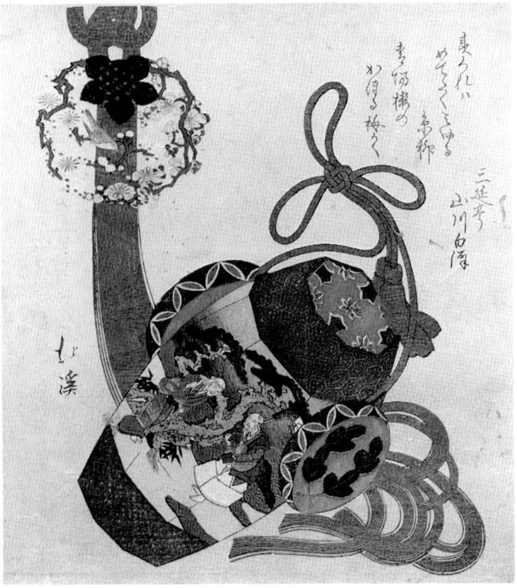

HOKKEI

138 A New Year pull toy

DATE ca. 1835
SIGNATURE Hokkei
FORMAT Shikishiban (20.8 x 18.0)
POET San'entei Yamakawa Shirozake
FLLW FDN 3017.062

A boy's pull toy is decorated for the New Year with the a scene from the propitious Nō play *Takasago*, which tells the story of the loving couple Jō and Uba. Another New Year ornament hanging behind it has a wreath of plum branches with the ubiquitous warbler in the center.

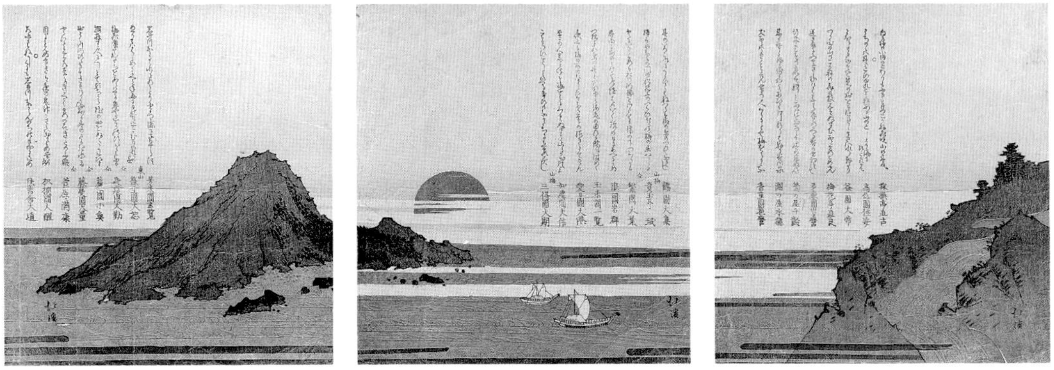

HOKKEI

139 Landscape triptych

DATE ca. 1835
SIGNATURE Hokkei
FORMAT Shikishiban triptych (19.8 x 17.9 each)
REFERENCES For a discussion of this design and a listing of all the twenty-four poets, see Keyes, *Beatty*, no. 146
FLLW FDN 3017.041-.043

The sun rises over the volcanic island of Kinkazan, which is located off the coast of Ojika Peninsula. To the right is Iwai River of Iwate Province, which in actuality lies quite far from the island.

Although a popular format for ukiyo-e prints in the 1850s, landscape triptychs in the surimono format are rare. This contiguous landscape scene is more closely allied to the compositional aesthetics of Japanese painting. Interestingly, this unusual surimono triptych is contemporaneous with Hiroshige's early experiments with this genre in his triptychs of the Sumida River.

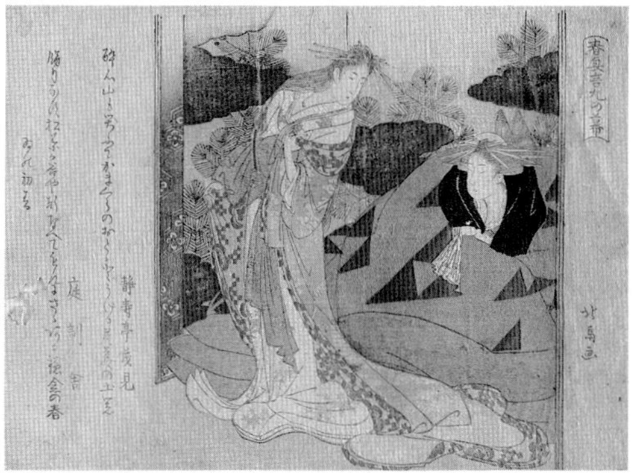

TEISAI HOKUBA
1771–1844

140 Courtesans beneath a quilt and standing before a screen

SERIES *Haru Kyōgen Ku no Maku;* Nine Acts of a Spring Play
DATE 1803, Year of the Boar, Spring
SIGNATURE Hokuba ga
FORMAT Koban yoko-e (13.8 x 18.6)
POETS Seijutei Shigemi, Teikinsha
FLLW FDN 3014.010

Haru Kyōgen in the title refers to Kabuki plays performed to celebrate the New Year. Customarily, plays based on the themes from the *Tales of the Soga Brothers* were staged, but the scene in this print has yet to be identified. This surimono represents one of Hokuba's earliest known prints and the portrayal of the courtesans demonstrates the artist's stylistic debt to his master Hokusai. This is one of two prints from the series in the Wright collection.

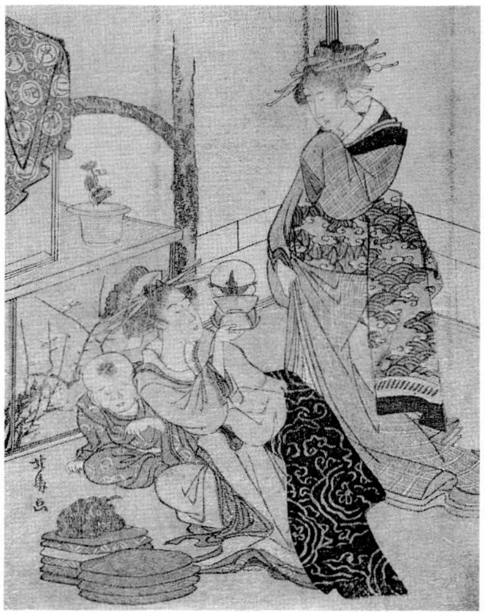

HOKUBA

141 Two women, one holding a *fukusuke* doll, with a boy

DATE 1805, Year of the Ox
SIGNATURE Hokuba ga
FORMAT Koban tate-e (12.8 x 10.2)
FLLW FDN 3014.005

The *fukusuke* doll was originally modeled after a merchant named Satarō who came to Edo and had great success. Later he changed his name to Fukusuke (*fuku* means luck). The doll, popular in the early nineteenth century, is readily identified by its huge head and large, lucky ears.

In the foreground is a *nadeushi,* a small ox talisman that was stroked for luck. A new pillow was placed under the *nadeushi* every time it granted a wish. The red cloth which partially covers a large box at the far left is decorated with circular motifs bearing the numbers for the long months—2, 4, 8, 9, 10, 11—for the year of the ox, 1805.

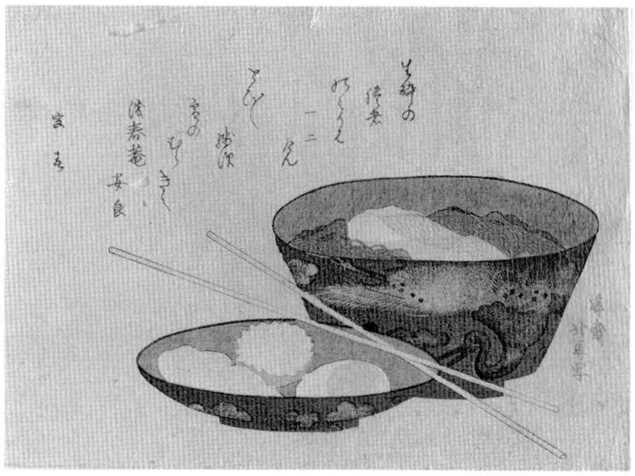

HOKUBA

142 A lacquer bowl and cover with noodles and other ingredients

DATE 1806, Year of the Tiger, Spring
SIGNATURE Teisai Hokuba sha
FORMAT Koban yoko-e (14.0 x 18.5)
POET Senshun'an Yasuyoshi
REFERENCE *UT, Bibliothèque Nationale,* p. 225, pl. 85. Another impression may be found in the collection of the Metropolitan Museum of Art
FLLW FDN 3014.008

An unusual green lacquer bowl is filled with green noodles and a piece of fish. A slice of egg, potato, and *yuba*, a special type of tofu, rest in the inverted cover. The exterior of the soup bowl is arrayed with the New Year motifs of a crane and plum blossoms. Green-colored lacquer originated in China and was relatively rare in Japan even as late as the mid-nineteenth century. For another example see a surimono by Hokkei (cat. no. 94).

While the vivid color scheme and intricate embossing suggest a later dating (plausibly dating to the next tiger year, 1818), the format and simplicity of the design point to the earlier year. The poet, who was affiliated with the Tsubo-gawa, was appointed a poetry judge of the group in the sixth month of 1805 (see "*Tsubo Sumire,*" 126); it is possible that he commissioned this print for the spring of the next year to commemorate the occasion.

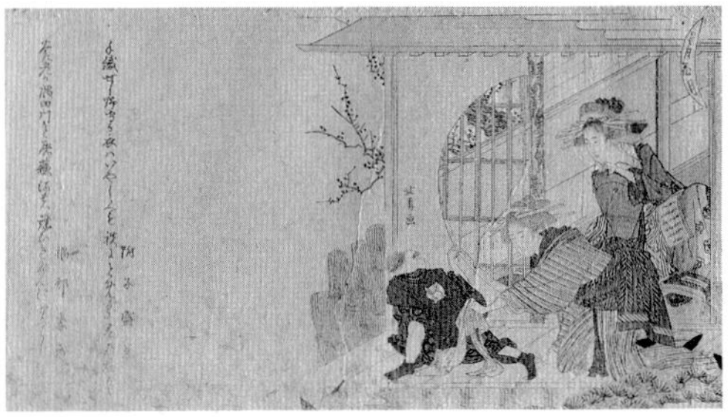

HOKUBA

143 A woman and her maid with a boy on a porch

SERIES [*Mochi*]*zuki Hanazuki*; [Full] Moon, Flower Moon
DATE 1806, Year of the Tiger
SIGNATURE Hokuba ga
FORMAT Koban yoko-e (trimmed; 13.4 x 23.6)
POETS Busu no Morikane, Fukube Suenari
REFERENCE *UT, Bibliothèque Nationale,* 226, pl. 87
FLLW FDN 3014.012

A maid fusses with a boy's obi as his mother waves to the child while reading. A white rabbit appears conspicuously as the design element on the back of the child's garment. The rabbit is traditionally linked to the moon, which is mentioned twice in the title cartouche. The visual pun of a moon-shaped window further alludes to that association. Despite these references to the rabbit, an untrimmed impression in the Bibliothèque Nationale is dated to the year of the tiger and has another poem, by Hyōtei Hyakunari, which mentions a tiger.

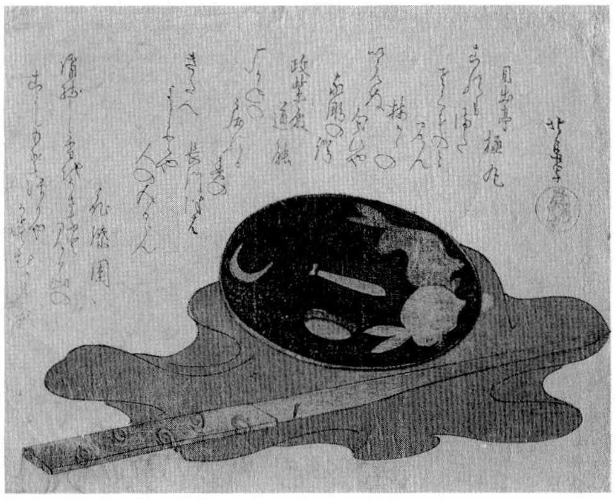

HOKUBA

144 A sword guard and knife

DATE possibly 1807
SIGNATURE Hokuba sha
ARTIST'S SEAL Undeciphered
FORMAT Koban yoko-e (14.5 x 17.8)
POETS Medetei Kiwamaru, Seishiden Michiyoshi, Kashitsuen
FLLW FDN 3014.004

A metal sword guard, with inlays of gold and silver representing two rabbits beneath a crescent moon, lies on a wrapping cloth together with a silver *kozuka*, or small knife, with a gilt metal handle. Both items are part of a set of sword fittings. In such an ensemble, the small knife slides into an opening on the sheath of a sword.

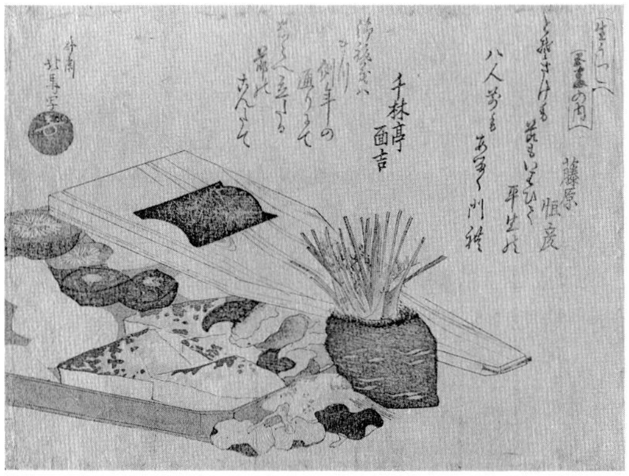

HOKUBA

145 Vegetables and a grater

SERIES *Shōutsushi Goban no Uchi;* Five Designs Drawn From Life
DATE ca. 1808
SIGNATURE Teisai Hokuba sha
ARTIST'S SEAL Uma
CARVER'S SEAL Undeciphered
FORMAT Koban yoko-e (14.2 x 18.6)
POETS Senrintei Tsurayoshi, Fujiwara Tsunehiko
FLLW FDN 3014.002

In this surimono, a grater or slicer is placed beside a tray containing various vegetables—dried shiitake mushrooms, raddish, carrot, and others—and decorated fish cakes. This type of special food is for the New Year. For another design from the series see catalogue number 27.

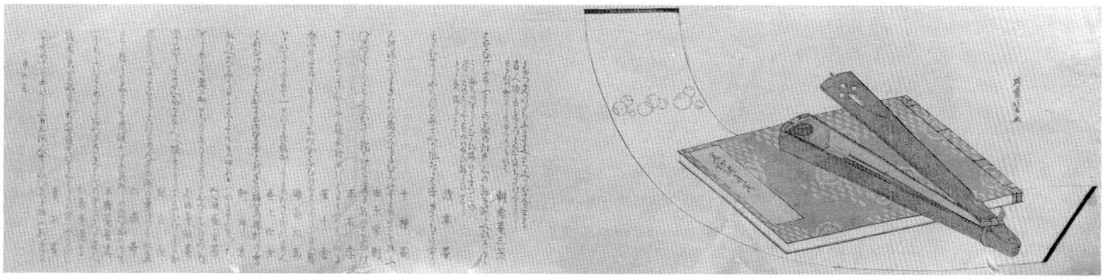

HOKUBA

146 A brush box, paper, and stitch-bound book

DATE 1812, Year of the Monkey
SIGNATURE Teisai Hokuba ga
FORMAT Yokonagaban (14.0 x 57.1)
REFERENCE *UT, Bibliothèque Nationale*, 202, pl.41
POETS Asakuraan Sanshō, Noki no Masukata, Chikusaan, Koryūan Otoyoshi, Tawara Tsunenori, Kasekitei Hakuboku, Taira no Ishisue, Aki no Nagayo, Tsuru no Sensha, Rokuzōtei, Teisai Hokuba, Suehiroan Nagakiyo, Makiage Tsugime, Jingidō Michimori, Masagoan (Michimori)
FLLW FDN 3014.013

An open, portable brush box was used by poets and writers when travelling, and thus made the ideal going-away present. This brush box lies on a blank sheet of paper decorated with the arc-in-a-circle emblem of the Asakusa-gawa. Between them is a stitch-bound book to be used as a travel journal for jotting down observations and poems.

This surimono, bearing poems by sixteen poets, represents a farewell present commissioned on the occasion of the departure of the poet Chōsōan for his hometown Mikawa (modern Shizuoka).

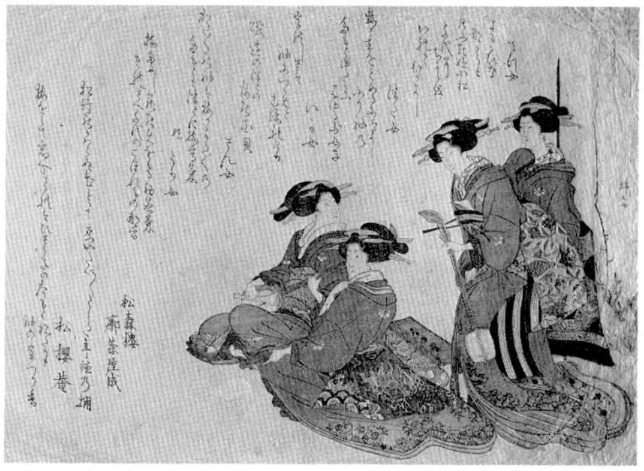

HOKUBA

147 Four women entertainers

DATE 1820
SIGNATURE Teisai (on screen of plum)
FORMAT Chūban yoko-e (20.5 x 28.6)
POETS Tetsume, Tsutame, Ikame, Samme, Torime (daughter of Samme), Shōshinrō Kuruwa no Chayanari, Shōōan
FLLW FDN 3014.017

Four geisha are dressed in formal robes adorned with paulownia crests, probably the mark of a Yoshiwara bordello. The two women in purple robes play shamisen; the other two in green kimono will accompany the performance. The prominently displayed dragon motif embroidered on the obi of the central figure indicates this print was issued in 1820, a dragon year.

The first five poems are signed with feminine appellations, perhaps the geishas' real names. Since the sixth poet's name includes a term for a teahouse (*kuruwa*), perhaps he was the owner of such an establishment and commissioned this surimono to present to his acquaintances and prized customers. This print and the following (cat. no. 148) are linked by their use of the paulownia-crest motif, and both bear a poem by the poet Shōōan in the honored position on the far left; the calligrapher is also the same. Since both prints are the same format and use the same exceptionally fine quality paper and pigments, it is reasonable to assume that they were issued together.

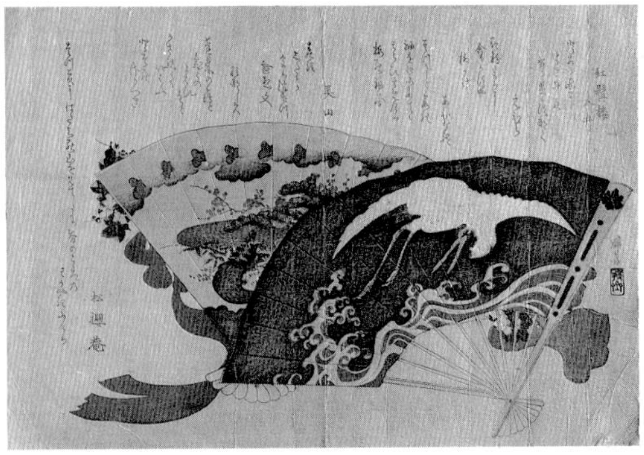

HOKUBA

148 Two folding fans

DATE probably 1820
SIGNATURE Teisai
SEAL Teisai
FORMAT Chūban yoko-e (20.0 x 28.5)
POETS Sekizenrō Ōi, Bizan, Shōōan
FLLW FDN 3014.018

Initially a student of Kanō-school painting, Hokuba reveals here his early training in the design of the fans. Both images are classical New Year represention of long life echoing allusions in the poems.

The folding paper fan in the foreground shows a crane flying over waves set against a gold ground. A gold paulownia crest appears on the wooden frame (see prior entry). The slats of the second fan are held together with red silk cord. The rear image includes a turtle, a symbol of longevity, against a traditional motif of pine, bamboo, and plum—the "three friends" of East Asian painting.

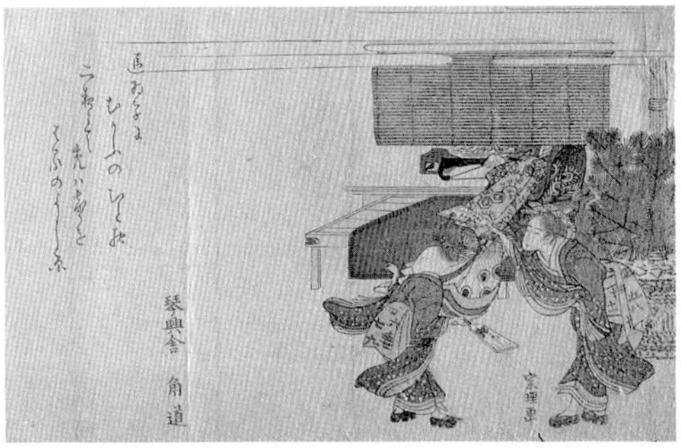

KATSUSHIKA HOKUSAI
1760–1849

149 Two children playing with battledores

DATE 1797
SIGNATURE Sōri ga
FORMAT Small koban yoko-e (9.6 x 15.0)
POET Kinkōsha Kadomichi
FLLW FDN 3002.123

Two children with paddles used in a game of battledore pause during their game. A courtesan sits hidden behind partially unrolled blinds. On the obi of the slightly older girl attendant are the numbers for the long months—1, 3, 5, 8, 10, 11, 12; the short months are on the younger child's obi—2, 4, 6, 7, 7I , 9. To the right stands a New Year's pine-tree decoration. The poem refers to *kamuro,* girl attendants to courtesans, of the Yoshiwara.

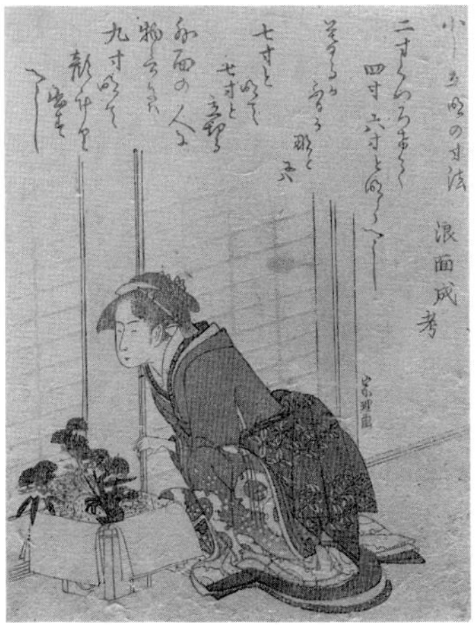

HOKUSAI

150 A woman with a New Year arrangement

TITLE *Shōji Toshiake no Sumpō;* Measuring the Beginning of the New Year
DATE 1797, Year of the Snake
SIGNATURE Sōri ga
FORMAT Small koban tate-e (13.2 x 9.7)
POET Nami no Tsuranari kō
FLLW FDN 3002.038

In this egoyomi, a young woman carefully opens a sliding paper door in order to bring in a New Year arrangement. The numbers for the short months are given cryptically in the text (2, 4, 6, 7, 7 I, 9) as the five increments by which a sliding door may be opened. The seventh month is listed twice to indicate an intercalary month.

The inscription was composed by Nami no Tsuranari and signed with the word *kō,* meaning "conceived by."

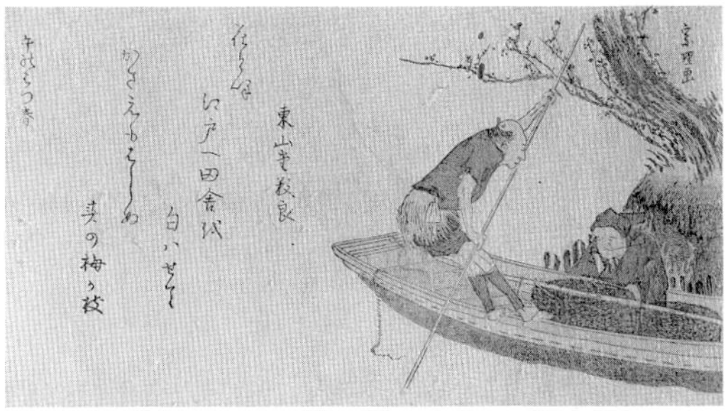

HOKUSAI

151 Two men in a boat

DATE 1798, Year of the Horse, Spring
SIGNATURE Sōri ga
FORMAT Koban yoko-e (9.5 x 17.0)
POET Tōzandō Kazuyoshi
FLLW FDN 3002.098

A man poles his boat as another prepares the fishing traps. Hokusai was apparently intrigued with the image and strong diagonal tension created by a boatman poling his vessel. He used this image repeatedly as a compositional element throughout his career.

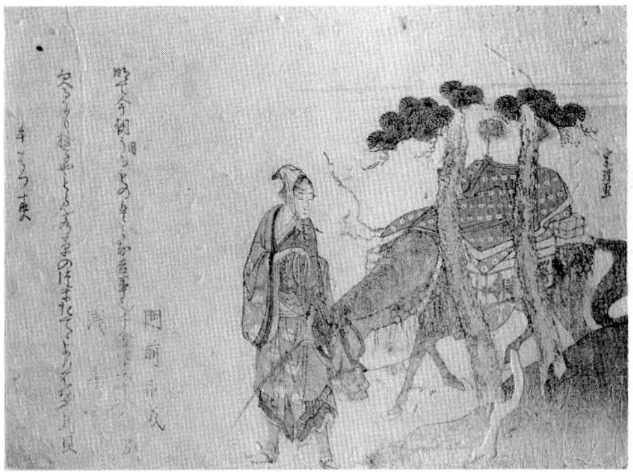

HOKUSAI

152 A man leading his horse past pine trees

DATE 1798, Year of the Horse, spring
SIGNATURE Sōri ga
FORMAT Koban yoko-e (13.8 x 18.4)
REFERENCES *UT, Bibliothèque Nationale*, 203, pl.43; NUK, *Pulverer,* 2-27
POETS Monzen Ichinari, Asakusaan Ichihito
FLLW FDN 3002.100

A merchant leads his horse along the pine trees. Observing a New Year custom termed *hatsuni*, merchants loaded and decorated their horse with goods to be delivered to their customers for the first time in the New Year.

As with all New Year surimono of 1798 bearing a "Sōri" signature, the attribution to Hokusai stands because he did not give that name to his pupil (Sōri III) until the eighth month of that year.

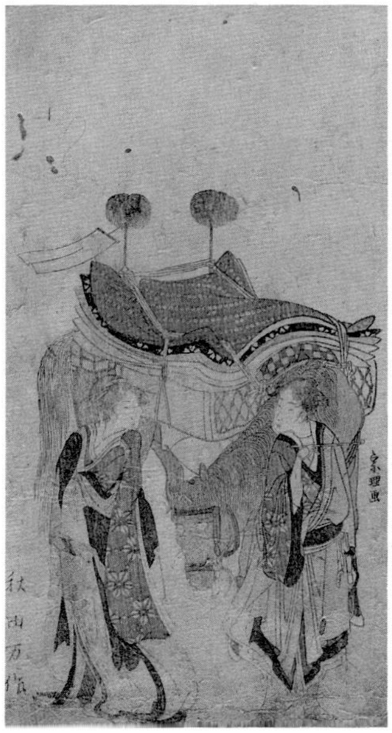

HOKUSAI

153 A fashionable young man and woman with a horse

DATE 1798
SIGNATURE Sōri ga
FORMAT Koban tate-e (20.0 x 10.8)
POET Akita no Mansaku (poem trimmed)
FLLW FDN 3002.122

A young woman and man stand before a horse laden with packages. In this *hatsuni* scene, the goods to be sold to a client at the New Year have been decoratively piled onto the horse. This design surely refers to the horse year.

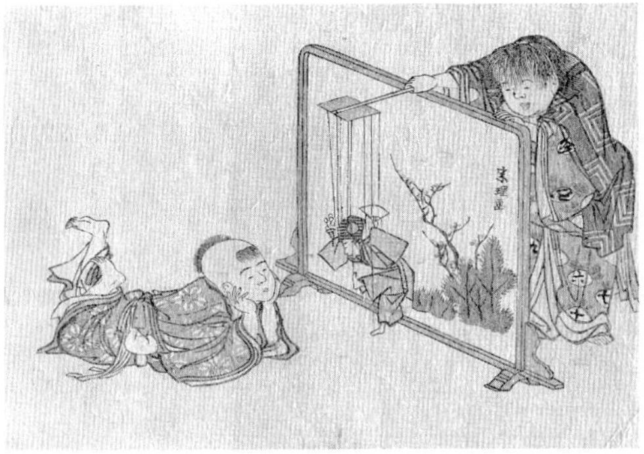

HOKUSAI

154 Two boys with a marionette

DATE 1798
SIGNATURE Sōri ga
FORMAT Small koban yoko-e (8.5 x 12.2)
FLLW FDN 3002.106

A boy gazes intently as his companion makes his marionette enact the Sambasō dance, traditionally performed at the New Year or at the opening ceremonies for new Kabuki theatres. The kimono pattern of the standing boy bears the numbers for the short months—1, 4, 6, 7, 9, 10. The artist's signature appears on the screen.

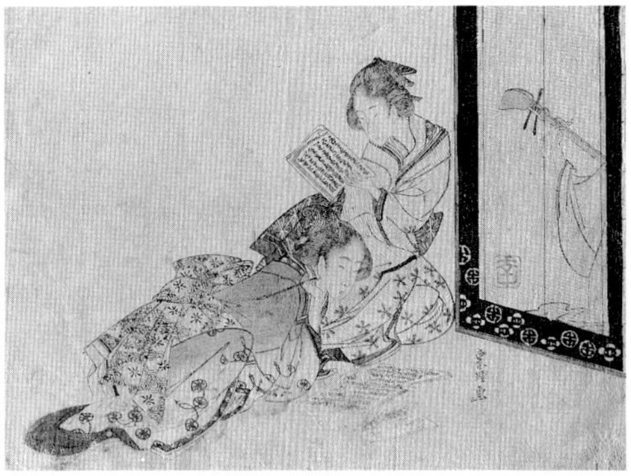

HOKUSAI

155 Two young women reading a Jōruri text

DATE 1798
SIGNATURE Sōri ga
SEAL Kō (or *sachi* meaning luck)
FORMAT Koban yoko-e (13.7 x 18.3)
FLLW FDN 3002.127

Two young women seem to be carefully studying Jōruri texts as a musician sitting on the other side of bamboo screen plays a shamisen. The months are cryptically indicated in the white circular motifs. The smaller four-petaled design is an abstracted form of the character for "small," and the larger circular form contains the character for "large." Thus, reading from right to left, the long months are 2, 3, 5, 8, 11,12; the short months are 1, 4, 6, 7, 9, 10. The collection includes another, slightly weaker impression of the same image (FLLW FDN 3002.128).

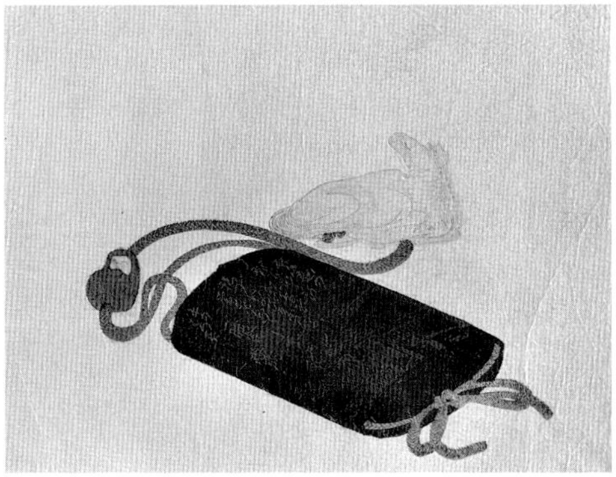

HOKUSAI

156 An inrō with a netsuke

DATE 1798, Year of the Horse, spring
SIGNATURE Sōri tō
FORMAT Koban yoko-e (11.2 x 14.2)
POET Issuisha Yumenari
FLLW FDN 3002.145

While the composition of this small-format print at first glance appears quite simple, a closer examination reveals that the inrō includes a poem in gold and a scene of a farm house with plum trees. Printed on a textured paper, this extremely small print is a tour de force of the printer's art. The inrō was burnished to create a lacquerlike effect and the ocher-colored horse netsuke has the appearance of aged ivory. The *ojime* bead is a typical representation of Daruma, shrouded in his red robe. The date appears following the poem on the inrō, while Hokusai's signature is written on the netsuke as if it were the carver's signature.

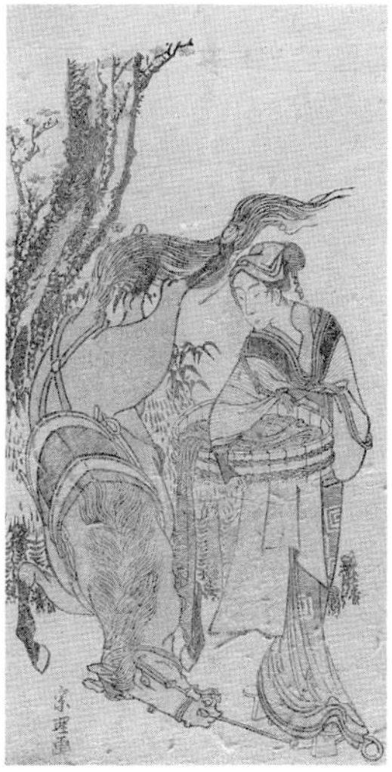

HOKUSAI

157 A washing woman stopping a horse

DATE 1798
SIGNATURE Sōri ga
HEIGHT 17.5
WIDTH 9.0
FORMAT Koban tate-e (17.5 x 9.0)
FLLW FDN 3002.053

An obvious subject for an egoyomi for a horse year, the strong woman of Ōmi, called Kaneko or Okane, managed to stop a runaway horse by stepping on its dragging tether. She is usually portrayed carrying a washing tub.

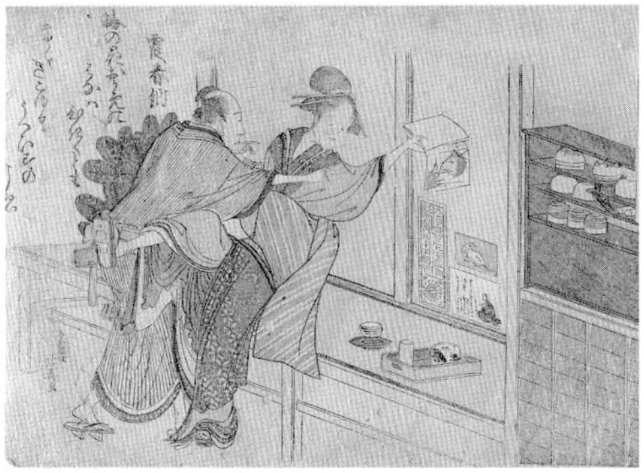

HOKUSAI

158 A man and a serving woman

DATE 1799, Year of the Goat
SIGNATURE Sōri Aratame Hokusai ga
FORMAT Koban yoko-e (12.8 x 17.8)
POET Kasumi no Haruami
FLLW FDN 3002.028

A man knocks over a serving woman as he reaches for a picture book, causing her kimono to open suggestively. The waitress resembles Okame, the goddess of mirth, also mentioned in the poem.

The book is open to a scene of the rising sun with plum branches. In the background, a picture of a goat is pasted on a sliding door, together with a listing of the long—2, 3, 4, 7, 9, 12—and short months—1, 5, 6, 8, 10, 11—revealing this print to be an egoyomi for 1799, a goat year.

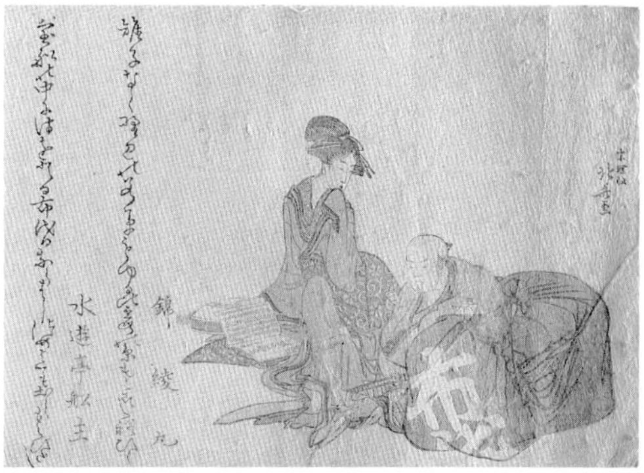

HOKUSAI

159 Hotei Ichiemon

SERIES Untitled series of the Five Thieves of Osaka (*Karigane Gonin Otoko*)
DATE ca. 1799
SIGNATURE Sōri aratame Hokusai ga
FORMAT Koban yoko-e (12.9 x 17.5)
POETS Nishiki no Ayamaru, Suiyūtei Funanushi
FLLW FDN 3002.131

A woman with a score and shamisen in her lap covers her smile as she looks at Hotei Ichiemon, one of the five thiefs of Osaka. In a parody of his namesake, the god Hotei, he holds a sack containing precious gifts on which is written "Hotei."

This series is based on the true story of five thieves active in Osaka, who were all captured, put in prison, and executed in 1702. Their lives assumed heroic proportions when their stories were later adapted into Kabuki and Jōruri plays. The collection has four of the five prints from the series; Kaminari Shōkurō is the missing design. See also catalogue numbers 160, 161, and 162.

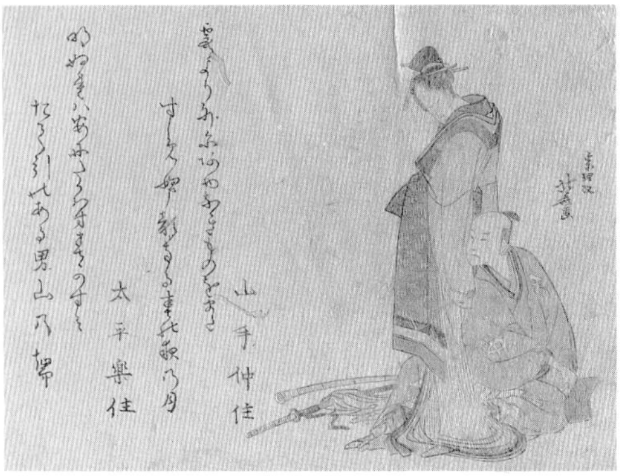

HOKUSAI

160 Anno Hirabei

SERIES Untitled series of the Five Thieves of Osaka (*Karigane Gonin Otoko*)
DATE ca. 1799
SIGNATURE Sōri aratame Hokusai ga
FORMAT Koban yoko-e (13.2 x 17.5)
POETS Yamate no Nakazumi, Taihei Rakuzumi
FLLW FDN 3002.132

A courtesan stands next to a seated man, the thief Anno Hirabei, whose flute and sword lie at the courtesan's feet. He can be identified by the character *an* in the crest of his kimono.

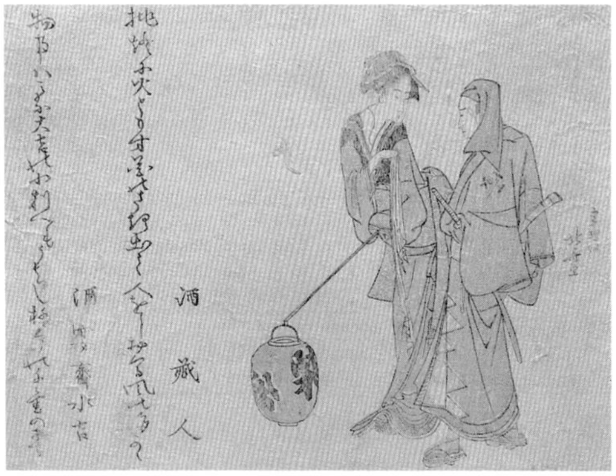

HOKUSAI

161 Gokuin Sen'uemon

SERIES Untitled series of the Five Thieves of Osaka (*Karigane Gonin Otoko*)
DATE ca. 1799
SIGNATURE Sōri aratame Hokusai ga
FORMAT Koban yoko-e (13.3 x 17.6)
REFERENCES Markus, *I Surimono,* p.28; *Collection Ernest Le Vèel (1re vente),* pl.142
POETS Sake no Kurōdo, Shuensai Mizuyoshi
FLLW FDN 3002.133

Holding a lantern, a woman stops to speak with a man who carries a flute and sword. The crest of crossed mallets on his robe identifies him as the thief Gokuin Sen'uemon.

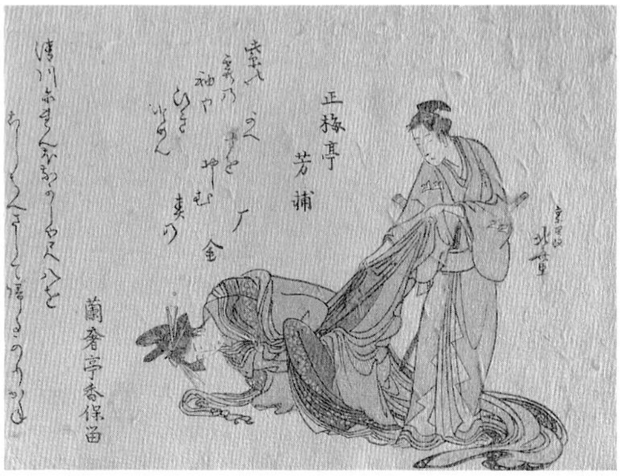

HOKUSAI

162 Karigane Bunshichi and Kiyokawa

SERIES Untitled series of the Five Thieves of Osaka (*Karigane Gonin Otoko*)
DATE ca. 1799
SIGNATURE Sori aratame Hokusai ga
FORMAT Koban yoko-e (13.3 x 17.5)
POETS Shōbaitei Yoshisuke, Ranjatei Kaoru
FLLW FDN 3002.134

A courtesan and a man have a playful tug-of-war with a kimono. His crest of two wild geese identifies him as the thief Karigane Bunshichi. He and his love for the courtesan Kiyokawa were a theme portrayed by numerous ukiyo-e artists, including Utamaro.

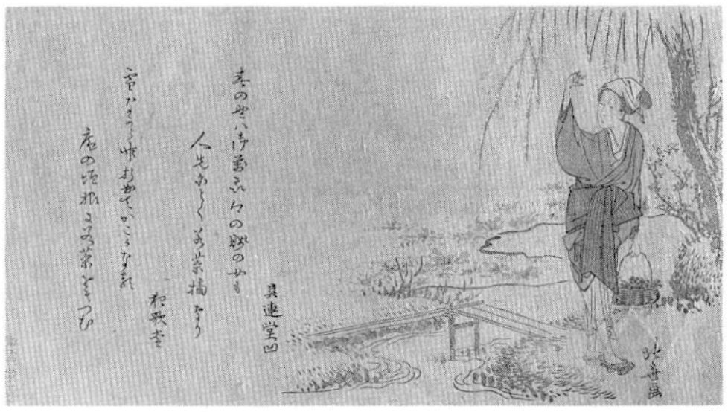

HOKUSAI

163 A woman collecting New Year herbs

DATE ca. 1800
SIGNATURE Hokusai ga
CARVER'S SEAL Horikō Nakaide Masuzono [?]
FORMAT Koban yoko-e (10.1 x 17.6)
POETS Gurendō Nakakubo, Kyōkadō
FLLW FDN 3002.126

A woman with a basket of herbs has just crossed a small wooden bridge and gazes off into distance. Both poems mention the New Year custom of collecting spring herbs.

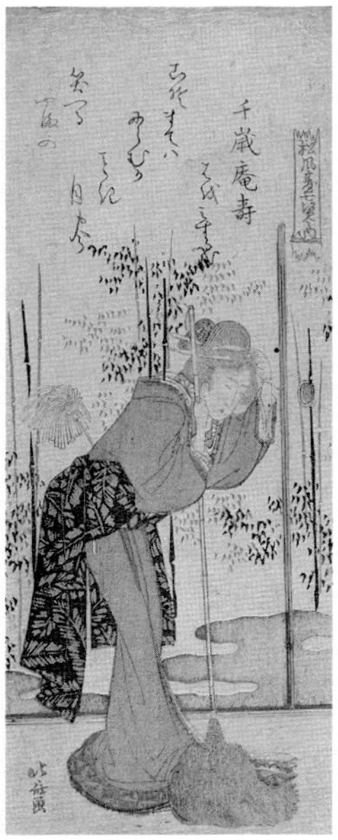

HOKUSAI

164 A woman leaning on a broom

SERIES *Shōfūdai Shichiken no Uchi;* Seven Sages of the Bamboo Grove for the Shōfūdai Club
DATE 1800
SIGNATURE Hokusai ga
FORMAT Koban tate-e (21.9 x 8.8)
POET Senzaian Kotobuki
FLLW FDN 3002.059

The theme of the Seven Sages of the Bamboo Grove originated in ancient Chinese lore and eventually became a popular pictorial subject in East Asian art. Customarily, the seven wise men are depicted conversing in a group, surrounded by bamboo. In this series of seven designs, the sages have been replaced with young women juxtaposed against a folding screen decorated with a bamboo pattern. Shōfudai in the title refers to the poetry circle headed by Shōfūdai, the older brother of the prominent kyōka master Bumbunsha Kanikomaru, leader of the Katsushika-ren. The set has been dated on the basis of the mention of the year of the monkey in one of the prints.

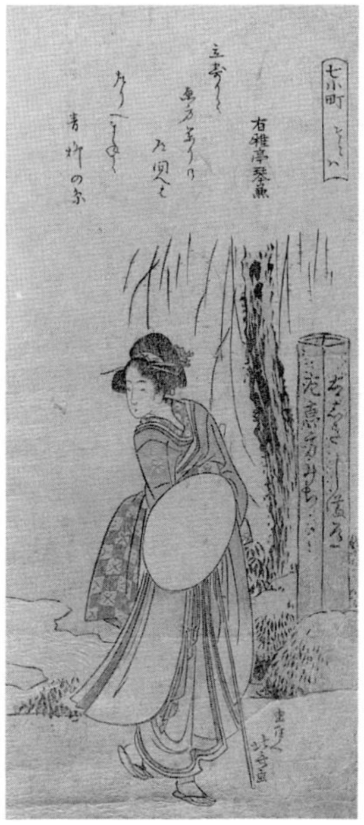

HOKUSAI

165 A woman with a pilgrim's hat and a walking stick

TITLE *Sotoba*
SERIES *Nana Komachi*; Seven Episodes in the Life of Komachi
DATE ca. 1801
SIGNATURE Gakyōjin Hokusai ga
FORMAT Koban tate-e (21.4 x 9.5)
POET Arigatei Kotokane
FLLW FDN 3002.055

In the story of Sotoba Komachi, the elderly Ono no Komachi met and conversed with a traveling priest while she leaned against a *sotoba* (stupa). In this parody, a young beauty carries a traveling hat and stick. She stands by a wooden signpost which reads *hidari ehō michi*, "the lucky direction is the left road." This refers to the New Year tradition of going to a shrine in the lucky direction (*ehō*). The other side reads *migi shikishima michi*, "the way of poetry is to the right."

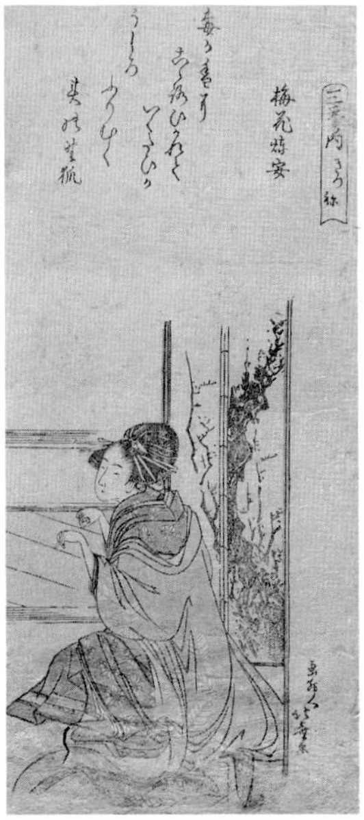

HOKUSAI

166 A crouching woman playing "fox charades"

TITLE *Kitsune*; Fox
SERIES *Samban no Uchi*; A Set of Three Designs
DATE ca. 1802
SIGNATURE Gakyōjin Hokusai ga
FORMAT Koban tate-e (20.2 x 8.8)
POET Baika Neriyasu
FLLW FDN 3002.056

Kitsune ken (fox charades) was once a popular amusement, especially among women. Three players adopted formalized poses and used hand gestures to represent the fox, hunter, and village chief. The Japan Ukiyo-e Museum has an uncut sheet containing the three prints in this series.

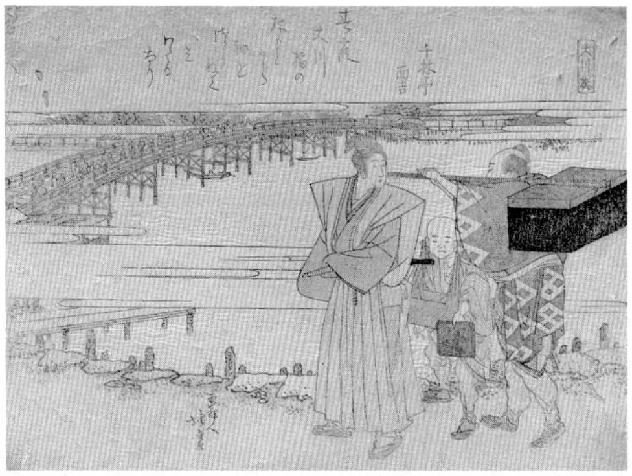

HOKUSAI

167 A samurai with a porter and a boy attendant

TITLE *Ōkawabashi*; Ōkawa Bridge
SERIES Untitled series of landscapes
DATE ca. 1802
SIGNATURE Gakyōjin Hokusai ga
FORMAT Koban yoko-e (14.0 x 18.8)
POET Senrintei Tsurayoshi
FLLW FDN 3002.101

Ōkawabashi was the original official name of Azumabashi, the last and most northern of the four large bridges spanning the Sumida River. In contrast to the more famous Ryōgoku Bridge, it was constructed entirely by public funds in 1774, and at one time a small toll was collected. Samurai, however, were exempted.

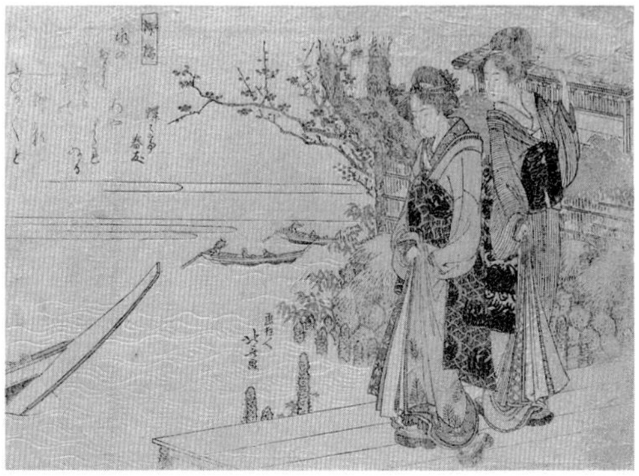

HOKUSAI

168 Two courtesans on a pier

TITLE *Yanagibashi*; Yanagi Bridge
SERIES Untitled set of landscapes
DATE ca. 1802
SIGNATURE Gakyōjin Hokusai ga
FORMAT Koban yoko-e (13.8 x 18.3)
REFERENCES Keyes, *Spencer*, cat. 96; *UT, Bibliothèque Nationale*, pl. 197
POET Chōchōtei Harutomo
FLLW FDN 3002.112

Two women walk to the end of a pier and watch for the approaching *chokibune* (boar's-tusk-shaped boat). This craft was used for swiftly ferrying customers to and from the Yoshiwara pleasure quarters district.

Yanagi Bridge spanned the Yoko Jukkengawa Canal, an east to west waterway in northeastern Edo.

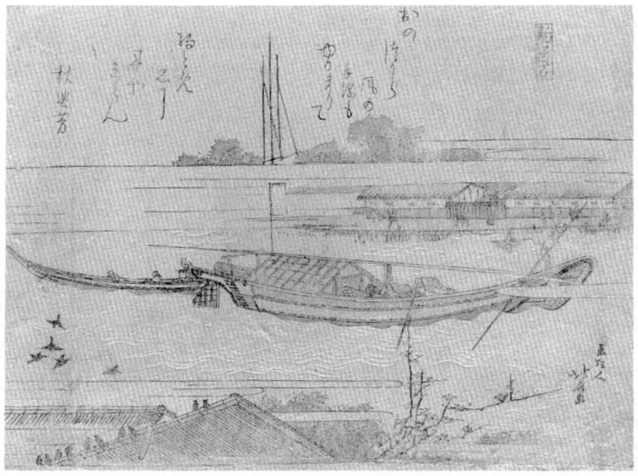

HOKUSAI

169 Departing fishing boats

TITLE *Komatomeishi*
SERIES An untitled set of landscape views of Edo
DATE ca. 1802
SIGNATURE Gakyōjin Hokusai ga
FORMAT Koban yoko-e (13.9 x 18.5)
POET Aki no Katayoshi
FLLW FDN 3002.015

Fishing boats set out in the morning, as crows swoop down in the lower left of the composition. On the opposite shore are warehouses; beyond them stands the framework for a well.

The Wright collection has three designs from this series including catalogue numbers 167 and 168, each of which bears a small red cartouche giving the name of the site. Typical of the surimono of this era, the coloration is quite delicate with only minimal use of gaufrage and brass.

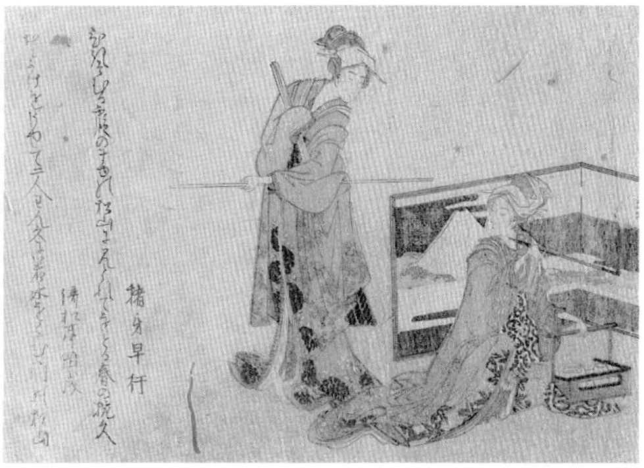

HOKUSAI

170 Two women before a small screen depicting Mount Fuji

SERIES *Odori Zukushi*; Dance Series
DATE ca. 1803
SIGNATURE Gakyō (on screen)
FORMAT Koban yoko-e (13.3 x 18.3)
REFERENCE *UT, Bibliothèque Nationale*, pl. 211 (with a series stamp, missing in this impression)
POETS Choki no Hayayuki, Kishōtei Okanari
FLLW FDN 3002.146

A seated woman who is smoking sits before a small two-fold screen of Mount Fuji, which bears the artist's signature, while a standing figure holds several poles. This print is a parody of the dance based on the tragic story of the lovers Wankyū and Matsuyama, who are both referred to in the poems. Wan'ya Kyūemon (whose name was contracted to Wankyū in stage versions), the wealthy merchant, fell in love with the courtesan Matsuyama. Infatuation turned into obsession, causing him to lose his fortune in attempting to win her, and finally he went mad and committed suicide.

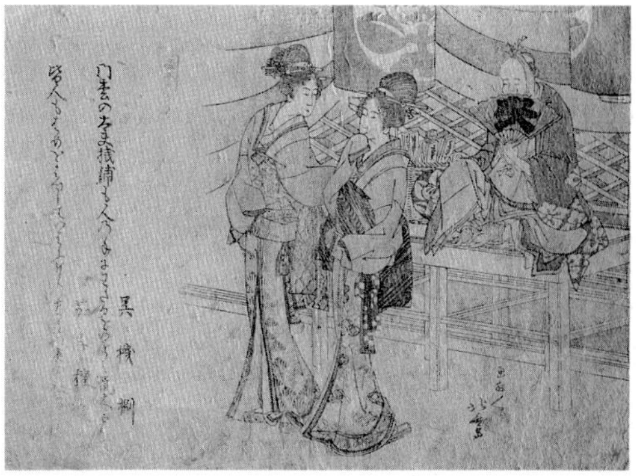

HOKUSAI

171 A hawker outside a theater

TITLE *Nezumi Kido*; Rat Entrance
SERIES *Nezumi*; Rat
DATE 1804
SIGNATURE Gakyōjin Hokusai ga
FORMAT Koban yoko-e (13.8 x 18.4)
REFERENCE *UT, Bibliothèque Nationale*, pl. 235
POETS Kure no Kihachi, Nasu no Tane[kazu]
FLLW FDN 3002.089

In this theater-district scene, a hawker baits customers with jokes and gives play summaries as young girls wait to enter. The title likens the small theatre entrance, which served to deter gate-crashers, to a rat hole, and dates the print to the year of the rat, 1804.

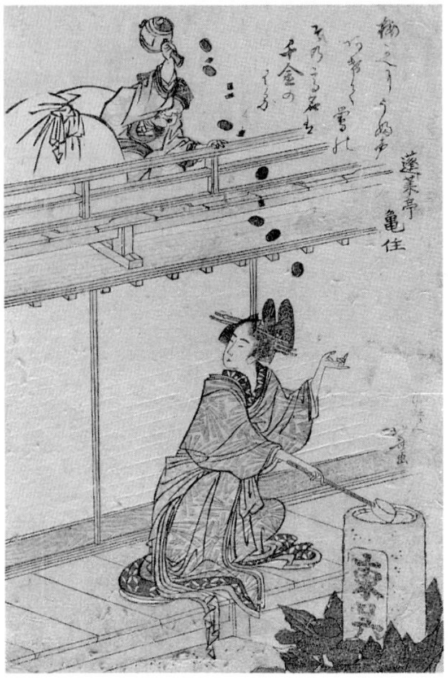

HOKUSAI

172 Daikoku tossing gold coins upon a woman drawing water

DATE 1804
SIGNATURE Gakyōjin Hokusai ga
FORMAT Koban tate-e (19.0 x 12.3)
POET Hōraitei Kamezumi
FLLW FDN 3002.062

According to legend, Daikoku, one of the Gods of Good Luck, carries precious items in his bag and has the ability to confer wealth with a mere wave of his lucky mallet. The date of the print is determined by the sequence of large and small gold pieces, starting at the top: the long months are 1, 3, 6, 8, 10, 11, and 12 and the short months are 2, 4, 5, 7, and 9.

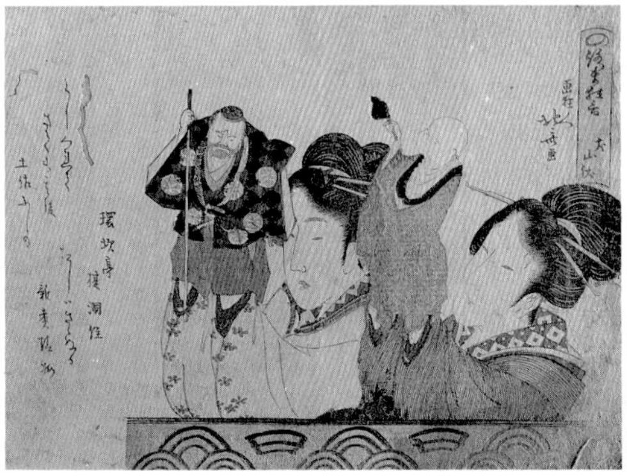

HOKUSAI

173 Two women acting as puppeteers

TITLE *Inu Yamabushi;* The Mountain Priest and the Dog
SERIES *Noroma Kyōgen*
DATE ca. 1804
SIGNATURE Gakyōjin Hokusai ga
FORMAT Koban yoko-e (14.0 x 18.8)
POET Kankantei Enoki no Horazumi
FLLW FDN 3002.020

Two women manipulate hand puppets representing the roles of a mountain monk (*yamabushi*) and a Shintō priest. The teahouse owner in this Kyōgen play, after listening to a long argument between the two priests, suggests that as a means of settling their dispute both attempt to quiet his ferocious dog with their respective prayers. Having secretly learned the command which calms the animal, the Shintō priest succeeds by intoning that word repeatedly within his prayers.

In addition to the example illustrated in color (cat. no. 31), the collection includes four designs from this series: FLLW FDN 3002.019, .023, .024, and .025. All are in the same format, although the title cartouche varies between white and yellow. Because the yellow-colored examples are slightly better impressions, it is possible that they represent an earlier printing. A still later edition is known in chūban format, with different poems (see Lane, *Hokusai,* pl. 67).

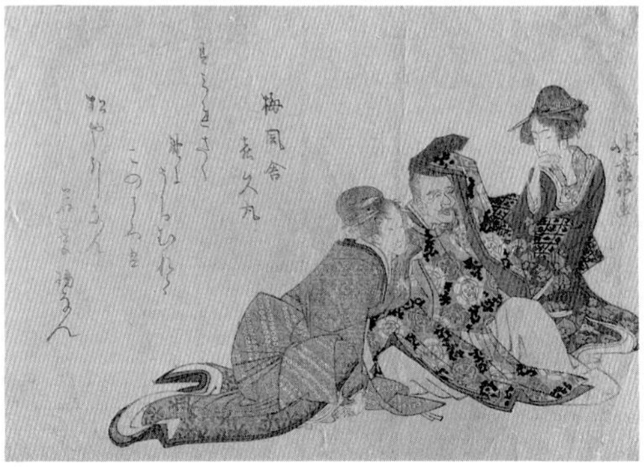

HOKUSAI

174 A courtier and two women

DATE ca. 1804
SIGNATURE Gakyōjin Hokusai suichū ga (drawn while drunk)
FORMAT Koban yoko-e (13.0 x 18.1)
REFERENCES *UT, Bibliothèque Nationale*, 222, pl. 80; Tōbu Museum of Art, ed., pl. 50
POET Baifūsha Kikumaru
FLLW FDN 3002.088

The poem alludes to a famous verse on the theme of violets by the ancient poet Yamabe no Akahito. The classical garb of the male figure suggests that Hokusai intended to create an imaginary portrait of Akahito. The women are dressed, however, in contemporary Edo attire.

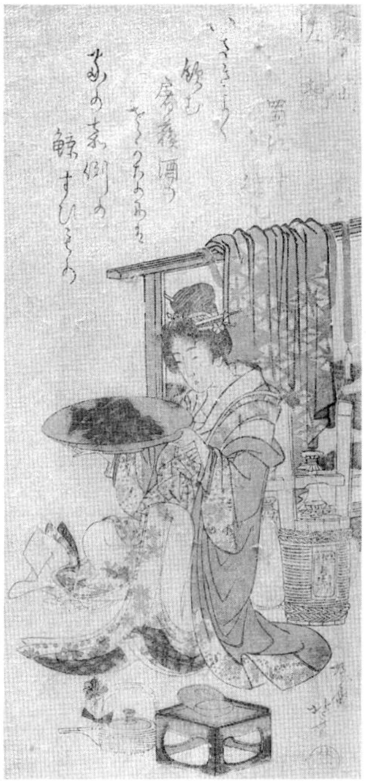

HOKUSAI

175 A woman with a large sake cup

TITLE *Sasō*
SERIES *Inchū Hassen*; Eight Immortals of the Wine Cup
DATE 1805
SIGNATURE Kyūkyūshin Hokusai ga
DEALER'S SEAL Hayashi Tadamasa
FORMAT Koban tate-e (19.5 x 7.0)
POET Shokkōtei Ayamaru
FLLW FDN 3002.054

In this scene parodying a Taoist immortal, an elegantly garbed woman holds a large ceremonial sake cup. The poem mentions drinking New Year's sake and a soup made of whale meat. The character in the cup appears to be *nishiki,* which might refer to the poet's other name, Nishiki no Ayamaru.

The signature on this print was one used by Hokusai only in 1805.

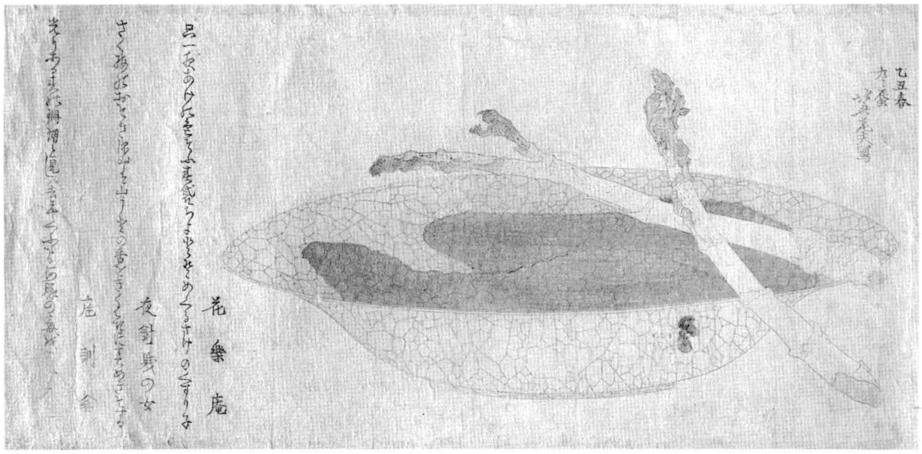

HOKUSAI

176 *Udo* and fish roe in a porcelain bowl

DATE 1805, Year of the Ox, spring
SIGNATURE Kyūkyūshin Hokusai Rōfu (Old Man) sha
FORMAT Small yokonagaban (14.0 x 28.2)
POETS Karakuan, Yahari Shizunome, Teikinsha
FLLW FDN 3002.063

In this still life, *udo*, a Japanese vegetable similar to asparagus, lies with fish roe, a symbol of fecundity, in a crackle-glaze ceramic bowl. The wonderful play of textural patterns contrasts the linear crazing of the glaze with the red, circular, soft form of the fish roe and the stiff *udo* spears.

The first poem puns on a maiden who serves medicinal wine at the New Year while the second alludes to the tough *yama udo* eaten at that time to strengthen teeth. The third poem deals with the potentially fatal but popular delicacy, blowfish.

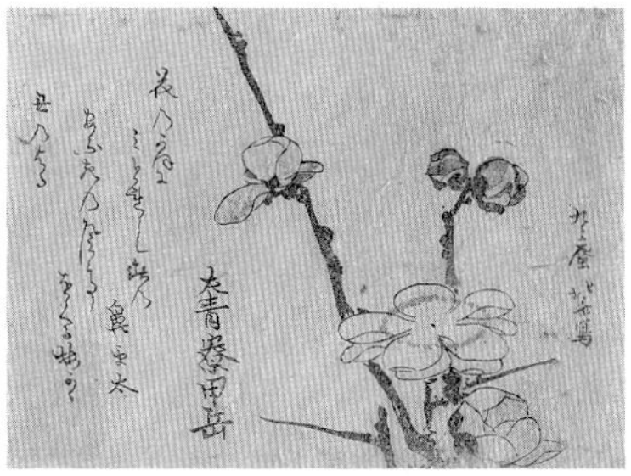

HOKUSAI

177 Plum branch

DATE 1805, Year of the Ox, Spring
SIGNATURE Kyūkyūshin Hokusai sha
FORMAT Koban yoko-e (9.0 x 12.0)
POET Saseiryō Kōgaku
FLLW FDN 3002.096

This signature was one used by Hokusai only in 1805.

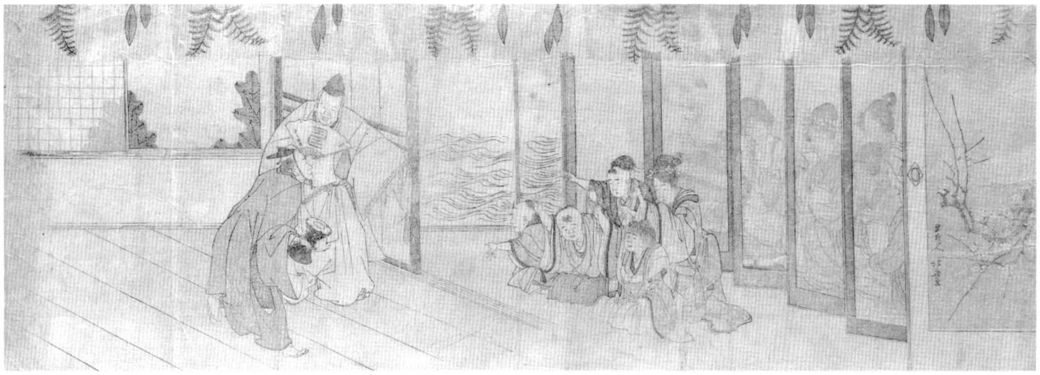

HOKUSAI

178 A *manzai* dance performance

DATE ca. 1805
SIGNATURE Gakyōjin Hokusai ga
FORMAT Yokonagaban (20.8 x 56.2)
FLLW FDN 3002.141

Several women watch from behind a mesh screen as children enjoy a performance by *manzai* comic dancers. A fan held by one of these performers bears a stylized rendition of the Chinese character *kotobuki,* meaning luck.

Hokusai's signature appears on a sliding-door panel as if it were that of the artist of the plum-tree painting. The text portion of the print is missing.

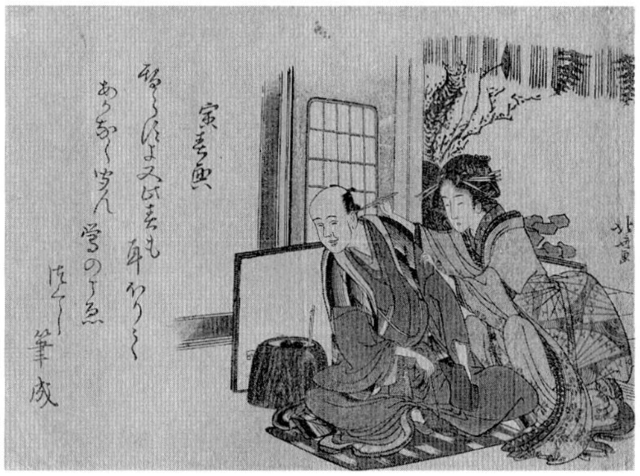

HOKUSAI

179 A young woman cleaning a man's ear

TITLE *Tora Shunkyō*; Spring Amusements in the Year of the Tiger
DATE 1806, Year of the Tiger
SIGNATURE Hokusai ga
FORMAT Koban yoko-e (13.8 x 18.5)
POET Tsukushi Fudenari
FLLW FDN 3002.027

This depiction of a patron lacks any trace of Hokusai's typical figure style of this period. Instead, the man's animated expression and individualistic countenance suggest that this may have been intended as a portrait, perhaps of the poet Fudenari.

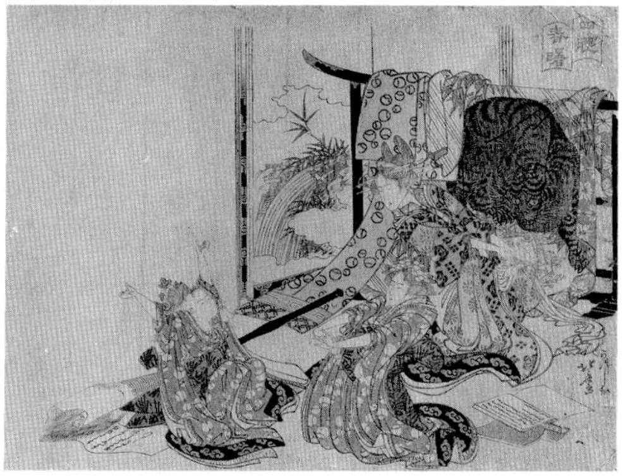

HOKUSAI

180 A courtesan and two attendants awakening

TITLE *Haru Akebono*; The Dawn of Spring
SERIES *Shisui;* Four Sleepers
DATE 1806, Year of the Tiger
SIGNATURE Katsushika Hokusai ga
FORMAT Yokonagaban (trimmed; 20.8 x 27.5)
REFERENCE *UT, Bibliothèque Nationale,* p. 225, pl. 85
FLLW FDN 3002.079

Several kimono are draped over a stand. One is boldly decorated with a tiger and bamboo motif, alluding to the zodiac year and the Four Sleepers, a subject of Chinese origin. An ideal image for a New Year surimono, the Four Sleepers symbolize perfect tranquility as the four dissimilar figures sleep peacefully together—Kanzan and Jittoku, the Zen monk Bukan who is their teacher, and a tiger. Here the monks are represented by a courtesan with her two girl attendants awakening at dawn.

The complete sheet, including the kyōka by thirteen poets, is in the collection of the Bibliothèque Nationale, Paris. The last two poets, Ryōsōtei and Ayabatei, are the same two poets who appear in the rare Utamaro surimono (cat. no. 288). They were the leaders of the Tsubogawa, whose emblem adorns the draped obi and robes the girl attendant.

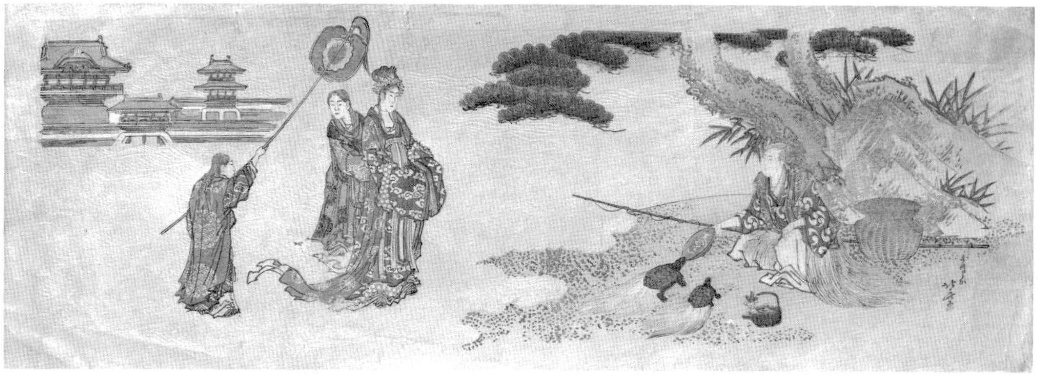

HOKUSAI

181 Urashima Tarō meeting Otohime

DATE ca. 1810
SIGNATURE Katsushika Hokusai ga
FORMAT Yokonagaban (19.8 x 54.6)
REFERENCE Ōta Memorial Museum of Art, ed., *Hatsukōkai Katsushika Hokusai Ten,* pl. 173
FLLW FDN 3002.143

Urashima Tarō meets Otohime, the daughter of the Dragon King, whose palace is visible in the background. Tarō feeds two auspicious turtles from a sake cup; only by riding on the back of a turtle was he able to approach this palace (see also cat. no. 105).

The poetry, program, or text section has been cut from this print.

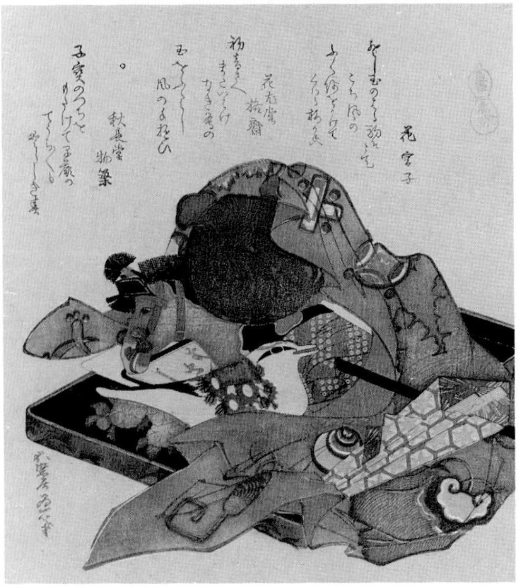

HOKUSAI

182 New Year presents

TITLE *Harugoma*; Hobby Horse
SERIES *Uma Zukushi*; The Horse Series
DATE 1822
SIGNATURE Fusenkyo Iitsu hitsu
FORMAT Shikishiban (21.2 x 19.0)
REFERENCES Rijksmuseum, *Hokusai*, pl. 38; Forrer, *Hokusai*, 103.1; *UT, Rijksmuseum*, pl.54
POETS Hana no Miyako, Kayūdō Kakusai, Shūchōdō Monoyana
FLLW FDN 3002.008

Inside a cloth decorated with motifs of the treasures of the Seven Gods of Good Luck are several toys. Most prominent is the horse-head stick, a child's toy which was used in dance performances for the New Year. The lacquer tray on which they rest bears the crest of a flying crane, the crest of the Shūchōdō poetry club, a subgroup of the Yomo-gawa.

There is another impression of this design in the collection, FLLW FDN 3002.009.

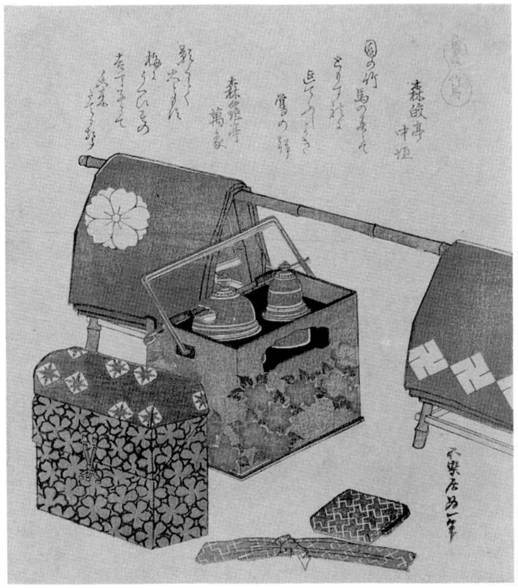

HOKUSAI

183 A bamboo horse with a smoking set

TITLE *Takeuma*; Bamboo Horse
SERIES *Uma Zukushi*; The Horse Series
DATE 1822
SIGNATURE Fusenkyo Iitsu hitsu
FORMAT Shikishiban (22.6 x 17.8)
REFERENCE Ostier, *La voix silencieuse*, pl.107.
POETS Shinkōtei Nakagaki, Shinratei Manzō
FLLW FDN 3002.007

A *takeuma* or "bamboo horse" is covered with two saddle blankets which have the reverse swastika crest of the Yomo-gawa subgroup and the symbol of the poet Shinratei. Beside them are a smoking set, a brown box covered with brocade, a tobacco pouch, and a wrapped pipe.

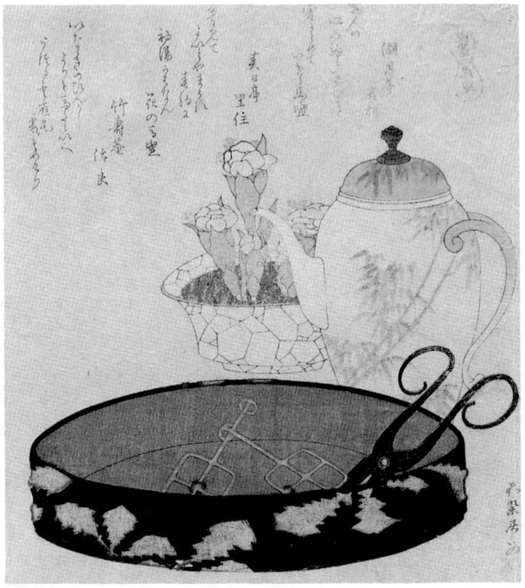

HOKUSAI

184 A lacquer tray with spurs and a scissors by a teapot

TITLE *Uma Tarai*; Horse Trough
SERIES *Uma Zukushi*; The Horse Series
DATE 1822
SIGNATURE Fusenkyo Iitsu hitsu
FORMAT Shikishiban (19.8 x 17.0)
POETS Kogetsutei Yoshimura, Kasugatei Satozumi, Chikujuan Haruyoshi
FLLW FDN 3002.003

Against an unusual light pink ground, silver spurs and a scissors lie in a lacquer tray decorated on the exterior with a dandelion motif in gold. A blue-and-white Arita porcelain teapot with a delicate bamboo pattern stands beside an adonis plant in a crackle-glaze bowl. The spurs provide the link to the horse theme.

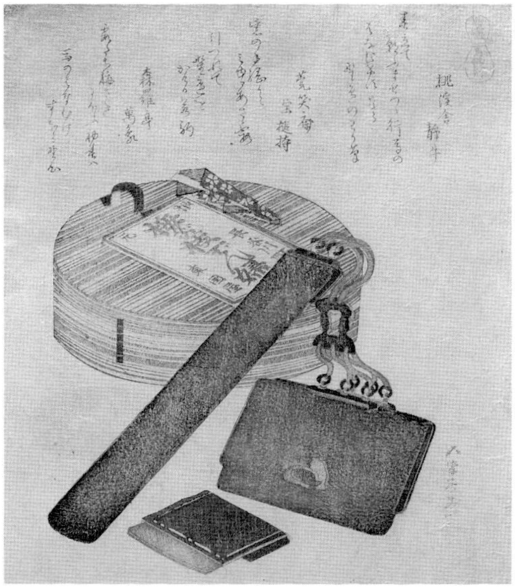

HOKUSAI

185 A pipe case with tobacco pouch and a box

TITLE *Uma no Sembetsu*; Farewell Gift for the Horse
SERIES *Uma Zukushi*; The Horse Series
DATE 1822
SIGNATURE Fusenkyo Iitsu hitsu
FORMAT Shikishiban (19.5 x 17.2)
REFERENCES Rijksmuseum, *Hokusai*, pl. 54; *UT, Rijksmuseum*, pl. 58
POETS Tōkeisha Seigyū, Kanshōsai Takara Tsuchimochi, Shinratei Manzō
FLLW FDN 3002.002

The tobacco pouch clasp, in the shape of a reclining horse, provides the linkage to the horse in this still life. The attached pipe case lies on a round box of mashed and seasoned fish (*dembu*). It is labeled "Umagae Dembu Hasegawa-chō, Tōgokuya," the name and address of the shop where it was sold. In the foreground is a small cloth case which is printed with gaufrage. A toothpick and its carrying case rest on the box.

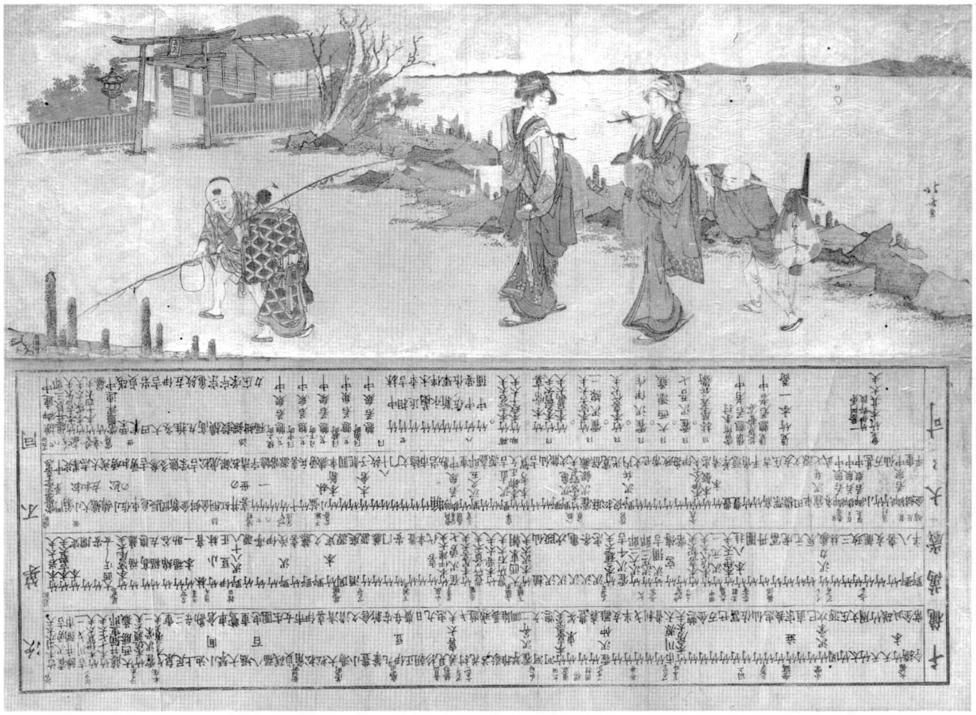

HOKUSAI

186 Two women and three boys with fishing rods

DATE ca. 1830
SIGNATURE Hokusai ga
FORMAT Yokonagaban (complete with text section; 38.4 x 52.8)
REFERENCES Tokyo National Museum, ed., vol. I, pl. 3704; Tōbu Museum of Art, ed., pl. 73; Ōta Memorial Museum of Art, ed., *Hatsukōkai Katsushika Hokusai Ten*, pl. 164
FLLW FDN 3002.140

This surimono was commissioned as a Jōruri program showing the schedule of performers. A name change is announced at the end. It states that the organizer of this event, Takeino, pupil of Ikkyō, changes his name to Takemoto Gidayū.

This impression is a reprint of a surimono which was originally issued circa 1804. The coloration and lack of detail in the printing points to a dating to the early 1830s.

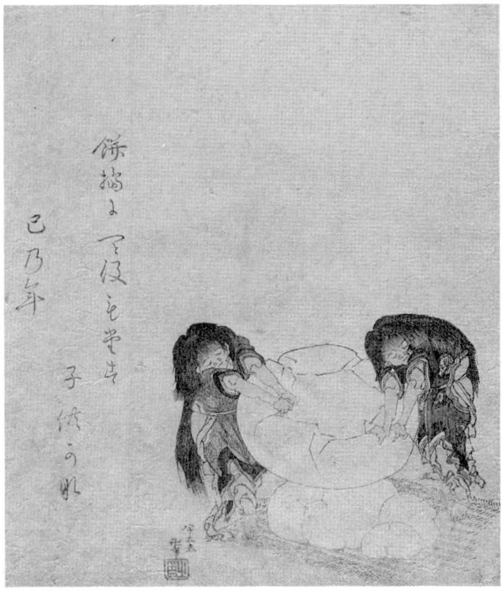

HOKUSAI

187 Two *shōjō*

DATE 1845, Year of the Snake
SIGNATURE Hachijū-go rō (age 85) Manji hitsu
ARTIST'S SEAL No in (seal of)
FORMAT Chūban tate-e (excluding mounting; 20.9 x 17.6)
POET Hokusai
FLLW FDN 3002.076

In this print, two *shōjō*, youthful red-haired gods of sake, pull apart dried rice cakes for the New Year. Perhaps Hokusai's last surimono, this unusually large example has both the charm and brilliance of line characteristic of the artist's late work. Two other variants of this design exist, one in small koban format (perhaps a trimmed impression), another as a key block impression in a miniature album in a private European collection (Lane, *Hokusai,* pls. 332–33).

The seventeen-syllable *senryū,* or comic poem, by Hokusai reads: *mochi tsuki ni / hitoyaku modosu / kodomo kana* ("We pounded the rice cakes, but we're back where we started, with the help of the kids!") The artist-poet humorously likens the children who tear apart rice cakes to the impish *shōjō* of the image.

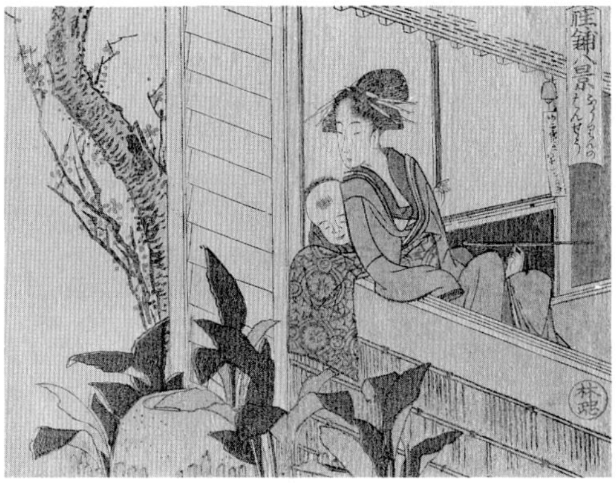

Attributed to HOKUSAI

188 A woman and a boy by an open window

TITLE *Fūrin no Banshō*; Evening Wind Chime
SERIES *Zashiki Hakkei*; Eight Views of the Parlor Room
DATE 1800
DEALER'S SEAL Hayashi Tadamasa
FORMAT Koban yoko-e (9.0 x 12.0)
FLLW FDN 3047.001

The title of this series of eight prints playfully refers to the traditional Chinese painting theme of the Eight Views of the Xiao and Xiang. While Japanese painters created their own variations on this theme, for example, the popular "Eight Views of Omi," ukiyo-e artists often created sets based on interior scenes in a Yoshiwara bordello. Here the setting cannot be precisely determined.

The standard theme of an evening bell at a distant temple is represented by the image of a wind chime swaying in the breeze. The ribbon sheet hanging from the chime lists the short months for 1800—2, 4 I, 6, 8, 10, 12.

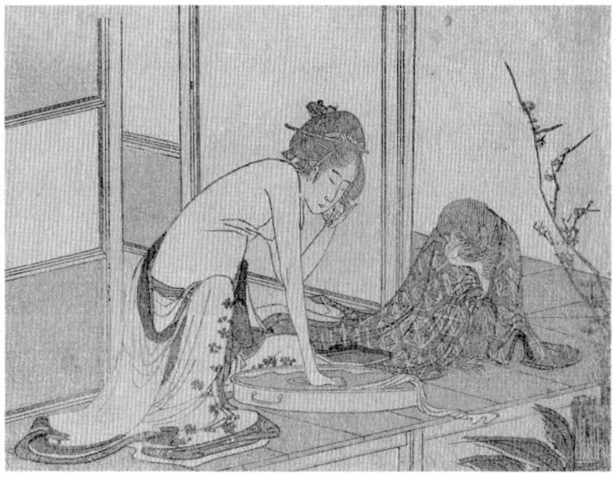

Attributed to HOKUSAI

189 A woman bathing herself, and a monkey

DATE probably 1800
FORMAT Koban yoko-e (9.2 x 12.0)
FLLW FDN 3047.005

The fluidity of the line and delicate naturalness of the figure suggest the hand of the Hokusai. The pose of the woman is reminiscent of a signed Hokusai surimono of about two years earlier depicting Yang Guifei bathing (see Lane, *Hokusai*, pl. 19). The monkey is draped in the woman's tie-dyed underrobe.

Since there is no clear calendar information given other than the monkey itself, it is possible that this impression is a reissued print.

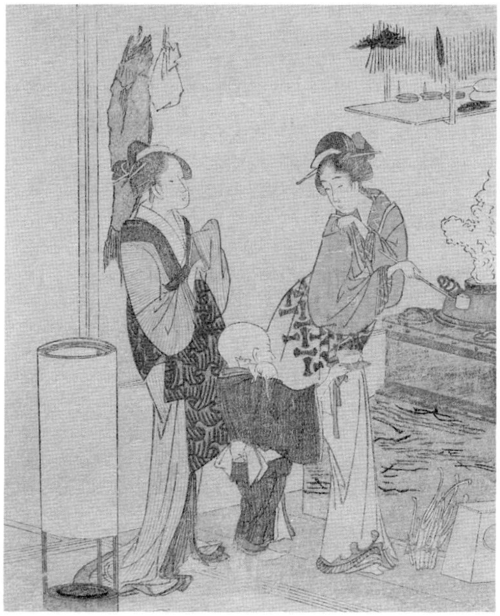

School of HOKUSAI

190 Two women and a boy in a kitchen

DATE 1804
FORMAT Koban tate-e (trimmed?; 14.0 x 12.6)
FLLW FDN 3047.003

This deceptively simple design is distinguished by a number of quite interesting details such as the hanging salted salmon, the metal stove, and the overhead shelf of a household shrine decorated for the New Year. In addition to the pet rat, the year is revealed in the dark wood-grain pattern on the base of the stove. The long months are 1, 3, 6, 8, 10, 11, and 12.

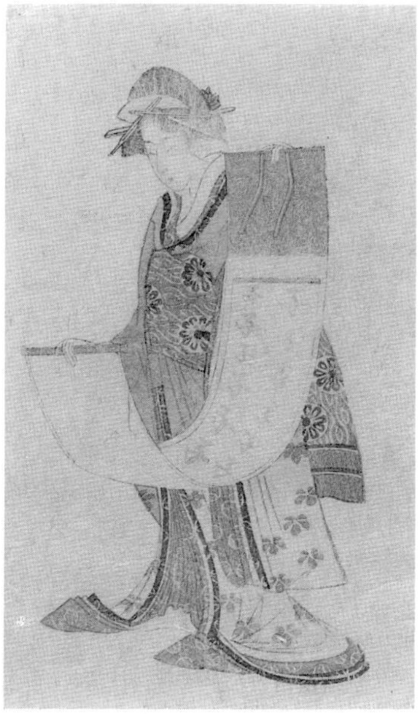

School of HOKUSAI

191 A young woman holding a hanging scroll

DATE 1804, Year of the Rat
FORMAT Koban tate-e (12.0 x 7.4)
FLLW FDN 3048.002

On the hanging scroll are twelve large and small identical characters meaning rat. The large characters indicate the long months—1, 3, 6, 8, 10, 11, 12; and the smaller ones the short months—2, 4, 5, 7, 9.

This character may be read as either *ko, shi,* or *ji,* (meaning "child") or *ne* (meaning "rat"). Since the words for "cat," *neko,* and "lion," *shishi,* can also be formed by combining the character's readings, the repetition of what seems to be the same word may be read as *neko no ko no koneko, shishi no ko no kojishi* (A cat's child is a kitten, a lion's child is a cub; see Lane, *Hokusai,* p. 28).

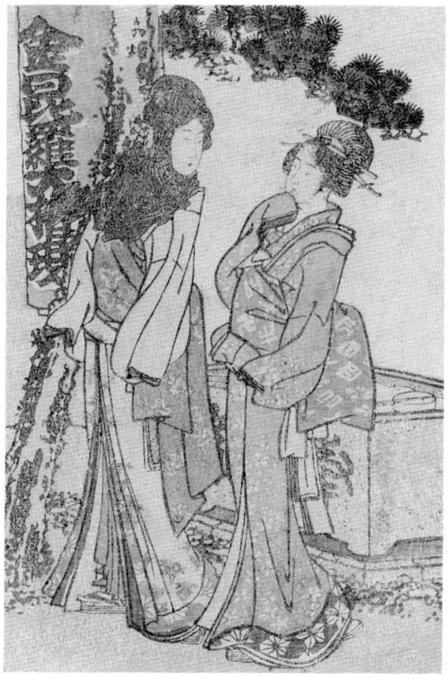

School of HOKUSAI

192 Two women at an entrance to a shrine

SERIES Untitled egoyomi set of women on outings
DATE 1804
FORMAT Koban tate-e (12.7 x 8.3)
FLLW FDN 3048.014

Two women stroll past a cistern used for the cleansing of one's hands before entering a shrine, on which the date of the issuance of the print is written in gold: *Bunka sho* [illegible] *no toshi* (Year of the [rat?] first year of the Bunka era).

Certainly in the style of Hokusai but somewhat lacking in refinement, this surimono is from an untitled set of small koban egoyomi which all illustrate women. The characters on the lantern mention Kompira Daigongen, a Shintō god worshiped in particular by sailors and fishermen.

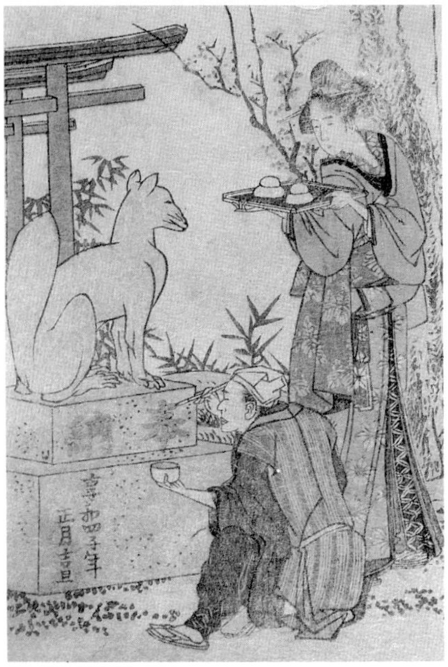

School of HOKUSAI

193 A woman carrying rice cakes by a shrine

SERIES Untitled egoyomi set of women on outings
DATE 1804, Year of the Rat
FORMAT Koban tate-e (12.7 x 8.3)
FLLW FDN 3048.015

A woman carrying a platter of New Year rice cakes pauses to watch an artisan paint an inscription on the statue of a fox which guards the entrance to a Shinto shrine.

At the base of the statue, the date has been written in red: first day of the first month of the rat year, Kyōwa fourth year. There are two others from the set in the collection (FLLW FDN 3048.012 and .017).

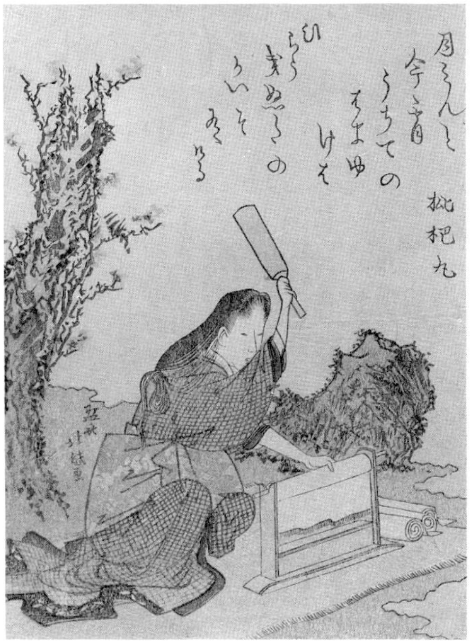

KATSUSHIKA HOKUTAI
ACT. CA. 1800–1825

194 A woman pounding cloth by the shoreline

DATE ca. 1803
SIGNATURE Eisai Hokutai ga
FORMAT Koban tate-e (14.5 x 10.2)
POET Biwamaru
FLLW FDN 3019.005

A woman fulling cloth, a theme derived from classical Chinese and Japanese poetry, was often depicted by ukiyo-e artists. As seen in this print, cloth was pounded on a fulling block with a wooden mortar to give it a sheen. The monotonous sound of the mortar striking the block was a traditional metaphor for a melancholic woman whose lover has left her behind. The presence of a few plum blossoms is the only sign of the New Year in this uncharacteristically somber surimono.

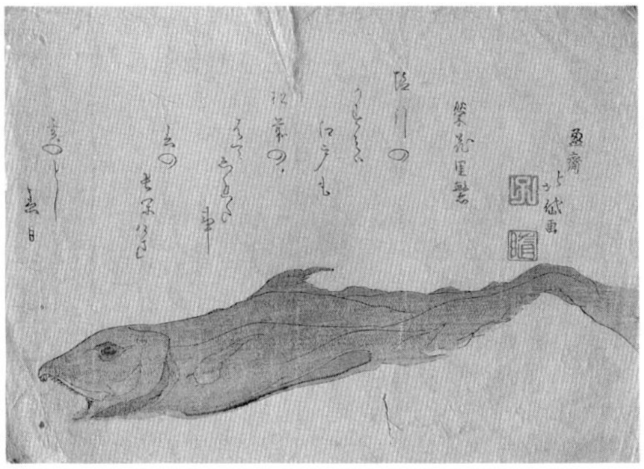

HOKUTAI

195 A salted fish

DATE 1803, Year of the Boar, Spring Day
SIGNATURE Eisai Hokutai ga
ARTIST'S SEALS Shi; Shin
FORMAT Koban yoko-e (14.0 x 19.0)
POET Eiga no Satoshige
FLLW FDN 3019.001

As an early pupil of Hokusai, Hokutai was strongly influenced by the style and technique of the master and in the 1830s received the name Raito. He made his living as a picture book illustrator, but was also known as a competent painter of beautiful women.

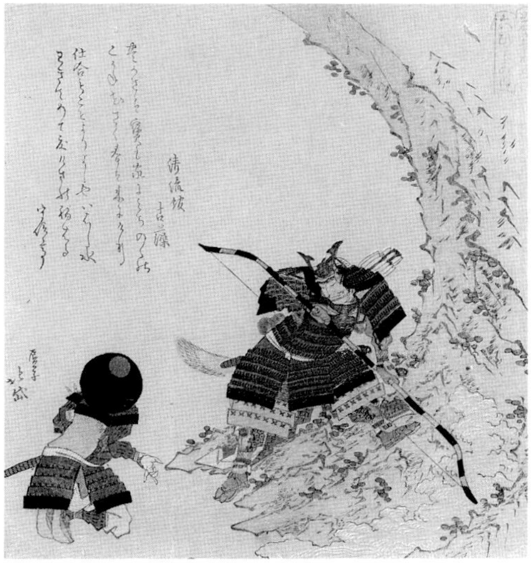

HOKUTAI

196 Minamoto no Yoriyoshi drawing water from a rock

SERIES *Iwagaki-ren Rokuhira no Uchi*; Six Sheets for the Iwagaki Group
DATE 1821
SIGNATURE Shinshinshi Hokutai
FORMAT Shikishiban (20.0 x 18.8)
POETS Seiryūkan Yoshimo, Shushintei (Okotaru)
FLLW FDN 3019.004

Of this series of six prints, four designs with figures are by Hokutai and two still lifes are by the poet Shushintei, who was probably the leader of the Iwagaki-ren. The unifying theme of all the prints is water. The Wright collection has the complete set.

The scene here illustrates an event that took place during a severe drought in 1052. After praying for his army, Minamoto no Yoriyoshi extracts water from a rock by striking it with his bow. His aide looks on in amazement.

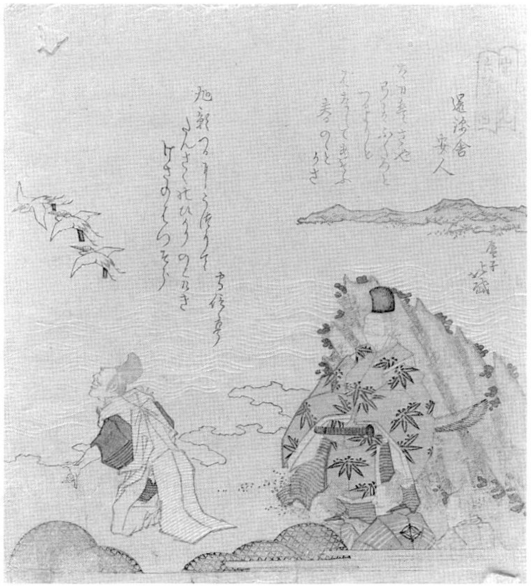

HOKUTAI

197 Minamoto no Yoritomo and his retinue watching three cranes

SERIES *Iwagaki-ren Rokuhira no Uchi*; Six Sheets for the Iwagaki Group
DATE 1821
SIGNATURE Shishinshi Hokutai
FORMAT Shikishiban (21.3 x 19.0)
REFERENCE Galerie Zacke, pl.13
POETS Genkinsha Yasuhito, Shushintei
FLLW FDN 3019.006

Three tagged cranes have just been released by an attendant to Minamoto no Yoritomo (1147–99), who looks on approvingly. The tracking of these birds became an obsession of Yoritomo and his fellow bird watchers. Legend holds that the three cranes were spotted repeatedly for centuries. An appropriate theme for a New Year surimono, cranes are auspicious birds and said to live one thousand years.

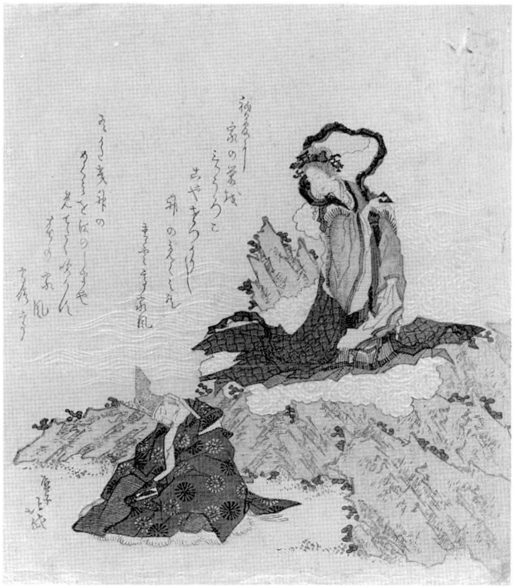

HOKUTAI

198 Hōjō Tokimasa dreaming of the goddess Benzaiten

SERIES *Iwagaki-ren Rokuhira no Uchi;* Six Sheets for the Iwagaki Group
DATE 1821
SIGNATURE Shinshinshi Hokutai
FORMAT Shikishiban (22.3 x 19.2)
REFERENCE Galerie Zacke, pl.12
POETS Seiuntei Iekaze, Shushintei
FLLW FDN 3019.007

Benzaiten, the goddess of learning and art, is worshiped at Enoshima (mentioned in the second poem), where she is said to have slain a serpent (see cat. no. 137). At the temple erected at the site of this feat, Hōjō Tokimasa (1138–1215) later prayed for success and wealth. Aided by Benzaiten, his family then ruled for over one hundred years, as mentioned in the poems.

The subject of Enoshima is generally associated with a snake year.

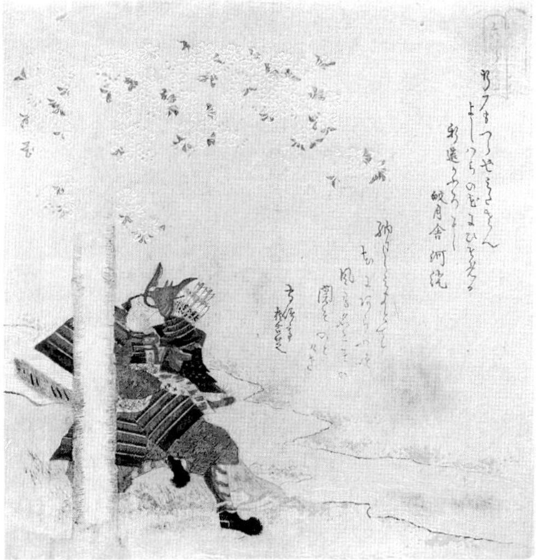

HOKUTAI

199 Taira no Tadanori beneath a cherry tree

SERIES *Iwagaki-ren Rokuhira no Uchi;* Six Sheets for the Iwagaki Group
DATE 1821
SIGNATURE Effaced?
FORMAT Shikishiban (19.8 x 18.5)
POETS Kōgetsusha Kawazumi, Shushintei Okotaru
FLLW FDN 3019.008

Taira no Tadanori (1144–84) is usually depicted as a warrior in full armor beneath a cherry tree, symbolizing his bravery on the battlefield as well as his sensitivity as a poet. When Tadanori realized his days were numbered, he beseeched Fujiwara Shunzei, poetry advisor to the Emperor, to grant him the ultimate honor of allowing one of his poems to be included in an imperial anthology. Tadanori was slain at the battle of Ichinotani in 1184, but since he was a member of the defeated clan, Shunzei was forced to include his poem anonymously. Tadanori's tragic tale is included in the *Tale of the Heike* and Nō plays and, in an ironic twist of poetic justice, he became all the more famous for not having his name recorded in the anthology.

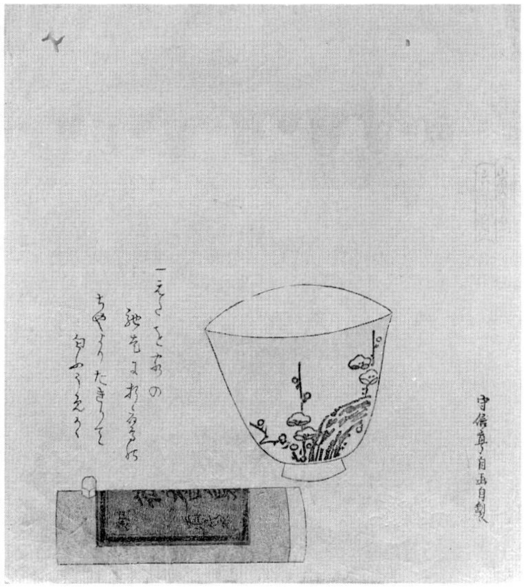

SHUSHINTEI OKOTARU
ACT. CA. 1810S–1820S

200 Tea cup and *kōsen* container

SERIES *Iwagaki-ren Rokuhira no Uchi;* Six Sheets for the Iwagaki Club
DATE 1821
SIGNATURE Shushintei jiga jisei (designed and produced by Shushintei)
FORMAT Shikishiban (21.1 x 19.0)
POET Shushintei
FLLW FDN 3019.009

Probably the cover sheet for the set, the title cartouche has been placed lower down and a faded drip pattern appears at the top. This surimono was designed and composed by the Shushintei, who was no doubt the leader of the Iwagaki-ren.

Kōsen powder is made from roasted barley flour blended with various spices and dissolved in hot water. A subtly embossed blossom which lies to the left of the signature is barely visible.

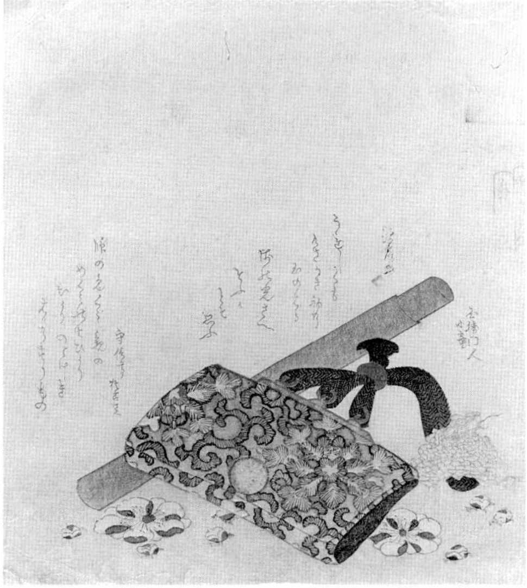

UNIDENTIFIED

201 Leather tobacco pouch

SERIES *Iwagaki-ren Rokuhira no Uchi;* Six Sheets for the Iwagaki Club
DATE 1821
FORMAT Shikishiban (20.0 x 18.0)
REFERENCES Shimizu, pl. 53; Ostier, *La voix silencieuse*, pl. 105
POETS Kunikatsu monjin Shōryū, Shushintei Okotaru
FLLW FDN 3019.010

This print is known in at least three states. One in a private collection shows the still life set against a dusty pink ground decorated with various crests. Another has different coloring and poems more appropriate to the subject matter (see Shimizu, pl. 53). The dragon netsuke relates to the theme of the Benzaiten surimono from this set (see cat. no. 198).

The placement of the right-hand signature seems to indicate that the author of the first poem may have been the artist. This identification, however, is tentative. The dark, partially effaced signature reading [Tsune] *fusa ga* appears to have been added later with a separate block.

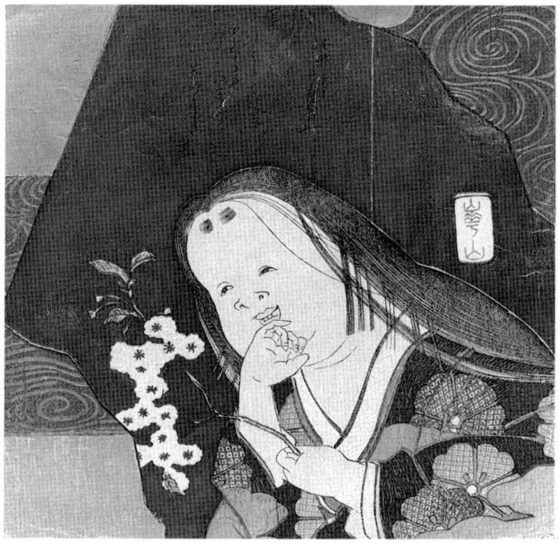

WATANABE KAZAN
1793–1841

202 A fan design of Okame

DATE ca. 1835
SEAL Kazan
FORMAT Shikishiban (trimmed; 18.3 x 18.3)
POET Kuretaketei Masugu
FLLW FDN 3041.001

Best known as a scholar and literati painter, Watanabe Kazan also experimented with a wide range of painting styles and techniques, including portraiture and Western-inspired landscapes. In the area of color printing, he designed a set of six commercial prints issued by the publisher Sen'ichi and a few surimono. This image reveals his familiarity with Rimpa decorative painting traditions.

A gold folding fan showing a smiling Okame with a cherry branch is juxtaposed against a stylized water design in silver. Okame, also known as Otafuku or Uzume, is the goddess of laughter and is customarily portrayed as a plump young woman with chubby cheeks and a sweet smile.

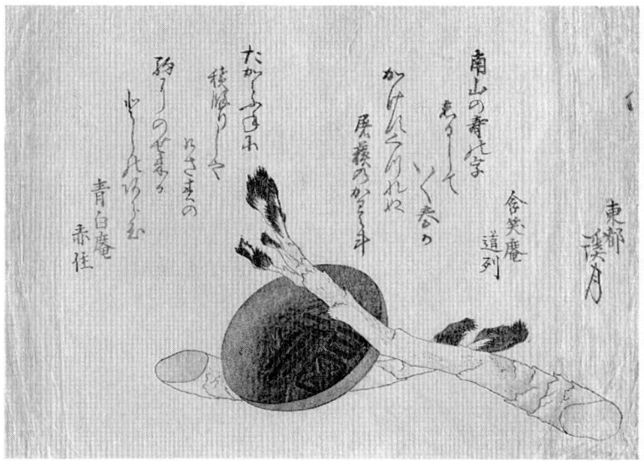

AOIGAOKA KEIGETSU
ACT. CA. 1818–30

203 Sake cup with *udo*

DATE ca.1820
SIGNATURE Tōto Keigetsu
FORMAT Chūban yoko-e (17.2 x 24.2)
POETS Ganshōan Michizura, Seihakuan Akazumi
FLLW FDN 3039.001

A lacquer sake cup with a character *fuku,* "good fortune,"printed in gold lies between two stalks of *udo,* an asparagus-like vegetable.

Keigetsu was a minor pupil of Totoya Hokkei, from whom he received his art name of Aoigaoka. The use of the appellation "Tōto," meaning Eastern Capital, refers to the city of Edo, where he worked, and suggests that the poets who commissioned it were from the provinces.

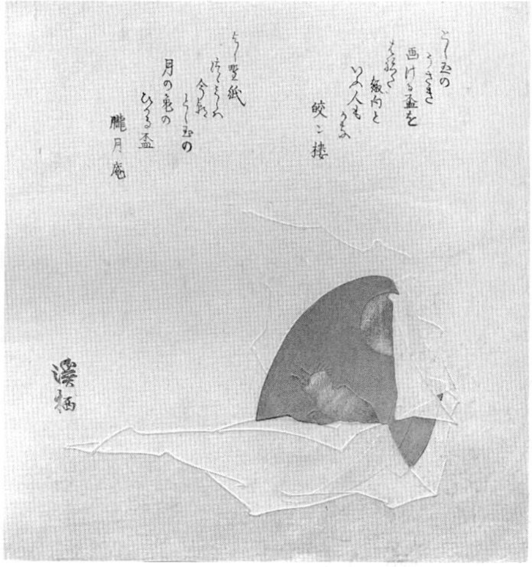

AOIGAOKA KEISEI
ACT. CA. 1818–1835

204 A lacquer sake cup with a silver rabbit design, wrapped with translucent white paper

DATE 1831
SIGNATURE Keisei
FORMAT Shikishiban (19.8 x 18.3)
POETS Kōkōrō, Rōgetsuan
FLLW FDN 3051.002

Probably from the same set as cat. no.38, this print presents a New Year subject also suggestive of a rabbit year—namely the rabbit which is said to live in the moon and pound rice cakes. Both poems are composed on the theme of *toshidama,* or gifts for the New Year. The second poem mentions a soft paper used for wrapping fragile objects such as lacquer sake cups. *Yoshinogami,* the name of the paper, alludes to Mount Yoshino, long associated with moon images.

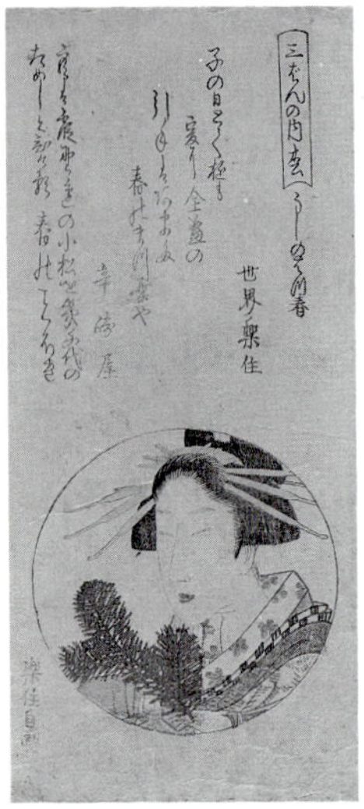

RAKUZUMI

ACT CA. 1800-1810

205 A bust portrait of a courtesan holding a pine branch

TITLE *Matsu;* Pine
SERIES *Samban no Uchi*; A Set of Three Designs
DATE 1805, Year of the Ox, Spring
SIGNATURE Rakuzumi jigasan (written and drawn by Rakuzumi)
FORMAT Koban tate-e (21.1 x 9.2)
POETS Sekai no Rakuzumi, Karasakiya
FLLW FDN 3050.001

This is an example of a surimono both designed and authored by an amateur poet-artist. The name Rakuzumi, meaning "living in ease," was not an uncommon artistic name, so it is difficult to ascertain if this is the same Rakuzumi who composed poems for prints by professional surimono artists (eg. cat. nos. 16 and 74).

This set is based on the traditional subject of the three friends, pine, bamboo, and plum. Here the pine bough alludes to a courtesan at the Matsubaya teahouse, referred to in the poem.

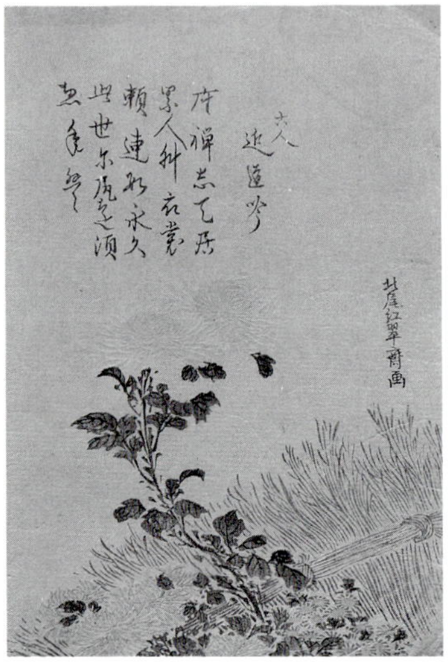

KITAO SHIGEMASA

1739–1820

206 Chrysanthemums by a fence

DATE 1803
SIGNATURE Kitao Kōsuisai ga
FORMAT Yokonagaban (trimmed; 19.5 x 13.2)
REFERENCE Entire surimono is illustrated in *UT, Bibliothèque Nationale*, p. 209, pl.55
FLLW FDN 3006.003

This long surimono commemorates the seventh anniversary of the death of the kyōka poet Chikamichi, who was a judge for the Yomogawa group. Because Chikamichi died in 1796, the print can be dated to 1803. (See Kondō, *Ukiyo-e Geijutsu*, no. 81 (1984) 16).

Chrysanthemums are shown by a brushwood fence with a Chinese-style poem. These flowers are customarily used to honor the deceased.

Shigemasa, best known as a book illustrator and a skillful calligrapher, designed a small number of egoyomi and surimono, and painted pictures of beautiful women.

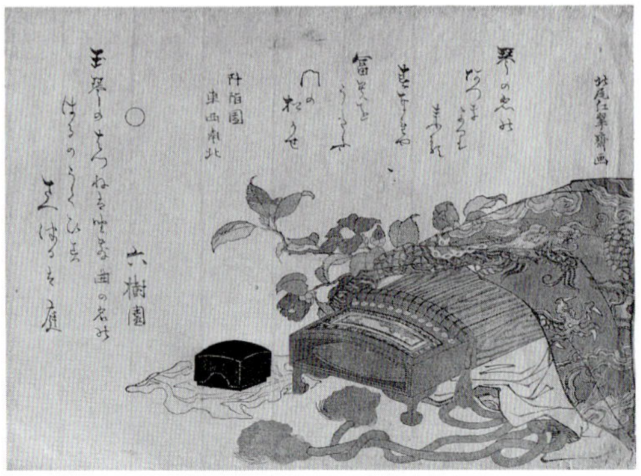

SHIGEMASA

207 A koto with a brocade cover

DATE 1808
SIGNATURE Kitao Kōsuisai ga
FORMAT Large chūban surimono (20.9 x27.9)
POETS Sembakuen Tōzai Namboku, Rokujuen
FLLW FDN 3006.004

A koto is partially covered with a brocade cloth decorated with a dragon design, indicating the year. A camellia branch and a lacquer box for picks lie beside the stringed musical instrument. There is a similar composition by Shinsai in the collection (see cat. no. 225).

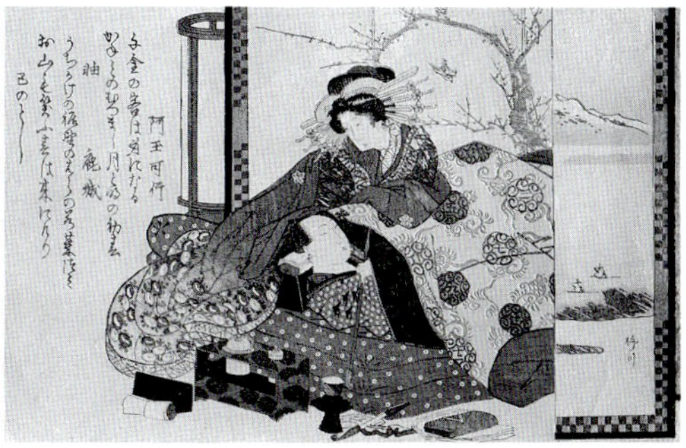

YANAGAWA SHIGENOBU
1787–1832

208 A courtesan leaning against her lover

DATE 1821, Year of the Snake
SIGNATURE Yanagawa
FORMAT Koban yoko-e (13.6 x 21.0)
POETS Atama Kayuki, Jiku no Shikashiro
FLLW FDN 3016.003

The lovers are shielded by a landscape screen which bears the artists's signature, "Yanagawa." On the heavy brocade quilt are the numbers for the long months—2, 5, 7, 9, 10, 12—which are integrated within circular medallions.

Another surimono using the identical blocks (with an extremely small variation to the key block) but in a shikishi format with a different poetry block is included in the collection (see fig. 5 and cat. no. 209). In this print, both poems mention courtesans and either paying for their services or sleeping with them at the New Year.

A pupil, later son-in-law, and then adopted son of Hokusai, Shigenobu started his artistic career as a book illustrator. By the late 1810s, he was already designing beauty prints, landscapes, and surimono. The year after the publication of this surimono, he traveled to Osaka and worked there, developing a market for these privately issued prints.

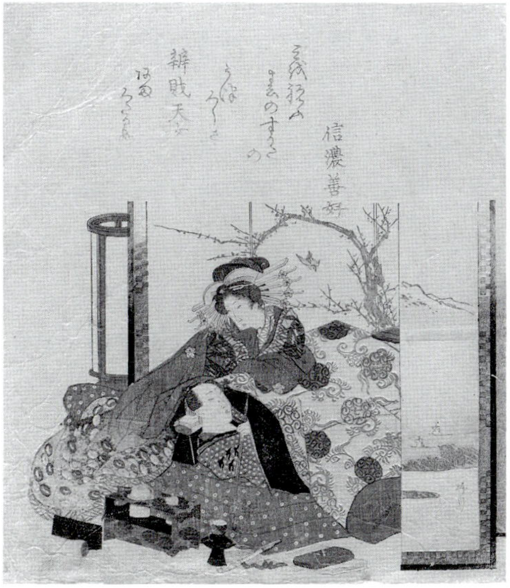

SHIGENOBU

209 A courtesan leaning against her lover

DATE 1821
SIGNATURE Yanagawa
FORMAT Shikishiban (21.4 x 19.5)
POET Shinano Zenkō
FLLW FDN 3016.006

This surimono, which is a shikishiban impression using the same pictorial blocks as the koban version illustrated in the previous entry, was probably from a slightly later printing of that same year for which the month designations would remain appropriate. Although the impression in this format is marginally sharper, the composition was clearly designed for the smaller rectangular presentation. For a more complete discussion of these prints see page 18.

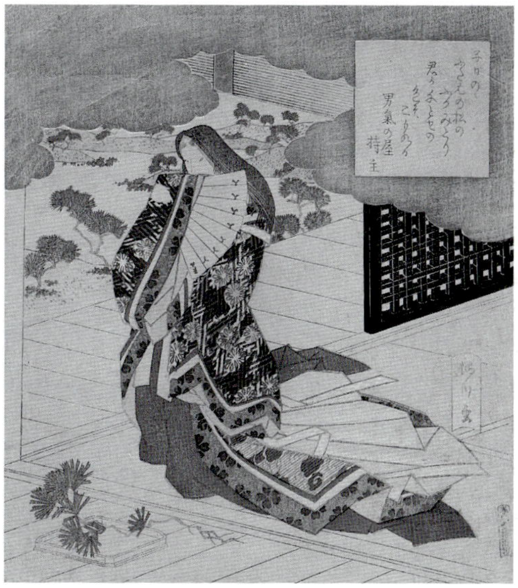

SHIGENOBU

210 A court woman on a veranda

DATE ca. 1824
SIGNATURE Yanagawa ga
PRINTER'S SEAL Shumpūdō Ryūko suri
FORMAT Shikishiban (21.0 x 18.4)
POET Otokoginoya Mochinushi
FLLW FDN 3016.004

The richly attired woman demurely covers her mouth with the sleeve of her kimono and a fan. The young pine trees in the garden may be seen through the open door. Before her lies a tray with pine saplings for the first rat day of the New Year, mentioned in the poem.

Shigenobu designed a number of surimono portraying court ladies in a palace setting which may have been issued as part of a series. For instance there is an image of a court lady facing right, on a veranda with a similar black lattice door, in the Duel Collection (cf. Polster, no. 384). However, its clouds are printed in gold, rather than silver as in the Wright example. In another related example of a court lady admiring plum blossoms, the clouds are printed in deep indigo (cf. Keyes, *Beatty*, no. 268).

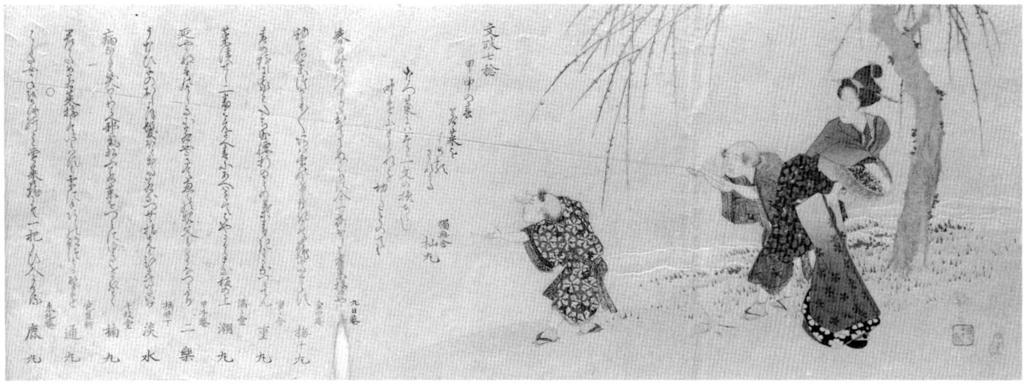

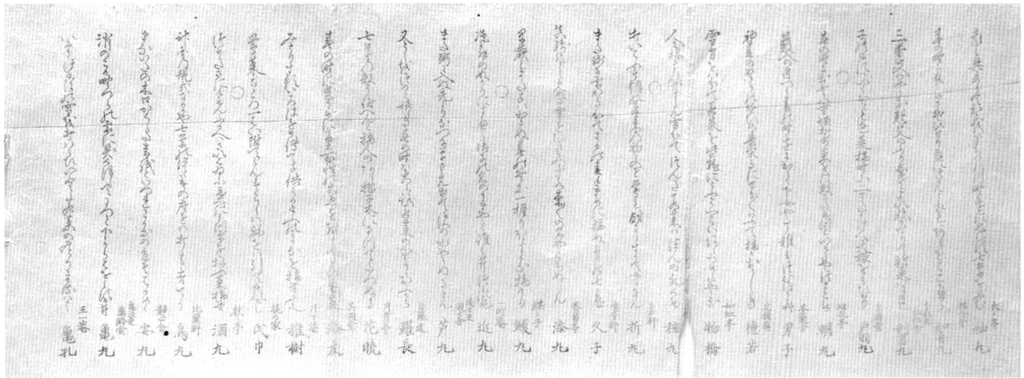

SHIGENOBU

211 A woman collecting spring herbs as two boys fly a kite

DATE 1824, 7th Year of Bunsei, Year of the Monkey, Spring
SIGNATURE Rinsai (Reisai)
ARTIST'S SEAL Yanagawa
PRINTER'S SEAL Seikō
FORMAT Double yokonagaban (each 19.4 x 52.6)
POET Dokumusha Somamaru
(poet of introduction)
FLLW FDN 3016.005

In this unusually long surimono—over half a meter in length—the kite string leads the viewer past an introduction and nine poems on the front of the surimono and another twenty-five on the back. The kite is not actually shown. Remarkably, the striped paper tie which joins the back half to the front is still intact.

The "Seikō" seal indicates that this surimono was printed in Osaka. In fact, Shigenobu did not return to Edo, which he had left in 1822, until the middle of 1826.

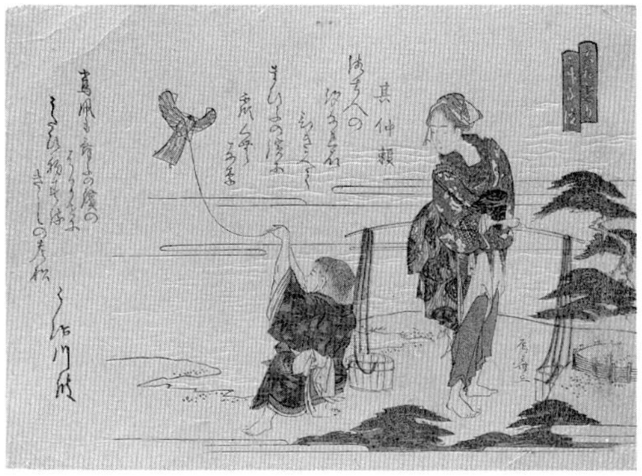

RYŪRYŪKYO SHINSAI
1764?–1820

212 Women with buckets and a boy flying a kite

TITLE *Maikonohama*, Maiko Beach
SERIES *Yamato Meguri*, Famous Places around Yamato
DATE ca. 1805
SIGNATURE Shinsai ga
FORMAT Koban yoko-e (13.7 x 18.4)
POETS Sono Nakayori, Uji Kawanami
FLLW FDN 3003.026

A woman with buckets for collecting brine for salt-making watches a boy with a kite in the form of a hawk. Kite flying is traditionally associated with the New Year. Maiko Beach, located near Kobe, was well known for its white beach lined with pine trees. Both poems mention Maiko Beach.

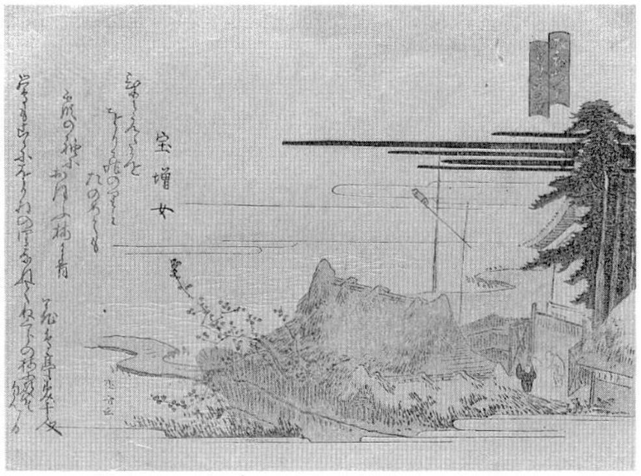

SHINSAI

213 A shoreline scene with figures by a gate

TITLE *Orii no Sato;* The Village of Orii
SERIES *Yamato Meguri;* Famous Places Around Yamato
DATE ca. 1805
SIGNATURE Shinsai ga
FORMAT Koban yoko-e (14.1 x 19.0)
POETS Takara Masume, Kachōtei Michibito
FLLW FDN 3003.040

This rural scene shows people standing at the gate to the village and the framework for a well protruding into the sky. Orii is the name of a famous family of drum makers who were based in Yamato Province (present-day Nara area).

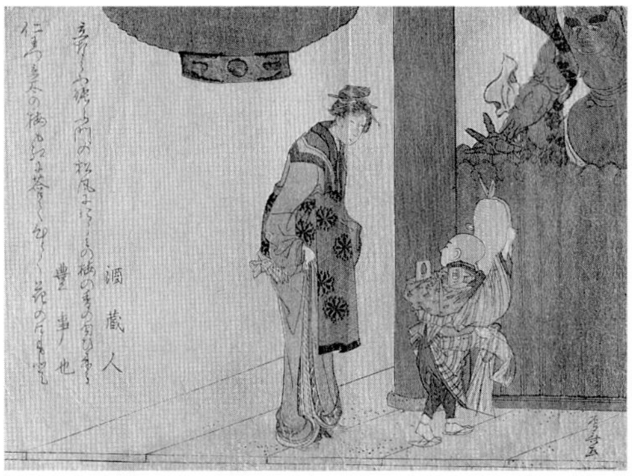

SHINSAI

214 A courtesan and a boy at the entrance to Sensōji Temple

DATE ca. 1805
SIGNATURE Shinsai ga
FORMAT Koban yoko-e (13.7 x 18.9)
REFERENCE *UT, Bibliothèque Nationale*, p. 222, fig. 79
POETS Sake no Kurōdo, Yutaka Kotonari
FLLW FDN 3003.020

A courtesan and boy attendant pause in front of a giant sculpture of the wind god at the Kaminarimon (Thunder Gate) at Sensōji Temple in Asakusa; unseen, the thunder god—the source of the name of the gate—stands on the opposite side. Above them is the large red lantern for which this temple remains famous. The boy carries a kite in one hand and, on his back, a stand for New Year gifts wrapped in cloth.

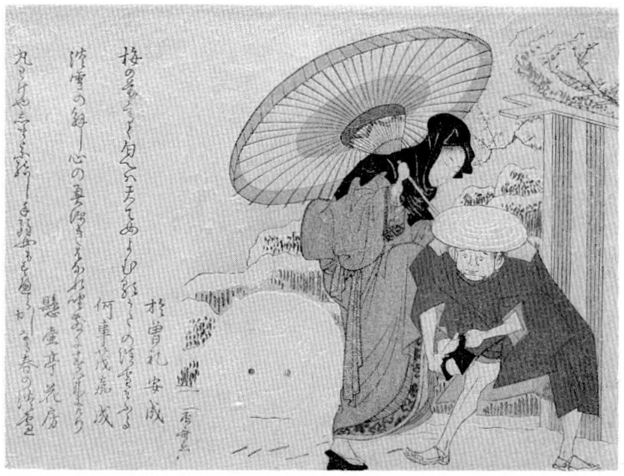

SHINSAI

215 A servant assisting a courtesan with her wooden sandal

DATE 1807
SIGNATURE Shinsai ga
FORMAT Koban yoko-e (14.0 x 18.1)
POETS Osore Yasunari, Nanigotomo Yoshinari, Kenkotei Hanabusa
FLLW FDN 3003.015

A servant bends down to help a young woman, whose wooden sandal is clogged with snow. She holds an umbrella to protect herself from the light snowfall. To their left stands a large snow sculpture of a rabbit.

All three poems are composed on the theme of *awayuki,* or "a light spring snowfall."

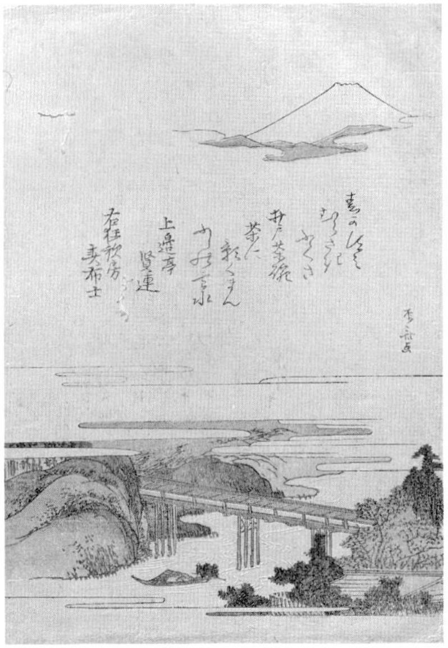

SHINSAI

216 A bridge over a river with Mount Fuji in the background

DATE ca. 1807
SIGNATURE Shinsai ga
FORMAT Large koban tate-e (21.0 x 14.0)
POET Jōbentei Katatsura
FLLW FDN 3003.033

Above a covered bridge in a tranquil river scene, Mount Fuji appears through the mist. The poem mentions an Ido tea bowl wrapped in a purple cloth and tea prepared with water from the melted snow of Mount Fuji. Such pottery tea bowls, which were produced by Korean potters in the fifteenth and sixteenth centuries, were highly esteemed by Edo tea connoisseurs.

The inscription to the left of the poet's name reads: *Migi, Kyokabō, Haru Fuji* (To the right, [a poem by] Kyokabō about Mount Fuji in spring). There is a similar print in same format with a poem by Kyōkabō in the Spencer Collection (see Keyes, *Spencer,* cat. no. 245).

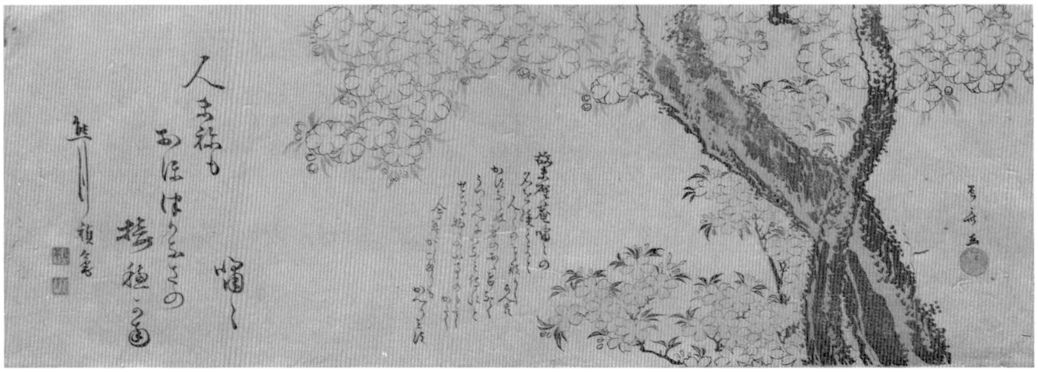

SHINSAI

217 A cherry tree in bloom

DATE ca. 1808
SIGNATURE Shinsai ga
ARTIST'S SEAL Undeciphered
FORMAT Yokonagaban (16.5 x 44.5)
POET Kumagawa Teiki
POET'S SEALS Kuma; Kawa
FLLW FDN 3003.063

The tree, laden with flowers, frames a seven-line poem—a tribute to the deceased poet Miken'an.

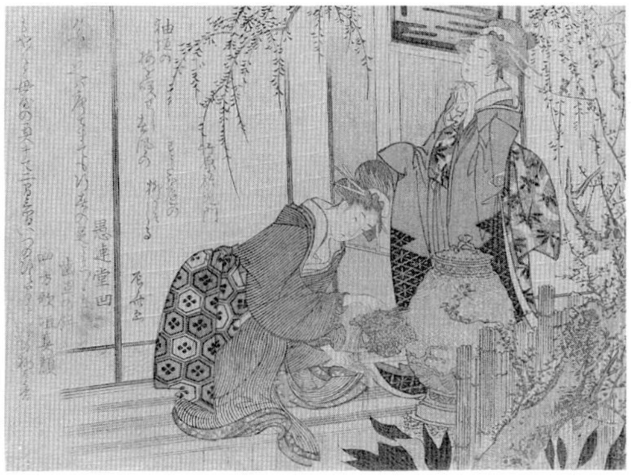

SHINSAI

218 Two ladies washing hands

DATE 1808
SIGNATURE Shinsai ga
FORMAT Koban yoko-e (13.5 x 18.6)
POETS Takehara Otokado, Gurendō Nakakubo, Yomo Utagaki Magao
FLLW FDN 3003.014

The hand washing depicted here perhaps refers to the annual New Year tradition of collecting fresh water on the first day of the year. The water was used for symbolic purification of the hands and mouth to expel evil spirits. Here the water is drawn from a dragon-spigot bronze vessel, a clue to the zodiac date.

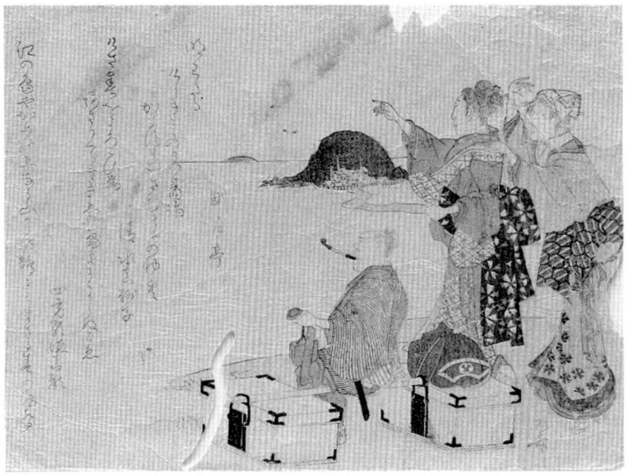

SHINSAI

219 Travelers pausing to admire the rising sun at Enoshima.

DATE 1809
SIGNATURE Shinsai
FORMAT Koban yoko-e (14.0 x 18.5)
POETS Jungetsutei, Shimizu Masako, Yomo Utagaki Magao
FLLW FDN 3003.067

Enoshima is associated with the worship of Benzaiten and snake legends. Here, the women travelers and their porters admire the view of the sunrise over the island of Enoshima as Mount Fuji may be barely seen at the far right.

This surimono was commissioned for the Yomo-gawa group led by Yomo Utagaki Magao. It was later reprinted in shikishiban format with other poetry blocks for another club (see cat. no. 220). The fan bears a "three comma" design which appears on the wrapping cloth and a woman's bandana, and is the emblem for this club.

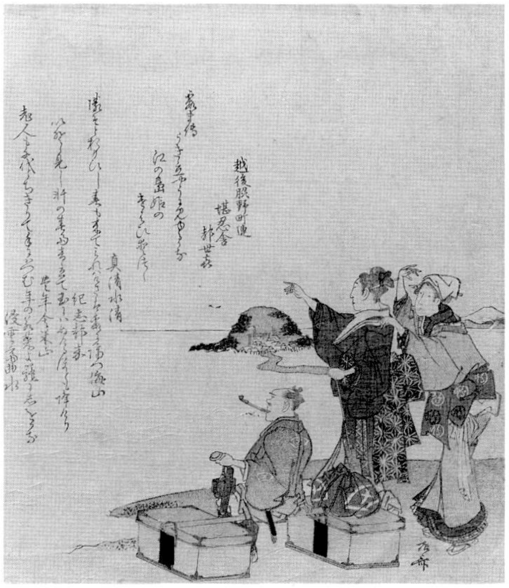

SHINSAI

220 Travelers viewing Enoshima

DATE Probably 1809
SIGNATURE Shinsai
FORMAT Shikishiban (20.8 x 17.8)
POETS Kanninsha Tsuyoki, Mashimizu Kiyoshi, Ki no Shizuki, Hōnensha Yoneyama, Shinsetsusai Kyokusui (poem trimmed)
FLLW FDN 3003.057

This is a second version of an earlier koban surimono (see cat. no. 219). Here the printer has opted not to include the rising sun and has made new blocks for the textile patterns, as well as for other sections. The poetry blocks have changed together with the emblem for the club, which appears on the wrapping cloth and as the crest on the garb of the resting porter.

The poets are all of the Echigo (modern Niigata Prefecture) group of the Wakinomachi-ren; each name includes a famous product from the region.

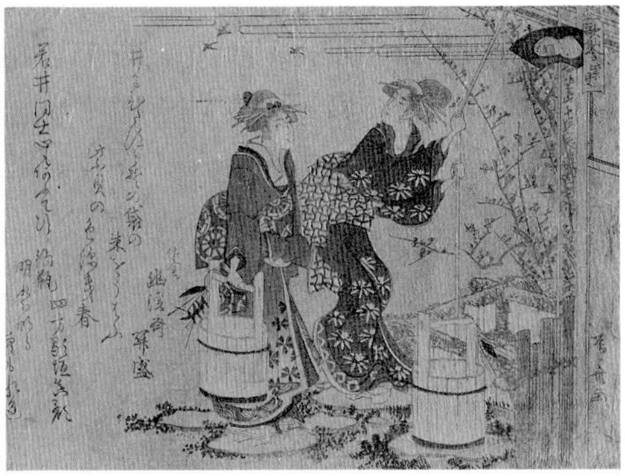

SHINSAI

221 Two women drawing water from a well

TITLE *Murasakigai*; Purple Shell
SERIES *Kasen Awase*; Contest of the Immortals of Poetry
DATE 1809
SIGNATURE Shinsai
FORMAT Koban yoko-e (13.8 x 18.3)
REFERENCE Rijksmuseum, *Hokusai*, p. 60, nos. 93–94
POETS Yūkeisai Sekimori of Sakura (Chiba Prefecture), Yomo Utagaki Magao
FLLW FDN 3003.023

This series of thirty-six prints, each based on shell themes, calls to mind Hokusai's more famous series of 1821. Surimono on shell themes were usually prepared for snake years, since shells were a famous specialty of Enoshima, which was connected to legends of Benzaiten and snakes. Like most other designs in the series, this print shows women engaged in everyday activities.

In the first poem, the color purple is linked to spring as it is the conventional description of the color of spring mists.The second poem centers on the New Year's custom of the first drawing of water.

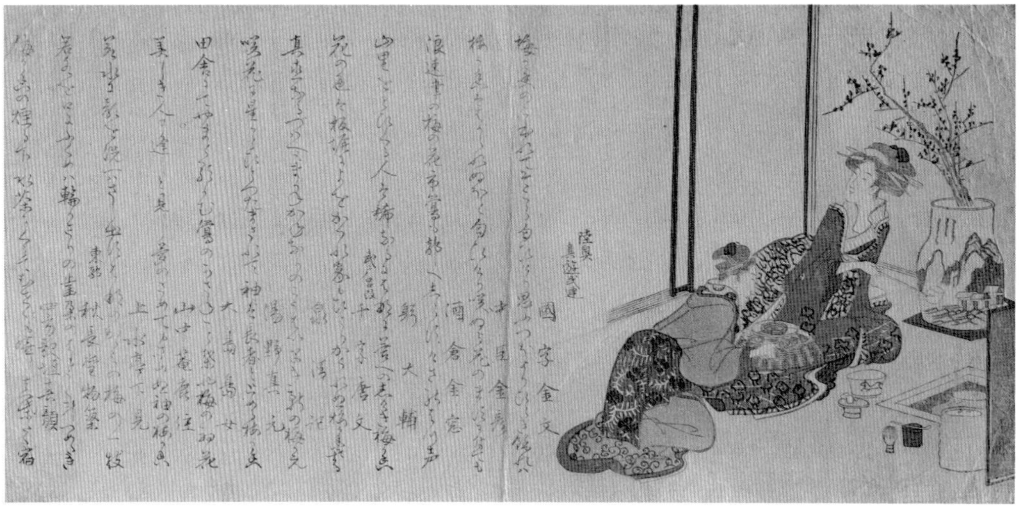

SHINSAI

222 A woman preparing tea

DATE 1810
SIGNATURE Shinsai (on back of screen)
FORMAT Yokonagaban (13.8 x 17.6)
POETS Kokuji Kanefumi (far right), Shūchōdō Monoyana (far left), Yomo Utagaki Magao (left) and ten other poets.
FLLW FDN 3003.070

A woman sits by a brazier with a water scoop for making tea. Beside her kneels a serving woman holding a basket with charcoal and a lacquer dish. The tea scoop, wisk, and other implements necessary for the preparation of tea surround the hibachi. On the bowl is a simple rendering of a horse, indicating the date.

Except for the last two poets, who were leaders of the Edo kyōka movement, the poets belonged to the Mayūmin-ren, a poetry circle affiliated with the Yomo-gawa based in Mutsu Province (present-day Aomori Prefecture).

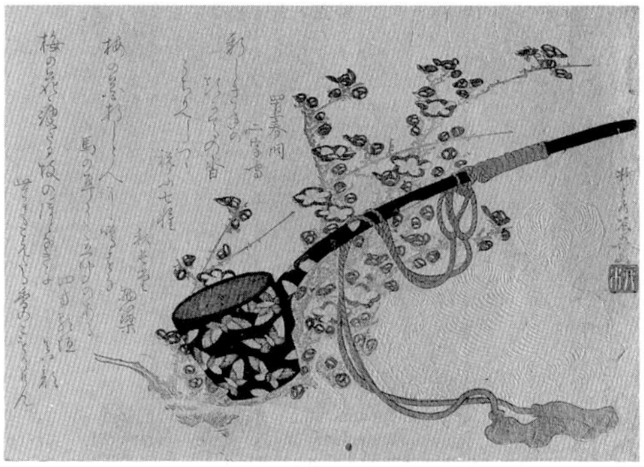

SHINSAI

223 A water scoop with a plum branch

DATE 1810, Year of the Horse
SIGNATURE Ryūryūkyo Shinsai ga
ARTIST'S SEAL Ryū (Yanagi)
FORMAT Koban yoko-e (13.4 x 18.6)
POETS Chishundō Nijimori, Shūchōdō Monoyana, Yomo Utagaki Magao
FLLW FDN 3003.001

A black-lacquer water scoop used for watering horses, adorned with a butterfly motif, is placed beside a plum branch and a heavily embossed pair of straw sandals used to protect horse hooves.

The first poem mentions making horse shoes and gathering the seven herbs of the New Year, while the second specifically mentions the year of the horse. This design closely resembles one by Hokusai from the series *Genroku Kasen Kaiawase* (A Matching Game with Genroku Poem Shells) based on the thirty-six shells, issued in 1821 (see Forrer and Keyes, fig. 3).

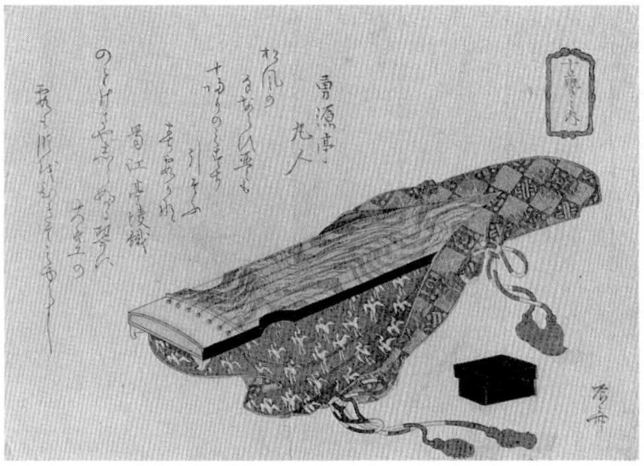

SHINSAI

224 A koto in a brocade satchel and a box for picks

SERIES *Jūgei no Uchi*; The Ten Arts
DATE ca. 1810
SIGNATURE Shinsai
FORMAT Koban yoko-e (13.6 x 18.8)
REFERENCES Preetorius, p.12; series illustrated in Ostier, *Les objets tranquilles,* pl. 13
POETS Yūgentei Maruhito, Shokkōtei Ayaori
FLLW FDN 3003.008

A small black box for picks rests beside a koto in a brocade satchel. Still lifes composed of these instruments with their cloth sacks were a common subject for many of the designers of surimono (see also cat. no. 207). Both poems treat the theme of playing the koto, which is considered one of the ten arts.

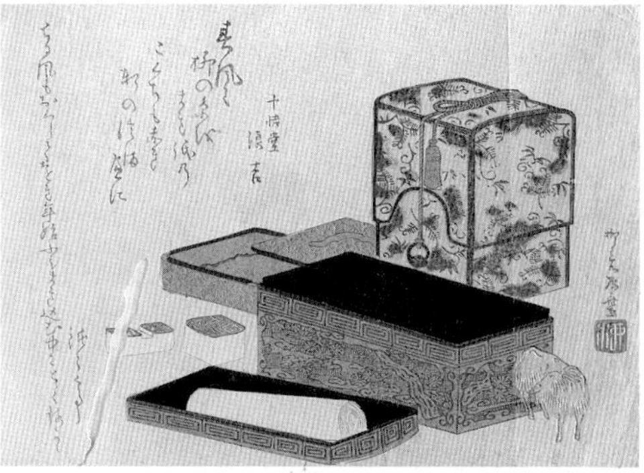

SHINSAI

225 Scholar's boxes with a small goat sculpture

DATE 1811
SIGNATURE Ryūryūkyo Shinsai
ARTIST'S SEAL Ryū (Yanagi)
FORMAT Koban yoko-e (13.8 x 18.8)
POETS Jūgodō Namiyoshi, Dondontei
FLLW FDN 3003.002

A carved red-cinnabar lacquer box for paper storage sits beside another of imitation-tortoise-shell lacquer, used for the storage of the seals. The red seal ink is contained in a small purple box. The miniature goat sculpture indicates the zodiac year.

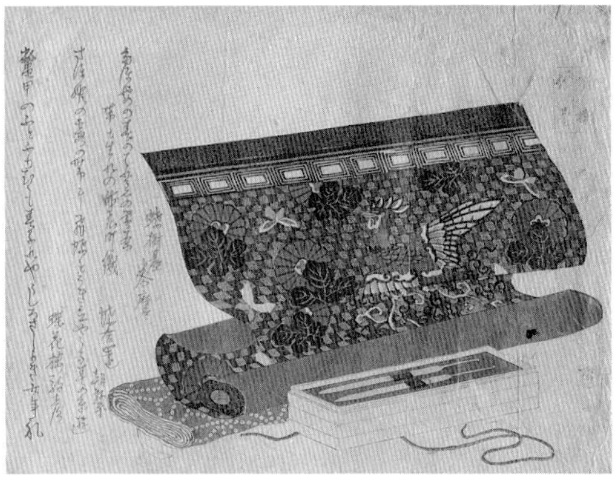

SHINSAI

226 A bolt of obi fabric with hair ornaments

TITLE Obi
SERIES Illegible
DATE 1813
SIGNATURE Shinsai ga
FORMAT Koban yoko-e (14.8 x 19.2)
POETS Chōjudai Yasumaro, Chōgōtei Asashige, Chōkarō Komahiko
FLLW FDN 3003.004

A roll of obi cloth decorated with a phoenix (indicating the zodiac year of the bird) and butterflies lies next to boxes holding hair pins. Originally a type of hair pick, these pins were used by nineteenth-century Edo women as hair ornaments. Beneath them is a bolt of tie-dyed cloth.

The name of each poet begins with the character for butterfly (*chō*), and each is graphically referred to by a butterfly on the bolt of obi fabric. The first poem mentions an obi and special products, while the second poem mentions Saohime, the goddess of spring, from whose obi the butterflies fly away. The third mentions the hair pins of a courtesan seen at a New Year's parade in the Yoshiwara.

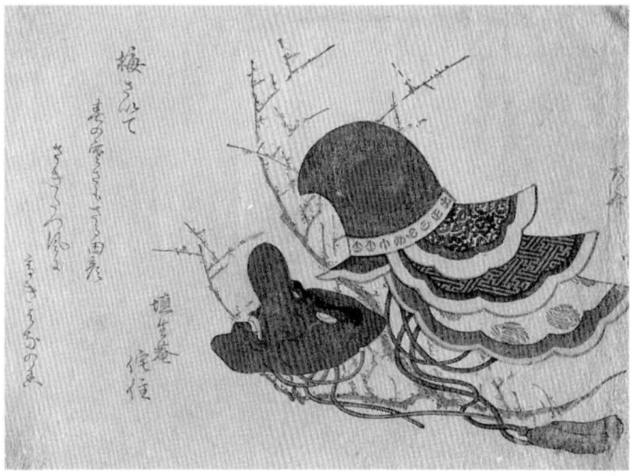

SHINSAI

227 A *torikabuto,* a *tengu* mask, and a plum branch

DATE 1813
SIGNATURE Shinsai
FORMAT Koban yoko-e (13.8 x 18.8)
REFERENCES Rijksmuseum, *Hokusai,* pl. 104; *Collection de Monsieur X . . . ,* pl. 534
POETS Haniuan Wabizumi
FLLW FDN 3003.006

This still life for a bird year is composed of two objects alluding to birds. The mask is in the form of Sarutahiko. The cap is a *torikabuto,* literally "bird's cap." Both were used in Bugaku, a form of court music and dance. The key to the print lies in the poem, which mentions Sarutahiko, a Shinto god known for his extremely long nose (see cat. no. 122). According to myth, Sarutahiko blocked the descent of the first emperor of Japan from heaven to earth, but was charmed by Okame, the goddess of mirth and obligingly moved aside.

The numbers for the long months—1, 3, 7, 9, 10, 11, 12—of the year of the bird, 1813, appear as a decorative band around the crown of the hat.

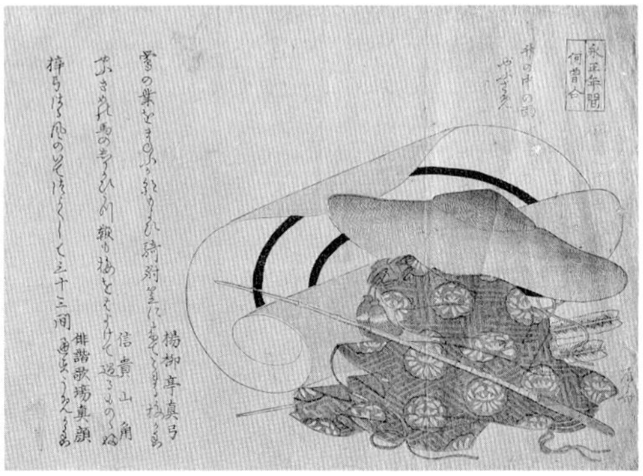

SHINSAI

228 Archery equipment

TITLE *Take no Naka no Ame Yabusame;* Rain in a Bamboo Grove: Archery on Horseback
SERIES *Eishō Nenkan Nazo Awase*; A Riddle Game in the Eishō Period
DATE ca. 1815
SIGNATURE Shinsai
PRINTER'S SEAL Ryūsai; undeciphered
FORMAT Koban yoko-e (13.8 x 18.6)
REFERENCE Hillier, "Still-life in Surimono," fig. 5
POETS Yōryūtei Mayumi, Shigi no Yamazumi, Haikai Utaba Magao
FLLW FDN 3003.009

The tradition of riddle games dates back to the Heian period when, as a court amusement, poems were improvised on themes provided by riddles based on wordplay. It is not clear why the title of the series refers to the Eishō period (1504–21), but perhaps the riddle topics were inspired by poems in the early sixteenth-century kyōka anthology *Eishō Kyōka Awase* (see Keyes, *Beatty,* no. 297).

Here, the riddle inscribed beside the title cartouche reads: *take no naka no ame,* "What do you call a grove of bamboo in the rain?" The answer is provided: *yabusame,* "archery on horseback," since *yabu* and *(s)ame,* can also mean respectively a "bamboo grove" and "rain." The image includes the accoutrements of a traditional equestrian archery contest: target and arrows, riding crop, brocade hunting cloak, and straw hunting hat.

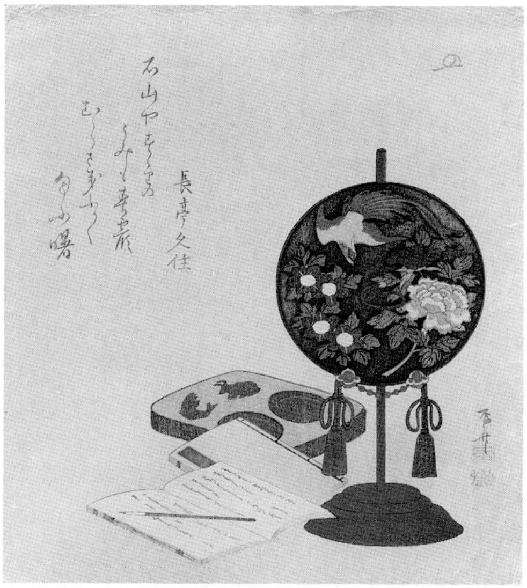

SHINSAI

229 A candle stand, books, a brush, and an inkstone

DATE possibly 1817
SIGNATURE Shinsai
ARTIST'S SEALS Shin; Sai
FORMAT Shikishiban (22.2 x 19.6)
POET Chōtei Hisazumi
FLLW FDN 3003.048

A candle stand is patterned with the motifs of a blossoming peony, bellflower, and phoenix. Beside it rest two books, one held open with a brush. To the left lies an inkstone with carved ox and fish designs. Perhaps the ox is the clue to the zodiac dating.

Alluding to *The Tale of Genji*, Shinsai has selected subtle references to its author, Murasaki Shikibu. She is said to have begun writing this novel by candlelight at Ishiyamadera Temple, which is mentioned in the poem.

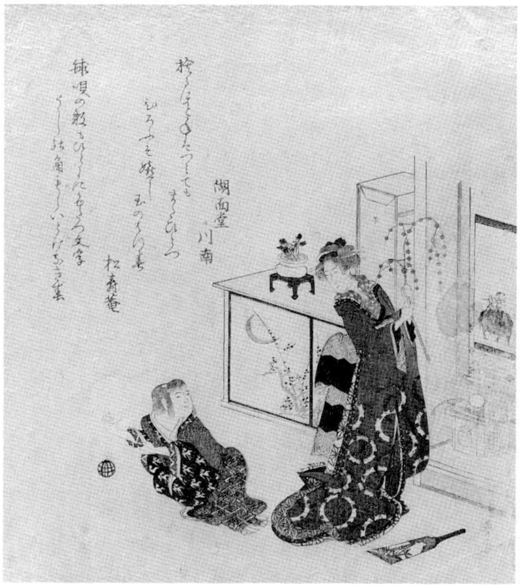

SHINSAI

230 A woman with rice cakes and a child with a ball

DATE 1817
SIGNATURE Shinsai
FORMAT Shikishiban (21.1 x 18.7)
POETS Komendō Kawaminami, Shōjuan
FLLW FDN 3003.050

A woman holds a willow branch decorated with rice cakes for the New Year as a child plays with a New Year ball made from different colored silk threads. In the alcove hangs a scroll of the oxherder boy, a recurrent motif in East Asian painting; on the mounting are embossed the numbers for the long months—1, 3, 4, 6, 8, 11—for 1817, an ox year. Other symbols for the New Year include the potted adonis plant, battledore, and painted panel of a plum tree.

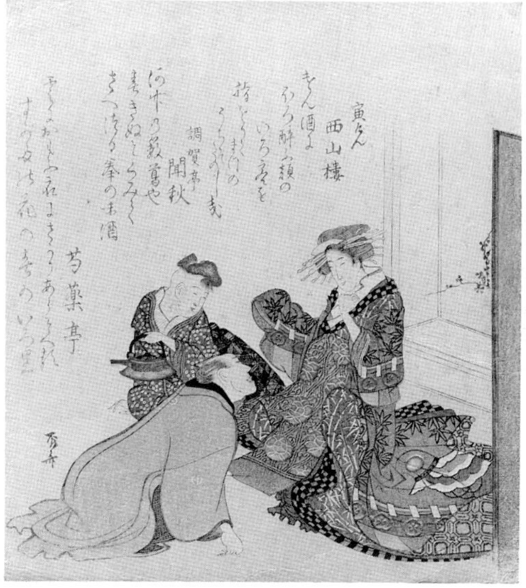

SHINSAI

231 A man and woman playing a game as a boy serves sake

TITLE *Tora-ken*; Tiger Hand Game
SIGNATURE Shinsai
DATE 1818, Year of the Tiger
FORMAT Shikishiban (21.6 x 19.0)
POETS Seizanrō, Chōgatei Kikiaki, Shakuyakutei
FLLW FDN 3003.058

A child attendant holds a sake pot, and a beauty cowers in mock terror as her patron impersonates a tiger. *Tora-ken* is a drinking game; the loser must drink sake. On the kimono of the courtesan is the emblem for the Shakuyakutei poetry group and a large "bird's cap" design.

The *tora-ken* game uses three basic hand gestures. Here, in the first gesture the beauty poses as if holding a staff, to ward off the man in the role of the crouching tiger, the second gesture. The third gesture is a raised fist. The staff beats the fist, the fist bests the tiger, and the tiger defeats the staff. Thus the beauty loses.

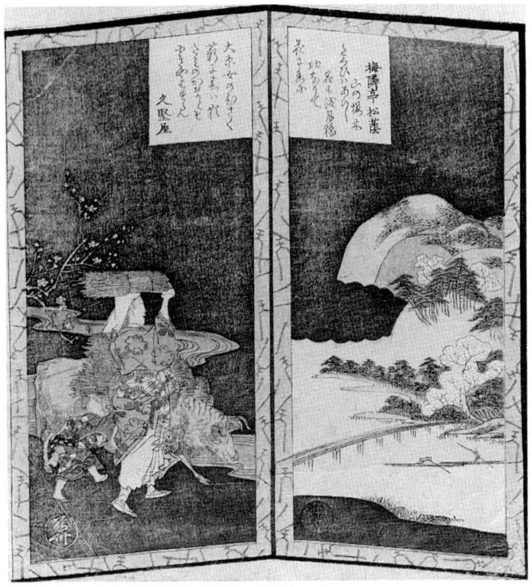

SHINSAI

232 Togetsu Bridge at Arashiyama with a peasant woman from Ōhara

SERIES Untitled set of six prints, each comprising two panels of a pair of six-fold screens
DATE ca. 1818
SIGNATURE Shinsai ga
ARTIST'S SEAL Shinsai
PRINTER'S SEAL Ryūsai
FORMAT Shikishiban (21.2 x 19.0)
REFERENCES Keyes, *Beatty,* no. 287; Schindler, pl. 40; Markus, *I Surimono,* 60. For the complete set see Rijksmuseum, *Hokusai,* pls. 97–102
POETS Bairintei Matsukage, Hisakataya
FLLW FDN 3003.059

In each print from this polyptych, a landscape panel is paired with a figure. The poems appear as shikishi poem cards at the top and contain classical references. Serving as a decorative motif on the band surrounding the screen panels, the koto bridges are the emblem of the Hisakataya-ren.

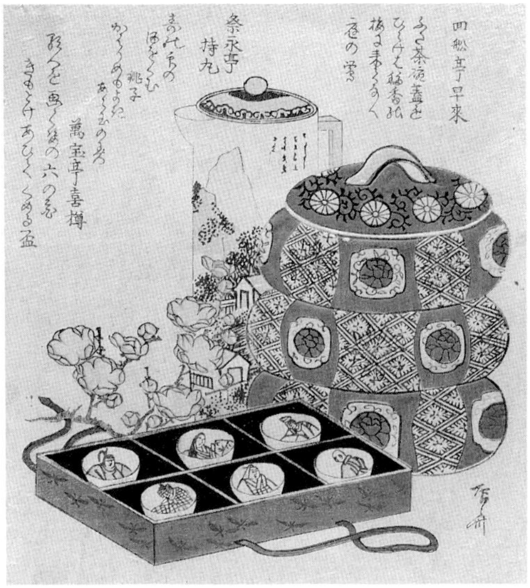

SHINSAI

233 A porcelain ewer, food server, and cups

DATE ca. 1820
SIGNATURE Shinsai
FORMAT Shikishiban (20.1 x 18.3)
POETS Kaisentei Hayaki, Saieitei Mochimaru, Mampōtei Kitaru
FLLW FDN 3003.044

A tiered Arita porcelain dish sits in front of a tall blue-and-white teapot. The tray contains six sake cups, each representing one of the Six Immortal Poets.

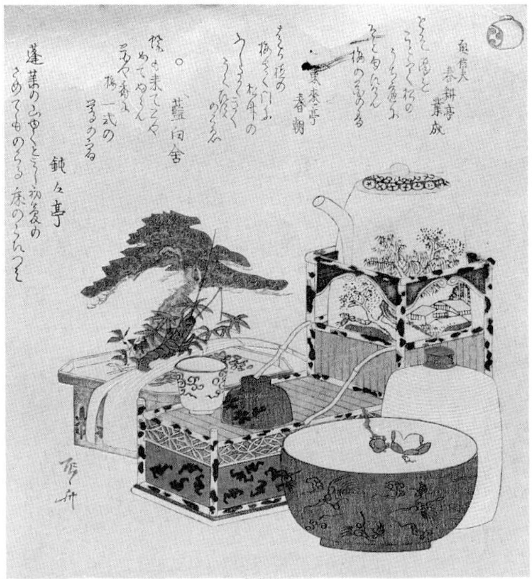

SHINSAI

234 A teapot and cups, with a New Year's arrangement

DATE ca. 1820
SIGNATURE Shinsai
FORMAT Shikishiban (20.2 x 18.5)
POETS Shunkōtei Narinari, Tōraitei Haruasa, Rankyūsha, Dondontei
FLLW FDN 3003.042

All the items are decorated with auspicious symbols—a Chinese phoenix, bats, and fungi. The folding stand for the porcelain teapot and cups is patterned after an incense tray used for Buddhist rituals. One poem refers to special spiced sake made for the New Year; another mentions a New Year's dream of traveling to Mount Hōrai, the mythical abode of Chinese immortals. The drum emblem indicates that this print was commissioned by the Taiko-gawa.

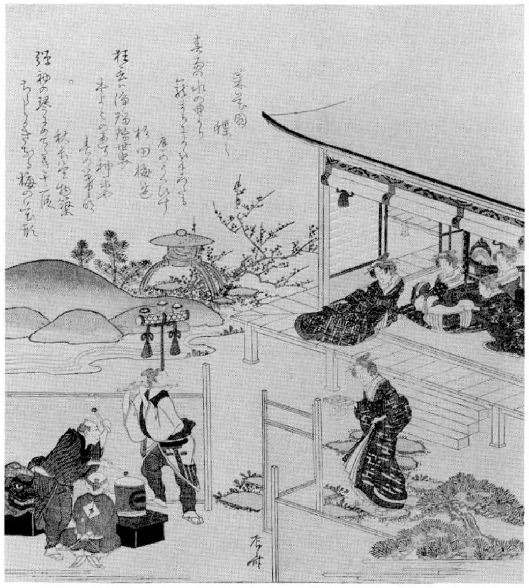

SHINSAI

235 Ushiwakamaru and Princess Jōruri

DATE ca. 1820
SIGNATURE Shinsai
FORMAT Shikishiban (20.9 x 18.6)
POETS Saikaen Chōchō, Sugita Umemichi, Shūchōdō Monoyana
FLLW FDN 3003.056

Based on a version of the sixteenth-century musical narrative *Jūnidan Zōshi*, this scene represents Ushiwakamaru (the young Yoshitsune) serenading Princess Jōruri. She sits on a veranda with her retinue as her servant delivers a message to him. Because of the popularity of Jōruri's tragic love story as musical narrative, her name was given to the popular dramatic form that later became the narrative of the puppet theater.

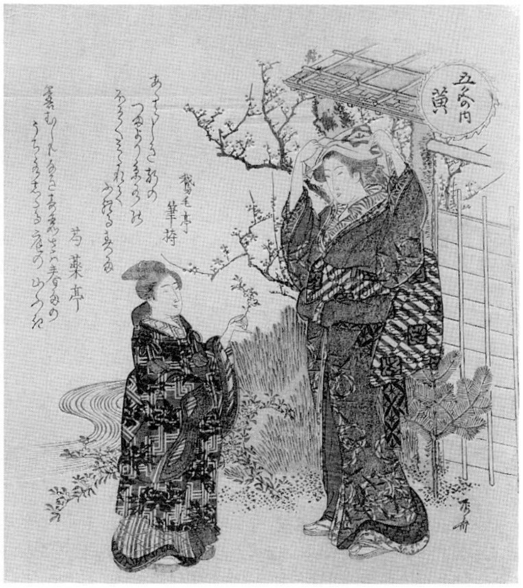

SHINSAI

236 A woman receiving a kerria rose

TITLE *Ki;* Yellow
SERIES *Goshiki no Uchi;* The Five Colors
DATE ca. 1820
SIGNATURE Shinsai
FORMAT Shikishiban (21.4 x 18.8)
REFERENCE Keyes, *Beatty*, no. 298
POETS Gamōtei Fudemochi, Shakuyakutei
FLLW FDN 3003.053

A well-dressed boy offers a branch of yellow *yamabuki* (kerria rose) to a woman who is adjusting her hat. On it is a stylized plum emblem for the poet Shakuyakutei.

This image alludes to the story of Prince Kaneakira, a prominent poet of the tenth-century Heian court Kaneakira is said to have offered a spray of kerria rose to a colleague who had asked to borrow a raincoat. This was his elegant way of apologizing for not having one to spare, because the phrase *mino nashi*, "no raincoat," can also be construed to mean "no fruit." Kerria rose, though a favorite spring flower of poets, does not bear fruit.

For another print from the series see catalogue number 43.

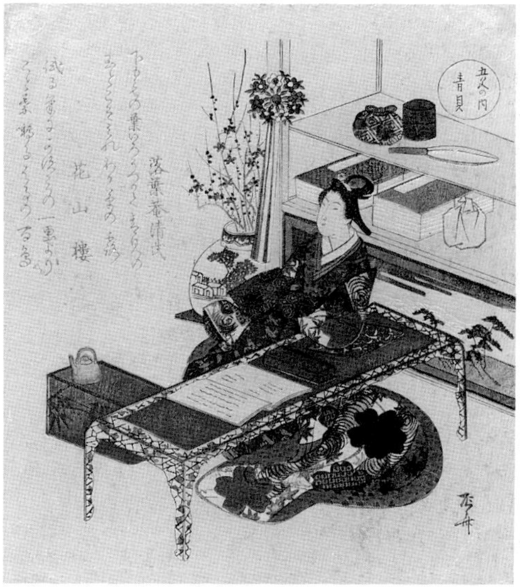

SHINSAI

237 A woman at a writing table

TITLE *Aogai*; Blue Shell (Mother-of-Pearl)
SERIES *Goshiki no Uchi;* The Five Colors
DATE ca. 1820
SIGNATURE Shinsai
FORMAT Shikishiban (21.2 x 18.3)
REFERENCES *Paul F. Walter Collection of Surimono,* no.126, pl.13; Polster, no. 406; for two others from the series see Polster, nos.417 ("Red") and 418 ("White")
POETS Rakuyōan Kiyotake, Kazanrō
FLLW FDN 3003.049

A sumptuously dressed woman sits at a writing table made with mother-of-pearl inlay. Behind her are books and tea ceremony implements. Below them is a small painted sliding door of pines by a shoreline

The theme of the five colors was often used as a theme by ukiyo-e artists.

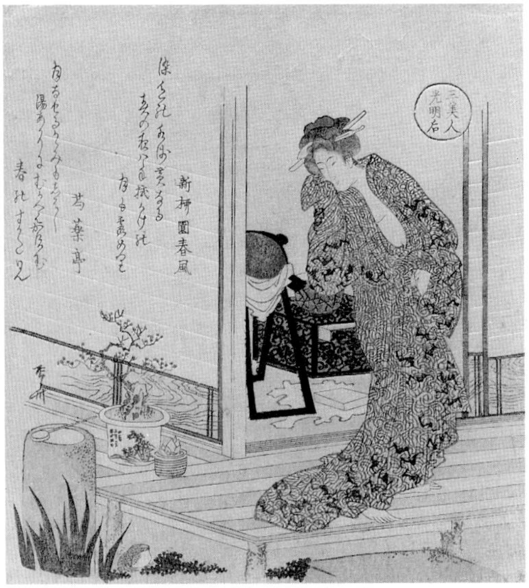

SHINSAI

238 A woman on a veranda

TITLE *Kōmyō Gō*, The Empress Kōmyō
SERIES *San Bijin*; Three Beauties
DATE ca. 1820
SIGNATURE Shinsai
FORMAT Shikishiban (21.6 x 19.2)
REFERENCES Schmidt, cat. no. 81; Rijksmuseum, *Hokusai,* pl. 106; Polster, no. 414.
POETS Shinryūen Harukaze, Shakuyakutei
FLLW FDN 3003.055

Empress Kōmyō, the wife of Emperor Shōmu, lived from 701 to 760. She inaugurated public baths and is said to have personally bathed the first thousand who presented themselves to her. According to legend, the last was a leper, here represented by the toad, whom she managed to bathe despite his repugnant appearance. In response to her kindness, the leper revealed his true form as a reincarnation of the Buddha.

Here Kōmyō is portrayed as a modern woman, emerging from her first bath of the New Year. She dries her face on the sleeve of her bath robe which is decorated with auspicious bats and a blue wave motif. As she pauses to look out at a toad, her robe opens.

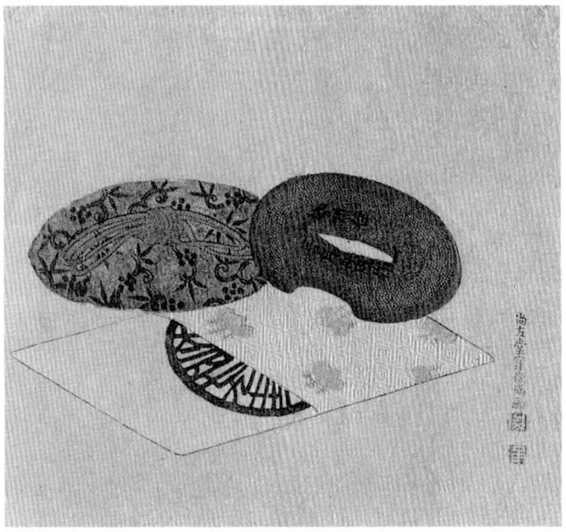

KUBO SHUMMAN

1757–1820

239 Two sword guards with pouches

DATE 1796
SIGNATURE Shōsadō Kubo Shumman ga
ARTIST'S SEALS Shun; Man
FORMAT Small koban egoyomi (13.0 x 12.0)
FLLW FDN 3007.031

Lying in a cloth folder embossed with the paulownia crest is an iron sword guard (*tsuba*) with the numbers for the long months—2, 4, 7, 9, 11, 12—pierced in positive silhouette. Another sword guard lies against it and a brocade pouch. Decorated with fish-roe stippling, this sword guard bears the name of a poet living in Sesshū, Mikazuki Funanari, as the maker (see catalogue number 241). This egoyomi is similar in composition to cat. no. 256.

There is another impression in the collection (FLLW FDN 3007.032)

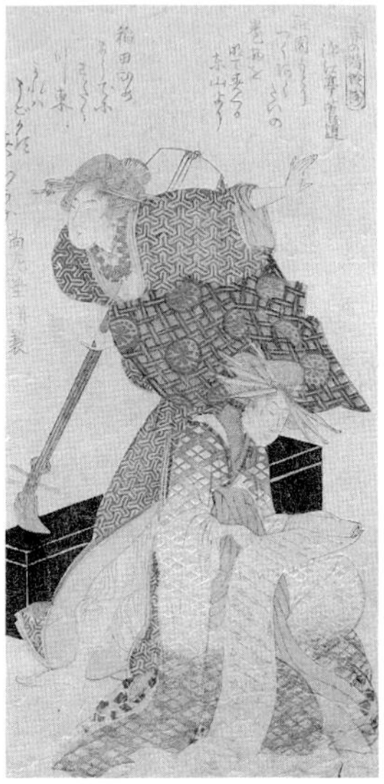

SHUMMAN

240 A lady holding a shamisen while another chants from a text

SERIES *Haru no Akizushima;* Spring in the Land of the Dragonfly
DATE ca. 1800
SIGNATURE Shōsadō hei sei (made and written by Shōsadō)
FORMAT Koban tate-e (19.1 x 9.1)
POETS Shinkōtei Sugamichi, Shōsadō
FLLW FDN 3007.005

"Land of the Dragonfly" in the title of the series refers to an ancient poetic name for Japan and suggests this print may belong to a series celebrating famous places. Here, the first poem mentions Gion in Kyoto, which is still famous for its geisha. In this design printed by the poet-artist Shumman himself are two geisha, one holding a shamisen and another chanting a song from what may be a Jōruri libretto.

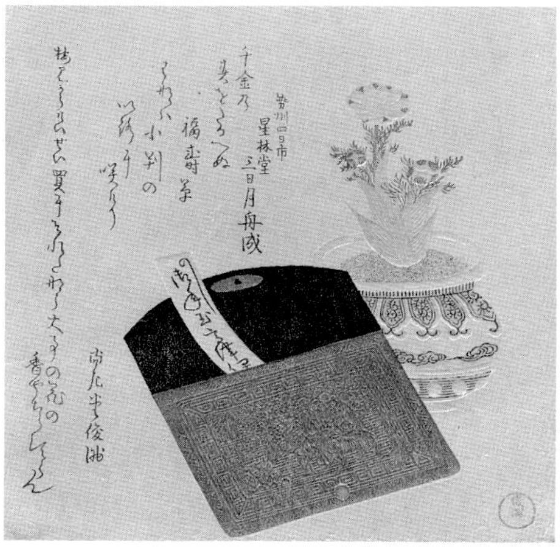

SHUMMAN

241 A coin pouch and a potted adonis plant

DATE ca. 1802
SIGNATURE Shōsadō Shumman (as the poet)
ARTIST'S SEAL Shumman
FORMAT Small square (21.0 x 17.5)
POETS Mikazuki Funanari of Seirindō of Yokkaichi in Sesshū, Shumman
FLLW FDN 3007.035

In front of a New Year's potted adonis plant rests an embossed leather coin pouch which contains a ribbon sheet indicating that it is a gift for children at the New Year.

In the poems the yellow flower of the adonis plant is likened to the golden color of coins.

There are three other fine impressions of this surimono in the collection (FLLW FDN 3007.033, .034, and .036).

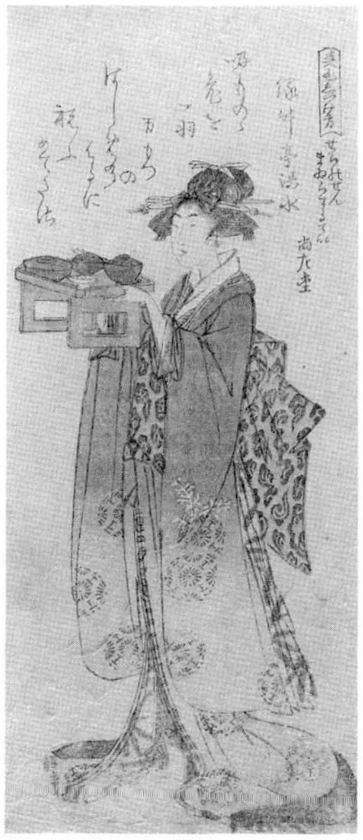

SHUMMAN

242 A woman with a tray of covered bowls of food

TITLE *Sechi no Zen Mairasuru Tei;* The Proper Way of Serving a New Year Meal on a Tray
SERIES *Shunshoku Shitsukekata;* Teaching Manners According to the Colors of Spring
DATE ca.1804
SIGNATURE Shōsado
FORMAT Koban tate-e (20.1 x 8.6)
POET Ryokuchikutei Yumizu
FLLW FDN 3007.001

Sechi in the title refers to *osechi ryōri*, an array of special dishes prepared for the New Year. In restaurants or wealthy households, formal meals such as those eaten at the New Year were served on wooden tray-tables with legs, as seen in the image.

The two-character word in the title of the series, *shunshoku,* literally meaning "the colors of spring," also conveys erotic overtones. There are six prints from this series in the Wright collection including catalogue numbers 243, 244, 245, and 246—and FLLW FDN 3007.015.

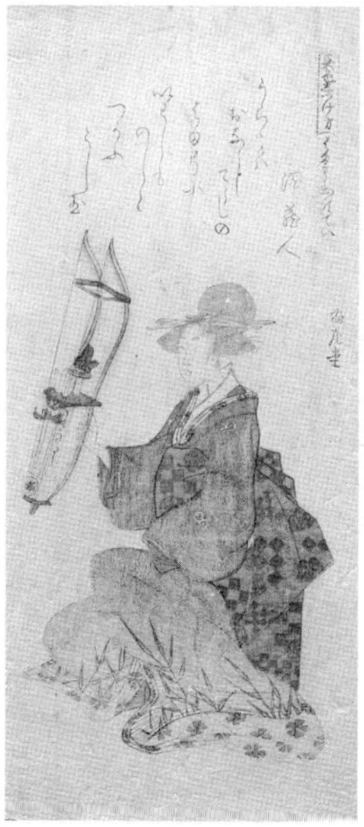

SHUMMAN

243 A woman with a toy archery set

TITLE *Hamayumi Idasu Tei*; The Proper Way of Presenting a New Year Arrow Set
SERIES *Shunshoku Shitsukekata;* Teaching Manners According to the Colors of Spring
DATE ca.1804
SIGNATURE Shōsado
FORMAT Koban tate-e (20.4 x 8.8)
POET Sake no Kurōdo
FLLW FDN 3007.002

A young woman is shown with a toy archery set traditionally presented as a gift during the New Year season. Compared to the more famous large-sheet portrayals of women by masters such as Utamaro, Choki, and other contemporaries, the small koban format of surimono does not seem to have been as conducive to the depictions of lovely women (for example also see cat. no. 288 by Utamaro and cat. no. 61 by Choki). Here, in series such as this, the faces of the women are stereotypical and attention is focused on their activities rather than their beauty.

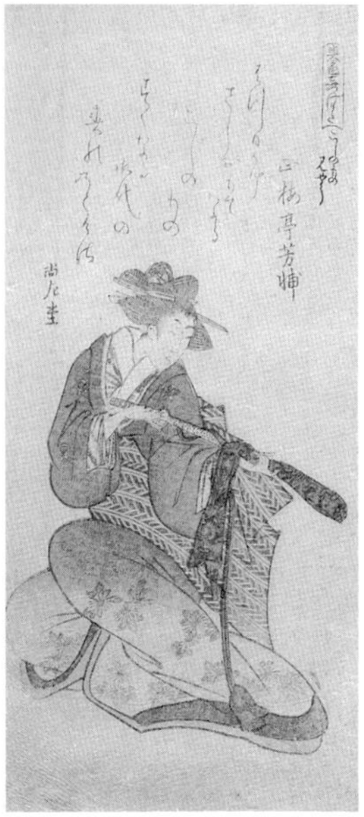

SHUMMAN

244 A woman with a sword

TITLE *Koshinomono Miyō;* How to Examine a Sword
SERIES *Shunshoku Shitsukekata;* Teaching Manners According to the Colors of Spring
DATE ca. 1804
SIGNATURE Shōsadō
FORMAT Koban tate-e (20.9 x 8.6)
POET Shōbaitei Yoshisuke
FLLW FDN 3007.003

During the long reign of peace that defined the Edo period, members of samurai households had little occasion to actually use a sword, but they were still highly esteemed as precious family heirlooms. At the end of this period, wealthy merchants were able to purchase permission to wear swords, thus erasing one of the few real distinctions that existed between these two social classes. Proper etiquette was required for the handling of swords.

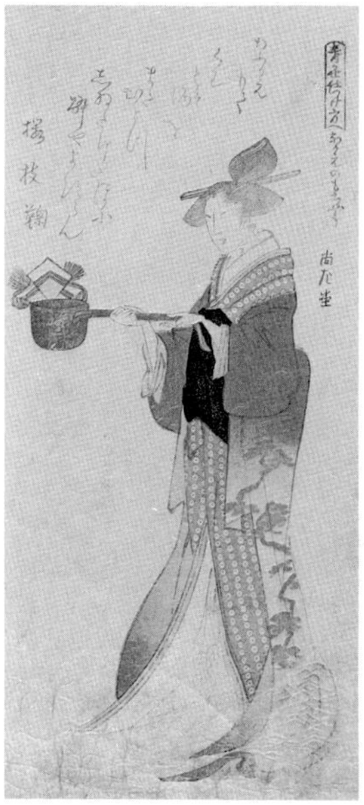

SHUMMAN

245 A woman with a ladle

TITLE *Nagae no Mochi-yō;* How to Hold a Long Ladle
SERIES *Shunshoku Shitsukekata;* Teaching Manners According to the Colors of Spring
DATE ca. 1804
SIGNATURE Shōsadō
FORMAT Koban tate-e (20.2 x 8.9)
POET Sakura no Edamari
FLLW FDN 3007.004

A woman holds a long ladle with a folded paper decoration for the New Year, (*noshi*) adorned with twigs of pine. The metal ladle is quite heavy and requires two hands to support it.

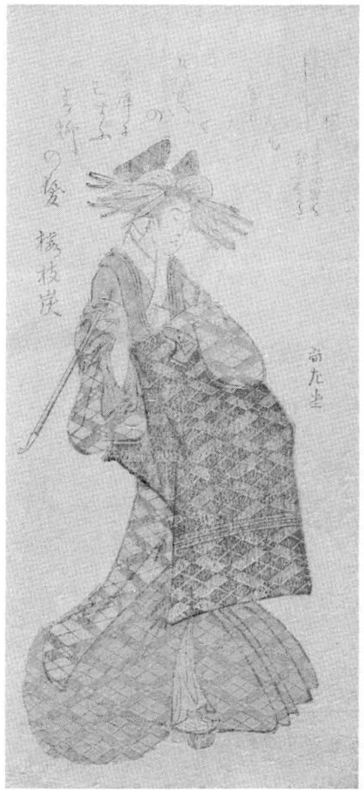

SHUMMAN

246 A courtesan with a pipe

TITLE *Nakanochō ni Kyaku o Mukau Sugata*; The Proper Pose for Greeting a Patron in Nakanochō
SERIES *Shunshoku Shitsukekata;* Teaching Manners According to the Colors of Spring
DATE ca. 1804
SIGNATURE Shōsadō
FORMAT Koban tate-e (20.5 x 9.0)
POET Sakura no Edazumi
FLLW FDN 3007.016

A courtesan in her finest New Year attire, with her obi tied in front and hair arranged in an elaborate coiffeur, strikes a coquettish pose to greet her client. Nakanochō, mentioned in the title of the print, refers to the main avenue of the Yoshiwara pleasure quarters.

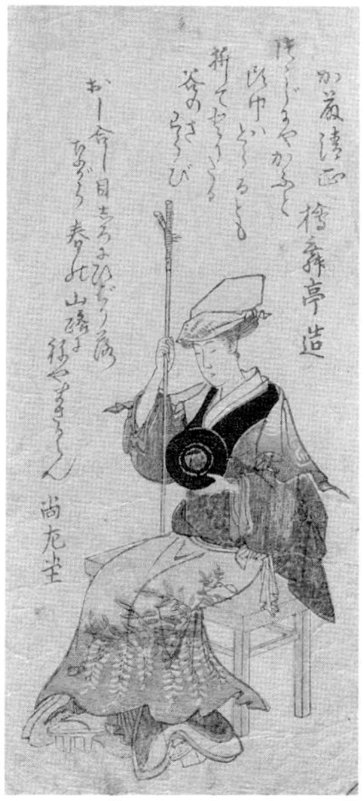

SHUMMAN

247 The warrior Katō Kiyomasa as a woman pilgrim

TITLE *Katō Kiyomasa*
SERIES *Ito no Yanagase Shichihon Yari Ume*; Parody of the Seven Spear-bearing Samurai at Yanagase
DATE ca. 1804
SIGNATURE Shōsadō (as poet)
FORMAT Koban tate-e (18.9 x 8.5)
REFERENCES *UT, Bibliothèque Nationale*, pl. 158; Markus, *I Surimono* 47; Polster, no. 428
POETS Hinokibutei Tsukuru, Shōsadō
FLLW FDN 3007.007

A woman holds a bamboo stick, parodying the spear used for hunting tigers. She also holds a disk, imitating the circular crest of Katō Kiyomasa.

Seven warriors established their reputations in this battle and became known as the "Seven Spear-bearing Samurai at Yanagase." From the series of seven parodies plus a cover print, there are five others in the collection: cat nos. 248 and 249, and 3007.011 and 3007.012, not illustrated.

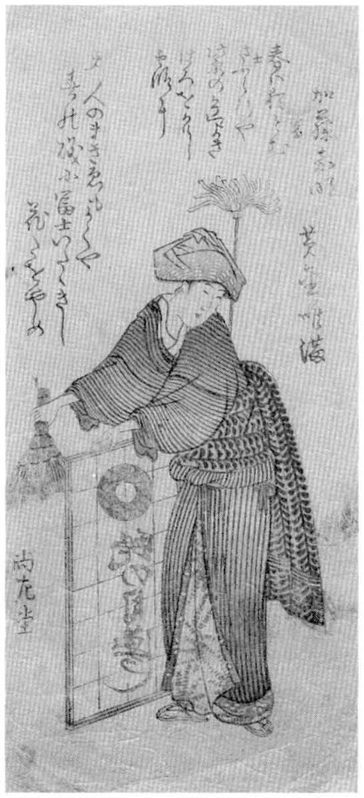

SHUMMAN

248 The warrior Katō Yoshiaki as a woman cleaning

TITLE *Katō Yoshiaki*
SERIES *Ito no Yanagase Shichihon Yari Ume*; Parody of the Seven Spear-bearing Samurai at Yanagase
DATE ca. 1804
SIGNATURE Shōsadō (as poet)
FORMAT Koban yoko-e (18.9 x 8.5)
REFERENCE *UT, Bibliothèque Nationale*, pl. 163
POETS Kogane Tadamitsu, Shōsadō (Shumman)
FLLW FDN 3007.008

A woman dusts a shōji screen on which is written "Janome Sushi" (meaning "eye of the snake," a name of a sushi restaurant). The eye imagery is carried further by the circular disk crest above the writing. This refers to the Katō family crest, as in cat. no. 247. Katō Yoshiaki was the head of the navy and commanded warriors under Tokugawa Ieyasu. See page 56 for a discussion of the poem by Tadamitsu.

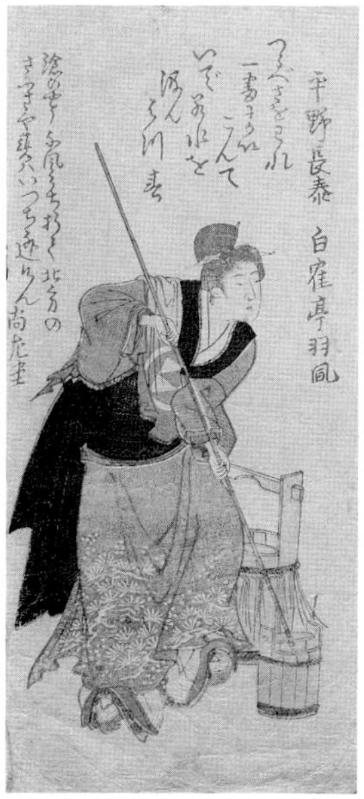

SHUMMAN

249 The warrior Hirano Nagayasu as a woman with a bucket

TITLE *Hirano Nagayasu*
SERIES *Ito no Yanagase Shichihon Yari Ume*; Parody of the Seven Spear-bearing Samurai at Yanagase
DATE ca. 1804
SIGNATURE Shōsadō (as poet)
FORMAT Koban tate-e (18.2 x 8.4)
REFERENCE *UT, Bibliothèque Nationale*, pl. 160
POETS Hakkakutei Hakaze, Shōsadō (Shumman)
FLLW FDN 3007.010

The spear in this print takes the form of a pole attached to a pail. The woman parodying the warrior Hirano Nagayasu is actually performing the ritual of drawing the first water for the New Year. The towel thrown over her shoulder bears the crest of three fish scales used by this famous hero.

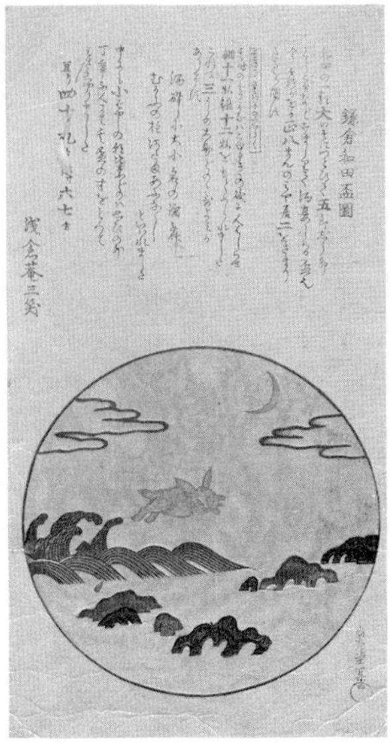

SHUMMAN

250 A design for a pink sake cup with decorations in gold and silver

TITLE *Kamakura Wada Sakazuki no Zu*; A Sake Cup Commissioned by the Wada Family in Kamakura
DATE 1807, Year of the Rabbit
SIGNATURE Shōsadō sha
ARTIST'S SEAL Shō
FORMAT Koban tate-e (21.4 x 11.0)
POET Asakuraan Sanshō
FLLW FDN 3007.043

In this design for a lacquer sake cup commissioned by the Wada family of Kamakura, a silver rabbit hops above the waves, beneath a crescent moon. Long associated with the moon and the New Year, the rabbit is said to conceive when running through the waves. The long months—1, 2, 3, 5, 8, 11, 12—and short months—4, 6, 7, 9, 10—appear in the prose in bold writing, integrated into the text.

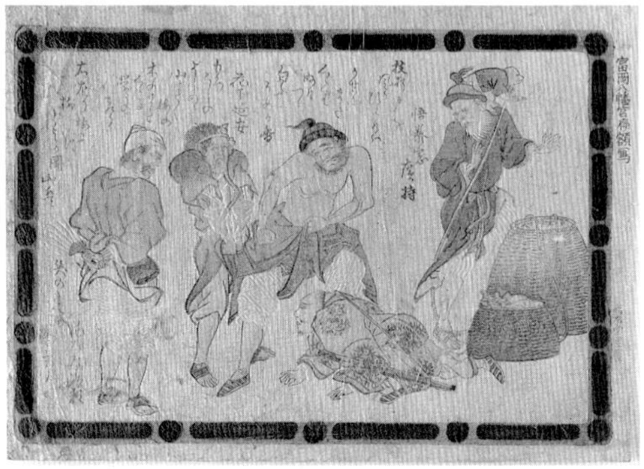

SHUMMAN

251 The humiliation of Hanshin

TITLE *Tomioka Hachimangū Hengaku Sha*; Copy of Wooden Paintings Dedicated to Hachimangū in Tomioka
DATE ca. 1808
SIGNATURE Shōsadō sha sei
FORMAT Koban yoko-e (13.5 x 18.3)
REFERENCE NUK, *Pulverer*, pl. 2-5
POETS Gotaisō Hiromochi, Hananoshita Nobiyasu, Hananoya Michiyori
FLLW FDN 3007.020

The youth Hanshin was disowned by his father, a prince of Han, in China. Living on the streets, he fished in the moat of his father's castle; eventually he was looked after by a poor woman. Once, when forced by a bully to crawl between his legs, Hanshin agreed to this humiliation rather than cause a disturbance with someone of low birth. Much later he became a general and prince; and he rewarded the old woman and took his tormentor into his service.

The same votive painting was copied by Utagawa Kuniyoshi (1797–1861) in a triptych format (see Springfield Museum of Fine Arts, *Utagawa Kuniyoshi*, 1980, pl. 91).

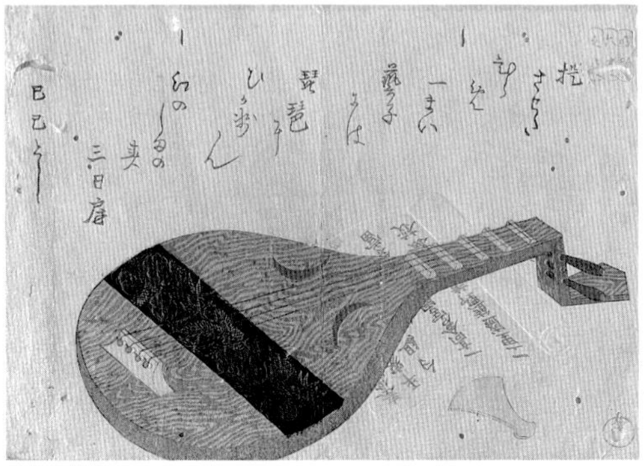

SHUMMAN

252 A lute

SERIES *Narimono Rokuban no Uchi*; Six Musical Instruments
DATE 1809, Year of the Snake
ARTIST'S SEAL Shumman
FORMAT Koban yoko-e (12.8 x 17.6)
POET Mikkabō
REFERENCE Ostier, *La voix silencieuse*, pl. 78
FLLW FDN 3007.026

A lute lies beside a chanter's text; a plectrum rests on the far right. Alluded to in the scroll, a Heike lute was a type played by a priest-minstrel in narrating *The Tale of the Heike* (*Heike Monogatari*). Taira no Shigemori and his Heike clan are specifically named on the scroll. The poem mentions spring in Enoshima, which is a further reference to the snake, because special ceremonies connected to the worship of Benzaiten were held at the shrine every snake year.

The Wright collection includes three other prints from the same series—catalogue numbers 253, 254, and 255.

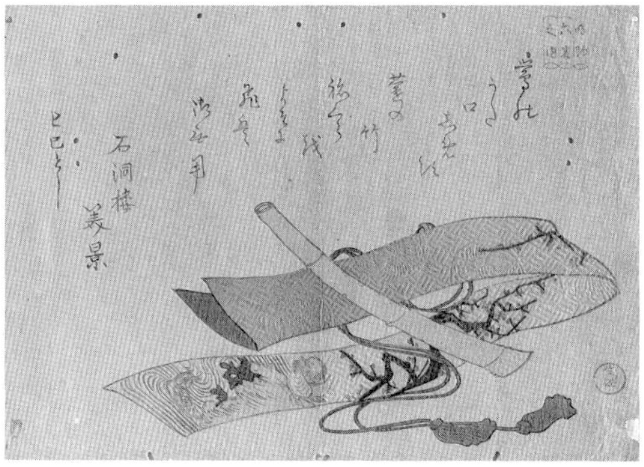

SHUMMAN

253 A flute

SERIES *Narimono Rokuban no Uchi*; Six Musical Instruments
DATE 1809, Year of the Snake
ARTIST'S SEAL Shumman
FORMAT Koban yoko-e (12.8 x 17.6)
POET Sekidōrō Yoshikage
FLLW FDN 3007.024

A *shakuhachi* flute lies with an obi cord on a folded obi that is decorated with a pair of mandarin ducks and embossed with medallions of a phoenix. Both of these bird images were traditional auspicious symbols and not necessarily linked with prints issued in a bird year.

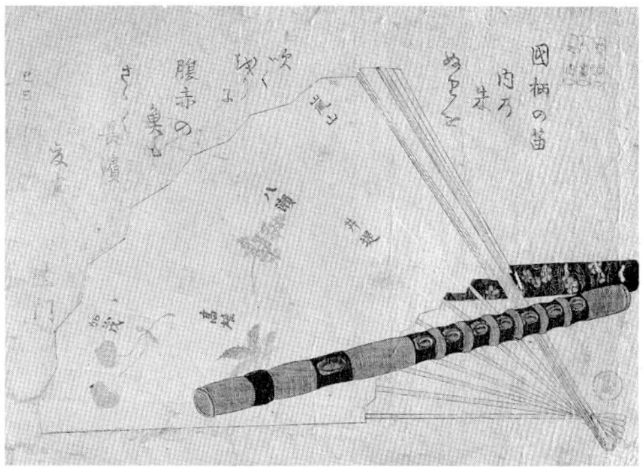

SHUMMAN

254 A fan with a flute

SERIES *Narimono Rokuban no Uchi*; Six Musical Instruments
DATE 1809, Year of the Snake
ARTIST'S SEAL Shumman
FORMAT Koban yoko-e (13.6 x 18.5)
REFERENCE Keyes, *Beatty*, no. 308
POET Kaanrin Fuku no Shigekado (in this impression, the poet's name is slightly abraded)
FLLW FDN 3007.023

A fan decorated with botanical specimens rests between a flute and its case. Five famous places in Kyoto and their most noted plant life comprise the theme of the folding fan: the cherry for Arashiyama, fern for Yase, water plantain for the Kamo River, maple leaf for Takao, and plum for Ide.

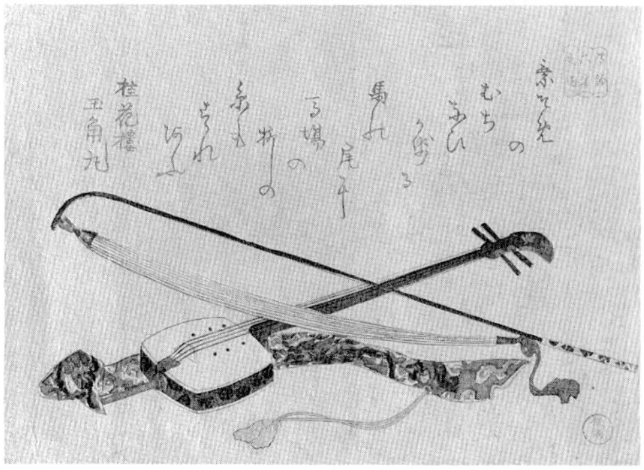

SHUMMAN

255 A Chinese fiddle

SERIES *Narimono Rokuban no Uchi*; Six Musical Instruments
DATE ca. 1809
ARTIST'S SEAL Shumman
FORMAT Koban yoko-e (12.8 x 17.6)
REFERENCE Forrer, *Surimono/Egoyomi,* fig. 31
POET Keikarō Tamakadomaru
FLLW FDN 3007.027

A *kokyū,* or "Chinese fiddle," rests on its brocade wrapping cloth along with its bow. Unlike the impression illustrated in Forrer, this print does not have the snake year date nor does the cartouche include the name of the club (Asakusagawa). The Wright impression is therefore most likely from a commercial edition.

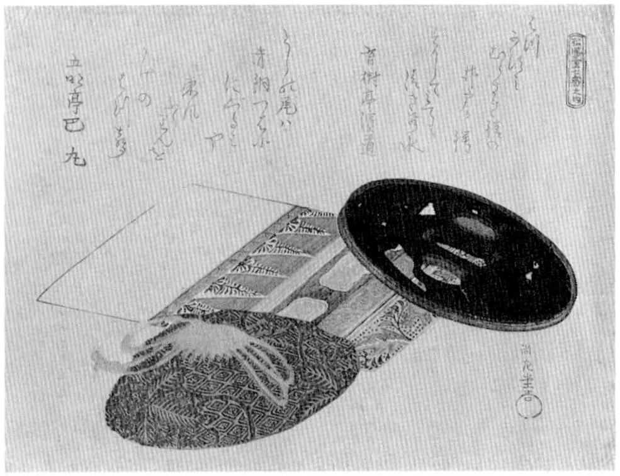

SHUMMAN

256 A sword guard with pouches

SERIES *Shōfūdai Shichiban no Uchi*; Set of Seven Designs for the Shōfūdai Group.
DATE ca.1810
SIGNATURE Shōsadō
ARTIST'S SEAL Shō
FORMAT Koban yoko-e (13.3 x 17.4)
REFERENCE Another print from the series in Keyes, *Beatty*, no. 366
POETS Ukitei Hamamichi, Gomeitei Hamaru
FLLW FDN 3007.028

Each of the prints in this series depicts sword furnishings. Here a sword guard lies beside its storage pouch and cloth folder made of Indonesian batik cotton fabric.

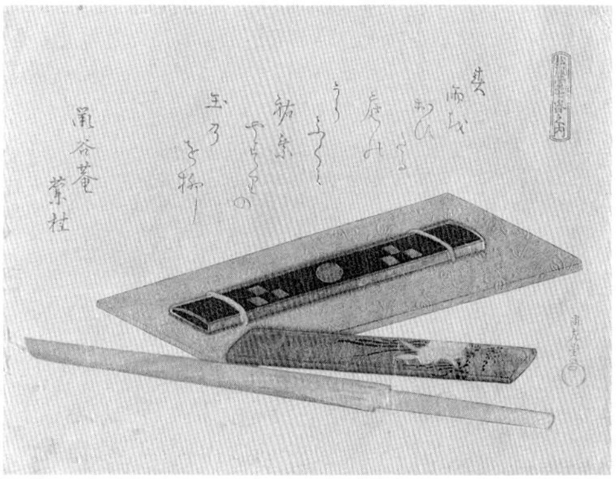

SHUMMAN

257 A file with sheath and handle

SERIES *Shōfūdai Shichiban no Uchi*; Set of Seven Designs for Shōfūdai Group
DATE ca. 1810
SIGNATURE Shōsadō
ARTIST'S SEAL Shō
FORMAT Koban yoko-e (13.9 x 18.0)
POET Sokokuan Chabashira
FLLW FDN 3007.030

A file and its handle lie in front of an embossed red lacquer board to which the sheath is tied. The handle is ornamented with a rabbit beneath a crescent moon. The rabbit, said to make rice cakes on the moon, is traditionally associated with the New Year.

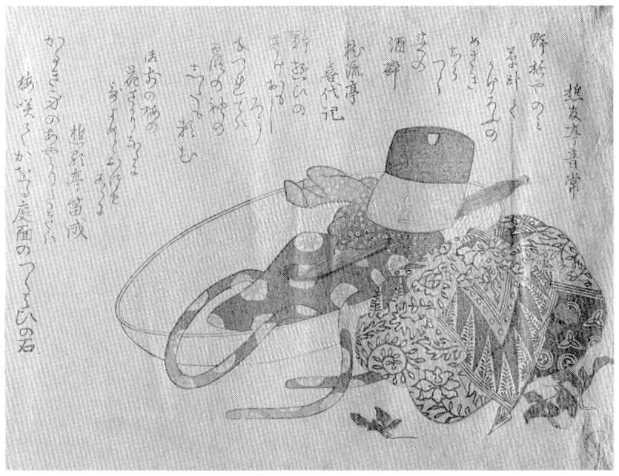

SHUMMAN

258 Items for a picnic

DATE ca. 1814
ARTIST'S SEAL Shumman
FORMAT Koban yoko-e (14.0 x 18.8)
POETS Shōyūtei Ototsune, Chinryūtei Kiyoki, Shōkatei Fuenari
FLLW FDN 3007.022

In this still life of picnic paraphernalia are a straw traveling hat, backpack, pipe, pink-and-green tobacco pouch bearing the name of the poet Shōyūtei, and a wrapping cloth which has an animal design, perhaps of a dog.

The first and second poems discuss a picnic outing in a spring field for the purpose of collecting the herbs for the New Year.

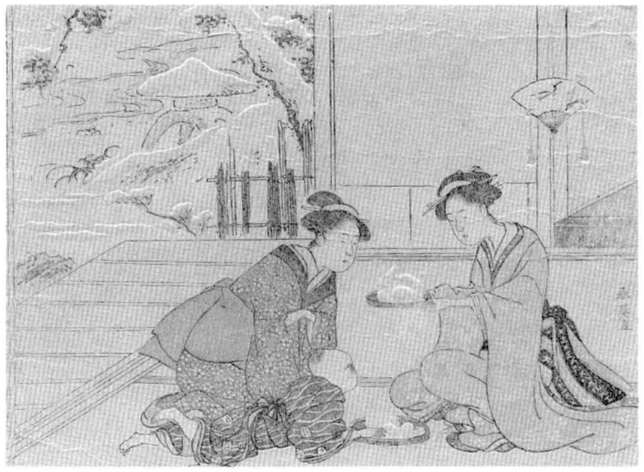

KATSUKAWA SHUN'EI

1762–1819

259 Two young women with a child and a rabbit snow sculpture

DATE 1795
SIGNATURE Shun'ei ga
CARVER'S SEAL Illegible
FORMAT Koban yoko-e (10.5 x 14.3)
FLLW FDN 3004.001

In this egoyomi for a rabbit year, a young woman and maid sit near an open doorway that reveals a snowy garden view. One holds a tray with a rabbit snow sculpture and shows it to the reclining boy, who plays with the remaining snow. On his robe are the numbers for the short months—2, 4, 5, 7, 10. The long months are indicated on the stripe design of the woman's obi—1, 3, 6, 8, 9, 11, 12.

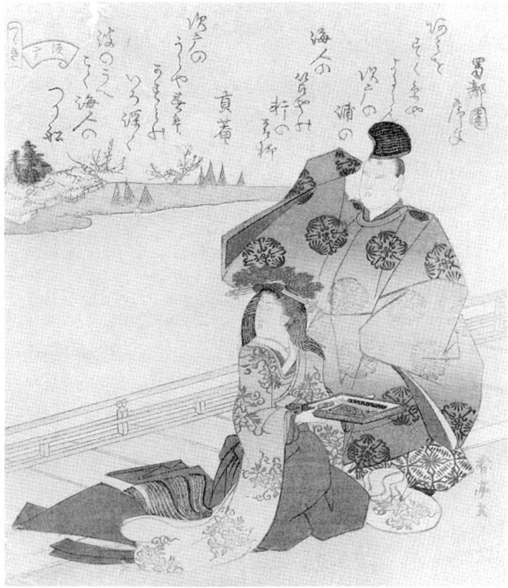

KATSUKAWA SHUNTEI

1770–1820

260 A Heian courtier and a woman of the court with a writing set looking out at the Suma landscape

SERIES *Suma Tsuzuki*; A Series on Suma
DATE ca.1818
SIGNATURE Shuntei sha
FORMAT Shikishiban (21.1 x 18.0)
POETS Shokutoen Jobun, Mitsugian
FLLW FDN 3012.008

Suma Bay, near Kobe, was the site of the exile of Prince Genji. According to *The Tale of Genji*, this coastline was nearly deserted save for the huts of the fishermen, which are shown here in the background together with their fishing nets.

A pupil of Katsukawa Shun'ei, Shuntei had a greater range of subject than his teacher, producing prints of warriors, beauties, and landscapes, as well as the actor portraits for which he is best known. Although he also acquired a name as a surimono artist relatively few of his designs have come to light. Fortunately, the Wright collection has some nine examples of his rare work in the genre (also see cat. nos. 55, 261–65).

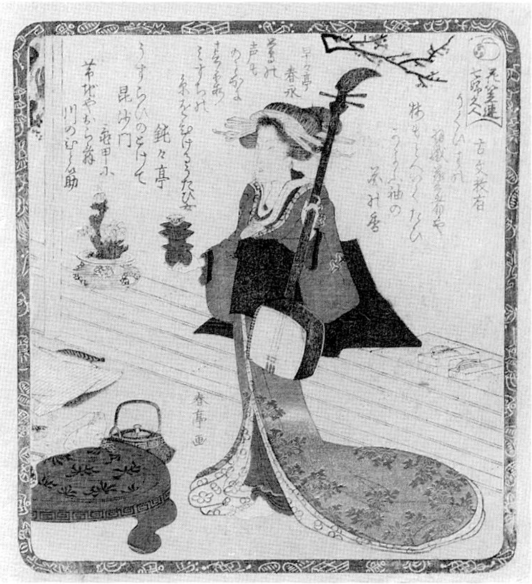

SHUNTEI

261 A woman holding a shamisen and a stack of cups

SERIES *Hanagasa-ren Shichifukujin*; Seven Women as the Gods of Good Luck for the Hanagasa Club
DATE ca.1825
SIGNATURE Shuntei ga
FORMAT Shikishiban (20.5 x 18.4)
REFERENCE Hempel, *Scheiwe,* pl.273
POETS Kobun Kazuari, Sōsōtei Harunaga, Dondontei
FLLW FDN 3012.001

A beauty holds a shamisen and a three-tiered set of sake cups as she enters from a veranda to entertain an unseen guest. An adonis plant for the New Year sits in a pot on the veranda and dishes of food have been placed on a low lacquer table. This is a parody of Bishamonten, the god of prosperity, who is traditionally shown holding a miniature pagoda in his right hand and a staff in his left hand.

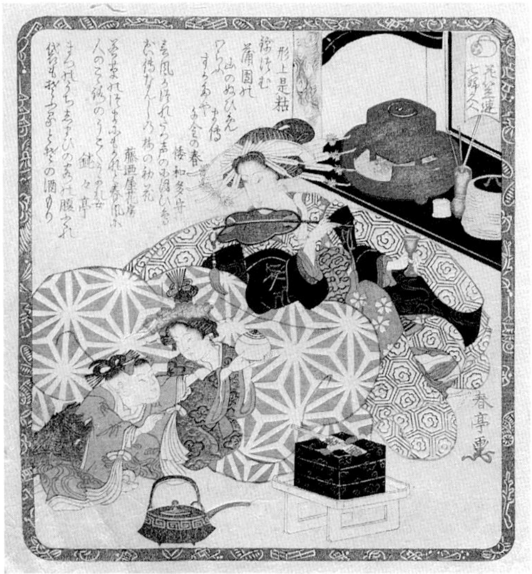

SHUNTEI

262 A woman with a Chinese fan and two children

SERIES *Hanagasa-ren Shichifukujin;* Seven Women as the Gods of Good Luck for the Hanagasa Club
DATE ca.1825
SIGNATURE Shuntei ga
FORMAT Shikishiban (20.4 x 18.4)
POETS Katanoue Koreneba, Yamato Watamori, Fujinoya Hanabusa, Dondontei
FLLW FDN 3012.002

In this parody of Hotei, the plump god of happiness, a woman holds a goblet and a fan. A boy and girl fight over a toy shaped like a precious jewel. The alcove is filled with tea-ceremony utensils, and in the foreground, stands a tray with a tiered lacquer food box on top of which lies a red and white paper decoration bearing the characters *ju* and *fuku,* meaning "long life" and "good fortune." Hotei is traditionally portrayed with his large sack of treasures, from which he offers precious items and toys for children. The ritual fan is another of his attributes.

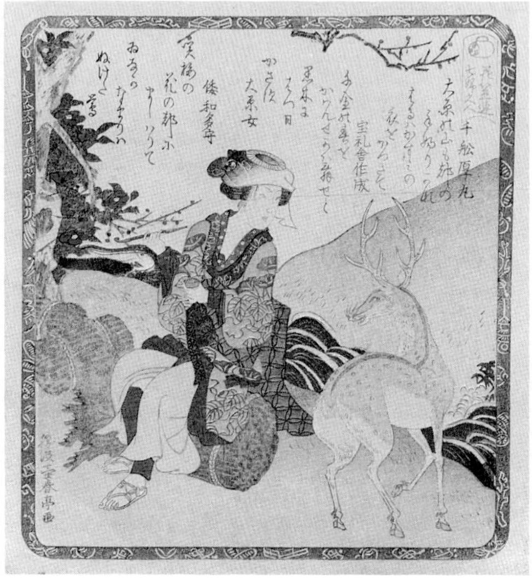

SHUNTEI

263 A woman with a stag

SERIES *Hanagasa-ren Shichifukujin*; Seven Women as the Gods of Good Luck for the Hanagasa Club
DATE ca. 1825
SIGNATURE Shōkyūko Shuntei ga
FORMAT Shikishiban (20.3 x 18.4)
REFERENCES Uhlenbeck, pl. 35; Hillier, *Japanese Prints and Drawings from the Vever Collection,* vol. 3, pl. 794
POETS Chifune Atsumaru, Hōreisha Sakunari, Yamato Watamori
FLLW FDN 3012.005

A woman from Ōhara prepares her tobacco pipe as she rests on her bale of firewood. A stag stops to watch her. Decorating her kerchief is the emblem of the poetry club, a drum. The circular ring on her head, made for supporting such bales, here symbolizes the god Jurōjin, often portrayed with a disc, representing the sun. The stag is one of the animals traditionally associated with this god.

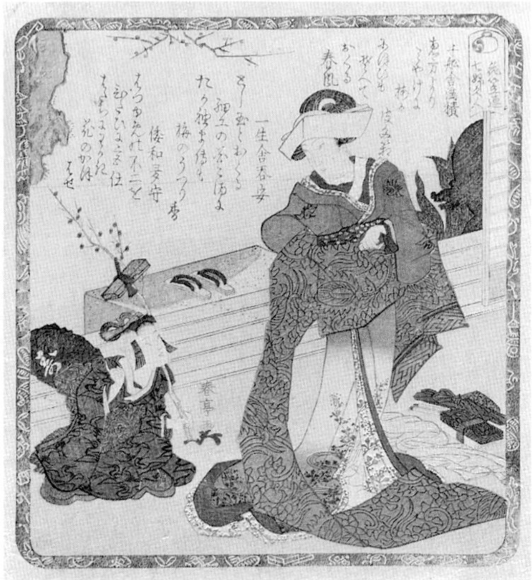

SHUNTEI

264 A woman tying her obi as a girl attendant holds a New Year's *mochibana* branch

SERIES *Hanagasa-ren Shichifukujin*; Seven Women as the Gods of Good Luck for the Hanagasa Club
DATE ca. 1825
SIGNATURE Shuntei ga
FORMAT Shikishiban (20.3 x 18.1)
POETS Chifunesha Mitsuzumi, Isshōsha Nomiyasu, Yamato Watamori
FLLW FDN 3012.006

The crane motif which appears on both the robes of the woman and the child is the symbol of the god Fukurokuju. Similarly, the form of the woman's hairstyle suggests the large head for which this god is well known. The word written on the packed cloth wrapper means luck and is a character used in the name of Fukurokuju.

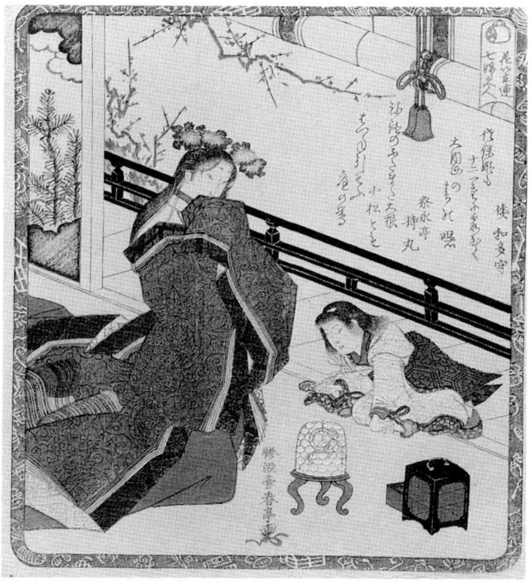

SHUNTEI

265 A woman and child watching a pet rat in its cage

SERIES *Hanagasa-ren Shichifukujin*; Seven Women as the Gods of Good Luck for the Hanagasa Club
DATE ca. 1825
SIGNATURE Shuntei ga
FORMAT Shikishiban (20.9 x 18.8)
POETS Yamato Watamori, Saieitei Mochimaru
FLLW FDN 3012.004

A court woman posing as the god Daikoku watches a white rat playing in a cage while a child looks on. Often depicted displaying his wealth to children, Daikoku is typically shown as a well-dressed courtier, so the woman here is appropriately attired in court costume. The animal symbol of this god is the white rat. For a discussion of this image and text see pages 54–55.

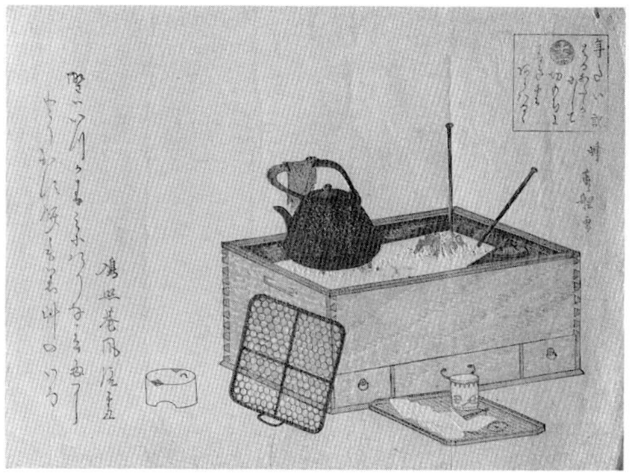

TEISAI SHŪRI

ACT. CA. 1804–1840

266 A wooden brazier with a kettle

TITLE *Jūni*; Twelve
SERIES *Nendaiki*; A Chronicle
DATE ca. 1810
SIGNATURE Hachi Shūri ga
FORMAT Koban yoko-e (14.2 x 18.3)
REFERENCE Ostier, *Les objets tranquilles*, pl.53 (without poem)
POET Nioteruan Fūryū
FLLW FDN 3025.001

Teisai Shūri was an amateur painter and print designer who studied briefly with Teisai Hokuba. He also studied kyōka poetry with Bembenkan Korifu, the head of the Biwa Poetry Circle. Although details of Shūri's biography are scant, his still-life compositions reveal the sensitivity of a man of letters who might have been active in literati circles (see cat. no. 268), but was also at home in the less stratified atmosphere of ukiyo-e and kyōka.

In this interior scene, a kettle rests on a stand in a wooden brazier. Metal chopsticks used as pokers for stirring coals protrude from the ashes. Rice cakes were grilled on the wire screen, which can be seen beside the tea cups on the green lacquer tray.

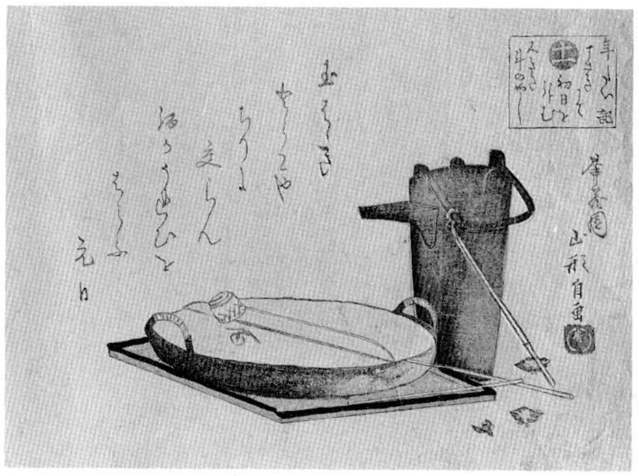

SHŪRI

267 Sake warmer with a covered skillet

TITLE *Jūichi*; Eleven
SERIES *Nendaiki*; A Chronicle
DATE ca. 1810
SIGNATURE Ryūkaen Yamagata jiga (drawn and composed)
SEAL Fusa
FORMAT Koban yoko-e (13.4 x 18.6)
POET Ryūkaen Yamagata (also the artist)
FLLW FDN 3025.004

Active in poetry circles, Shūri used the name Yamagata Ryūkaen as a poetry name and here as his artistic appellation as well. This surimono illustrates everyday cooking implements. A sake cup rests on the wooden pot cover which bears the emblem for the Biwa Club. The cartouche cites the New Year tradition of watching the first sunrise at Susaki on the coast near Shinagawa. Perhaps the round yellow cover of the pot and copper surface of the ewer allude to this theme.

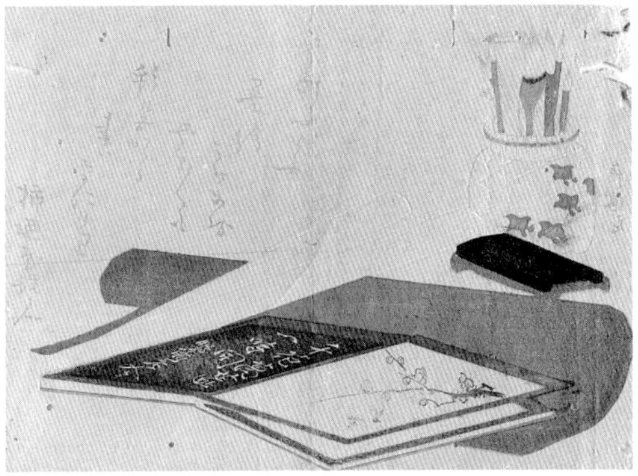

SHŪRI

268 A brushpot, inkstone, and album

DATE Early 1810s
SIGNATURE Shūri ga
FORMAT Koban yoko-e (12.8 x 17.6)
REFERENCE Ostier, *Les objets tranquilles*, pl. 7
POET Kakinoya Tanehito
FLLW FDN 3025.003

A poem on the theme of ink painting provided the artist with the inspiration to compose a design that starkly contrasts the bright red of the felt writing mat with the black of the inkstone and the page of poetry in the album created through an ink-rubbing technique. A flock of silver plovers adorns the crackle-glaze brush pot. The ink painting of the plum branch is accompanied by a line of Chinese poetry: *Senka banzui ichiji kai,* "A thousand flowers, ten thousand grasses, burst forth, all at one time," which is signed Bōsai Rōjin sha, "Written by Old Man Bōsai." This refers to Kameda Bōsai (1751–1826), a well-known Edo literati painter, calligrapher, and Confucian scholar.

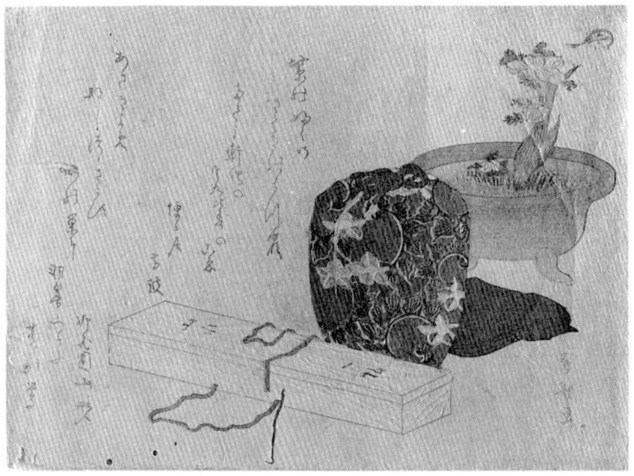

SHŪRI

269 A scroll box, tea caddy, and adonis plant

SERIES Untitled set of still lifes on the theme of colors
DATE Early 1810s
SIGNATURE Shūri ga
FORMAT Koban yoko-e (14.1 x 18.8)
POETS Bembenkyo Takanami, Ryūkaen Yamagata (also the artist)
FLLW FDN 3025.002

An untied wooden box for a small hanging scroll is inscribed *sansui ippuku* (one landscape scroll). Behind it sits a tea caddy wrapped in a brocade draw-string sack and a potted adonis plant.

Both poems contain color allusions—one to purple, the conventional description of the color of spring mists and Edo, but also the color of cloths used for the tea ceremony; the other to pale blue. The red emblem of the Biwa-ren group appears in the top right corner.

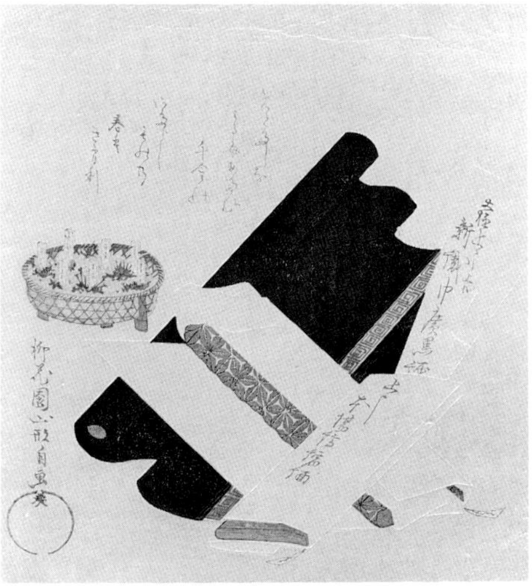

SHŪRI

270 A basket containing the seven herbs with packages of wrapped fabric

DATE ca. 1820
SIGNATURE Ryūkaen Yamagata jiga (drawn and written by)
ARTIST'S SEAL Fusa
FORMAT Shikishiban (19.3 x 17.2)
REFERENCE Ostier, *La voix silencieuse,* pl.64
POET Ryūkaen Yamagata (also the artist)
FLLW FDN 3025.005

Lying diagonally across one another are three bolts of fabric, one black, another gray and the central package containing a tie-dyed red fabric. The shiny silver-colored cloth and the dark iron-colored material create a striking contrast with their white paper protective wrappers. In the background, a round basket contains the seven herbs of the New Year, which are individually labeled.

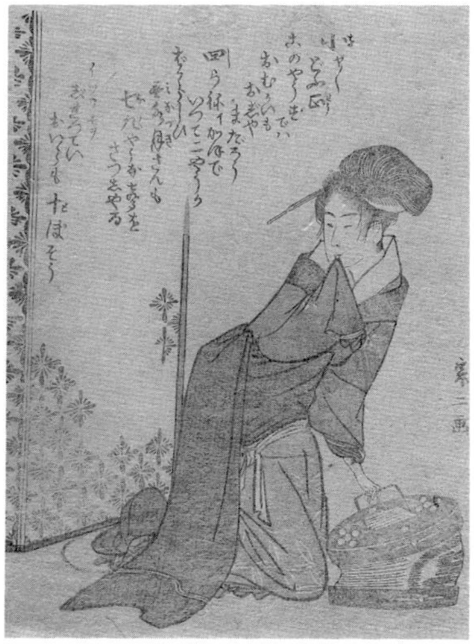

HISHIKAWA SŌRI III

ACT. CA. 1797–1813

271 A woman with a paper lantern

DATE 1798
SIGNATURE Sōji ga
FORMAT Small koban tate-e (13.0 x 9.4)
FLLW FDN 3008.062

A woman coyly glances around a screen while holding a collapsed paper lantern. In this egoyomi, references to the numbers of the short months of the year appear in the inscription—*shō* 1, 4, 7, 9, and 10—allowing the print to be dated to 1798. This was, in fact, the year Sōji received the name Sōri, formerly used by his master Hokusai (Sōri II).

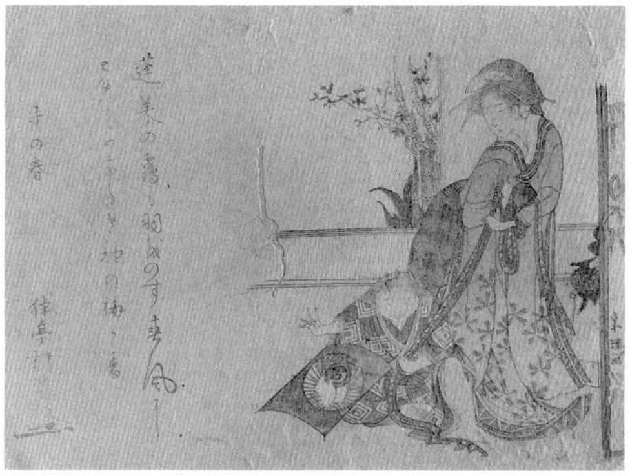

SŌRI

272 A woman and a boy in a game of tug-of-war

DATE 1799, Year of the Goat, Spring
SIGNATURE Sōri ga
FORMAT Koban yoko-e (12.4 x 16.5)
POET Sarutei Kaki no Narieda
FLLW FDN 3008.041

A boy in a kimono with a design of three concentric squares and a courtesan play a game of tug-of-war using a tie-dyed cloth. The kite at his feet bears the crane emblem of Asahina no Saburō. This image is a parody of the famous "pulling off the armor" scene from a Kabuki play based on the legend of the Soga brothers in which Soga no Gorō, a man of great strength, has his armor ripped off him by the equally strong Asahina during an altercation over a breach of etiquette.

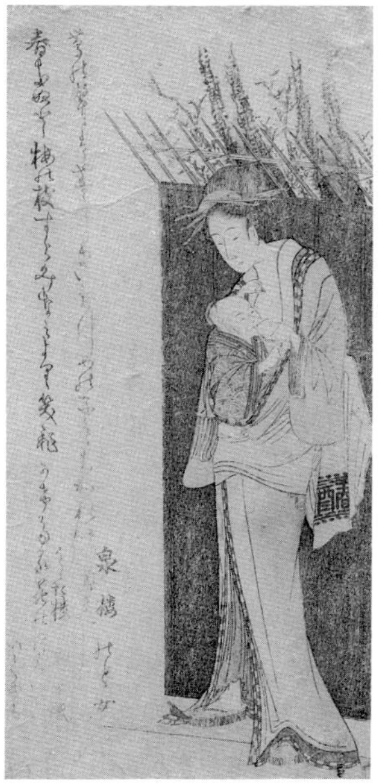

SŌRI

273 A mother nursing her child by a fence

DATE 1801, Year of the Bird, Spring
SIGNATURE Sōri ga (trimmed off in this impression)
FORMAT Koban tate-e (19.8 x 9.4)
REFERENCE Yoshida, 3:227
POETS Senrō Notome, Momotarō Mitsuyoshi, Ikume sho (calligraphy by Ikume)
FLLW FDN 3008.059

A woman standing by a fence nurses a little boy. At the hem of her obi are the characters indicating spring of the zodiac year of the bird. Strongly influenced by his teacher Hokusai, Sōri reflects those lessons in this sensitive portrait of maternal affection.

Impressions bearing clear signatures are in the collections of the Arthur M. Sackler Museum, Harvard University Art Museums, and the New York Public Library. This print is discussed in greater detail on pages 53–54.

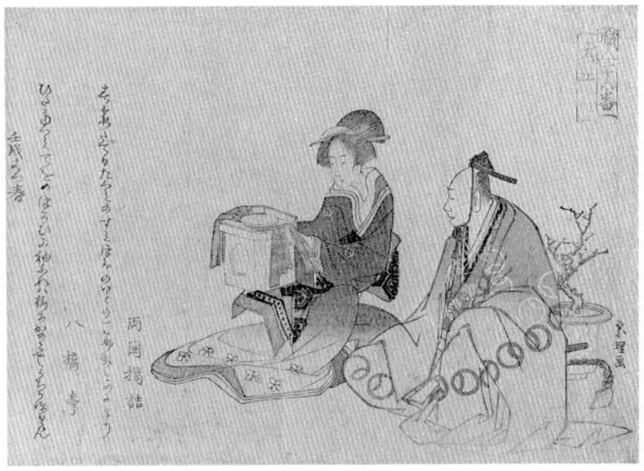

SŌRI

274 A woman and craftsman

TITLE *Daiku;* Carpenter
SERIES *Shokunin Sanjūrokuban;* Thirty-six Craftsmen
DATE 1802, Year of the Dog, Spring
SIGNATURE Sōri ga
FORMAT Koban yoko-e (14.0 x 19.2)
REFERENCE Keyes, *Spencer*, cat. 219.
POETS Ryōgoku no Hashizume, Yatsuhashitei
FLLW FDN 3008.038

A young woman holds a newly made tray-table bearing a large sake cup as a craftsman, perhaps a shrine carpenter, looks on. His tools lie behind him. Integrated into the textile pattern of his robe and the crest of the woman's kimono is the emblem for the Asakusa-gawa poetry group.

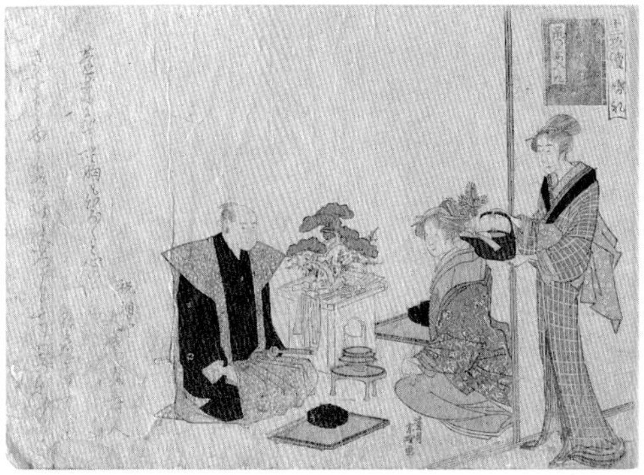

SŌRI

275 A woman serving wine to a couple

TITLE *Nezumi no Yomeiri: Ku;* Marriage of the Rat: Number Nine
SERIES *Jūni-mai Tsuzuki: Konrei*; Series of Twelve Sheets: Marriage
DATE 1804
SIGNATURE Hishikawa Sōri ga
FORMAT Koban yoko-e (14.5 x 18.0)
POETS Shukushitei Amano Manjujin, Shinratei Manzō
FLLW FDN 3008.037

A waitress serves sake to a bride and bridegroom who sit before a set of three ceremonial wedding sake cups. To the side is an arrangement with plum, pine, and bamboo. The reverse swastika crest on the samurai's formal robes is that of the poet Shinratei Manzō, suggesting that this may have been intended as a portrait. Since Manzō I (1754–1809) was still alive at this time, perhaps it is a depiction of him rather than his pupil Manzō II, whose poems are commonly found on surimono.

An occasional nickname for a rat is the word for "bride." This originated in a folktale about the wedding of a rat whose parents hoped she would marry the sun or moon; instead, she had to settle for a rat as a husband.

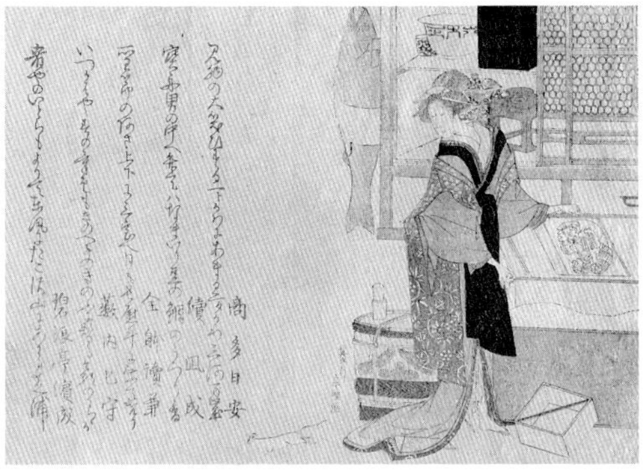

SŌRI

276 A kitchen scene of a woman with a picture of Daikoku

DATE 1804
SIGNATURE Hishikawa Sōri ga
FORMAT Koban yoko-e (14.0 x 18.5)
POETS Akinai Tabiyasu, Tsuzuki Naginari, Zentai Yomikane, Yabuuchi Sajimori, Hekirōtei Hamanari
FLLW FDN 3008.036

A woman holds a picture of Daikoku and turns toward a fleeing white rat. Some of the numbers for the long months are visible as a decorative band on the porcelain bowls on the top shelf. In addition to the obvious reference to the god of good luck, the large salmon and sake barrel are also New Year allusions.

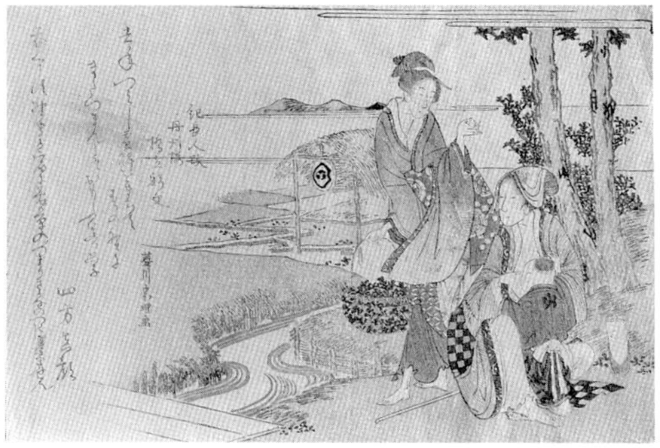

SŌRI

277 A woman nursing a boy as another woman collects herbs

DATE ca. 1804
SIGNATURE Hishikawa Sōri ga
FORMAT Koban yoko-e (13.0 x 18.6)
REFERENCE Keyes, *Beatty*, no.331
POETS Ki no Nagahito *aratame* (changed name to), Tanshūrō Hashidate Mifumi, Yomo Magao
FLLW FDN 3008.050

A farming woman has dropped her hoe in order to nurse her child. Another, more elegantly dressed woman watches while holding a basket of spring herbs. Hanging from the hut in the background is a medallion with the three-comma logo of the Yomo-gawa.

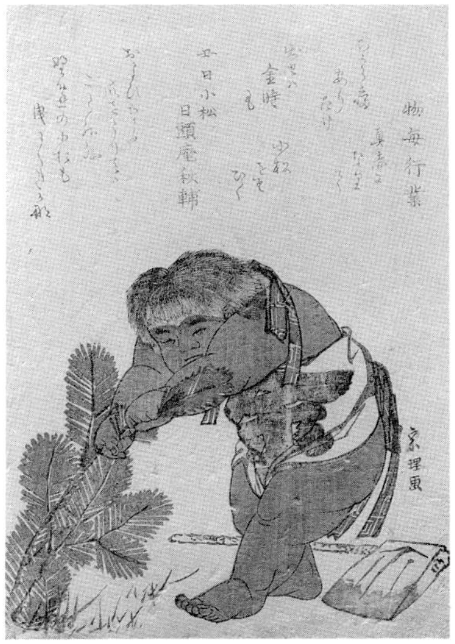

SŌRI

278 Kintoki dropping his axe to pull out a pine sapling

DATE 1805, Year of the Ox
SIGNATURE Sōri ga
FORMAT Koban tate-e (18.6 x 12.8)
POETS Monogoto Yukinari, Nittōan Akisuke
FLLW FDN 3008.049

According to the folk tale, Kintoki was a child lost in a forest and raised by the mountain woman, Yama Uba; he was also called Kintarō. Known for his enormous strength, he learned his skills through wrestling and playing with the animals of the forest.

Both poems mention collecting young pine trees, a popular New Year activity. This scene actually parodies one of Kintoki's famous feats of strength. Instead of ripping out an enormous tree to be used as a bridge, as the legend goes, here he pulls at a young pine sapling, which is more appropriate for a New Year surimono.

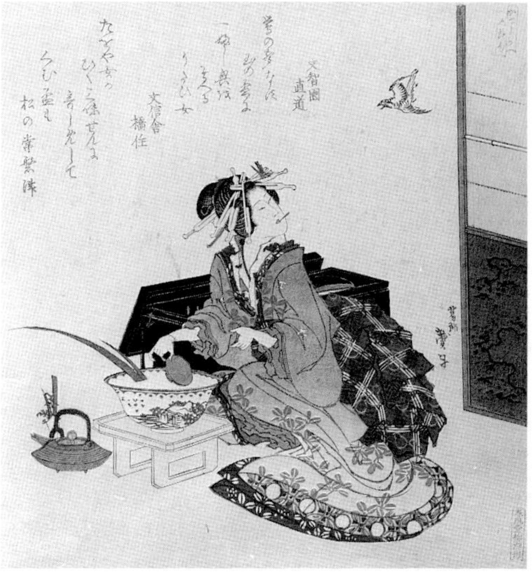

KATSUSHIKA TAITO II
ACT. CA. 1810–50

279 A geisha dipping a sake cup

SERIES *Katsushika Gosekku*; Five Festivals for the Katsushika Circle
DATE ca.1833
SIGNATURE Katsushika Taito
PRINTER'S SEAL Shumpūdō Ryūko suri
FORMAT Shikishiban (20.5 x 18.6)
REFERENCES Keyes, *Beatty*, no.338; Rijksmuseum, *Hokusai*, pl.120; Kruml, 1989, pl.37; Tokyo National Museum, ed., pl. 3738
POETS Bunchien Naomichi, Bunshinsha Hashizumi
FLLW FDN 3036.003

This set for the Katsushika group, whose *bun*-character emblem appears on the geisha's kimono, takes the five festivals as its theme. Depicted here is a New Year scene (first day of the first month), in which a geisha dips her sake cup into a porcelain bowl while she gazes at the warbler. Beside the stand is a kettle for the seasonal spiced sake and in the background is the storage box for her shamisen. Taito's surimono date mostly from the late 1820s to the mid 1830s.

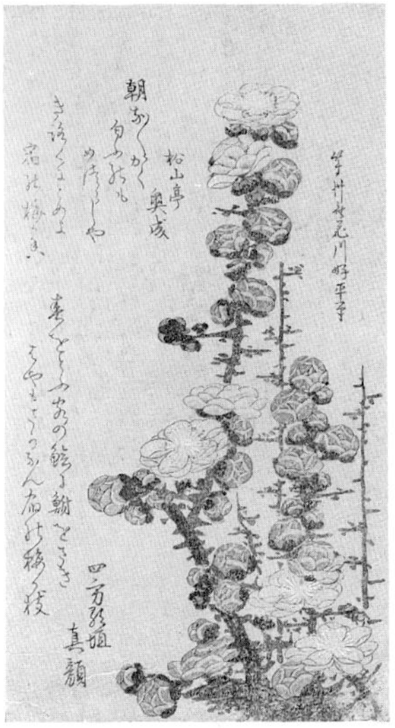

TŌSHŪ

ACT. CA. 1790–1825

280 A branch of plum blossoms

DATE ca. 1800
SIGNATURE Tōshūsai Hanakawa Kōhei hitsu
FORMAT Koban tate-e (19.3 x 10.3)
POETS Shōzantei Okunari, Yomo Utagaki Magao
FLLW FDN 3035.001

This image of a branch laden with both open and closed blossoms is quite similar to small surimono by Hokusai of plum branches (see cat. no. 177).

According to *Ukiyo-e Ruikō*, Tōshū was a pupil of the artist Tsutsumi Tōrin II (act. mid-to late-eighteenth century), lived in the Nihombashi section of Edo, and used the artistic name Kazan.

In addition to the three surimono illustrated here, the Wright collection includes several designs by him from a kyōka book of fifteen Nō scenes done in collaboration with Shinsai (Tōshū: FLLW FDN 3035.003-.008; Shinsai: FLLW FDN 3003.060-.062).

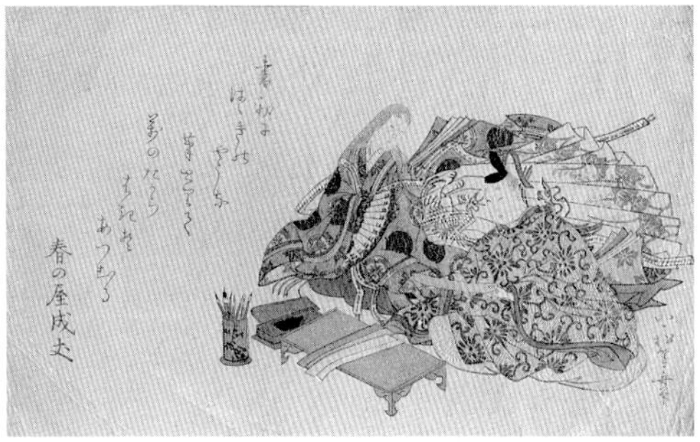

TŌSHŪ

281 A courtier and a court lady at a writing table

DATE ca. 1818
SIGNATURE Agematsu Tōshū hitsu
FORMAT Koban yoko-e (13.9 x 22.0)
POET Harunoya Naritake
FLLW FDN 3035.010

Seated before his writing desk, a courtier holds a poem card. The inkstone and writing brushes sit on the floor. A luxuriously dressed court lady sits to his right, holding a large folding fan.

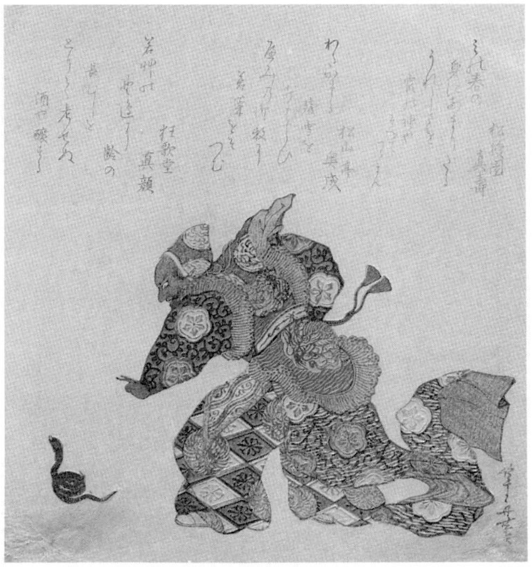

TŌSHŪ

282 A Gagaku performer with a wooden snake

DATE 1821, Year of the Snake
SIGNATURE Tōshū hitsu
FORMAT Shikishiban (20.6 x 18.8)
POETS Shōjuen Masu, Shōzantei Okunari, Kyōkadō Magao
FLLW FDN 3035.009

Gagaku is a slow-moving dance form which includes instrumental and vocal music. It originated in the Nara period and has roots in Chinese and Korean court music and dance. *Genjōraku,* a staple of the Gagaku repetoire, tells of an Indian king who rejoices over the defeat of a dangerous snake.

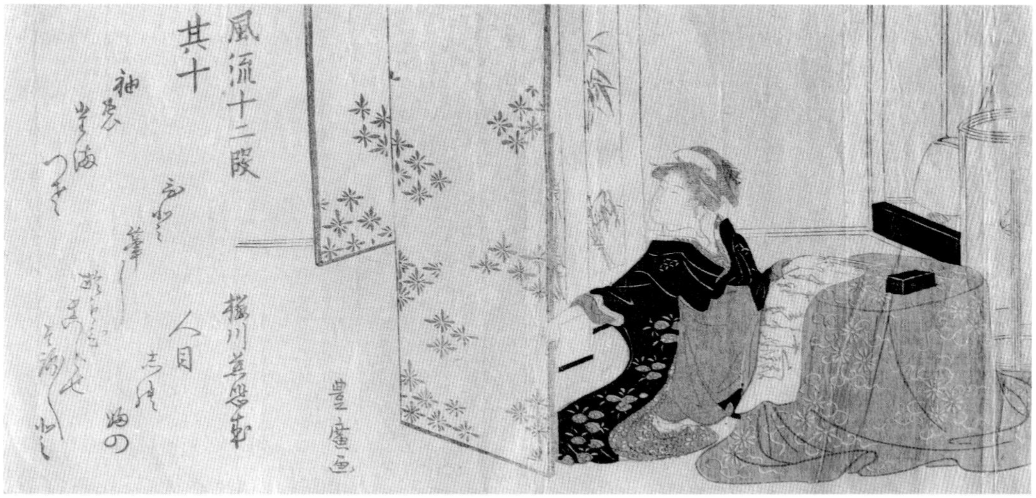

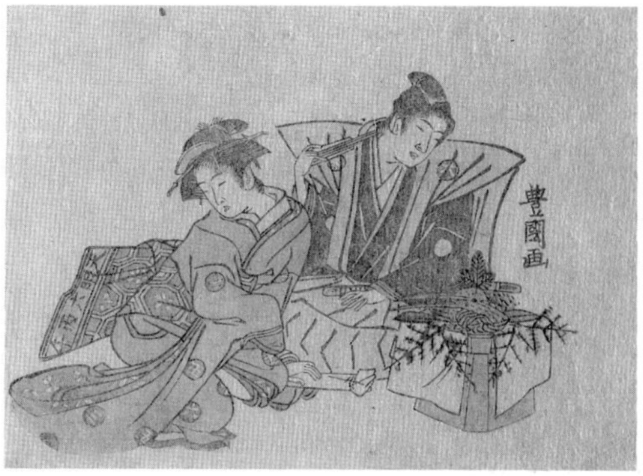

UTAGAWA TŌYŌHIRO

1773–1828

283 A woman with a scroll behind a screen

TITLE *Sono Jū*; Number Ten
SERIES *Fūryū Jūnidan;* Twelve Fashionable Views of Jōruri
DATE ca. 1803
SIGNATURE Toyohiro ga
FORMAT Long koban yoko-e (12.6 x 25.6)
REFERENCE Polster, no. 496 (without poetry)
POET Sakuragawa Jihinari
FLLW FDN 3015.014

One of the originators of the landscape print, Toyohiro is perhaps best known for his surimono and prints of beautiful women and as the teacher of Utagawa Hiroshige.

This surimono is from a series based on the *Jūnidan Jōruri* (Twelve Chapters of the Story of Princess Jōruri), a play based on the legend of Minamoto no Yoshitsune and his love for Lady Jōruri which was made popular by early Edo storytellers. According to tradition, Lady Jōruri was famous for her skill at the koto. In this fashionable version, she is presented as a courtesan whose shamisen is in the far alcove. She is seated at a table heater covered with a floral motif, and she peers beyond a screen painting of bamboo.

The poet Sakuragawa Jihinari was a close friend of the Kabuki actor Danjūrō VII and an enthusiastic patron of the theatre.

UTAGAWA TOYOKUNI

1769–1825

284 A couple with a New Year arrangement

DATE 1786, Year of the Horse
SIGNATURE Toyokuni ga
FORMAT Koban yoko-e (9.9 x 13.9)
FLLW FDN 3011.016

A man scratches his neck with a closed fan as a beauty coyly passes him a sealed package. Before them is a New Year still-life arrangement.

This surimono is an extremely early and rare dated example of the artist's work. Serving as a decorative motif on the hem of the woman's obi is the date—*Temmei roku hinoe uma*, indicating 1786, year of the horse. On her kimono are the short months, 1, 3, 5, 6, 8, 11.

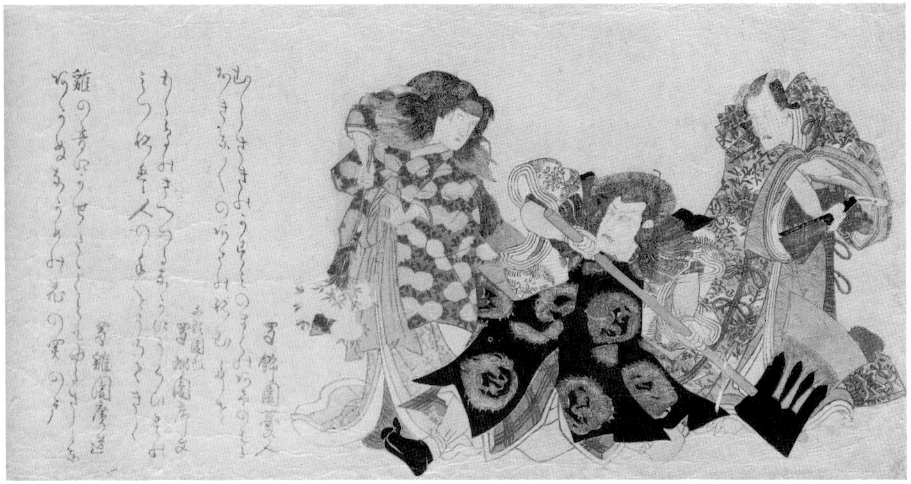

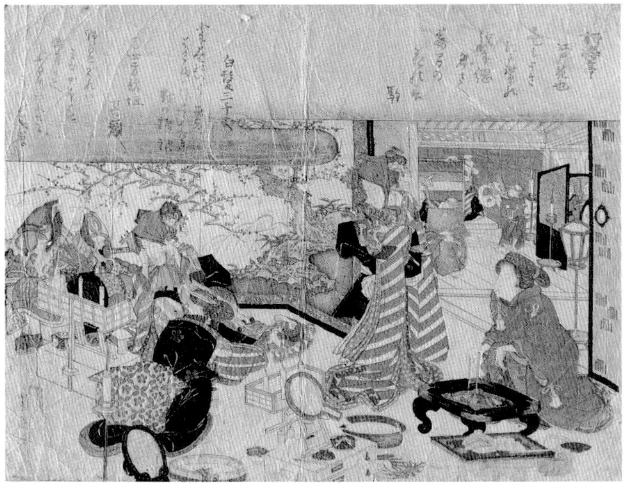

TOYOKUNI

285 A Kabuki scene from *Seki no To*

DATE 1821
SIGNATURE Toyokuni ga
PRINTER'S SEAL Shinzendō
FORMAT Yokonagaban (20.6 x 37.8)
REFERENCE Rijksmuseum, *Hiroshige*, pl.168
POETS Shokkin'en Tsuruhito, Senkaen aratame (changes name to) Shokutoen Jobun, Shokkeien Hiromichi
FLLW FDN 3011.003

In this scene from the Kabuki play *Tsumoru Koi Yuki no Seki no To*, Sekibei, the central figure with axe, is played by Ichikawa Omezō (1781–1833). The female spirit with the cherry branch, Komachi Zakura, is the actor Segawa Kikunojō V (1802–32), and the man with a fan, Yoshimune Munesada, is played by Ichikawa Danjūrō VII (1791–1859).

The signature is quite difficult to see in this impression but is quite clear in an example in the Duel Collection (1933.4. 2487). The example illustrated in Rijksmuseum, *Hiroshige,* plate 168 is a trimmed impression that is erroneously ascribed to Kunisada but the entry accurately discusses the date of the performance. In addition, the dragon pattern on the costume of Omezō refers to the zodiac year (1821).

TOYOKUNI

286 Preparations for a spring dance

SIGNATURE Utagawa Toyokuni ga
DATE ca.1823
FORMAT Chūban yoko-e (21.0 x 27.2)
POETS Ryūōtei Edo no Hananari, Shiraga Michitake, Yomo Utagaki Magao
FLLW FDN 3011.004

The interest in the backstage activities at a private residence is more closely aligned with traditional ukiyo-e and the triptych format than the poetic art of surimono. Behind the scenes of the stage, which is partially visible to the far right, are two beauties attired in the costumes making preparations for the New Year horse-head stick dance. One adjusts her kerchief in a theatrical mirror borrowed from an actor seated to her right.

The screen at the right bears silver and gold crests according the chapters of *The Tale of Genji,* which do not seem to refer to the zodiac.

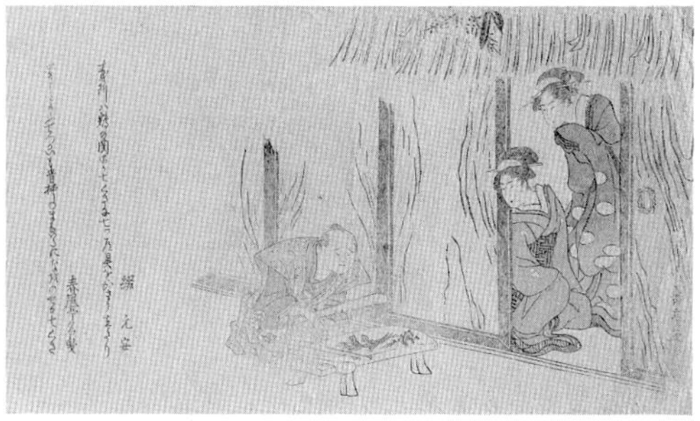

UTAGAWA TOYOMARU

ACT. CA. 1785–1802, D. 1817

287 Two women watching a man chop spring herbs

DATE ca. 1798
SIGNATURE Jutei ga
FORMAT Koban yoko-e (slightly long; 10.9 x 19.2)
POETS Tsuzuri Motoyasu, Shumpūtei Nabiki
FLLW FDN 3052.001

Toyomaru was initially a pupil of Utagawa Toyoharu and Katsukawa Shunshō. In about 1795 he received the name Shunrō from Hokusai, becoming Katsukawa Shunrō (Shunrō II). This print is in the style of Hokusai and his followers.

The theme of the image and both of the poems is the seven herbs of spring. Two women watch with amusement as a formally attired samurai attempts to perform this mundane domestic task. The crest on his robes is the character *bun*, but the early date of the print rules out any connection to the prominent kyōka master Bumbunsha, who also used this character for his personal emblem.

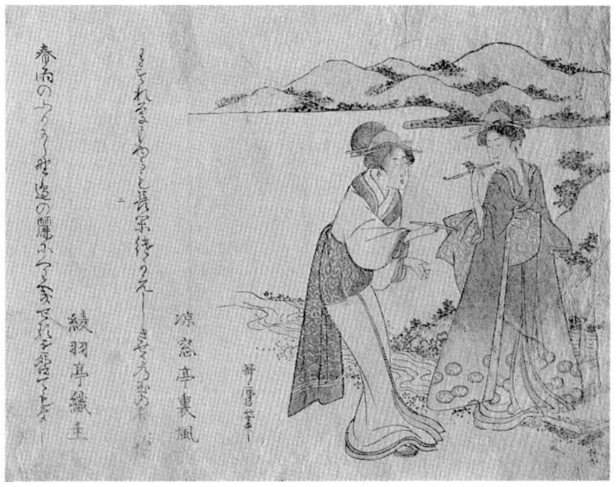

KITAGAWA UTAMARO

1753–1806

288 Two women with pipes chatting by a stream

DATE 1800
SIGNATURE Utamaro hitsu
FORMAT Koban yoko-e (12.5 x 16.0)
REFERENCE *UT, Bibliothèque Nationale,* 203, pl. 43
POETS Ryōsōtei Urakaze, Ayabatei Orinushi
FLLW FDN 3001.009

Despite the art-historical significance of this print—one of the very few surviving egoyomi by Utamaro—the portrayal of the women here lacks the brilliance that earned the artist his reputation as the greatest master of prints of beautiful women.

This print dates to 1800, since the short months of that year—2, 4, 6, 8, 10, 12—appear as the design motif on the obi of the right-hand figure.

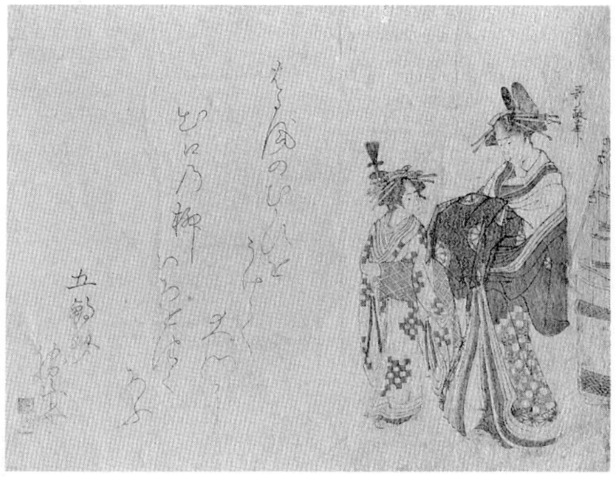

UTAMASA

1775–1824

289 A high-ranking courtesan with her young attendant

DATE ca. 1800
SIGNATURE Utamasa hitsu
FORMAT Koban yoko-e (12.3 x 16.7)
POET Gochōsai Katsunari (with two undeciphered seals)
FLLW FDN 3022.002

Early in his career, Utamasa was a pupil of Utamaro, from whom he received this name. The image of the elegantly attired courtesan with her young attendant is clearly influenced by the style popularized by Utamaro and other Edo ukiyo-e artists of the 1790s (see cat. no. 288).

Under the name Maki Bokusen, the artist was active as a designer, engraver and publisher of prints in Nagoya. When Hokusai visited in 1812, Utamasa assisted him with the preparatory drawings for his famous illustrated book, the *Manga*.

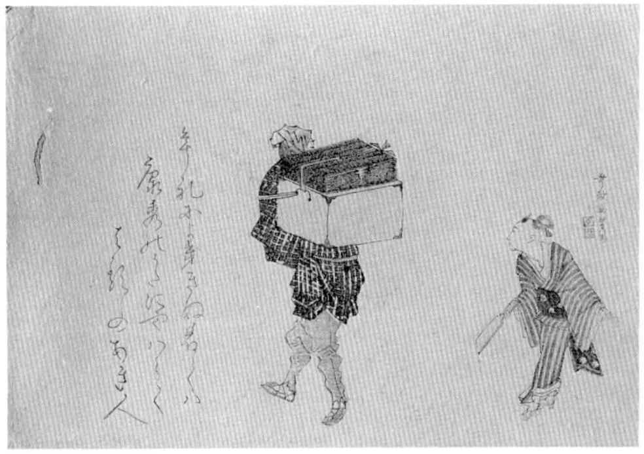

UTAMASA

290 A vendor and a boy with a battledore

DATE ca. 1802
SIGNATURE Utamasa gasan chō (designed, written, and carved by Utamasa)
ARTIST'S SEAL Gekkō
FORMAT Koban yoko-e (12.4 x 17.8)
POET Utamasa
FLLW FDN 3022.005

A vendor glances backward just as a errant shuttlecock lands on the bundle on his back. The boy is enjoying a game of battledore and shuttlecock, a New Year's amusement similar to badminton that was popular among young people.

The poem, by the artist himself, is on the theme of the vendor making a New Year's visit.

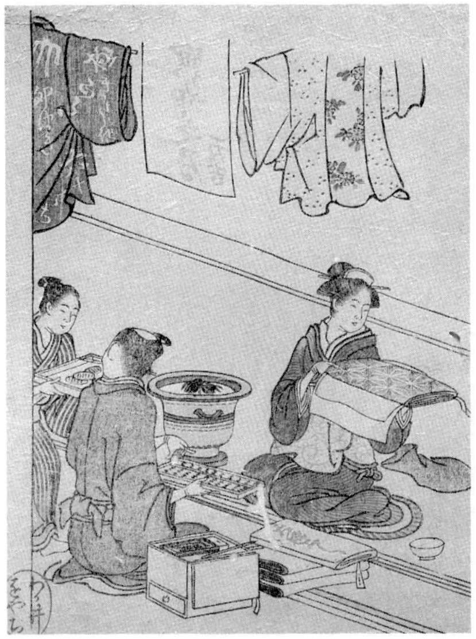

ANONYMOUS

291 A woman at a fabric shop

DATE 1782, Year of the Tiger
DEALER'S SEAL Wakai Oyaji (Old Man Wakai)
FORMAT Koban tate-e (13.7 x 10.2)
FLLW FDN 3031.009

In this egoyomi, the earliest print in the Wright collection, a woman examines a bolt of cloth as the merchant totals the sum on his abacus; a boy assistant brings a tray containing the three gold coins. The long months of the year may be discerned in the pattern of the white characters on the red robe hanging at the left. Some characters are numbers, others are common alternative names of the months: *shōgatsu*(1), *kisaragi* (2), *uzuki* (4), 6, *hachi* (8), 10, *goku* (12). Stylistically, the print can be dated to the last quarter of the eighteenth century; both 1782 and 1789 had these long months. But since the banner hanging between the robes has a spring greeting that puns on the word tiger (*tora*), this print was no doubt issued in 1782, a tiger year.

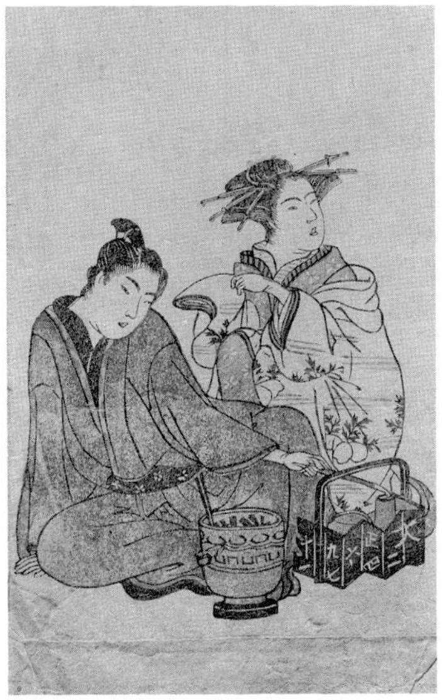

ANONYMOUS

292 A couple at a brazier

DATE 1784
FORMAT Koban tate-e (16.4 x 11.4)
FLLW FDN 3031.014

A courtesan and her customer are seated beside a brazier. He taps his pipe against a black lacquer smoking set that is decorated with a sequence for the long months—*shō* (1), 2, 4, 6, 7, 9, 11—which accords with 1784.

Although similar in aesthetic to the traditional ukiyo-e prints by artists such as Kitao Masanobu, the lack of sophistication in the carving, the inexpensive materials, and the simplicity of the design argue for an attribution to a minor or amateur artist.

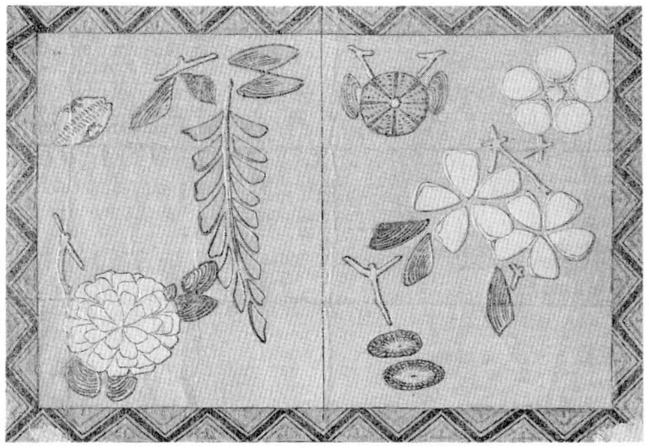

ANONYMOUS

293 A miniature shell screen

DATE 1797
FORMAT Koban yoko-e (9.2 x 13.3)
FLLW FDN 3031.012

This miniature two-fold screen of flowers constructed from shells is actually an egoyomi. Such screens were decorated with shells in a collage, often in floral patterns, and sold as souvenirs at Enoshima. Shells are traditionally associated with Benzaiten, the goddess worshiped at this site. Benzaiten is associated with the snake, suggesting that this egoyomi dates to that zodiac year. Furthermore, the right side of the screen appears to cryptically portray at least some of the numbers for the long months—5, 8, 10, 11, 12; and the left panel bears the short months—2, 6, 9 and others which have yet to be deciphered. A very similar screen is illustrated in Jan H. W. Gosling, "Calendar Prints: Egoyomi and Surimono" (*Andon,* vol. 10, no. 40, 1990, fig. V). Another shell screen is the central image of a shikishiban surimono by Hokkei (Paul F. Walter Collection, no. 126, pl. 12).

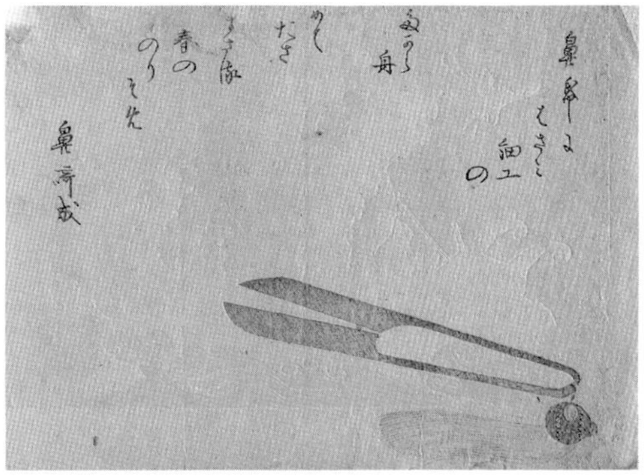

ANONYMOUS

294 The treasure ship for the Seven Gods of Good Luck

DATE ca. 1800
FORMAT Koban yoko-e (12.3 x 16.7)
POET Hana no Sakinari
FLLW FDN 3030.011

The silhouetted treasure ship of the Seven Gods of Good Luck together with a silver scissors is set against a pale yellow ground. Close examination of the image reveals that the outline of the ship and waves is constructed of one continuous line. Making paper cutouts was a traditional New Year pastime.

Paper cuttings also served as decorative ornaments for New Year shrines. Typically the themes were related to happiness and prosperity. This rectangular form is one of three styles; the others are the ritual folded and cut sacred papers (see cat. no. 114) and intricate streamers from which are hung symbols of good fortune.

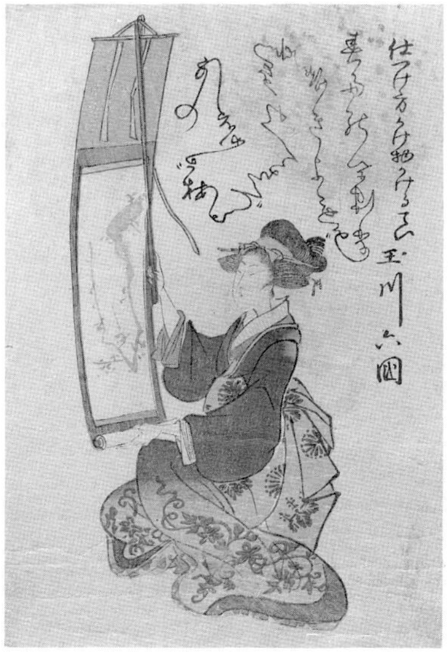

ANONYMOUS

295 A woman unrolling a hanging scroll of a plum tree

TITLE *Shitsukekata: Kakemono Kakeru Tei;* Manners: How to Hang a Scroll
SERIES *Shitsukekata*; Manners
DATE ca. 1805
FORMAT Koban tate-e (18.6 x 12.7)
POET Tamagawa Mukoku
FLLW FDN 3028.005

The name of the poet puns on the theme of the Mutamagawa, the Six Jewel Rivers known for the clarity of their water and a recurrent point of departure for both writers and painters. The poem has been written in a continuous string of calligraphy. For a translation of the poem see page 46.

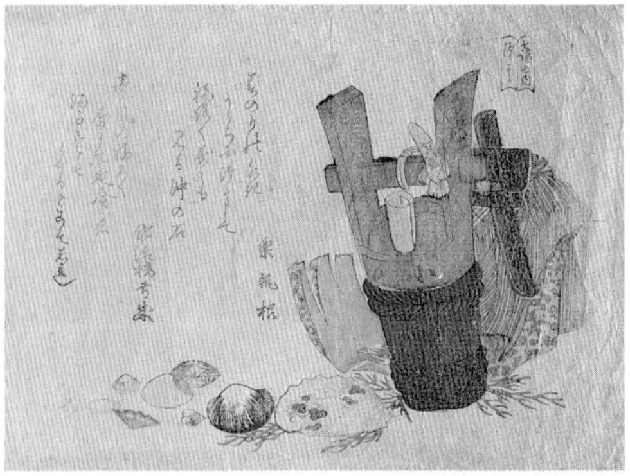

ANONYMOUS

296 A bucket and shells

TITLE *Shiohi*; Shells at Low Tide
SERIES *Shichifuku no Uchi*; Seven Lucky Things
DATE perhaps 1811
FORMAT Koban yoko-e (14.3 x 19.1)
POETS Raku no Tsukune, Taijirō Yuminari
FLLW FDN 3027.008

This still life consists of shells and a sake bucket, which bears the character for "small," meaning short months, as its emblem. Designed as an egoyomi, several of the short months are listed on the handle of the bucket, but due to abrasion only 5, 8, and 11 are visible. They are the final three short months of 1811.

Serving as a pin for the cord is a carving in the shape of Fukurokuju, one of the seven Gods of Good Luck whose name literally means "luck, prosperity, and longevity." The first poem alludes to gathering shells or small rocks on the beach (*shiohi* is an abbreviation for *shiohi-gari,* "gathering shells at low tide"), while the second poem specifically mentions a bucket for *tosozake,* New Year spiced wine.

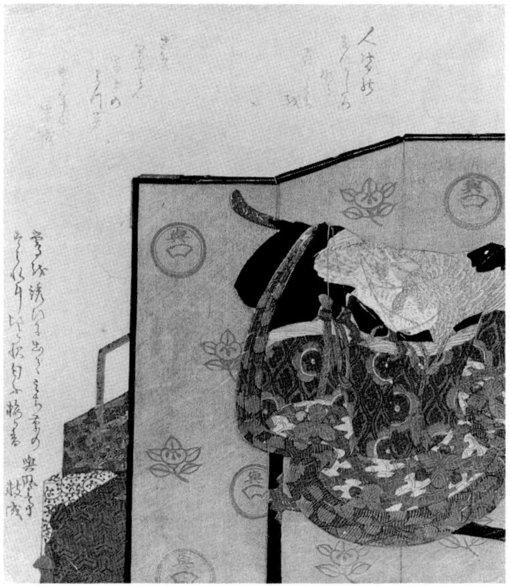

ANONYMOUS

297 The first dream of the New Year

DATE ca. 1825
FORMAT Shikishiban (22.1 x 18.8)
REFERENCE Rijksmuseum, *Hokusai,* pl. 282.
POETS Hōnensha Yonenari, Yohōtei Edanari
FLLW FDN 3027.004

An ever-popular theme for New Year images is that of the first dream. This print presents images of Mount Fuji, a hawk, and an eggplant, each of which was considered auspicious if seen in a New Year's dream. Mount Fuji, appearing only in gaufrage, juts out from behind the screen, which is decorated with the emblem of the Yomo-gawa and the first character in the name of the second poet. A large hawk on a perch adorns a draped kimono, which has a border pattern of eggplants on its brocade hem. For a further discussion of this theme and an illustration of this design see Matthi Forrer, "Dreaming of Fuji, Falcon and Eggplant" (*Andon,* vol. 6, 1986, 14–18, fig. 5).

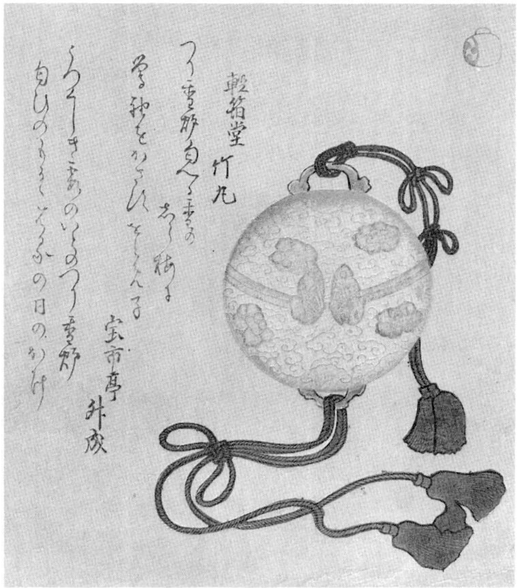

ANONYMOUS

298 A hanging silver incense burner

DATE Late 1820s
FORMAT Shikishiban (20.3 x 18.9)
REFERENCES Ostier, *La voix silencieuse*, pl. 51
POETS Keihakudō Takemaru, Hōshitei Masunari
FLLW FDN 3033.004

This delicately printed surimono was commissioned by the Taiko group, whose drum emblem appears in the upper right corner. A latch in the shape of a butterfly adorns the incense burner which is patterned in a peony-in-cloud design. The unusual blue ground serves to contrast with the silver of the incense burner and the gold in which the poems are printed.

Both poems are based on the theme of a hanging incense burner, the first comparing its fragrance to the scent of white plum blossoms.

In a second printing of this image with the same poems but lacking the club crest, the printer has changed the background to ochre and printed the poems in black. For an illustration of this printing see Markus, *I Surimono*, page 15.

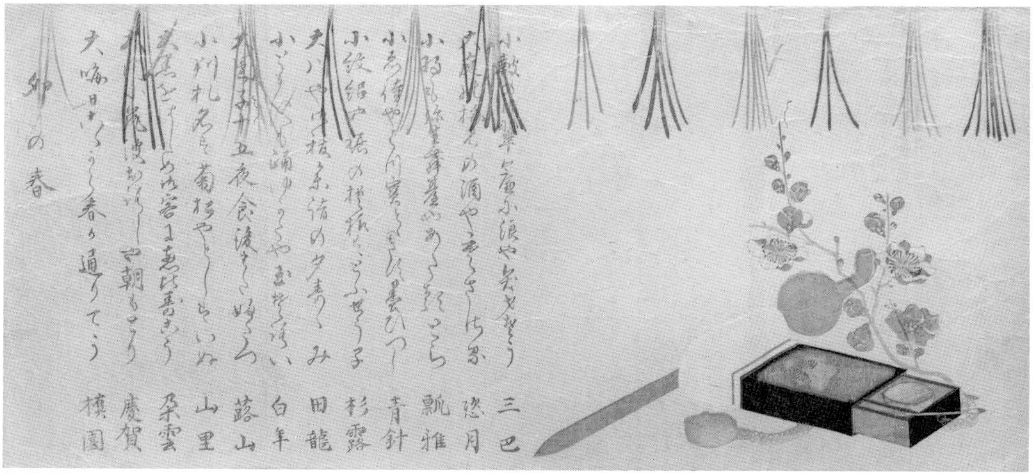

ANONYMOUS

299 A make-up brush-container with a cup and a brush for lip rouge

DATE 1831, Year of the Rabbit, spring
FORMAT Yokonagaban (18.3 x 39.8)
POETS Samba, Shigatsu, Hyōga, Seishin, Sanro, Denryū, Hakunen, Rozan, Sanri, Daun, Keiga, Shin'en
FLLW FDN 3030.005

Surrounded by a silver hairpin and a plum branch, a black-lacquer make-up brush contains a small lip-rouge cup and brush, recessed in its box-like handle. Across the top of the design is a silver and gold sacred straw gate decoration used for the New Year.

The haikai poems are the key to dating this print, as each begins either with the character for a short or long month. According to this scheme, the long months are 2, 6, 8, 10, 11, 12, and the short are 1, 3, 4, 5, 7, and 9, which accords with 1831, a rabbit year.

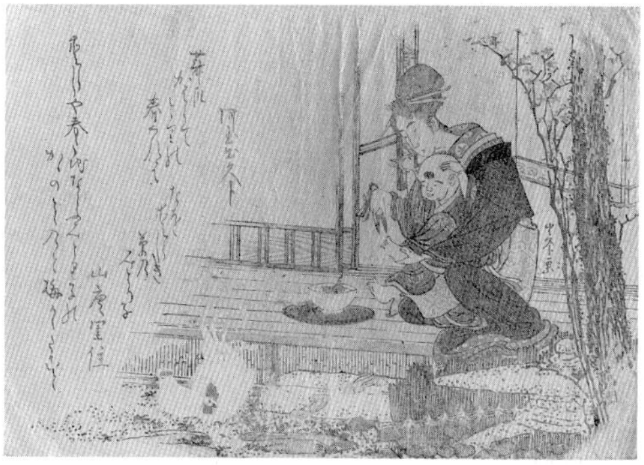

UNIDENTIFIED

300 A mother cutting her son's toenails

DATE Probably 1801
SIGNATURE Dekuboku ga
FORMAT Koban yoko-e (13.4 x 18.6)
POETS Atama Dekuboku, Yamakara Satozumi
FLLW FDN 3054.001

Both poems deal with the theme of *midorigo*, a word used to refer to a toddler; the literal meaning of the word, "green child," provides the appropriate vernal allusions.

Although the biography of the artist, who is also the author of the first poem, is obscure, it is possible that Dekuboku may be a poetic name used by Katsukawa Shunzan (act. ca. 1782–1800). In any case, the refined composition and elegant line points to an attribution to a professional artist rather than an amateur poet.

APPENDICES

SELECTED BIBLIOGRAPHY

For a list of reference works relating to the study of kyōka, see the introduction to the Index of Poets.

WORKS CITED BY ABBREVIATION IN THE CATALOGUE

NUK, *Pulverer*
Nihon Ukiyo-e Kyōkai, ed. *Purubera Korekushon: Ukiyo-e Hanga Meiten* (Masterpieces of ukiyo-e from the Pulverer Collection). Tokyo: Asahi Shimbun, 1990.

Rijksmuseum, *Hiroshige*
Rappard-Boon, Charlotte van, et al. *Hiroshige and the Utagawa School: Japanese Prints c. 1810–1860.* Catalogue of the Collection of Japanese Prints, Part 4. Amsterdam: Rijksmuseum, 1984.

Rijksmuseum, *Hokusai*
Rappard-Boon, Charlotte van, et al. *Hokusai and His School: Japanese Prints, c. 1800–1840.* Catalogue of the Collection of Japanese Prints, Part 3. Amsterdam: Rijksmuseum, 1982

Rijksmuseum, *Utamaro*
Rappard-Boon, Charlotte van, et al. *The Age of Utamaro: Japanese Prints, c. 1780–1800.* Catalogue of the Collection of Japanese Prints, Part 2. Amsterdam: Rijksmuseum, 1979.

UT, Beatty
Narazaki Muneshige, ed. *Hizō Ukiyo-e Taikan.* Vol. 13, *Chestā Bītei, Kerun, Amusuterudamu* (Ukiyo-e masterpieces in European collections. Vol. 13, The Chester Beatty Library; Museum für Ostastiche Kunst: Köln; Rijksmuseum, Amsterdam). Tokyo: Kōdansha, 1991.

UT, Berès
Narazaki Muneshige, ed. *Hizō Ukiyo-e Taikan. Beresu Korekushon* (Ukiyo-e masterpieces in European collections. Berès Collection). Tokyo: Kōdansha, 1991.

UT, Bibliothèque Nationale
Narazaki Muneshige, ed. *Hizō Ukiyo-e Taikan.* Vol. 8, *Pari Kokuritsu Toshokan* (Ukiyo-e masterpieces in European collections. Vol. 8, Bibliothèque Nationale). Tokyo: Kōdansha, 1990.

UT, Pulverer
Narazaki Muneshige, ed. *Hizō Ukiyo-e Taikan. Purubera Korekushon* (Ukiyo-e masterpieces in European collections. Pulverer Collection). Tokyo: Kōdansha, 1990.

UT, Rijksmuseum
Narazaki Muneshige, ed. *Hizō Ukiyo-e Taikan.* Vol. 13, *Chestā Bītei, Kerun, Amusuterudamu* (Ukiyo-e masterpieces in European collections. Vol. 13, The Chester Beatty Library; Museum für Ostastiche Kunst, Köln; Rijksmuseum, Amsterdam). Tokyo: Kōdansha, 1991.

OTHER WORKS CONSULTED

Asano Shūgō. "*Dure Kyūzō Surimono-chō no Gaiyō to sono Igi*" (The surimono albums from the Duret collection and their significance). *Hizō Ukiyo-e Taikan.* Vol. 8, *Pari Kokuritsu Toshokan* (Ukiyo-e Masterpieces in European Collections. Vol. 8, Bibliothèque Nationale), edited by Narazaki Muneshige. Tokyo: Kōdansha, 1990.

Bowie, Theodore, in collaboration with James T. Kenney and Fumiko Togasaki. *Art of the Surimono.* Bloomington, Indiana: Indiana University Art Museum, 1979.

Collection de Monsieur X . . . : Estampes, Dessins, Pochoirs du Japon. Salle No. 1, Les 12, 13, 14, 15; Décembre 1977. Paris: Drouot Rive Gauche, 1977.

Collection Ernest Le Véel (1re vente). Salles 12 et 13; 15 Novembre 1979. Paris: Drouot Rive Gauche, 1979.

Collection Ernest Le Véel (3e vente). Salles 5 et 6; 5 Novembre 1981. Paris: Nouveau Drouot, 1981

Collection Hayashi: Dessins, estampes, livres illustrés. Paris: Hôtel Drouot, 1902.

Forrer, Matthi. *Egoyomi and Surimono: Their Development and History.* Uithoorn, The Netherlands: J.C. Gieben, 1979.

______. "History and Development of Edo Egoyomi and Surimono." *Proceedings of the First International Symposium on Surimono,* Tokyo: International Surimono Society, 1977.

______. *Hokusai: A Guide to the Serial Graphics.* Philadelphia: The Heron Press, 1974.

______. *Surimono/Egoyomi.* Düsseldorf: Ukiyo-e Galerie Herbert Egenolf, 1978.

______, with texts by Edmond de Goncourt. *Hokusai.* New York: Rizzoli, 1988.

______, and Roger Keyes. "Very Like a Whale?—Hokusai's Illustrations for the Genroku Poem Shells." *A Sheaf of Japanese Papers: In Tribute to Heinz Kaempfer on his 75th Birthday,* edited by Matthi Forrer, Willem R. van Gulik, and Jack Hillier. The Hague: Society for Japanese Arts and Crafts, 1979.

Le fou de peinture: Hokusai et son temps. Paris: Centre Culturel du Marais, 1980.

The Frank Lloyd WrightCollection of Japanese Antique Prints. Public Exhibition from Wednesday, December 29th, 1927. New York: The Anderson Galleries, 1927.

Galerie de l'Imagerie. *Japon: Estampes surimonos xviiie-xixe siècles.* Paris, 1979.

Galerie Zacke. *Japanische Surimono.* Vienna, 1987.

Goslings, Jan H. Willem. "Calendar Prints: *Egoyomi* and *Surimono.*" *Andon* 10/4, no. 40 (1990): 105–109.

Green, William. "Dr. Arthur B. Duel (1870–1936): An American Collector of Japanese Prints." *Andon,* no. 13 (Spring 1984): 1–10.

______. "A Peerless Pair: Frederick W. Gookin and Frank Lloyd Wright and the Art Institute of Chicago's 1908 Exhibition of Japanese Prints." *Andon,* no. 14 (Summer 1984): 14–19.

______, comp. *Japanese Woodblock Prints: A Bibliography of Writings from 1822–1993 Entirely or Partly in English Text.* Leiden, Holland: Ukiyo-e Books, 1993.

Gunsaulus, Helen C. "Japanese Surimono." *Bulletin of the Art Institute of Chicago* 27 (February 1933): 37–39.

Hall, Manly P. "The Art of the Surimono." *PRS Journal* (published by the Philosophical Research Society, Los Angeles, California) 23, no. 4 (Winter 1963): 69–80.

______. "Surimono: The Little Japanese Prints." *PRS Journal* 34, no. 1 (Spring 1974): 41–57.

Hempel, Rose. *Ukiyo-e: Die Kunst der Heiteren Vergänglichen Welt, Japan 17.-19. Jahrhundert, Sammlung Scheiwe.* Recklinghausen: Verlag Aurel Bongers, 1972.

Hillier, J[ack]. *The Japanese Print: A New Approach.* Rutland, Vermont: Charles E. Tuttle, 1960.

______. *Japanese Prints and Drawings from the Vever Collection.* 3 vols. London: Sotheby Parke Bernet, 1976.

______. "Still-life in Surimono." *A Sheaf of Japanese Papers: In Tribute to Heinz Kaempfer on His 75th Birthday,* edited by Matthi Forrer, Willem R. van Gulik, and Jack Hillier. The Hague: Society for Japanese Arts and Crafts, 1979.

Japanse prenten met muziek (Japanese woodcuts with music). The Hague: Haags Gemeentenmuseum, 1975.

Japanese Prints and Drawings From the Collection of the Late Theodor Scheiwe, Part 2. New York: Christie's, October 26, 1989.

Japanese Prints, Paintings, Illustrated Books and Drawings From the Collection of the Late Theodor Scheiwe, Part 1. New York: Christie's, March 21, 1989.

Jenkins, Donald, ed. *The Floating World Revisited.* Portland, Oregon: Portland Art Museum, 1993.

Kanagawa Prefectural Museum, ed. *Ukiyo-e Meihin 500 Sen* (500 masterpieces of Ukiyo-e). 1991.

Keyes, Roger. *The Art of Surimono: Privately Published Japanese Woodblock Prints and Books in the Chester Beatty Library, Dublin.* 2 vols. London: Sotheby, 1985.

______. "Copies of Square Surimono." *Ukiyo-e Studies and Pleasures,* edited by H.M. Kaempfer. The Hague: Society for Japanese Arts and Crafts, 1978.

______. *Surimono: Privately Published Japanese Prints in the Spencer Museum of Art.* New York: Kodansha, 1984.

______. "The Van Reed *Surimono* Album." *The Stanford Museum* 3 (1974): 2–12.

Kondō Eiko. "*Pari Kokuritsu Toshokan zō: Mihappyō Surimono Arubamu Sankan ni tsuite*" (Three unpublished surimono albums in the Bibliothèque Nationale, Paris). *Ukiyo-e Geijutsu,* no. 80 (1984): 28–30; no. 81: 3–20; no. 82: 15–23.

Richard Kruml. *Surimono Prints: Catalogue 15.* London: Richard Kruml, 1975.

______. *Surimono: Catalogue 23.* London: Richard Kruml, 1989.

Lane, Richard. *Hokusai: Life and Work.* New York: E.P. Dutton, 1989.

______. *Images of the Floating World.* New York: G.P. Putnam's Sons, 1978.

Markus, Helena. *I Surimono.* Milano: Japanese Works of Art, 1992.

______. *Surimono: Stampe augurali nel giappone del'700 e' 800.* Florence: Giusti, 1983.

Meech, Julia. "Frank Lloyd Wright and the Art Institute of Chicago." *Orientations* 23, no. 6 (June 1992): 64–76.

______. *Rain and Snow: The Umbrella in Japanese Art.* New York: Japan Society, 1993.

______. "The Artist's View of Ukifune." *Ukifune: Love in The Tale of Genji,* edited by Andrew Pekarik. New York: Columbia University Press, 1982.

______. "Early Collectors of Japanese Prints and the Metropolitan Museum of Art." *Metropolitan Museum Journal* 17 (1982): 93–118.

______. "Frank Lloyd Wright and Japanese Prints." *The Metropolitan Museum of Art Bulletin* 40, no. 2 (Fall 1982): 48–56.

Meech-Pekarik, Julia. "Frank Lloyd Wright's Other Passion." *The Nature of Frank Lloyd Wright,"* edited by Carol R. Bolon, Robert S. Nelson, and Linda Seidel. Chicago: Chicago University Press, 1988.

Meissner, Kurt. *Woodblock Prints in Miniature: The Genre of Surimono.* Rutland, Vt.: Charles E. Tuttle, 1970.

Mirviss, Joan B. "Jewels of *Ukiyo-e:* Hayashi's *Spring Rain Collection* of *Surimono* Albums." *Orientations* 20 (February 1989): 26–37.

_______. *Surimono.* New York: Joan B. Mirviss, Ltd., 1985.

Narazaki Muneshige, ed. *Hizō Ukiyo-e Taikan* (Ukiyo-e masterpieces in European collections). 16 vols., including 3 supplement vols. Tokyo: Kodansha, 1987–91.

_______, ed. *Oranda Kokuritsu Raiden Minzokugaku Hakubutsukan, Shiiboruto Korekushon: Hizō Ukiyo-e* (The Siebold Collection of the National Museum of Ethnology, Leiden: Ukiyo-e). Vol. 1. Tokyo: Kōdansha, 1978

Nihon Ukiyo-e Kyōkai, ed. *Genshoku Ukiyo-e Daihyakka Jiten* (Full-color encyclopedia of ukiyo-e). 11 vols. Tokyo: Taishūkan, 1980–82.

Nute, Kevin. *Frank Lloyd Wright and Japan: The Role of Traditional Art and Architecture in the Work of Frank Lloyd Wright.* New York: Van Nostrand Reinhold, 1993.

Okada, Barbra Teri. *Netsuke: Masterpieces from the Metropolitan Museum of Art.* New York: The Metropolitan Museum of Art, 1982.

Ostier, Janette, ed. *Les objets tranquilles: Natures mortes japonaises xviiie-xixe siècles.* Paris: Galerie Janette Ostier, 1978.

_______, ed. *La voix silencieuse des choses: Natures mortes japonaises xviiie-xixe siècles.* Paris: Galerie Janette Ostier, 1989.

Ōta Memorial Museum of Art, ed. *Hatsukōkai Katsushika Hokusai Ten: Pītā Mōsu Korekushon* (Katsushika Hokusai Exhibition: The Peter Morse Collection). Tokyo: Ukiyo-e Ōta Memorial Museum of Art, 1988

_______, ed. *Ukiyo-e Yan Būru Korekushon: Hiroshige to Kihin* (The Jan Buhl Ukiyo-e-Collection: Hiroshige and other rare prints). Tokyo: Ukiyo-e Ōta Memorial Museum of Art, 1986.

The Paul F. Walter Collection of Surimono, Privately Commissioned Japanese Prints. New York: Christie's, October 23, 1992.

Polster, Edythe, and Alfred H. Marks. *Surimono: Prints by Elbow.* Washington, D.C.: Lovejoy Press, 1980.

Preetorius, Emil, and Roger Goepper. *Zehntausendfaches Glück: Farbige Bildergrüsse aus Japan, 16 Surimono aus der Sammlung Emil Preetorius.* Munich: R. Piper & Co. Verlag, 1959.

Proceedings of the First International Symposium on Surimono. Winter Park, Florida: International Surimono Society, 1979.

Riccar Museum, ed. *Surimono: Privately Published Prints from the Spencer Museum of Art / Surimono: Edo Bunkajin no Asobi* (Surimono: A pleasurable pastime of Edo literati). Tokyo: Riccar Art Museum, 1991.

Schack, Gerhard. *Surimono: Japanische Glückwunschblätter aus der Sammlung Gerhard Schack, Hamburg.* Lübeck: Ausstellung in der Overbeck-Gesellschaft, 1970.

Schindler, Werner. *Egoyomi et surimono.* Geneva: Musée d'Art et d'Histoire, 1983.

Schmidt, Steffi, and Setsuko Kuwabara. *Surimono.* Staatliche Museen Preussischer Kulturbesitz, Berlin: Dietrich Reimer Verlag Berlin, 1990.

Seigle, Cecilia Segawa. *Yoshiwara: The Glittering World of the Japanese Courtesan.* Honolulu: University of Hawaii, 1993.

Shimizu, Christine. *Portraits de femmes et surimono: Estampes japonaises des collections du musée Turpin-de-Crissé d'Angers.* Angers, France: Musée d'Angers, 1985.

Surimono, Sammlung Theodor Scheiwe, Munster. Wiesbaden: Kunstamt Wilmersdorf, Städtisches Museum, 1963.

Suzuki Jūzō. "*Edo Kyōka Surimono no Kaishaku to Kanshō.*" *Ehon to Ukiyo-e: Edo Shuppan Bunka no Kōsatsu* (Ehon and ukiyo-e: A study of printed pictorial art of the Edo period). Tokyo: Bijutsu Shuppansha, 1979. [For a translation, see "Interpretation and Appreciation of the Edo Kyōka Surimono." *Proceedings of the First International Symposium on Surimono.* Winter Park, Florida: International Surimono Society, 1979.]

Tanaka Tatsuya. "Hōtei Gosei no Kenkyū" (Research on Hōtei Gosei). *Azabu Bijutsukan Kenkyū Kiyō,* no. 1 (Spring 1986): 8–56 (English summary, ii-vi).

_______. "*Kubo Shumman no Kenkyū*" (Research on Kubo Shumman). 3 parts. *Ukiyo-e Geijutsu,* no. 107 (January 1993): 3–31; no. 108 (July 1993): 3–43; no. 109 (October 1993): 3–28.

Tōbu Museum of Art, ed. *Edo ga Unda Sekai no Eshi: Dai Hokusai Ten* (A world-class artist, born in Edo: The great Hokusai exhibition). 2 vols. Tokyo: Asahi Shimbun, et al, 1993.

Tokyo National Museum, ed. *Ukiyo-e Hanga Hen* (Catalogue of Ukiyo-e prints). 3 vols. Tokyo: Tokyo Kokuritsu Hakubutsukan, 1971.

Uhlenbeck, G. C., ed. *The Poetic Image: The Fine Art of Surimono.* Leiden: Galerie Burcht, 1987.

Ward, Sidney C. *One Hundred Surimono in the Collection of Sidney C. Ward.* Winter Park, Florida: Privately Printed, 1976.

Wright, Frank Lloyd. *Antique Colour Prints from the Collection of Frank Lloyd Wright.* Chicago: The Arts Club of Chicago, 1917.

_______. *The Japanese Print: An Interpretation.* New York: Horizon Press, 1967.

Yasuda Gōzō. "*Kondō Eiko Joshi no Surimono Kō ni tsuite*" (Comments on Kondō Eiko's essay on three surimono albums in the Bibliothèque Nationale, Paris). *Ukiyo-e Geijutsu,* no. 84 (1985): 7–9 (English summary, i).

Yoshida Teruji. *Ukiyo-e Jiten* (Dictionary of ukiyo-e). 3 vols. Tokyo: Gabundō, 1972. Each poet in the index is listed under his or her full pen name, given in the order found in signatures

INDEX OF POETS

COMPILED BY JOHN T. CARPENTER

Each poet in the index is listed under his or her full pen name, given in the order found in signatures on prints; listings of the second part of the name are keyed to the main entry. Often poems on surimono are signed only with a studio name—e.g., Dondontei, Hisakataya, or Sairaikyo—but for the convenience of students of kyōka and surimono, both parts of the poet's name have been included when known from prints in other collections or early sources. When there is any doubt that two different names refer to the same person, they are listed separately and cross-referenced.

Generally a poet's studio name (usually suffixed with *-tei, -sha, -an,* or *-en*) is read with a "Chinese" (*on*) reading, and the second part with a "Japanese" (*kun*) reading, but this is not an inviolable rule—especially when the studio name includes a common phrase or proper noun. Names ending with *-hito* can also be read as *-bito* or *-'ndo;* e.g., Ichihito may also be read Ichibito or Ichindo. Similarly *-zumi* and *-sumi* are equally acceptable pronunciations for this common kyōka-name suffix. The feminine name suffix *-me* can also be read as *-jo.*

Artists' names and plate numbers for prints are found in parentheses following each main entry. Biographical data have been provided when available, but usually the most we can determine about a poet is the *gawa* or *ren* with which he or she was affiliated. These two terms, both meaning poetry club, were used somewhat interchangeably during the Edo period but, generally speaking, a *gawa,* "group," was made up of a number of *ren,* "circles." Bibliographical sources, also scanty, have been cited below.

SOURCES USED FOR COMPILING THE INDEX OF POETS

Asō Isoji and Koike Tōgorō. *Senryū Kyōka.* Vol. 23, *Nihon Koten Kanshō Kōza.* Tokyo: Kadokawa Shoten, 1958.

Azuma Asobi (Entertainments of the East). Illustrated by Katsushika Hokusai with a preface by Asakusaan (Sensōan Ichihito) Edo, Kansei 11 (1799). Collection Japan Ukiyo-e Museum, Matsumoto. This kyōka anthology provides a rather comprehensive list of poets affiliated with the Tsubo poetry group around the turn of the century, with each poet listed according to his or her circle (*ren*). N.B., later editions were abridged and lack most of the poems included in the first edition.

Goslings, J.H. Willem. "Poetry Clubs and the Publication of Surimono in Series." *The Poetic Image: The Fine Art of Surimono.* Edited by G.C. Uhlenbeck. Leiden: Galerie Burcht, 1987. Includes a handy chart of the major poetry circles and their emblems.

Hamada Giichirō. *Senryū Kyōka.* Tokyo: Kyōikusha, 1977.

Kanō Kaian, comp. *Kyōka Jimmei Jisho* (Dictionary of kyōka names). Tokyo: Bunkōdō and Hirota Shoten, 1928. Barebones biographical data, but many times the only source of information about minor poets.

Kasuya Hiroki. *Ishikawa Masamochi Kenkyū* (A Study of Ishikawa Masamochi [Rokujuen]). Tokyo: Kadokawa Shoten, 1985. Includes chronological listing of activities of Rokujuen, the leader of the Go-gawa poetry group, and many of his literary acquaintances.

Kenney, James T. "A Brief History of Kyōka and the Edo Kyōka Movement." *Art of the Surimono,* edited by Theodore Bowie. Bloomington, Indiana: Indiana University Art Museum, 1979.

Keyes, Roger. *The Art of Surimono: Privately Published Japanese Woodblock Prints and Books in the Chester Beatty Library, Dublin.* 2 vols. London: Sotheby, 1985. Pioneering work in surimono studies. Index of poets includes Japanese characters.

Koike Tōgorō. *Edo Joryū Kyōka Hyōshaku* (Notes on female kyōka poets in Edo). Tokyo: Ōfūsha, 1971. Unsatisfactory work in scholarly terms, but does bring together much information about women poets found in contemporary sources.

Kubota Kazuhiro, comp. "*Katsushika Hokusai: Surimono Nempyō*" (Katsushika Hokusai: Chronological list of surimono). Unpublished manuscript, 1992.

Kyōbun Kyōka Shū (Collection of kyōbun and kyōka). Vol. 19, *Nihon Meicho Zenshū (Edo Bungei no Bu).* Tokyo: Nihon Meicho Zenshū Kankōkai, 1929.

"*Kyōka Bosho Ichiran*" (Inscriptions on gravestones of kyōka poets). Undated Meiji period manuscript compiled by Emaya (IV) Gakusuke (1856–1901). Collection Iwase Bunko, Nishio Municipal Library, Aichi Prefecture. Records inscriptions on gravestones of many noted kyōka poets. In some cases, it is is the only biographical information we have for a poet.

Kyōka Gazō Sakusha Burui (Portraits of kyōka poets according to groups). Compiled by Ishikawa Masamochi (Rokujuen), illustrated by Hōtei Gosei, with preface by Rokujuen. Edo, Bunka 8 (1811). Collection Japan Ukiyo-e Museum, Matsumoto. Anthology of poems, many by poets of the Go-gawa, but other groups as well; the portraits by Gosei seem to be faithful at least in representation of gender and social class. In the preface, Rokujuen mentions that each poet was consulted about his or her portrait. Important resource for the study of Edo kyōka movement of about 1810.

Kyōka Genzai Kijin-dan (Present-day tales of exceptional kyōka poets). Written and illustrated by Yashima Gakutei. 3 vols. (in 6 parts) with separately bound introduction. Edo, Nihombashi: Ōsakaya Shigeyoshi, Bunsei 7 (1824). Collection C.V. Starr East Asian Library (1 vol. missing). Provides phonetic readings for many names.

Kyōka Gojūnin Isshu (Fifty kyōka poets, one poem each). Illustrated by Ryūryūkyo Shinsai with a preface by Kubo Shumman. Edo, Kyōwa 3 (1803). Collection C.V. Starr East Asian Library, Columbia University, New York. Polychrome woodblock-printed portraits of fifty poets, each accompanied by one of their poems.

"*Kyōka Hanja Keifu*" (Lineages of kyōka poets). Meiji period manuscript compiled by Emaya (IV) Gakusuke (1856–1901). Collection Iwase Bunko, Nishio Municipal Library, Aichi Prefecture. Traces the lineages of certain kyōka teachers down to the Meiji period.

Kyōka Kei (Lineages of kyōka poets). Edited with preface by Shikitei Samba. Edo, Kyōwa 3 (1803). Collection Iwase Bunko, Nishio Municipal Library, Aichi Prefecture. Listing of the most prominent kyōka poets of the period, listed under the group (*gawa*) they were affiliated with at the time of publication; includes representative poems, samples of their signatures, seals, and crests, etc. Useful resource for the study of the history of Edo kyōka.

Kyōka Saiken-ki (Rankings of kyōka poets). Preface by Shakuyakutei Nagane. Edo, Bunka 2 (1805). Collection Waseda University Library, Tokyo. Includes a breakdown of the membership of various kyōka circles in the format of Yoshiwara guidebook. Also includes emblems associated with the leader of each kyōka circle.

Kyōka Sanjūrokkasen (Thirty-six poets of kyōka). Illustrated by Katsushika Hokusai. Edo, 1804/1805. Imaginative portraits of poets, accompanied by poems. Richard Lane in his recent *Hokusai: Life and Work* lists two other anthologies illustrated by Hokusai published under the same title in 1800 and 1824.

Nihon Koten Bungaku Daijiten Henshū Iinkai, ed. *Nihon Koten Bungaku Daijiten* (Encyclopedia of classical Japanese literature). 6 vols. Iwanami Shoten, 1983–85. Provides entries only for major figures in kyōka movement.

Shinsen Kyōka Gojūnin Isshu (New edition of the fifty kyōka poets, one poem each). Selected by Rokujuen Meshimori, edited by Rokkyokuen Namboku, illustrated by Kyōsai Hokkei. Preface by Rokujuen. 2 vols. Bunsei 2 (1819). Private Collection; photo-reproduction courtesy of Christies, New York. Similar in format to the *Kyōka Gazō Sakusha Burui* compiled by Rokujuen eight years earlier (cited above).

Suga Chikuho. *Kinsei Kyōka Shi* (History of Edo period kyōka). Tokyo: Nisshin Shoin, 1940. (1st ed. Tokyo: Nakanishi Shobō, 1936).

______, comp. *Kyōka Shomoku Shūsei* (Listing of kyōka anthologies). Kyoto: Hoshino Shoten, 1936. Includes a list of kyōka poets who were editors of kyōka anthologies; pronunciations provided.

"*Tsubo Sumire*" (Miscellany of the Tsubo poetry group). Preface by Kurokawa Harumura. Manuscript, Tempo 8 (1837). Reprinted in *Zoku Enseki Jisshū,* vol. 3. Tokyo: Chūōkōronsha, 1980. Miscellaneous notes on prominent judges and other members of the Tsubo-gawa (Asakusa-gawa).

Ward, Sidney C. "The Extraordinary Sakuragawa Jihinari." In *Proceedings of the First International Symposium on Surimono.* Tokyo: International Surimono Society, 1977. A consise but spirited essay on a major figure in Late Edo cultural circles.

釈堂 丸記 Shakudō Maruki
Circle of Sairaikyo (Hyōtan-ren).
(Hokkei 17)

鵲巣庵 Shakusōan
Circle of Shakuyakutei.
(Shinsai 40)

芍薬亭 長根 Shakuyakutei Nagane
Wrote popular novels under the name of Kisanji (II); head of his own circle of kyōka poets (Shitaya-gawa). Most influential kyōka master during the 1830s. Emblem was a stylized plum blossom. Seventh generation descendant of Hon'ami Kōetsu. 1767-1845. Kanō, 160; *Kyōka Gazō Sakusha Burui* (1811); *Nihon Koten Bungaku Daijiten*, 3:257; *Kyōka Kei* (1803).
(Shinsai 43, 44, 231, 236, 238)

三味 角製 Shami Kakusei
Tsubo-gawa. Portrait/poem included in Hokusai's *Kyōka Sanjūrokkasen* (1804/05).
(Hokuba 28).

芝の屋 山陽 Shibanoya Sanyō
Studied kyōka with Manzō I; became a judge of the Yomo Group in 1796. Designed a number of surimono. See Keyes, *Beatty*, no. 259, where he signs himself Shibanoya Kamon 芝馬の屋嘉門 followed by the phrase 准法眼 *junhōgen*, an honorary title. Also used the name Sanyōdō 山陽堂. Judge of the Shibahama-gawa. d. 1836. Kanō, 83; *Kyōka Kei* (1803); Suga, *Kinsei Kyōka Shi*, 340.
(Hokkei 103; Hokusai 32)

司馬の屋 Shibanoya.
Variant of above name.

司馬住 Shibazumi
(Hokkei 128)

恣月 Shigatsu
Haikai poet.
(Anonymous 299)

繁門 Shigekado.
See Kaanrin Fuku no Shigekado

茂見 Shigemi.
See Seijutei Shigemi

繁成 Shigenari.
See Shinshōtei Shigenari

茂留 Shigeru.
See Shōryūtei Shigeru

茂利 Shigetoshi.
See Kudanami Shigetoshi

信貴 山角 Shigi no Yamazumi
(Shinsai 228)

鹿城 Shikashiro.
See Jiku no Shikashiro

此花園 Shikaen (or Kono Hanazono)
(Hokkei 124)

史喬 Shikyō.
See Arakitei Shikyō

注連丸 Shimemaru.
See Fukusaitei Shimemaru

七五三好 Shimezuki.
See Natane Shimezuki

清水 真砂子 Shimizu Masako
Yomo-gawa. Perhaps same poet as Seigaen Masako 青峨園真砂子. Kanō, 212; *Kyōka Genzai Kijindan* (1824), vol. 1.
(Shinsai 219)

霜解 Shimodoke.
See Chikusaan Shimodoke

森富亭 満葉 Shimputei Mitsuba
Circle of Shinratei (Manji-ren).
(Hokkei 137)

信濃 善好 Shinano Zenkō
Shinano refers to Shinano Province (present-day Nagano Prefecture); Zenkōji 善光寺 is a temple in Nagano City.
(Shigenobu 209)

槙園 Shin'en
Haikai poet.
(Anonymous 299)

新玉亭 年波 Shingyokutei Toshinami
Yomo-gawa. *Kyōka Saiken-ki* (1805), 9.
(Hokusai 32)

森蔭亭 春秋 Shin'intei Haruaki
Yomo-gawa, circle of Shinratei.
(Gakutei 66)

神葵堂 Shinkidō.
See Jōsai no Sanjin Shinkidō

森皎亭 中垣 Shinkōtei Nakagaki
Yomo-gawa, circle of Shinratei.
(Hokusai 183)

深江亭 菅道 Shinkōtei Sugamichi
(Shumman 240)

森羅亭 萬象 Shinratei Manzō (or Banshō)
Shinratei Manzō (II) was a confectioner by trade. A reverse swastika, manji 卍 is the emblem used by poets of his circle, sometimes called the Manji-ren, which was affiliated with the Yomo-gawa. Shinratei at first used the pen name Shitchin Mampō 七珍萬寶; later he adopted the name Shinratei Manzō. He sometimes used a seal composed of a manji and a stylized elephant (*zō*), which was earlier used by his teacher Manzō I (1756?-1810?; Morishima Chūryō 森島中良, Takezue no Sugaru 竹杖爲輕). Shinratei II's dates: 1758-1831. Kanō, 216; *"Kyōka Bosho Ichiran"*; *Kyōka Kei* (1803); *Nihon Koten Bungaku Daijiten*, 3:215.
(Gakutei 65, 66; Hokusai 183, 185; Shinsai 39; Sōri 275)

森林亭 木守 Shinrintei Komori
(Hokkei 135)

森柳園 春風 Shinryūen Harukaze
Circle of Shakuyakutei.
(Shinsai 238)

弥生菴 雛丸 Yayoian Hinamaru
Studied kyōka with Yomo Utagaki Magao; low-ranking Bakufu official. Also used the pen names Shungetsudō 春月堂 and Momonomoto Hinamaru 桃の本雛丸. 1764-1830. Kanō, 189; *Kyōka Kei* (1803); Suga, *Kinsei Kyōka Shi*, 343 n. 7..
(Hokkei 131)

與鳳亭 枝成 Yohōtei Edanari
Yohōtei II; judge of the Yomo-gawa. Kanō, 29.
(Anonymous 297)

讀兼 Yomikane.
See Zentai Yomikane

四方 瀧水 米人 Yomo Takisui Komehito (or Komendo)
Active in circle of Ōta Nampo during the Temmei period, and joined Nampo's "Wabun no kai." His other pen names include: Kyōkabō 狂歌房 and Goyūken 吾友軒. Also used Sakazuki, written 酒月 or 坂月. Takisuirō 瀧水楼 and Yomo Takisui were names he used in his latter years. Influential judge of the Yomo-gawa and editor of a number of kyōka anthologies. Hamada, 19; *Kyōka Kei* (1803); *Nihon Koten Bungaku Daijiten*, 3:3; Suga, *Kinsei Kyōka Shi*, 341 n. 2..
(Shumman 52)

四方 歌垣 真顔 Yomo Utagaki Magao
Studied under Yomo no Akara 四方赤良. Also known as Haikai Utaba 俳諧歌場, Kyōkadō Magao 狂歌堂真顔, Yomo no Yamabito 四方山人, Shikatsube Magao 鹿都部真顔, etc. Prominent kyōka master who, as head of the Yomo-gawa, helped spread the popularity of kyōka beyond urban centers. Magao often contributed poems to surimono. 1753-1829. Kanō, 214; *"Kyōka Bosho Ichiran"*; *Kyōka Kei* (1803); *Nihon Koten Bungaku Daijiten*, 3:53-54.
(Gakutei 66; Hokusai 33, 163; Shinsai 45-47, 218, 219, 221-23, 228; Sōri 277; Toshū 280, 282; Toyokuni 286)

米人 Yonehito (or Komehito).
See Yomo Takisui Komehito

米守 Yonemori (or Komemori).
See Kashōan Yonemori

米成 Yonenari.
See Hōnensha Yonenari

米山 Yoneyama (or Komeyama).
See Hōnensha Yoneyama

楊柳亭 真弓 Yōryūtei Mayumi
(Shinsai 228)

美景 Yoshikage.
See Sekidōrō Yoshikage

吉藻 Yoshimo.
See Seiryūkan Yoshimo

吉村 Yoshimura.
See Kogetsutei Yoshimura

嘉成 Yoshinari.
See Nanigotomo Yoshinari

芳輔 Yoshisuke.
See Shōbaitei Yoshisuke

四辻 門守 Yotsutsuji Kadomori
Tsubo-gawa. Kanō, 40. *Kyōka Sanjūrokkasen* (1804/05).
(Hokuba 28)

勇源亭 丸人 Yūgentei Maruhito
(Shinsai 224)

幽渓斎 闕盛 Yūkeisai Sekimori
Yomo-gawa. Native of Sakura 佐倉 (Chiba Prefecture).
(Shinsai 221)

行業 Yukinari.
See Monogoto Yukinari

夢成 Yumenari.
See Issuisha Yumenari

弓成 Yuminari.
See Taijirō Yuminari

弓農屋 喜月 Yuminoya Kizuki
(Eisen 2)

湯水 Yumizu.
See Ryokuchikutei Yumizu

豊 事也 Yutaka Kotonari
(Shinsai 214)

善好 Zenkō.
See Shinano Zenkō

全躰讀兼 Zentai Yomikane
(Sōri 276)

INDEX

Numbers in italic typeface refer to illustrations.

The "weathermark" identifies this book as a production of Weatherhill, Inc., publishers of fine books on Asia and the Pacific. Editorial supervision: Jeffrey Hunter. Book and jacket design: Mariana Canelo Francis. Production Supervision: Bill Rose. Photography: Michael Mertz. Printed and bound at Oceanic Graphic Press, Hong Kong. The type faces used are Perpetua for the text and Gill Sans for display.